Technically Speaking

Chris Wilkinson

Traders Press, Inc.®
PO Box 6202
Greenville, SC 29606

Serving Traders Since 1975

http://www.traderspress.com

ISBN: 0-934380-39-2
Published by: Traders Press, Inc.®

This publication is designed to provide accurate and authoritative information with regard to the subject matter covered. It is sold with the understanding that the publisher is not engaged in rendering legal, accounting, or other professional advice. If legal advice or other expert assistance is required, the services of a competent professional person should be sought.

Teresa Darty Alligood
Editor and Graphic Designer
Traders Press, Inc.®

Traders Press Inc.®
PO Box 6206
Greenville, SC 29606

Phone: 800-927-8222 or 864-298-0222
Fax: 864-298-0221
http://www.traderspress.com

To Eddy Compton,
my first broker
for introducing me to technical analysis

PLANS FAIL FOR LACK OF COUNSEL,
BUT WITH MANY ADVISERS THEY SUCCEED.
PROVERBS 15:22

TABLE OF CONTENTS

ACKNOWLEDGEMENTS

First and foremost, I am indebted to each and every analyst featured in this book for taking time from their hectic schedules to help bring this project to fruition. Their complete willingness to share their time-tested methodologies and market insights with others was greatly appreciated and will prove valuable to readers. In addition, their continuous support and encouragement in this endeavor made the going a lot easier.

Working behind the scenes as liaisons and editors were the wives and office staff of several contributors. I would like to acknowledge Yolanda Ferguson, Jenny Graziano, Dorit Anne Kehr, Roberta Silveus, Nancy Tillman, and Rita Weinstein for their assistance.

Special thanks to Ed Dobson of Traders Press for sowing the first seeds. I am grateful to all at Traders Press for allowing me more liberties and voice than most authors are afforded.

Many thanks to Kewal Krishan at Mansfield Chart Service, who went the extra mile to reproduce charts spanning designated time periods.

I would like to recognize the artistic efforts of the individuals who participated in the creation of this book cover. The graphical layout was designed by Madeline Cripe and Nancy Wilkinson.

Last but not least, many thanks to unnamed family and friends whose interest and feedback helped fuel this achievement.

PUBLISHER'S FOREWORD

Of the many books and courses published over the years by Traders Press, this title stands right at the top of the list of those with which I am most proud to have been associated. Originally published nine years ago, this book has received well deserved kudos and praise from those who recognize its true value…and among those lavishing such comments are some of the most well-known and highly respected technical analysts in the world.

The true professionals in the field of technical analysis, the members of the Market Technicians Association, have made this book required reading for those who seek their coveted designation as a Chartered Market Technician.

This book came into being because of the diligent work and painstaking efforts of Chris Wilkinson, one of the most avid and diligent technical analysts I have ever known. Working with Chris in making this project come to pass was truly an enjoyable and educational process. Being her friend and knowing her during the time since we first discussed making this book "happen" has been an honor and a privilege. Her passion for technical analysis and for trading parallel my own.

Edward Dobson

Edward Dobson, President
Traders Press, Inc.®
Greenville, SC
January 2, 2006

ABOUT THE AUTHOR

Chris Wilkinson

Although her educational background and training are in the field of medicine, Chris Wilkinson holds the equivalent of a Ph.D. in the area of technical analysis of the markets. She has been an enthusiastic amateur investor for many years and has studied technical analysis in great detail. She has read virtually every worthwhile book on the subject, employed it in her own market analysis for many years, and observed it firsthand through market action. This rich experience makes her exceedingly well-qualified to choose the "all-star cast" of technical analysts contained in her first full-length book, *Technically Speaking.*

INTRODUCTION

Making money in the financial markets is a tough game, but based on personal experience, technical analysis offers a winning edge to those who use it. The following pages contain interviews with sixteen prominent technical analysts who have made money for themselves and investors who followed their advice. Remembering what a tremendous help their instruction was to my investing early on, I asked them to share with you their methods and strategies, which have proven successful over the years.

I discovered technical analysis by sheer coincidence. After opening my first brokerage account in 1985, I was assigned a broker who believed that when it came to making money, technical analysis held a distinct advantage over fundamental analysis. A series of initial trades using technical analysis were successful, convincing me also of its merits. From that point on, no investment decision was made without first consulting a chart. Later, I felt obligated to learn the basics of fundamental analysis but for no other reason than to become conversant in the dominant "language" spoken on Wall Street. Today, I believe the tide has turned. With each year that passes, technical analysis is gaining more and more converts. Although loath to admit it, even the most die-hard fundamental analysts feel compelled to use technical analysis to some extent or at the very least, inquire about the technical state of the markets. They have learned that price movements can be driven and exacerbated by the technical forces at play.

With interest in technical analysis growing by leaps and bounds, there has been a commensurate increase in the number of books devoted to this subject. In the early 1960s, one could count on two hands the number of books dealing with technical analysis. Now there are over 400 hundred titles and counting. Between the books touting trading systems that lead to the pot of gold and sophisticated software programs that virtually deliver instant buy or sell signals at the push of a button, it's no surprise that technical analysis has attracted scores of novices who, in their naivete, believe technical analysis is little more than artificial intelligence. But as seasoned analysts will attest, technical analysis is more than just a reflex reaction to a computer generated signal. An aspiring technical analyst cannot hope to become proficient by blindly following a set of rigid rules, any more than a first year medical student can hope to successfully remove a patient's gall bladder following a diagram in an anatomy book. Technical analysis goes beyond book knowledge or state of the art analytical programs. It involves a "feel" for price behavior, the intuitive ability to interpret a multitude of indicators in context of various market conditions, and the flexibility to reverse course when caught on the wrong side of a trade or investment.

My objectives in writing this book were twofold. First, I wanted to expand the reader's existing knowledge of technical analysis. Secondly, I wanted to disclose many of the attendant caveats linked to particular indicators. To achieve both goals, I called on the expertise of men whose market research and predictions are a cut above the rest. My choice of contributors bring to the table a wealth of experience. Surviving multiple bull and bear markets have left these analysts with above average instincts that supercede the best indicator any day. On average, each has been involved in market analysis over twenty-eight years. Unlike the transient popularity of the here today, gone tomorrow gurus, all have good, long-term track records. These analysts prevail because their forecasts are conservative and supported by logical, concrete evidence. They are independent thinkers and contrarian in that they are not pressured to fall in line with Wall Street's expectations or the forecast du jour. In addition to their daily routine of closely monitoring market activity, they also find time in their busy schedules to do research, consult, write and edit newsletters, lecture, and manage money. Many are published authors and I would point out that the information included here should be viewed as a supplement to their original work, not a substitute.

From an analytical perspective, each technician has his own unique style. The forthcoming interviews explore the nucleus of each analyst's work. Emphasis is placed on pet indicators which each believes to be the most valuable in assessing the broader markets as well as individual stocks. Given the fact that a wide array of analytical methods do exist, many contributors expressed concern that some of the material may present conflicting views, which would be more confusing than helpful to readers. While different views were expressed, none were inherently contradictory. Among these sixteen analysts, the only major point of contention was whether price or volume is the first to lead a move. From an investing standpoint, disagreement over this issue is as innocuous as the debate between which came first, the chicken or the egg. Based on the successful track records of each analyst, it appears that accepting either viewpoint doesn't compromise the ability to make money. However, despite the subtle differences in thought among these analysts, there were four critical points on which they unanimously agreed; 1) there is no perfect indicator 2) emotional input will destroy the effectiveness of any indicator 3) cut losses quickly and 4) stay with the trend.

Most of the interviews were conducted between June and September 1996, a time of increased volatility in the financial markets. For those who missed the action, charts are included in Appendix I. Knowing that it would date the book, my original intention was to eliminate any conversation relative to this time period. However, such unusual activity created a perfect backdrop for discussing the reliability of particular indicators; therefore, I retained certain references to this period.

When all is said and done, there are two ways an investor can learn. One is through first hand experience, otherwise known as the school of hard knocks. Although effective, this route is time consuming and expensive. An alternate and more expedient approach is to learn from the trials and errors of others. This book attempts to zero in on technical strategies and indicators with a proven track record. Having experimented with nearly every technique and methodology known, these experts have narrowed down what actually works in the real world of technical analysis. Based on numerous years of market experience, they share their individual insights, methodologies, and observations, providing you with a solid technical platform upon which to launch your own analysis. Follow their lead and success will ensue.

Stan Berge

With a degree in electrical engineering, Stan Berge was managing a plant for General Electric in 1957 when he decided to begin investing seriously for early retirement. Already a General Electric shareholder, he was interested in portfolio diversification. While on a lunch break one day, he stopped by a brokerage firm for some stock suggestions. Based on the recommendations of the broker, he bought a few hundred shares in five different securities. This was March of 1957. By June, his portfolio was up 12%. About the same time he reasoned he could make as much money in the stock market as on the job, the market turned on a dime and headed south. In short order his investments were below their original cost. He placed a call to his friendly broker to find out what sparked this sudden negative turn of events. The broker's response was "don't worry." When pressed for an explanation, the broker said that his firm believed the decline was nothing more than a shortterm correction. Four weeks after the first conversation, the market had fallen another 5%. The second worried call to his broker was met with the same glib reassurance as the first—"Don't worry. Go back and do what you were doing." Mr. Berge pointed out to the broker that incoming orders to General Electric had slowed and layoffs seemed inevitable. Given the gloomy scenario developing at the manufacturing level, he envisioned a general economic slowdown occurring soon. He asked the broker to look into the matter. Another week passed before the broker called back to say that his firm's research department admitted that the market had fallen more than they had expected and the possibility of a recession loomed on the horizon. They were advising their clients to "sell." This was now October and the overall market had declined 25% and Mr. Berge's account had suffered a 15% loss. On October 23, 1957, relying on the judgment of his brokerage firm, Mr. Berge liquidated all of the stocks in his account. The very next day, October 24, 1957 marked the exact bottom of that decline. He had sold at the very lows almost to the exact day. For the next six months, stocks meandered sideways before gaining enough momentum to resume their uptrend. It wasn't until the market was well underway on the upside that Mr. Berge witnessed a recovery in orders at General Electric.

This experience made Mr. Berge realize that there were forces in the market which he didn't understand. Why did the stock market decline before business conditions deteriorated and then rally while the economy was still in the doldrums? His early suspicions that the stock market discounts events in advance were later confirmed. A loss of hard earned capital is a potent catalyst for seeking a new system of investing. Mr. Berge embarked on a mission to learn everything he could about the stock market. He began subscribing to *Business Week, Barron's*, the *Wall Street Journal*, and several market newsletters. He read every book pertinent to investing. In his free time, he sought personal counsel from such prominent market analysts as John Magee, Hamilton Bolton, George Chestnut, and Ray Mansfield.

At the end of this period, from 1957 to 1961, Mr. Berge realized that his original motivation for understanding the markets—to preserve capital—had evolved into something more. He actually enjoyed market analysis and in fact, was becoming a rather proficient technician. He side-stepped the bear market in 1960 by selling out in January and then re-entering in December of that same year. This maneuver did not go unnoticed. A partner in the brokerage firm of Davis and Davis, where his trading occurred, asked Mr. Berge for his source of information. An explanation that he was the source of information and that the market was a hobby for him elicited an open invitation to join the firm at any time. He never considered the offer again until 1962.

When General Electric asked Mr. Berge to transfer for the seventh time, he said "no" and accepted a position as Executive Vice President and Chief Operating Officer of Haveg Industries in 1957. In 1962, Hercules Corporation made a tender offer for Haveg Industries. Intent on establishing a permanent home for his family, he declined an offer from Hercules to relocate and reconsidered his earlier option to become a broker. After deep deliberation, he cut his ties with industry, accepted a 60% reduction in pay, and went to work for Davis and Davis. This brokerage firm was too small to meet Mr. Berge's objectives. His goal was to attract institutional clients such as banks, mutual funds, and insurance companies. A merger later with Tucker Anthony provided this opportunity.

Though a latecomer to the financial markets, Mr. Berge was a pioneer in the field of analysis in the sense that at this time, he was probably the only analyst to combine technical analysis with the economic and monetary forces at play in the market. He became extremely successful as he exploited this undiscovered market niche. His well-respected advice earned him recognition within the financial community. Among institutional analysts, his market newsletter has been ranked #1 by Market Timer on several occasions. During the early years, Mr. Berge quickly discovered that his institutional clients were not receptive to technical rationale. Even though his market calls were based on technical analysis, he found it necessary to temper his technical proclivity during presentations to institutions. For such occasions, he substituted economic and monetary explanations for the technical.

After a few years of research and experimentation, Mr. Berge created the Primary Trend Index in 1961, a model designed to position clients ahead of a bull or bear market in excess of 16% to 20%. Intermediate term corrections are anticipated through a second model, the Intermediate Trend Index, which signals an eminent rally or decline in the range of 10% to 16%. He uses the same technical indicators that other technicians use but as he will reveal shortly, his manipulation of the data is a little unique. Periodic modifications are incorporated into the model to stay in step with the evolutionary changes in the markets. Through his own admission, his market models have "missed a couple of points" but anyone capable of reading a chart can see they have been right on the money for the really big moves. Going back to the 1960's, a graphic depiction of the PTI level superimposed on a chart of the DJIA demonstrates amazing accuracy at major turning points.

In 1982, when Mr. Berge was Tucker Anthony's largest stockholder, the firm was acquired by John Hancock. Six years later, in 1988, after several top management changes, some of which were not to his liking, he, his daughter Susan, and son-in-law, Ronald Kent, resigned to establish an independent family enterprise. Their shingle swings from a branch office of Dominick and Dominick, Inc. in Providence, Rhode Island where they produce the ***Berge-Kent Report*** and continue to provide research for institutional clients, many of whom have been with them for twenty-five years or more.

At first glance, one could argue that Mr. Berge's success was a result of being in the right place at the right time and in fact he modestly refers to his good fortune as "dumb luck." But upon closer inspection, he had prepared himself in advance to such a degree that when the opportunity emerged, he was qualified to seize it. He views his involvement with the market as a wonderful experience and "wishes that everyone could experience some of what he has experienced."

From the 1960's until his semi-retirement, Stan Berge was a household name among institutions. On several occasions, he was voted as one of the top three market timers by ***Institutional Investor*** magazine. In those earlier years, his market comments were featured frequently in such publications as ***Barron's*** and the ***Wall Street Journal,*** but now he shuns interviews because journalists pry and his models are proprietary. Also, he has ethical reservations about giving out free advice to the media when his private clients pay well for his superior, unpublicized research. However, remembering the helpful guidance he received as a market novice, Mr. Berge has agreed to reveal the basic construction of his Primary Trend Index but understandably is unable to disclose the details. The information provides a good starting point and presents a great challenge for those who wish to climb to the heights of Mr. Berge's success. I am extremely grateful to him for sharing his knowledge and experience.

So that he can divide his time up among his two passions, the stock market and golf, more and more of his activities are being taken over by his daughter, son-in-law, and youngest son Tom.

After your market experience in 1957, what influenced your decision to focus on technical analysis rather than fundamental analysis?

I read John Magee's book *Technical Analysis of Stock Market Trends* and discovered there was a lot to technical analysis. You could read through his book and see the various technical formations that were occurring in individual stocks and determine whether they were going to go up, down, or base. I became interested in the technical work. A friend of mine, who was a doctor and owned his own plane, shared a similar interest in the stock market. After reading John's book, we decided to go visit him. He flew us up to Springfield, Massachusetts. We talked to him in a room with no windows. There was nothing but charts all over the wall. John was a wonderful man. I also found that when I started talking about the market to other people like John Magee, they would tell me to only stay with the technicals; don't get into the fundamentals. But I went up to see Hamilton Bolton in Toronto, Canada, who wrote the *Bank Credit Analyst*. He told me that you have to understand what the Federal Reserve system is doing because they are responsible for monetary policy. When they are easy, the stock market goes up. When they tighten, the stock market goes down. So I began studying monetary policy and subscribed to the St. Louis Federal Reserve figures. I visited Ray Mansfield in Newark, New Jersey. Mr. Mansfield told me that the technical stuff was very good but you have to know something about economics. He suggested that I subscribe to some of the government periodicals such as *Business Conditions Digest* which is now called *Business Cycle Indicators*. So I subscribed to these things to learn something about how the economy worked. I began to develop this as a hobby putting various statistics together.

In general terms, would you run through the construction of the Primary Trend Index (PTI)?

Primary Trend Index includes many economic factors in the leading, the coincident, and the lagging business indicators. It becomes bearish when the leading indicators drop below 50% expanding and the lagging indicators rise above 50% expanding. It normally means that the probability of an economic slowdown has increased. But this indicator can lead a recession by several months. Sometimes it is just a slowdown as in 1966 or 1995 and sometimes it actually results in a recession. As the leading indicators rise through 50%, we say that is now ranked as a +1 in the PTI. When it gets up to 100% expanding, we say that is now neutral. In other words, it has reached a point where the economy is being operated under full steam so to speak. Then when it turns around and comes back down again, and drops through 50% expanding, we put that in -1. When it gets down to zero expanding, which it generally does, it then goes back to zero, and as it turns up from zero and starts back up to 50% it becomes bullish. So you go from +1 to zero to -1 to zero to +1 to zero and so forth. Same thing is true with the coincident indicators but with the lagging indicators—it's just the reverse. When we go to the monetary factors, like interest rates, bonds, free versus borrowed reserves, money supply, and things of that nature, we are involved in rates of change. How fast is the money supply expanding? When it is expanding rapidly, that is a plus for the economy and a plus for the stock market so we rank this as +1. When it begins to slow down, it becomes neutral. When it turns down it becomes negative and ranked -1. Of course, as it keeps on going down it gradually gets down to the point where we can rank it as being neutral again. When it hits bottom and is ready to turn up, we decide that is where we should be bullish again. The same thing is true with the Free Reserve picture. If the economy is moving along under a free reserve basis, in other words, there is not any tightness on the part of the Fed—they are perfectly willing to make reserves available to the banks—that is positive. But if the Fed begins to tighten, and we see a shrinking reserve position and interest rates begin to rise, these become negatives for first the stock market, and later for the economy. The reason for having so many different factors and then condensing them down to 17 for the PTI is that there are times when the money supply contracts and the stock market goes up. That is one of the things that is happening right now and the reason behind that, which is unusual, is that people are moving money from their checking and savings accounts into the stock market. That is sustaining the stock market. In the meantime, they are running up huge debt on their credit cards. From the monetary factors we go to the technical factors. Here we are talking about such things as the put/call ratio. When put/call ratios are very low it indicates the market isn't going to go up very much. When the put/call ratios are very high, as they were at the low in July 1996, it says that the market is going to rally. We do the same thing again—if the put/call ratio is very high, we say that is +1 for the index. If it is very low, we say that is -1 for the index. When it is some place in the middle, it's zero. We use the same principle with new highs and new lows, the advances and declines, total trading volume, upside trading volume versus downside trading volume, and the rate of change of the S&P 500 on a 20 week moving average basis versus a 40 week moving average basis. We measure the stocks that are trading unchanged for the day. That incidentally, on a 10 day basis, was at the highest level in history in June 1996, which said the market was unlikely to go much higher. After the June-July correction was completed, it again rose to still higher levels without a correction.

Is there a good way to detect the number of stocks that are inconspicuously moving from the advancing camp and hiding out in the unchanged figures?

There are several ways of doing that. One way is called DISART. It is the plurality of advances minus declines ignoring the sign. In other words, you take the difference of the stocks that are up for the day from the stocks that are down—forget the sign and add those up for 25 days. It is a measure of volatility. When the number is very low it is at a market top. When it is very high, volatility is high and we are at a market bottom. Volatility got very high in mid-July of 1996 and the market bottomed. Now the spread between advances and declines is narrowing so volatility is coming down. Twenty five years ago when I started to work with it, the total number of issues traded were maybe around 1500. Now the total number of issues traded is 3300. For this reason, it takes a lot of experience to properly interpret DISART.

If I understand you correctly, each indicator oscillates from bullish to bearish, passing through zero or neutral on its way up or down?

Yes. Let's take the difference between advances and declines. We normally see this top out before the stock market tops out. If we see this indicator on a 10 day basis down below minus 7000 to minus 10,000 we think that is very bullish and if we see it above plus 7,000 or plus 10,000 we think we are getting way overbought and that is bearish. Let's say this is the only factor we are looking at. Now when that tops out first, if everything is in gear on the way up and bullish, once we get a decline and then rally back up, if the advances and declines lag, as they do now, then that gets to be neutral. If we go to a new high and then turn down but the breadth doesn't go to a new high and turns down, then that particular factor is ranked bearish, or -1. The criteria is what's important. Another

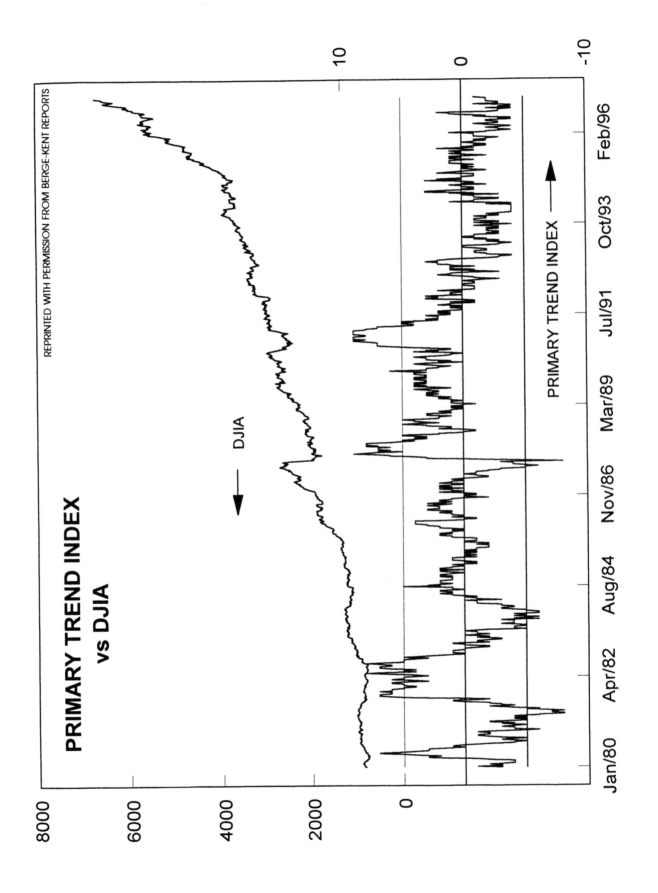

PRIMARY TREND INDEX
vs DJIA

DJIA

PRIMARY TREND INDEX

REPRINTED WITH PERMISSION FROM BERGE-KENT REPORTS

Jan/80   Apr/82   Aug/84   Nov/86   Mar/89   Jul/91   Oct/93   Feb/96

example is let's say the market is at a new high and the number of stocks making new highs are say 600 and that is the highest that we have had for the entire move. If we have some sort of a pullback, when we go back up again and if the market goes to new highs, the number of stocks making new highs is going to be way down from where they were. That makes the new highs versus the Dow bearish. That would be ranked -1. So we build this up for 17 factors condensed from about 110 indicators.

Would you explain the methodology behind the model?

We make a composite index from the distillation of everything else. We have a computer set up that says this particular factor is bullish when it's in this position, it is neutral in this position, and it is bearish in that position. The methodology is going again from -1 to zero to +1 to zero to -1. Since it has to cross zero on the way up from -1 to +1, and cross zero on the way down from +1 to -1, it just works like a pendulum telling us whether we should be bullish or bearish in the stock market. We do this with the economic, monetary, and technical factors and then just add them up. Anybody can set something like this up. If we get to the -5 or -6, we say we are in the area of a market top. If we get to +5 or higher, we say we are in the area of a market bottom. Again, those numbers have to go from being above zero or positive, through zero on the way down, which is neutral, and into negative positions at -7 or -8. We have never had a negative position since they turned bullish in 1990. We have been bullish since the 1990 lows. In 1994, our indexes got very close to bearish positions. It almost looked like we were going into a recession and for all practical purposes the industrial sector was in a recession. Industrial production in 1995 was almost flat but the service sector was enough to offset that so gross domestic product didn't actually turn down. In 1994, the S&P 500 index fell only 8.9%. At the present time, we are of the opinion that the stock market has not seen its final high, but it's entirely concievable that a decline close to or beyond 10% may begin in the third quarter of 1997.

What type of move is the Primary Trend Index designed to capture?

Normally we would expect a move about 20% in either direction and it should last six months to a year or longer. Our Intermediate Term Index (ITI), which has to get to +7 or -7 is designed to indicate to our clients that there will be a correction of less than 16-20% and would last a minimum of six weeks to six months or longer. The ITI has not been bearish since October 1990. But then there are occasions like 1965 which only took about 6 weeks for the market to decline 12% or 13%. The ITI is not supposed to affect the PTI, which it didn't in 1965. The market went down about 12% then the ITI turned bullish and in December 1966, the ITI and PTI gave sell signals.

Is the model set up to correlate best with the larger cap S&P 500 type stocks?

We essentially measure the broad market indices, like the S&P 500, NYSE, and the Dow Industrials. But then beyond that we have group work which tells us what groups to be in for various stages of the stock market cycle. Then we will recommend in that group maybe four or five stocks strictly on a technical basis. We do no fundamental analysis whatsoever. What we do is look at a stock and make a determination as to whether it is going to go up or not. Then we look at a group, whether it be steels, aluminums, papers, chemicals, airlines—whatever it happens to be—and make that determination as to whether it is going to outperform the stock market on the way up or going to underperform the market on the way down so that people lose less money in a downtrending market than they would if they had stayed with the cyclical stocks or something like that. About eight years ago, we developed a methodology to compare our own raw performance against the S&P 500 and we are consistently beating it on the upside and downside by being in the right groups.

Is the NASDAQ Composite index included in your PTI model?

There is a separate PTI for the NASDAQ type stocks. We were very bearish on NASDAQ in the fall of 1995 because market breadth topped out. We monitored this situation very carefully to see if that divergence still existed when the NASDAQ averages came into new highs. When NASDAQ came into new highs in 1996, breadth didn't confirm. Our PTI was at -4 and very close to a -5 indicating that we were going to have a pretty good size decline. Also, on a relative strength basis the NASDAQ was outperforming the NYSE, Dow, and the S&P 500 after the February 1996 consolidation began. That stretched the rubber band so tight at that point that we could forecast that the OTC market would go down more than the Dow or S&P would go down. We advised people to get out of the NASDAQ type stocks. By the end of July NASDAQ had fallen over 20% while the S&P had fallen less than 10%.

You look at as many as 110 different types of indicators. Why did you develop a model rather than looking at each indicator separately?

We developed these composite indexes because we know that a single factor, whether it be volume, advance/decline, or highs versus lows doesn't always give you a precise answer in so far as timing a market top or bottom. Sometimes one indicator is very early, sometimes it is late. For instance, a cumulative advance/decline line almost always tops out on major declines prior to the top in terms of the Dow but that didn't happen in 1976. The Dow topped out in August/September 1976 and breadth didn't top out until July 1977. If you relied strictly on the breadth in 1976 to tell you that you were getting divergences against the popular averages, you didn't get any. This is why we use a conglomerate of various factors. We want to be certain that if one isn't working enough others are working to offset it.

Do you segregate your indicators into different categories?

When I started getting interested in the market back in the 1950's I probably had only 40 different factors. I characterize each factor under sentiment, volume, monetary, economic, etcetera. As new things came along that would impact the stock market, I would incorporate that into the appropriate category. For example, the rate of change of upside volume versus downside volume. Is this a volume characteristic? Yes. Is the market rallying because upside volume expanded? Yes. Over the last 30 days, upside volume was up an average of 5 million shares a day. But the interesting thing is that the downside volume, the volume on the stocks that were going down, declined by 11 million shares a day. The reason we had this rally is not because of strong buying but because nobody wanted to sell anymore. When that happens, we start to get a high level of unchanged volume and you need to get ready because we are going to go down again. Factors like odd-lots, puts and calls, short selling, open interest, and *Barron's* numbers of percentage bulls and bears are all measures of sentiment. As we develop new techniques and as new information becomes available, we constantly try to upgrade the ability of the index to be accurate.

Do your indicators receive equal weighting?

Yes, they do. Of course if we are talking about volume for instance, there may be many different individual volume factors involved in making a determination about the volume characteristic which we rank only as one point in the PTI. The volume characteristic would include everything to do with volume—upside volume, downside volume, rate of change of upside versus downside, and various moving averages of that. We will take into account the total trading volume and the rate of change in total trading volume. When we get through with each indicator, we make a decision that the total volume characteristic is now bearish, which it is now, and rank that -1 in the PTI.

Would you run through your list of the 17 components in your Primary Trend Index?

When an indicator is bullish we rank it "plus one" (+1). If it is neutral it becomes zero and if it is bearish it is "minus one" (-1). The first indicator we use is 30 day volume. That is up volume minus down volume divided by the up volume plus the down volume. We run an oscillator on that. When it gets up to a very high level it indicates that the market is overbought. When it gets to a very low level it means the market is oversold. The second is what we call the trading ratio, also known as the ARMS index. It is advances divided by declines and upside volume divided by downside volume. The volume ratio is then divided into the advance/decline ratio. The third one is the 60 day ratio of advances over declines. When the number gets very low, as a result of the advances being low and the declines being very high, that is normally very bullish because the market is oversold. The reverse is true. When the advances are very high and the declines are relatively low then the market is overbought and it becomes more bearish. The fourth indicator is one we refer to as money flow. It is a longer term index and it is based on the price changes in the Dow times daily trading volume. The next one is the P/E ratio of the S&P 500 versus its dividend yield. There would be certain criteria here that determines when the P/E ratios are too high and dividend yields are too low and therefore bearish. The reverse, of course, is true. Another indicator has to do with a shift in Treasury bill yields; not bonds but bills. If it rises a certain percentage from a low—let's assume bills are yielding 6% and they go to 7%—we would then say this is now becoming bearish. If they were to go from 7% down to 6% then we would say this is more bullish because rates are coming down. As other people have observed in the past, shortterm rates, particularly Treasury bills, have a lot more influence on what's going to happen to the economy, and in many cases the stock market, than longterm rates. The next has to do with the annual rate of change of the Dow or the S&P 500. When that gets up to a very high level, say 35%, that says that we are beginning to push into an area that would have to be ranked as neutral. In other words, it had been ranked bullish because we had a low level at the market lows in 1990 and also in December of 1994. Most of the time we don't make the final market top with a maximum position there. It goes from a bullish position because it is very oversold through a neutral position because it has gone above zero and continued to climb and then it starts to roll over and when it begins to roll over that then says that the momentum on the upside is beginning to be lost and it would then be ranked as bearish. We think the percentage of stocks that are over their 30 week moving averages is a very important indicator. We refer to this as, "How far can you stretch the rubber band?" When we have a big gap on the upside it says we are reaching an overbought condition in the

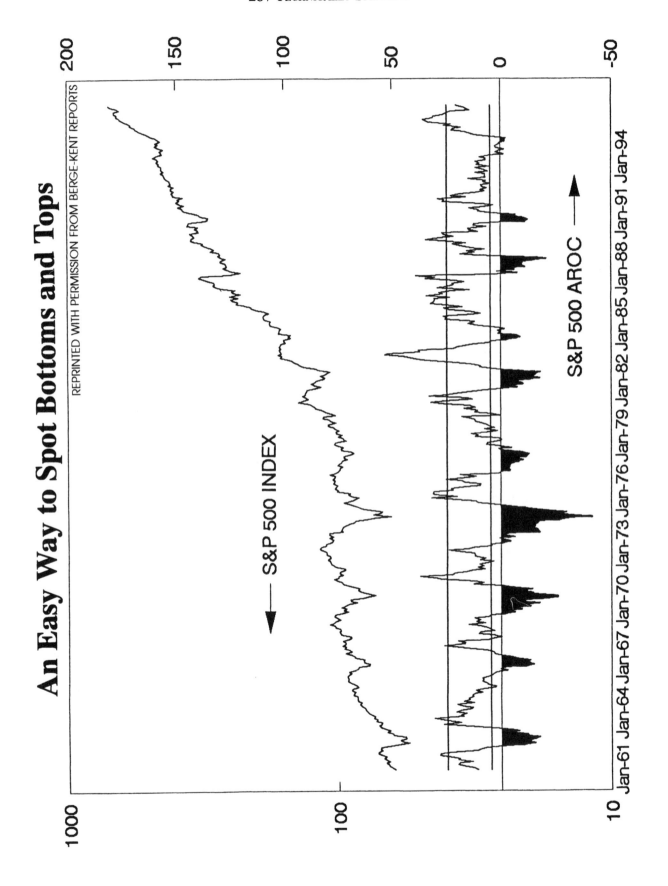

An Easy Way to Spot Bottoms and Tops

REPRINTED WITH PERMISSION FROM BERGE-KENT REPORTS

S&P 500 INDEX

S&P 500 AROC ⟶

market and the reverse, a big gap on the downside means the market is oversold. When it is very low, we rank it as +1 then when it goes through the neutral position it gets ranked zero, which means we are losing a point in the primary trend index, and when it turns fully bearish we lose a total of two points. The eighth one is an indicator of volatility. This is a 10 week total of advances less declines. We just forget the sign.

Is that similar to the DISART?

No. The DISART is a 25 day figure. This is a 10 week figure and it is more useful from a longterm viewpoint. The DISART is important but we use that more from an intermediate term viewpoint. Here again if we have a very high level it says that the market is too strong. There is no indication of any distribution because the volatility is very high. When we start to get distribution, as we did in May 1996, this number begins to drop because we reach what we call a state of balance between buyers and sellers with the market up. When that happens, it means that the selling pressure is beginning to increase in the stock market. People are willing to take profits at that point and that causes this index to drop down. When it gets to a relatively low level, the next significant move will be down.

What are you accomplishing by ignoring the sign?

You are measuring volatility. Let's assume this week there are 2,000 stocks up and 1,000 down so we have a plus 1,000. The next week it is reversed, 1,000 up and 2,000 down. If we were subtracting the advances and declines on a weekly basis, we would have zero. Ignoring the sign allows us to measure the volatility in the market. Volatility gets very high at market bottoms because there is panic. When people are liquidating stocks down near a bottom, it is emotional. People are saying, "I don't care what the price is, get me out." Normally, that gives us big, big numbers—maybe 2,000 stocks down, only 500 up, and the rest unchanged for the week. When we are getting to a market top and the spread narrows, whether it is up or down, it's indicating that people are making an unemotional judgment to liquidate stocks. Next, we use the weekly rate of change in the S&P 500 over a 20 week period to measure how far the S&P 500 average has dropped or increased over a period of time. If it drops to a very low level obviously under that basis, we have to be bullish and so we rank it a +1. As the market rises, that indicator is going to go through zero which makes it neutral. When it gets up to a very high level, we say it is overbought and has to be ranked as being bearish or minus one. The next has to do with the gap between the 20 week moving average and the 40 week moving average of the S&P 500. Whenever this gap is rising, particularly when it is from a very low level, we are going to rank it as being bullish. Somewhere along the line the gap between the two begins to narrow and it becomes neutral. When it finally crosses after being neutral, it becomes bearish.

Don't you measure gaps between moving average lines of individual stocks also?

Yes. A lot of the things we are mentioning here we put into a computer and run it through for individual stocks. This is very helpful because if we see a preponderance of stocks exhibiting the same characteristics that we are seeing in the S&P 500 we have further confirmation. Another important consideration of following individual stocks is that there will be times when some stocks, like the cyclicals, may be vulnerable to market declines while others may buck the trend and go up. Next year, if the market as a whole starts down, we may see the gold stocks moving upward. Maybe it won't be like 1929-32. At that time, the market went down about 90% and Homestake Mining went from $40.00 to $400.00 per share. For the next indicator, we run a ratio of cyclical issues versus defensive issues. There are about eleven cyclical groups and eleven defensive groups. The cyclicals would be the steels, papers, chemicals, aluminum, copper, airlines, autos, machinery, electrical equipment—those groups which would be vulnerable to declining profits during a recession. The defensive issues would be like foods, food chains, banks, insurance companies, oils, gold; the necessities of life, so to speak, that generally resist the decline. You can forego buying a new car but you can't go without energy or food. Then we look at what the Federal Reserve position is. We have had a net free position for several years now so Federal Reserve policy is still easy.

Do net free reserves correlate with the stock market or the economy?

Let's say the economy has slowed down. If I look at net free reserves and see that there are plenty there, the slowing economy is a case of higher interest rates rather than low reserves. The banking system can be in a net free reserve position, but if people don't want to borrow a lot of money, the money just stays in the bank. If people are borrowing enough money, banks can go into a net borrowed position. The market can still go down, as it did in 1990, without a negative borrowed reserve position. If we were to go into a net borrowed position I would really run for the hills because it hasn't happened in so long. The fifteenth indicator, mutual fund equity cash positions, is important. If cash levels are very high, we are down near a market bottom and if they are very low, we are near a market top. The sixteenth indicator is the annual rate of change in 30 year bond yields. We calculate this on a monthly basis. When the rate of change begins to rise very rapidly over an annual basis, it is telling us that we have to be watching out. That is going on now. I think we will end 1997 somewhere around 7.25%, maybe 7.50% to 7.75% in 1998.

That will be a shocker to some people.

Well, I can't find anyplace where the stock market has gone down without 30 year bond yields going up and also 90 day Treasury bill yields going up. Maybe this time will be different but if it is, then something else is going to have to take over in its place. The last indicator has to do with money supply, M1 and M2. If they are rising from below zero, we would consider that to be very bullish. Right now, I would say the money supply figures are negative because they have been contracting for quite a long period of time.

Your PTI signals are generated after the summation of pluses, minuses, and zeros of these seventeen indicators?

That's right. We add the plus ones, zeros, and minus ones to get a total. We were around +10 or +12 at the 1990 bottom and it has never been bearish since. At the present time, we are at -3 in the PTI. If we go to -5 or lower, we would tell our clients that we have reached the area of a significant top. From this area of the top, we would expect a decline of 16-20% or more. My own feeling now is when we get there, which I think will be by the end of 1997 or early 1998, we will probably be saying 16-20% would be the absolute minimum. We could possibly think in terms of maybe 50%.

The market in 1996 certainly gave a lot of confusing signals.

This frequently happens when we are coming to the end of a secular bull market. If you go back to early 1929 as an example, you would see that the market went up to 320 back down to 291, back up to 321, back down to 287 and it did this three or four times before we finally hit bottom and went up to 386 which was a very big blow-off move in 1929. A somewhat similar pattern happened in 1972— back and forth over the same territory, occasionally making minor new highs, as we have done since February. This is a distribution period. It is also a period where the percentage of bulls and the percentage of bears begins to narrow to the point where they are almost equal. This is generally another warning sign that we are getting close to some sort of a significant market top. It is very difficult to predict in advance where the market is going to top out. With the distribution patterns that have been developing, particularly in the OTC market, people have asked me quite a bit lately, "If the market does go down 50%, what's it going to be like? Is it going to be like 1987 or is it going to be like 1973-1974?" The answer that I have given is, "It's going to be both." It will be 1987 first and then 1973-1974 later, after the bear market rally.

Are current economic conditions similar to those of 1929?

What is happening now is exactly the same sort of thing that was happening near the end of the 1920's. If we go back and study the period around 1880 to 1929, we find a period in which the country was emerging from being an agricultural economy to an industrial economy. During the latter part of the 1920's, we had created a tremendous ability to grow grains, cotton, and all of the other things with considerably less manpower because the machinery age came into play. The farmer had to come in off the farm and learn how to run an industrial machine in some factory. That was a tremendous upheaval for labor at that particular time. There was also a period in the late 1920's where growth in the economy was not very much better than it is right now. We had a tremendous expansion until 1981 or 1982, when we gradually began to change over from an industrial economy to an information economy. This is disruptive because the people who worked in a steel mill are not trained in conveying information over the Internet or in using computers. With industrial production now having dropped well below its normal uptrend, which is 3.4%, I see the present time as very similar to the tremendous upheaval that we had in the late 1920's. I think the result will be essentially the same. The Federal Reserve will try to prevent a recession occurring and we will find that the free market forces are unable to do so because adjustments have to be made. This is why I think we are going into a major bear market that will last until at least 1998. From 1946-1949, after the war, we had a lot of adjustment to go through. We had to convert all of our factories to produce consumer goods rather than war goods. The normal growth rate of industrial production over the last hundred years or so was 3.4%. For a while, the economy performed well below this. Of course, when we finally got things in the right position, the stock market did very well during that period because we had more than excess capacity. Everything went along very well until 1966. During 1965-1966, we began to rise above that trend of 3.4% and that was the beginning of the inflationary period. The Fed was continuing the same policies it had before, not realizing they were creating this tremendous inflationary period. So for 15 or 16 years from say 1949 up to 1965, the market did very well. The bond market was

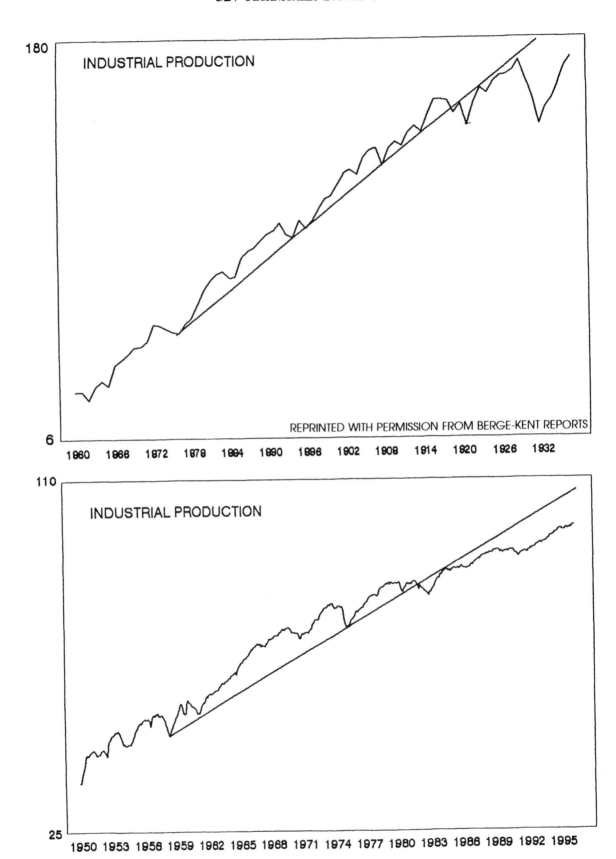

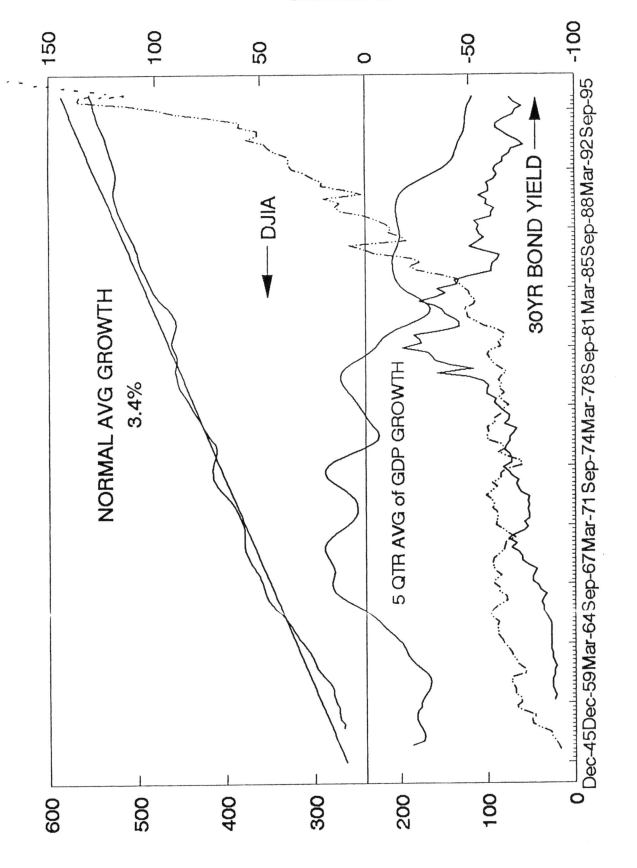

subdued and interest rates and the inflation rate were low. When we started 1966, the stock market couldn't get through the 1,000 level by more than 50 points until 1982, another 16 years. During that period of course, we had rising inflation, we had interest rates going up, and the attention was shifted over to the bond market. People were saying, "I will buy longterm bonds because they used to yield 3% and then it was 5%, then 8%, and then 14%. So this constantly attracted money to the bond market rather than the stock market. The stock market went through a plateau period and then after we finished the plateau period, the market hit bottom in 1982. By that time inflation had slowed. All through this next period, inflation and interest rates came down because we had reached a secular peak in inflation. As a result of that, we had the big move in the stock market from 1982 to 1996. 1920-1921 was our peak of inflation during that period, and after we slowed the inflation in 1921, the market went up from 63 to 386 in 1929. This time it has taken longer because we are not on a gold standard anymore. We can print all the money we want now but back in the 1920's we couldn't do that, because we required 40% backing of our currency in gold.

In terms of a cycle, sixteen years seems to recur with amazing consistency.

Yes, we are in that same time frame again—15 to 16 years. I think the market may top out in late 1997.

Volume in general is one of the 17 components of your PTI?

Yes, that would be volume whether it be upside versus downside volume on a 10 day basis, 30 day basis, 60 day basis or the total trading volume. When we get through making the analysis of all of the factors concerning volume which is one factor in the PTI index, we say, "Okay, volume is now bullish or bearish." The STKS or ARMS index, developed by Richard Arms, is very valuable for shortterm work but then when you move it into the category of a six month rate of change, it becomes a valuable tool for the longer term aspects. But that still counts as just one factor. We can use the alphabet as an example. Let's say we use ABCD as the first factor and the EFGH as the second factor and so forth. We don't make a determination just based on A, or B, or C, or D. We have to look at all of those factors in the first four letters of the alphabet to make a decision as to how we want to rank that particular factor.

Is your work done on a weekly or daily closing basis?

We do it on a daily basis but there are weekly figures involved which we get out of *Barron's*. We follow how many stocks advanced and declined on a weekly basis, upside and downside volume for the week, and the weekly new highs and new lows and combine these with the daily figures.

Since your models are geared more for the intermediate to longer term time frame, how closely do you monitor the market on an intraday basis?

I have never found a way of making a calculation of our indexes based on what happened intraday. All of our work is calculated on the basis of closing prices but there is value in being alert to what's going on within the day. Let me give you an example. On July 15, 1996, the market had turned down very dramatically. It was down over 100 points. The next day it was down 165 points during the

Parabolic Blow Off Moves in Dow Jones Industrials 1919 to 1929 and 1974 to 1996

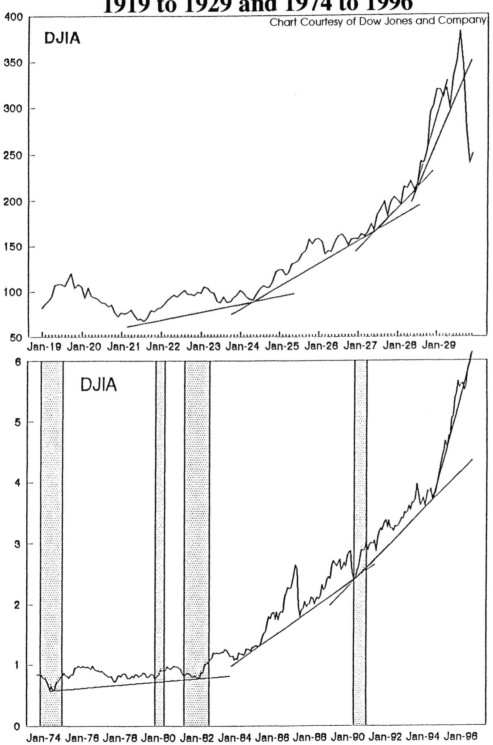

day. We looked at where the advances and declines were at that time and they were extremely negative. The highs and lows were extremely negative. We looked at the upside versus downside volume for that day which was 10:1 on the downside. We said this rubber band is going to snap back. We started calling clients. The market went down another two points before we could finish our calls, turned around and closed up 9 points for the day. The following week it went back down and tested the low by dropping 3 points below its previous low. Since then, we have rallied to a new high. On an hourly basis on July 16th, we were down 10% at one point in the day but then we closed up. We have to wait and see what happens at the end of the day for our indexes but we can make an occasional judgment call during the day to say buy or sell.

What are some of your GRTS (Get Ready to Sell) indicators?

New lows exceeding new highs would be one of the "Get Ready to Sell" signals. Certain moving averages that have dropped down below much longer term moving averages indicating that we are beginning to lose momentum would be another. Breadth would be a third. As I mentioned before, breadth normally peaks out before the market top. The exception to that was 1976-1977. The year to year rate of change would be another. We have been up 35% in the year and now we are up only about 17% against a year ago. This is the same sort of thing that happened in the early part of 1987, the early part of 1990, and almost throughout 1972 before the 1973 top. We are telling our clients to expect a major decline to start sometime in late1997 and are advising them to make their sell lists out early before we get to the top because when we get to the top this time, there aren't going to be many buyers on the way down.

Your GRTS components primarily include momentum and breadth indicators?

Yes, and volume. We have always had a peak in volume prior to the time that we have had a peak in prices. We have always had a peak in issues traded before we have had a peak in the stock market if the decline is going to be 20% or more.

You mentioned earlier the rate of change in upside versus downside volume? Do you calculate this on a weekly or monthly basis?

We normally use a time frame of six to twelve weeks and measure it on that basis to see if there is a definite trend developing. In July 1996 when the market turned around after being down 167 points we had a 680 million share day. Out of that volume, over 400 million shares were on the downside and less than 40 million were on the upside. That is a very big rubber band pull, something like a slingshot that turns the market around and pushes it back up again. If you use something like a 6, 12, or 25 day moving average on the rate of change in upside versus downside volume it might be helpful from a very shortterm viewpoint but it doesn't help too much for moves of more than 5%.

Is it helpful on a shortterm basis to look at the differences in the upside:downside volume?

I think it is but again, if you are trying to make a call on one day it has to be very extreme in order to qualify for a reversal move. You can stretch the rubber band a little bit and let it relax and stretch it and let it relax but when you really stretch it to the point where it almost breaks, that is the important consideration in so far as reversal moves. The purpose of moving averages is to try to get away from whipsaws on a single day's move. There is no question that single days are important, particularly when they become so extreme as they did on July 16, 1996.

Do you use any fundamental factors?

Some people refer to monetary and economic factors as fundamental, as I do. If you will notice, I mentioned nothing at all about P/E ratios, book value, dividend yields or anything like that. There are times that people completely ignore that sort of thing—normally when we are nearing the end of a secular bull market. This was very true in 1929 and it was true to some extent in 1987. In circumstances of extreme over and under valuations, concentration on the technical work is about the only way I see that you can possibly identify a top or a bottom accurately. What we have right now is a mania. We have a lot of people saying, "I don't care, I am going to put my money in the stock market because my friendly broker tells me I can get 9% a year and last year I got 35%." I said the same thing to myself in 1957 before I got killed.

When calculating the rate of change of particular economic indicators, what is the optimum time period to use—monthly, quarterly, or yearly?

We don't take a rate of change. We take the last three months and if the net of the last three months is down compared to the previous three months, that would be like 4, 3, and 2 compared to 3, 2, and 1 then we say that indicator has now turned down. Each month, when the figures come out, we take a look at the numbers of the eleven leading indicators. We rank each one as plus, minus or neutral. The indicators can change of course in one month. If you take these eleven indicators and divide them into 100, you get about 9 for each indicator. We convert this into percentage terms. If we had all of the eleven indicators moving upward, we would have roughly 100% (9% x 11). Right now we have ten out of the eleven expanding. The rate of change in manufacturer's unfilled orders is coming down a little bit so that would be ranked as negative or -1. We multiply the ten that are expanding times 9%, which equals 90%, and then subtract 9% for the one that is going down. We are at 81% expanding. Each month you just rank each indicator based on what the index has been doing over a three month period and then add them up. If everything is going up you get 100%. If they are all going down you have zero. It is just an oscillator if you will.

So the term "50% expanding" refers to the plurality of the eleven indicators which are still in positive territory?

Yes. If we had five of them going down and four of them going up, and two neutral we would be under 50%.

Looking at a rate of change on a yearly basis is not very helpful then?

I don't think so. The newspapers have a tendency to report that, "The average work week is now up above where it was a year ago," and most people think that is positive. Well, it still could be above where it was a year ago but the last three months may have been declining. The year to year rate of change is too long a period of time. The shorter term aspect is more important.

Could we go into the nuts and bolts of your leading, coincident, and lagging economic indicators?

When the Fed tightens, that immediately impacts the stock market but there is a time delay before it begins to impact the economy. It takes time for the economy to adjust to a change in Fed policy. Leading indicators are a measure of input to the economy, coincident indicators are a measure of output to the economy, and lagging indicators measure the excesses that build up in the economy. We have to monitor each individual factor in these economic indicators. Just slowing their pace could get us to 50% expanding because if none are expanding and none are contracting you would be in the 50% range. The leading indicators dropped rather rapidly in the first quarter of 1995 as a result of the Fed tightening in 1994. We came very close to having a recession in industrial sector of the economy in 1995. Then as they reversed that policy and eased, all the leading indicators recovered and turned back up again. As they did, the stock market stopped going down. In some cases certain leading indicators haven't reached the highs that they had earlier. The average work week here is considerably below the peak that we had in January 1995; however, it is still expanding. We don't know whether it is going to reach that peak. The second quarter of 1996 showed the average work week up 4.8% but the recovery was due to snowstorms, floods, government shutdown, and the General Motors strike. It is a concern of ours that we haven't been able to exceed the peak we had in 1995. That indicates a weak economy. Then when we look at vendor performance, it is saying that things are expanding. Deliveries are getting a little slower than they have been but we haven't reached anywhere near the number that we had in December 1994. When we look at sensitive price changes they dropped like a stone in 1995. They are nowhere near the high that we had in October 1994 but they are expanding and that is the important thing. As long as the leading indicators continue to expand and remain above 50% expanding, there is no chance that we are going to go into a recession. Now if the leading indicators start to flatten out or falter, that is, turning around and going down, that says the lead time before the coincident indicators start to go could be anywhere from three months to six months, and in some cases nine months. In the meantime, when the leading indicators begin to falter we have to monitor what is happening to the lagging indicators. When the lagging indicators start to move up and the leading indicators start to come down, we have the economy in a squeeze. That means there is a slow down in the *input to the economy* at a time when we are *building excesses* in the economy. So when the leading indicators drop below 50% expanding and the lagging indicators go up through 50% expanding, it says we are either going to have a mini-recession like 1966 or a very sharp slow down in industrial production the way we did in 1995, or we are actually going to go into a recession. You will hear from economists that *"the business indicators have correctly identified 11 of the last 6 recessions."* The business indicators make mistakes and we understand that but there has never been a recession without these things happening. We

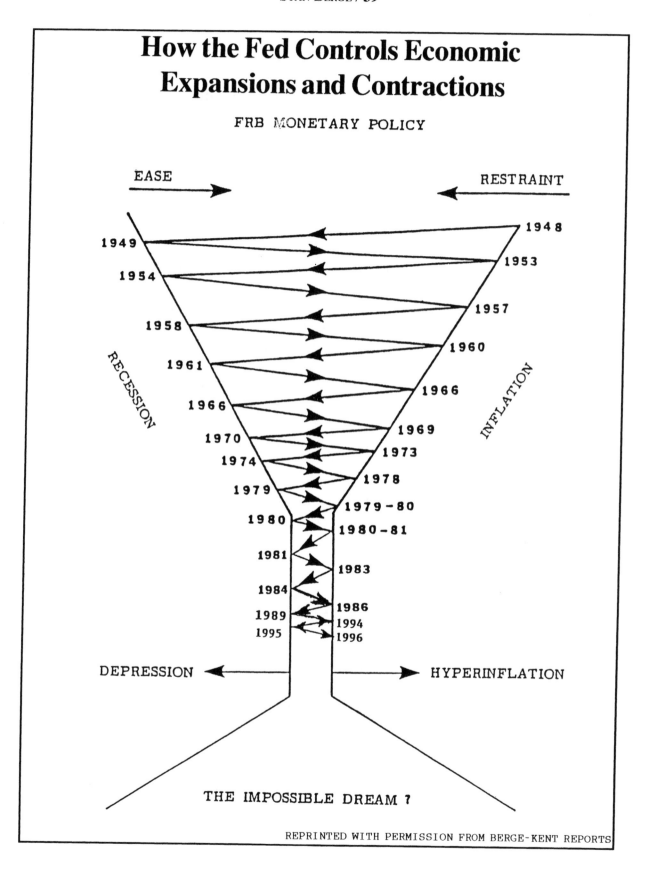

How the Fed Controls Economic Expansions and Contractions

FRB MONETARY POLICY

EASE →

← RESTRAINT

1949
1948
1954
1953
1957
1958
1960
RECESSION
1961
1966
INFLATION
1966
1969
1970
1973
1974
1978
1979
1979-80
1980
1980-81
1981
1983
1984
1986
1989
1994
1995
1996

DEPRESSION ←

→ HYPERINFLATION

THE IMPOSSIBLE DREAM ?

don't say once the leading indicators drop below 50% and the lagging go above 50% that we are going to have a recession. We look at a lot of other things too that would give us some idea of a recession. In other words, some of these things, like manufacturing and trade inventories as a ratio to sales, are not even in these indicators. When that starts to move up, it's saying not that inventories are too high but that sales are slowing down. We will put a lot of emphasis on things like this to come to a conclusion about what is happening in the economy. Of course, when the leading indicators start to come down through 50% expanding and the lagging indicators go up through 50% expanding, the coincident indicators haven't even gone down yet but the stock market begins to worry about it. That is why we get stock prices topping out most of the time before the recession starts—not always, but most of the time. There are times when the stock market has topped out at exactly the same time the recession has started, such as 1957 and 1990. Lead times vary.

Typically, does the stock market lead a recession or slowdown anywhere from 3 to 9 months?

Yes, I would say 3 to 9 months. We do know that during a presidential election period, the Federal Reserve tries to have the economy and the stock market up. We can then have our recessions after the elections. This is why we have the four year economic cycle and stock market bottoms in 1958, 1962, 1966, 1970, 1974, 1978, and 1982. 1987 was delayed because we had portfolio insurance which really didn't protect us from a 36% decline. There was another bottom in 1990. We came close to a recession in 1995. I expect that we will go into a recession in 1997, maybe 1998.

The four year business cycle seems to be a very accurate indicator.

It is a very reliable warning that you generally don't worry too much about recessions in a presidential election year. Of course, we did have a recession in 1960. After the elections are over we really start concentrating on the business indicators, the monetary policy, and the technical condition of the stock market.

What are your leading economic indicators?

The leading business indicators are essentially the kinds of things that are input to the economy. There are eleven leading indicators. This includes stock prices, average work week, consumer expectations, vendor performance, plant and equipment contracts, sensitive price changes, unfilled orders, new orders on consumer goods, unemployment claims, money supply, and building permits. Unfortunately there is always about a 2 month lag.

For clarification, you analyze your economic indicators in the context of a three month time frame even though the actual monthly figures could be higher or lower than they were six months to one year previously?

Yes. Now the government uses a six month span. I don't care for that too much because there is a delay in the trend changes. For the leading indicators, I get a little different reading than they do in a composite of

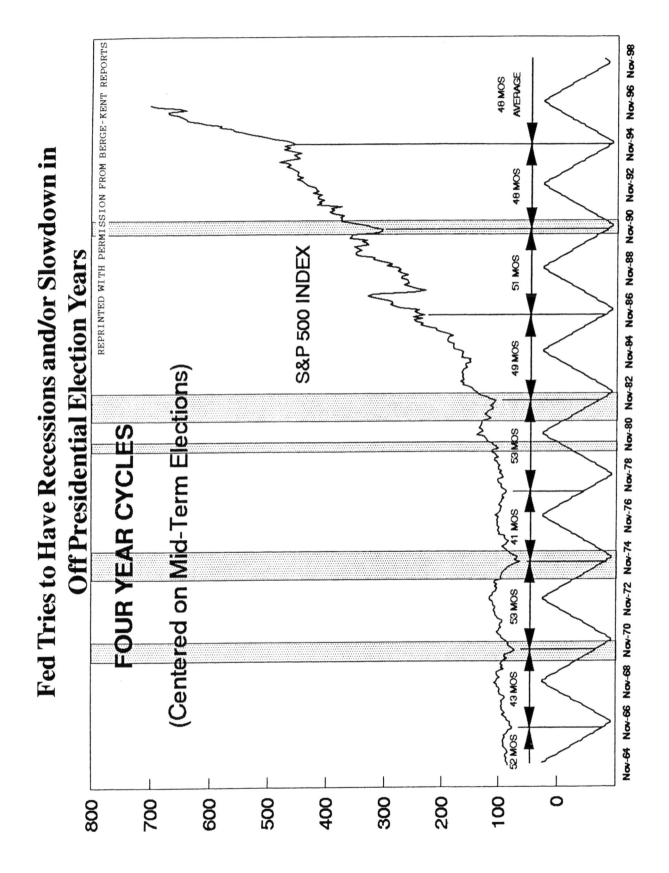

Fed Tries to Have Recessions and/or Slowdown in Off Presidential Election Years

FOUR YEAR CYCLES

(Centered on Mid-Term Elections)

S&P 500 INDEX

REPRINTED WITH PERMISSION FROM BERGE-KENT REPORTS

the diffusion indexes but I think it is more sensitive. On occasion I get a false signal because of a temporary influence—like a General Motors strike.

For example, would you look at the trend in the figures from June through September?

Yes, but then you average those and plot that for August. In other words, if you take the average of those three months, and plot it, you are really looking at something that supposedly occurred in August. Then what you have to do is ask, "What is the trend within these three months?" We have to go back 3 months and ask, "What was the number four months ago compared to what it is now?" The trend for the three month period is up but the trend for the monthly figure is starting to turn down compared to what it was four months ago. We are looking at both of these things so we can make a determination to say, "Yes, for this last three month period it is still up but the number for the past month compared to four months ago is lower." The number for the month we are deleting, June, was higher than the number we are adding, September, even though the three month trend is up. This is what's wrong with the statistics that compare what happened a year ago with today. Retail sales may be up 5% from where they were a year ago but if they are up only 2% from where they were last quarter, and last quarter they were at 4% and the quarter before that it was 6% and the quarter before that it was 8%; even though we are still up against a year ago, the trend is essentially down.

If the average work week lengthens, what is the implication?

If it lengthens, it means that a lot of corporations are employing people to work overtime so therefore business is very good. That was the case up until the end of 1994 when the Fed began to tighten. The average work week just fell apart because interest rates were going up. At the present time it is 41 which says we are working very little overtime right now. We are talking here about manufacturing hours, not service hours.

Are the hours broken down between manufacturing and service?

Yes, there is a difference between the work week for services and the work week for manufacturing.

Vendor performance sounds a little vague. Could you explain what that is?

Vendor performance figures essentially measure how long it takes for somebody to receive delivery after they place an order. If vendor performance is declining that means that manufacturers are able to meet more readily the demands of their customers—the delivery time is shortened. If the average work week begins to decline at the same time the vendor performance figures decline it is saying that the pipeline is backed up now to the point where at the end of the pipeline, people are cutting back. In other words, the consumer is saying, "I don't think I want to buy another new car." If that lasts long enough then it begins to impact the average work week because General Motors and Ford will have to cut back. When that happens, the vendor performance or delivery time, begins to improve. Steel may deliver within shorter time frames to the automobile manufacturers because the demand has begun to slacken. When all of these things begin to impact the leading indicators and they all roll over, and the lagging indicators are all going up, this is bad news for the economy. Of the leading indicators, I consider the average work week and vendor performance to be the most important.

What is the normal range for the average work week?

The highest we have had in the last 40 years was at the end of 1994. It plunged right after that from a little over 42 down to 40 in January 1996, which was hurt badly by snowstorms, the government shutdown, and the General Motors strike. Unions don't go on strike when the economy is bad because they are worried about their jobs. They strike when business is humming along.

Let's hypothetically assume we are emerging from a recession and suddenly orders pick up. Businesses who laid people off have not had a chance to re-hire. Wouldn't this situation also produce a large gap in delivery time?

Yes. During a recession, vendor performance is always very low and shipments can be made quickly. Manufacturers have the inventory and they want to ship a product the very next day so they can get paid. When the recession ends, demand picks up and it takes time to hire people and get them trained—to get output running as fast as demand. For a while it doesn't happen and vendor performance shows slower deliveries because they can't build fast enough to meet the demand. When I was with General Electric, this is one of the reasons I advocated expanding capacity or renovating equipment during a recession. Prices will be lower and there will be less interruptions to your plant. Don't expand after the economy has expanded for a long time because then we are coming to the end of a move where orders have picked up and it is going to take longer to get deliveries. When vendor performance starts to turn down it means that the pipeline is full and manufacturers are able to make deliveries in less time. It is a valuable tool to watch because when it starts to go down, it is warning us that the economy is going to slow down.

If the vendor performance numbers are increasing, can that be interpreted as bullish for the economy?

That is saying that the demand is so great for a product that the supplier can't get it out fast enough. As a result of that, we start to get a build up of unfilled orders.

Are there any normal numerical ranges for vendor performance?

No, I don't think so. It varies all over the place. On a diffusion index, it reached a high of 95% in 1973 just before the recession started in November 1973. In other words, this is saying that deliveries are getting slower and slower relative to when people placed the order. It is saying that 95% of the deliveries are coming in slower. Now just before the recession ended we came down to about 15%. In other words, if you called someone up and said, "I need 10,000 widgets," they would be on your doorstep the next day. These people had inventories they couldn't liquidate. Low inventories mean slower delivery. High inventories mean faster delivery. When inventories to sales are low, the economy is expanding fairly close to peak capacity. The Fed moves in to slow things down before problems start to occur, otherwise we will have inflation and high interest rates.

Would you define diffusion index?

It is very similar to the work that we do on the Primary Trend Index except that it applies not to the stock market but the economy. There are eleven leading business indicators. You rank each one if it's bullish, neutral, or bearish. If all eleven are going up you obviously have 100% expanding. If they are all going down, you would have a -11, so that would be zero. That is the diffusion index.

Can your eleven leading economic indicators be individually classified as leaders or laggards?

Not really, it varies all over the lot. For instance, in April 1960, vendor performance topped out over a year before the economy went into a recession. If you look at the recession of 1973-1974, vendor performance topped out after the recession started. So you can see the lead times are quite variable and they wouldn't be reliable. It is the weight of the evidence, so to speak, that tells you whether you are in a declining economic situation or an expanding one.

How many coincident economic indicators do you follow?

I use the four business cycle indicators put out by the Conference Board. These are the same indicators the government uses to identify when a recession starts and ends. One is industrial production, another is manufacturing and trade sales. The third is personal income less transfer payments; in other words, they back transfer payments out on the basis that it is not considered personal income. The last one is the number of employees on non-agricultural payrolls. Most of the time, but not all of the time, these indicators turn down or flatten out at the beginning of the recession. Lead time is virtually nonexistent. A recession starts when these four turn down and ends when these four turn back up again. Currently, they are all at the highest levels in history. These indicators are of no great importance to us from the viewpoint of predicting what the stock market is going to do. Most of the time the stock market will top out before these four factors turn down.

Do you pay attention to capacity utilization?

No, not particularly. When it is very high, labor is in relatively short supply and we see all kinds of price increases. A high capacity utilization rate worries the Federal Reserve because we are getting close to a peak in the economy. That is when interest rates go up. The capacity utilization rate now has dropped from 85% in late 1994 to about 82% now and it has been moving sideways since the first of the year. The fact that it is down below its 1994 peak and hasn't been able to get back up to it, and probably won't, is a warning that we are headed toward some sort of recession. Now, if it were to turn around and go back up through 85% or 86% from the current 82%, then I would say that would have to come down before we have a recession. We are not going to have a recession with capacity utilization up above 85% and under those circumstances the Fed might tighten. Excess capacity also develops by an increase in capital spending on new plant and equipment but as I said, people generally expand capacity pretty close to the top of the business cycle because that is when business is most profitable. The peak in the capacity utilization rate is about 90% and that was back in 1973 just before that recession. It eventually dropped to about 72%. Capacity utilization almost always tops out before the recession starts. The only exception to that was in November 1973.

High capacity utilization translates into higher prices for consumers?

Yes. If business is very good, you can have two things happen. One is that prices can rise. Number two is that you can have rising wage rates.

What are the lagging indicators that you follow?

Labor costs, consumer price index (CPI), producer price index (PPI), inventories, and the prime rate charged by banks. The lagging indicators are measures of excesses developing in the economy. As lagging indicators rise, it means that the economy is going to find it more and more difficult to grow because of the rise in bank loans, a rise in the inventory to sales ratio, labor costs, interest rates, inflation, and things of that nature. That becomes a deterrent to economic expansion so that then becomes negative. Consumer installment credit to personal income is a lagging indicator and it is at the highest level in history right now which is scary. People have used their credit card to buy food and things they want for their home while putting their savings and 401 K's into the stock market. When the stock market goes down, they are going to be pressured to sell stocks in order to pay off their debt. If they do it soon enough they will be all right. If they don't, they may be bankrupt.

Are you using installment credit because it excludes mortgage debt?

Yes. Lately, delinquencies have been going up while we are in an economic expansion. This is not a good sign. What's going to happen when we go into an economic contraction? The problem that we are running into now is very similar to what we ran into in 1929. Then, people were going into debt and their means of paying off that debt were their savings they put in the stock market. That is why there were so many bankruptcies and why the recession lasted so long. People couldn't pay off their bank debt. Bank loans were extinguished and that extinguished the money supply. The money supply contracted from September 1929 all the way into the bottom of 1932. I hope something like that doesn't happen but the only way that I see it can be prevented is by the Fed going to the printing press and if they do, you better own some gold stocks. If the government tries to reflate the situation this way they will depreciate the dollar. When people start to worry about the value of the currency or the banking system, they are apt to hoard currency. Each time we have more inflation in the money supply figures, the worse it is going to get.

Is a contraction in the money supply recessionary?

I think so, although a lot of money formally held by banks has now gone into money market funds. If interest rates take a big dive that normally would correspond with an increase in the money supply. Since the 1990 bottom, this has been one of the most sluggish recoveries that we have ever had after a recession and is very similar to what happened after 1927. We had very little real solid growth from the mid-1920's to 1929. As I mentioned before, we were going through that transition period from an agricultural economy to an industrial economy. It took time to accomplish this after the great inflation of 1920-1921. Of course, we finished a period of great inflation in 1980-1981. When the market hit bottom in 1982, we were in a decided downtrend in longterm government bond yields and corporate rates. The stock market was a more attractive place to put money, just as it was after the 1920-1921 period. But when we got into the latter part of the 1920's, there was very little expansion of the money supply and the economy was very sluggish. The Fed dropped the discount rate in 1927 and then raised it a few times going into 1929. About a month or two after they made the last increase in rates in 1929, just before the 1929 stock market top, the Fed turned around and started to loosen which brought rates down all the way into 1932. The Fed doubled Federal Reserve credit in 1930 and 1931 but by that time it was too late. They couldn't get things going. So we had a situation where the funds were available but the banks wouldn't lend to the credit risk individuals or corporations. That is the way the system finally breaks down. People with debt can't borrow money and people who don't have debt don't want any loans. That is essentially what I think is going to happen again. I am looking over my shoulder every minute because I am very worried about late 1997 and 1998.

Lagging economic indicators and leading economic indicators move inversely, right?

That's correct. The leading indicators go up first, the coincident indicators go up next, and the lagging indicators come up last. On the way down, the leading indicators go down first, the coincident go down second, and the lagging indicators come down generally very close to the end of the recession.

How does the inventory to sales ratio fit into your economic model?

The inventory to sales ratio will start to go up when sales start to dry up. You will hear a lot of people saying inventories are under control. They are under control as long as sales stay up. If inventories are increasing at about the same rate as sales, then the inventory to sales ratio will flatten. When it turns up, it is a warning. It isn't a case that inventories are out of line. It is a case of sales, the denominator of this equation, starting to slow. Manufacturers have too much inventory relative to their sales. When this happens the inventory to sales ratio will turn up.

Is unemployment a lagging indicator?

It is more of a coincident indicator. It is related to some extent to what is happening in the average work week. As the average work week goes down, people are going to get laid off so the unemployment rate will start to go up. When the unemployment rate starts up the economy has already topped out and it is too late to use this indicator for the stock market.

Given that the PPI and CPI figures are lagging indicators, wouldn't the CRB provide much earlier clues of inflation?

I think so.

Earlier you referred to sensitive price changes as one of the leading indicators. Would you define sensitive price changes?

Commodity type things like crude oil. The CRB index is the one that we use more than any other to try and determine what is going on with commodities. Obviously there are going to be fluctuations. One of the things that has been very helpful in the past was the price of copper. When copper prices got very high, we were near the top of an economic expansion. When they were very low we were near the end of the recession. I haven't followed it for years. In the 1920's, people used inner tubes in automobile tires. When the demand for inner tubes declined it meant that there were going to be some problems insofar as the economy was concerned.

Any increase in commodity prices will translate into higher prices for the end product?

Most of the time that's right and that keeps the CPI going up. The wholesale price index or the producer price index moves first and then after it has been going up for a while, we would expect to see the CPI going up also. Sometimes there is a temporary blip. When we had the Gulf War, oil prices went up and then came right back down after the war was over.

Is it worthwhile to analyze some of the economic figures in context with previous historical highs and lows?

I think that it makes a lot of sense to do that. For instance, when initial claims for unemployment rises it is bearish for the economy. Initial unemployment claims always reaches a high right near the end of the recession. These claims are plotted inversely on the charts. This peaked in 1969. At that time, about 200,000 people were seeking unemployment insurance whereas now we have 350,000 unemployment claims. Here is a case where something has been going down now on a chart for a period of almost 30 years, which means in actual terms it is going up because it is inverted. I hate to think of what it's going to be like in 1998. I can see that figure going to maybe 700,000 or 800,000.

Natural disasters and strikes obviously act as an unexpected stimulant on the economy. How long does it take for these effects to filter down through the economy and what are the long-term economic consequences?

I would say it takes about six months, sometimes a little longer, for the rebuilding process to pass through the economy. Keep in mind that it also represents a consumption of capital. The balance sheets of insurance companies start to deteriorate a little bit. The individual who doesn't have any insurance has to replace his home so his ability to purchase goods goes down. Let's say I have $500.00 and decide to buy a new suit, shirt, tie and pair of shoes. I find out that when I go in to buy, prices have just gone up 10%. This is all the money I have so I will have to forget maybe the pair of shoes. Inflation is defined as a rapid rise in money supply. As a result of that we get rising prices. Rising prices are not inflation but everybody accepts that as inflation. If the Fed is unable to expand the money supply and you have these disasters hitting, the money supply is going to decrease.

Do you follow the figures on imports and exports?

No, I don't follow them at all but from a technical viewpoint, investor responses to these reports will show up in the action of stocks.

Let's say investors don't have time to track all of the leading, coincident, and lagging indicators that you keep. Could they use the monthly figures from the National Association of Purchasing Managers (NAPM) as a reasonably good gauge of economic activity?

That would be helpful but they ought to subscribe to *Business Cycle Indicators* put out by the Conference Board. It comes out once a month and is very reasonable at $120.00 per year for first class mail service. In this particular issue I am looking at, they talk about the cyclical indicator approach. It has explanations on how composite indexes are weighted. It also has all of the charts of the leading indicators and coincident indicators—employment, unemployment, sales, orders, wages, consumer attitudes, capital investment, and things of that nature.

You consider *Business Cycle Indicators* a good source of data?

I would say that it is an excellent source of data. It certainly would be worthwhile for people to subscribe to this. When I decided to leave industry and go into the brokerage business, I got everything I could possibly put my hands on about Fed policy and I also subscribed to this.

Reading economic textbooks is not compulsory?

I don't think so. I think if they study this booklet they are going to get an education. It would be a redundancy to do anything else. Some of the economic preaching out of Harvard and other schools is very socialist. It is not really what we can call the free enterprise or capitalistic system. Henry Hazlitt, whom I met twenty years ago, wrote *Economics in One Lesson*. This is a good book and the 15th anniversary edition is out with a forward by Steve Forbes. There is a marvelous book written by Michael Novak called *Business As a Calling*. It is subtitled, *Michael Novak Tells Why Capitalism is Essential for Free, Democratic and Virtuous People.* What he says essentially is that if people want to be free in a democratic society they have to support the capitalistic system because it is this system that created the wealth for the majority of people in the United States. The other book that I like is one by a very smart guy named Tom Sowell. I happen to agree with him so well, that's why I think he is great. He has a book out titled *Knowledge and Decisions.* The subtitle is, *Why Government Makes Bad Decisions*.

Are there any final comments you would like share with readers?

Now having told you all of the foregoing, I want to repeat something I always tell our clients—"I may be wrong, but I don't want to be misunderstood."

Ralph Bloch

Market Commentary on Long Term Treasury Bond

February 15, 1996

Using pure and simple technical analysis, an argument can be made that it has been taking on the configuration of a multiple "head and shoulders" top. Another pattern, not that it really matters, would be a symmetrical triangle. The bottom line would be if bonds closed at 118¾ or lower—that would complete a distribution pattern, which suggests a shot at 116-116½.

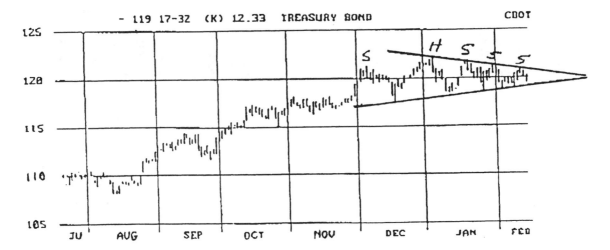

Ralph Bloch is chief technical analyst at Raymond James and Associates. He began his career on Wall Street in 1956 entering Merrill Lynch's Junior Executive training program along with fellow classmate Jack Hemingway. During this early period as a trainee, he watched the financial markets recover from a 20% bear market despite the fact that the country was still in the midst of an economic recession. Puzzled by this incongruity, he eventually reached the conclusion that "the primary purpose of the stock market is to anticipate and discount the future." It was this revelation which prompted him to later choose technical analysis over fundamental analysis. His very first introduction to technical analysis came from an older gentleman at Merrill Lynch who spent his days charting commodity prices by hand. Taking Ralph under his wing, he passed on the techniques of charting. This first glimpse into the world of technical analysis made a great deal more sense than anything else he had been exposed to thus far in the trainee program. From that time on, he has focused his attention on technical analysis although admittedly, he prefers that the fundamentals confirm the technicals. In that way, it *improves your odds of being right.*

I would describe Mr. Bloch as a technical "purist." He doesn't clutter his analysis with a multitude of indicators. The scope of his work is limited to about six indicators which he uses in conjunction with tape reading. Evidence suggests that he is one of the last souls practicing the dying art of tape reading. He scoffs at new-fangled indicators and sophisticated computer software analysis programs. In fact, he so wholeheartedly endorses and believes in the effectiveness of Technical Analysis 101 that he issues the challenge that he will match his record with anybody on Wall Street. In his estimation, analysts who follow hundreds of indicators are deliberately avoiding a decision. It is this paucity of indicators which I believe accounts for his success. His simple and basic approach makes him immune from "analysis paralysis," a condition of mental immobility resulting from too many indicators generating conflicting signals.

Mr. Bloch's track record is outstanding. He hasn't made a major mistake calling market turns during his ten year tenure with Raymond James. Of all the technicians interviewed, Mr. Bloch is the only one I have met personally, and that was nearly ten years ago. In 1987, while visiting St. Petersburg, Florida, I made an appointment to meet Mr. Bloch. As it turned out, that visit had great significance for me. I sat outside his office waiting for him to finish penning his weekly newsletter titled "Sell New Highs." His bearish views on the market during our conversation prompted me to immediately place a call to my broker selling every share of stock I owned. That day was August 20, 1987. The exact market top occurred four days later, on August 25, 1987. Precisely catching the August 1987 top was a remarkable feat in my opinion. After the crash of 1987, while popular gurus of the time were calling for Dow 400 and 1200, Mr. Bloch went against majority opinion four days after the October 1987 low declaring that the broader market had finished its decline. He was on the money. The list goes on. He called the July 1990 stock market top. In October of that same year, he reversed course 180 degrees. Despite the pessimistic national tone surrounding the United States' controversy with Iraq and subsequent military confrontation, Ralph Bloch was so bullish in October of 1990 that "he couldn't see straight." Most recently, he locked horns with prominent bond traders and analysts calling for a bear market in bonds in February 1996. The consensus had bond yields pegged to decline between 5 ½% and 5 ¾%. What edge did Ralph have over the thousands of brilliant minds on Wall Street? Technical Analysis 101. He simply spotted the textbook formation of a multiple head and shoulders distribution pattern. His call proved to be accurate. Five months later in July 1996, he became bullish shortterm and issued a "get ready to buy" signal on bonds based on an inverse head and shoulders pattern. Bonds broke through the neckline at 110 and took

Market Commentary on Long Term Treasury Bond

August 1, 1996

For four months, the long bond market has been in a pattern of accumulation known as a multiple head and shoulders bottom. This long trading range, bounded by roughly 106 on the low end and 110 at the high end, has broken the downtrend that has been in place since February of this year.

The 110 area of resistance has turned the bond market back on four separate occasions this year. A breakout above this 110 area would suggest an initial measured move to 112½-113. This bottom is almost a mirror image of the top in the bond market that developed in late 1995—early 1996, before its drop.

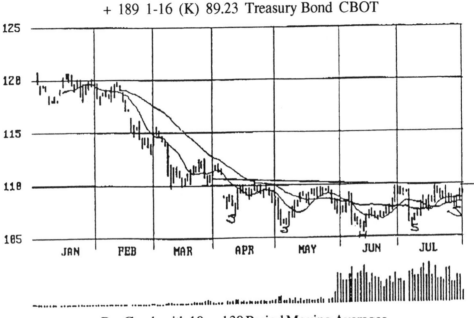

Bar Graph with 10 and 30 Period Moving Averages

off with great momentum to the upside just as he finished sending his "buy on the break above 110" message across the wire. You can't get much closer than that.

This dual play in bonds aptly demonstrates two things. Number one is that technical analysis is alive and well and two, don't get locked into longterm forecasts. He avoids longterm forecasts like the plague because psychologically they lock you into a mind-set which is often inescapable. Long term forecasting is the precise mechanism that entraps so many gurus, derailing their credibility when such forecasts never materialize. They become "locked into a situation where they have a vested interest which ultimately clouds good judgment." Take the downfall of prominent analysts as a warning. If you find yourself dogmatically adhering to your own preconceived notions of what the markets "should" do, you are headed for trouble. Inflexibility can destroy you financially. According to Mr. Bloch, neither "technical analysis or any other discipline has the tools to make longterm calls." Thus his reasoning behind focusing on the shortterm picture and calling the shots from day to day as he sees them. Go with what the tape, trend, and charts are telling you.

Always the contrarian, Mr. Bloch recalls that the best market calls he ever made were contrary opinion calls. His view is "the market has been placed here to confound and confuse the majority and accommodate the minority." Contrarians usually comprise the minority; therein lies his comfort in being a contrarian.

At Raymond James, Mr. Bloch writes a daily market letter which is disseminated internally among brokers and traders. For the firm's clients, he produces a weekly market letter titled the *Bloch Letter*, which is an encapsulation of the week's daily market activity as well as his short term views on the market. His market views also appear weekly in Mansfield's Chart Service. He is unique in that he is probably the only technical analyst with a major brokerage firm who still writes on a daily basis. Though these daily commentaries create extra work for him, he finds that they produce a psychologically different attitude toward analyzing the markets. This daily routine is an asset in terms of producing discipline and forces him to be accountable for his predictions. As he puts it, when you are in print every day, your predictions are exposed and "you don't have any place to hide." Writing also helps him develop and maintain a feel for what is happening in the market.

Mr. Bloch has quite a few literary achievements to his credit. He was an original contributor to the *Encyclopedia of Stock Market Techniques* and at the request of the *Financial Times* of London, wrote a chapter on the put/call ratio for their book *The Global Guide to Investing.* One year ago, he wrote *Technical Tactics for Investing,* a booklet that outlines twenty do's and don'ts for successful stock market investing. Some of the questions in this interview are derived from information in his booklet. While this booklet is currently distributed only to clients of Raymond James, it may be reprinted and made available publicly at a future date. Mr. Bloch has made guest appearances on CNBC and is called upon frequently by major financial newspapers and magazines for his market commentary. He speaks at seminars worldwide and gained such recognition and popularity in France that they decided to feature him on the magazine cover of *La Vie Francaise.*

The dialogue in this interview reveals the select few indicators Mr. Bloch follows and also stresses the significance of the psychology of investing. In his opinion, one's psychology is equally, if not more important than one's methodology. Having the right indicators and tools is only half of the equation. The other half is understanding your emotions. I would point out that the indicators mentioned are to be used in conjunction with one another and are not designed to be used or interpreted singularly. Forget pinning Mr. Bloch down to specific parameters when it comes to the interpretation of the indicators he uses. Technical analysis is an art, not a science. His market expertise has been derived from nothing less than years of practice and experience watching price and volume movement minute by minute, hour by hour, and day by day. As a refresher course on the tactics of tape reading, he will periodically read his favorite financial book, ***Reminiscences of a Stock Operator*** by Edwin Lefevre. As for the interpretation of chart patterns, he refers readers to the best source—Edwards and Magee's ***Technical Analysis of Stock Trends.***

With over forty years of market experience to his credit and an intense passion for his work, Mr. Bloch aspires to be the "George Burns of Wall Street." Although he views his goal purely in terms of longevity, I found his sense of humor to be on a par with that of Mr. Burns.

For those who desire to simplify their analytical approaches but have reservations about relinquishing their dependence on so many indicators, fear not. Mr. Bloch is a living testimonial that the "KISS" (Keep It Simple Stupid) approach works. Further, he has the track record and net worth to prove it.

How did you get started in technical analysis?

I realized that Wall Street is not a world of numbers. Think about it. If Wall Street had nothing else to do but numbers, everybody would pretty much come to the same conclusion. Stock X's earnings are this, their sales are this, the multiple is this, the outlook looks pretty good for Stock X. Go out and buy it except there is one problem. Everybody is dealing with the same set of facts. If numbers were the only ingredient in stock market analysis, the people who are long the stock would be seeing the same thing. Why would they sell it? In effect, you wouldn't have an auction market. Nobody every thinks of that.

Having said that, you do want the fundamental picture to confirm the technical picture, right?

Yes, I do. What is a chart? All a chart is are people's perceptions of what they think the fundamentals are when they put their money where their mouth is.

That is the best and most unique definition I have ever heard.

It's original. When they put their money where their mouth is, that's when technical analysis takes place. They create volume and they create price movement. If I can find out that the fundamentals on stock X look attractive, I have improved my odds a little bit. Both disciplines, technical and fundamental, confirm one another.

What do you look at in regard to fundamental analysis?

We have in-house coverage. If our in-house research department doesn't follow a stock, then I go to an outside source for the information. After 40 years in the business, there isn't a research department on Wall Street that I can't get into for a quick opinion. I don't need an in-depth analysis. All I need to know is does a decent analyst like it or not like it. What I don't understand is why most fundamentalists don't check with the technicians. There is an opening joke which I often use when I speak. There is an American taking a leisurely auto vacation on the back roads of New Zealand. He has to stop his car because there is this huge herd of sheep crossing the road. The shepherd walks over to the American and says, "it will be a few minutes and they will be across the road." The American said, "I am in no rush." They start to chat and the American looks at the herd and says to the shepherd, "I'd like to make you a bet." The shepherd says, "What?" The American said, "I bet I can guess exactly how many sheep you have in your herd." The shepherd says, "I don't think so, this is the largest herd in New Zealand, but if you want to make the bet, fine. If you should win what do you get?" The American said, "I love lamb, I get one of your sheep to keep." The shepherd says, "Fine. I will just tell you that I have five grades of sheep, from the lowest quality to the finest quality. Go ahead." The American walks around and comes back a little while later and says "You have 10,248 sheep in your herd." The shepherd goes nuts. "That's exactly right," he said, "How did you know?" The American said, "I am very good with numbers." The shepherd said,

"Pick your sheep." The American looks around and points to the back and said, "I'll take that one." The shepherd walks over, picks it up, and starts to bring it to his car. The shepherd then said, "I'd like to make you a bet in turn." The American said, "What?" The shepherd said, "I bet I can guess your occupation." The American thinks, gee I have never been to New Zealand before and there have to be a million occupations on this planet. He'll never guess. "If you are right what do you get?" asked the American. The shepherd replied, "I'll get my sheep back." "It's a bet," said the American. The shepherd looks at him and says, "You're a Wall Street Securities Analyst." The American goes crazy and said, "How did you know that?" The shepherd said, "It was really quite simple. You are obviously very good with numbers and then you picked the worst one." Why can't the fundamental analysts go to the technicians and ask, "Do the technicals match my perception of the fundamentals?" Most of them don't. I think fundamental analysts and technical analysts should work together.

For those who don't have such connections in high places, what's the next best thing?

They can do business with a full-service brokerage firm like Raymond James or use a service such as Standard and Poor's or Value Line.

You were quoted in Investors Business Daily as saying "Technical analysis is a tool for short term planning. It is a mistake to use it for anything longer." What did you mean by this?

I don't believe technical analysis has the tools to make a long term call. And then again, neither does any other discipline. People just think they can do that. Clients and reporters constantly want to know "where do you think Stock X or the market is going?" My answer is, "I don't know where it is going in terms of points." Then they ask, "How long do you think it will take?" I say, "How the hell does anybody know that." Nobody knows. My job, as a technical analyst, is very simple. I tell our brokers, and in turn our clientele, the market is healthy or not healthy day by day and go through the reasons why. I think I am better able to do this than my contemporaries because I am the only one who writes every day. Some of the analysts out there get locked into a long term call and they have a vested interest in the call. People who make long term calls usually go down with the ship. "I'm right, the tape is wrong." Even 100 years ago, Jesse Livermore knew the same thing- The tape is never wrong, we are frequently wrong. Why is that so difficult to understand?

What are some of the advantages of technical analysis?

Technical analysis does a pretty good job of outlining to you a market that may be in the process of changing direction. Most of the money is made and lost in markets changing direction. People tend to stay with the pre-existing trend too long. The 1982-1987 bull market was never going to end and when it did end, the 1987 bear market was never going to end. One prominent analyst was looking for a continuation of the decline to 400; another was looking for 1200. If you are going to buy something, technical analysis can help you with a decent entry point. One thing I insist is that technical analysis will get you out 99 out of 100 times before the fundamentals will. The fundamentalist needs to see something change. By the time he sees the numbers change, the stock is down 20% because people are always anticipating.

Anticipating what?

If I am going to make money in a stock, I have to pay $50, and I have to hope you pay 50 1/8 and Charlie pays 50 1/4 and so on. How do I get in ahead of you? I make certain assumptions about the future from a fundamental point of view. If the fundamentals are good and institutions are believing it, they will behave in very repetitive patterns. If a fund manager is going to go out and buy a million shares of stock, he can't put down an order, "Buy me a million shares."

Because an order that size will drive the price up?

Yes. He buys 25,000. He buys 50,000. He stops. Maybe he will let the offer build up again. All of this is reflected in chart patterns as accumulation or distribution. All of the people who were bullish from January to June of 1996 because of all the money coming into mutual funds weren't looking at the next step. OK, we got 123 billion bucks in the first six months of 1996, what did it do? The answer was it did nothing after the first 400 point run within 13 days from late January to February. It was being met by selling. You had all these rallies with token new highs then a sell off, token new highs then a sell off. That is distribution. The problem is as a technician you never know how long this stuff takes to unfold. That is why it pays to write every single day. That's the way you build your case.

For the benefit of those who may not get to read the wisdom of your booklet, what is the markets primary role in life?

To anticipate and discount the future. This is what I learned in the 1957-1958 period. The market did things then that were not explicable to my satisfaction and is what really sent me into the world of technical analysis. Why did the market drop 20% in August 1957 while we were in an economic recovery, back and fill, and then start to rally while the economy was still in a recession? The market fell because it anticipated the recession and then the rally anticipated the recovery. Not a difficult concept once you let it into your mind.

So a current stock price or market index level won't always mesh with the fundamental realities of the situation at the time.

Let me give you an example. A fundamental analyst comes to me and says he has just visited company X. It looks like a great buy. He rattles off a half dozen reasons, all of which make sense to me. I go to my chart. I see the stock in a free fall. What's reality? Obviously the free fall is reality. I come to one of two conclusions. Either the analyst is wrong or because the analyst is good, he or she is early. How do I know when to buy this stock if it is a good early call? Simple. I see the stock ending its decline and starting to undergo a pattern of accumulation—a rally, then a sell-off, a rally then a sell-off producing higher highs and higher lows.

What was one of your most memorable trades related to a stock's price anticipating the future?

IBM in 1993. The stock had fallen from around 172 in 1987 and the fundamentals were terrible. The bottom in IBM took 4 months to unfold. It stopped 3 times over a four month period at 46 3/8. I bought options on IBM the minute it printed 46 ½ and it's still moving up. It was textbook.

I have seen IBM produce some great textbook charts before.

Correct. This is a classic example of why I like to stay with big name, big cap stocks because they do perform better technically than low-priced stocks.

What is the theory behind large cap companies rendering more classic chart patterns? Is it because of the institutional influence?

Yes, it is very, very important. Institutional money managers tend to behave in very repetitive manners.

When looking at charts of individual stocks is there a particular time period you prefer using?

My initial work is done on the daily chart. Most of the time a six month chart should give you enough technical information for the trade. If not, I will go to a weekly two year chart to see whether there is a larger picture at work. For example, I was looking recently at Kellogg. Cereal prices have been coming down. If you look at the daily chart, you will see a small head and shoulders top pattern forming. Probably a close below 72 or 72½ would complete this small top which would measure you down to about 70. Then I went to the two year weekly chart. Looking at the weekly chart, you see a much larger potential head and shoulders pattern at work that has to break beneath 70. So you have a small picture within a larger picture. If you are dealing with a market or a stock that may be in the process of changing direction from bull to bear or bear to bull, the weekly chart sometimes gives you a much better long term picture. But once a stock has broken out and is in a good uptrend or a good downtrend, six months is enough because then you are dealing with a trend. Let's say a stock has a breakout. What will you be looking for? The first flag pattern- the first pause after the initial breakout. There should be two, three, or four days of this flag-type pattern. Buyers have stopped. Few sellers are in there. Volume dries up into the flag. You know it's going to start again because there weren't any real sellers and the buyers just paused because the stock had a run. Look for a flag or pennant pattern. In a downtrend, you are looking for the same thing.

Can you spot potentially problematic overhead resistance on a 6 month chart?

Very often you can. You know when that shows up a lot? In a period like this where the Dow has fallen 7½ %, NASDAQ has fallen almost 20%, and you are now getting some rally tries. In my June 13, 1996 Mansfield issue, the title was "Raise DJIA Stops." In the conclusion of that issue I said, "aggressive trading accounts should sell some stock if the Dow closes beneath 5650. If it then closes beneath 5600, you want to sell more stock." If you were in the tech stocks and you sold when it cracked 5650 and sold more and more size at 5600, then you got out well in the tech stocks.

Didn't the tech stocks, on a technical basis, turn over and head down before the Dow did?

Sure they did but you still got out a lot better than where they eventually went to, which is what technical analysis is supposed to do. Now, if you look at a bunch of the tech stocks you will see many of them banging into supply pretty soon at their respective equivalents of 5650 and 5600.

If you look at a six month chart but you don't see any resistance, will you keep going further back until you find some?

I'll go back to a two year chart. Much beyond that I have some doubts whether support or resistance is very effective. My overall view on something like that is that those levels have probably already been taken out.

I use Mansfield's' three year charts and it is surprising how stocks will rally and meet overhead resistance from two years prior and then back off a little bit, even after that length of time.

Absolutely. The real question evolving in all of these questions and one which I try to think about every day is "where do I think I am in the overall market?" 1993 was a choppy uptrend—a technician's dream. Buy the dips and sell the flips. If I am in a choppy uptrend, I am in what I call a "rape and pillage" market. I am going to buy it, hope I'm right, take the initial shot out, and I'm gone. If I am in 1995, I am dealing with a fully in gear stock market. By that I mean the Dow Industrials are running, the Transports are in gear making new highs, NASDAQ's confirming and very important, the advance/decline index is confirming. It is kind of an expanded version on the Dow theory. When a market is fully in gear you are in more of a buy and hold market. The first question is "where do you think you are in the overall market trend?" That helps me decide my trading posture. Rape and pillage—I'm in and out. Buy and hold—I'm liable to stay a little bit longer.

Given that the majority of stocks tend to move with the overall market, do you ever try to buck the trend?

It's crazy. In a downtrend somebody will ask me, "Is there anything that looks good?" Even if I think there is, my response is "The stock market is a place of percentages." One of the signs signaling the end of a lengthy decline is when the strong stocks finally start to break down. If you believe Wall Street is a place of percentages and you think you are in a legitimate downtrend, why are you looking for that one stock or one group that could buck it? Why don't you go with the trend? There's the old saying, "When the cops raid the brothel, they take the piano player." That poor guy wasn't doing anything but entertaining the customers. He wasn't breaking any laws but they are going to take him anyway. It's a perfect analogy. You have to stay with the percentages. The rules of Wall Street intellectually are very simple—adhering to them is almost impossible.

You mentioned the flag pattern earlier. What are some of your other favorite chart patterns?

The classic ones. All chart patterns are what? They are either accumulation patterns, continuation patterns, or distribution patterns—no mystery. The flag or pennant pattern is the continuation of a trend already in force. They are among the most reliable of patterns. The most popular pattern—I think simply because of its dopey name—is the head and shoulders pattern. It may be the one pattern that can trick you more often than any other pattern.

I would agree with that. I have watched many head and shoulders patterns waiting for a break. They will break through the neckline and then before you know it, they reverse course.

Exactly, they do something different. You very rarely, if ever, anticipate the completion of a head and shoulders pattern, either top or bottom, until it happens. I'd rather pay "X" percent higher if by doing so I have increased my odds of being right. People will say, "Ralph, why do you tell me to buy a stock at 50 if it's 48½?" I tell them, "Because it has to get through the supply at 50." If it does that, odds have improved that the trend will be enforced. "What do I have to do to improve my odds?" I had rather pay the point and a half higher. The best cartoon I ever saw about Wall Street was when I was a trainee. Merrill Lynch had a cartoon which showed a boardroom. There was a big clock in front of the boardroom which said 6:00 p.m. There was a cleaning woman sweeping up. There was a customer sitting in a chair next to his broker's desk looking very dejected with his head in his hand. The caption read, "Waiting for the Last 1/8." It was perfect. That's what people do. When I was a broker, I had clients that depending on whether they were buying or selling, would up or lower the quote I gave them by 1/8 or 1/4. Do you know what I used to do? I would cuff a quote just to make him do something because I knew his pattern. He had to get that last 1/8 or 1/4 because he was beating somebody. If the bid/ask was at 50 x 50 1/8 and we were looking to buy, he would have said buy it at 50. I'd say, "Charlie, it's 50 1/8 x 50¼." He'd say, "OK, pay 50 1/8" and the quote was really 50 x 50 1/8. That comes under Rule 405—know your customer.

Did your affinity for technical analysis help you as a broker?

I started to fool around with the charts while still in the training program. In those days, you didn't have Trendline and you didn't have computers. You had to hand post your charts. My first wife and I would sit down after dinner and hand post 150 charts every night. She would rattle through my list giving me the high, low, close, and volume. It took maybe an hour and a half every night. In a way it was good because it gave you an extra feel. After graduating from the training program in April 1958, I lasted about 9 months as a broker with Merrill Lynch. The reason I left is because things were very slow. When I got started in this business average daily volume was about 3 million shares a day. I remember very clearly one of our weekly meetings. The manager, a little guy, pounded his fist on the desk and said, "I don't give a damn what that market is doing. You men are not investment counselors, you are salesmen. You get out and sell what Merrill Lynch is pushing." I didn't know if I would ever make it in this business but I knew I was not a Fuller brush salesman. I wanted to be something better than just a salesman. I wanted to be the equivalent of a counselor. I wanted to advise people to do the right thing because if you do the right thing you build up a big business. I quit a month later and went to Shearson. My business started to grow. I wanted to write a market letter to build up a really big business but Shearson said no. There was a small member firm who was trying to expand a bit and wanted my production. I said, "I will come if you let me write." They said, "Fine." I started to write a weekly letter as a sales device.

Based on technical analysis?

Yes. I wrote about the market and made stock recommendations. The first market letter I ever wrote had five short sales in it including AT&T at 127 3/8. My second letter was in early May 1962. The market had already topped and was starting south. The market crashed into late May 1962 when Jack Kennedy forced the steel companies to roll back price increases. Three weeks later, AT&T was something like 98 and change. I was getting a little press because I was one of the very few writing about it. My business doubled as a result of that. I was a partner in a small member firm at age 34.

How did your 18 year tenure as a broker prepare you for what you are doing now?

I think having worked as a broker for 18 years helps me do a much better job. To my knowledge, I am the only working technical analyst who was in the trenches for so many years. None of the rest of them know what it's like to be at a desk and making a phone call to a client or a prospect. I think that is why my daily market letter is so practical. I am a believer in the Ernest Hemingway school of writing. I try not to write in a highfalutin' way. My job is to impart information and opinion in as simple and effective a form as possible. I think I know better than most of my contemporaries what information a stock broker needs to pick up a phone and make a client or prospect call and tell them something that sounds reasonable and intelligent and may help them.

As a broker, you were probably able to witness first hand the fear and greed of your clients almost before these emotions showed up on the charts.

People don't change. I have charts that go back to 1885. If I cover the scale and cover the date, you couldn't tell me whether it was 1885 or 1985. People unfortunately do not change. What did the philosopher Santayana say? "Those who ignore the past are doomed to repeat it." That's what people do because they are dealing primarily from emotions. The average person unconsciously feels more comfortable in a crowd even if the crowd is wrong. He doesn't feel quite so stupid because everybody else around him was as stupid as he was. Stepping away from the crowd is what the technical analyst has to do. The best calls any of us have ever made are almost always contrary opinion calls. It is our job to try and figure out what consensus thinking is among the public and among institutions. We have some sentiment indicators to help. If you can statistically verify what consensus thinking is and then you have the ego, nerve, and more importantly, the experience to go contra the crowd, you are probably going to be right. People want to be led. That's how you get a Joe Granville who rises and then crashes and burns, and you get a Prechter who does the same thing and then a Garzarelli. People want to believe that somebody much smarter than they have figured out they have the "open sesame." What insanity. Every one of these heroes crashed and burned. Like a shooting star, really bright for a while, and then they just disappear. How you go from market mover to total failure I will never know. I don't want to ever get that high if the net result is you fall off the cliff.

In their day, they could move markets but not anymore.

No, not at all. I was a guest lecturer for a graduate school class at NYU in 1980-81. Joe Granville was just in the process of burning. I finished my presentation and went to question and answers. Somebody raised his hand and asked, "Can you explain to me how a Joe Granville rises to a position where he can move markets?" I said, "Before I answer your question, let me ask the class a question." These were very bright students but I set them up by telling them it was going to be a very hard question. I said, "The average IQ in this country is 90 or 100. Can anybody explain to me why it is so low?" A hand goes up. "We have a lot of sociologically disadvantaged people in this country." I took two or three answers like that before I said, "Well, I told you it was a tough question—you are all wrong." I said, "The reason the average IQ in this country is so low is because there are a lot of stupid people out there." People want the Messiah. They want to believe somebody out there knows. That's how Joe Granville rises. Nobody knows. There will never be the "open sesame." Jesse Livermore made millions four times and lost it and then finally blew his brains out.

The market can be a very humbling experience.

Of course it is. I very often start a speech by saying, "Ladies and gentlemen, I am six foot two. When I started in this business, I was six foot eight." How others ignore their shortcomings is probably the most classic case of denial for psychiatrists. I read Bernard Baruch's life story. What impressed me, and I have never forgotten it, is how he described periodically selling out everything and going away. It was a kind of cleansing. No matter how good you are, you get swept up and sometimes you have to get away.

What is your secret for success?

It's done by hard work. Every single day you have to be smart enough and experienced enough to know where you are in an overall market trend. Once you come to that conclusion, assuming you are right, you can choose which indicators to give additional weight. If I am in a healthy uptrend, I am going to look at this. If I am in an unhealthy trend, one that is down, then I am going to look at this. If I am in a market that may be changing direction, I am going to look at this. That is the way you do your work. It is a never ending battle.

Is your initial starting point determining the trend of the overall markets—that is the Dow, NYSE, and NASDAQ?

Actually, I look at the individual stock charts first and then the indicators next. The overall trend becomes my conclusion based on all the other charts and indicators.

A bottom-up approach rather than a top-down approach?

The first thing I do on Sunday when my Trendlines come is go through the individual charts. The bottom line of all technical analysis is the tape. It tells you whether a stock is doing what it is supposed to be doing. Are there more good-looking charts or are there more negative charts? If there are more good looking charts, how good-looking are they? Are they real legitimate patterns of accumulation? Are they breaking out? If they are breaking out, are they fulfilling their technical implications, namely, are they going up or down? Sometimes you get too bogged down with indicators. When I get confused about the market, I go back to square one and try to figure out exactly what is going on. Square one is "let me go through my charts." How do the charts look? Do they look good? Are they breaking out? Are they following through on the breakout? The tape is the final arbiter of all your analysis.

How do you gauge the health of the overall market?

It is very important for me to decide where I think we are in a market trend. Is it a healthy uptrend, a choppy or sporadic uptrend, a downtrend or more importantly, is it a market that may be in the process of changing direction? A market that is fully in gear, as I call it, is when the Dow Industrials are making new highs, the Transports are confirming, and the A/D index is confirming and making new highs also. That is a buy and hold market. If the market is in a choppy uptrend with some indicators lagging a bit, that is a rape and pillage market. You're in and out. A negative breadth non-confirmation is when the Dow makes a new high and breadth not only is no where near confirming but is actually heading the opposite direction.

You give a lot of weight to the advance/decline index, right?

The first time I ever learned about non-confirmations was in 1962, after the market had rallied off of a May reaction low. It rallied rather sharply into June and July as I recall. All the stocks went into flags. I bought the flags because that is what you are supposed to do and they all broke down. I lost my shirt. A guy who used to write for Forbes and Barron's, John Schultz, who died in 1995, showed me about non-confirmations. He said the A/D index did not confirm this run. It was very narrowly based and it wasn't healthy. The husband of a former secretary of mine was getting his master's degree at NYU and wanted to do his thesis on something to do with technical analysis. He asked me for suggestions. I responded instantly. Check out the validity of breadth divergences—negative ones at the top and the converse at the bottom. His professor approved the idea. I took out my Trendline charts and went back about 10 years showing him every non-confirmation—negative at the top and positive at the bottom. He fed the data into a computer to see if it signaled direction changes. The track record of non-confirmations was frighteningly high. He decided to go back even further, another 10 or 15 years, for a total of 20 or 25 years. The bottom line is that he got an A+ on his thesis and the track record of non-confirmations was in excess of 98%. His professor called to say that it was the first master's thesis in years he had worked with that amounted to a hill of beans in the real world. He invited me up to talk to his graduate class. I did that for years.

In the event of a non-confirmation, do you give the A/D line some leeway, say 2-4 weeks to play catch-up?

It all depends when it happens. I have seen breadth non-confirmations work the same day. I have seen them take weeks. July 1990 was the top and the market turned down almost immediately. When you get a breadth non-confirmation the way you did in July of 1990, which was an extreme divergence between the Dow and the A/D index, I will wait a week or two for the A/D index to play catch up. If it doesn't, the Dow will almost always turn down very quickly. Now, when you get non-confirmations, a lot of people will say, "The Dow just made a new high, NASDAQ failed to confirm, the A/D index failed, sell short." That is wrong. There is a little trick you have to be aware of.

What's the trick?

If you start to get a move where the Dow is running ahead of breadth, the trick is that you have to be aware that all three, industrials, transports, and breadth, do not have to confirm one another at the same time. If they are doing that, you are dealing with a particularly healthy market. But let's say the Dow makes a new high on a Monday and the following Monday, the A/D index confirms. That's OK. What you have to watch for during a run is when one is moving more rapidly than the other. Is the A/D index moving in line with the Dow on a day to day basis the way it did yesterday, they way it did today? If we were up 65 points today and the A/D index showed 700 net advances, I would say "no." If there were over 1300 net advances then the answer is "probably." You have to look at the rate of advance of the Dow in relation to the rate of advance of the A/D index. The A/D index can lag for a while but then three to five days down the road it can catch-up and confirm. A lot of people don't seem to be aware of this and it is very, very critical. You don't want to go short just because you have a non-confirmation set in place.

What else do you look for other than the rate of advance?

I just look at the trendline and I use a 10 day moving average of the A/D index which is what everybody uses for confirming new highs.

There are several components of the Dow Theory. Do you think the part where the Dow and Transports have to confirm one another is still a viable indicator?

Not really because if you look at most calls Dow Theory signals come really late. We have improved on it by adding the advance/decline index which Charles Dow didn't have. The A/D index is the most broadly based of all the measuring tools. The July 1990 top was a screaming breadth non-confirmation.

Because of the advance/decline line?

Yes. The three oil stocks in the Dow, because of the confrontation in Iraq at that time, carried the Dow to new highs. They were the only group doing that. I remember very clearly the Dow making a new high while the A/D index was going the other way. A classic breadth non-confirmation. Plus, at the end of a lengthy uptrend, when the oils are rallying and are about the only game in town on the upside, that is late in trend stuff.

Strength in oils in the latter stages of a bull market is a sign that the end may be drawing near?

Yes. In 1990, I think the last 80 or 90 points in that run were basically the three oils.

Do you monitor the individual Dow components on a daily basis to determine which issues are participating in a rally or correction?

I am looking at that all of the time. The other day United Technology was up 4¼ points and another stock, maybe Boeing, was up 2¼. Those two stocks accounted for ½ of the Dow's gain that day. That is something I will put in my letter. That is something that a stock broker can utilize to make a prospect call or if the client calls us and says "Charlie, the market is up 30 points and my stock didn't do anything" the broker can say, "Yes, but what you have to understand is that just two stocks accounted for 18 points." The Dow in that case overstated market strength. The S&P, NYSE, and A/D index were not nearly as strong.

What characteristics do you look for in accumulation and distribution?

The accumulation/distribution patterns are vintage John Magee. Look at a stock's trading characteristics. For example, in 1993, IBM was in a big inverse head and shoulders pattern. It hit 46 3/8 three times over that four month period. The left shoulder went down to 41, rallied to 46 3/8 then fell back down to 40 5/8 making the head. The head was 3/8 below the left shoulder. It went back to 46 3/8, came back down to about 41 forming the right shoulder then back up to 46 3/8. The last time it didn't come back down. As I recall, it hovered for 3 or 4 days right beneath 46 3/8 and volume disappeared as it is supposed to in a head and shoulders pattern. Volume with head and shoulders should be declining throughout the head and shoulders pattern. The highest volume should be on the left side of the pattern, head lower volume, right shoulder lower yet. In the IBM pattern, the right shoulder volume disappeared and the price of the stock did not go down back to prior reaction lows telling me that the selling was about over. It printed 46½ and she was off to the races. Same thing with the bond market in July 1996. It had a perfect multiple inverse head and shoulders pattern. Every time bonds got close to 110 they were turned away. They got up to 109 ¾ but did not come back down nearly as deep as they had on other prior lows. The selling pressure was less and this told me the pattern was changing. These are the kind of things that you have to look at every single day. When you see a pattern evolving, you have to pay attention to it. Sometimes when you hand post your own charts, you are forced to look at it very closely.

IBM Jan 1994

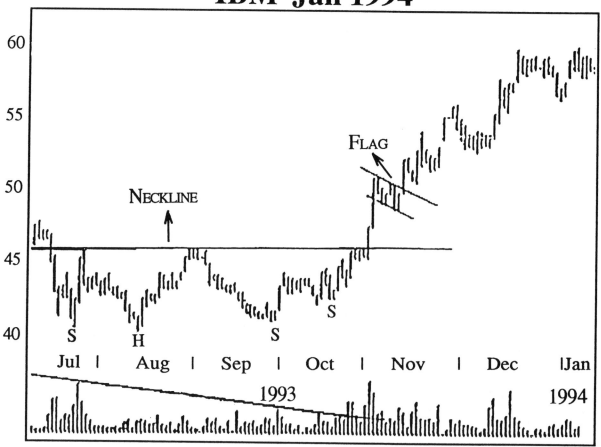

A lot of guys don't do that. The volume configurations in any pattern are very, very critical.

Having said that, what is your opinion of point and figure charting?

I was once asked about the use of point and figure charting at a big conference. I said, "Now think about this—why would you want to utilize a service that ignores one of the most important technical characteristics and tools we have—volume?" Nobody on the Street uses point and figure charts anymore. Why do you think that is? Bar charts will beat a point and figure chart 99 out of 100 times simply because the discipline is better. If you are using a one point reversal or a three point reversal, I am going to get a break-out on IBM; for example, at 46½. Point and figure chartists are not going to be doing IBM on a ½ point reversal chart. The discipline is inferior. Volume is very, very critical. It helps you spot aggressive buying. Let's say you are in a good uptrend and you have a little pause which forms a flag or pennant. Volume is supposed to trail off very dramatically. If a stock is in a good healthy uptrend and you see volume drying up to where it can't get any lighter, you are able to buy the stock into that low volume before it moves up again. Volume is a critical indicator.

Given your 40 years of market experience, what characteristics allow a chartist to differentiate between a dead cat bounce, short covering, and the start of a new uptrend?

The most recent classic example of the start of a new uptrend was in April 1994. Since February of that year, the market had dropped 9.8%. April 4th was the low in a classic multi-swing session. That day, the market opened 84 points lower, and shortly after 11:00 a.m., the 10:30 and 11:00 put/call figures were through the roof. They had been very benign on the way down. By 11:00, the Dow had rallied to minus 33. I sent out a special memo commenting on the put/call ratios and saying that this could be the start of a multi-swing day (down 84 points and then the recovery to down 33). One more sell-off into the 2:00-3:00 p.m. time frame would be a buying opportunity. The market fell to minus 69 at 3:00 p.m. and turned up. I caught the day and the hour of the low, something I will never do again. But it was one of those perfect down-up, down-up multi-swing days. Now, because of the bearish sentiment that started to explode I was very bullish. But what got me even more bullish and made me comfortable about my bullishness was the fact that the rally of the next three days did not show the characteristics of a dead cat bounce rally which is merely a pause in the resumption of a downtrend. A dead cat bounce is shallow and short-lived and then the downtrend resumes. It displays two very distinct characteristics. Number one, volume is very light during the bounce. Number two, the advance/decline statistics can be strong the first day of the bounce but then breadth starts to lag almost immediately with a dead cat bounce rally. On April 5th, 6th, and 7th of 1994, two things happened. Bearish sentiment stayed high via the put/call ratio and the A/D statistics were spectacular. On the first day there were something like over 1800 net advances. The market was up big. On April 6th, the market was up modestly but the A/D index was vastly stronger than its relationship to the Dow. Same thing on April 7th, a modest up day with vastly superior breadth readings. I said, "This is not the way technical rallies behave; this rally is for real." Those three days had three very significant characteristics telling me this is not just a dead cat bounce rally. Volume was good, breadth was good, and the high put/call ratios indicated that investors believed that the rally was just a dead cat bounce.

So for the start of a new uptrend, you match the expansion in the put/call ratios with key reversal days. How about short covering rallies?

Short covering rallies are usually very violent, very dramatic. They run up spectacularly but volume is not that euphoric and breadth may not be that euphoric either. I call a short covering rally a "vacuum filling rally." You get this huge big break down, shorts are in there and they turn it around for whatever reason. You have this explosion in price for one or two days on the upside and then it peters out. If there is nothing else behind the short covering rally it tends not to last very long.

Do you see more volume or less volume?

You see less.

Typically, aren't blue chip stocks the strongest at the beginning of market moves and at the end of market moves?

I don't know. They usually are certainly at the beginning. One thing I know for sure, when the oil stocks are the primary source of upside fuel, that's late in trend stuff. I don't do a lot of work with "We're in such and such a market so I want to buy the consumer stocks or I want to buy cyclical stocks." That's a strategist's job. I have never found much success with that. I spend my time looking at things on a stock by stock basis. I don't spend any time at all doing sector analysis. We are here; therefore this group is supposed to lead the way. If a group is leading the way, sooner or later I am going to spot the leadership by just looking at the charts. It's almost a little esoteric for me.

When a stock penetrates resistance or breaks support, do you buy it immediately or will you wait for a re-test or pullback first?

I buy immediately. As I recall Edwards and Magee suggested waiting for the stock to move 3% before you buy it. If I am in a big, fat healthy market, I am a believer that the break-out is going to play, so I really do it. I am a very big believer in putting all my eggs in one or two baskets and then watching those baskets very closely.

When you put all of your eggs in one basket, do you set your exit points based on support and resistance levels or in terms of percentage gains or losses?

When I buy large positions, I let the stock run up and take profits when I think they should be taken based on technical and psychological indicators. That's how you make money. I believe that when I buy a stock, it's going to start moving immediately whether I am long or short, particularly if I have waited for what I consider to be a valid break-out. Therefore, if I think a stock is going to start moving immediately and it doesn't, I am wrong. Run like a thief in the night. I bought 10,000 shares of an oil stock and paid 42 5/8. Then the thing wouldn't print anymore— 42 5/8, 42 5/8, 42 5/8. Then it prints 42 1/2, 42 3/8, 42 1/2. I said, "Something's wrong." This breakout is not following through. An hour after I had bought 10,000 shares at 42 5/8, I sold them at 42 3/8 taking a 1/4 point loss per share. It closed at 42 1/4 that night. The next morning there was good news and the stock opened 2 ½ higher. I left $25,000 on the table. Reciprocally, six months ago I was long 15,000 shares of a stock I paid 23 for. It closed that night at 24 1/4. I told myself I had a winner. The next day it comes back down again, starts drifting and drifting, and then broke 23. Something was wrong. This should not be happening. It broke out yesterday and now it's pulling right back and a little volume is coming back in. I sold 15,000 shares at the market. Some got filled at 22 ¾, the rest at 22 5/8. Dan Dorfman came on CNBC and mentioned this stock as a potential takeout by Computer Associates. It looked like it is going to be bid at 28. 2500 shares actually traded at 25. I thought I had just left $100,000 on the table. I was going out of town. Before they reopened the stock, the company came out with earnings. They were a monster disappointment and the stock opened 8 points lower. When I got to my hotel room and saw it on CNBC at 18 and something, I thought it was a misprint.

Eight points lower. Had you not gotten out when you did, you would have been staring at a $70,000 loss.

The point of these two stories quite clearly shows that you must stick with your discipline. If you are wrong, you get out. Over a period of time, it balances out.

Your decisions to get into and out of a stock are based on the action of the tape?

Always the tape. I understand that the average client is unable to do this. They can't make the IBM trade; that is, buy it at 68 and then sell it the next day at 66 even though its going 25 points lower. This is what you are supposed to do. The main point is to protect your working capital. It's probably the hardest decision that an investor or trader can make.

What are your views on day trading?

Fastest way to intensive care I know. It's insane. The minute I hear the word day trading I know I'm staring at a loser. It can not be done. You know how I describe day trading? Best day trades I ever made were by accident. I bought a stock that looked good and I happened to get lucky that day and if I got lucky that day, odds are that I should probably stay.

Because there will be a follow through?

Probably.

Do you rely on technology stocks as a proxy for the overall health of the stock market?

Yes. I have used it particularly in the past couple of years.

Can you explain the theory which supports tech stocks as being market leaders?

Tech stocks function very well from a technical point of view. Most of the big ones fit the characteristics of the stocks institutions are interested in, i.e., very liquid. If the institutions are willing to be buyers in size of tech stocks, this to me is a proxy for market health overall. Why? Tech stocks carry high betas so they are scary stocks. Very volatile. They also tend to carry the highest P/E ratios. So if institutions are pouring billions of dollars into stocks with high betas and very high P/E ratios, that is another plus outlining the overall health of the stock market. It has worked extremely well.

Wouldn't it also be an indication of speculative activity?

Yes, when they get down to the garbage. When the IPO market goes nutty and the $2.00 stocks run to $5, $6, $7, and $8 over very short periods of time. When they are running Microsoft, Sun Microsystems, or Intel, I am not worried about that kind of speculative fever. When it gets down to the proverbial cats and dogs, now you are talking about something else.

Can you generalize and say that tech stocks are leaders at tops and bottoms.

Absolutely. Certainly during this most recent cycle.

Do you follow technology indexes and sectors or do you look at each individual tech stock?

I tend to go with each individual issue. All of these big brokerage firms come up with all this fancy sector analysis. I think it is much ado about nothing. If I see Sun Microsystems acting well and Oracle acting well and Microsoft acting well that's good enough. How long does it take to pick up your Mansfield chart and go look at a sector. Two minutes?

How about the technology indexes? Which ones do you monitor?

I always watch the SOX index for the semiconductors. I watch the NASDAQ 100 which is comprised of the really big names.

Bonds play a role in your analysis, right?

Sure. That is such a key indicator, particularly in the past couple of years because the primary source of fuel in this rally has been the best of all worlds—low inflation, moderate growth, and an accommodative Fed. If you wanted to describe the last 2100 points from a fundamental backdrop, those would be the reasons. So yes, I want to be really aware of directional changes in the bond market.

Do bonds usually lead stocks?

Usually.

But you can't depend on it?

Once again, you don't want to take one indicator by itself. It's just one indicator. If there is other stuff acting dicey, you are building the case. You need more than just one indicator and you have to know where you are in the market trend so you know which indicators you might want to give some extra weight to.

When stocks and bonds diverge, what is your strategy?

If bonds and stocks are diverging, I am going to go back to my other indicators. If the market indicators I rely on are still acting well and stocks have separated themselves from the bond market, I am going to put the bond market in the back seat. There are many, many periods where stocks and bonds diverge. It is not a lock step all the time. It's just like the utilities. Utilities are usually precursors to directional changes elsewhere but in late June of 1996 they had a nice move without stocks following. Then they turned around and completely gave up that wonderful run. You have to understand that bonds and stocks do diverge very often. Are your other indicators bullish or bearish? Go with the weight of evidence. That's how you play it.

The put/call ratio has served you well, demonstrating a high degree of reliability and it is in fact your most important indicator. What are your parameters?

There aren't any real parameters. People want parameters. Like if the put/call ratio is such and such a number it means the following...—that's not what it is about. What you have to do is live with the market, live with the put/call ratio. You have to follow the market trend. The put/call ratio has to be utilized in terms of the direction of the market and how speedily the market is moving. There aren't any hard and fast rules. One of the things that helped me catch the low day on April 4, 1994 was the put/call ratio. When the market started down off its early February top, the put/call figures were rather benign. About two days before the eventual bottom, which was April 4, the put/call ratios exploded. The boys had waited until the market had fallen almost 10% and then they started buying puts. This type of activity occurs close to a bottom. On April 4th, you had a classic multi-swing reversal day—down-up; down-up. In the first three days after that reversal, April 5th, 6th and 7th, two things kept me very bullish. Number one, the put/call ratios went through the roof. Secondly, the A/D index was extremely powerful. One of the characteristics of a lousy technical rally in a down market is that the A/D index lags and lags badly because there isn't any real buying. The selling just stops for a couple of days but there is no real buying out there. Throughout the rally, the level of bearish sentiment was incredibly high. I remember seeing the put/call ratios over 300% in the middle of the day. I think it took four or five months before there were three down days in a row during that initial part of the run. When the market had a little corrective phase of one, two, or three down days in a row, the put/call ratio got even higher. The bears were fighting the rally with high put/call ratios. It was perfect textbook stuff. The reciprocal occurred in 1987. From the first day of January, 1987 until mid-August of that year the put/call ratio was very high indicating high levels of skepticism during that powerhouse rally. Then in mid-August, sentiment began to shift and the put/call ratio began to decline. The market high occurred about three weeks after this shift in sentiment. You don't want to see a dramatic drop or rise in the put/call ratio in the morning and then see it reverse later in the day. One-half hour doesn't make a trend. You need two or three days of extreme readings.

It is the relationship of put/call ratios relative to the movement in the Dow rather than actual numerical values. If it is moving inversely and at extreme levels, then that is significant?

Of course. We are looking at numbers but not by themselves. What is the market doing? These guys who are trying to write a book, well, if the put/call is 103 it means this and if it's 84 it means that. That's nonsense.

Most of the work you do with the put/call ratio is intraday?

That's right. The C.B.O.E. gives you put/call ratios every half hour. I get the 10:30 a.m., the 11:00 a.m. and the 12:00 p.m. You usually don't get a lot of changes after that. If we have a very free swinging day, then I might get a 2:00 p.m. or 3:00 p.m. reading just to see. Of course, I always look at the closing figures.

Do you look at all the C.B.O.E. option data?

I only look at the indexes. I use the figures the C.B.O.E. provides for puts and calls on just the indexes. This includes the OEX 500, the OEX 100 and a couple of relatively insignificant indexes. These other smaller indexes have such few contracts outstanding that it rarely affects the ratio. Combining the OEX 100 with the OEX 500 supplies me with a more complete picture.

You don't include equity options in your data?

No. First of all, equity put/call ratios can be skewed by one stock attracting a huge amount of calls or puts. The OEX is what? People making a bet on the market. I don't care about the individual stocks. I'm trying to use that indicator to help me gauge market sentiment.

For readers who are unable to retrieve intraday data, will closing data suffice?

Yes, it will be a good clue.

Do you use odd lot and short selling activity as indicators?

No. In my opinion, they are not clean anymore. There could be hedging involved.

If short selling produces aberrations as a result of hedging, can't you make the case that institutions buy index puts and calls as a "hedge" and therefore the possibility of aberrations exists also in the put/call ratio.

Sure, but when are they buying them? When they are bullish or bearish? I was on CNBC a couple of years ago. The anchorman asked me at the time if there was anything in particular that I wanted to talk about and I said, "Yes, I'd like to talk about the put/call ratio." They fed me the line and I did my little spiel on it. He comes back to me, "Roy Blumberg, our technical guy, doesn't give the weight to the put/call ratio that you seem to." I was a little confused and said, "Really, why?" He said that institutions use options as hedges. And I said, "Well, so what? When do they buy puts to hedge? When they are nervous, right?" What difference does it make who's doing it? All I am interested in is their sentiment. Are they bullish or bearish? I don't care if a specialist is doing it or an institution is doing it.

One of your other primary indicators is a contrarian indicator, the consensus sentiment figures from Investors Intelligence?

Yes. The primary sentiment indicators I use are the put/call ratio and the Investors Intelligence figures. The Investors Intelligence figures are another good confirming tool.

What numerical values do you use to pinpoint extremes in optimism and pessimism?

Mid to upper 50's on the bullish side and nicely below 30%, mid-20% for the bears. Another indicator that I give a lot of weight to but it doesn't "talk," if you will, all the time, is mutual fund cash. It talks only on rare occasions but when it talks, it has an awfully good track record. It worked perfectly in October 1990. That has helped me make some great calls.

This figure is available from the Investment Company Institute on a monthly basis?

Yes. I gave it a lot of weight in May 1996 when the figure was 7.0%, the lowest since October 1978. Then the May figures were reported in June at 6.7%. They were very, very, helpful then. It worked for me also, like pure gold in 1990. In July of 1990, the market made a peak and then promptly fell 600 points or 20% until October of 1990 when I turned very bullish. I went to Minneapolis and had dinner with some institutional people at IDS and presented a very bullish scenario. They weren't going to buy stocks because consensus at the time was that the war in Iraq was going to start and the market would drop 200 or 300 points and then they would buy. What an absurd concept that was. In October of 1990, mutual fund cash was at 12.9%, a record figure since they had been keeping the data. Now, when I talk to trainees or brokers or clients I tell them, "Look these mutual fund people are supposed to be the smartest ones out there, right?" They all nod their head. Well, what's wrong with this picture? If these guys are so smart, shouldn't it be that their cash levels were at record highs in July at the top of the market and at record low levels in October at the bottom? They are flat out bullish at the top, no cash at the top, and loaded with cash at the bottom on the way down. And these guys are considered smart? The mutual fund cash levels, put/call ratio and Investor's Intelligence numbers are the three primary sentiment indicators that I use.

For the Investors Intelligence numbers, will one extreme reading suffice for a signal or do you wait for a couple of readings?

No, you generally only need an extreme. You can watch the trend in relation to the direction of the market. Does the bullish percent go through the roof when the market takes off? Does the bearish percent explode when the market corrects? The correction camp are the real cowards, not committing to either side. There is a one to two week time lag on those Investor's Intelligence figures because it takes some time to get all of the market newsletters in and collate the stats.

So in two or three weeks time, the figures could shift and give a totally different picture?

Well, it really takes 3-4 weeks because the newsletter writers won't respond to what we are seeing in the market today for another 2-3 weeks then it's another week or two for Investor's Intelligence to put everything together.

Do you follow foreign stock markets?

No, I rarely comment on foreign markets. I have enough trouble with our own market.

Do you use indicators like MACD and stochastics?

A bunch of years ago, the editor of *Technical Analysis of Stocks and Commodities* saw my letters in Mansfield and decided to feature me in one of his issues. He asked me a question that I had never been asked before. He said, "How would you describe yourself, what kind of a technical analyst are you?" I took a few minutes to think about it and came back with, "I'm a ham and egger. I'm a basic technical analysis 101 guy." He said to me, "Do you use stochastics?" I said, "Number one, I haven't a clue what it is, and number two, I'm not even sure I can spell it." The vast majority of the technicians today, with the advent of the computer and "systems" have gotten away from the basic work. I describe myself as an expert in Technical Analysis 101.

I have noticed that in the last 3 to 4 years, stocks break out with such incredible thrust. Aren't momentum players using technical analysis?

Yes, that's right and also because there are more mutual funds now then there are effective stocks so money is concentrated in a relatively small number of stocks. I mean everybody is long Microsoft and Intel, aren't they? Everybody. So when Microsoft had that little head and shoulders top recently, it broke down. In a matter of three days, Microsoft was down 11 and Intel was down 6. When the buying stops, and seller goes to seller—bang, everybody is doing the same thing at the same time to the same stocks.

Does the average investor have to take a shorter term approach to investing now because that is what the institutions are doing?

We are now seeing all of these violent moves, particularly on the way down. Why? Because all of these momentum players and all of these performance funds are doing the same thing at the same time to the same stocks. That exit door gets very, very narrow. In July 1995, NASDAQ fell 5.3% in 3 days. When I got started in this business, market movements evolved. The 1961-1962 top took a very long time to evolve. The 1973-1974 bear market was a 48% bear market and took 18 months to uncor. 1987, the 3rd worst bear market in history using intraday figures, which I generally use for measuring purposes, had a 41% drop in 7 weeks.

So these swift moves are trends we will continue to see?

Absolutely. The current period is a little more old-fashioned. In late January 1996, the Dow punched through a double top at 5250 and 13 days later it was 400 points higher. Every trip to new highs subsequent to that move was a token new high followed immediately by a sell-off. If you look at a chart, you see this rolling top. The bottom line is that it was a momentum loss staring you in the face.

When the market indexes have these major swings, either up or down, such as we had on July 16th, 1996, is it healthy for them to reverse quickly and retrace their losses?

In the old days, that wouldn't happen but since the time periods have become so compact and so condensed that is the new reality. We no longer get those long, lengthy drawn out bottoms and tops. Old timers, such as myself, had better adjust to the new rules and there are new rules.

With such drastic moves, it's difficult to evaluate when trends stop and start.

Don't fight it. That is the way the market has been functioning. 1987 is and will be the classic example for decades to come and maybe forever—41% down in 7 weeks. Scary. Those are the new rules.

One of your investment rules to which you strictly adhere is taking your losses early. You can always re-enter your position.

Probably the hardest thing for John Q. Public to do is to take a small loss. People do all the homework possible on Stock X, the broker does all the homework possible on Stock X, and then they go out and buy the stock because they like it for "the long term." I hope that the long term investor who paid $94¾ for Micron Technology in 1995 was about six months old. (Micron Technology was trading at $20.00 at the time of the interview). When people buy a stock for the long term in effect what many of them do is turn their back on the stock. What they have to do is say to themselves, "If I have made an error, what has to happen for me to realize that I have made an error?" You have to play devil's advocate. Nobody ever does that. That is one of the things I think about every morning on my way to work. I come up with an opinion, I finish my market letter, and then I start beating up on myself. When I give a talk to the public, I walk investors through the following scenario. You buy a stock because you like it for the "longterm." The stock goes down 2 or 3 points. You say to yourself, "No big deal, just a little correction, it will come back." The stock drops another 2-3 points. Now your palms are getting a little moist and you think that maybe if it gets back to my price, maybe I will get out. Then the stock drops another 2-3 points. Now you are long term investor. People fall in love with stocks. These are inanimate objects. I always tell people, "Don't fall in love with a stock." It can't even kiss you and make you feel nice.

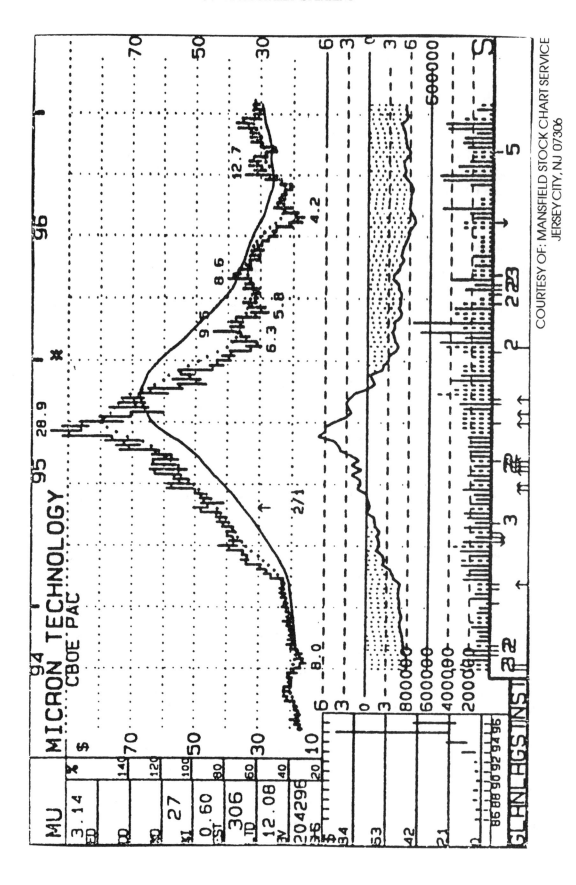

Taking small losses early allows you to stay in the game.

I guarantee you the people who bought the top in Micron Technology are still long because the loss is too big to take. Technical analysis can help get you out of a bad stock. It can help you avoid becoming an unwilling long term investor. 1993 was the best trading year of my life.

Why was that?

I was up almost 300%. A couple of really good option trades is the only way you can get that kind of performance. However, the smartest and most professional trade of the year was buying IBM one day at 68 and selling it the next day at 66 on its way to 40 5/8. You have to take the small loss so you can come back for round two.

John Bollinger

John Bollinger has always been interested in the financial markets but this was not his first pursuit. After high school, he attended the School of Visual Arts majoring in cinematography. For four years he worked in New York as a cameraman, on documentaries and commercials. There was even a stint with "60 Minutes" before he became restless to branch into feature films. This goal necessitated a move to Hollywood. Fourteen hour days at non-union wages were not the greener pastures he had envisioned. During the transition, he had missed the window of opportunity to become a union member on the West Coast, which would have ensured higher wages. This unfortunate timing was a stroke of luck as tough work conditions spurred him to consider alternate career paths which eventually led to the financial markets.

In the early 1970's, Mr. Bollinger entered into a business partnership with a friend, renting grip trucks to movie studios as an additional source of revenue. For those unfamiliar with this term, a grip truck carries lighting equipment and cables used on movie sets. The duo decided a computer would be handy to keep track of inventory, so in 1977, Mr. Bollinger not only resourcefully built his own computer, but in addition, wrote his own software program. The business was later dissolved and he inherited the computer. So special was this first computer that the motherboard now hangs, enclosed in a frame, on his study wall. Prior to this time, he had been dabbling in the stock market. Spying an opportunity to maximize the full potential of an idle computer, he wrote another software program, this time relating to technical analysis, which would allow him to develop a reliable trading system. No question about it, he was ahead of his time. In 1973-1974, a severe bear market occurred as many will remember. Although Mr. Bollinger was not invested in the markets at the time, he witnessed first hand the financially and psychologically devastating blow the market dealt to his co-workers and friends. Not only did that event make a lasting impression upon him, but it also motivated him to study the markets extensively before investing.

By 1979, Mr. Bollinger had gained sufficient knowledge and experience in the stock market and his investments had been successful enough to allow him to divide his time between freelancing as a cameraman and trading. In 1981, he was given a desk in a small brokerage firm to trade his personal account. The brokerage house had a motto: "Pick a system, any system, and then use it." According to Mr. Bollinger, "There is no perfect system. There is no perfect approach." Success depends on "finding a methodology that works for you." In this same firm, the benefits of discipline became clear as he watched two traders continue trading until they lost every penny, causing the collapse of the firm.

In 1983, Mr. Bollinger had a chance encounter with a doctor and trader who happened to be a good friend of Earl Bryan, then chairman of the Financial News Network (FNN). At the time, FNN was looking for someone who understood both the markets and computers. Mr. Bollinger fit the bill and the doctor recommended him to Earl Bryan. Mr. Bollinger accepted the position with the understanding that he would never have to be an anchorman. For a while, he stayed in the background doing research and analysis for the program's anchors. This opportunity was proving to be an invaluable learning experience. Then one day he arrived at work to find a union picket line. Since FNN was still a fledgling network that was not yet profitable, he did not see the rationale of unionizing, so he went to work. The network was desperate for material and under protest, he found himself facing thousands of television viewers as an anchor. In the early days, production was still a bit primitive at FNN. Viewers heard the responses of guest analysts via the telephone and in order to put a name with a face, their photograph was displayed during the interview. But what FNN lacked in presentation, they made up for in content.

While nurturing the dream of one day managing money, Mr. Bollinger moved toward this goal while working at FNN. He enrolled in the demanding and intensive three year program to become a Chartered Financial Analyst (CFA). In 1986, he became a member of this small and elite group. At this same time, as an outgrowth of his work at FNN and in response to viewer requests, he started writing a newsletter called the *Capital Growth Letter*, still published today. Given the terse coverage of topics on FNN, the *Capital Growth Letter* was begun with the original intention of filling in the information gaps left vacant by FNN and providing expanded coverage on particular subjects. In short, it was an educational tool.

Mr. Bollinger stayed with FNN for ten years as Chief Market Analyst. A change of command occurred when CNBC acquired FNN, forcing a relocation of the network. Mr. Bollinger was asked to stay on but declined a move to the East Coast. He viewed the existing circumstances as an opportunity to pursue his long awaited goal—money management. In 1993, he founded Bollinger Capital Management, a money management firm that deploys asset allocation and technical analysis as a basis for investment decisions.

In addition to being a CFA, also he is a Chartered Market Technician (CMT). He is the creator of Bollinger Bands, a technical indicator now integrated into virtually every technical analysis software program available. He is a frequent contributor to *Technical Analysis of Stocks and Commodities* and to the Market Technician Association's newsletter; and is invited to speak at both national and international seminars. He is currently under contract to write a book so keep your eyes peeled for its debut.

John Bollinger exhibits the kind of versatility of which most people only dream. In general, his functional style is technically oriented. Even as a cameraman, he enjoyed solving the technical difficulties that cropped up. Technical analysis was a natural extension of his aptitude for problem solving, analysis, and mathematics. For someone who describes his entire life as "being in the right place at the right time," Mr. Bollinger certainly was prepared for the challenges that lay at hand.

Bollinger Bands, as you developed them, have been in existence how many years?

Thirteen years, since 1983.

What prompted you to modify the already existing concept of trading bands?

Trading bands certainly existed before I created Bollinger Bands. The earliest reference that I have been able to locate comes from a book called *The Profit Magic of Stock Transaction Timing* by J. M. Hurst. The book detailed an approach to creating bands around the price. The fixed width trading band evolved from that work—the idea of taking a moving average and shifting it up and down on a chart by some given percentage. The book was published originally in 1973. For the next ten years, that work really dominated. In the early 1980s, a number of people recognized that there were some basic problems involved with fixed width trading bands. The first was that for a given stock the band width might be different than for another stock. For instance, a very quiet trading utility might have a band width of 1½% or 2% whereas a very volatile, high-flying OTC issue might have a band width of 20% or more. So one had to fit by eye or by hand whatever the appropriate band width was for that item. If that band width needed to change over time, there was really no method of doing so. I was very familiar with the options market and it was very interesting to study market volatility. In the options market, there are a couple of different concepts of volatility. One of them is the actual volatility that a stock experiences and another is the estimate of volatility that option traders put to the option's price. I had spent a lot of time looking at those variables and trying to figure out what effect they had on the market and trying to use them as forecasting tools. Literally, it just popped into my head one day that the ideal way of setting band widths would be via some measure of volatility. I examined about seven different measures of volatility and the consistently most robust was standard deviation. Going back to the work of J.M. Hurst and others, it had been demonstrated that for things financial, such as stock market averages, a 20 or 21 day moving average was a very good time period to use if you were looking for a moving average that was descriptive of the price structure. So I started with a 20 day moving average because it is the number of trading days in a month. I then tried the idea of using standard deviation as the measure of the band width. Initially, I tried a standard static deviation but that didn't work well. It wasn't until I had experimented further and came upon the idea of a moving standard deviation coupled with a moving average that I found the key that worked.

How long did this empirical experimentation take place?

It is hard to say. I had been working on the idea of improving trading bands for a couple of years before I came up with the idea that I finally implemented. Then I used them myself without really ever showing them to anybody for another year or so. I was Chief Market Analyst for the Financial News Network before I finally presented them on air. They actually didn't have a name. I just showed them on air one day and Bill Griffeth asked me what they were called and I said, "I guess they must be Bollinger Bands".

What is your definition of a Bollinger Band?

The base case for Bollinger Bands is a 20 day moving average where each data point on the moving average is shifted up or down by two standard deviations using the same 20 data points that we use to calculate the moving average. Now that is simply the base case. If one wishes to shorten the moving average, then one needs to reduce the number of deviations used. For instance, at about 10 periods, the standard deviation should be set to about 1.5. If one wishes to lengthen the moving average out to 50 periods or so, then one should expand the number of deviations used to about 2.5 standard deviations. So there is a relationship between the length of the moving average and the number of standard deviations one should use. By the way, statistically, that is a non-intuitive statement. That relationship had to be derived empirically.

To reiterate, you use 1.5 standard deviations with a 10 day moving average, 2 standard deviations with a 20 day moving average, and 2.5 standard deviations with a 50 day moving average. Given these different relationships, under what circumstances would you use each of these periods?

More intermediate term to longer term traders would use the 50 day moving average whereas the 10 day would be for quite a shortterm trader. I myself use the 20 day moving average and two standard deviations because most of the things that I deal with seem to work well within that framework. We are money managers and primarily invest in stocks and things related to stocks, although occasionally we take some positions in bonds. For stock market oriented items, 20 days and two standard deviations work very well. I am not really in favor of over optimization. I suppose you could find the perfect combination of an average and bandwidth for each individual item, but an 18 or 19 day average works more or less as well as a 20 or 21 day average. Just as bands that are 1.5 or 2.0 or 2.2 standard deviations all seem to work very well. Rather than try to find the optimal circumstance, I took these initial values that were quite robust. Sometimes when you try to get overly tricky about optimizing, you can have your head handed to you. The relationship breaks down. Coming out of the box, it seems that a 20 day moving average and 2.0 standard deviations are a very robust set of parameters.

What is your definition of short, intermediate, and longterm?

I personally define shortterm as less than one month. I would define intermediate term as some place between one and six months and longterm as something beyond there, but that is really a matter of personal choice. For some people, shortterm would be the next two or three minutes whereas intermediate term would be half an hour and longterm would be several hours. Warren Buffett would define longterm as 50 years which is quite useful from his perspective but would leave me a little anxious.

Since you have had experience trading options, would you suggest using a 20 day moving average or something shorter?

It has become my opinion over the years that the options market is so fairly priced at the important turning points, that at least in the time frames I trade in, it is very hard to make money. One of the things that we see time and time again at important market bottoms, which the bands are very helpful in diagnosing, is that you will get a huge surge in implied volatility. So even if you can identify the bottom correctly and purchase call options, you are going to pay a lot for them, and over the next four or five trading sessions those volatility estimates are liable to be reduced by 25% or more. Therefore even if you are right on the direction of the market, the market has to move quite a ways just for you to stay even. Although I haven't really made the transition from the options market to the futures market for that type of trading, I have become ever more and more convinced that one needs to trade those types of setups with items that are not strongly impacted by the decay of time premium.

Of the three moving averages you mentioned, is there one which produces a fewer number of whipsaws than another?

I don't think that question is germane. People often ask me how to select a moving average for use in this type of work. Mine is an interesting approach. What you want is not a moving average that gives the best crossover type buys and sells, nor a moving average that gives the best change of direction buys and sells. What you want is a moving average that is descriptive of the intermediate term trend. By intermediate term trend I mean the trend that you trade. All traders should have access to a time frame shorter than and longer than the time frame they trade in to be able to bracket their decisions with shortterm and longterm information. So what you are looking for is a moving average which is descriptive of the trend that you trade. The easiest way to find that is to identify an important turning point in the market where either an "M" type top or a "W" type bottom was formed.

When you say market, are you speaking in general terms?

Yes, a stock or whatever it is you trade. To find several important turning points where either "M" type tops or "W" type bottoms were formed, the correct moving average will be the one that offers resistance to the middle of the "M". There is another test that you can make which is the first pullback after the first rally away from the bottom. In other words, you form a "W" bottom and on the right hand side of the "W" you get a strong rally that say carries you up to the upper band. The first pullback will find support at the moving average if the moving average is properly specified. So, there are two points that you can check there. The middle of the "W" will generally find resistance at the moving average and then the correction of the first rally will generally find support at the moving average. If those are continually violated, then you are using a moving average that is too short. If they are continually not touched, then you are using a moving average that is too long.

Those are excellent guidelines. What are your recommendations regarding the use or application of Bollinger Bands?

There are two popular uses of Bollinger Bands. I don't particularly recommend this, but some people use them to identify overbought and oversold areas. That is, if price declines and tags the lower band, they look for a reversal to occur at that level. The problem with that is that you get a lot of run-throughs. In fact, part of the elegance of the band approach is that in a protracted uptrend the bands will essentially walk up the upper band or in a protracted downtrend the bands will essentially walk down the lower band. I use bands primarily to define, on a relative basis, the answer to the question of whether prices are high or low. At the upper band, by definition, prices are high. At the lower band, by definition, prices are low. We can then check a confirming indicator, hopefully an indicator that involves an independent variable such as volume or sentiment, to see whether there is a divergence. If there is a divergence then we can think about selling high prices or buying low prices. If there is confirmation, then that is an indication that prices will continue to remain high or continue to remain low. If that is the case, both the average and the bands will continue in the direction of the move. The other thing that Bollinger Bands are really useful for is identifying "W" type bottoms and "M" type tops. In many circumstances, the left hand portion of the "M" or "W" will be outside of the bands and the right hand portion of the "M" or "W" will be inside the bands. Take the example of the "W" bottom. By definition, even though prices may have drifted to an absolutely lower level, the fact that they were outside of the bands on the first push down and are inside of the bands on the second push down means that they are relatively higher even though they are absolutely lower. This allows correct and proper diagnosis of "M" and "W" reversal formations.

Will these "M" and "W" formations occur at major tops or major bottoms respectively or can they be found at shortterm and intermediate term points also?

You can find them on five minute bar charts. They are reversal patterns so you generally won't find them in the middle of a trend, but it is not impossible.

You said that you use Bollinger Bands primarily to determine when prices are high or low. How well does this strategy work for the S&P 500 index or the NYSE Composite?

I use the bands to determine if prices are high or low on a relative basis. It doesn't matter what type of security it is, whether it is a composite or an individual stock. Composites are probably a bit better-behaved in that the diversity of their components would suggest that they tend to have a greater inertia than an individual security, so they probably tend to work a little bit better. But the idea is the same regardless of whether it is a future's contract, a stock traded on the NYSE, or a volatile NASDAQ issue.

Bollinger Bands can be used in all types of markets for the same purpose?

Yes, more or less. I think it would be pretty evident if you tried to use them on things for which they are not suited. For instance, thinly traded issues which have large spreads can have fairly decent size percentage moves in terms of the reported last price without having the price of the bid and ask changed. It is simply the trades rattling back and forth between the bid and ask, not an actual change in price. For those securities, Bollinger Bands would be relatively inappropriate unless you looked at the midpoint between the bid and ask rather than the closing price.

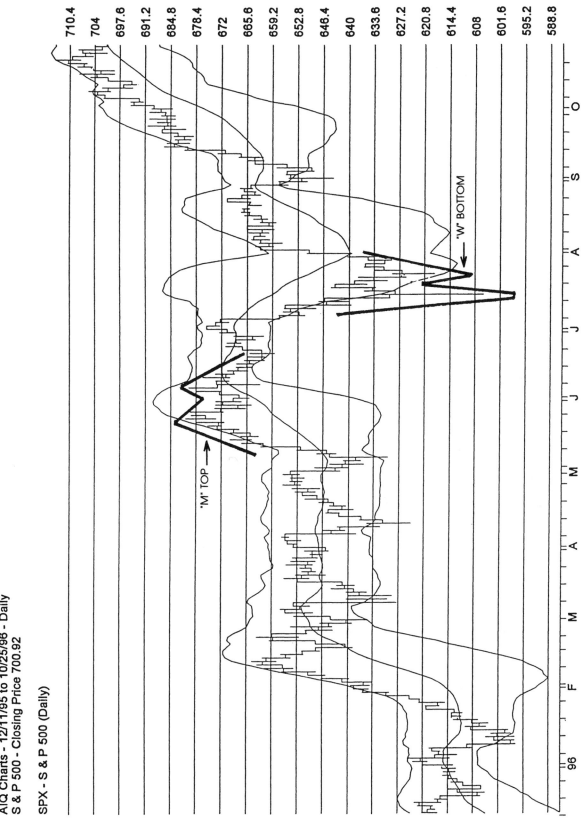

AIQ Charts - 12/11/95 to 10/25/96 - Daily
S & P 500 - Closing Price 700.92

SPX - S & P 500 (Daily)

Can you give me an example of how you would use Bollinger Bands to determine whether a price is relatively high or low?

If price is at or near the upper band, by definition the price is relatively high. If price is at or near the lower band, the price is relatively low. What you would look for is confirmation of that price. If your indicators were very strong when prices were at the upper band, one would consider that to be a confirmed status. Conversely, if a price went up and tagged the upper band and perhaps even pressed through it and the indicators were neutral at best, then one would think that a setback in the price of that security was in the offing.

When you look at Bollinger Bands, you often see prices moving from the upper band back to the lower band and so on. This movement can go on for quite some time. Should readers confirm these movements using other indicators?

Yes, but prices don't necessarily have to move from the upper band to the lower band. For instance, the S&P index essentially walked up the upper band for the first six months of 1995. There is nothing in the theory or practice of the bands that requires that prices vacillate back and forth between the bands. One of the things that you often see—and I would suspect that this was truer in commodities than in stocks although I couldn't prove that—is in an extended move you will see prices remain in contact with either the upper band in an up-move or the lower band in a down-move for extended periods of time while a primary trend is in place.

Would you consider the S&P 500's move up in the first six months of 1995 an example of an extended move?

Yes and using that particular example, if you were to take specifically that move from the November-December "W" bottom—the first part of the bottom was in November, 1994, and the second part was in December—price didn't contact the lower band from the time it left the band in December until a panic day in July 1995. In fact, I don't think price ever even closed below the middle band during that entire period. A volume based indicator like money flow percent was strongly positive all during that period suggesting that although the market was very strong, there was little technical deterioration going on.

Typically, when the bands narrow, that implies low volatility, correct?

If standard deviation is the definition of volatility, then volatility is low by definition. However, there are many other definitions of volatility. In order for the bands to narrow, standard deviation has to have been reduced.

Let's assume you have had a two to three month period of low volatility producing a contraction in band width. At some point, you know that prices will either break out to the upside or to the downside. Will Bollinger Bands offer any early clues as to the direction of the break?

AIQ Charts - 10/05/94 to 08/22/95 - Daily
S & P 500 - Closing Price 559.52

SPX - S & P 500 (Daily)

I don't know that they really do. I have studied the case for the S&P 500 a few times and there is a general pattern. Unfortunately, most of the period we studied was during a bull market. The reason is that we didn't want to take the study back before the birth of the OEX and S&P futures. We feel that those instruments have changed the character of trading in the market—especially from a volatility perspective because so many people use them to hedge. Taking volatility studies of big indices back prior to 1982 doesn't seem to make a lot of sense, at least from an intuitive point of view. So we have studied squeezes— we call periods of low volatility "The Squeeze"—in the S&P; specifically where the bandwidth for the S&P get below 2%. A typical pattern following that contraction has been for a sell-off tagging the lower band and then a marked rally. That pattern has broken down only two or three times. One of those breakdowns in the pattern was 1996, just before the July correction took place. There was a tightening in volatility but it didn't meet the rigorous definition because it didn't fall below the 2% bandwidth, which may have been the problem. The rule says that for "The Squeeze" the bandwidth has to fall below 2% and it only got to about 2.1%. We got the sell-off to the lower band, and then you got the rally, but it failed at the upper band and almost from exactly that point the correction set in and the S&P dropped nearly 10% from there. It is not certain that given another market environment whether that pattern would be reversed. For example, if we were to examine a real bear market, I don't know whether we would see a tightening of volatility and then a rally to the upper band followed by a collapse in prices of greater magnitude. One would suspect that might be the case, but many things in the market are not symmetrical so I would not assert that would be the case.

So it's best not to rely on using the bands in this capacity?

We know for a fact that volatility is cyclical; we can demonstrate this very clearly. By observing the bandwidths, we can observe a contraction in volatility and we can expect the extension in volatility. But the bands by themselves are not going to tell you much about which direction that expansion in volatility will occur. The fact that you have volatility severely reduced on a shortterm basis is *highly* significant.

Can you say more about the 2% band width rule for the S&P 500?

I have worked it out only for the S&P 500 and I think I told you everything I know about it. I would assume that there are similar levels and patterns to be found in other vehicles but the S&P 500 has been the primary focus in my research as far as trading bands are concerned.

Prices don't always move directly from one band to another. Sometimes they will pause at the moving average line and then continue up or down. Does this have any particular meaning?

The object of selecting the moving average that you want to use in trading bands is not to select one that produces the best buy and sell crossovers but to select a moving average that produces the best description of the intermediate term trend, which is the trend you are going to trade. To test if the average you are using is correct, in a move when you make a primary bottom and rally back and prices fall back again, the first pullback after the breakout should find support at or near the correct moving average.

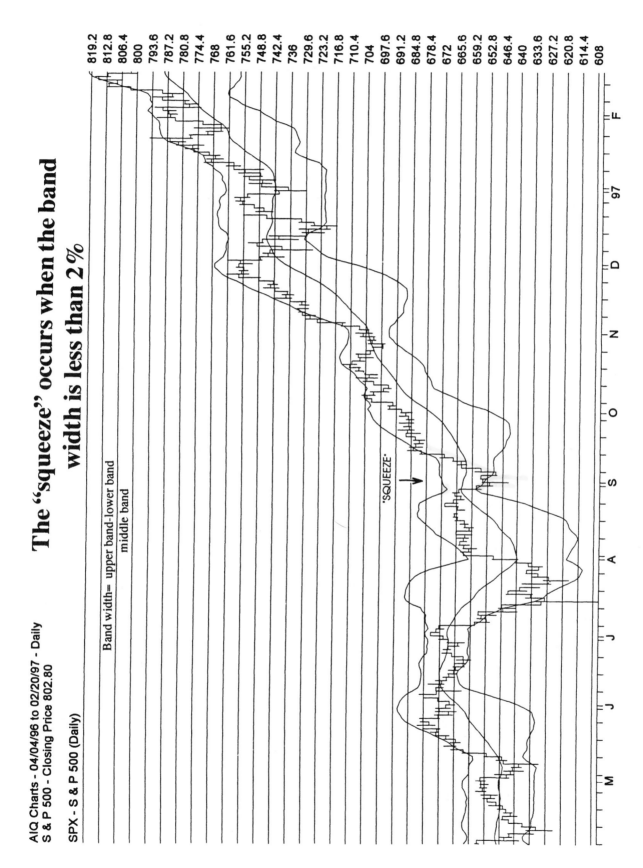

The "squeeze" occurs when the band width is less than 2%

AIQ Charts - 04/04/96 to 02/20/97 - Daily
S & P 500 - Closing Price 802.80

SPX - S & P 500 (Daily)

Band width= upper band-lower band
middle band

"SQUEEZE"

In other words, after you make a bottom, you rally and then you have a failure. You don't go straight to the moon, generally you pullback. Well, in many cases, a properly specified intermediate term average will provide support for that failure. It is almost flat at the time of the re-test. It should provide support.

Are penetrations of the upper or lower bands likely to be continuations of a move that was in progress?

That is correct.

Are there other conditions which should be met to justify the continuance of the trend or will penetration alone suffice?

The whole purpose of trading bands is to allow you to evaluate indicators. The indicators you are using ought to support a trend. If they don't then as soon as you get back inside the bands you have a reversal signal on your hands.

There are obviously different degrees of penetration. Are there any rules of thumb?

I don't particularly worry about it as there is nothing exact about this. One of the great evils of trading is false exactness. I always tell the story about the fellow who's guru was 99% right. Unfortunately, it was the 1% wrong that caused the fellow to stumble and this is the way it goes. The guru predicted that the XYZ market average would rally until it reached 1,622.13 and that would happen in 312 trading days from the day in which the prediction was made. By golly, 312 trading days later, the average stopped at 1,610.00 and immediately fell like a stone. The fellow who took the guru's advice never sold because the average never reached the projection. I think this is very, very typical. There lies a false precision that we do not have available to us in our work. People focus on the forecast rather than the market and that causes a great loss of money. If one relies on the forecast, then one has a great deal of trouble recognizing where the forecast is inaccurate. In other words, there is some margin of error there that is belied by the great precision of the forecast. If you get to within one or two percent of the target, that's enough; let's give up and go home. Rather, people are left hanging on for the last tick. If it doesn't happen what do they do? Our entire business is relative. Nothing ever repeats exactly. There is no finite answer. There is no best stock. There is no best fund. There is no best commodity. There is no best trader. There is no perfect trade. All we try to do is find the best opportunity that we can at a given time and exploit as much of it as we can, and then walk away and look for the next opportunity. Bands are like that. We say that 20 days is the base for Bollinger Bands plus or minus two standard deviations. Those numbers happen to work well in fairly many circumstances and thus they are what we call robust. Trading is a fuzzy process and I mean fuzzy in the best sense of the word. That is, as in fuzzy logic, as in the willingness to accept the idea that things aren't exactly quantifiable and to forge ahead anyway.

I am sure people abuse the premises of Bollinger Bands in the sense that they try to force them to give trading signals when they are not designed for that.

That's right. I feel sorry for those people because they are literally trying to do what I believe is impossible. If the S&P went up and tagged the upper band and 21 day money flow was negative, I would say that the probabilities of an ensuing decline were extraordinarily high. But all that has happened is that you have found a situation in which the probability of a coming market move is high. There is no certainty.

What are the most common mistakes you see inexperienced investors or traders making when using Bollinger Bands?

I think the precision error is probably the greatest error—but, without a doubt, I can predict that it will be psychology that levels the investor, not Bollinger Bands. What makes or breaks an investor is not the tools that he or she uses, but the mind and the emotions with which they use those tools. Bollinger Bands, the various volume indicators, the industry group structures that we like so much and find so valuable, and some of our market and individual stock modeling work are very helpful, but I would point out that in July 1996, we went through a very large correction in terms of the market; a correction that terminated in a "W" bottom. That "W" bottom was a classic formation. On each point of the "W," at each spike down, a major guru capitulated and sold out their portfolio. That was caused by psychology; not by the failure of the systems or approaches that those two quite capable gurus advocated. Whatever tools you pick, whether they be the tools that I use and advocate or whether they be the tools that someone else uses and advocates, they are absolutely meaningless unless you first enter the arena with your emotions in control so that you can follow the system you have chosen to follow.

Can you think of a situation where the Bollinger Bands could be used alone?

The "W" bottom and its cousin, the "M" type top. The "W" bottom that I just described was classically defined by the bands. There is some information that is thrown off by the price action in and around the bands that is useful in-and-of itself. It's not a whole approach but this "W" bottom was perfectly constructed. The first leg down produced a low that was made outside the bands. The rally carried it about halfway back to the moving average. The second low was made inside the bands and the subsequent rally broke the 20 day moving average and carried to the upper band where it failed for a period of 10 days and consolidated. Now the rally has resumed again. Just in terms of the descriptive powers of the bands, they have worked very well in terms of how you would expect them to work. It's not that simple all the time, but there are occasional setups and bits of information and such that become very clear simply by adding the bands to a price chart.

Let's say stock XYZ moves to the upper band indicating that the price is relatively high. In your own work, would you use your other indicators to determine whether to continue holding the stock or selling it?

Yes. For instance, the S&P 500 was in contact with the upper band for the first half of 1995 but the indicators were strong and never generated a sell signal during that entire time.

If you were going to select a stock for purchase, which indicators would you use in conjunction with Bollinger Bands to make your final selection?

For confirmation I would use the RSI, On-Balance-Volume, money flow, positive volume index, and our industry group work. The more indicators that confirm, the more confidence I have in the trade.

Moving to a broader viewpoint, I believe you place a great deal of emphasis on group and sector analysis.

Yes, this is extremely important and forms a core piece of our philosophy. When making investment decisions, I think most people place two-thirds or more of the weight on an individual stock and a third or less of the weight on the market as a whole. Then there are some pure market timers who place most of the weight on just the market. My feeling is that there are a couple of very important interim layers that are generally ignored. Each successive layer is an agglomeration of the prior. You can think of it as a pyramid with the pinnacle of the pyramid being the market. If you slice the pyramid horizontally, the first slice below the top is the "sectors." The next slice down is the "industry groups" and the bottom slice is all of the "individual stocks." So, a proper approach would be to put roughly equal weight on the market, the sector, the group, and the stock. For instance, the market has been very strong recently, the communications sector has been strong, the international telephone group has been strong, and BCE, which is the old Bell Canada, has been quite strong. When you have that combination of factors, you stand a much higher chance of initiating a successful trade. I often compare this to a scull being rowed by four rowers. If the rowers are in rhythm and well coordinated, the scull will make tremendous and very graceful passage through the water. But, if one of the rowers is out of sync with the other rowers, the scull is likely to go nowhere. A lot of energy will be expended but the scull's progress will be halted.

In order to gain some perspective on group and sector performance, where would you suggest readers begin?

The first place you have to start is with a group structure and there are several group structures that readers might use. The traditional ones are the Security Industry Codes (SIC), the Standard and Average you will see all kinds of stocks; while they meet the generic term "utilities," their lines of business are wildly different. There is little internal consistency. I don't think that you can treat the Baby Bells as utilities anymore. They are becoming entrepreneurial companies. Increasingly, their real revenues are derived not from their regulated base but from their non-regulated activities and that is what Wall Street analysts look at when they are forecasting. They belong in their own universe with their own co-equal units so we have pulled them out and put them in a communication sector with seven other groups.

The general rule is that the Dow Jones Utility Average will lead the broader market usually by eight months. Do you find that the group you have assembled gives you a better lead time?

Poor's group structures, and the Dow Jones group structures. Those are the most common and best known but they all suffer from various problems. The structures themselves were created a long time ago and although they have been updated, they haven't received the total overhauls that they really need in order to model the current market correctly.

That doesn't sound too encouraging.

We have taken the traditional idea of groups and sectors and made a pass through a universe of 2,000 stocks. Based on the current role of companies in the modern economy, we have set up a group sector structure that consists of 15 sectors and 130 industry groups. We call this a Rational Industry Group Structure because we did this from two different points of view—technical and fundamental. That is, we asked what businesses these companies were in and using a correlation coefficient, we also checked to see that the groups were internally consistent. We went through each of the groups and eliminated the outliers. Now the groups have a great deal of internal consistency which dramatically helps results from a trader's point of view. Therefore, I would recommend our "Group Power" over any other group structure; however, using any group structure is far better than using none.

How is your "Group Power" constructed?

We developed several rules for "Group Power" that all have to do with familial relations, like parents and children. Any groups' parent is its sector but it also has uncles and aunts because there are related sectors and related groups. Let's use IBM as an example. IBM'S group is mainframe computers which has uncles or aunts, depending on how you look at it, which would be computer parts, computer PC's, and so forth. When they are properly constructed, these groups can be used in relation to other groups. By association, when you have all the stocks in a group pulling together and all the groups in a sector pulling together and all the related sectors pulling together, then the market is going to do well.

What constitutes "properly contructed"?

Bob Brogan, while he was with Bomar, developed an index of 50 electric utility companies that he used as a forecasting tool for the broad stock market. When we reconstructed our utility sector, we followed his lead and moved the communication stocks into their own sector. Taking it one step further, we looked at the electric utilities and said, "The correlations are very poor between the bulk of these utilities and the nuclear utilities," so we stripped out all the nuclear utilities and put them in their own industry group. Now we have an electric utility group that is *very* useful for forecasting movements in the broad stock market and a utility sector that is cohesive.

More useful than the traditional Dow Jones Utility Average?

Much more so because this is a pure electric utility group. If you look at the Dow Jones Utility

Crude oil, gasoline, and, heating oil topped in Dec. 1996
The energy stocks topped in Jan. 1997

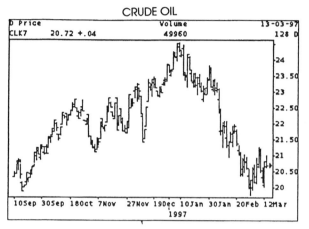

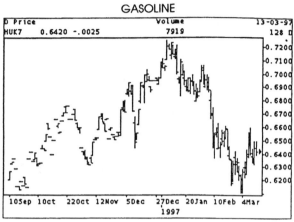

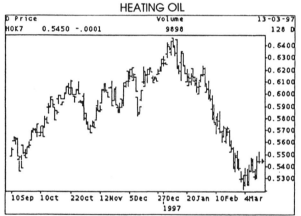

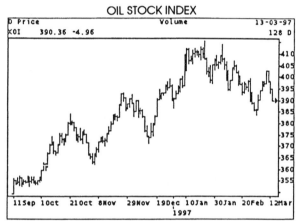

Knight-Ridder MoneyCenter

I have never compared the lead times of the pure electrics to the Dow Jones Utility Average in that sense. I rely primarily on the testing and research that Bob Brogan did and he found that a pure electric utility index was a superior forecasting vehicle to the Dow Jones Utility Average. My contribution was to delete the nuclear utilities from the group because they really do trade to their own drummer and I think they will increasingly do so because many of the security analysts believe that many of the nuclear utilities are structurally bankrupt. Another important relationship exists between the energy sector and the energy futures. We break up the energy sector into its logical components and then compare the action of those industry groups to the action of the energy futures, leaving you way ahead of the people who are looking at the energy group alone.

What is the relationship between the energy group and the futures? Will one lead the other?

In the energy area, the relationship is not consistent. Energy stocks usually lead the futures but that is not necessarily true at all times. In other areas where you have related commodities, often the commodity will lead the stock. In late 1996, we had a very long topping out process in the energy area with virtually no downside pressure on the stocks. However, in late January 1997, the two leading groups; drillers and producers, turned down and accelerated to the downside. Right after that, the energy futures themselves broke down.

In that situation, the stocks broke down in advance of the futures.

Yes. This intermarket analysis goes back to Bill O'hama's 3-D and 4-D rules. The 4-D rule suggested that you needed to look not only at the front month of a futures' contract (where everybody focuses their attention), but also at all the back months and the chart patterns had to confirm in all of those months. If they didn't, then you had a possible divergence on your hands and you had to analyze that divergence. His 3-D rule suggested that related commodities or futures had to confirm. In other words, the price of oil, heating oil, unleaded gas, and natural gas all had to be moving in the same direction. I have extended O'hama's rules to include my industry groups so that we have a version that runs from the futures markets all the way through to the equity markets. For example, you have the metals complex—gold, silver, platinum, palladium—and you have the various gold stock groups, such as the South African gold mining companies, the North American companies, on down to the more speculative penny mining shares.

Confirmation from a majority of related markets translates into a higher level of confidence for a particular move.

That's right. "Catching a hickey" is a phenomenon that occurs in sculling when one of the rowers doesn't get his oar out of the water fast enough. Because the oar has such huge leverage, the river just picks the rower up and tosses him out of the boat. It's like an eject seat. That image illustrates exactly what will happen in the market if you don't have a confirming relationship between groups, sectors, and equities in a narrow sense or with the related markets in a broader sense. There is a company called Acme Analytics that is in the process of developing a couple of Internet products to forecast stocks and mutual funds. They use a fuzzy logic model to drive those analyses. The model uses the traditional technical rules and pattern matches but one of the big factors it keys in on is group structure. It looks for positive relationships between stocks and groups and unless a group is going in the same direction as a stock, the model won't rate it highly.

Haven't there been academic studies which have documented that while an individual stock may appear strong on a chart, if its related industry group is weak, then you really can't expect too much from that stock in terms of performance?

There have been a lot of performance attribution studies, as they are called, and they have been all over the board with their results. Some studies have suggested that 2/3 of the performance of a stock can be attributed to the market and 1/3 to its own characteristics. Other studies have suggested that as much as ½ of the performance might be attributable to the market, ¼ to the group, and ¼ to the stock. I don't have the mechanics to perform attribution analysis so we came up with ¼ weighting for each and when you implement that in a model, it works very well. One of the signs of a good model is that if your unoptimized naive parameters plug in and work well, then you are probably doing the right thing.

Of course, negative performance from several groups in one sector could undermine the entire sector. A computer model would completely gloss over that sector despite the fact that it might happen to contain one or two stellar performing groups.

Yes, absolutely. There will always be the one stock in a group that goes to the moon while the rest of them do not go anywhere but, also there will be the one stock in the group that crashes while the others do not. In certain phases of the market, you are going to get whole sectors of the market that are going down while other whole sectors are going up. We call that rotation. You are going to miss opportunities this way but any disciplined approach to the market is going to miss opportunities. This type of market discipline will present you with a set of opportunities that you can understand and rationalize and therefore, take advantage of.

Regarding sectors or groups, are there any specific parameters to which you adhere in determining whether the market is healthy or unhealthy? In other words, do you require that 12 out of 15 sectors have to be in gear to the upside for a sustained, broad uptrend?

No, but it is an input into my overall market analysis. We don't see things as black and white, that is, we don't have any specific requirements. If we have 15 sectors in the market and 15 of them are in gear, that's great. If 12 of them are in gear, that's still great but not so great. If 10 of them are in gear, it's okay. If only 5 of them are in gear, that's not very good and if 2 of them are in gear....

The risks have increased tremendously.

Yes, but it's a curve. We evaluate things in a continuous manner. Going back to the sculling metaphor, the more rowers that we have in the scull, the more speed we have and the more confident we are. For instance, if our pure electric utilities are rising, that's good. If they are flat, that's ho-hum, and if they are falling, that's bad. We look at them in a continuous manner. So if they are rising slightly, that is a small positive input into our market opinion. I think one of the greatest fallacies is this idea that there are such entities as crisp buy and sell signals. They simply don't exist. Everybody is always looking for the "buy signal" or the "sell signal" that takes us from 0% invested to 100% invested or from 100% to 0%. In fact, nothing in life works that way. What you want to do is gradually transition from a period in which you should be short to a period in which you should be flat to a period in which you should be long to a period in which you should be flat and so on. We take a fuzzy logic approach in our analysis because a multifactor fuzzy approach is very robust.

Would you clarify what you mean by fuzzy logic approach?

When you build a fuzzy logic inference, you are using a set of fuzzy rules to map the underlying mathematical function that is behind the market. That's what the fuzzy approach is all about and if you properly specify the rules, ultimately you will be able to draw out some underlying function. Now, if you make those fuzzy rules adaptive, which is very easy to do, as it goes forward it compares its results to what has actually happened and will adjust itself accordingly. The system will actually tailor itself to what is going on and will continuously re-evaluate its performance. If you do this, then your system will adapt from bull market to bear market to trading range market—back and forth.

Allowing you to phase in and out of positions automatically.

That's right. Now, this is not the same as continuous optimization in any way whatsoever. The math is not as complicated. The math for fuzzy logic, while not trivial, is not rocket science by any means. Adaptive fuzzy logic looks at the weights of its rules. If a certain set of rules aren't working, it will reduce the weights of those rules and if another set of rules is working very well, it will add some weight to those rules.

For those who want to learn more about fuzzy logic, what references would you recommend?

If someone wanted to get a quick, non-technical introduction to the world of fuzzy logic and how it works, there is a book called *Fuzzy Logic* by Daniel McNeill and Paul Freiberger. It's a good survey of what has been done in the field. From there, you will want to go to the more technical books written by Bart Kosko or Earl Cox, which actually tell you how to get things done.

What other analytical tools do you use in your assessment of groups?

One thing that we do in "Group Power," which I find to be very valuable, is calculate the new highs and new lows for industry groups. We calculate new highs not only for the traditional 52 weeks, but also for 26 weeks and 13 weeks. It turns out that the 13 week new highs list is essentially an early warning list for the 52 week new highs list.

What is the rationale for that occurrence?

Groups tend to be very trendy. These days the stock market is full of momentum players. When a group shows up on the 52 week new highs list, momentum players go out and buy all the shares they can. What you have in a 13 week and a 26 week new highs list for industry groups is essentially a roll call of what's going to be on the 52 week new highs list before it gets there. You can buy groups that appear on the 13 week new highs list and then watch as they get lifted through the rotation. When groups finally appear on the 52 week new highs list, often you will see them take off as a lot of money flows into them from momentum players.

Will this system work for individual stocks as well?

Yes, we find that this works for stocks too. We calculate 13 week and 26 week new highs and new lows. Let's take a stock that is basing after some type of disaster and it starts to emerge out of the base. If the base is any decent size at all, as *soon* as the stock breaks out of the base, it is going to show up immediately on the 13 week new highs list. So, the chart patterns of stocks that you see on a 13 week new highs list will either be emerging out of a base or consolidating. You can then look at all the important technical variables—relative strength, money flow, On-Balance-Volume—and make an assessment about whether you want to own those issues or not. If you have a good eye for charts and for the indicators, you are going to find stocks that will be on the 26 week new highs list in a couple weeks and on the 52 week new highs list sometime after that.

Scrutinizing a 13 week new highs list would give you a fantastic lead over everyone else.

Yes, we think this is very important. Another thing which we do in "Group Power" is to count the number of stocks over key moving averages. We took Abe Cohen's (Chartcraft) idea and modified it. First we use industry groups instead of individual stocks and secondly, we use days instead of weeks as our time periods—10 days, 50 days, and 200 days. We have found them to be *extremely* reliable overbought and oversold tools. For instance, at the market highs on January 23, 1997, all three time periods had readings above 90%. You tell me that 90% of the groups are over their 10, 50, and 200 day moving averages and I am going to tell you that you ought to own some puts. For the broad market, it's probably the best pure overbought and oversold tool that there is.

Does 90% represent an overbought level for stock groups?

There are so few occurrences of that nature, I would hesitate to speculate. People underestimate the importance of groups and the information that can be derived from them. Most people think "Group Power" is only about stock selection but when you include the intermarket relationships, the moving averages, and the new highs and lows, you end up with a lot of stock market forecasting variables. The "group" principle works in the commodity world just as well. It's one thing to be long beans when they are flying through the prices while none of the other grains are moving. It's another thing to be long when all the grains are moving. In one you tend to rather nervous, and the other you have a great deal more conviction. The CRB calculates commodity sector indices for energy, meats, grains, and metals.

Are you speaking about something other than the CRB index?

Yes, these are separate indices, like a CRB energy index, a CRB grain index—there are seven of them in all.

Can these indices be found in the Wall Street Journal?

No, I've only seen them on the front inside page of the CRB chartbook and in the Market Week section of *Barron's* labeled "Key Commodity Indexes." They are very poorly distributed and underutilized, but they are very important. So, whether it is stocks, commodities, or countries, this whole "group" area is a gold mine.

To wrap things up, would you name three or four investment books which helped broaden your understanding of technical analysis?

Extraordinary Popular Delusions and the Madness of Crowds by Charles Mackay, *Smarter Trading* by Perry Kaufman, *New Concepts in Technical Trading Systems* by Welles Wilder, and *Technical Analysis Explained* by Martin J. Pring.

```
Return-Path: <gg@margin.margin.com>
Date: Tue, 11 Mar 1997 15:39:43 -0800
From: gg@margin.margin.com (Bollinger's Group Grope)
To: bbands@ix.netcom.com, bbands@margin.margin.com, data.entry@telescan.com,
      s.jacobs@telescan.com
Subject: Group Power for Tuesday, March 11, 1997 (text version)
```

```
             John Bollinger's Group Power

Welcome to Group Power for Tuesday, March 11, 1997.

>From a short term perspective,
the trend of the market is flat and the market is overbought.

>From an intermediate term perspective,
the trend of the market is up and the market is overbought.

>From a long term perspective,
the trend of the market is up and the market is very overbought.

70 groups advanced on 28.545 million shares.
61 groups declined on 30.368 million shares.

The Group Power Arms index is 1.22.

There were 33 52-Week New Highs & 1 52-Week New Lows.
There were 37 26-Week New Highs & 1 26-Week New Lows.
There were 39 13-Week New Highs & 2 13-Week New Lows.

81% of groups are over their 10-day average.
80% of groups are over their 50-day average.
90% of groups are over their 200-day average.

Group Power list ranked by short term momentum:
```

(handwritten note in left margin: "When all 3 time periods > 90% !! OB !!")

GROUP NAME	SHRT MOM	MOM CHNG	INTR MOM	$$ FLOW RANK
Retail,Apparel	12.26	0.73	17.99	37.60
Airlines	9.37	1.05	13.17	35.20
Tobacco	8.21	0.82	17.79	84.00
Retail,Specialty	8.03	0.68	11.05	39.20
Employment Services	7.93	1.34	10.37	52.80
Pollution/Waste Management	7.66	0.37	13.44	37.60
Office Supply Stores	7.55	3.82	9.09	57.60
Clothing and Fabrics	7.31	0.36	14.80	89.60
Healthcare Providers	7.27	0.41	13.16	57.60
Savings & Loans	7.25	-0.07	20.66	72.80
Insurance,Life	6.62	-0.26	18.04	100.00
Banks,East	6.47	-1.01	18.67	98.40
Aluminum	6.07	1.65	10.57	73.60
Insurnace,Diverse	6.06	1.60	12.38	98.40
Banks,South	6.05	-0.21	17.56	98.40
Retail,Broadline	6.03	-0.28	7.59	43.20
Banks,Central	6.01	-1.29	17.66	93.60
Home Supply Stores	5.99	-0.92	0.56	13.60
Diversified Technology	5.99	0.08	14.11	87.20
Household Products	5.72	-0.22	11.57	80.80
Soft Drinks	5.66	0.74	13.15	52.00
Air Freight/Couriers	5.53	0.83	12.77	91.20
Insurance,Prop.&Cas.	5.50	0.75	12.15	99.20
Insurance,Full Line	5.27	0.11	14.21	96.00
Retail,Drug	5.18	0.26	13.10	78.40
Oil Equipment	5.17	0.09	6.98	68.80
Broadcasting	5.10	-1.14	6.67	28.80
Precious Metals	5.04	1.83	9.03	80.00
Banks,Money Center	5.03	-2.37	17.21	96.80
Recreation,Other	5.01	0.20	7.23	46.40
Food Retailers	4.97	-0.40	8.71	81.60

Footwear	4.94	-1.74	12.79	56.00
Pharmaceuticals	4.59	-1.03	11.75	79.20
Computer Services	4.49	-2.67	9.40	36.00
Metals,Non-ferrous	4.43	3.44	6.19	66.40
Household Products,Durable	4.28	-0.03	11.11	79.20
Textiles	4.24	-0.60	10.55	80.80
Banks,Western	4.23	-0.81	15.74	59.20
Financial Services	4.22	-0.93	10.92	72.00
Africa	4.06	-0.13	8.44	56.80
Publishing	3.96	-0.37	8.71	81.60
Railroads	3.89	0.31	7.00	89.60
Brokers	3.76	-0.47	19.69	95.20
Lodging	3.58	-1.40	7.78	44.00
Machinery,Heavy	3.52	1.31	6.89	48.00
Coal	3.48	1.23	12.80	84.00
Europe	3.47	-0.66	7.34	68.80
Advanced Medical Devices	3.27	0.18	8.06	68.80
Printers	3.24	-0.25	8.08	68.00
Cosmetics/Personal Care	3.23	0.66	10.59	95.20
Chemicals,Specialty	3.21	0.77	5.84	68.80
Newspapers	3.08	-0.14	8.19	54.40
Chemicals,Commodity	2.98	0.81	5.39	52.80
Tires	2.96	-0.68	8.98	56.80
Trucking	2.96	0.06	6.27	52.80
Retail,Electronics	2.86	-0.34	-0.49	20.80
Home Furnishings	2.77	-0.14	9.51	48.80
International Telephone	2.66	-0.55	8.48	80.00
Oil,Drilling	2.65	0.01	2.21	71.20
Diversified Business	2.61	-0.19	5.80	77.60
Containers & Packaging	2.59	0.61	3.46	52.80
Commercial Services	2.54	-0.86	4.12	34.40
Real Estate Investment	2.49	0.13	8.82	100.00
Transportation Equipment	2.48	0.12	6.56	65.60
Industrial,Diversified	2.47	0.61	6.95	79.20
Studios	2.44	-0.45	3.88	72.80
Food	2.21	-0.22	6.99	80.80
S&P 500 Index	2.19	-0.22	8.50	100.00
Latin America	2.15	-0.74	9.27	43.20
Building Materials	2.05	0.43	7.48	82.40
Alcoholic Beverages	1.99	-0.93	7.37	59.20
Machinery	1.88	-0.29	7.40	94.40
Manufactured Housing	1.82	-0.16	1.20	44.80
Cement	1.75	0.43	7.12	92.80
Appliances	1.72	-0.17	2.00	24.80
Canadian Oil	1.71	0.77	6.04	92.80
Office Equipment	1.63	-0.27	8.70	55.20
Industrial Services	1.45	0.61	4.34	41.60
Pipelines	1.39	0.67	4.17	68.80
Electrical Components	1.31	-0.01	7.77	94.40
Stock Funds	1.27	0.57	4.04	80.00
Factory Equipment	1.21	-0.00	7.16	43.20
Instruments	1.16	-0.60	5.39	22.40
Semiconductor Equipment	1.14	1.60	23.20	61.60
Construction	1.10	-0.13	4.67	80.80
Cable Television	1.06	1.17	3.82	17.60
Bond Funds	1.04	-0.39	2.42	38.40
Telephone Systems	1.04	-0.31	4.09	91.20
Auto Parts	0.97	0.52	4.45	81.60
Biotech	0.70	-3.01	16.80	36.00
Oil,International	0.57	-0.70	4.12	76.80
Semiconductor	0.49	1.18	13.57	40.80
Machinery,Agricultural	0.45	0.63	4.99	87.20
Restaurants	0.38	-0.20	1.38	28.00
Gold,South Africa	0.35	-0.64	2.97	55.20
Forest Products	0.29	0.01	0.89	80.00
Electronics	0.24	-0.83	6.83	68.80

Metal Fabricators	0.05	-0.54	2.92	75.20
Water Companies	0.05	0.51	5.70	51.20
Gas Companies	0.04	0.35	1.75	74.40
Home Construction	0.01	0.88	5.12	70.40
Advertising	-0.06	-0.32	1.76	36.80
Consumer Services	-0.08	0.01	-0.41	56.80
Mining,Diversified	-0.10	1.31	1.86	93.60
Medical Supplies	-0.11	-0.08	5.58	39.20
Marine Transport	-0.12	0.98	2.30	45.60
Paper Products	-0.13	0.12	1.16	80.00
Food Wholesalers	-0.33	-0.32	3.92	66.40
Electric Utilities	-0.38	-0.16	0.58	35.20
Steel	-0.41	2.54	2.17	48.00
Computers,PC	-0.47	-0.48	9.25	32.80
Aerospace/Defense	-0.61	0.14	2.35	52.80
Industrial Technology	-0.79	0.69	3.53	48.80
Recreation,Toys	-0.86	-1.77	2.22	31.20
Wireless Commun.	-0.93	0.14	-1.03	16.80
Pacific	-0.99	0.61	-0.28	39.20
Fertilizer	-1.17	-0.59	-3.03	31.20
Long Distance Comm.	-1.43	-1.17	6.03	95.20
Automobile Mfg.	-1.59	-1.69	1.77	60.00
OTC Composite Index	-1.79	0.02	2.57	75.20
Oil,Domestic	-2.01	-0.63	0.48	76.80
Computers,Mini	-2.14	-0.22	4.59	44.00
Computers,Mainframe	-2.17	-1.37	5.41	56.00
Software	-2.20	-0.06	0.42	29.60
Commun. Technology	-2.35	-0.16	-0.83	33.60
Oil Producers	-2.55	-0.00	-3.87	77.60
Nuclear Electric Utilities	-3.56	-0.48	-3.58	50.40
Casinos	-3.83	0.32	-6.12	16.80
Computer Components	-6.76	0.17	8.11	61.60
Internet	-9.14	-1.30	-10.86	7.20
Networking	-9.65	0.05	-12.56	18.40

Top Ten Relative Strength Groups:

GROUP NAME	REL STR	SHRT MOM	INTR MOM	$$ FLOW RANK
Retail,Apparel	100.0	12.26	17.99	37.60
Office Supply Stores	95.8	7.55	9.09	57.60
Home Supply Stores	94.7	5.99	0.56	13.60
Precious Metals	93.9	5.04	9.03	80.00
Tobacco	91.5	8.21	17.79	84.00
Retail,Broadline	90.9	6.03	7.59	43.20
Airlines	87.9	9.37	13.17	35.20
Retail,Specialty	87.2	8.03	11.05	39.20
Computer Services	87.1	4.49	9.40	36.00
Recreation,Other	83.2	5.01	7.23	46.40

Bottom Ten Relative Strength Groups:

GROUP NAME	REL STR	SHRT MOM	INTR MOM	$$ FLOW RANK
Nuclear Electric Utilities	36.0	-3.56	-3.58	50.40
Oil Producers	34.6	-2.55	-3.87	77.60
OTC Composite Index	34.1	-1.79	2.57	75.20
Brokers	32.7	3.76	19.69	95.20
Commun. Technology	27.6	-2.35	-0.83	33.60
Semiconductor Equipment	22.7	1.14	23.20	61.60
Casinos	19.1	-3.83	-6.12	16.80
Networking	2.7	-9.65	-12.56	18.40
Computer Components	2.2	-6.76	8.11	61.60
Internet	0.0	-9.14	-10.86	7.20

Top 10 Persistency of Money Flow Groups:

GROUP NAME	$$ FLOW	SHRT MOM	INTR MOM
Real Estate Investment	100.0	2.49	8.82
Insurance,Life	100.0	6.62	18.04
S&P 500 Index	100.0	2.19	8.50

Insurance,Prop.&Cas.	99.2	5.50	12.15
Insurnace,Diverse	98.4	6.06	12.38
Banks,East	98.4	6.47	18.67
Banks,South	98.4	6.05	17.56
Banks,Money Center	96.8	5.03	17.21
Insurance,Full Line	96.0	5.27	14.21
Long Distance Comm.	95.2	-1.43	6.03

Bottom 10 Persistency of Money Flow Groups:

GROUP NAME	$$ FLOW	SHRT MOM	INTR MOM
Restaurants	28.0	0.38	1.38
Appliances	24.8	1.72	2.00
Instruments	22.4	1.16	5.39
Retail,Electronics	20.8	2.86	-0.49
Networking	18.4	-9.65	-12.56
Cable Television	17.6	1.06	3.82
Wireless Commun.	16.8	-0.93	-1.03
Casinos	16.8	-3.83	-6.12
Home Supply Stores	13.6	5.99	0.56
Internet	7.2	-9.14	-10.86

Largest Gains in Short Term Momentum:

GROUP NAME	SHRT MOM	MOM CHNG	$$ FLOW
Office Supply Stores	7.55	3.82	57.60
Metals,Non-ferrous	4.43	3.44	66.40
Steel	-0.41	2.54	48.00
Precious Metals	5.04	1.83	80.00
Aluminum	6.07	1.65	73.60
Insurnace,Diverse	6.06	1.60	98.40
Semiconductor Equipment	1.14	1.60	61.60
Employment Services	7.93	1.34	52.80
Machinery,Heavy	3.52	1.31	48.00
Mining,Diversified	-0.10	1.31	93.60

Largest Declines in Short Term Momentum:

GROUP NAME	SHRT MOM	MOM CHNG	$$ FLOW
Banks,Central	6.01	-1.29	93.60
Internet	-9.14	-1.30	7.20
Computers,Mainframe	-2.17	-1.37	56.00
Lodging	3.58	-1.40	44.00
Automobile Mfg.	-1.59	-1.69	60.00
Footwear	4.94	-1.74	56.00
Recreation,Toys	-0.86	-1.77	31.20
Banks,Money Center	5.03	-2.37	96.80
Computer Services	4.49	-2.67	36.00
Biotech	0.70	-3.01	36.00

52-Week New Highs:

GROUP NAME	SHRT MOM	INTR MOM	$$ FLOW RANK
Insurance,Life	6.62	18.04	100.00
Real Estate Investment	2.49	8.82	100.00
Insurance,Prop.&Cas.	5.50	12.15	99.20
Insurnace,Diverse	6.06	12.38	98.40
Banks,South	6.05	17.56	98.40
Insurance,Full Line	5.27	14.21	96.00
Cosmetics/Personal Care	3.23	10.59	95.20
Air Freight/Couriers	5.53	12.77	91.20
Clothing and Fabrics	7.31	14.80	89.60
Coal	3.48	12.80	84.00
Tobacco	8.21	17.79	84.00
Building Materials	2.05	7.48	82.40
Auto Parts	0.97	4.45	81.60
Publishing	3.96	8.71	81.60
Household Products	5.72	11.57	80.80
Industrial,Diversified	2.47	6.95	79.20
Household Products,Durable	4.28	11.11	79.20

	SHRT MOM	INTR MOM	$$ FLOW RANK
Retail,Drug	5.18	13.10	78.40
Aluminum	6.07	10.57	73.60
Savings & Loans	7.25	20.66	72.80
Chemicals,Specialty	3.21	5.84	68.80
Printers	3.24	8.08	68.00
Transportation Equipment	2.48	6.56	65.60
Banks,Western	4.23	15.74	59.20
Healthcare Providers	7.27	13.16	57.60
Footwear	4.94	12.79	56.00
Newspapers	3.08	8.19	54.40
Soft Drinks	5.66	13.15	52.00
Machinery,Heavy	3.52	6.89	48.00
Industrial Services	1.45	4.34	41.60
Retail,Specialty	8.03	11.05	39.20
Retail,Apparel	12.26	17.99	37.60
Pollution/Waste Management	7.66	13.44	37.60

52-Week New Lows:

GROUP NAME	SHRT MOM	INTR MOM	$$ FLOW RANK
Internet	-9.14	-10.86	7.20

26-Week New Highs:

GROUP NAME	SHRT MOM	INTR MOM	$$ FLOW RANK
Real Estate Investment	2.49	8.82	100.00
Insurance,Life	6.62	18.04	100.00
Insurance,Prop.&Cas.	5.50	12.15	99.20
Insurnace,Diverse	6.06	12.38	98.40
Banks,South	6.05	17.56	98.40
Insurance,Full Line	5.27	14.21	96.00
Cosmetics/Personal Care	3.23	10.59	95.20
Air Freight/Couriers	5.53	12.77	91.20
Clothing and Fabrics	7.31	14.80	89.60
Tobacco	8.21	17.79	84.00
Coal	3.48	12.80	84.00
Building Materials	2.05	7.48	82.40
Publishing	3.96	8.71	81.60
Auto Parts	0.97	4.45	81.60
Household Products	5.72	11.57	80.80
Industrial,Diversified	2.47	6.95	79.20
Household Products,Durable	4.28	11.11	79.20
Retail,Drug	5.18	13.10	78.40
Aluminum	6.07	10.57	73.60
Savings & Loans	7.25	20.66	72.80
Chemicals,Specialty	3.21	5.84	68.80
Printers	3.24	8.08	68.00
Transportation Equipment	2.48	6.56	65.60
Banks,Western	4.23	15.74	59.20
Healthcare Providers	7.27	13.16	57.60
Africa	4.06	8.44	56.80
Footwear	4.94	12.79	56.00
Newspapers	3.08	8.19	54.40
Chemicals,Commodity	2.98	5.39	52.80
Soft Drinks	5.66	13.15	52.00
Machinery,Heavy	3.52	6.89	48.00
Recreation,Other	5.01	7.23	46.40
Industrial Services	1.45	4.34	41.60
Retail,Specialty	8.03	11.05	39.20
Retail,Apparel	12.26	17.99	37.60
Pollution/Waste Management	7.66	13.44	37.60
Airlines	9.37	13.17	35.20

26-Week New Lows:

GROUP NAME	SHRT MOM	INTR MOM	$$ FLOW RANK
Internet	-9.14	-10.86	7.20

13-Week New Highs:

GROUP NAME	SHRT MOM	INTR MOM	$$ FLOW RANK
Real Estate Investment	2.49	8.82	100.00
Insurance, Life	6.62	18.04	100.00
Insurance, Prop.&Cas.	5.50	12.15	99.20
Insurnace, Diverse	6.06	12.38	98.40
Banks, South	6.05	17.56	98.40
Insurance, Full Line	5.27	14.21	96.00
Cosmetics/Personal Care	3.23	10.59	95.20
Air Freight/Couriers	5.53	12.77	91.20
Clothing and Fabrics	7.31	14.80	89.60
Tobacco	8.21	17.79	84.00
Coal	3.48	12.80	84.00
Building Materials	2.05	7.48	82.40
Publishing	3.96	8.71	81.60
Auto Parts	0.97	4.45	81.60
Household Products	5.72	11.57	80.80
Industrial, Diversified	2.47	6.95	79.20
Household Products, Durable	4.28	11.11	79.20
Retail, Drug	5.18	13.10	78.40
Aluminum	6.07	10.57	73.60
Savings & Loans	7.25	20.66	72.80
Chemicals, Specialty	3.21	5.84	68.80
Printers	3.24	8.08	68.00
Transportation Equipment	2.48	6.56	65.60
Banks, Western	4.23	15.74	59.20
Healthcare Providers	7.27	13.16	57.60
Africa	4.06	8.44	56.80
Footwear	4.94	12.79	56.00
Newspapers	3.08	8.19	54.40
Chemicals, Commodity	2.98	5.39	52.80
Employment Services	7.93	10.37	52.80
Soft Drinks	5.66	13.15	52.00
Machinery, Heavy	3.52	6.89	48.00
Recreation, Other	5.01	7.23	46.40
Retail, Broadline	6.03	7.59	43.20
Industrial Services	1.45	4.34	41.60
Retail, Specialty	8.03	11.05	39.20
Retail, Apparel	12.26	17.99	37.60
Pollution/Waste Management	7.66	13.44	37.60
Airlines	9.37	13.17	35.20

13-Week New Lows:

GROUP NAME	SHRT MOM	INTR MOM	$$ FLOW RANK
Nuclear Electric Utilities	-3.56	-3.58	50.40
Internet	-9.14	-10.86	7.20

Marc Chaikin

Marc Chaikin received his license as stockbroker on the precise day the bear market of 1966 ended. For the first two years of his career, he relied on fundamental analysis to guide his investment decisions in a market that seemed to know only one direction and that was up. The bear market of 1969, however, altered his faith in fundamental analysis as he watched in disillusionment prices of sound companies entangled in the selling deluge, slashed by half. Obstinately fighting the "tape," fundamental analysts continued to recommend stocks, waiting only until prices were near their lows before capitulating to the trend in progress. This experience combined with a developing interest in trading forced him to face the necessity of finding a more efficient means of timing the market. To rescue him from this inherent limitation of fundamental analysis, he turned his attention toward technical analysis.

An integral element of Mr. Chaikin's interest in the financial markets is research and his first project involved relative strength analysis. Using an expanded time period of eight years and incorporating a wider universe of stocks, he attempted to verify the doctoral dissertation of Robert Levy, who earlier had maintained that stocks which displayed strong relative strength over a 26 week period would continue to demonstrate strength for another six months. Today, relative strength remains one of his most valuable and reliable technical tools. Mr. Chaikin's aversion to emotional investing was the impetus behind his quest to find technical indicators which would lead to disciplined investment approaches. Over the last 27 years, he has spent much of his time creating, adjusting, and testing indicators which would give him an edge over the market. The results of his labor include such technical indicators as Bomar Bands, accumulation/distribution, the Chaikin oscillator, money flow percent, and persistency of money flow, all of which are designed to anticipate price movements.

In the summer of 1969, Mr. Chaikin left the brokerage arm of the business to start an investment partnership but returned in late 1970 to market research to institutions. In 1989, he founded Bomar Securities, L.P. and began marketing to institutions and traders an analytical workstation he had developed earlier which utilized technical analysis. In 1992, Instinet acquired the company and the workstation's capabilities were enhanced to allow fundamental screening and real-time electronic trading.

Mr. Chaikin is Senior Vice-President and Director of Research at Instinet. With regard to picking stocks, he favors a multifactor approach combining pattern recognition and earnings momentum. Recognizing the need to remain in step with constant market transformations, his last five years of research have focused on using genetic algorithms and neural networks in the development of new trading systems. Some are functional while others are still in the experimental stages.

Please walk us through the conception of Bomar Bands.

I had noted back in the early 1980's that it was important to get a sense of how high is high and how low is low and some sense of the normal trading behavior of a given stock. I don't think Bollinger Bands had been developed, or they were not popularized; certainly the public did not know about them yet. I didn't find any tools at that time to enable you to quantify price movement in terms of ordinary behavior. Basically, the Bomar Bands were developed with the idea of containing price movement most of the time but not all of the time because if you developed bands that contain price movement all the time, they would rarely be reached or tagged. In the technical vernacular, when you tag a band you have touched it. In other words, price has reached the band value either up or down. The work began in the late 1970's analyzing the Dow Jones Average going back to 1920. I was trying to find a way to define normal price behavior using the theoretical Dow price, which was what the world was looking at in those days. In other words, the Dow never actually got to that high or that low in the course of the trading day because they used the highs of each stock and the lows of each stock. Now when they quote the high and the low for the Dow, it was the actual reading that was achieved. After toying with a lot of fixed bands, it became apparent that bands positioned 4% percent above a 21 day moving average and 4% below a 21 day moving average contained the Dow most of the time. That would equate to a 3% band based on the current way the Dow's highs and lows are reported. I picked the 21 day moving average because it represented a month of trading and a month was a unit that people were comfortable with. Then I said, "There are a lot of stocks that are more volatile than the Dow. Without looking back at the price history of each one, maybe we can compute a beta computation and if a stock is twice as volatile as the Dow, then it should have 8% bands above and below a 21 day moving average." We experimented with that and used that technique for a while but it really didn't take into account stocks that were in sharp uptrends or sharp downtrends. Finally, I resorted to a technique that just said, "Let me look back for each stock over the last 250 days, or year of trading basically, and just empirically fit bands that would contain—and I just picked a number that I felt was valid—85% of all the price movement in that one year period." What happened was we came up with a set of bands which did some wonderful things in terms of technical analysis because the bands could be flexible, they could change if the volatility of the stock changed. They were not the same on the upside above the 21 day average as they were on the downside. If a stock was in a sharp uptrend the upper band would be much wider than the lower band because there weren't very many sell-offs so you didn't have to contain much negative price action. Again, what that did was it made the bands much more useful in terms of helping to define short term tops and bottoms.

How are Bomar Bands calculated?

You compute a 21 day moving average of the closing price then look back 250 trading days and create bands which contain 85% of all the closing prices above the 21 day moving average and 85% of all the closing prices below the 21 day moving average. The Bomar Bands don't breathe as much as Bollinger Bands, which are standard deviation bands that really contract and expand dramatically in the shortterm. The Bomar Bands are more stable. They could change on any given day but they won't necessarily because there would have to be a big shift in the trend of the stock or the volatility.

What is the primary advantage in using the Bomar Bands?

Basically, the Bomar Bands are a function of the trend of the stock and the volatility of the stock. So for instance, if you had a stock like one of the regional "Bells," which are fairly stable and usually trade within a range, the percentage width will be the same on the upside or the downside and price movement will tend to reverse pretty reliably at the upper band or the lower band. That is the purpose for which I felt bands were necessary. Whether you are trading stocks or investing, it is important to not get caught up in the emotions of the marketplace. One of the ways I felt both visually and mathematically that you could help rein in your emotions was by knowing when a stock was at the upper range of its normal trading pattern and when a stock was at the lower range. For instance, right now, Bell South (BLS) has a trading band of 10%—5% above the 21 day moving average and 5% below. Typically, if Bell South makes a low near the lower band, you can expect a 10% rally to the upper band and that 10% rally, once it has happened, is not really a good place to buy the stock. Unfortunately over the years, what I have observed, both in my own decision making and in others, is that people are reluctant to buy a stock when it has been weak, which is normally the time you should buy it, especially if there is a good reason to be buying it from either a bigger technical point of view or a fundamental point of view. The bands help you buy stocks on weakness because visually they give you some confidence that what looks like a decline that might be endless may be about to reverse. More importantly, after a stock has moved up to the upper band, one should be discouraged from buying it, but that is typically when people have more confidence. They have observed the recent price action, which is positive, or they feel they have been left behind and they are kicking themselves, so they just throw in the towel and say, "I'm just going to buy it up here. I missed it, I should have bought it." So the bands do serve a purpose as a frame of reference for the normal price activity for the shortterm trading pattern of a given stock.

I never realized that Bomar Bands gave you the capability of projecting price.

We never viewed it as projecting price but then we realized that it gives a target because it represents the normal trading pattern. If you add up the upper and lower band widths, that tells you that in any two to four week period the stock will typically fluctuate in a range based on that percent. If I pull up IBM on my computer screen, I see that the upper band is 11% above the 21 day average and the lower band is 5% below. If I add up eleven and five I get sixteen, and it's reasonable to say that in any four week period, IBM will fluctuate in a 16% range. This is all empirically derived which I love because you are looking at the real world. It's not theoretical. You are saying, "Okay, in the past 250 trading days this is what IBM has done." The assumption is that it will continue to behave this way in the future. Now the caveat is that all things change and when a stock gets into a very strong trend, its trading pattern will change. We have to be looking at other technical indicators to help us know when there is a very strong trend in force which may change the trading pattern or cause the rules to be suspended. But, these rules work so much of the time that you really have to follow them.

That is how you earlier concluded that Bell South would fluctuate 10%?

Looking back, the bands were 5% above the 21 day moving average and 5% below and if you add them up, five and five is ten and it is safe to say that in any four week period it would trade in a 10% range. The point is, if it has already rallied 10% in the last two weeks then what are your odds of buying it here and having a profit a month later? That is more important if you are a trader than if you are an investor. If you are going to hold a stock for one to five years, paying a percent or two more, or even 5% more, may not be as critical than if you are a trader where paying too much adds up over time.

If you use the upper and lower bands as strategic exit and entry points respectively, what is the risk of getting whipsawed?

The bands were constructed to contain 85% of the price movement so logically going forward one would expect that 85% of the time, when price approaches the band, that the bands will then turn back price or serve as a point of reversal and that about 15% of the time or one in seven, the price will continue in the same direction instead of reversing. It's not an automatic system. It was meant to have a twofold benefit to traders or investors. Number one, the Bomar Bands were meant to help you rein in your emotions so that you weren't buying on strength or selling on weakness unless there was a very good reason to do it. Number two, they serve as a reference point where one should look at all the other technical indicators to decide if price is going to reverse. Sometimes the stock will trade to the upper band and you will look at all the other technical indicators—the interest rate picture, the overall market, and the group that the stock is in. You may determine that even though the stock has rallied its normal two to four week rally of 10% or 15% or whatever the band widths are, there is no reason to sell it here because everything looks great. Maybe we are in a bull market and the group is doing well, the company has a new product, and it is probably going to keep going higher. I may not want to buy" it at this price. I may want to watch it for a few days and see if it pulls back but I don't want to sell it here. Then there are other times where a stock has rallied and it's at the upper band but everything else about this stock looks terrible so I take advantage of the strength and sell because I shouldn't be holding this stock, or I want to buy something else, or I am nervous about the market. So the bands serve as a frame of reference where other technical indicators are then analyzed and a decision is made to buy, sell, or do nothing. If a decision is made to do nothing, it is because everything looks okay or in the case of a stock that is going down, everything still looks terrible so there is no reason to be buying the stock.

Do you get a penetration of the upper band and lower band of the Bomar Bands as you do with the Bollinger Bands?

Oh sure. Fifteen percent of the time you are going to get the penetration and then it will either continue dramatically or it may ultimately reverse and come back within the band. We found that almost all important highs and lows come within the bands. Even if you go back in the market to 1987, for instance, and you look at the Dow Jones Average, the first lows in October were made well outside the Bomar Bands and the actual closing low I think was 1738 on the Dow. Ultimately, you went sideways for about a month and a half. In December of 1987, you made a low at 1767 which wasn't a new closing low but if you look at the chart, you would see that this was within the bands and a much more stable time to buy stocks. Typically, if you are buying stocks which have been going down outside the band, or if you are selling stocks on the way up which are outside the band, you get a better opportunity and usually a better price, certainly at a more stable price. A lot of the work that I did from a technical analysis point of view was based on my own need to be unemotional in trading. I was just like everyone else sitting in front of a quote machine all day long. You get very susceptible to every little blip in stock prices so you become much more emotional. I found that if you bought stocks at a time when they were highly volatile on the downside and outside the trading bands, the likelihood that you would be forced out of your position was greatly increased whereas if you bought stocks in a quieter time, when they were bottoming within the trading bands, particularly if that was a re-test of a previous low, the likelihood of being shaken out of a position because of an emotional reaction to the volatility was greatly diminished. Again, it is a technical approach that tries to take some of the emotions out of the decision making process and also tries to anticipate future emotional reactions. The worst thing that happens to an investor is they go into a position for a very good reason and then they lose heart either because the market doesn't accommodate them, or the market does something unexpected. The stock they bought goes down or the stock doesn't do what they thought it would do in the shortterm. It may be because they bought it at the wrong place. If you buy a stock after it has rallied 15% and then it drops 15%, you are pretty nervous. It may just be that this is the normal trading pattern for that stock. The worst things people do is either chase fads or become emotional. The case in point is a stock that has run up dramatically. There is lots of news in the paper and everybody is talking about it. That probably means that it has already made a significant move based on smart money having seen the events unfold. To buy it and watch it go down makes your stomach start to churn. That is why you need these technical indicators. They are like antacid—they coat your stomach.

Bollinger Bands, at two standard deviations, contain 95% of price data. Most commercial technical analysis software packages allow users to construct Bollinger Bands. Can these programs be adjusted to contain 85% of the price data as with the Bomar Bands?

No and there is no publicly available software. You have to write your own program and it is highly computational. The closest thing to Bomar Bands are in the AIQ software. The bands that they have in their software are built around a 21 day exponential moving average. A lot of what they did was based on the technical work that I had put together and I think Jerry Smith did an incredible job of putting together a set of technical indicators which led to disciplined decisions.

In periods of lower volatility, would Bollinger Bands be a better choice than Bomar Bands?

Bollinger Bands do some interesting things in terms of volatility. They will contract when there is low volatility and typically after a period of low volatility, the market breaks in one direction or the other. Bollinger Bands serve two purposes in low volatility markets. Number one, the Bomar Bands will not be reached in a low volatility period. In other words, the stock won't trade to the upper or the lower band. They are not meant to adjust as quickly as Bollinger Bands. In a low volatility period, the Bollinger Bands will be tagged by stock price. For instance, in June of 1996, the Dow Jones Average went into a sideways period with low volatility and the Bollinger Bands were tagged the last week in June on the upside and then dropped dramatically. The Bomar Bands were no where near being tagged at that point. They were at the 5875 level and the closest the Dow came was about 5720. The downside of that is that the Bollinger Bands will be tagged very early in a move. In May, the Bollinger Bands were tagged at 5638 and the Dow went all the way to 5838 before the Bomar Bands were tagged so you had 200 Dow points where you might have been bearish or cautious. The two can be used together but it takes a seasoned analyst to figure out the nuances of which bands are likely to be more important in terms of turning back price. Remember, all the bands are meant to do is give you a clue that price may be changing direction or may be too high or too low on a shortterm basis.

Are Bomar Bands more ideal for traders?

No, Bomar Bands and Bollinger Bands are both for traders and investors. They are used differently and at different times. It takes a seasoned analyst to figure out which one to use at a given point in time. The biggest difference is that Bollinger Bands will adjust to shortterm changes in volatility. People refer to the Bollinger Bands "pinching." That pinching represents a contraction in volatility. One of the real values of the Bollinger Band is when volatility contracts, you have a clue that there is going to be a big move in one direction or the other. When you reach a band extreme with volatility contracting, the trick is to know whether that is a potentially meaningful turning point. Bands are only useful if you have some disciplined way to analyze the price activity at the bands. So for instance, if you get to an upper trading band, the real decision should be, "Is this stock likely to reverse back to the downside and if I have a position in it, do I want to sell it? If I am thinking of shorting it, is this a good spot to short it?" The band is meant to take the emotions out of the decision making so that you don't buy on strength and sell on weakness and find the stock reversing because you have acted emotionally. The question with Bollinger Bands is, if volatility has contracted and you now reach a Bollinger Band, is that going to turn back price? Or, is volatility now in the process of expanding and therefore, will the stock go to the more normal bands based on a longer time period? Bollinger Bands just look at the last month of trading whereas the Bomar Bands look at a year of trading. The Bomar Bands say, "Okay, based on the last year of trading, here is what the normal extremes of the shortterm price activity are likely to be." There is a nuance there. You just have to have a sense of whether or not this is a point in time when you should be anticipating a turning point and then looking at other technical indicators to see if in fact, they are supporting a turning point decision or not.

You don't ever get pinching with the Bomar Bands?

No, rarely. They weren't created to do that.

For Bomar Bands, you mentioned the 21 day moving average but don't you also use a 50 day moving average?

I use a 50 day moving average to create intermediate bands which are more for investment purposes. The intermediate bands present a set of price targets which would reflect the way an investor might look at the world. They are constructed the same way as the 21 day bands but they are much wider. Looking at Intel right now, the 21 day band width is 6% and 10% for a total of 16%. The 50 day band width is 9% and 17% for a total of 26%. That is 50% wider and reflects the way Intel trades on a three month basis whereas the 21 day bands mirror a one month trading pattern.

Your intermediate time frame is three months?

Yes, three months at a minimum.

Is there anything we have left out regarding Bomar Bands?

I created a concept called breakout bands which is really important. Early on, I said that there are times when the bands will function less well because a stock has gone into a very steep trend, either up or down. I created a set of bands that would give one a clue as to whether or not there was a very sharp trend in progress and named them breakout bands. Basically, breakout bands are built around a 90 day average. It could be a 90 day average of price, it could be a 90 day average of the relative strength line compared to a market average, or it could be a 90 day average of money flow. I wrote a program that said, "Compute 21 day band widths, take those percentages and multiply them by 1.5 and then apply those percentages to the 90 day average." That ends up giving you a series of slow moving bands built around a 90 day average. When they are violated, in other words, when price closes above them for two days or more, it tells you that there is an unusual price movement in progress and to be cautious about applying the normal reversal rules and to anticipate further price movement in that direction. So when you apply it to price, you basically get a clue as to whether a very strong market movement is in progress either on the upside or the downside. When you apply it to a relative strength line and to money flow, you end up finding some of the stronger stocks in the marketplace. When the breakout bands applying to money flow or relative strength are violated, it's telling you that something really significant is going on. When both of those conditions are true, that is a stock tip-off that is really going to help your portfolio's performance. The concept of breakout bands was an attempt to help define very strong stocks in very strong trends, either up or down.

You have another indicator which you developed called the money flow indicator. Is this also referred to as accumulation/distribution?

Yes it is. The derivation of the money flow work and the resulting indicators is the most important work I have done in the technical analysis area. It builds on the pioneering work done by four technicians over the years—Joe Granville, R.W. Mansfield, Larry Williams, and David Bostian— all of whom looked at volume in relation to price movement as a way to assess the supply and demand situation for a given stock. If you look at the various forms of technical analysis, they really break down into just two broad areas. One is trend type analysis—a stock versus its moving average or ADX or my breakout bands or whatever—some way to measure the trend of a stock because the favorite expression on the floor of the exchange, "the trend is your friend," is really true. Getting in on a trend early and staying with it for the longterm is how the really big money is made. The second area of technical analysis is the oscillators; the people who are trying to guess

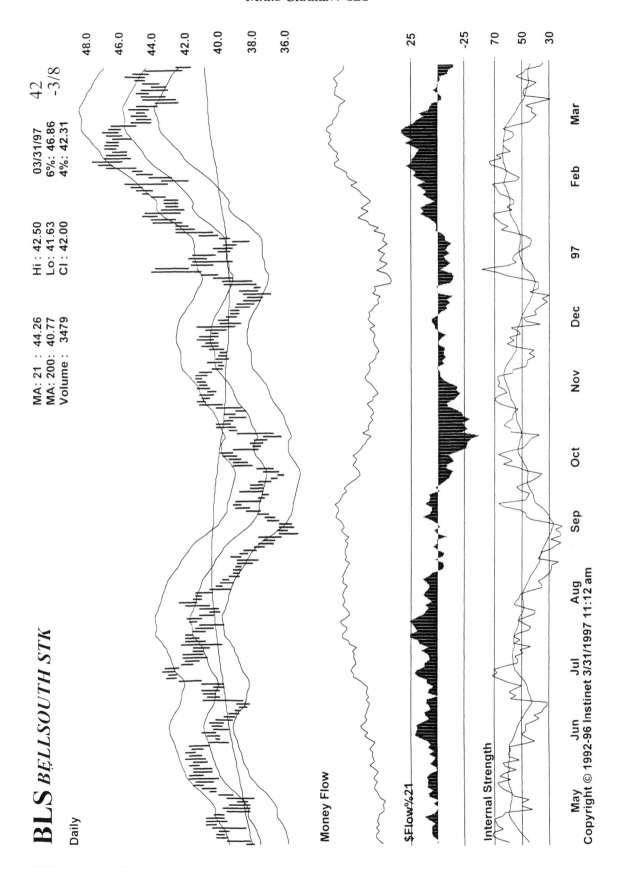

BLS *BELLSOUTH STK*

Daily

MA: 21 : 44.26
MA: 200: 40.77
Volume : 3479

Hi : 42.50
Lo: 41.63
Cl : 42.00

03/31/97
6%: 46.86
4%: 42.31

42
-3/8

48.0
46.0
44.0
42.0
40.0
38.0
36.0

Money Flow

$Flow%21

25

-25

Internal Strength

70
50
30

May   Jun   Jul   Aug   Sep   Oct   Nov   Dec   97   Feb   Mar

Copyright © 1992-96 Instinet 3/31/1997 11:12 am

tops and bottoms. We all probably put in too much time on that form of analysis because it leads to trading and it leads to shortterm decisions which look great and feel great for a day or two, sometimes for more than that, but then often results in performance that is very inferior to just staying with something that you really like. The oscillator approach is sort of a short cut. The bands are really oscillators. They are just a different form of measuring oscillations but whether you are looking at Welles Wilder's RSI, the Commodity Channel Index, the Williams %R or any of these overbought/oversold measurements, they are almost a lazy man's approach to stock selection. If you are trading with oscillators, you don't have to know anything about a company to buy it at the lower band or sell it at the upper band or sell when the internal strength is above 70 or if there is a divergence. Staying with the trend assumes that you know what's going on in the company even though you may have just found it from a technical point of view. An intelligent person putting his money on the line is going to want to know why he is in that stock. If it has gone from 20 to 40 and you are still staying with it, a prudent person says, "Okay, what does this company do? Is it really going to keep going up? Is it just a function of some fad in the marketplace?" I want to know what a company does whereas if you are trading oscillators, buying low and selling high, that sounds great but sort of too easy. Most of the work in technical analysis has gone into looking at those types of indicators and they all measure what is happening, and what you can see—price is up, price is down—price is up sharply in a few days, price is up gradually over a few months. The only thing that gives you a look under the surface is volume analysis because a stock can double and volume can be dropping in the latter stages of a move or a stock can double and volume can be tripling and quadrupling. They represent different supply/demand characteristics. That is why I spent a lot of time looking at volume and price and came up with these money flow indicators. Granville developed the On-Balance-Volume concept and then Larry Williams developed a volume accumulation approach which compared the close to the opening. The theory was if a stock closed above its opening price for the day, then there was net accumulation. When all of us were doing technical analysis by hand in the 1960's and 1970's, the newspapers published the opening price. Starting in 1974, the Associated Press, which distributed the stock prices to all the newspapers, decided to cut the opening price out of the newspapers because of space limitations. I had to find a substitute for the work I had been doing based on Larry Williams' volume accumulation work so I started experimenting with different techniques. David Bostian, who is still practicing technical analysis, had what he called his "intraday intensity index." He looked at where a stock closed in its range as a guide to whether it was healthy and in demand or weak and under distribution. Basically, you are trying to figure out if the buyers are stronger than the sellers. I came up with a formula which compared the closing price to the midpoint or mean price for the day. All the volume work that I have done since then, and the supply/demand and money flow work, has been based on the relationship of the close to the mean.

What is the theory behind your money flow indicator?

The theory is that if a stock closes above its midpoint consistently, especially on the high volume days because this is all related to the volume of trading, then it was under accumulation and going into strong hands. You could have strong stocks closing below their midpoint because it was a very weak day in the market. That is why you have to create oscillators and ways to look at money flow and supply/demand over extended periods of time, but the general theory was that stocks with strong supply/demand characteristics tend to close high up in their trading range for the day and stocks with weak supply/demand characteristics, where the sellers are stronger than the buyers, tend to close in the lower portion of their range. What came out of that was what is called either accumulation/distribution or money flow. Starting in the late 1960's and early 1970's, there were people with powerful computers who measured every tick to see if it was at a price higher than the previous price, which they called an uptick. If the price was lower, it was a downtick. They multiplied the price change times the volume. The theory was that strong stocks will trade on upticks with heavier volume and weak stocks will trade on downticks when there is heavy volume. They called that money flow; it was the money flowing in or out of a stock. I realized that the analysis that I was doing was also a way to measure the money flowing into and out of a stock so I called it money flow. The building block is the one day number arrived at by comparing the closing price to the mean and relating that to the trading range. By multiplying that fraction times the volume, you get a picture of what percentage of the volume represented net buying and selling. From those one day numbers, I created what is either called accumulation/distribution or the money flow line. It is just a cumulative line, similar to the Granville On-Balance-Volume line, that measures the flow of money in or out of a stock. The basic theory was that if a stock was making a new high, the money flow line should also be making a new high. If it wasn't, that meant that the supply/demand characteristics were deteriorating under the cover of strong price action. You can sort of take volume as the fuel that powers the engine. If you think of a stock like an automobile—accelerating and braking and going at high speeds—you need gasoline in the engine. You can be going 90 miles an hour but if you are on your last drop of gas, I can predict with 100% certainty that within a minute or so you are going to be going zero miles an hour. The analogy in the stock market is that you can be making a new high today in price, but if volume is dropping, that is telling you that the money going into the stock is drying up. It may be on its last leg and about to peak. Volume analysis and money flow analysis is really the only analysis which looks under the surface of price action.

Some technicians think price leads volume, others think volume leads price. What is your opinion?

I think volume leads price, definitely. H. M. Gartley, who wrote the seminal book on volume in 1935, proposed the original volume rules and they have been repeated over and over since then. A stock should go up on increasing volume; that's bullish. If a stock goes up on decreasing volume, that's bearish. On the downside, the initial downward move typically is on light volume and then as the downward move picks up, volume will pick up as people panic and sell and the buyers start to view the stock as more attractive at lower prices and are willing to buy more shares. Typically, you will get some sort of panic low on heavy volume, then you will rally and come back down and either make a new low, or test the low on lighter volume, and that will be your final bottom. Those patterns are pretty reliable. Granville's On-Balance-Volume approach basically assumed that volume led price. In the case of our money flow line, if money flow makes a new high ahead of price, that is bullish and the assumption is that volume will pull price up to a new high. Now, of course, none of this works all the time but over a broad group of stocks, or over ten or twenty years, this will be true much more often than not.

Investors Business Daily **uses an accumulation/distribution rating system. Is that based on**

your indicator?

Yes and they basically categorize stocks between A and E based on a moving window of money flow. It is more similar to my 21 day volume accumulation oscillator which AIQ has as their volume accumulation (VA) percent.

I have noticed that signals sometimes come late with IBD'S lettering system. In other words, on a few occasions stocks with an "A" rating have collapsed for whatever reason and yet it seems to take two weeks for the rating to change to "D."

Money flow will sometimes do that. There are stocks which peak with very powerful money flow because there is no warning. Micron Technology is an example of that. Micron made a high in September of 1995 and money flow was just as powerful because investor enthusiasm was at its peak and people were chasing earnings momentum stocks. There was just no clue. There are going to be situations like that. In those cases, where stocks are really accelerating on the upside or the downside, you have to apply other ways to get out. The money flow will not help. If the top takes a long time to form you may get the kinds of divergences and deterioration in money flow that will give you a clue. If a top comes on very spiky price action, then money flow is likely to be at its peak.

You mentioned earlier that people used to do tick analysis. Will the money flow line yield similar results?

I think it actually works better because of the way it's computed, but when you create some of these other oscillators, like the 21 day money flow percent or the VA% in the AIQ system, you have a way to normalize the money flow to the trading volume and then compare stocks to each other. One of the problems with tick by tick analysis is that you really don't have a way to compare stocks to each other because the trading volume and the price has a big impact over the stocks that appear to have the strongest money flow. Big capitalization stocks with heavy volume will always over-weight small names. When you get into the other money flow indicators that I developed, you have the ability to compare stocks in a portfolio and that is very important. I think the money flow does a better job than the tick by tick analysis.

How will your other money flow indicators give you the ability to compare stocks in a portfolio?

Money flow typically is a function of the volume of trading and the price of a stock. In conventional money flow analysis, which has been going on in one form or another since the 1960's, the stocks with the large market capitalizations are the ones with a high volume of trading and high share prices. Market capitalization is defined as price times the number of shares outstanding. So for instance, in the computer group, the large capitalization stocks would be Microsoft, IBM, and Intel—high share prices and lots of shares outstanding. Whatever measure you use for money flow is greatly affected by large capitalization stocks that trade heavily. Therefore, if you were looking at a list of 100 computer stocks and you were just looking at pure money flow, positive or negative, the top of the list would invariably be the large cap names because a small capitalization stock that has either a lower price or fewer shares outstanding, or doesn't trade as actively, is not going to generate the kind of absolute money flow numbers to get it to the top of the list. The 21 day money flow oscillator and VA percent normalizes the money flow to the volume of trading for each individual stock. You get something that fluctuates between plus 100 and minus 100 because it is always a function of volume. So, if the stock closed in my work at its high price 21 days in a row, then the 21 day money flow oscillator would be at plus 100. That means that a small capitalization stock can have as high a reading from a money flow point of view as a large capitalization stock. Therefore, you can take a universe of stocks or a portfolio and rank them based on the money flow oscillator or on the persistency of money flow. A small capitalization stock could be at the top of the list even if the large capitalization stocks also have positive money flow. That is a big step forward because it enables you to look at any list of stocks, whether it is a portfolio, or a buy list, or an industry group and find the stocks that are truly in the best supply/demand situation. That is really the concept behind that.

How do you calculate the money flow line?

You take the daily money flow number, which is the close minus the low, then the high minus the close, divided by the high minus the low. Then you multiply that times the volume. That is the single day money flow number. You then start at some arbitrary number and keep adding and subtracting every day moving forward; it's cumulative.

This indicator is incorporated into the AIQ and Metastock software programs, right?

Yes, it's on AIQ and Metastock. It's in almost every software package.

Earlier, you mentioned using breakout bands with money flow analysis. Would you expand on that thought?

One of the things I did with regard to the cumulative money flow line was to build these breakout bands and I really think that has provided another level of analysis. It has enabled me and anybody else using this to see which stocks truly have the strongest money flow because it basically measures the slope of the money flow line in a very objective way. If the money flow line moves above its upper 90 day breakout band, that is telling you this is a stock that is in very strong hands and the supply/demand picture is very positive. Conversely, if it drops below its money flow lower breakdown band, something is wrong. Trying to guess a bottom in that stock is going to prove to be painful and costly.

Is the Chaikin oscillator an extension of money flow analysis?

The Chaikin oscillator basically is a way to look at the shortterm money flow versus the slightly longer term view. I use the difference between the 3 day moving average and the 10 day moving average of the money flow line. The Chaikin oscillator is a way to measure shortterm money flow movements by looking for divergences between price action and money flow and although it still has validity; again, it leads to very shortterm trading decisions. I found a much more powerful way to look at money flow and that was to create what we call the money flow percent or the 21 day money flow oscillator. Again, this is in AIQ and Metastock. I took the 21 day total of the single day money flow numbers and divided it by the 21 day total of volume. That created an oscillator that in theory could go between plus 100 and minus 100. It would be plus 100 if a stock closed at its high every day for 21 days, which obviously is unlikely. It would be minus 100 if it closed at its low every day for 21 days but the practical limits are plus 25 and minus 25. One of the things we found was that when the money flow percent got above plus 25, there was likely to be more price action in a positive direction because the money flow oscillator had gotten very overbought. More importantly, this led to a much more powerful kind of analysis. I found that in strong stocks, even when there was a 10% or 15% sell-off in price on a shortterm basis, the 21 day money flow oscillator would stay green or positive even though you got a sharp sell-off in price. The reason for that was likely to be twofold. Either the sell-off was coming on light volume or, on the down days in price, the stock was still closing above its midpoint. We developed a form of analysis which said that if a stock trades down to its lower band and the 21 day money flow oscillator stays green or positive, that is very bullish because it should be going red or negative.

Red or green refers to the color patterns integrated in the software program?

Yes. The normal pattern on a sell-off in a weak stock would be for the 21 day money flow oscillator to go negative or red because the stock is closing weak and volume is picking up. We had a way to then find buy points in stocks that was a twofold technical approach—a) look for weakness and you could measure this by looking for a sell-off to the lower band or wait for some oscillator to get oversold and then b) look at the 21 day money flow oscillator to see if that had stayed green or positive. If it did stay green, you had a very powerful and successful entry method. I had a partner in Philadelphia, Bob Brogan, who helped develop a lot of this work. He used to spend hours and hours on the weekends just going through charts looking for this pattern. One day he called and said "Marc, I'm burned out. I can't do this anymore. You have to computerize this." I said, "Tell me what you do." He said, "I just look for charts where the money flow is green and the price is down." I said, "Green over what time period?" When we came up with the first analysis it only had to be green or positive on the day that you made the new low. As it turned out, he was looking at about six months of data. What we found was that the strongest stocks over the past twenty years were the stocks where the 21 day money flow oscillator was predominately green. These stocks were not necessarily going straight up. Whether the stock was trading up or down over the last six months, for most of the days, not necessarily every day, the money flow oscillator stayed green or positive. I developed an approach and an indicator called persistency of money flow. This is now in the AIQ software and it is in my own software that we market to institutions at Instinet. Basically, it is the percentage of days in the past six months that the money flow oscillator was positive or green. You could have a stock with a persistency of money flow of 90. That means that 90% of the days in the last six months, this 21 day oscillator was green or positive. When you looked at the reasons for this, it became apparent that these were stocks where the earnings were increasing at an above average rate, where analysts were raising their estimates, and where reported earnings were better than expected. So you had positive earnings surprises and basically a bullish consensus on Wall

Street about the fundamentals. These are the same stocks that William O'Neil finds in his institutional service by looking at relative strength and earnings momentum. He calls them the "90-90" stocks. I think the accumulation/distribution figures in *Investor's Business Daily* are based on a three month time framework and I am looking at a six month. The "A" stocks would equate to the stocks where over three months the money flow was positive almost every day. The reason that the money flow stays green day in and day out even when the stocks are selling off in price is because of supply and demand and human nature.

I understand the reasoning behind supply and demand but how does human nature fit into the picture?

Let's say you have a stock with a very positive earnings picture. People are doing quantitative screening and it comes up on the top of the list as the strongest growth stock or the stock with the biggest estimate increases by the estimate services. Then there are other firms that like it just from a fundamental point of view. Let's say the stock is IBM and let's say that on a given day, there are six institutional money managers out of the hundreds that exist who decide they want to buy the stock because it has positive earnings characteristics. First, they call their trading desk and say they want to buy 100,000 shares of IBM. Let's say that all six of them place the same order. Now the trading desk calls the brokerage firm and says, "I have a big order to buy IBM." The trader usually says, "Well, how much do you have to buy?" The trading desk says, "Take 25,000 and I have more behind it" or he may say, "I have 100,000 to buy. You manage it." The broker that he talked to calls his trading desk and says, "I have IBM to buy. Take 25,000 and there is more behind it" because everybody is trying to be a genius and do a good job. Then the trader calls the floor and says, "We have IBM to buy." So now six brokers are running into the crowd and they are all trying to buy IBM. Now the price starts moving up because there are no sellers left. Everybody on the floor sees that there are buyers and the people watching the tape or what have you all see buying in the stock. Now the stock is up one point and it is reported as active. Of the 600,000 shares that the portfolio managers were to buy, maybe 100,000 have been bought—maybe. At about 11:00 a.m., the portfolio managers look at their machines and see that IBM is up two points and they say, "Oh great." They go into their trading rooms and say, "How much IBM did we buy?" The trader calls the brokerage firm and reports, "We only bought 25,000 shares." Now the trader at the institution yells at the broker and the portfolio manager yells at the trader and says, "Why are you masterminding this order? We should have just bought it at the opening. I told you never to mastermind my orders." So one or two of those guys get really angry and tells the broker he did a terrible job and he had better buy the rest of it. The stock keeps moving up. Finally at three o'clock, some portfolio manager somewhere comes in and says, "What do you mean we only bought 50,000 shares. I told you to buy this thing. It's up three points. Just buy it at the market. We never should have masterminded it." At the end of the day, there is buying and nobody to sell except the specialists so this stock will tend to close near its high for the day. This happens day in and day out on Wall Street. Now what happens in a weak stock? 600,000 shares to sell, sellers everywhere, the buyers get filled. The sellers are thrilled that there are buyers. The buyers get filled early in the day and the sellers can't sell enough stock, so by the end of the day it's reversed. The broker is now being berated by the trader who is being berated by the portfolio manager saying, "Why didn't you just sell it on the opening? It is down two points." Strong stocks are hard to buy because there is not enough supply and there is too much demand. Human nature causes someone to throw in the towel at the end of the day and say, "Damn it. We should have bought it. I am never going to let you mastermind an order again." That is why the strongest stocks, the stocks that are going to outperform the market over the next 6 to 12 months, have money flow persistency ratings between 90 and 100. Because day in and day out, they are hard to buy. When you are measuring supply/demand this way, you are measuring fundamentals without actually knowing what the fundamentals are. This analysis picks up the strongest stocks.

Let's say the persistency of money flow for a stock is +80. If it's measuring a six month window of time, won't you possibly be taking a position late in the stock's trend?

Stocks with strong earnings patterns tend to move anywhere from 6 to 24 months. Very often the money flow persistency number will be high even before the price has moved. You could be in a bear market or you could be in a correction in the market so that is inhibiting the price movement of the stock. You have two or three different scenarios. One is that the market has been weak but there are some stocks that are still in demand because they have strong earnings pictures. Those may not have moved yet so you won't be late at all in those. You will have another situation where the stocks have moved up somewhat but they haven't really exploded yet. Then you will have a third group, which is what your question is pointing toward, where the stocks have really moved up. They may have doubled, but if you look at William O'Neil's work, a stock that doubles is his favorite stock. In these stocks you run the risk that you are buying at the top but typically these stocks move for anywhere from 12 to 24 months. If it is only six months into the move, there may be a lot more to go. When I started looking at stocks with high persistency of money flow, I discovered two things. It didn't matter whether you bought stocks at the upper band or the lower band if you were going to hold them for 6 to 12 months. In fact, sometimes you never got a lower band tag because they were so strong or the lower band tag came at a much higher level. The persistency numbers of 80 or higher are really the good ones. Fifty to eighty is normal, below fifty is weak, and below forty is very weak. Let's say you are looking at only those stocks with a persistency of money flow number of 80 or higher. If one of those stocks has gone from $20 to $40, then you identify it based on the persistency of money flow analysis as a potentially very strong stock. It may not sell-off to the lower band and give you a better entry point. Let's say you buy it at $40. With a normal stock, if you buy it after it has doubled at the upper band and the persistency of money flow isn't great, the odds are it's going to sell down to $35 or $32—somewhere between a 10% or 20% sell-off. With a stock that has high persistency of money flow, the odds are that it's not going to sell-off more than 5% or so unless the market gets very weak. The first big sell-off may come from the $60 level. It may go from $60 down to $50, but you are still paying a lot more than it was at $40. What I learned was that if you are an investor and you are going to hold the stock for a long time and you want to be in stocks with positive earnings momentum and sharply increasing estimates, it doesn't matter if you pay up and buy it at the upper band. If you are trading, it makes a big difference for all the reasons that we discussed before.

What is the best application for persistency of money flow?

For traders, the persistency of money flow is a way to identify stocks to buy on weakness but you may not want to wait for a move all the way down to the lower band. If you were looking at Intel right now, which has been strong since early July 1996, you would see that it rallied from a low of 64 to 83 in about one month, between July and August. It then started a sideways sell-off. It never got to the lower band. It really only got down to its 21 day moving average. That is what you find in very strong stocks. You don't sell off to the lower band, you only go down to the 21 day moving average. If a person is a trader and they have a stock with very strong earnings and fundamentals and therefore, the persistency of money flow is very high or the O'Neil accumulation/distribution is an "A," you want to buy the stock on weakness but maybe not at the lower band. You may have to buy it at the 21 day moving average. If you are an investor, you can buy that stock at the upper band because the risk of missing a big move is too great. Obviously, if you get the chance to buy it at the 21 day moving average or the lower band, that is all to the good. If you are initiating a position in a stock with very positive earnings and you are a longterm investor who plans on holding for six months to a year or longer, it really doesn't matter if you buy it at the upper band. Too much technical analysis research is focused on oscillators—the idea that you only buy on weakness. Usually it is good to wait to buy on weakness but not with stocks with very strong earnings and fundamental pictures or very high money flow persistency.

Previously, you outlined three conditions that justified high readings in the persistency of money flow. One involved a situation where a stock was moving up gradually but had not exploded yet to the upside. Under these circumstances, will the money flow line be green for six months prior to the explosive move?

It could be. Basically, those are stocks that are being accumulated by knowledgable investors. They could be insiders or just someone who follows the company who knows about a new product or thinks that there is going to be a change in the earnings picture. There are stocks that seemingly, out of nowhere, start to move but have very positive persistency of money flow. In the 1980's, a lot of the takeover stocks had very high persistency of money flows and were doing nothing. There were knowledgable people either guessing or who were in the know that there was going to be a takeover announcement. You could track them day in and day out just by looking for these stocks that were all green for persistency of money flow. It was uncanny. There was a takeover of Bally in 1996. The stock had been doing nothing in October, November, and December of 1995 and yet it had very high persistency of money flow. Over a period of 5 months, it sold off from about 11 to 8½ and the money flow persistency was enormous. Ultimately, the deal was announced in the 20's and it went up to 30. It's now trading at 28 with high persistency of money flow all the way so, obviously, people knew or felt that this stock would be taken over. When Paramount or Lotus were acquired, you could see it. It could have been rumors. It didn't necessarily mean insider activity. It just could have been people who said, "This company is likely to be sold. The company can't make it on their own; they need a big partner." So there were people willing to bet or there were just no sellers left. Remember, the pattern is that you get high persistency when there are a lot of buyers and very few sellers and therefore the stock closes strong. That pattern is pretty reliable.

Can you program analytical software to search for companies that have shown a specific

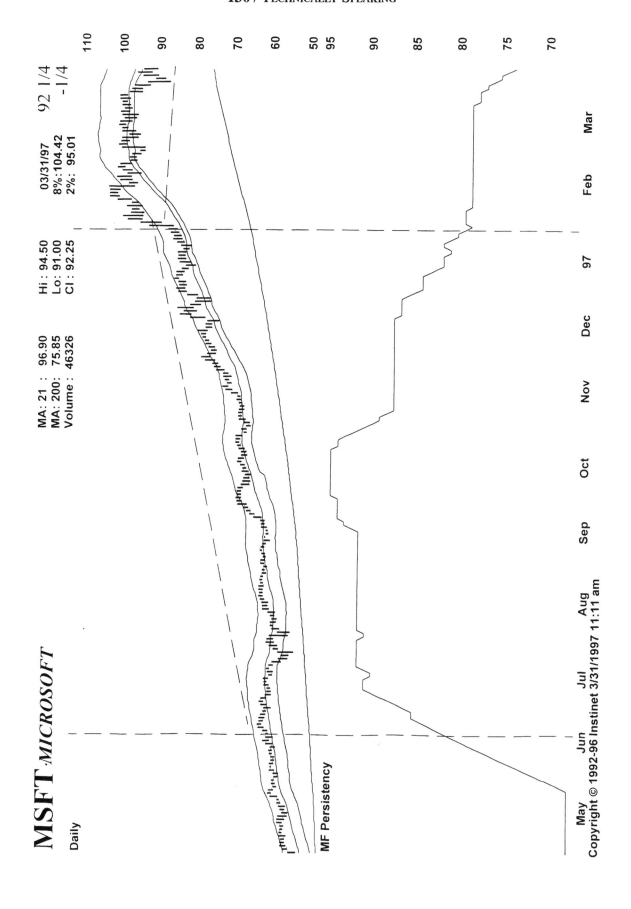

MSFT *MICROSOFT*
Daily

MA: 21 : 96.90
MA: 200: 75.85
Volume : 46326

Hi : 94.50
Lo: 91.00
Cl : 92.25

03/31/97   104.42
8% :104.42
2% : 95.01

92 1/4
-1/4

MF Persistency

May Jun Jul Aug Sep Oct Nov Dec 97 Feb Mar
Copyright © 1992-96 Instinet 3/31/1997 11:11 am

level of persistency of money flow, say eighty and above, over the last six months?

Absolutely. They all have screening programs which enable you to do that and a lot of the on-line packages will enable you to do that. That is the power of the R&A workstation that Instinet sells— the ability to monitor these indicators in real time and come up with a short list of attractive names. Computers have put the public investor on an equal footing with institutional investors because the public can do this relatively inexpensively. You don't need wildly expensive computer systems to do these screens overnight. There is other screening in real time where you do have an edge if you are looking for shortterm trading patterns or opportunities, but just to screen for stocks with high persistency of money flow, it's certainly sufficient to do that overnight because things don't change that often on a day to day basis. Things like Metastock and AIQ are perfectly capable of enabling you to do that.

If I understand you correctly, a high persistency of money flow equates with strong earnings momentum?

Yes, that usually happens in stocks where there is a consensus about the earnings. Now, people could be dead wrong. In fact, the money flow is very strong at the top because everybody is bullish and nobody is skeptical. There are no sellers and that happens periodically when you get these big fads and people are just playing follow the leader. That can happen, but usually it happens in stocks where there are very positive earnings and everybody is bullish.

We have primarily been talking about the persistency of money flow in bullish terms. Is it possible to short stock or buy puts using the persistency of money flow?

Absolutely. You would screen for stocks that had persistency numbers less than 50 and then look at other technical factors. In the markets that we have been in for the last 10 or 15 years, that is a sign of weakness. You would see only 40% of the days in the last six months where the money flow line was positive more often in a bear market.

If you had a situation where the persistency of money flow line was red for six months and the stock was trading sideways, is this distribution?

Absolutely. It works in reverse.

You look at both the relative strength index (RSI) and relative strength.

Yes. The more important one is relative strength, relative to some market index.

Since you use both, does this become a little confusing in conversation?

I solved that problem by referring to Wells Wilder's relative strength index as "internal strength"

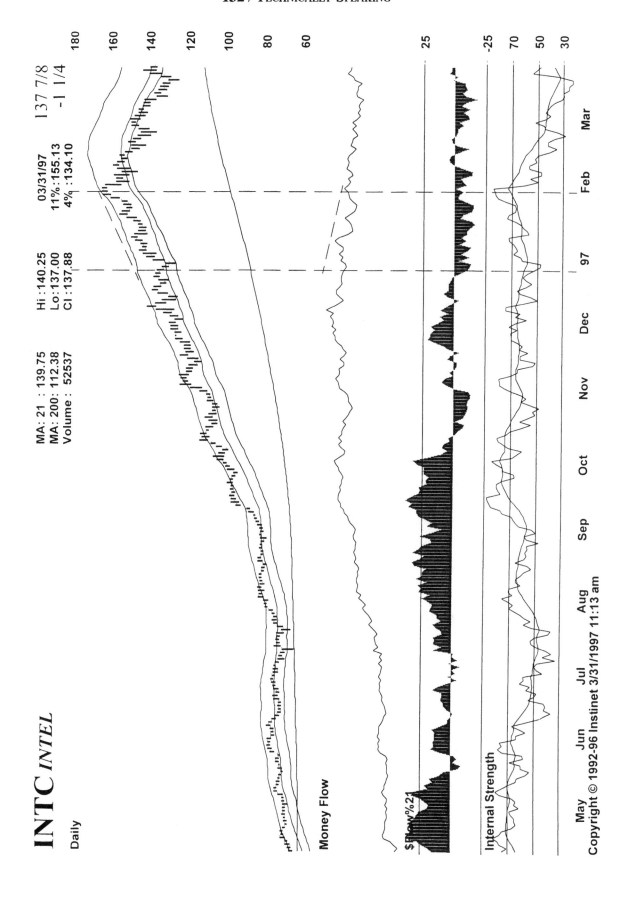

INTC *INTEL*

Daily

MA: 21 : 139.75
MA: 200: 112.38
Volume : 52537

Hi : 140.25
Lo : 137.00
Cl : 137.88

03/31/97
11% : 155.13
4% : 134.10

137 7/8
- 1 1/4

Money Flow

$ Flow % 21

Internal Strength

May   Jun   Jul   Aug   Sep   Oct   Nov   Dec   97   Feb   Mar

Copyright © 1992-96 Instinet 3/31/1997 11:13 am

180 160 140 120 100 80 60   25   -25 70 50 30

because that is what it really is. You are measuring a stock's internal strength so you are really looking at each stock's individual price action. Since it's very confusing for people, I just refer to that as internal strength.

Would you differentiate between the two?

Relative strength, the old relative strength which I think is a very crucial thing for people to look at, measures a stock relative to a market average, typically the S&P 500. The relative strength line compares the stock's price action to the market. That would be the relative strength line on William O'Neil's charts, Trendline, or Mansfield. Usually, they are looking at a six to nine month time period. Typically, it's relative to the market average. You are looking for the stocks which have gone up the most. That is a critical piece of the technical puzzle. Absolutely critical. You can't look at money flow in isolation. Money flow has to be analyzed in relation to relative strength activity. Think of a scenario where money flow is very strong but price is not moving up. What does that mean? It means that some very powerful buyers have very strong feelings about a stock and they are willing to put their money where their mouth is, but the rest of the world doesn't yet agree with them. It is not until the relative strength line starts to trend upward, has a positive slope, and moves above its 90 day average that you know that you have a stock that is now likely to perform very well. All of those things have to happen. I recommend to people in seminars that you must look at both the relative strength line relative to the market and a stock's supply/demand characteristics, as embodied in the money flow and persistency of money flow, in order to get a true indication that this is a stock that you want to own very aggressively.

The trend and slope of the relative strength line seems self-explanatory but what about the 90 day moving average you just referred to?

Trend analysis can be pretty subjective. To help quantify the trend, I create a 90 day moving average of the relative strength line. I got this from the *"Encyclopedia of Stock Market Techniques"* published in 1963. Sedge Coppock, who published a market letter out of Texas, said in an article, "If you want to have a very easy, but effective way to analyze the relative strength line, just put an 18 week moving average on it." If a relative strength line is above its 18 week moving average, that is bullish. If it is below its 18 week moving average, that's bearish. I have been doing that now for years and it really works. It is simple but so powerful. It is the combination of relative strength compared to its 90 day moving average and the persistency of money flow or money flow compared to its 90 day average that really helps you find the big winners. Think of it this way, if only one is positive, you only have half the picture. It's like two people who go out dating. One of them is in love and the other couldn't care less. You don't have much of a relationship. You need both people to really care. Relative strength is actually a dual indicator. Remember in the beginning I said there were two forms of technical analysis and the most important one is the trend? Trend analysis takes two forms. Is the stock in an uptrend? The theory is that if a stock is in a positive trend, that is bullish and you want to own that stock, but there are two ways to look at this. The stock can be in an uptrend and you may not want to own it. Why? Because it may be underperforming the market. In other words you may have a market like you did in 1995, where technology stocks were up, on average, over 50%. Do you want to be in a stock that is up only 6%? Probably not, unless you are very conservative. If you are an aggressive investor, you want to find stocks that are not just in uptrends, but the stocks that are in uptrends and also outperforming the market. In other words, you want to buy the best stocks. If you were hiring for a company and you wanted some bright people, you would look at all college graduates so everybody you are interviewing is positive from that point of view. But, the people with the best grades, in theory, are the smartest people and the best achievers. It is sort of the same with relative strength. The stocks that are going up would equate to college graduates. The stocks with very strong relative strength lines would equate with the people with the best grades. If that is your goal, to hire the best and the brightest or to invest in the best and the brightest stocks, then relative strength takes the concept of trend analysis to a second level. It basically says, "I don't want just stocks in uptrends. I want stocks in uptrends that are outperforming the market." It is not that hard to follow relative strength because William O'Neil publishes these numbers in *Investors Business Daily* or you can get it from a Mansfield or Trendline chart. Anybody who has a computer can find screens that help identify the strongest stocks from a relative point of view. It really does fine tune the analysis to the point where you are getting much better stocks to trade or invest in.

You modified the name of Welles Wilder's RSI but didn't you also reduce the time period from fourteen days to nine days?

Yes and I did that in 1982. I had read Welles Wilder's book in the late 1970's but, of course, you couldn't compute this very easily by hand then. It wasn't until the Computrac software came out that I had an easy way to follow RSI on a lot of stocks. Computrac software was originally developed by, and for, commodity traders. I was trading stocks. They were using a 14 day Welles Wilder index as a default and I said, "This is great for commodities, which are volatile and where you get big swings up and down, but for stocks, if you want to use the 70 and 30 reference lines as overbought and oversold indications, you are just not going to get a lot of stocks that will get to 70 or 30 because stocks are not as volatile as commodities." After playing around with the numbers, and a lot of this was really just trial and error, I decided that 70 and 30 would be reached if you used a 9 day time framework. Of course, since these are exponential averages, 9 days is not quite as short as it sounds. Even now, if you look at very strong stocks, you will see that only once or twice a year does Welles Wilder's relative strength index get down to 30. Even using 9 days, a very strong stock may not reach an oversold reading of 30. In fact, a number of people have now developed floating overbought and oversold points for this indicator. They basically figured out that a strong stock isn't going to give you a reading of 30 very often, therefore, you have to adjust your bands upward. So in a very strong stock, the OB/OS extremes for the RSI may be 40 and 80 instead of 30 and 70.

It's prudent to factor the strength of the trend into the equation.

Yes. There have been articles published in *Technical Analysis of Stocks and Commodities* and indicators that are now being developed which look at past readings and say, "Okay, this stock is in a very strong trend. It's not going to get to 30 so use 40 as an oversold reading."

I would think fewer signals would mean fewer whipsaws.

If you are trading that's true, but going back to what we were just talking about, let's assume you only want to be trading the strongest stocks. If your methodology says, "I want to buy strong stocks when the Welles Wilder's RSI gets under 30," well, you are not going to get that happening very often. If, in fact, you want to be trading the strong stocks, you have to adjust your oversold level in order to get oversold indications and the 40 level may be very reliable. In doing this kind of analysis, it is critical not to use just the standard break points. If you do, you are going to sit on the sidelines or you are not going to be in the stocks you really want to be in. You don't have to adjust the parameters, but it is beneficial because you will pick up more great opportunities. Now, the risk is that you will get a few more whipsaws and losses, but that is a small price to pay for zeroing in on opportunities when they present themselves.

Given that 30 and below is oversold and 70 and above is overbought, what adjustments do you recommend for these standard parameters in bull and bear market conditions?

You have to look at each stock. If you are in a bear market for an individual stock, then 20 and 60 would be right, or 40 and 80 in a very bullish market. You really need a computer program to do that. You could eyeball and figure out that this is what's happening but people have published articles that purport to do this automatically by analyzing the volatility and the price action and what it has done over the last period of time. That seems to be a promising area of research.

What guidelines can you offer in terms of using the RSI?

It's first purpose is to look for overbought and oversold levels. The second purpose is to look for divergences. Divergences are much more important typically on the upside than on the downside because usually stocks will bottom in a "V" pattern in some sort of panic selling, especially in the kinds of markets we have been in the last 10 or 15 years. Tops tend to be made more slowly and take more time. The first overbought indication is not usually a good time to sell and so you want to look for divergences. If you get a divergence at the bottom, that's great, but you don't always get one. Whereas at the top, especially in the kinds of markets we have been in where we haven't had a protracted bear market, you want to look for one or two divergences before you get bearish on a stock. The bottom line is that if you are an investor with money to put to work and the stock gets oversold and Wells Wilder's index drops below 30, just buy it.

Do you include the Commodity Channel Index (CCI) in your analysis of stocks?

Yes. We renamed that overbought/oversold because a lot of institutional stock investors get nervous when they hear the word "commodity." Basically, that is just another oscillator. Depending on the time frame that you choose, it could be better or worse than Welles Wilder's. We look at two time frameworks, a 13 day and a 45 day. I use it in a very simplistic way. If a stock looks good from a technical point of view—supply/demand, money flow persistency, relative strength is strong, and the 13 day CCI goes to minus 100—that is a buying opportunity.

The CCI measures when a price is relatively high or low. How is this different from Bomar Bands which also measure when prices are high or low, relatively speaking?

It's not really. The computation might be different but it accomplishes a similar thing. That is why we use the 21 day bands, then the 50 day bands, and then we use the oscillators. Occasionally, you will pick up something that you don't see in the bands. That is another problem technical traders have. They sometimes fool themselves into thinking that they are looking at a lot of different indicators and that is going to improve their analysis, but in fact, they are really looking at the same analysis in five different indicators. For instance, if your only tools were the Bollinger Bands, Bomar Bands, Welles Wilder's RSI, and the CCI, you are really looking at one thing four different ways. You are not helping yourself and you are fooling yourself into thinking that you have a really great system. You are looking at four different indicators and they are all telling you the same thing when in fact, they are all measuring the same thing. Now, if you change the time frameworks and look at the short and intermediate-term, this is a little better but not really good enough. These all measure the same things; they just do them slightly differently and for different time frameworks.

Regarding the CCI, would you comment on some potential trouble spots that could lead investors astray?

If you just assume that a plus 100 rating is a time to sell and a minus 100 rating is a time to buy, you are going to get in big trouble. You just can't apply a sort of rote approach to overbought/oversold. That is assuming that every time the light is green, you can safely cross the street. If you live in New York City long enough, you know that you have to be watching what's going on more carefully. Not everybody respects the rules—same thing with overbought/oversold. You can't just automatically buy an oversold or sell an overbought. You have to understand the time framework that the indicator is based on. If you are a longterm investor and a shortterm oscillator gets overbought, that is meaningless. Let's say you are a longterm investor and you like to buy stocks and hold them for a year or two years. You buy a stock at 20 and it goes to 25. Well, the commodity channel index is going to go to plus 100. Do you want to sell the stock there? No. Do you want to buy it there? Maybe not. If you automatically assume that anytime a stock you own gets a reading of 100 or even 100 with a divergence—maybe it's the second time it's rallied—if you are a longterm investor, selling is not a good thing to do. If you are a trader and you are looking for spots to take profits, then this may all make a lot of sense. It really depends on the time framework of the indicator and also what your goals are. For instance, I also look at a 5 day commodity channel index and I use it in a totally different way than what we have just been describing. If the five day index gets up to +160, that basically tells me that there is a very powerful shortterm move in progress and I want to stay with it. With a very shortterm overbought/oversold indicator like a five day commodity channel index, an overbought reading on a shortterm basis is actually very bullish. It is sort of like when a thermometer reads 101 degrees, you know the patient is really sick. In this case, if it reads +160 you know the patient is super healthy. It is a good way to find stocks that on a shortterm basis are going to continue up.

Is the opposite true—a reading of -160 means the stock is terminally ill?

Terminal is not the appropriate word. This is for very shortterm purposes. But yes, it does work on the converse. It is just an indication that whatever moves spawn that reading will continue for a bit. It can be one day or three days but it basically says it is too early to fade the move. In fact, if you are a very aggressive shortterm trader, you may just want to get on board and stay with that move.

All of the indicators which we have discussed can be used for either shortterm trading or intermediate-term investing.

That's right. It depends on the time framework. A 45 day, 50 day, or 90 day commodity channel index would give you some intermediate-term guidance.

Let's assume you were going to buy a stock or recommend a stock for purchase. Can you define how you would go about making your selection?

If you were limiting me just to technical analysis factors, I would look for stocks in positive trends, with strong relative strength versus the market, that have very powerful money flow persistency. If I were a trader, I would try to buy those stocks on some sort of pullback in price either to a 21 day average or a lower band. If I were an investor and I was dying to put money to work, I would just buy them. You are basically trying to put four different technical disciplines in place—trend analysis, relative strength, supply/demand in the form of money flow persistency, and some sort of oscillator approach. Now, if you said, "Okay Marc, you can throw in a fundamental factor," I would say look for the stocks which have two characteristics—consistency of earnings gains over a three to five year period. In other words, companies that year in and year out are increasing their earnings and companies with the strongest earnings momentum—companies where the estimate for the current year and for next year are the highest percentage gains versus the previous year. I would cull a list of names that have very positive earnings momentum and earnings consistency and then I would filter them by the same four technical approaches.

Do you prefer to begin your analysis from a fundamental perspective?

Absolutely, because it puts the odds on your side. It means that you are not guessing bottoms in stocks that are making new lows for all the reasons that we talked about. I mean, if you are in a bear market some of these stocks are going to be weak. Basically it is like panning for gold. You try and get rid of the rocks and start with the nuggets. Then you throw out the small nuggets and stay with the big ones. That is what this whole technical approach does for you. I absolutely start with fundamentals in the form of earnings momentum stocks because year in and year out, investors pay for growth and earnings. You can also take the Benjamin Graham approach or the Warren Buffet approach to value, where you don't pay too much for stocks, but you want to monitor them technically because that is your safety net. You don't want to blindly own these stocks. If things start to deteriorate or if the technical picture changes, get out. Given the tools we have been talking about, the investor should be able to do an excellent job of making money if he just follows these guidelines and disciplines.

Suppose readers are not willing to devote a lot of time to fundamental analysis. Can they use the earnings per share ratings from *Investors Business Daily* and if so, what guidelines would you suggest?

Oh sure, it's real easy. You just look for the stocks that have a 90 earnings rating or higher.

***Investors Business Daily* also has numerical rankings for relative strength. What number would you look for there?**

That would be 90 so these would be the 90/90 stocks. You can shave it down a little but basically that gets a lot of the job done. The public really has access to these tools. It is just a question of the institutions having the ability to monitor things more closely on a real time basis, but it doesn't always buy you better performance. Sometimes it is a lot of noise and distracting.

A lot of technicians are tape readers and chartists. Other than reducing the emotional aspect of investing, what advantage will these indicators have over more traditional forms of analysis?

It gives you a different level of analysis. If you are looking at a chart you are really just looking at the price action. With the supply/demand work and the relative strength, you are looking under the surface of price action and that is really critical.

What have you observed to be the necessary traits of a successful technical analyst?

Not second guessing the indicators, which is really discipline, and being flexible enough to look for new indicators because the markets are changing all the time. What works today for one reason or another may not work tomorrow. If you just stick with the same set of tools you will find that you are left behind. I think you have to be open to new ideas and new ways of looking at things but not be seduced by every new idea. It takes a lot of discipline and the ability to know whether something is going to improve on what you have been doing or just create noise. I think discipline and an open mind are really the two most important characteristics.

Does an indicator stop working because too many people follow it?

No. Actually, I have never seen an indicator that stopped working because everyone followed it. I think indicators stop working if there has been a major change in the structure of the marketplace. The indicators that are based on human nature will always work and most of what we are talking about is based on human nature.

Everything changes but human nature. Supply and demand factors never change.

Yes, and the fact that people tend to overreact to events and they like to jump on a bandwagon.

That is what trend analysis is all about. People are sheep. They will follow the leader. Over the years, it has been proven that this is a profitable way to invest and make money. As long as what you are looking at is based on human nature, it will continue to work. If it is based on some quirk in the marketplace, it may not work. For instance, you asked me about trade by trade money flow and whether that was the best way to look at supply and demand. For a lot of years, it probably was. Once program trading became a reality where people with computers could find small discrepancies and flood the market with orders, I think that trade by trade analysis became a lot less accurate. Very often you would get big trades on downticks. When these sell programs hit the market, it didn't really reflect anybody's opinion about the prospects for that stock. People were just taking advantage of a shortterm inefficiency in the marketplace. That would show up as negative money flow but 20 minutes later, the stock could be back above its mean or up on the day. When program trading became a reality, I think a lot of the tick by tick money flow analysis became less valuable. That is an example of where a new type of trading took place in the market and something changed. When 24 hour trading becomes a reality, do you look at just the trades within the exchange hours or do you look at the 24 hour trades? That has created a problem for technicians. Something like that could make certain indicators less valuable.

S&P 500 futures contracts trade 24 hours don't they?

Yes, but so far I think the general reaction is that what happens outside of trading hours is noise and ignore it, but that may change over time. Anything that is based on the types of money flow analysis that I have been talking about, as trading gets diffused in different markets around the world, as with the S&P futures, then some of these analyses could be different.

Do you have any advice for beginners who might run out and buy a software program for technical analysis?

If they just go out and buy a program and expect to turn it on and follow just the ordinary rules, they could get into big trouble. I do think that with a little thought, a program like Metastock, which is reasonably priced, can be a very valuable tool by helping people organize information. If they view technical analysis software as a way to organize information and sift through it, then I think ultimately it is a very profitable decision and I would encourage people to do it. If they expect the world without putting in some work, then they are kidding themselves.

Would you advise beginners, before they actually put money where their mouth is so to speak, to play with the indicators for a while and get a feel for how they work in the real world?

Absolutely, and really over and above that, they have to know what their goals and objectives are and what time horizons they are comfortable with. I think that is the biggest mistake that people make. They don't analyze what their own risk tolerances are and what their own goals are so they enter into a strategy which might be very shortterm and high risk when their goals and their risk tolerance are really longterm oriented. It is a twofold process. They have to get comfortable with the indicators but even before that, they have to know what their goals are. These indicators will work differently and be used differently if someone is a longterm investor versus someone who is a trader. Someone may think they are a trader but not have the psychological makeup for trading and yet making a lot of decisions under stress and high volatility. You could have a technical analysis package which would do wonders for you if you use the indicators in one way, but you may embark on a different course. If that is what you are limiting yourself to, then you may have very unsatisfactory results, not because the technical analysis package was bad or deficient, or even that you didn't understand the indicators. You may just have embarked on the wrong course for what your real and true goals are. I think it is really important to analyze your objectives and then choose the tools which will help you accomplish those objectives. Maslov said, "If the only tool you have is a hammer, you tend to treat everything as if it were a nail." I think that is so true. If you only have a shortterm oscillator, everything is going to look like a trading opportunity. If you are not a trader, if your true goal is not trading profits, then that software is useless. You have to understand the indicators and what they are meant to accomplish and then you have to understand your goals. If you mesh the two, then software is invaluable.

Paul Desmond

Paul Desmond is president of *Lowry's Reports*, a technically oriented investment advisory firm which has the distinction of being the oldest in existence within the United States. Founded in 1938 by Lyman M. Lowry, *Lowry's Reports* provides timely market analysis to both institutional and individual investors.

Mr. Desmond inherited his fascination for the financial markets from his father, an avid investor. Helping his father research stocks in Value Line and elsewhere fostered a strong interest in the markets during his youth and influenced his decision to seek a career in that direction.

After receiving his degree in banking and finance, Mr. Desmond realized that analyzing corporate balance sheets would not produce the kind of market profits he envisioned so he embarked on a mission to find a viable system that would consistently make money in the markets. Frequent visits were made to the Miami Public Library, combing the shelves for any related information. One of the available resources was *Lowry's Market Trend Analysis*. The content and technical orientation of this newsletter made more sense to him than anything else he had encountered previously. Published in Miami, he copied the address with the intention of looking into employment opportunities with the firm. When he went in search of the Key Biscayne address, instead of finding an office building, he discovered a palatial three story home situated at the end of a long, picturesque drive lined with palm trees. The slightly intimidating presence before him and the residential location called into question the validity of the address so in doubt, he drove away. As it turns out, it was the correct address and after regaining his courage, he made a second attempt. Upon arrival, he noticed a man in old work clothes and felt hat pruning shrubs and walked over to inquire if there was anyone on the premises connected with the Lowry organization. Emerging from the bushes, the gentleman introduced himself as Lyman Lowry. The two men conversed for four hours before Mr. Lowry's wife, who had come to investigate her husband's disappearance, interrupted them. Now confident that he had finally found a methodology that would lead to profits, Mr. Desmond offered to work for free in exchange for an apprenticeship. Impressed by this genuine demonstration of interest and initiative to learn, Mr. Lowry hired him on the spot, with pay.

Mr. Desmond had been with the firm eight years and was essentially running the office when Mr. Lowry's age invited questions from concerned clients who wanted assurances that the same quality standard of service and analysis would continue in the event of his retirement or untimely death. The question continued to surface so in an effort to resolve the issue, Lyman Lowry sold the business to his protégé in 1972, continuing to actively work for the organization another seven years.

In 1933, Mr. Lowry developed a unique formula to assess the forces of supply and demand as they relate to stocks listed on the New York Stock Exchange. The Buying Power Index and Selling Pressure Index, as the indicators are called, is Lowry's trademark and incorporates four distinct variables which collectively determine whether buying or selling predominates. For this and other outstanding achievements in technical analysis, he was the very first recipient of the Market Technician's Association annual award. The fact that this indicator has survived 58 years with relatively few modifications demonstrates the constancy of the law of supply and demand.

Lowry's Market Trend Analysis is still published in its original format but in order to meet the growing needs of institutional clients, additional services have been added through the years. More comprehensive in nature, *The Institutional Report* includes an extensive analysis of 50 groups and 3,000 individual stocks. Abstracts from *Lowry's Market Trend Analysis* are occasionally featured in the Market Watch section of *Barron's*.

Technical analysis certainly was not in vogue when Lyman Lowry launched his technical advisory service, Lowry's Market Trend Analysis. What sparked this unconventional choice?

Back in the early Thirties, Lyman Lowry was working as a new junior executive in the trust department of a bank in Coral Gables, Florida. The depression was on and the market was dropping rapidly. All day long, senior bank officers would pace up and down the hallways. One would say, "I don't understand what's going on." Another officer would say, "Who can find fault with the way we have managed the portfolio? We invested in good quality stocks." That went on day after day and the portfolio kept going down and down. Mr. Lowry realized that these guys were not doing anything to preserve the assets of their clients. In 1933, he left the bank and started doing some independent research. All of the textbooks talked about how critical the laws of supply and demand were but he didn't see it being used at all in the stock market. He tried to figure out how to measure supply and demand as it applied to individual stocks and the general market and decided it came down to two basic factors, price and volume. He broke those two factors down into price gains, price losses, upside volume, and downside volume. Using the *Wall Street Journal*, he went back to January 1933 and calculated those numbers for each stock listed on the NYSE. It was a gargantuan effort. In those days there were no computers or data bases, just hand cranked adding machines. With a five year hypothetical back record, he started publishing the Lowry Report in 1938.

There have been monumental changes in the market since 1933. Has the original methodology for measuring supply and demand survived these changes?

The methodology has stayed the same but our ability to read the data and our ability to view it in a series of different contexts has improved over the years. In an environment that has changed so dramatically, people wonder how something like this can stay the same and still have validity. I keep relating our system to a weather barometer. Invented back in the 1600's, the weather barometer is essentially the same today as it was hundreds of years ago because it is such a basic measurement. Changes in the ozone layer and air pollution haven't distorted the accuracy of the barometer. The law of supply and demand is the first thing you learn in Economics 101 and is the foundation of all macroeconomics. Lowry's tries to determine whether there is greater buying enthusiasm or a greater desire to sell and to do that, we measure supply and demand. With the sophistication of today's investors, all of the electronics that exist, world markets opening up, trading day lengthened, and the advent of mutual funds; all of those various things haven't really changed that basic indicator. Just as barometric pressure is an ideal starting point for any analysis of weather, supply and demand is a logical and essential starting point for any serious analysis of the stock market.

Can you describe the technique that Mr. Lowry developed to measure supply and demand in the stock market?

Visualize taking the stock listings in the Wall Street Journal and laying them out in front of you. Start at the top and every time you see a plus sign in the change column, accumulate the amount of the change. For example, if the first stock is up 3/8, add 3/8. If the next stock is up ¼, add ¼. The next stock is up 1½, add 1½. You just add all of the positive price changes for the day. Let's say you add all of the fractions stocks gained on an individual day and it equals 300 points. That total is what we call "points gained." Then you do the same thing with the number of points or fractions of a point that were lost per stock—accumulate the negative net change for each stock and then add all the minus signs together. You come up with a total of "points lost." You do the same thing for upside and downside volume. In other words, any stock that has a plus sign in the change column, its volume is totaled as upside volume. Any stock that has a minus sign in the change column becomes downside volume. When you get down to measuring supply and demand, the specialists, the odd-lotters, the institutions, the foreign investors—whoever it might be that is doing the buying and selling—their activity is encompassed in those basic numbers. You can break it down further but I don't think you really want to because the smaller the sample, the more likely you are to get distortions.

After completing your supply/demand analysis of the NYSE, you are left with four variables: points gained, points lost, total upside volume, and total downside volume. Do you look at each variable individually or collectively?

Depending on what you are trying to accomplish, there are a number of different ways to look at them. The first thing to do is compare points gained to points lost. Which one is stronger? Just subtract one from the other to get a net positive or net negative number for the day, then you can accumulate that on a continuous basis. That's one way of doing it. Another part of it is to look at the ratio of upside volume to points gained. You can take the difference between the upside volume and the downside volume or calculate the ratio of upside volume to downside volume. Let's use a comparison to make this a little clearer. Suppose you and I are running a department store. The department store has several different departments such as clothing, jewelry, socks, gloves, household wares, and home appliances. Parenthetically, the NYSE has different stock groups- technology, drugs, automobile, steel, etcetera. We want to determine how well our department store is doing on a day by day basis. What would we do? I would propose that the first thing we do is count the cash register receipts at the end of the day so that we can see how much money came in. That would be comparable to points gained. Then we would have to see how much money the creditors took away with them because we have to pay off our suppliers on a daily basis. That money going out the back door needs to be counted. Let's say we had $10,000.00 coming in the front door and $5,000.00 going out the back door. By subtracting the money coming in versus the money going out, we have a $5,000.00 positive inflow of capital. Another important measurement to look at would be the number of customers buying things in our store on a day by day basis. If we had 1000 customers and we took in $10,000.00, the average customer bought $10.00 worth of goods. We do the same thing for money going out. How many creditors were there? For the sake of discussion, let's say there were 500 creditors taking money away, so they each took away $100.00. Now you have four numbers. You have money coming in the front door, money going out the back door, the volume of customers coming in the front of the store, and the volume of creditors taking money out the back of the store. What else could we do to measure what's going on in our store? We could stand around and get public opinions from people but those types of things are not going to mean nearly as much as what is actually in the cash register. We can break down what's going on in the store by departments, such as the jewelry department or the glove department, but the smaller sample we get, the less likely it is to be significant. Let's say we have $10,000.00 in the cash register at the end of each day for five straight days. That number is consistent but the volume of customers

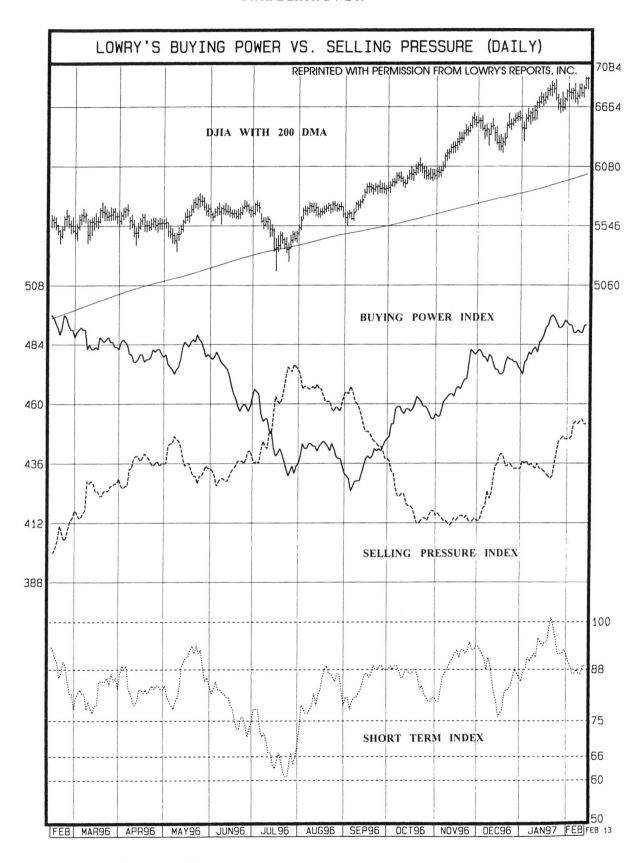

LOWRY'S BUYING POWER VS. SELLING PRESSURE (DAILY)

REPRINTED WITH PERMISSION FROM LOWRY'S REPORTS, INC.

DJIA WITH 200 DMA

BUYING POWER INDEX

SELLING PRESSURE INDEX

SHORT TERM INDEX

buying drops off. We had 1,000 customers and over a period of time it has dropped off to 500 customers. Now you have 500 customers buying $10,000.00 worth of goods. What is going on? We quickly find that there is nobody in the sock department or household department. They are all in the jewelry department or the home appliance department. The customers are spending big money but only in a particular segment of the total store. That is not a good sign. The changes that occur between the money coming in the door and the volume of customers bringing that money in the door—the ratio of those two numbers—is extremely important. The same thing is true on the back end. You want to look at the number of people taking money out the back door. So the interplay between all four of those numbers are supplying you with an extremely simple, but significant snapshot, of what is going on inside the store on a daily basis. We are doing the same thing with the stock market. We are looking at the amount of money that customers are putting into the market, that is points gained. We are looking at the volume of transactions at which that is occurring, that is upside volume. We are looking at the amount of money that is being extracted by sellers and that is points lost. We are looking at the volume of trading that is going on in the process of that extraction which is downside volume. All of the buying and selling is encompassed in those four numbers regardless of who's doing it—institutions, individual investors, or specialists.

Does distribution occur when supply exceeds demand?

It actually begins earlier than that. We use some longer term measurements of supply and demand in order to get a picture of the real trend. Supply and demand fluctuates from day to day. If you look at it on a single day basis, you often can't tell what the market is doing but if you look at it over a period of time, you see some patterns develop. That is the reason that we use the longer term indicators. At market tops, you tend to see weakening demand and increasing supply taking place over a period of months so that you are forewarned. It isn't something that happens all of a sudden—one day supply exceeds demand. It is a gradual process. This is not necessarily true at bottoms. Bottoms tend to be much more sharply defined. The market simply comes crashing down and then reaches a point where everybody that wanted to sell has done so and buyers come rushing in to take advantage of the opportunities. In the case of a market bottom, you are watching for a total exhaustion of sellers and a new emergence of buyers that had been virtually absent up until that point; whereas at market tops, you see distribution taking place over a much longer period of time.

At tops, there is usually plenty of advance warning.

If you go back to mid-February 1996, our buying power index topped out and started to suddenly decrease. It had been in a strong uptrend since late 1994. The papers were full of stories about people's insatiable desire for stocks and the market kept going higher. The general perception was that money was pouring into the market at an incredible rate but in actuality, it was slowing down. From mid-February 1996 until early September, we saw less money flowing into the market and fewer trades overall. If you go back and look at mutual fund net purchases at that time, you will find that indeed they started to slow down significantly in February. They weren't reported as slowing down but the Buying Power Index was saying someone, someplace, is putting less money into the market now then they were back in December 1995. The stock market peaked in May 1996, so you had months of advance warning. Then in October 1996, it appeared as though the storm clouds suddenly blew away and renewed buying enthusiasm emerged, sending the market off on a new leg.

Despite the market's deterioration into June 1996 and subsequent sharp sell-off in July, a bear market never materialized.

Every year in south Florida we go through the hurricane season. The hurricane trackers are constantly on the news warning of impending storms. We go out to the stores and buy up bottled water, canned goods, and candles. We close all of the shutters. In a lot of cases they tell you to evacuate. Then they will come back and say, "The storm turned around and blew away." Each time the storm approaches you have to go through the same process of closing the shutters and buying water even though you know in advance that the vast majority of those storms are not going to hit. If a storm is threatening, you have to take a defensive posture because if you don't and the storm hits, it will cause damage that will take years to repair. The market is somewhat the same way. Many times we will see signs of distribution, diminishing demand, diminishing volume, weakening momentum, selectivity, and so on. It is warning that something is wrong and it could develop into a significant decline. Even though you know that the vast majority of threatened bear markets never materialize, you have to take a defensive posture to make sure you don't get hit by a real bear market.

Do you look at the supply/demand equation for several indices or just the NYSE?

We have done the analysis back to 1933 on the NYSE. We shifted over to computers in 1972 and at that point we picked up the American Exchange and did the same kind of analysis, but the American Exchange has become less and less significant and the numbers more subject to distortion. In the meantime, the NASDAQ has become a massive exchange and major market. NASDAQ lists some of the key stocks of the future but there are also thousands and thousands of issues listed which have very little substance to them. From a liquidity standpoint, probably only 150 to 200 stocks, out of several thousands listed on the NASDAQ, are issues that an institutional investor could get into and out of relatively easy. For this reason, we have not been rushing to include a lot of illiquid stocks in our analysis because they can create distortions, though we will probably include the NASDAQ sometime in the near future. The NYSE really provides a strong surrogate for all stocks, regardless of the exchange. In fact, we have quite a large number of Canadian subscribers who say the relationship between the NYSE and Canadian Exchange is so close that they can use the NYSE analysis to manage money on the Canadian Exchanges. The same thing is true with the NASDAQ. There will be times when the NASDAQ acts differently than the NYSE but those times are generally limited. I think the most significant divergence between the two goes back to 1977. During 1977, the NYSE went down for most of the year while the AMEX and NASDAQ, what there was of it then, went up rather strongly for the year.

Lowry's Buying Power and Selling Pressure Indexes measure the supply/demand situation of the entire group of stocks listed on the NYSE. Is it feasible to use this procedure for individual issues?

Originally, we were operating on closing numbers because that is all there was at the time. For an individual stock, all you would have at the end of the day was that it was either up for the day, down, or unchanged. If it was up for the day, 100% of the volume would have been allocated to upside volume and that is obviously inaccurate. During the day, it may have ticked up and down one hundred times but there is only one closing price and one closing volume. It wasn't until the late 1960's that trade by trade numbers became available but then the computer equipment necessary to analyze those tick figures for all the stocks listed on the exchange wasn't available. One day we would like to be able to do a complete supply/demand analysis on individual stocks.

So the holdup toward implementation is an equipment problem rather than a conceptual problem?

Yes. In the mid-1960's, we were still essentially doing everything by hand. The numbers were being calculated on adding machines. Now we are to the point where computers are getting fast enough to wade through all of that information. We may be able to go back and do some serious experimentation. In the meantime, we do a full supply/demand analysis on the general market and then when it comes to individual stocks, we are forced to rely on relative strength analysis until we can get computers fast enough to do the same thing for individual stocks that we do for the general market.

When a change is occurring in the supply/demand picture of the NYSE, are the signals leading or coincident?

It is coincident but some aspects are projectable by looking for particular patterns to emerge. Once a pattern develops, based on past experience, you have a higher probability that it is going to lead to a certain conclusion. You see buyers go through periods where they slowly accumulate stocks and then as crowd psychology comes into play, the frenzy grows and grows. Once that frenzy starts to fade, you can to some extent project its conclusion. The Lowry Market Trend Analysis has 63 years of history. We publish that back record in graphic form as well as related statistics so people can go back and compare the current situation with similar situations in the past. It allows people to say, "We have seen this pattern 25 times and here is what happened in each one of those cases." You develop a table of probabilities, similar to what an insurance company uses. When insurers look at the hurricanes on the east coast of Florida, there is a certain probability that applies to the months of June through October. Insurance companies have to allow for the risks that occur during that time period. The stock market is the same way. If you see a certain pattern repeating over and over again, it allows you to be prepared for the next eventuality.

With program trading, buy or sell signals are generated by a computer programmed to detect and take advantage of price discrepancies between stocks and an underlying index. Since this buying and selling is a result of a mechanical decision rather than an emotional one, will this distort the true supply/demand picture?

It is a mechanical process rather than an emotional process but once the money is plunked down, then the emotion is gone and now we are measuring dollars coming across the table. We never know for sure why any investor bought or sold, only that they did. From that standpoint, their money being spent looks exactly the same as any other investor's money being spent; therefore, program trading does have a relationship to supply and demand in that we pick those numbers up as net buying or net selling. Investors are constantly up against various influences. Years ago, the Japanese started pouring money into the U.S. market unconcerned about what they were buying. Everybody wondered what kind of distortions would be caused by foreign investors. For years, Garfield Drew wrote about odd-lot trading and what influence they would have. From time to time, short sellers have been looked upon as a great distortion. It is always one thing or another but all of those things go into making up the markets. We still have foreign investors and now realize that they are not as great a threat as we thought, so we don't pay much attention to them anymore. Over a long period of time, the significance of any single group diminishes. Even if it did bring to bear a different attitude, that attitude would still work out to be net bullish or net bearish—it doesn't change the basic equations of supply and demand. If there is more money trying to flow into stocks than there is trying to leave, you have a bullish market. If you have more people getting out of stocks than getting in, you have a bearish market. When you look at it over a period of time longer than a few days, these trends seem to be as clearly defined now as at any other point in history. We haven't seen any real distortion other than on a short term basis. If you look at program trading on a daily basis, it has created a significant amount of problems but over a longer period of time, its significance becomes minimized.

Obviously readers will not have the capability to generate the kind of supply/demand analysis that Lowry's does but even if they tackled something manageable, such as the 30 components of the Dow, would that be helpful?

If that is all you had available to you, that would probably be a pretty good 30 stocks to use. We have done some work on that basis and it is a start but the broader the sampling that you use, the truer the picture. Sometimes you run into situations where the blue chips act much stronger than the average stock. If you add up just the 30 Industrials and then confine your buying and selling to those 30 stocks, that would be valid. But, if you measure those 30 stocks and then go out and buy some small cap stocks, it's not going to work, and that is typically what people want to do. The average small investor wants to get a general idea of where the market is headed and then buys a radical stock, something that probably has a lot of expectations for the future but at present it doesn't have any earnings.

An original indicator developed by Lowry's is the 90% downside day. Would you describe what this measures and how it is used?

It is a very helpful way of identifying major market bottoms. For years, people have tried to come up with some way to identify a market low. Edson Gould defined what he called the "classic V bottom;" a market that declined sharply early in the day on big volume and then at some point during the day, stabilized, and then rallied on expanding volume, closing up for the day. We found that when you applied that concept, it didn't always work. For example, many times the market would sell-off sharply throughout the entire day and it wasn't until the next day that it reversed to the upside. That threw people off because Gould had identified it as being something that occurred in the middle of the day. There were a lot of cases where you did indeed have this "V" bottom, but it didn't last. We went back to 1933, looking at all of the major market bottoms for something that would help us hone the idea of the classic "V" bottom. What we found was that major market declines generally contained 90% downside days, which simply means that 90% of all the volume and 90% of all the price movement during a particular day is on the downside.

This indicator includes both price and volume?

Yes, and we found that as you approached the final lows, these 90% downside days became more frequent. During the course of the bear market they would be 30 days or so apart, but as the market came closer and closer to the lows, the 90% days would become more frequent. All this represented was panic selling. The "90%" isn't as important as what's going on from a supply and demand standpoint. During a bear market, investors panic and sell their stocks. That panic tends to intensify and feed on itself as the market works lower. A point is finally reached where everyone who has wanted to sell does so and that creates the final 90% downside day, which tells you that the market has reached a point of capitulation. There are no sellers left. The only people left are those who have been on the sidelines in cash waiting for an opportunity to buy. When they step in and start buying, that produces a 90% upside day.

Are you saying that a market bottom occurs when a 90% downside day is followed by a 90% upside day?

During the big declines, you will see several 90% downside days followed quickly by a 90% upside day. That is what we define as a true selling climax. We went back through our records to 1933 and looked at all the major market bottoms and found that this pattern was consistent. You have a complete panic and then the opposite, buyers recognize that incredible bargains exist and jump back in giving you a 90% upside day. Going all the way back to 1933, whenever you see two or more 90% downside days, that tells you that you are in involved in a market climate that is more serious than a normal market correction. As their frequency increases, you are probably coming closer and closer to the final lows. You simply wait for that last 90% downside day, whenever it is, to be followed by a 90% upside day, and that is your signal that something has changed. It is one of the more important indicators of a major market bottom because it has been extremely consistent and because it occurs so quickly. Generally, in over 50% of the cases, you have a 90% downside day followed immediately by a 90% upside day. In most other cases, the 90% upside day will occur within 1 to 3 days of a major low, which is the last 90% downside day.

If you get a 90% downside day followed by a 90% upside day, is it possible that the signal will lead to a bear market rally rather than a true trend reversal?

Sure, there are a few cases on record where the market turned around and went back down again but those are very rare Generally, it is a good place to at least recognize that a significant event may have occurred and that you need to change your attitude toward the market.

How is the 90% downside or upside day calculated?

For a downside day, you would divide downside volume by the sum of upside and downside volume. If that number is 90.0% or more, then you have a 90% downside day. For a 90% upside day; you take upside volume divided by the sum of upside and downside volume. It should be 90.0% or higher. Interestingly, we found that close doesn't count.

In other words, 89.9% is not close enough for government work.

No, and we also go an additional step in our own work of calculating the percentage changes of price as well as of volume, but I think if people did it just on the basis of volume, they would be 95% correct.

Investors could match the 90% downside and upside days with sentiment figures or use other indicators to confirm that a major bottom was occurring.

Yes, and it doesn't have to be a mad dash to become totally reinvested immediately It should be a green light that says, "change your attitude." You have been bearish and the market has been going down confirming that you are right, so you are not going to be inclined to change your attitude quickly. You need something to come along and say, "Now is the time for an attitude adjustment" and this indicator is probably one of the first signs that you will get. It doesn't necessarily mean that you rush in and buy, but it does mean that you have to start thinking differently than you have been up to that point.

With regard to your analysis of total volume for the NYSE, you filter out the volume of unchanged issues leaving what you define as "active" volume, upside volume plus downside volume. What does this accomplish?

We exclude unchanged volume because it is not telling us anything that the upside and downside volume isn't already telling us. About the only thing that you can get out of unchanged volume, particularly on a short-term basis, is that sometimes you can see an indecisiveness on the part of investors. It is only worthwhile from a day trading basis.

At times, can you see a pattern evolving in unchanged volume?

Yes. On any given day, if unchanged volume is very high relative to what is normal and high relative to upside and downside volume, it tells you that investors are very unsure of what they are doing. It is more of a trading environment; one bull is being offset by a bear and so nothing is happening. Generally after periods of indecision, something big happens immediately so you always want to watch those periods very closely. They are warnings of a breakout.

Can we expect total volume to have any value with regard to detecting changes in the trend?

Total volume by itself isn't going to tell you a whole lot because you don't know whether total volume is a lot of downside volume and a little bit of upside volume or vice versa. You can say that total volume should expand with a market advance but you can get fooled if that is as far as you go with it, because it could be covering up some heavy selling. You need to ask, "What kind of volume is going into the equation?" If people are selling into a rally and you are looking just at total volume, then you are never going to see that truck coming at you. If you take a closer look and the total volume is mostly upside volume, then the uptrend is confirmed.

Active volume will detect signs of distribution and accumulation better than total volume?

You can take a general position that increasing volume during any trend tends to confirm that the trend is strong, but at significant tops that is not true. At significant tops you get distribution. If you don't break it down and look at upside volume versus downside volume, you won't see that the expanding volume is really sellers instead of buyers. To be sure that we are looking at demand numbers in terms of both price and volume, we also compare points gained versus upside volume Then you can see churning or selectivity. With churning, there is expanding upside volume but price is not going anywhere. The reverse is true for selectivity; you see price expanding rapidly without an expansion in volume. If you were using just total volume or total active volume, it would be much more difficult to see. The further you come towards the end of a market advance, the more downside volume will dominate. In other words, as you approach a market top in an uptrend or in the final stages of a bull market, upside volume starts to taper off and downside volume, which has been expanding, continues to expand. Volume may still be expanding in terms of total volume but that total volume is now made up of shrinking upside volume and expanding downside volume. On the surface, the total volume picture could be very bullish whereas breaking it down into upside and downside volume could tell a completely different story. If you don't know whether active volume is made up of buyers or sellers, you could be making a really significant mistake.

If investors are going to monitor "active" volume, what time period do you recommend using?

If you are going to use a single time period for the shorter term trends of the market, 30 days is a good, simple, single time period. It is not perfect but we use it rather consistently all the way through our work, running 30 day moving averages on many things such as total volume, active volume, points gained, points lost, upside volume, downside volume, and price indicators. Its weakness—and this is a weakness not just of 30 days but of moving averages in general—is that most people calculate a moving average based on one single time period. They pick out 10 days, 30 days, or 200 days. The problem with that is that on any given day, 50% of the net change is caused by whatever happened at the back end of the time period. Half or more of the net change in the 30 day moving average of today was caused by what happened 31 days ago. If something really dramatic happened 31 days ago, it can distort the picture of what is going on today. One way around that is to use a series of moving averages around a time frame that has some significance. For example, you might decide 30 days is an appropriate time period and run a 30 day moving average but you could also run a 27 day moving average and a 33 day moving average. Now you have three different moving averages clustered around 30 days. The result is an index that is much less likely to be distorted by whatever happened 28, 31, or 34 days ago.

Lowry's publishes a stock's price as a percent of its 10 week and 30 week moving average based on an index of 100. For example, if the number is 110 for the 10 week moving average, then that indicates a stock is 10% above its 10 week moving average line. If it is 96, then it is 4% below its 10 week moving average. Are you using these percentages to gauge overbought and over-sold conditions of individual stocks?

We use that as an indication of price trend. One of the big mistakes that investors make is to blindly hang on to a position not because the evidence supports them hanging on, but because they don't want to accept the fact that they could be wrong. Their position is, "I'm right, the market is wrong." You need to surround yourself with indicators that force you to recognize that you are wrong and give you the chance to reverse your position. The 10 week and 30 week moving averages are part of that overall process of forcing yourself to recognize that changes have occurred. Mr. Lowry used to always say, "If somebody locked me up in prison and I could have one thing to operate on, it would be the 30 week moving average of price." If you didn't have anything else to function with, a simple 30 week moving average of price would go a long way towards allowing you to participate in all of the major market advances and to avoid all of the major market declines. There would be whipsaws along the way, but that is just inevitable.

If a stock is 30% above its 10 week moving average, does that signify an overextended move?

Well, it can be overextended based on how that particular stock looks relative to the vast majority of other stocks. There is no absolute number. It is always a case of being relative to what other stocks are doing. If you get into a crazy speculative binge, you are going to have the vast majority of stocks showing rare numbers. You shouldn't be taken out of a stock just because it's going up fast but it is a warning because generally the stocks that go up the most tend to have the most violent reactions, and you need to be prepared for that.

Could you use this information as a timing tool?

Not by itself, but you can tie it together with the trend of the general market. For example, if you are invested in stocks that are 50% above their 30 week moving average and the trend of the market has turned negative, then that would be the kind of stock you would take faster defensive action on as opposed to a stock that was 15% or 20% above its moving average. Whether an individual stock should be sold or bought is heavily influenced by the condition of the general market at the time. In a major market decline, 85% or more of all stocks go down. In a bull market, an even higher percentage go up. It doesn't make any sense to look at individual stocks in a vacuum because statistics indicate that stocks are far more dependent upon the trend of the market than on their own unique internal characteristics. Whether you sell a stock that looks overextended on an individual basis depends on what the overall market is telling you to do.

The Buying Power and Selling Pressure Indexes measure supply and demand but can you also say they are measures of market momentum?

There are momentum characteristics to it but all momentum really does is measure a change in the pattern, not a reversal in the pattern. Trendlines can be a measurement of momentum. If you see trendlines bending further and further to the right, which is a case that the momentum of the trend is changing but it hasn't necessarily reversed. If you shoot a rocket into the air, for some period of time it goes in a straight line but then the further it goes, the more gravity starts to affect it and it arcs over. It hasn't really started to drop yet, but its rate of ascent is slowing. That is all momentum is and a change in momentum generally proceeds a change in trend. Going back to our department store example, if we see the number of customers coming into the store or the amount of money in the cash registers slowing down or speeding up, that is the momentum characteristic of supply and demand. We use a whole series of technical indicators and some fundamental indicators to refine the supply and demand side of the Buying Power and Selling Pressure Indexes. If you are using a weather barometer and you see the barometric pressure dropping in March, April, or May. It doesn't have anywhere near the significance that it has if you see the barometric pressure dropping in July, August, or September, because that is when all the hurricanes occur. They don't occur in March, April, or May In the stock market, you have to put buying and selling into context. You have to ask, "What are the surrounding circumstances?" If P/E ratios and book to price ratios are at very high levels and dividend yields have been at extremely low levels, the market has moved to a point of extreme valuation. Then if you start to see some deterioration in the supply/demand analysis, it means a lot more than if you saw a deterioration and the background fundamental numbers were at moderate valuations.

What other technical indicators do you use in conjunction with the Buying Power and Selling Pressure Indexes?

We use relative strength, volume studies, and basic momentum indicators like MACD, RSI, and stochastics to give us an advance warning of when a change might be occurring. We don't use the momentum indicators as a buy and sell mechanism by themselves because momentum very often can give premature signals. Markets can slow down for a period of time in which case stochastics or MACD will give a sell signal, but the trend hasn't reversed. So we use momentum indicators as an early warning of a loss in upside momentum. That is a danger signal and we need to be on our toes watching it very carefully, but we don't act on it until we not only see the market slow down, but also begin to reverse. Relative strength has a limited application.

Doesn't the correct use of MACD and stochastics require that the market or individual stocks be in a clear uptrend or downtrend?

Yes, that's right. You start out with this relatively crude analysis and then keep adding refinements and adding refinements. So you can't really use MACD and stochastics without also using ADX to give you some indication as to whether you are in a trading market or a trending market.

Why does relative strength have a limited application?

Relative strength, which is what most people use for individual stocks, can be very deceptive. People get hung up on the idea of watching relative strength ratings but what they need to realize is that during an extended market decline, stocks with the highest relative strength are the ones that go down the least. In other words, everything could be going down and you would still have some stocks rated stronger than others on a relative strength basis simply because they went down less You can't look at relative indicators and have a strong, clear picture of exactly what is going on without relating it to the general market. Too many investors follow individual stocks thinking they don't have to look at the general market but there is just too strong a body of statistics that says stocks do not operate in a vacuum. You need to recognize that and the faster you recognize that, the quicker you can get down to the business of making money.

The bottom line is that investors should always determine whether the trend of the general market is up or down and then turn to the individual indicators for confirmation or timing.

I don't know of anything that can be used as a solitary indicator. To use a single indicator would be the equivalent of saying, I am going to be a carpenter and I am only going to use a hammer. You need to have a full range of tools available to you and keep working with all of them in order to have a really clear picture of what you are trying to accomplish. Relative strength is a very important tool if you use it in a realistic framework. Relative strength looks at individual stocks relative to all the other stocks, but if you don't know what all the other stocks are doing, then you can't relate it.

With regard to stochastics, you use a 14 week and 14 month time period for measuring overbought and oversold conditions. Is there some significance attached to the number fourteen?

Actually we use a 14 day, 14 week, and a 14 month. There seems to be a cyclicality to certain indicators Some time periods work better than others and this is consistent all through the market. We talked about 30 day moving averages and actually if you went back and idealized it, you would probably conclude that a 33 day moving average is better than a 30 day moving average. Why, I don't know. A lot of research has been done on the stochastic indicator and the conclusion has been that 14 is a good time period to use.

How does a 14 "month" stochastic oscillator help in pinpointing overbought/oversold market conditions?

I use it for confirmation of a trend, nothing more. You would not use that in any way, shape, or form as a timing tool.

Do you use the full range of overbought/oversold indicators?

Yes, we use MACD, RSI, and a number of our own indicators to confirm or deny the basic trend of the market. The Short-Term Index, which is a shortterm version of our Buying Power Index, has overbought/oversold characteristics to it. If we see stochastics, RSI, or MACD all turning negative, then that alerts us to watch the longer term indicators more closely to see if that is going to influence the market significantly. But, momentum indicators turning negative won't tell you anything other than the fact that the degree of momentum has slowed. If a market has been advancing at a certain angle of ascent and then starts to advance at a lower angle of ascent, that will be enough to cause momentum indicators to turn negative. That doesn't necessarily mean the trend has turned negative.

With respect to RSI, what alerts you to changing market conditions?

We look for divergences in momentum. While the market is continuing to decline but approaching a low,

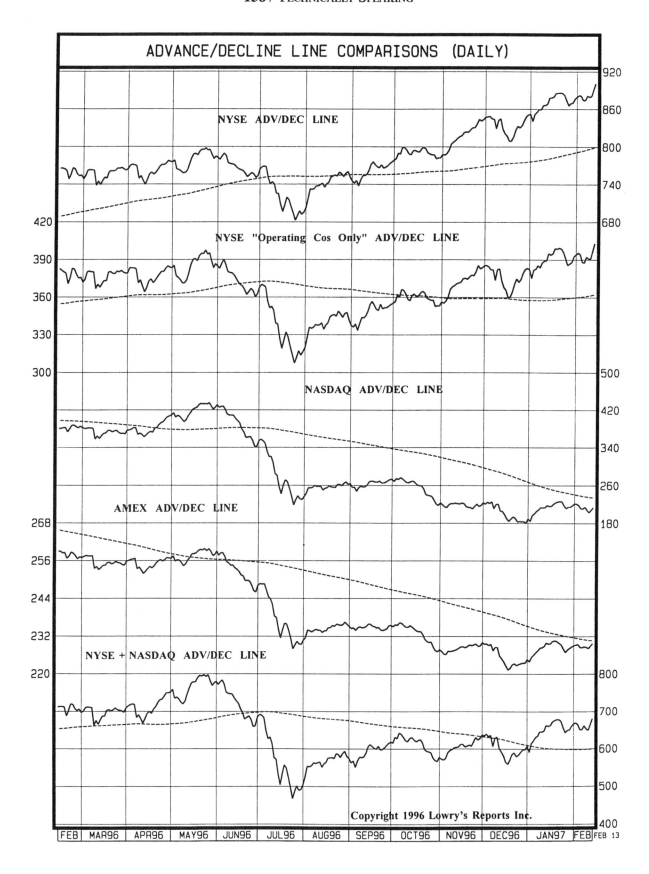

ADVANCE/DECLINE LINE COMPARISONS (DAILY)

NYSE ADV/DEC LINE

NYSE "Operating Cos Only" ADV/DEC LINE

NASDAQ ADV/DEC LINE

AMEX ADV/DEC LINE

NYSE + NASDAQ ADV/DEC LINE

Copyright 1996 Lowry's Reports Inc.

you will very often see the RSI begin to turn up. The same thing is true at market tops. If a market makes a new high and the RSI fails to make a new high or turns down during a rally, that is a warning that a change in momentum has occurred. We apply RSI to the general market because our concentration is on first defining the trend of the general market. I use tides as an analogy. Whether the tide is coming in or going out goes a long way toward determining whether you are going to get out of the harbor or not. The boat that you are going to use to get out of the harbor is not nearly as important as the fact that either the tide will take you out or keep you from getting out. A great percentage of our time is spent trying to determine which way the tide is flowing rather than trying to pick an individual boat.

Do you use the parameters of 30 and 70 for RSI?

Those overbought and oversold zones can be helpful but in my opinion, the divergences are more important than anything else. Reaching an overbought or oversold zone doesn't necessarily mean that you should be selling or buying. You need to reach an overbought zone and then see a deterioration in the indexes before you actually take any action or you need to reach an oversold level and then watch for the indicators to diverge from the price index. Like so many other indicators, used one way they can be very helpful; used another, they can be dangerous. Overbought/oversold zones can be dangerous if people assume that because something is overbought that it can't go any higher, or, if it is oversold it can't go any lower. That is simply not the case. Overbought and oversold are relative terms. An overbought market can keep getting more and more overbought. Don't take action simply because overbought or oversold levels are achieved. Be certain that a change in momentum is followed by actual evidence of trend weakness before you sell; otherwise, you may find yourself having sold into a market that is continuing to rise but at a slower rate than before.

Or the stock could be consolidating, waiting to take off again.

Exactly. When you take a cursory look at these indicators, they look as though all you have to do is wait until these little lines cross and then you can buy, sell and sell short with abandon but that is simply not the case.

Lowry's has developed a unique way of looking at the advance/decline data of the NYSE, using what you term operating-companies-only (OCO), which excludes 1,100 issues relating to closed-end bond funds, foreign shares, and preferred stocks. It seems that this method would project a more accurate view of breadth.

It gives you an edge. The operating-companies-only numbers won't give you a bullish picture when the consolidated numbers are giving you a bearish picture, but it does give you a refined way of looking at the advance/decline statistics and determining if they are being unduly influenced by interest rates or distorted by foreign securities being bought or sold in the domestic market.

What instigated the revision?

A number of years ago, everybody was pouring money into ADR securities like Sony and Panasonic. The number of ADR's registered on the NYSE was increasing at a tremendous rate and we were concerned about what influence they would have. We were trying to measure the interest in domestic securities and these were foreign securities. The other influence was the mad rush in the mutual fund industry to run out and create closed-end funds and register them on the NYSE. A great percentage of those were closed-end bond funds. These new types of securities being registered on the NYSE got us around to the point where we felt we should try to deal with it. We didn't know if we would find dramatic distortions, but we wanted an indicator that would allow us to determine if indeed a distortion was occurring.

Are the equity closed-end funds excluded?

Yes, because people are buying and selling individual stocks and then if you also include what the mutual funds are buying and selling, that is double counting. The biggest distortion in the advance/decline statistics comes from closed-end bond funds. There could be a run on closed-end bond funds and you might see advancing issues increase, but bonds have absolutely nothing to do with equities.

If you compare the OCO advance/decline line with the traditional NYSE cumulative advance/decline line, are there blatant differences?

Most of the time the two measurements move in unison. But, there have been times, such as from late 1993 through most of 1994, when the NYSE A/D line showed a positive pattern while the OCO A/D line was in a negative trend, and the result was a very difficult, unsettled market for almost a year. The goal of watching two indicators instead of one is to ensure that investors do not get misled.

In your analysis, do you use both the OCO A/D line and the traditional cumulative A/D line?

Yes, we use what we refer to as a consolidated NYSE advance/decline line, which is what you see in the Wall Street Journal. We really run four different advance/decline lines, including the OCO, NASDAQ, and the AMEX.

How much history do you have on the OCO advance/decline index?

We took the numbers back to about 1985. Going back historically is an incredibly difficult job because you have to look at each individual stock listed on the NYSE and make a determination as to which camp it belongs in. Our ability to extend that record back to the 1940's is rather restricted.

Most technicians use the cumulative difference between new highs and lows, either on a weekly or daily basis. Rather than tracking the difference between the two, Lowry's uses two separate charts, one for new highs and the other for new lows. Does this system more accurately reveal the true trend?

I think so because when you are in a strong uptrend, you don't expect new lows to be a factor at all. The only thing you typically see at a major market top is a deterioration in the number of stocks making a new high. Generally, new lows are not a factor until the market has declined for some time. At a market bottom you are watching for some lessening in the number of stocks making new lows. New highs don't have anything to do with a market bottom because virtually nothing would be at a new high at a real market low. Norman Fosback, who wrote *Market Logic*, did a thorough analysis years ago on new highs and new lows and concluded that taking the difference between new highs and new lows or a ratio of new highs to new lows is one of the most worthless indicators. I was never able to make heads or tails out of the number of new highs and lows until I started looking at them individually. Why would you expect the number of stocks making new lows to be increasing near a market top or the number of new highs to be increasing at a market bottom? It just isn't going to happen. If you separate them and look at the number of new highs after the market has been advancing strongly or you look at new lows after the market has been declining strongly, you get a clearer picture. These indicators also have to be viewed in relation to the market averages themselves. For example, at a major market top, you will often see a series of declining tops in the number of stocks making new highs while you have a series of rising tops in say, the S&P 500. That can go on for a prolonged period of time. A lot of people say, "If I see that kind of negative divergence, I will sell," but you are often selling far too early. The best thing to do is watch for the divergence and that is your warning sign but don't actually sell until some of the other indicators show actual weakness setting in. At that point, trendlines and moving averages become increasingly important as confirmatory tools because negative divergences can go on for a long time. Watch very closely for evidence that the market is actually weakening. It is important to make a distinction between a "lessening of strength" in the market and an actual "weakening."

That is an excellent point.

For example, we saw an interesting phenomenon in mutual fund net purchases during 1996. Net purchases made their highs in January 1996 at close to $30 billion a month. By November 1996, they were about $13 billion and had been weakening for the last three consecutive months. People could have looked at that and said, "Mutual fund money is drying up so we better get out of the market." It indicated a lessening of strength, not actual weakness. You don't get actual weakness until that number becomes zero.

Or until mutual funds show net redemptions.

Right. The new highs and new lows are very much the same. The divergence itself is not sufficient to yield a worthwhile buy or sell signal. It is divergence plus an indication that an actual change of trend has occurred.

Would a trendline break in the NYSE or S&P 500 qualify as a sign of weakness?

I have always had a problem with trendlines because they are so arbitrary. You see people drawing trendlines all different ways. There are some printed rules that price is supposed to touch the trendline at least three times but there are a lot of trendlines drawn that don't fit that rule. I personally prefer using moving averages more than trendlines. I will use a trendline with the recognition that it's arbitrary but I prefer to have tools that allow me to keep the emotions out of my work. I can always draw a trendline three or four different ways, depending on the case that I am trying to prove to myself, whereas, a moving average is factual and takes out the emotional factor.

Are you referring to a moving average of an index like the S&P 500, or are you smoothing the number of news highs and lows with a moving average?

You would apply moving averages to a price indicator, like the S&P 500, so that when you have a divergence in the number of stocks making new highs, you can see if that is actually causing some weakness in price. There are some broad general rules that you can apply to using moving averages on new highs or new lows, but we haven't found any specific crossing level that qualifies as an absolute buy or sell signal. What we have found is that if you run a 60 day moving average of new highs or new lows, if they round over during a period of market advance and drop below a previous low, that is usually a significant warning sign, but warning signs are very different from actual sell signals. Part of that difference is the arbitrariness of the situation and again, I try to avoid having sell signals based on something that I know in advance is relatively arbitrary.

What constitutes a sell signal using new highs?

New highs can be a very helpful indicator, particularly in an old bull market but if you don't tie it back to price, it will lead to a false conclusion. To actually get a sell signal, we watch for the daily new highs to diverge from the pattern of the S&P 500 In other words, we would look for the number of stocks making new highs to be make a series of lower tops while the S&P 500 is making a series of higher tops. Then we would apply a moving average to the S&P 500. Sooner or later the divergence will cause some actual weakness in the market, but you don't know when. The moving average on the S&P 500 says "when." For example, the number of stocks making new highs on a daily basis peaked in December 1995, and until November 1996, that high was never challenged. It wasn't until August, September, and October of 1996, that new highs showed a strong uptrend pattern. Prior to that, new highs had been making lower and lower tops. That by itself is evidence of diminishing strength. It is not evidence of actual trend weakness. When you applied a 200 day moving average to the S&P 500 it said, "Stay in, don't act on the warnings." The warnings are there and you need to be aware of them, but don't actually do any selling until you see a deterioration in price.

Lowry's uses relative strength ratios for various indexes, but one in particular is the ratio of the DJIA to the S&P 500 index. Do you use the DJIA/S&P 500 ratio to spot a narrow based rally or to determine which one is outperforming the other?

It is a case of trying to determine where the money flows are going. We are trying to see whether money is flowing into a broad list of big cap stocks, small caps, mid-caps, or blue chip stocks. That is the whole purpose of that exercise and if everything is moving positively, then you know that you have a nice broad market advance. In addition to comparing the market averages, we also break the market down into ten major sectors for the same reason, to determine where the buying enthusiasm is emerging. The general rule is that once group leadership is established early in a move, it generally continues throughout the market advance. The move in the finance stocks, for example, started back at the 1990 bottom and became clearly established right off the lows and continued unabated all the way up. You are going to go through corrections from time to time but the leadership usually comes right back again.

From an analytical perspective, what is your starting point?

I always start with the general and work down to the specific. Number one, where are we from an overall standpoint? Is the market in a downtrend or an uptrend? Then we start to become increasingly specific. At a market bottom, after a climactic period of selling when the market starts back up again we would say, "Okay, the tide has turned. Which boats are we going to get into to ride this tide?" We start looking at the broadest breakdown of the market which we view as 10 sectors. Once we take a look at the 10 sectors, and see a picture, then we move to an analysis of our 50 different industry groups. We have a series of charts comparing certain categories of assets such as cyclical stocks versus non-cyclical, industrial stocks versus technology stocks and so forth for the purpose of narrowing down where the buying enthusiasm is concentrated. From industry groups we break it down into individual stocks and then look at them in a series of superlative or summary tables of the best acting growth stocks, the best acting high dividend stocks, the best acting high P/E stocks, and so forth.

Is there an advantage in starting the analytical process with ten large sectors first and then working down to 50 industry groups?

That is very debatable. A lot of people take a bottoms-up approach analyzing individual stocks first and then if a bunch of stocks are all in a certain sector, then they know where they are going. I have always preferred to start with a top-down approach. If you start from the bottom-up, many times you are overlooking what the general market is doing. Studies show that about 80% of the change in the price of a stock is due to changes in the market rather than to anything unique about a particular company. If 80% of the influence of a stock's price is based upon the general market, then I better take a look at what the general market is doing before I pick an individual stock.

When a bear market occurs, will the majority of stocks move with the trend in progress?

There have been a lot of studies done by universities around the country that have said 85% or more of all stocks go down in a major downtrend. I think the number is substantially larger than that. The fundamentalists don't particularly like that number because it says that you really can't find a needle in a haystack. If you go back and look at the markets of 1946 to 1949, 1962, 1966, 1973-1974, or 1987, those numbers stand up fairly well.

Would you advise beginners to stay away from the more sophisticated indicators until they have the basics of technical analysis down?

I really think so. A man was recently telling me about his investment philosophy. He said, "I take a couple of thousand dollars every month and send it to my broker to put into growth mutual funds and that is my retirement program. How does that sound to you?" I said, "Let me put this in a different context." Let's say we are farmers sitting around an old pot-bellied stove in the general store and a guy in citified clothes comes walking in and starts telling about his approach to farming. Every day of the year, rain or shine, snow or sleet whatever the weather conditions, he loads up his seeder and plants a bunch of seeds. I asked, "What would you think of him as a farmer?" He said, "Well, I wouldn't think he would be in the farming business too long." I said, "That is exactly right and yet you are proposing precisely the same thing." Every month you take a couple of thousand dollars and throw it into the market regardless of the time of year or the circumstances under which you are operating. You don't have to be a farmer to know that early springtime is when it pays to throw seeds in the fields. You can continue to throw seeds in the fields during the summer but you are not going to get the same results. The best thing to do is plant seeds in the early spring and then in the summer months, pull out the weeds and the weak crops, clearing the way for the good crops to really grow. Fall is the time to harvest the crop. Don't wait until they start to rot. Harvest them while they are at their peak then stop trying to plant, stop trying to harvest, stop trying to do anything except protect your assets. Get in a sheltered position and stay there until the spring arrives again so that you are in a position to take advantage of the opportunities that the new springtime has created. We all see seasons in the weather but we don't see them in other things around us. All of life moves through seasons. The stock market goes through seasons and you need to be able to learn to recognize those seasons. For some reason, people think there is an eternal springtime to the stock market and sometimes they think there is an eternal winter. You need to step back and say, "Wait a minute, don't worry about what is going on today or next week or next month." An individual investor needs to concentrate first on determining where they are in the overall market cycle. Is the market in the spring, the summer, the fall, or the winter? Because even if you don't plant your seeds correctly in the springtime, chances are that what you plant is going to grow. If you try planting seeds in the autumn, no matter how hard you try, it is not going to work very well. The average investor wants to plant their crops in the fall and harvest in the dead of winter and then they can't figure out why it's not working. So timing is the first part of it.

What is the second part of it?

The second part of it is that an individual investor needs to deal with their own personal psychology. Why doesn't an individual investor make more money? Why aren't their investment experiences more positive? The answer is not because other traders are taking advantage of them or the specialists on the floor of the exchange are cheating them. It is because they don't have control of their emotions. They are buying or selling based on hope, fear, and greed. Until an investor learns to deal with their emotions, they haven't got a chance in the market. They could understand all the indicators in the world and yet still continue to lose money because they are not capable of controlling their emotions. It's not just the rules but the ability to follow the rules that is really the critical part.

Are you saying the biggest obstacle to an individual's success in the markets is temperament?

If you could take a group of experienced investors and sit them down and say, "Tell me about all of the times when you have lost money," they would unravel stories about how they got caught up emotionally in situations—they were swept along by mob psychology, they became overly negative or overly enthusiastic or they were paying attention to what some expert was saying—something that was clearly an emotionally controlling factor. They were not looking at the numbers; they were looking at what their heart was telling them. If you can conclude that 10 out of 10 of your major investment mistakes have been caused by your emotions becoming entangled in your investment decisions, then you could substantially improve your overall score if you recognize that the biggest problem you have is not analyzing the market or picking individual stocks; it's keeping your emotions out of the equation. If you will deal with that issue before you start dealing with all of the other issues about which indicators are the best indicators, you will be a lot better off. You find people buying a charting package or subscribing to a newsletter thinking that is going to be the answer to all their problems when the answer to all of their problems is getting control of their emotions. A lot of people will ask me, "What indicators are the most important indicators to watch? The best indicators in the world aren't going to do you any good unless you can approach them from a factual, unbiased, unemotional standpoint. If potential investors look at their emotional makeups and determine that they can't keep their emotions out of the stock market, then they need to accept that and hire someone who is capable of keeping emotions out of the decision making process. They will save themselves a substantial amount of money by spending the time to do that analysis before they start analyzing anything else.

Since many people start investing before they have a good understanding of their emotions, can you offer any advice as to how they can develop an unbiased or detached attitude toward investing?

I always tell people to take a couple of days off and go sit under a great big tree and don't get up until they have come to terms with themselves. The first part of it would be to do an honest inventory. Am I an emotional person? To what extent am I an emotional person? What gets me overly enthusiastic? What gets me overly negative? What are my strengths? What are my weaknesses? What things do I need to avoid? A lot of people say, "I just can't be around chocolate cake." Well, that is an important thing to know because until you come to terms with your weaknesses and learn to avoid those things, you will continue putting yourself in harms way. If you say, "I know that every time I see a chocolate cake I start to salivate," then at that point you can develop an internal discipline that throws up a red flag the minute you see anything dark brown. That kind of internal discipline comes from a real understanding of your strengths and weaknesses, particularly your weaknesses. You have to know yourself before you can start trying to figure out how to control yourself.

Isn't it true that your weaknesses become more prominent once you start investing?

Sure, you have to expose yourself to the game. Over the years, I have seen many situations in which people were really good analysts but were no good managing investment portfolios for other people. They could pull the trigger for their own portfolio but they found it extremely difficult to pull the trigger for someone else's portfolio. That is part of the process. A lot of books have talked about investing on paper first—don't put any money at risk until you try it on paper for a while. Maybe that works but I think the game changes radically once the money starts hitting the table. Hopefully an investor will start out investing with very small amounts of money so they can learn those lessons without being wiped out. But generally their first experience is to open an account with a futures broker and start trading S&P's and get wiped out instantly. They don't understand the risks. What they are really doing is saying, "I am going to ignore the risks because this is a chance for me to get rich." It's the same thing with people buying lottery tickets. They don't want to hear that the odds are against them.

Investors seem to come to the market with the preconceived notion that they will always be right.

The perceptions that people have about what's going on in the market and what's really happening when you start measuring the internal conditions of the market can be distinctly different. Back in February, March, and April of 1996, the general perception that people had, without really looking at the statistics, was that mutual fund investors were still pouring money into the market with abandon, therefore, there was no way the market could possibly go down and yet, the internal statistics were saying that buying enthusiasm had slowed down substantially. Investors should be flexible rather than taking the position of being bullish or bearish and say, "If buying enthusiasm is stronger than supply, I will be enthusiastic. If supply exceeds demand, I will be on the sidelines." A lot of investors find it very difficult to be wrong. They abhor anybody saying, "you were wrong" and yet a realistic approach to the stock market says that a significant percentage of the time, you are going to be temporarily on the wrong side of the market. That is just a fact of life. We don't have perfect knowledge. Rather than getting caught up in the egotism, you have to accept the idea of being wrong and adjust to changes as they occur. From time to time you are going to be on the wrong side of the equation but be willing to recognize when you are wrong and reverse yourself quickly so that the vast majority of the time you will be on the right side of the market. That is about all you can really hope for. A lot of people aren't willing to accept that but overcoming your own psychology is the real determinant as to whether you are going to make money in the market or not and to a large extent, it is a matter of training.

Thinking back to your own market experiences, have there been many instances in the past where you ignored your gut instincts and followed your model or indicators, only to discover in retrospect that your gut instinct was right?

There have been times but when you add up the number of times your gut instinct has been right and the number of times your gut instinct has been wrong, it comes out very close to 50-50, but then it goes beyond that. Your emotions cause you to magnify your mistakes and minimize your good calls. If the market goes against you, your emotions are constantly telling you, "I don't want to admit that I was wrong so I'll wait until I get even." If you are right, you tend to say, "If I get a 20% gain I am going to take my profits." Automatically, you maximize your losses or minimize your gains. I had a really wonderful mentor, Mr. Lowry, who taught me very early on that this is a business of probabilities and you need to get those probabilities working for you. To do that, you have to get rid of the emotion and recognize that there are certain repetitions in the market that you can take advantage of. You want to find a situation where you can go back historically and say eight out of ten times this pattern has led to a conclusion. Allow those probabilities to work for you rather than letting your emotions take control. Emotions have a tendency to fall in line with hope, fear, and greed. Fear always comes in at a time when you should be the most courageous and enthusiasm comes in at exactly the time you should be more cautious. Your emotions are almost exactly the opposite of what they should be and in order to make money in the stock market, you have to put them aside.

To successfully put emotions aside, would you suggest that people develop a model or system to follow so that they are not making emotional decisions?

No single indicator consistently tells the right story, but you can pick out a series of indicators that have a good batting average and put those probabilities to work for you. Rather than letting emotions dictate one's actions, an individual investor could settle on probably 10 indicators using the preponderance of evidence pointing in one direction or the other.

Do you have any favorite book titles that have helped you in the market?

The Richest Man in Babylon talks about the principles that are necessary to be successful, particularly in business but also in life. *Reminiscences of a Stock Operator* by Edwin Lefevre is an important book. *Where Are All the Customer's Yachts* is an old book but it addresses the point of establishing your emotional makeup before you start worrying about analyzing the stock market.

Peter Eliades

Peter Eliades took a circuitous but fascinating route to the financial markets. To begin with, he is an accomplished pianist and singer. His father, an attorney, recognized his son's musical gifts and aspirations to be in "show business" but asked that he first complete his formal education before becoming a "bum." Accepting his father's advice, he received his undergraduate degree from Harvard and then entered Boston University Law School where he received his law degree. Having fulfilled his educational commitment, he immediately left for the bright lights of Manhattan where he performed in off-Broadway shows and entertained in night clubs. About four months into his new lifestyle, he received notice that he had passed the bar. Instead of returning to Boston to practice law, he decided to continue his music and acting career in New York.

After four years in New York, he migrated to Los Angeles in search of fame and fortune. He knew Hollywood was "dying to make him a star." By 1968, he had accumulated a tidy sum to invest in the stock market. Following the crowd, he decided to participate in the mutual fund mania. As it so happens, his foray into mutual funds was almost the exact day of the market top in December 1968. In short order, he faced a loss of 15%. Determined to prevent further losses, he spent his days in the library learning the intricacies of the market and his evenings earning a living.

Two years later, Mr. Eliades became a stock broker only because it was a means to an end. In fact, the last thing he ever wanted to be was a broker. The story of his path to success started with routine daily telephone calls to a Los Angeles brokerage firm to obtain stock quotes for updating his charts. During these exchanges, he would voluntarily pass on his market prognostications to a female broker, who noticed that many of his forecasts materialized as predicted. After about six months, she leaked word of his remarkable calls to her boss, who was head of a brokerage firm that bought airtime at station KWHY. He asked Mr. Eliades to present stock market analysis on television during his firm's time slot; however, the invitation came with a proviso attached. Accepting the position was contingent upon becoming a licensed broker. This "dangling carrot" appealed to Mr. Eliades' sense of stardom, as well as his interest in the markets. But when not on the air, he had the same responsibilities as any other broker and on more than one occasion he was asked to put away his charts and pick up the phone. In early 1974, the brokerage firm went out of business but due to his popularity, he managed to negotiate an arrangement with KWHY to continue offering independent market commentary. This was the year of a great bear market and most people were losing money "hand over fist." It was in this year that Mr. Eliades gained his initial public notoriety. In the fall of 1974, he repeatedly predicted on KWHY that a major bottom in the stock market would occur during the week of December 9th through the 13th. The exact bottom occurred on December 9, 1974. In retrospect, this market call had great significance because the 1974 bottom turned out to be the most important market bottom of the past several decades.

Mr. Eliades' analysis may be classified as unconventional and original. He is challenged by the prospect of discovering and creating new and unique indicators. Run of the mill indicators are of little value to him. If he does use a common market indicator, it is only after stringent modifications. You could call him a history buff in that he enjoys searching as far back as his computer data bases will reach for recurring patterns and historical market comparisons. To compensate for the market's periodic metamorphoses, I would call your attention to the fact that he uses ratios rather than the raw numbers in the majority of his work. Using ratios will allow you to compare current indicator readings with those of the past.

Though known for his cycle work, price projections are the one aspect of his analysis that separates Mr. Eliades from 99% of the other technicians and is the technique which allowed him to make such remarkable forecasts beginning in the early 1970's. Given the complexity of the subject and the difficulty in articulating the methodology, we have decided to forego a discussion of his price projection analysis.

Mr. Eliades is currently publisher and editor of *Stockmarket Cycles* which made its debut in 1975. This newsletter provides timing signals for mutual fund switchers who have an intermediate to long term focus. Daily telephone updates are available for short term traders. *Stockmarket Cycles* has received numerous accolades. *Forbes* magazine rated it the "Best Mutual Fund Advisory" and Mark Hulbert rated its Fidelity Select Portfolio number one among mutual fund newsletters in the last ten years through June 30, 1996. Up 16.5% on an annualized basis, it was the only mutual fund portfolio that beat a buy and hold approach. Mr. Eliades has also received "Timer of the Year" award from *Timer Digest*. Aside from appearances on CNBC, Wall Street Week, and the Nightly Business Report, Mr. Eliades was a regular panelist on ABC's weekly Sunday broadcast of Business World before it was discontinued.

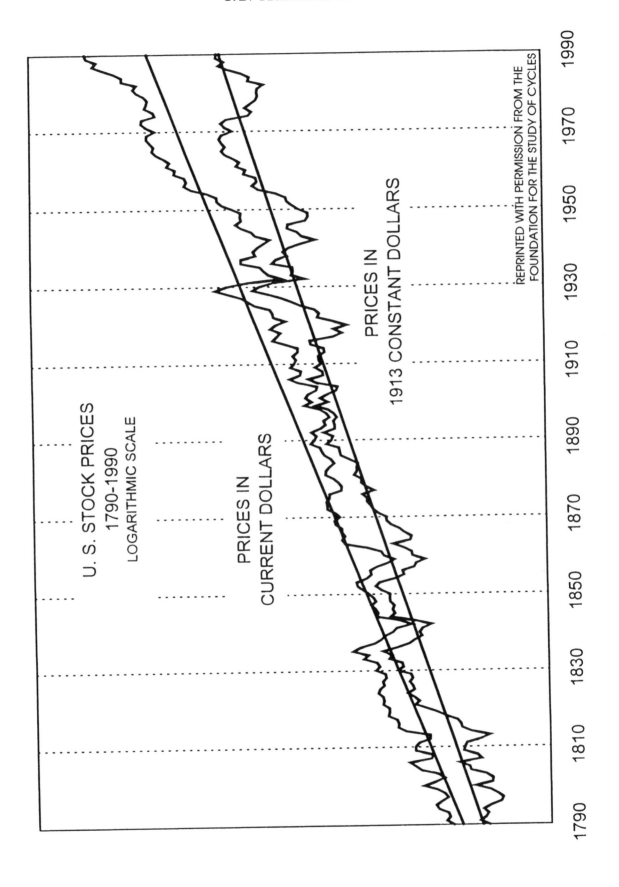

U. S. STOCK PRICES
1790-1990
LOGARITHMIC SCALE

PRICES IN
CURRENT DOLLARS

PRICES IN
1913 CONSTANT DOLLARS

REPRINTED WITH PERMISSION FROM THE
FOUNDATION FOR THE STUDY OF CYCLES

You are perhaps best known for your cycle work. Does your entire market analysis revolve around cycles?

In many ways it distinguishes the work I do from what most other people do. I think it is probably the most important element of my work. For a general answer to your question, I usually begin most of my analysis from a broad, overall, cyclic viewpoint. If I find a particular technical or historical pattern then I will go back and find out how many times that has happened historically in the last 23 to 40 years. For example, let's say the McClellan oscillator has fallen lower than minus 140, a very rare reading. I will try to determine what happened after such a reading and use that in my current analysis. Now, strictly speaking, that is not a cycle, but it is a technical pattern that has taken place in the past. If the pattern repeats itself and there is a strong correlation between what happens afterwards, then that might overrule some kind of cyclical pattern that I see.

I believe you look at quite a wide range of cyclic periods.

Yes, from one minute charts of the Dow and stock index futures to the longest practical cycle I have discovered- what I call the 60 year cycle. In fact, this was the cycle that allowed me to predict in the early 1980's that we were due for a spectacular bull market. The Foundation for the Study of Cycles has data for the market back to 1789, a little more than 200 years. If you de-trend that data and take a look at it, it's amazing how a cyclic period of around 60 years just stands out with important lows within a year or two of 1800, 1860, 1920, and then, of course, one was due in 1980.

When you speak of 60 year cycles, are you speaking about Kondratieff cycles?

No, the Kondratieff wave is something a little bit different. This is just an observation that I made in looking at the data from the Foundation for the Study of Cycles and detrending it. In the late Seventies and early Eighties, I pointed this out to people on the old FNN, now CNBC. I showed the chart and said, "Though it may not be statistically significant, because we only had three prior occurrences—1800, 1860, 1920—we are due for a very major stock market bottom within a year or two of 1980 and there was a pretty good chance that the Dow could get to the 4700 level." Of course, people thought I was crazy at the time.

Excellent forecasting.

It was dead on. In fact, looking back at the prior cycles you could have looked forward to a move of somewhere between 8 to 10 years on the low side to as long as 13 to 15 years on the high side. It wasn't the perfect sinusoidal or sine wave cycle because it didn't go up for 30 years and down for 30 years. The pattern indicated that every 60 years you had a very major market bottom and then you would see a spectacular stock market rally that would last anywhere from 8 years on the low side to 12 to 15 years on the high side. Of course, we are now in the 14th year from 1982. One could argue that the bottom occurred in 1980 because the Dow saw slightly lower prices intraday in 1980 than in 1982. Then we would be in the 16th year. So it is very long in the tooth now in terms of the prior history from 60 year cycle bottoms.

Are you saying that within these 60 years cycles there are 8 to 16 year cycles?

No, that wouldn't work. Let me try and clarify it. From 60 year cycle bottoms, there is a tendency to see very strong upward movements for at least the next 8 to 10 years and as many as 12 to 15 years. I am saying that is how long the rally lasted from the prior low of the 60 year cycle. That doesn't make it a cycle in and of itself because a cycle would imply that it would return to where it started in 8 to 10 years.

Is it possible to do price projections from the bottom of a cycle?

Only to the extent that it is a repeatable pattern. I went back and figured what percentage gains had been made in the prior rallies from the 60 year cycle bottom and projected that forward for this particular cycle bottom. I came up with a number around 4700 which is what I put in my letter back in 1982 when the Dow was still around the 1,000 level. If you go back in a time machine to 1982 and heard anyone talking about 4700 in the Dow, they would have laughed you out of town. You could have argued that we didn't necessarily have to see a high in this market at 4700. When we look at cycles, we tend to look at the last experience. Well, the last experience was in 1920. Depending on whether you used 1920 or 1921 as the bottom, the market rally lasted only 8 or 9 years. So there was a tendency to bring that into the current time and say that this 60 year cycle might do the same thing and last 8 or 9 years. That is why I started to get more bearish around 1988 to 1989. If you went back to the bottom that was reached in 1800, a top didn't occur for about another 15 to 16 years.

So back in 1800, the bull market rally lasted 16 years?

Yes, I think the bottom from 1800 saw a pretty concerted rally for at least the next 15 to 16 years. That is not to say that we came down and went to new lows after that. It simply means that the initial thrust off this cycle bottom of 60 years has always been a very impressive one. In the year 2040, we can look for another very important market bottom.

Let's say the stock market has finished its 8 to 16 year bull market run. Is there a predictable course of action during the subsequent 45 to 50 years?

No. I looked for that but there really isn't any consistency to it. You can't come up with a typical scenario. It's just that the greatest part of the advance seemed to come in that first 10 to 16 years. I'm looking back at 1800 right now. If you say the advance started around 1802, the fastest and biggest part of the advance ended somewhere around 1818 so that was about 16 years. It then moved sideways with an upward bias for about 20 years and then a big decline in 1840; another move up and then a big decline into the cycle bottom of 1860. The one in 1860 had an initial very sharp advance for about 10 to 12 years and then continued upward again with a much slower bias. There was a pretty good decline into the 1896 time period then the rally continued. There was a decline into 1920, which was the cycle bottom. We had the big hard, fast advance for the next nine years, from 1920 into 1929.

So the 60 year cycles are more adept at pinpointing major market bottoms and are rarely useful in terms of predictive value after the first bull market run.

Yes. You could make general rules but that is all they would be. Usually the biggest part of the advance out of the 60 year low comes in the first 10 to 15 years. The most important thing is figuring out where the bottoms have occurred.

What originally sparked your interest in cycles?

In December of 1968, I made my first stock market investment. I didn't know the first thing about the stock market. For those who don't remember back that far, it was a craze almost as great in its time as the current craze is although if you look at the actual money numbers involved, the current craze really makes that one look minuscule. That year mutual funds and individual stocks were going up 300%, 400%, 500% in a few days and everybody was making money. It was the old story about the shoe shine boys and the waiters giving you stock tips. In December of 1968, in the full heat of the battle, I said, "My goodness, where has this wonderful stock market been all my life?" I took all my fortune, $2,000.00 that I had saved, and put it into a mutual fund which so far that year was up 300%. I figured that would be wonderful if it just continued at that pace. Some day I would love to find my initial confirmation slip because I have a feeling that I made this investment either at the top day or within 2 or 3 days of the exact stock market top in December of 1968. Of course, from that point, the average share of stock, not the Dow, went down about 75 to 80% over the next six years, from December of 1968 to December 1974. Within a month or two I watched my $2,000.00 dollars go down first 2%, then 3%, then 5%, then 8% and I think it finally was down 10%. I couldn't believe that I lost the whopping grand total of $200.00 in just a period of one month. I thought that I had better do more research on the stock market. Back then, I had the days free because I was working four to five hours a night as a night club performer, playing the piano and singing. I started going to the library every day and reading about the stock market. Because I majored in physical sciences at Harvard, I tended towards the mathematical side of analysis. Even though I started out reading books about the fundamentals, I was always attracted to the technical side of the market. A friend of mine in Los Angeles invited me to his beach house in San Clemente for the weekend. There was a book in the beach house called *"The Profit Magic of Stock Transaction Timing"* by J. M. Hurst. Hurst was one of the real pioneers of cycle analysis in the market. There is a great lyric from a popular song written by Jimmy Webb and the lyric is, "sometimes a single moment changes all the ones that follow." I happened upon this book after I had been doing several months of research and study in the library. I took it home and read it. That may have been the single moment that changed every one that followed in my life because from that point on I became very hooked on the whole concept of cycles. Hurst said in his book that the day to day movements of the stock market have nothing to do with the news or listening to media reports about the Federal Reserve and things like that. At that time, I was quite a novice in terms of the market but I had always felt intuitively that these movements from day to day in the market didn't really have to do with what the media was telling us it had to do with— "the stock market was down 17 points today due to investor fears of...." The very next time that there should have been investor fears the stock market was up so they had to run a different story. The Hurst book was of immediate appeal to me for the reason that he said news had nothing to do with timing the market. That appealed to me on an intuitive level. From that moment on, I promised myself I was going to get more serious with this book. It tends to be mathematically oriented. In fact, when you first look at it, it might even scare you away a little bit. I looked at it a couple of times and said, "I don't want to go through this; this doesn't do anything for me." So I sat down and really concentrated and put it to work. I challenged myself with that book. The stock market became an obsession with me. I started buying charts and counting the days or weeks between market bottoms and finding these little patterns in the market that I thought were fascinating. That started my whole study of cycles.

Before you read Hurst's book, did you have some general knowledge of technical analysis?

Yes, but not too much. It was only in that year or so leading up to this that I had even gotten interested in the market so I was quite naive when it came to different phases of market analysis. I was immediately drawn to the technical side as I said, because of my interest in math and trying to quantify everything with formulas and numbers.

What type of charts were available then?

Mansfield had both daily charts and weekly charts. The weekly charts were eventually taken over by William O'Neil in terms of the Daily Graphs. I think one set of charts was maybe $15.00 or $20.00 just for each exchange. At the time, that was prohibitively expensive for me so I ordered them every couple of months. I would look at different stocks or market averages and start counting time periods between bottoms. Incidentally, cycles tended to be more reliable when you counted between lows rather than between highs. Most of the cycle counting that I did, if not all of it in those days, related to counting periods between market lows. Hurst got that idea going in my head.

Will particular stocks trace out cyclic patterns between highs and lows which are individualistic and repetitive? In other words, one stock bottoms consistently every 12 weeks while another bottoms every 20 weeks.

Yes and no. Each stock does have its own individual pattern and rhythm and there is an amazing uniformity but I think it probably relates to the fact that there is uniformity of cyclic movement within the market itself. All stocks move with different relative strengths but they tend to move with the stock market. So, if you were to see a 34 or 54 day cycle in the Dow, chances are you would see that same pattern in most stocks. Now that is the "no" part of the question, where you cannot make the assumption that they are all different. On the other hand, each stock does have its own individual fingerprint. You could find a completely different pattern in some that might not show up in others. There are yes's and no's in terms of individual stocks.

In terms of your cycle work, are you short, intermediate, or longterm oriented?

Ideally I would like to think that I work from the longterm down to the very shortterm. I will give you an example. The longterm at this point has me obviously quite bearish although I must say that I have been prematurely bearish not only for several weeks or months, but over a few years here.

With that overall background of longterm bearishness, I told people on Friday, in my daily telephone update, that I had some price projections for closes on the NYSE Composite index and the S&P 500. I thought that the typical scenario would be to see the market rally for the next day or two into those closing highs and then turn down again, perhaps fairly dramatically from there. I gave them a time cycle and a time period that resolved yesterday. I said, "We noted yesterday that the time pattern from our 30 minute S&P cash chart called for a turning point focused on 11:00 a.m. to 12 noon Eastern time today, but as early as 11:00 a.m. to 11:30 a.m. yesterday, Monday, and as late as 3:30 today, which is Tuesday." In this case, this is about as shortterm as I ever get and I think anyone ever gets.

So your analysis allows you to pinpoint price targets as well as time frames?

Well, it certainly allows you to attempt to do that. As I said, that was from a 30 minute S&P chart. Now a 30 minute S&P chart has 13 bars during the day because there are 6½ hours so for every week there would be 65 bars. This particular cycle ran approximately 172½ bars which meant it lasted about 13½ trading days. It has just been incredibly consistent and successful over the past year. They are not always tops or bottoms, they are turning points. I had neglected it for several months and a couple of weeks ago I picked up a chart that I had done and checked to see where the particular cycle was in the current time period. The consistency had remained and because I was very confident about its resolution, I told people when to look for an important top. Sure enough, right exactly in the time period that I gave, they both reached the top and now they are down. Not meaning to imply that this happens each and every time but it's the kind of success you can enjoy with this type of analysis.

What sort of books are out there now on cycles?

There are two books that got me started. The first was the Hurst book. The second one was *"Investing for Profit with Torque Analysis of Stock Market Cycles."* The author's name is William C. Garrett. It was an interesting book and I got a lot of insight from it. In fact, a lot of techniques I use today came from that book but again, it is very mathematically oriented.

Do you use your cycle analysis to time entering positions strictly at tops and bottoms or will you take a position in the mid-phase of a cycle?

There isn't any one way I tend to use them. Mostly, what I attempt to do with them is pick tops and bottoms. Once I pick out a top or a bottom, the other technical indicators I use in my cyclic arsenal allow me to follow these trends. I do price projections from a technique that I think was originated by Hurst but I have worked a lot of my own little derivations from it. Once a top or bottom is picked, then I have a tendency to start using these price projection techniques that give me clues in terms of how far it is going to go. I don't tend to trade the cycles because in my experience they have not been uniform in terms of their time periods. For example, instead of going up 30 years on an idealized basis, a 60 year cycle may only go up 10 or 12 years and then come down and go up but you don't know where the peak is going to be in between. I am more inclined to pick tops and bottoms rather than saying, "This is a 30 week cycle so it should be up for 15 weeks or at least 7 or 8 so I will get in and stay in for 7 or 8 weeks and I won't pay attention to anything else." I will get in at a point that I think is the bottom and then stay in until either my price projections or technical indicators get me out.

Approximately how many indicators do you follow?

It's hard to answer that because I don't have a list of like twelve technical indicators that I look at every day. There is a certain ritual that I go through every day in terms of the work that I do. There are indicators that I use and look at religiously, one of them being the trading index which is now called the ARMS index, named after Richard Arms. This has always been one of my favorite indicators.

At one time you used a cumulative 10 day TRIN.

Yes, but that was not by any means my own discovery although I have made some modifications to the 10 day moving average of the trading index which have worked out pretty nicely. One of them, the Open 10 trading index, I didn't discover but I did name it. This was invented by a man named Harvey Wilber, or at least I have always given him credit for inventing it. I read one of his articles about the trading index in an old computer magazine. The formula for the simple trading index is that you divide "up" stocks by "down" stocks and call that "A." Then divide "up volume" by "down volume" and call that "B." Then you divide A by B. So it is a ratio of two ratios. That would be the TRIN or simple trading index. To do a ten day moving average, you simply do that calculation each day and then at the end of 10 days, you just add the last ten days of the simple trading index and divide by 10 and you have your simple 10 day moving average of the trading index. Instead of calculating it each day, I thought it might be a good idea if you could somehow smooth it out and perhaps even make it a little volume weighted by adding up each of the four components individually over 10 days, calculating the trading index only once.

So the Open 10 TRIN is your cumulative computation of the simple trading index (TRIN)?

Yes, I gave it that name because you use the whole open universe of the last ten days. You add all of the "up" stocks over 10 days, all of the "down" stocks, all the "up volume" and all the "down volume" and then you use those four sums to calculate the trading index. That is the Open 10 trading index. That's what distinguishes it from the simple one. With the simple trading index, you do the TRIN calculation every day. With the Open 10 TRIN, before you do any divisions or calculations on a single day period, you simply add the last 10 days of each component together and then you can do your divisions.

In terms of application, what is the advantage in using the Open 10 TRIN versus the simple TRIN?

Back in the 1985 to 1987 time period when I first started following the Open 10 trading index, it was working marvelously. Anytime the Open 10 trading index moved higher than 1.00 it was almost certainly a good buying opportunity. In fact, in September 1987, I wrote an article in *Barron's*, after the top but before the top had led to the crash, about the Open 10 trading index.

What other variations of the trading index have you created?

I follow the TRIN, which is the single day trading index, the 10 day moving average, the 40 day moving average, the weighted 10 day moving average, the exponential 10 day moving average, the exponential 40 day moving average, the 50 day moving average, then the Open 30 and the Open 10. The latest twist I invented about eight years ago is something I call the "New 10 TRIN" for lack of a better name. It was just a 10 day trading index that I put a new spin on. That has actually been one of the best overbought/oversold indicators over the last couple of years in this bull market. It has been a lot better than the Open 10 or the simple 10 trading index. What distinguishes it from the other ones is that it is very much volume weighted. I input these numbers—advancing stocks, declining stocks, up volume and down volume—by hand but the computer does the calculation. I still do a lot of charts by hand but there is a lot less chance of mathematical error if you let the computer do the calculations.

I am interested in the fact that you still do some charts by hand.

Even though most of my charts are computerized, I still like to do several charts by hand every day to maintain that feel. I do some cycle lines, which I get off my spreadsheet, on a daily closing price chart on the Dow. I do trading index charts by hand, some little oscillators, and another bar chart on the Dow with a high and low and also some cyclic patterns.

Is it the physical exercise of going through the motions that makes it more memorable?

I think so. It's that tendency for "feel" and actually putting the numbers down. It may be psychological but whatever it is I think it allows you to maintain a better feel or intuition about the market.

Regarding the Open 10 trading index, what numerical parameters have you set to generate overbought and oversold conditions?

Generally 1.00 should be considered a neutral number. I think because we have been in a bull market for so long, when you get to that neutral number it tends to be an oversold condition rather than neutral. Maybe if we had some really bad market periods of five to ten years rather than just a year or two at a time, then those things might balance out. Generally speaking, on the Open 10 TRIN, a numerical reading higher than 1.00 would be an oversold condition.

What about an overbought condition?

As a general rule, it is a number below 0.80. There have been a lot of criticisms about the trading index moving averages and the open trading index moving averages, the criticism being as follows. If you use it arithmetically, then you are assuming that a reading of 1.75 is the same as a reading of 0.25 because they are both 0.75 away from the neutral level of 1.00. In reality, that is not the case. One reading is the reciprocal of the other. That is the true equivalent. For example, if the TRIN for the day were at 1.75, in order to find the low equivalent of that, you would have to place 1.00 over 1.75, so the true reciprocal of 1.75 is 0.571.

That is an interesting point.

I bring this up because a lot of technicians recently have been criticizing trading index readings for that very reason. They say the low numbers do not represent the same in terms of their distance away from a neutral 1.00 reading as the high numbers do. You can figure that out because you know that the TRIN can go from a neutral reading of 1.00 to a high reading of 3.00, 4.00, 6.00, or higher whereas it can never go below zero. In fact, I don't think there has ever been a single day reading lower than 0.10 and that, of course, is not even one full number away from the neutral reading of 1.00. So for example, if you had an extreme situation where you have incredible buying power come in for 10 days in a row and you had a .20 10 day moving average of the TRIN, which I don't think I have ever seen, and then on the other hand, if you had very strong selling for 10 days in a row and you had a 3.00 or 4.00 or higher, which actually occurred in the crash of 1987—they don't line up with each other. That is why some people have criticized them. I see the mathematical truth of the criticism and yet I don't pay too much attention to it. In real time these numbers, as I calculate them and use them, have served my purpose very well and there is no reason for me to think that I should change them.

Is your "New 10 TRIN" a proprietary indicator?

No. In fact, I am trying to think if I have anything that is proprietary. I have a rule—"the value of an indicator is inversely proportional to the tendency of the person wanting to keep it proprietary." This game is difficult enough as it is without people playing games about these proprietary indicators. No one has the holy grail or lock and key to the secret of the market. I think the more you can share with people in terms of this business, the better off you are.

Would you explain your latest invention?

What I have attempted to do is to take the best features of the simple 10 day TRIN and the Open 10 TRIN and combine them. The strength of the Open 10 is that it is in effect volume weighted. An extreme high or low daily reading of the TRIN will have little effect on the Open 10 TRIN unless there is heavy volume accompanying the reading. The strength of the simple 10 day TRIN is that very high single day readings seem to have significance regardless of volume. The New 10 TRIN is calculated by taking a ratio of 10 day down volume to 10 day up volume then dividing that ratio by the 10 day moving average of the simple TRIN. I guess you could abbreviate it by saying the 10 day DV divided by 10 day UV and call that "A." Then you divide that result, "A," by the 10 day moving average of the simple TRIN.

How do you interpret the results?

The results usually range from a low of around .60 or .70 to a high of around 1.50 to 1.70. There are obviously extremes too. This has been a wonderful indicator during times when the typical TRIN readings have not been very helpful.

How long have you been working with the New 10 TRIN?

At least four or five years. I learn more about it all the time, especially lately I have become more impressed with its effectiveness as opposed to some of the more orthodox trading index readings. I think at the May 1996 top, the New 10 TRIN was the only one that got convincingly overbought. We topped on Friday, May 24, 1996, at an all-time closing high for the NYSE and the S&P 500 and I said that a shortterm sell-off appeared inevitable because the New 10 TRIN gave a sell signal by moving from a reading of lower than .80 to a reading of higher than .80. That's the little trick that I use for sell signals. It's not just moving to overbought levels. It can go from .80 to .70 to .65 to .62 and stay there for as long as it wants, but once it has moved into that overbought territory below .80 and then comes back again numerically higher than .80—even if it is .805 or .81 or whatever—that constitutes a shortterm sell signal.

So you are looking at the number in isolation as overbought but rather than reacting at the first sign of an overbought market, you wait until the reading moves back above .80?

When you get lower than .80 and then you go higher, the signal is given. On May 16th, 1996, the New 10 TRIN was .809 and on the 17th it finally got overbought. The reading was .76. Both the Open 10 and the simple 10 gave overbought readings prematurely. They got overbought on May 21st and May 22nd. The New 10 also got overbought but didn't move higher than .80 until Friday May 24, 1996, when it had a reading of .807. That constituted a short term sell signal. The New 10 TRIN also gave a sell signal on February 13th, the day after the NYSE topped out on February 12th. The February 13th reading was the highest for the NYSE over the next 3 or 4 months. There was another sell signal again on April 25, 1996. The NYSE Composite went up another point and then there was a pretty sharp decline over the next week.

Do you strictly adhere to these rules and parameters or is subjectivity sometimes involved?

The signal for the New 10 TRIN is very objective. You go from an overbought reading below .80 and reverse and go above .80. That is the signal. There is no subjectivity in terms of the signal being given but that doesn't mean that I would do anything based on that. You have to put that in the whole mix of all the other things you are looking at. There is no question that subjectivity is involved with the other things I do with the trading indexes. I like to massage the data and look at it in different ways from how other people would look at it. This is just one among many in terms of the formulas and things that I look at. Remember these are shortterm signals. These would be more for people trading futures and options. I wouldn't use these to switch mutual funds unless they were backed up by some other signal. As a general rule, I actually use the New 10 trading index for specific buy and sell signals. I use the other trading indexes as ancillary indicators. If they tell me the market is very overbought then I will look for some other indication of a change in trend to the downside or vice versa for oversold readings. I have found the New 10 TRIN is one of the few trading index readings that I have been able to use that actually gives shortterm sell signals. I wouldn't use it for much more than a shortterm sell signal.

Are there times when your TRIN indicators conflict with your cycle analysis?

Yes. If you are using them for very important turning points, then you have to be pretty confident what those numbers mean in terms of a longer term history. I will give you an example. Back in August of 1982, when the market was bottoming, I actually got some lower cycle projections for the market on August 6th or 9th. In my newsletter, I said that there has never in the history of the trading index been a reading in the simple 10 day moving average of higher than 1.50 that was not at or within several days of a very major market bottom. And that is what happened on August 9, 1982. We had a 10 day moving average of the simple TRIN of 1.51. At that time, I had historical data back probably 10 or 15 years. Several months later, *Barron's* wrote an article about how technical analysis had failed everyone at the market bottom in August because none of the technical analysts had picked out the bottom. I sent them a copy of my newsletter section referring to the simple 10 day TRIN and they published it in full.

What constitutes a buy signal for the simple trading index?

As a general rule, if you get two consecutive readings higher than 2.00 or greater, the odds are very high that you have hit a very tradeable market bottom. There were two days in October 1987, the 16th and 19th, that the readings were incredible. They were 5.276 on Friday and 10.781 on Monday. Then about a week later, on October 26th, there was a reading of 11.97. So the 10 day moving average at that time was just unheard of. On October 26th, the 10 day moving average was 3.55. Now, we have gone probably six or seven years without a single day reading above 3.00; never mind a 10 day moving average. Single day patterns can be important. There is a remarkable technical statistic that we stumbled upon while examining our trading index spreadsheet. Single day trading index readings are usually not very useful for longer term analysis of the market. Extremes and single day readings, especially high single day readings, can be informative, however. For example, since 1950, any two consecutive single day readings greater than 2.00 have invariably marked excellent buying opportunities. Some of them have marked within a week or two of very major market bottoms. Here are the times since 1950 when there were two or more consecutive daily TRIN's higher than 2.00. There aren't too many of them—May 19, 1951, Sept. 14, 1953 (3 consecutive readings), Dec 15, 1957, June 21, 1962, August 29, 1966 (3 readings), May 20, 1970 (the bottom was 6 days later), August 20, 1975, December 3, 1975, August 4, 1982 and October 19, 1987. Those are the only ones in the last 45 years. Additionally, since 1950, there has never been a period of time longer than 19 months without seeing a single day TRIN reading higher than 2.00. As of July 1996, we had gone 27 months without one single day reading greater than that. That tells you something. If you are in a bear market, you are going to see 2.00 at least once every few weeks. On the other hand, if you don't see them in a month or two, or three or five, or you don't see them for a year and a half—no great squalls of selling—that bespeaks of great complacency in the market. The last reading we had above 2.00 was back in February 1994. If you take that one out, you can go back three years ago to April 1993, and we've had one reading over 2.00 since then. It's a monumental display of investor complacency. There hasn't been any real selling pressure or liquidation and the longer that builds up, the greater the final selling pressure should be when it comes in. Is it a coincidence that the only two prior periods since 1957 to see stretches longer than 15 months without single day readings higher than 2.00 occurred in the vicinity of two of the most important market tops of this century? One string ended in late June of 1965, just 7½ months before a major top in February 1966. The other string ended in May 1973, four months after the major top in January 1973. I use some of these things in ways that I would like to think no one else uses them. I have a data base for the trading index that goes back to at least 1940 although I must say that I don't have too much faith in the numbers before the 1950's and 1960's because they were calculated by hand. The NYSE did not officially compile up and down volume until 1962. There were a lot of guys in this business who were curious enough to pay someone to compile up and down volume. You had to look through the NYSE every day and add the volume of all of the stocks that were up and all of those that were down. You would have to go through the whole list and do that every day. Of course, it was a lot easier 40 or 50 years ago because there were fewer stocks listed.

Sounds like a very intensive process and I can understand why you question the reliability of the figures. What do the overbought numbers look like for the simple trading index?

Generally speaking, for all of these trading indexes, a reading of about .80 and below. You have to be very careful because it is a much more effective bottom tool than it is a top tool. You can get readings of .80 on all these things for days and sometimes weeks on end and although they will eventually work, that doesn't necessarily help you with your market timing.

In other words, you don't want to short the S&P index futures just because you get a reading below .80?

Absolutely.

Are the intraday levels of the TRIN critical?

Sometimes I will watch the TRIN intraday for clues for the short term. If it's a very high number and you start seeing it come down, that indicates you probably have a rally going on. There are calculations I do during the day for the TRIN but I don't take them seriously. There is no need for anyone to look at the intraday figures. The close is not only sufficient but I believe the best number.

Are you using the longer term trading indexes for confirmation?

The Open 30 is one of my favorites. Some of the readings on these things are objective. When you get readings on the Open 30 higher than 1.10 or 1.15, you can almost bet that you are at or very close to market bottoms. The reason I like the Open 30 is that it isn't influenced by a single day's reading of TRIN.

For example, I am going back to 1987 again. The Open 30 TRIN on October 16th, the day before the crash, was at 96.6. It wasn't anywhere near oversold despite the fact that on this day you had a single day reading of 5.276. On the day of the crash, it moved to 1.092. This is just a smidgen away from 1.10, a benchmark reading. There is more research to be done on some of these trading index numbers, but it used to be that a reading above 1.10 for the 40 day moving average of the TRIN was almost always a benchmark reading unless you are in the heart of a real terrible bear market like 1973 to 1974. Those are the times when you have to be a little bit careful for any of these "mortgage the house and the children" readings.

We never see the TRIN used on any exchange other than the NYSE.

No. I played around with it on other exchanges like the NASDAQ. I don't know whether I did enough research to give a knowledgeable opinion but I think by far the most effective one is the NYSE. If you get yourself into a position where you are acquainted closely with the numbers then you are not thrown off. If I had two or three different exchange numbers for trading indexes in my head, I might see one reading, say at 1.30, and think, "boy, that's really bullish" and then realize that it was for another exchange. I have found that you get good indications from the NYSE Composite because the majority of institutional volume still goes on there.

Which breadth indicators are in your arsenal?

I follow the advance/decline indicators, both daily and weekly. I think they are important. There are also advance/decline oscillators which are calculated from breadth readings, like the McClellan oscillator, which has become quite popular recently.

What are the parameters of the McClellan oscillator?

The general guidelines are -100 and +100. Those are oversold and overbought conditions respectively. There is an interesting thing about an indicator like this that maybe a lot of neophyte technicians aren't aware of. One of the lessons I learned a long time ago, particularly in some of the very strong market moves off bottoms, is that oscillators, such as the McClellan, can go into what I call "out of bounds" territory. You move out of normal boundary lines and go into abnormal boundary lines. Usually when they do that they are giving you an important message. For example, if overbought on the McClellan has been +80, +90, +100 and then all of a sudden it gets up to +150 or +200, then you know that there is something going on. Usually this will happen in times of a kickoff from a bottom, like 1982 or 1990, especially the January 1991 low. Those kickoff breadth moves produce very overbought situations very quickly. A neophyte at technical analysis will have a tendency to think that the higher you got the more overbought you got and that would be a great sign to go short or buy puts. Of course, it is just the opposite. When they go that far overbought or oversold, it is giving you important information. In 1982, the McClellan oscillator moved to +203, with six consecutive prior days reading above +100. This was perhaps one of the most overbought readings the McClellan oscillator has seen in its history. If you had been following it, you would have thought it was overbought when it was really a big kickoff move.

So it would be a mistake to just blindly follow the numbers. They require some interpretation.

You see these parameters going higher and higher because there are that many more stocks to influence it. On an absolute basis, there are so many more stocks trading today. I know Sherman McClellan fairly well who developed the oscillator with his wife Marian. Their son Tom, is now writing a very good newsletter called *The McClellan Market Report.* Where I tend to disagree with the McClellans and a lot of people that use the indicator is that they don't adjust it for the current market period. It is a completely different universe because of the number of issues trading. My contention is that a +100 reading on the McClellan now has nowhere near the meaning of a +100 reading of 10 or 15 years ago. That is why I have a completely separate spreadsheet on the McClellan oscillator with what I call the adjusted McClellan oscillator but I don't get too deeply into analysis of the McClellan oscillator unless I see something that is really interesting.

What is the adjusted McClellan oscillator?

I have worked out what I call an adjusted McClellan oscillator that is based just on advance/decline ratios rather than advance/decline differentials. It kind of neutralizes and normalizes the McClellan oscillator so you can compare it with any other period in market history. Forty or fifty years ago, if you had a 2:1 positive day, there may have been 600 stocks up and 300 stocks down so the difference between them would be 300. As you add those up over a period of time, a plus 300 reading would be very high. If you come into today's world, a 2:1 positive reading would be something like 1600 and 800. Now you have a differential of 800 different issues. If you did that 10 days in a row, you would have +800 as opposed to the +300 reading you would get from an equivalent period several decades ago. So the numbers are not comparable at all and if you compare today's readings on the McClellan oscillator with those of 30 years ago, you are making a mistake in terms of comparisons. The oscillators change a lot over a period of time but if you did them by ratios, they wouldn't. If there were twice as many stocks up as down thirty years ago and today there are twice as many up than down, then there wouldn't be any change. If you get yourself to the point where you use ratios rather than raw numbers, that is instead of using advances minus declines you divide advances by declines, then that gives you a number which you can compare with any other number in market history, whether you go back 5, 10 or 100 years.

Is the McClellan oscillator better suited for short term signals rather than long term signals?

Yes, I think so although the McClellans themselves have found some significant longer term patterns, especially in the Summation Index, the oscillator's companion tool.

I recall reading that you discovered a churning pattern which seemed to identify market tops. What do you look for in such a pattern?

In 1992, I discovered a pattern that qualifies as remarkable in its ability to discern approaching market tops. When I find something like this, it doesn't mean anything to me until I go back to my computer and ask, "How many times has this happened in the past?" When I went back and looked, this had happened either two or three times in the past thirty to forty years and every single one of them was within maybe two to six weeks of a very major market top. As it turns out, it did not work at all in 1992. In 1994, there wasn't any major top but it worked, we had about a 9.8% decline. What I also found was that if you went back beyond 1966, the 1962-1966 time period, there were a whole group of churning patterns that didn't lead to any tops either. When you get into a real concerted bull market like they had from 1962-66 and like 1990 to the present, I think you get so many false signals that you just get frustrated trying to use it. So, I don't know how useful it is but I do know that it has pointed out some very important market tops in the past and I have a feeling it will in the future too.

For the adventuresome, would you describe what you saw?

In November 1992, I was struck by the apparent lack of volatility in the daily advance/decline statistics on the NYSE. I examined the daily A/D ratio and discovered that over the prior 21 market days in November of 1992, the highest ratio was 1.84 to 1.00 and the lowest was .71 to 1.00. I used 21 market days because there are that many "trading" or "market" days in the average month. Rather than use these exact limits as a precedent, we arbitrarily widened the limits somewhat to .65 and 1.95. We then searched our computer data base for other time periods of 21 market days when similar trading patterns occurred in the market, periods that were noteworthy for their lack of volatility. We started by going back to 1965, when the Dow made its initial move to the 1,000 level. We were stunned by the results. From November of 1966 to November 1992, there were only three other periods when the conditions were satisfied—namely the highest A/D ratio over a 21 market day period was less than 1.95 and the lowest one was greater than .65. Here are the dates—four days in January 1966, the 25th through the 28th, six days in October 1968, the 17th, 18th, 21st, 22nd, 24th and 25th, and four days in December 1972, the 6th, 7th, 8th, and 11th. Anyone even marginally acquainted with stock market history should recognize those dates immediately. In each case, the dates preceded very major market tops by no more than five weeks. You would think that from 1972 to 1992, you could find 21 consecutive market days within that period when the ratio was not higher than 1.95 or lower than .65 and yet it never showed up again until twenty years later in 1992. I was truly stunned and very excited when I found it.

That is remarkable. Did you stumble upon it or were you looking for it?

I stumbled upon it because we were not getting any big up/down days nor were we getting any real little ones. There was no big wide spread and there was no great amount of weakness. We were getting days of maybe 1100 up, 1000 down —900 up, 800 down —1200 up, 1100 down. They were coming one after another. I thought that it was amazing that we would go this long, this far. Then I started putting parameters on it. I found that the two extremes over that period of time were 1.84 and .71. Then I decided to give a little more leeway on the up and downside. I moved the parameters to 1.95 and .65, wrote a little formula on Excel, and told my computer to show me every day since 1966 where for any 21 day period there was no ratio higher than 1.95 or lower than .65. These three dates appeared like a gold mine. I got curious about it and continued to go back prior to the 1962-1966 period and I discovered that indeed, prior to that time period, there were also excellent results—December of 1952, January 1953 for about 4 days, and September 1955. I think I went all the way back to either 1940 or 1950. For now, let's throw out the two periods of 1964 and 1965 and observe the average results for the remaining six periods. The Dow on average advanced 1.7% from the close of the first day in the churning pattern, in other words, 21 consecutive days of less than 1.95 and greater than .65, to the highest subsequent intraday high after the pattern emerged. It then took 10 market days to reach that high on average and the subsequent decline averaged 15.2%. I deem those results significant and impressive. In the past when you found that kind of pattern, with only a couple of exceptions in that 1962-1966 time period, it led to an average decline of 15.2% within a month or two. Most recently, I decided to go back before 1940 to see where churning patterns may have appeared. I was stunned to find that the first churning pattern prior to 1940 occurred in July 1929, just 6 weeks before the top that led to the crash. In doing additional research, I also found that 19 or 20 consecutive days could also be considered as completed churning patterns. (In December 1996, a 20 day pattern completed.)

Let's revert back to our discussion of cycles. Other than the 60 year, what other cycle periods do you study?

Over the last couple of decades—I almost hate to say that because it makes me sound old—my thinking has turned to different areas trying different things on "cycle wise," but it seems like I keep coming back to what I call "static" time cycles. Some people will look at a cycle and then start taking Fibonacci multiples on it and trying to make the market work out that way. Indeed, I have done that and tried it myself but I keep going back to good old-fashioned time cycles that have worked for me so well in the past. One of the things that got me started in my career was a 212 week cycle that I discovered back in the 1960's. In 1974, I was doing television commentary on the stock market in Los Angeles. I showed a chart with this 212 week cycle to the people in the fall of that year saying that because of this cycle, the Dow was scheduled to see a very important bottom the week of December 9th through 13th. I repeated this most of that fall as I showed the chart. Sure enough, on exactly December 9th of 1974, the Dow hit a low that it has never seen since. In fact, one could argue that we have been in a bull market for the last 22 years. My point is that even though I keep experimenting with other things and looking for new ways to attempt to locate bottoms in the market, a lot of times I keep going back to these static time cycles that seem to work so well. Sometimes they will work very well within a certain period of time and then they tend to disappear. I think what happens is what I call "interference" patterns in cycles. For example, if you have two cycles that are very, very close to each other but one is reaching a top and one is reaching a bottom at the same time, they will tend to cancel each other out for a while. I think that is the reason these cycles apparently disappear. Most technicians who are serious about doing cycle analysis at one time or another get very frustrated or give up on the whole idea of cycles because they say, "Yes, I can see three repetitions here but then what happened after that?" The 212 week cycle has dissipated and in fact, over the last decade or so, nothing really important has come from that and that frustrates a lot of people.

They want the cycle patterns to be exact.

Yes, but I have to say that I want it to be exact also. In fact, the one thing I didn't like about Hurst's work is that he gave cycles plus or minus two or three weeks. I would find a 20 week cycle bottom occurring anywhere from 16 weeks to 23 weeks. I don't want that kind of cycle. That doesn't help me very much in terms of finding bottoms in the market. For most of my cycle work, I have tried to show that there are some very exacting cycles in the market, some of them in fact almost to the day.

Are the cycle time periods measured from peak to peak or trough to trough?

I started measuring them bottom to bottom and I found out that this is always the most reliable way to do it. In fact, that fits in with Hurst's theory, that the most reliable way to count cycles is from bottom to bottom. I sent out a challenge once to anyone who could find a consistent cyclic period from top to top. Since then I have found a few but I must say that the great majority of cycles that have been reliable over time have been cycles measured from bottom to bottom.

Are we talking about cycle time periods as they relate to the NYSE Composite?

Most of the things I look at are the NYSE. Once in a while, I may notice something different on the OTC or some other index, but for the most part, all of the cycle work I do is on the NYSE.

Do you have any theories as to why cycles work best from bottom to bottom?

I am not really sure although I think there is a tendency for stocks to bottom out together and there is a tendency for tops to be a lot more scattered. For example, one industry group will top out in February, the next one in April, and the next one in June. Also, there is another potential explanation but I don't know how logical or rational it is. If you are at a very important bottom, and you have a high momentum move off that bottom, there will be a tendency, especially at the real kickoffs from bear market lows going into a new bull market, for things to get overbought very quickly in terms of magnitude. This is one of the reasons that overbought and oversold indicators don't always work so well for people who are just looking for a level of 70 to sell or a level of 30 to buy on the Relative Strength Index (RSI). We talked about the McClellan oscillator earlier. The McClellan oscillator generally might reach an overbought reading at +80 or +100. During one of these kickoff moves, it might go all the way to +150 or +180 or +200. A novice might think this a great place to sell short because it is so overbought and exactly the opposite is true. Usually, when overbought/oversold indices become very strong they are giving you information about the magnitude of that move saying that this is not going to be just a little move up or down but probably a much larger one. As an example, I use a space shuttle being lifted into the air but you can just as easily use a baseball. If you throw a ball up into the air and were to measure the speed of the ball with a radar gun, the greatest speed in the whole measurement would be as it just started off the bottom. The bottom is where the greatest speed is and the speed determines how high it's going to go. The higher it goes, the slower it gets. When it reaches as high as it's going to go, there is an instantaneous moment where it actually stops and changes direction. If you think about that as being the top of a market, momentum is slowing down significantly before it reaches the top and starts coming down again. That might be one explanation for the difference between tops and bottoms in the market. If you think of how that ball reaches its top, it gets up there very slowly. If you watched it in slow motion, you would see the ball getting to the top, doing a little curve, stopping, and then starting to come down. When that ball comes down and it hits the ground, it turns very, very quickly. All of a sudden it's down and then it's up again. On August 18th, 1982, the McClellan oscillator reached its first reading over +100. Then it went to +126, +116, +158, +188, +176, +195, + 203, +150, +130, + 150, + 115, + 128, +142, and then below +100. That +203 is a very rare reading and if a novice technician had only worked with the McClellan oscillator a little bit and saw that, he would say the market was overbought and look for a short sale. On that day, the Dow was at 892.41. The next day there was a little tiny pullback—it was down about 8 or 9 points. It was interesting because any pullback we had over the next month came almost exactly down to the reading. We pulled back on September 30th to 896 on the close and then that's all she wrote. Another time period where you had a real big kickoff was at a market bottom in October of 1990. The market rallied and then stalled a little bit with the big panic into January 1991 with the Iraq situation. We entered a very overbought condition off that bottom too which led us into the present time, a five or six year bull market. On February 6, 1991, the McClellan oscillator got to +171.

Your point is that you can't look at overbought/oversold figures in a vacuum. Intuitive judgment is necessary for correctly identifying market tops and bottoms.

Yes, but sometimes they will tell you where you are. It's difficult to use McClellan now because there are so many more issues traded on the NYSE. That's why I have developed an adjusted McClellan where I use advance/decline ratios. This is a good comparison basis because you are using a ratio rather than the raw figures. That way you can compare any one period in history with any other. As a general rule, if you see a McClellan oscillator of +200 or greater, that is not a move that is going to die in the next week or two. That is an important upside move with a lot of thrust to it and it is going to take quite a while for it to dissipate, especially the series of readings over +150 in 1982. You can almost look at it as being a space shot. 1982 was a space shot that had such an initial thrust that 14 years later, we are still floating up in the air just from the initial thrust of that shot. It is something that took us off into another galaxy somewhere. Checking back into 1987, after the crash, the McClellan oscillator was the lowest reading in history, a -260. Although the Dow bottomed on October 20th, the overall market took another 6 weeks or so before it bottomed in early December. And at that December bottom, the reading on the McClellan oscillator was -71 or -72 as opposed to a -260 in October. At that time, if you had looked at a chart and compared the NYSE Composite index on October 20th to the NYSE Composite index on December 4th, you would have seen a massive divergence. The NYSE Composite had gone to a lower low on December 4th while the McClellan oscillator reading was a higher low of -71. Especially when the McClellan oscillator had started to turn up from there, it was a confirmation that you had probably seen a very important low.

Can you name some other market periods where the 212 cycle worked?

That particular cycle was running really well with bottoms in October 1962 and October 1966. There was a big move up after the cycle bottom during the week of November 20, 1970. These were the three 212 week cycles I had spotted prior to showing people the charts of the Dow Industrials and Transports on the

Los Angeles TV station KWHY in 1974. The next low was due the first week in January of 1979. As it turned out, not a bad time to buy. The Dow had gotten down to the 800 level and it subsequently rallied all the way up to the 900 level but it took a long time to do it. It was about a 12% advance then the Dow had a very quick decline into the March 1980 bottom. After that, the cycle started getting a little bit more diffuse. On FNN in November 1982, I told people that the next cycle low was due on January 24, 1983. As it turned out, we had bottomed five months before that in August 1982. From August to November we had this huge rally and I kept telling people on FNN that despite the huge rally, we were due for a cycle bottom on January 24, 1983. Everyone said, "You are crazy. How can you have a cycle bottom when we just exploded to the upside?" I was just telling people when it was due. This particular call got me a lot of notoriety and fame because I repeated it so often in late 1982, early 1983. What happened was the Dow had reached a new rally high of 1105 on January 12, 1983. Now mind you, the Dow had gone 16 years without being able to close above 1067. On January 10, 1983, we got up to a close of 1092 and broke through that barrier which we had not been able to break through in 16 years. And at this time, I was looking at the market and saying, "This is crazy. We are at a new all-time high and in two weeks we are due to see a cycle bottom." Guess what? On January 24th, the Dow gapped down. The Dow had been as high as 1105 intraday and it went down to a low of 1013 intraday. It closed at 1030. In a period of 8 market days the Dow declined 10%. Another 212 week cycle was due in early 1987. We had a spectacular move of about 500 points, another 20%, from February 1987 up until the August high. The next one that was due was in March 1991. Again, it was an excellent time to be buying the market but if you were to look at a chart you would say that doesn't look like any kind of a low. In fact, the Dow was moving up into that time period. But again, it was a great time to be buying the market. The same thing happened in April 1995. We had just made a new all-time high. Another lesson about cycles is that cycles don't necessarily have to have a price move down into them. That is how they typically resolve themselves but they also depend on the underlying cycles. If you have very strong underlying cycles, that is, cycles which are longer or stronger than the one you are looking at, prices may simply go sideways or even be forced to the upside before they really accelerate. If I were to show you a chart of these cycles, you would see that for the last three or four resolutions, there was a kind of acceleration to the upside rather than finding a bottom on the chart.

Will cycles occurring in the Transportation Average coincide with the cycles in the Dow and NYSE Composite?

Yes and no. In 1962, I think that the Industrials went to a double low in June and October whereas the Transports didn't really make a double bottom. They held or made a much lower bottom. At times like that you will see these particular cycles, some of them at least, show with a lot more visibility on one chart than another. This tells me that there may be slightly different cycles, certainly for individual stocks but maybe even for stock indices and averages. One cycle may be more important to one average than to another.

Do you follow cycles in individual stocks?

I do very little with individual stocks. If I find a pattern, say a 35 week cycle, I might save it so in the future if I happen upon it, I can see how it turned out.

If you don't get a cycle confirmation from both the Dow and the Transports, or other indices, how do you resolve the conflict between the two?

I am not that concerned about confirmations with the Transports and the Industrials. One of the important theories of cycles, as Hurst put forward, was that there was a tendency for stocks to move together. So even though it is a market of individual stocks, it is amazing how they really move together. For example, I challenge anyone to find 7%, 8%, or at most 10% of stocks that went up during the great bear market from December 1968 to December 1974, where the average share of stock was down 75%. I can guarantee you there were stocks whose fundamentals were great but because they were in the midst of what was a great bear market at the time, they didn't go anywhere simply because they moved with the overall market. I am not concerned with the differences between the Industrials and Transportations. I usually prefer to see the Dow confirm because although it's only 30 stocks, it's an index that a lot of people identify with and it is such a great psychological indicator. In 1987, I had a down side projection on the Dow Transports and one on the Dow Industrials. On December 4th, 1987, the Transportation Average met its cycle projection almost exactly while the Industrials were 100 or 200 points away from their projection. The fact that one of them had hit almost exactly was pretty strong evidence that we could have been at a bottom but I kept looking well into 1988 and even late into 1988 for the Dow to make a lower low because it had lower projections. It ultimately invalidated those projections but it threw me off in 1988. Subsequent to that, one of the lessons I learned was that if one of them meets the price projection, don't seek perfection. If you have one of the major indices apparently meeting all projections and not giving any further projections, then you have to take into consideration the possibility that it is a potentially important turn.

In other words, one index alone meeting your price projections is a sufficient signal.

It's just saying, "These are two major averages and one of them has fully met its downside projection." Because it has done that, you have to give the benefit of the doubt that perhaps this is a turning point coming. There are two main possibilities. The Transports have bottomed and the market will move up from there but there will be a test in the next month or two at which point the Industrials will go down and meet there projection and the Transports will stay above the prior low. That is one way of satisfying both projections. The other way is that the Transports meet their projection and they both just take off and ultimately the Industrials will invalidate their projection. That is of course what happened in 1987. But I have learned that when you have a major average that has reached its downside objective on a long term price projection, you should give that the benefit of the doubt. Maybe that is telling us something important is happening and the other index is not going to meet it.

You mentioned earlier that you had spotted a couple of cycles that can be measured from top to top. Are they reliable enough to merit mentioning?

No, because I don't feel strongly enough about any of them that I could say this is the pattern to watch for in the future. Something that we might discuss is turning points rather than just tops or bottoms. It is something that I am still a bit uncomfortable with in terms of the concept. I am not quite sure how practical it is to have this information. Sometimes turning point analysis is confusing. Turning points are cyclic patterns that resolve with a top or a bottom but you never know ahead of time which its going to be. Generally speaking, a lot of them have worked out pretty well for 1996 in particular. I have been paying a lot more attention to turning points, in either calendar days or market days although most of the shortterm turning points I do are usually market days. For example, on my update on July 18, 1996, I told subscribers that this day should mark the resolution of a 31 day turning point pattern. Because we had rallied up to it in three days on a pretty strong rally, that should have been some kind of top, at least shortterm. As it turned out, it was. The market went down 120 points from there on a closing basis. I wasn't too happy with the prior resolutions. The thing that is important to me is real time. If I tell you there is a 31 day turning point pattern that should resolve tomorrow, I expect it to occur. If the market has been bouncing up a little and down a little for three or four days, you are going to ask, "Is it due to be a top or bottom?" My answer is, "I don't know but it will be one or the other." Sometimes it is pretty clear. If you have had a rally for two to three days that has gone up a hundred points, and you close on that turning point day right there, then the implication is that this is going to be a top. On the other hand, if you have come down for a few days, especially if it has been more than 100 Dow points or so and it is due to resolve that day, then the implication is that it is going to be a bottom. But there are times when it is not as clear as that. This particular 31 day turning point pattern has been very successful in the past but has not been as consistent lately. In 1994, for example, there were a stunning series of highs pinpointed to within one market day on this pattern—February 2, March 18th, May 4th, June 17th, August 2nd, September 15th, and October 28th. Those are all exactly 31 days apart. If you check it out, its like a Who's Who of closing highs in the Dow that year. It is just unbelievable how they came one after another. One or two of them may have been a day off but none of them was more than a day off. When you spot a pattern like that, those could be very helpful. As I said, sometimes if you are up 6 points, down 7 points, up 6 points, or whatever and the turning point is supposed to resolve that particular day, if it hasn't been a good move into that particular time, then you can run into problems. In retrospect it will be easy to say whether it was a top or bottom.

If I understand you correctly, a lot of the cycle periods you have picked are based on trial and error?

Trial and error is a little too vague and general. A lot of them are empirically based. You eyeball a chart and say, "This period from here to here looks like a turning point." I'll give you an example, one that I based my opinion on that we were at a very major turning point the end of May 1996, especially because some of the other technical factors fell into place. Martin Armstrong, who is on the Board of Directors for the Foundation for the Study of Cycles, has a company called Princeton Economics. They do stock market analysis, commodity analysis, and all kinds of other things. When I went to deliver a speech for the Foundation for the Study of Cycles in April 1996, Martin talked about an 8.6 year economic confidence model and a turning point that was due on May 25, 1996, which was a Saturday. The last resolution of that particular phase of the cycle was due on October, 1987, the closing low date for the Dow Jones Industrials after the 1987 crash. At the time of the conference in April, the preferred scenario for the stock market, according to Princeton Economics, was to see a decline into late May around this cycle date, and a generally rising market until 1997. Alternatively, they theorized that if the market advanced into late May, especially if the Dow approached the 5800 level, a 1987 crash like situation would be possible. That last statement attracted our attention. After calling Martin and discussing the 8.6 year cycle with him, I had mixed emotions. I was excited on the one hand that a fellow cycle analyst perceived the possibility of an imminent decline of significance. On the other hand, I was frustrated because I saw nothing in my own cycle analysis that suggested a possible turn of importance in late May. The evening of my phone conversation with Martin, I was scheduled to speak to some local doctors about the stock market. In reviewing some material, I came across a chart I had constructed in February 1996, depicting a 276 week pattern with major turns in December 1974, March 1980, September 1985, and October 1990. The next turn was due Monday, February 12, 1996. What drew our attention at the time, however, was that we could see by eyeballing the chart that if you moved the resolution of the pattern to the April 1980 low rather than the March low in 1980, some new and equally compelling market turns would be pinpointed. The March 27, 1980 low on the Dow was 729.95 on a theoretical intraday basis and 759.98 on a closing basis. The April 21, 1980 low was only 751.37 intraday but the closing low of 759.13 was actually fractionally lower than the March 27th closing low. So then, I theorized that the April 1980 low was a legitimate bottom to use even though it didn't go as low intraday as the March low, but it did go to a new closing low on the Dow. If you now use December 9, 1974 and April 21, 1980 as the first two points on the pattern, the period of the pattern moves from 276 weeks to 280 weeks and the subsequent resolutions of the pattern change to Monday, September 2, 1985 and Monday, January 14, 1991. In my May 24, 1996 newsletter, I had a chart on the front page that had 1,960 calendar days which works out to exactly 280 weeks between patterns. Now prior to this year, these cycles were all at lows or bottoms, points that marked dramatic moves to the upside on the Dow Industrials. The 1985 date was the only one of the four that did not see an exact resolution. It fell on Labor Day 1985, and was almost exactly between a double bottom on the Dow of 1312.50 on August 19th and 1298.20 on September 17th. The next resolution of the pattern was due on January 14, 1991. It was perfect. For those who don't recall, it fell on the exact low day of the so-called Iraqi War crisis at a time when sentiment was gloomy and bearish. Within two months, the Dow was up over 20%. The next one was due on May 27, 1996, three days after my newsletter and a Memorial Day holiday. When I realized that the resolution date of my cyclic pattern corresponded virtually exactly with the 8.6 year resolution of the Princeton Economic's confidence model, I became very excited. Here were two completely different cyclic patterns derived in completely different ways that were pointing to May 25th 1996, a Saturday and May 27th, 1996, a Monday holiday, as potentially important market turning points. Either or both could be considered exact resolutions if a closing or intraday high occurred on Friday, May 24th or Tuesday, May 28th.

On what day did the market top actually occur in May?

What happened was, on May 24th, both the S&P 500 and the NYSE Composite Index closed at new all-time highs and subsequently fell 7.2% and 9% respectively. On the Dow, the closing highs actually came a couple of days earlier, on May 22nd, but on the 23rd, we went a little bit higher intraday.

So just a minor adjustment of one month, from 276 weeks to 280 weeks made a tremendous difference.

It was originally 276 and I looked at it and said, "If you change this one a little, it moves this one over and that one over and it turned out to be 280 weeks or 1,960 calendar days." I did a big thing on the Internet because I wanted to go on record as saying I thought we were at a potentially important market top and give the reasons for it. I also showed the S&P channel chart. We hit the top of that channel in February 1996 and the May 1996 high hit it almost exactly. This was happening plus, if you drew a trendline on the Dow at its greatest rate of ascent on an arithmetic chart, not logarithmic, through the period of 1983 to the 1987 high, the Dow was hitting that line exactly at the same time the S&P was hitting its channel line.

So you had sufficient confirmation.

Yes, and the two charts have nothing to do with one another. One of them is based on a 60 year pattern, the other is based on a pattern that is about 14 years long. One of them was hitting that line for the first time in 30 years and the other one was hitting the line for the first time in 8 years and they were both occurring within one or two market days of the resolution of these patterns. It was just very powerful evidence that something significant could be happening.

You seem to make a distinction between turning points and cycles. Would you clarify the difference?

Yes, that is something that I have changed my mind about a little bit over the years. What I used to call a cycle was either bottom to bottom or top to top. Now I realize that a lot of times when you find some kind of pattern, let's say the 31 day pattern, sometimes it will be a top and sometimes it will be a bottom. It is really inconsistent. Rather than call that a cycle, I have had the tendency lately to call it a turning point pattern. So the distinction between what I normally call a cycle and what I normally call a turning point pattern is that cycles have all the same resolutions, either tops or bottoms. Turning points can be either a top or a bottom. A turning point pattern is just that; it's a pattern whereas when I use the word cycle, I try to make it refer to either all tops or all bottoms. I tend to use the word "pattern" with turning points as opposed to turning point "cycle." For example, the 280 week one we just talked about—I refer to that as a turning point pattern rather than cycle. Cycles talk about tops to tops and bottoms to bottoms measured in terms of the length of the cycle whereas turning points could be top to bottom, top to top, top to bottom, or a combination of tops and bottoms but the pattern is there in a rhythmic fashion.

When measuring 31 day turning points, how do you choose your starting point?

Actually, it is easy to do now with computers. Before, I would have gone back and just found a turning point. For example, I would say, "Here is a top in May and count a certain number of points backwards to a prior top. Oh, look at this, 26 days back to this prior top. Let me try going back another 26... no... another 26... no nothing there." I'll try again maybe 31 days from the top. If I go back 31 days... yes, that was a top... look at this, another 31 days, that's right head on,... and another 31 and you have exactly a bottom. A lot of it is empirical work. Now with computers, all you have to do is anchor on one day, move the mouse a certain number of days and watch the whole thing fan out in front of you. You can spot six or seven of them at a time and see important turning point patterns.

Do you typically use your computer to count your cycles for you rather than performing the task by hand?

I still count some of them by hand although I use the computer a lot more now than I used to. I used to go blind counting cycles on these tiny little charts. I don't do very much of it by hand anymore because the computer enables you to do it a lot more quickly and is less likely to make counting mistakes. In fact, it won't make any counting mistakes at all. If there is some bad data in there, like an extra day or if you are missing a day, that might make a difference but otherwise it wouldn't.

So far, we have discussed the 212 week cycle, the 280 week cycle, the 60 year cycle and the 31 day turning point. Are those the primary cycles you rely on?

No, I am giving you examples. I don't want to set these cycle periods up as the be all and end all of the work that I do. On my Dow chart, I have written probably at least six to eight different turning point patterns. Shortterm ones that run from maybe 26 days to as long as 50 days are sprinkled all over my chart. Two or three of them may be real close to each other and I use those mostly as guidelines. If we are hitting one of those at the same time as all my other technical work says I have met all upside or downside projections and there is an indication that we may be at a top or bottom, then that gives me a lot more confidence that we may be seeing a turn there. I don't use those specifically to predict or project turns in the market.

Thanks for making that distinction. Certainly for technicians starting out, they can get into a great deal of trouble trying to follow so many different turning points.

Yes, it would just get very confusing.

Can you offer any advice to novices who might take a position at a 212 week cycle resolution thinking it is a top or bottom and action doesn't occur until the 280 week cycle period? That is a pretty large span of time to be early or late.

Yes, and that is why people get confused with cycles. People ask, "Which one do you pay the most attention to?" If this one says you have a bottom here and you don't expect another bottom for two months, do you buy here or wait for two months? It gets very confusing. I think the most important lesson to learn from any of the cycle patterns is first of all, the longer I work with them, the more respect I have for them. But also, the important thing to learn is to use them as guidelines. I would never make a recommendation for people to buy or to sell a group of stocks or the market as a whole based on just one particular cycle. I would have to look at that cycle in relation to all the other technical work that I do. And that is an important point to remember because sometimes people will get excited by cycles. They will find one and say, "Okay, look at this, 8 weeks, 8 weeks, 8 weeks." Usually the first time you commit money to a cycle after discovering it, that's the time it's not going to work. That's one of Murphy's laws.

Stocks, bonds, mutual funds, commodities, and stock indexes are the most common types of investments. Based on your experience, does one respond better to cycle analysis than another?

As a general rule, the best work in cycles is done on market indices and averages—something where you are not dealing with a single entity, like an individual stock. A mutual fund would be different because there are groups of stocks in there so that might work equally as well. I would much prefer to base my decisions of my analysis on market indices and averages as opposed to individual stocks.

Do you perform cycle analysis on individual mutual funds?

I don't too much analysis on mutual funds per se. I do my analysis on the market and translate that analysis into investments in mutual funds. There is a difference. The analysis is done on the market itself because I believe the market does have a degree of predictability to it. If there is a particular pattern there, having found that pattern I will act on it. Action will be taken in mutual funds rather than individual stocks because mutual funds tend to perform like the overall market. Let's say you are absolutely right about the market. You think it has reached a bottom and so you tell people to jump into General Motors and all of a sudden the market goes straight up 10% but it just so happens that General Motors has a strike or bad earnings and it actually goes down as the market goes up. There is nothing worse to the psyche. You are right about the market but you lose money on what you are investing in. I learned a long time ago that I believe the best way to invest is using mutual funds because 99% of the time, a fairly well diversified mutual fund will move like the market moves.

Isn't diversified the key word? Wouldn't it be a little tricky if someone were in a sector fund?

I still make specific recommendations for Fidelity sector funds because so many people are in the Fidelity group of funds. In that case, I will make a quick analysis. I will make a decision on the market first and then translate that decision into a mutual fund which has been performing well on a relative strength basis. For example, today we went to a new closing low in a lot of these indices and averages. If I wanted to recommend a mutual fund, what I would do is find one that maybe closed at a higher low than last week. That would mean that it was stronger on a relative strength basis. So I might do some quick technical analysis and maybe even some cyclic analysis in terms of price projections but most of the market work is directed toward timing. Turning that timing into investments becomes a move into mutual funds. Again, I won't do too much individual analysis of mutual funds, just kind of a group thing. I try to find an individual one within a quality sector that is performing well.

Are there any more cycles which you follow?

There is one more cycle we should discuss because it really has been consistent. It's the one where the bottom occurred in December of 1994. I have honed it down a few times but it is right around 108 weeks. In our March 18, 1994 newsletter, I said that there was another cycle due to resolve in late 1994 and the results of this particular cycle have been nothing short of spectacular. We wrote about this same cycle in our newsletter of September 18, 1992 and before that in our October 5, 1990 newsletter. I generally calculate cycle lengths to an exact number of days and or weeks including the fractional lengths thereof. With this cycle, within one to two weeks on either side of an approximate 108.5 week cycle, some of the most important bottoms of the past decade or so have occurred. The dates of the important lows are April 3, 1978, April 21, 1980, June 9, 1982, June 18, 1984, August 4, 1986, August 23, 1988, October 1990, and November 1992. The 1992 bottom though was several weeks after the October 1992 climactic low but only 1.8% above the closing low of October 9th. Using the November 1992 low as an anchor for measuring the next potential bottom and using the average cycle span of 763 calender days or 109 weeks, we came up with a tentative cycle low around December 21, 1994. Of course, that was within a week or two of that very important low in 1994. And that is now due to come in the last week of December 1996 or first week of January 1997. As we approached the early January 1997 potential resolution, we theorized in our newsletter that the upcoming resolution could well mark an important market top.

It seems difficult to understand how cycles can repeat themselves with such regularity when human behavior is so unpredictable and erratic. New players enter the market while older ones exit. Do you have a theory as to why cycle analysis works so well?

The theory is a very easy one to explain. If you could follow an individual around all day long and watch his behavior and actions you'd say, "There is absolutely no order whatsoever to what this person is doing." There is no cyclic activity unless you want to say they rise at a certain hour of day and go to sleep at a certain hour of night. You see absolutely no pattern of activity. On the other hand, markets are the sum of all people acting at once on the markets. If you were to go to a crowded stadium to a football or baseball game and watch from one side of the stands to the other, you would see people jump up, yell and scream at the same time, sit down at the same time, and leave the stadium at the same time. You would see that groups of people, especially large groups of people, tend to act together. That is one of the basic theories behind how cycles work. You can not predict an individual's behavior but there seems to be cyclic patterns to the behavior patterns in mass groups.

You mentioned that you go through a ritual every day. Can you describe what you do?

I have a lot more flexibility during market hours than I do after the market closes. When the market closes, then I have a ritual I go through. During the day, if the market is in a critical area, I just follow it very closely to see if there are any clues in terms of its behavior that would precipitate a decision on my part in terms of money management. I have to make that decision about 40 minutes before the market closes as to whether we want to get out of our position or get into a different position.

Why forty minutes before the market closes?

Because the positions are based on mutual funds. For mutual funds, in order to get the closing price for that day, you have to make a decision anywhere from 15 to 40 minutes before the market close.

Sometimes you get some crazy activity in the last 15 minutes of market trading.

Absolutely, something wild can happen in the last 10 or 15 minutes, even the last couple of minutes. If there is something important going on in the market or I am waiting for an indicator to flip or something to happen, I try to get as close as I can to the cut-off point.

During the day, do you pay close attention to indicators like the intraday values of TRIN and the McClellan oscillator?

It depends. Let me give you an example from today. The New 10 TRIN went to .78. It went below .80. That is a full-fledged overbought position. All you look for now is a move back above .80 numerically and that is theoretically a shortterm sell signal. It is a shortterm sell signal, not a long term one by any means. As it turned out, the last time the signal was given was at the market top on May 24, 1996 which was the exact day for the highs in the NYSE Composite and the S&P 500. It was a great signal but it's not always going to be that good. When I get something like this I look at it and say, "Can this turn into something more significant than just a shortterm signal?" So that's part of my analysis.

Let's say the New 10 TRIN is at .78 and "intraday" it rises above .80. Do you act on that signal if it is intraday?

No, absolutely not, because the New 10 TRIN is very dependent on final up and down volume and you don't get that until the end of the day. Any other figure would be misleading. For the simple trading index, once it stabilizes midday, unless you get a real big rally decline, it will generally stay the same. If it is a real volatile day, that's not true but if the market has a stable day that trades within a relatively small range, the simple trading index will not move much. But even in a situation where the trading index itself stays stable, the New 10 TRIN could change dramatically because of the volume. Let's say early in the day the ratio of up and down volume stays the same but later on in the day that ratio, even though it's the same, shows a much higher raw number that could dramatically affect the New 10 trading index. So the intraday readings are not important.

What about end of day chart analysis?

The first thing that I do is sit down and look at the charts on the screen. I'll look for new patterns or things that I am interested in that I have been looking at for several days. For example, I look at the intraday charts on the S&P futures. You can draw a parallel channel for the S&P 500 using the July 16, 1996 low and the secondary low on July 24th. Draw just a simple trend line up through those two bottoms and then draw an exact parallel line above that bringing it through the high of July 18th, the interim high between the bottoms of the 16th and the 24th. We stopped exactly on that line on August 2, 1996 and August 5th. I have grown to have more and more respect for little channels like this. As a technician, I can say that the channels would be better if there were three points on either the top or the bottom of the channel. That would give it better definition.

Do you prefer that your trendlines have three points?

Yes, a legitimate trendline for a technician should have at least three prior points that were turning points. If not, then any line is a trendline—you could pick two bottoms and say, "that's my trendline." Now a parallel channel is a little bit different. For a parallel channel, if you can draw a simple trendline between any two points and you have a corresponding two points on the other side, then you have enough to define a good parallel channel. Now that we have two bottoms and two tops exactly on a parallel line, it has become a well defined parallel channel that should have some power into the future. If we rally back up to it again, it would be a great place to short.

This is from an intraday chart of the S&P 500 futures?

Yes, I am looking at a five minute chart. On the futures, I tend to use different charts than most people. I use a 5 minute and a 15 minute but after that I go to 27 minutes, and either 45 minutes or 81 minutes because they divide evenly into the market day. I don't like to have a bar that does not complete at the end of the market day. There are exactly five 81 minute bars in the stock index futures day because the day is 405 minutes or 6 and ¾ hours. You want a chart that divides evenly- 6.75 times 60 is 405 minutes. If you did a 10 minute chart, the last bar of the day would be only 5 minutes and it would put the other 5 minutes into the bar of the next morning. To me, that would be deceptive because it's not a continuation of behavior there. So I like to use intraday charts that fit exactly even into a day of 405 minutes. That is one reason I use a 27 minute chart with the stock index futures as opposed to a 30 minute chart. The cash charts are a little bit different because the cash doesn't trade that extra 15 minutes at the end of the day. They only trade 390 minutes. So on a cash chart, I would use a 65 minute chart instead of an hourly chart because the cash day is 6 ½ hours long and a 65 minute chart goes exactly 6 times into a 6½ hour day.

I assume that any signals generated from 5 minute and 27 minute charts would represent shortterm moves?

Well yes, but it's just like the New 10 TRIN I told you about. As far as I am concerned, everything starts with a shortterm move. If you are in an area where you are looking for the possibility of a very important turn, then that shortterm move may become something a lot bigger. Otherwise, yes, that's all it is, a shortterm turn and that's what you look for.

In other words, if the S&P 500 broke out of the parallel channel to the upside or downside?

Yes, if something big like that happened, absolutely, that would be something of significance.

Considering that cycle analysis is just one aspect of your work, could we talk about how you integrate your other technical indicators, such as the TRIN, with your cycle analysis?

A lot of what I do is kind of intuitive. I don't want to make it sound like this is the exact procedure that I go through every day but I will try and objectify it as much as I can. If there are things that I am watching for in terms of price projections or particular technical levels, maybe we are close to some important moving average, then those could rule what I am watching. For example, over the last week or so, I knew we were very close to getting shortterm sell signals from two of the trading index indicators, the New 10 trading index and the Combination 10 trading index.

We didn't talk about the Combination 10 trading index.

That is just an average of the simple 10 day TRIN, the Open 10 trading index, and the New 10 trading index. I have found in looking back on that historically, when that moves from lower than .80 to higher than .80, it tends to be a pretty good sell signal, at least for the shortterm. It doesn't necessarily mean it's a long term signal. The times when I am waiting for something like that, then that can tip the scales in favor of the positive or negative side. This is really a difficult time for me because even though I am getting some technical negatives, some of my projection numbers show significantly higher prices. This is one of those time periods where things are being called both ways so you have to be careful.

Without question, the market is flashing conflicting signals.

The problem is that tops are formed sometimes agonizingly slow and other times, but not very often, they are inverted "V" shaped tops. You tend to get "V" bottoms, but an inverted "V" top, where you just go up and come down, is very rare. What tends to happen is that one stock after another gets weak. As more and more stocks get weak, there is a tendency, especially for large institutions, to start putting their money into more and more highly capitalized stocks—what they consider to be safer territory. That has a way of holding up the "nifty-fifty" so to speak, you know, the top 50 or 100 stocks. The secondaries start getting worse and worse and then finally the house of cards falls. But sometimes it takes a very long time. I think in March, April, and May of 1996 we started to finally see some internal deterioration. Now, it is not as serious as it has been at other market tops, especially given the fact that at the May top, the daily advance/decline (A/D) line and the weekly A/D line both confirmed that high. There was no divergence at that high in May. There have been only a couple of times historically where we didn't get a divergence from the A/D line at a market top. One of them was really important because it was December of 1968. In fact, there were analogies to the other two times that it happened. December 1968 was the last real mutual fund craze that we had and I remember it well because it was the first investment I ever made. There was a craze then for mutual funds and individual stocks. It wasn't anything like the mutual fund craze now. The craze then looks like real child's play compared to what's going on now but it was truly a craze at the time and it ended very abruptly because there was no divergence at the top in December of 1968. The only other time that there was a fairly significant top and no divergence in the A/D line was in May 1946. 1946 is interesting historically for a couple of reasons. In 1946, the market declined about 20% in about a month. It was a very precipitous decline in a short period of time. The other thing that happened in 1946 was that it was the record holder, prior to the 1995-1996 rally, for the longest rally without an intervening correction of 12% or greater. It went from April of 1942 to May 1946, 4 years and a month, before the top was in. Now, we have not only broken that record with this rally from October of 1990 but we have beaten it by well over a year or so. Although we don't have that many times to go back and say that it is statistically significant, another thing we have learned is that rallies which last for long periods of time without corrections tend to be followed by pretty important market tops when they finally come. 1946 was the record holder and although that wasn't a monumentally important top, it was a top that held for a few years. The record holder now is 1990-1996. 1966 was another time we had a long, uninterrupted rally, without a 12% or greater decline. After the 1966 top, the market didn't really see a significant new high for almost 16 years. Another one was from the 1984 low to the 1987 high, well over 3 years without a correction. Of course, that led to the crash where we went down 40% in a couple of months. So if we go back historically and look at these periods of time when we saw very longterm rallies without normal or average corrections taking place, they tend to be relatively important tops when they are reached. Unfortunately, it doesn't tell you anything about when they are going to be reached.

That's where your technical indicators come into play.

So at this point, I must tell you very frankly, the message is confusing now (August 1996). We have sell signals from the Combination 10 and the New 10 TRIN. On the other hand, there are some cycle projections that are arguing that we could see significantly higher prices. If these cycle projections come to pass, we are talking about a Dow at 6100 or 6200. They are numbers I have to pay attention to because my projection techniques call for it. So at a time like this, what I do on a daily basis is to go through all the numbers and if I have higher projections, then I look for the possibility of where things can go wrong with those projections. How could they be invalidated or what could turn the market to the downside? Because we got these shortterm sell signals on the trading index indicators, they bear watching fairly closely but unless I have other confirming information, I would not act on these simply by themselves. I would need to see other things happening.

Do you place your indicators within a particular hierarchy?

It is a very general hierarchy. In terms of my work, my cycle projections take mild precedence over other things simply because I think it is an edge I have that most people don't have.

What other unique indicators do you have in your arsenal?

There are some other A/D oscillators, or they are like A/D oscillators, which I call advancing issues oscillators. I track several from very short ones, like 4 and 5 days, up to longer ones, like 27 days or 54 days. All the advancing issue oscillator does is look at the number of advancing issues over that time period. I do it two ways on the computer spreadsheet. I have it either as a moving total or as a moving average. In other words, if it is a 4 day, you just look at the last four days and add up all the advances on the NYSE over a four day period. It is very similar to an A/D oscillator except the declines are not in the equation. This can give you good feedback in terms of the market internals and whether things are being confirmed or not to the upside. The interesting thing about the daily A/D line now is that it is at a recovery high since the July 1996 bottom but if you look at some of the A/D oscillators, they are nowhere near recovery highs. Some of them made their peaks and now we are seeing some divergences. Now that tells me one of two things. Either the market is going to turn itself around and go down because it doesn't have the internal momentum going or else, in order to generate that internal momentum, we are going to get some real smashing breakout to the upside. I can't rule that out simply because this market has really gone higher than it should have gone if this was going to be a typical rally in a bear market.

Why do you leave the declining issues out of the picture in your advancing issues oscillator?

It started out with what I ultimately called the "cycle indicators" (CI) and "neutral cycle indicators" (NCI). This is something I kind of originated at least twelve or thirteen years ago and, in fact, this is in the top right hand corner of my newsletter every time it comes out. I write CI, NCI, and then the ratio of CI to NCI. I just kept track of the total advancing issues on the NYSE over a 189 day period. The reason I used 189 days was because that is the closest number of days to 39 weeks and 39 weeks was an important cycle—39 weeks was the half-span of the 78 week cycle. So because that was an important cycle relative to price projections, I thought it might also be an important cycle in terms of these technical indicators. I devised something that kept track of the total number of advancing issues. I could have done it as a moving average but as it turned out I didn't. The CI just takes the moving total of the last 39 weeks or 189 days of advances on the NYSE. As I did this over a period of five or ten years, I discovered that there was a pretty good correlation to market tops and bottoms. When the cycle indicator reached a certain number on the upside, the market tended to be topping out. When it reached a number on the downside, there were two general areas. In one area you might see some kind of intermediate-term bottom and the other one, if it got down that low, maybe a longer term bottom.

So that is how the advancing issues oscillator was conceived?

Yes, I was just using the advances and I ignored the declines and the unchanged and it seemed to work very well. So that got me started on that concept. Now subsequent to that, I realized that the number of issues trading on the NYSE changes every year. As it turns out, the number of issues trading on the NYSE exchange has increased dramatically over the past several years. For example, a neutral day now is almost 1200 advances and 1200 declines. Well, if you had 1200 advances seven or eight years ago, that was a great up day. If you had 1200 declines, that would have been a big down day. Now you can have 1200 of both and it is a neutral day. So that required bringing in the other part of the equation, which was, how many stocks declined over this period of time? That phenomenon is measured indirectly by my CI/NCI ratio. First of all, the CI, which stands for the cycle indicator, measures the average number of advances on the NYSE exchange over a 39 week period. Now as it turns out, as of July 26, 1996, the CI was at 1,198 and all that means is that over the prior 39 weeks the average number of advances each day was 1,198. The NCI was 1,180. Well, we know that the CI is 1,198. The neutral reading is 1,180. That tells us that there has been a slight upside bias over the last 39 weeks because we have had on average 1,198 advancing issues each day over that period. To get the neutral cycle indicator, you would add together all the advancing issues and declining issues for the last 189 days, divide by two and that would tell you what a neutral day would be. What you are doing is ignoring the unchanged issues. In other words, if the NCI is 1,180 today, a neutral day based on the advances and declines of the last 39 weeks, would be 1,180 stocks up and 1,180 stocks down. If you multiply 1180 by two you arrive at a figure of 2,360 issues on average that change price each day on the NYSE over the prior nine months. Here is how the 2,360 compares with other time periods over the past few decades: in 1978 it was 1,496 and in 1981 it was 1,516. In 1987 we had reached 1,614 and from there into 1990 there was a decline. By 1990, it was down to 1,522. Of course, you had the crash occur in 1987 and you had the recession and a bad market for part of 1990. From 1978 to 1990, a period of 12 years, it hardly changed at all—1,496 to 1,522. In 1992 it was 1,730 and in 1994, the number was 2,156. The dramatic jump took place from 1990 to 1994; it went from 1,522 to 2,156. It tells you something about the character of the market. When you are in a bull market, more and more stocks want to be listed on the NYSE. If you go all the way back to 1949, the number is 742 so a typical or unchanged day in 1949 would have been half of that, 371 issues up, 371 issues down. Since that time we have almost tripled that number.

The ratio is derived by dividing the CI by the NCI.

To get the ratio, you simply divide the 1,198 by the 1,180 which is 1.015. I started working with the ratio rather than the raw numbers themselves because of the changes in the number of issues traded each year. You get numbers that can be compared with any other time in market history because you are using a ratio. I wanted to go back historically and see if there was some kind of consistency as to where market tops and bottoms came in. Indeed, I noticed that high risk intermediate to longterm tops generally form between readings of 1.035 and 1.08 on the CI/NCI ratio. We reached this level in May 1996. We got to 1.03 and change. Neutral territory would be between .995 and 1.034. Now, intermediate-term bottoms tend to come in at .980 to .995. Generally, you won't get a major market low occurring between .980 and .995. Usually, it takes a reading between .925 to .965 to get a major market bottom. On that big climactic day of July 16th, 1996, we got down to 1.003 and then we went down to 1.003 again on the 24th, but we didn't get below 1.00. So as great as that decline was, over the prior 39 weeks leading up to it there were still more stocks up than down over that time period. There are a couple of other things to watch for that give you very important information but historically, they come very seldom. A move above 1.08 is very important because that is kind of an "out of limit" move to the upside and that is telling you that there is great upside momentum and because of that great upside momentum, generally you are going to see a market rally that lasts for well over a year and often several years beyond when you see that reading occur. A lot of people might perceive this as being a top because the market is so overbought both on a short, intermediate, and longer term basis. On May 10, 1983, the CI/NCI ratio reached 1.102, its highest reading in 32 years. This reading characterized the very rare period of great upside momentum. There was every reason to believe it had the same implications then as it had in 1943 and 1950; in other words, a very longterm and consistent market advance. So that move up in 1983, because of my research, was telling me this was not a market move that was going to end in the next six months. Generally, when you get that kind of upside momentum, it is a multi-year market move.

Similar to what we talked about earlier with the McClellan oscillator.

Exactly. On a longer term basis, exactly the same thing, these "out of limit" moves.

Don't you have to use some judgment as to what stage the market is in? In other words, if you get a reading of 1.08 in the late phase of a bull market, should you ignore it?

Generally a top is formed between 1.035 and 1.08. If you get above 1.08, then you are no longer looking for a top. You may get a shortterm top or a top that lasts for a few months, but almost always, without fail, any time we have had readings above 1.08 that's telling you that there is incredible upside momentum here that is not going to dissipate in the next 6 months or even one year. Now the same thing is true of the downside too except we haven't seen one of those readings in a long time. When "out of limit" moves occur on the downside, the ratio is simply telling us that downside momentum is so great that no new all time high will follow on the popular averages at the next major top. There have been five such bottoms since 1932—1932, 1938, 1966, 1970, and 1974. Each one of these lows, which were "out of limit" to the downside, never made a meaningful all time high at their next important top. In March 1980 and again in March 1982, we had the first bottom readings in 20 years that were low enough to qualify for a major bottom but also high enough to propel the Dow to new all-time highs over the next few years. In other words, they didn't go out of limit to the downside and there was a good indication at that time that these were typical major, oversold levels so now you could start looking for new highs on the upside. In fact, that is exactly what happened after the 1980 and 1982 bottoms.

You use the raw number rather than a moving average for the CI/NCI ratio.

Yes. At that same time that I was doing the CI, I started doing work with the shorter term ones too because there is a tendency for them to reach limits. If you look at just the 5 day advances on the NYSE, you will notice that when they get above probably 6,500 or 7,000, there is a tendency for the market to turn around, at least shorterm, and start moving to the downside.

So you simply add the total advancing issues from the previous five trading days?

Yes, so 6,500 would be an average of like 1,300 a day. It is another way of judging market internals in terms of whether the whole universe of stocks on the NYSE is going up or just a select few.

The 5 day advancing issues oscillator is obviously a shorterm indicator. What is a suitable application?

I will give you one way of using it which actually ties in with the 189 market day cycle. This little interesting technique is not my idea originally. It comes from *"Investing for Profit with Torque Analysis"* by William C. Garrett. In fact, I got part of my idea for the CI/NCI ratio from Garrett and I like to give attribution when something like that happens. Garrett took the five day total of advancing issues and charted it on a piece of paper on top of the five day total of advancing issues from 189 days back. You could do it in different colors or one of them could be a line and the other one a dash—anything to distinguish them. His reasoning was that when the current five days of advances are above the five days of advances from 189 days ago, the market should be in a positive configuration. I think you stretch it a little to call it a buy signal. I have wanted to go back and test this out as some kind of system to use, although I am sure it would give several whipsaws because sometimes it will just go above and below and above and below over a very short period of time. Let's say you took the last 189 days of advances, like the CI, and kept a moving average or a moving total of that. There is no way that the CI could move up unless this most recent period is above that period from 189 days ago. Carrying that one step further, if the market is going up, chances are the CI is going up too. Garrett just used it as a positive/negative confirming indicator. It is kind of input and output from 189 days ago compared with the current five day total. If the current one is above the one of 189 days ago, then you can assume that the 189 day one is going up. That is basically the way he used it and it has been very helpful to me a lot of times. That is one of the indicators I chart by hand and look at every day. If we are below where we were 189 days ago, generally the market is not in a situation where it can have a meaningful rally and vice versa. If it is well above where we were 189 days ago, then chances are we are not going to have a significant decline until we get into a position to move either below or be below the total from 189 days ago. So that is one of the ways that the 5 day advancing issues is used.

As you said, a computer would be required to generate this data.

No question about it. It would be very painstaking if you didn't have one.

Is there a way readers could construct something similar to the CI/NCI ratio?

The formula for it is very simple and it is not proprietary. I am happy to give it to people but it is something you would not want to do unless you had a computer and a spreadsheet. You simply add up the last 189 days of advancing issues on the NYSE and divide that number by 189. The moving average itself would be the cycle indicator or what I call the CI. I use 189 days because that allows for holidays and that is as close as you come to 39 weeks. In order to get the NCI, or neutral cycle indicator, you add the last 189 days of advances and the last 189 days of declines. Adding those two together and dividing by two gives you the neutral reading or NCI. To get the CI/NCI ratio, you divide the cycle indicator number (CI) by the neutral cycle indicator number (NCI).

For theoretical purposes, let's say someone jumps in and starts tracking the CI/NCI index during a week when the market experiences a series of overbought or oversold days which will produce extreme levels in the daily advance or decline figures. Over a period of time, will this distort the ratio?

No, it won't distort it at all. It doesn't make any difference when you start as long as you gather or have gathered 189 prior days worth of data. Nowadays, most people have access to computer data bases and they can just download the information from the prior 189 days. I would certainly encourage them to go back a lot further than that so that they have some kind of feel for the history of the indicator and how it moved in different historic periods.

Can we talk about your work with speed resistance lines?

They are quite interesting and I still use them. You should give attribution to Edson Gould because I think he is the one that invented them. You can use them on any chart at all, a daily chart, a weekly chart, and in fact, I was using speed resistance today on tick charts and they really work quite well. You can use any bottom and any top. Now obviously the more important the bottoms and tops you use the more significant the lines will be. For example, let's say we are looking at a Dow chart from 1982 into the present. There are a lot of bottoms you could use measuring up to the tops. One of them would be the 1982 low. The others would be the 1984 low, the 1987 low after the crash, and the 1990 low. All those bottoms are legitimate points to work the speed resistance lines from. The shorter term they are, the less significant they are and the less information they will give you once they are broken.

How do you construct speed resistance lines?

You draw horizontal lines off both the low and the high. Looking at the chart, you would draw a horizontal line at the 627.46 low, and a horizontal line at 958.12. Then draw a vertical line from 958.12 all the way down to the bottom line at 627.46. You are attempting to measure the complete distance from bottom to top and that is why you have that dashed line. The top is 958.12 and the bottom is 627.46 so you subtract the smaller from the larger and that tells you how large a move it has been. In this case it is 330.66. Now we want to break that into thirds. We divide the 330.66 by three which equals 110.22. Now divide that vertical line coming down from 958.12 to 627.46 line into exact thirds. Those broad horizontal lines mark those exact levels. So if you subtract 110.22 from 958.12 you should get 847.90. Then you would add that same number, 110.22 to the low of 627.46 and you would put little crosshatches on that rising dashed line. Those two little crosshatches would tell you where your line should come through from the bottom. So then you go back to the bottom at 627.46 and draw a line through those crosshatches. The steeper of the two, the one that is moving up the fastest, is the 2/3 speed resistance line. The less steep of the two, the one that goes toward the 790.67 low in November of 1971, is the 1/3 speed resistance line. Now the general rule is once the 2/3 is broken, it should move down to the 1/3. Notice a couple of interesting things happened which are typical. See how you broke the 2/3 line pretty decisively. You rallied right back up to it but couldn't get above the trendline again and then when you turned around you came very quickly down to the 1/3 speed resistance line. It held there and that was a very important low. From there we advanced almost 300 points. Looking at the other example with the speed resistance lines coming down, you measure from 1067.20 which was the high in January of 1973 to that first low that was made at 845.50. Draw a horizontal line at 1067.20 and a vertical line up from the 845.50. Now that line defines the decline in points so in this case it would be 1067.20 minus 845.50 so that is 221.70 points. You divide that by three and it gives you 73.90. That vertical line coming down should be divided into three equal segments of 73.90 points apiece. If you take 73.90 points and subtract that from 1067.20 you come up with 993.30. That is where the little crosshatch is made and that is the 1/3 speed resistance line. Then if you add 73.90 to the low of 845.50, that gives you 919.40 and that will be where the second speed resistance line intersects. Then you draw your speed resistance lines through the point at 919.40 and 993.30. Now mind you, if we had continued down after a couple of weeks of rally, your speed resistance lines would change. Once you go to a lower low then you base the lines on that new low that is has made.

So in other words, you could have drawn new speed resistance lines when the market tried to rally to 1,000 and then fell back to 780?

Absolutely, you could do the same thing all over again. The other thing to notice about speed resistance lines is, unlike trendlines, prices will often move above or below the line but not decisively. Notice the move after the market went from 1067 down to 845.50 and had that big rally up to about 1,000 again. One of those weeks we closed above the speed resistance line. If you had looked at the market at the end of that week you might have said, "Well, we broke above it. That is very bullish. That means we are going back to the old high." One of the guidelines to use is that in order to have what you might call a convincing break you should probably have the whole bar for that period—whether it be a daily, weekly, or monthly—completely above the speed resistance line. Notice that this didn't happen when it broke through. In the rally up to the 997.59 level, we closed pretty well above the speed resistance line but notice that the complete line for that week still showed the lower part of the line below the speed resistance line. Even the next week the market went a little bit higher at the beginning but then came down very quickly and closed beneath the speed resistance line. So you never had a full week that was completely above the line. That is not a magic rule but it is a guideline to use. If you do have a complete week above the speed resistance line, then you have had what I would call a convincing move and the implications would be that the market should go back to the old high.

The period of time that we are looking at here is 12 months. Would you advise anyone measuring a longer period of time to draw several sets of speed resistance lines?

It depends on where you are in the overall picture. We can do a little exercise together. If I were to look at this whole chart I would say the lowest point on the chart was at 627.46 and the highest point at 1067.20. We'll do a speed resistance between those two. Draw a horizontal line through the low of 627.46. Now you want to draw a vertical line directly under the bar at 1067.20 coming down to the horizontal line at 627.46. We want to break that vertical line into three equal parts. The complete distance between those two points is 439.74. We divide it by three and that comes to 146.58. Add 146.58 to 627.46 and that gives us 774.04. Make a little crosshatch there and draw the 1/3 speed resistance line from the 627.46 bottom to the vertical line. The first time down it held there, went above it, came down again, held and went above it and now just at the end of this chart it is down below it and sitting there. We don't know by looking at the chart which way the market goes but it looks like it has broken rather decisively below in that one week although mind you there was one week in between there where it was completely below the line. Counting from right to left at the end of the chart, notice how the 15th bar is completely below the speed resistance line. After the general rule I just gave, you would say, "Wait a minute, this looks like a convincing break." So that one week was a complete week below but first of all, notice that we closed right near the high on that week too. In a situation like that you would say, "Let me see what happens next week." Very quickly the next week you climbed back above the line again and you stayed above there about 12 weeks. The 13th week you broke below and the next week was also completely below the line. The implication is that the market should go lower. I'm looking at another Dow chart. After that, there was another rally for about one to two weeks and then we went straight down to below 600. So we not only broke that low on the left hand side of the chart but we broke it pretty decisively. The Dow went down another 30 or 40 points which at those levels is another 7% to 8%. To draw the 2/3 speed resistance line, subtract 146.58 from the high of 1067.20 which is 920.62. Something interesting happens when you draw that one in. The 2/3 speed resistance line is almost a shadow of the prior 1/3 speed resistance line. This happens quite often. From a high of 1067.20 the Dow fell, held on there for a few weeks, broke pretty

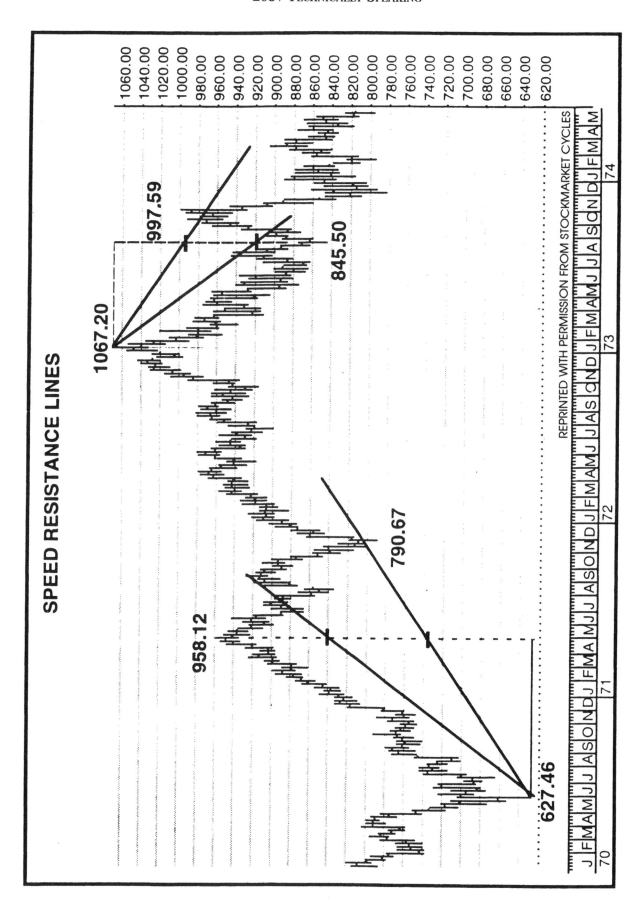

SPEED RESISTANCE LINES

1067.20

997.59

958.12

845.50

790.67

627.46

convincingly and almost came down to the 1/3 but didn't. Then we attempted to come back to the 2/3 resistance line again with the rally up to 997.59. The point that I am making here is that on the first decline from 1067.20, we tried to hold on that line for 3 or 4 weeks and then it broke down and almost got down the lower speed resistance line but didn't quite make it. It looks like it misses it by 20 or 30 points, then has the big rally up to 997.59 which just happens to be underneath this 2/3 speed resistance line. So you had two things going on with speed resistance line analysis. You had come up to the top of the declining 1/3 speed resistance line and you had come up right underneath the 2/3 speed resistance line from the 627 bottom. So you knew that there was a lot of resistance in that area. As it turned out, you turned down, and down you went to the 1/3 line. So you see how breaking the longer term speed resistance lines is even more important than breaking the shorter term ones. Now, what I haven't experimented with are the real longterm charts. Say if you go back to the 1932 low and the high in 1973. In those cases I don't know whether you are better off using logarithmic chart or an arithmetic one but it would interesting to look at those. If you are going to do really longterm work, I would put in a proviso and say that for charts over a 20 to 40 year period, you best use both the arithmetic and the logarithmic, and see which one works better.

Is it feasible to use speed resistance lines for price projections?

You can use them for price projection to a certain degree if you follow the general rules. The general rules are that once the steeper of the two lines, the 2/3 speed resistance line, is broken then the projection would be for you to decline or advance, depending on whether you are using declining or advancing speed resistance lines, to the next line, which is the 1/3 speed resistance line. Now, that line is moving so it would be a dynamic projection. Once the 1/3 line is broken, the presumption is that you are going to go all the way back to the original low from which you measured the lines. In that respect you have a projection but because the line is moving, that projection changes from day to day. When the market came down from 958.12, it broke the 2/3 speed resistance line. At the time you broke the 2/3 speed resistance line, the 1/3 speed resistance line was at the 760 level. By the time the market touched the 1/3 speed resistance line, the Dow was closer to 790 or 800. So, you could have projected that you would come down to that line; unfortunately, you don't know when that line will be touched. Without both time and price it is hard to make a price projection. You can use this technique on closing price charts too. When you have really climatic days like we had on July 16th where the Dow was down almost 180 points and actually closed up for the day, do you use the low that day or do you use the close? If you are looking at a closing chart, in order to get a signal you would have to close above or below the speed resistance line. On intraday charts theoretically all you have to do is get above or below it although I would allow for being completely above or below the line before you consider a signal having been given.

Just to clarify what you said, if someone is using a chart with just closing prices then they should draw the speed resistance lines on the close and if they are using a daily high-low chart, they should use the intraday low or high.

Exactly.

Is there a particular advantage cycle analysis has over pure technical analysis?

Oh yes. I would like to consider that the work I do has a very major advantage, especially the price projection work in terms of time and prices. The big advantage you have in cycles is that you can anticipate tops and bottoms in the market. Now a lot of people will say, "Don't anticipate the market, let it tell you what it's going to do." I prefer to have a ballpark figure for either a time or price and if it is both, all the better. To give you an example, in July 1996, on a closing basis from a closing price chart, I had downside projections on the Dow somewhere around the 5350 level, give or take 30 or 40 points. We were in the RYDEX fund to take advantage of the downmove. The Dow got down there initially on July 15th and then we had that real climactic day the next day but then we came down and closed slightly lower on the 23rd and that is when we got out of the RYDEX mutual fund. I think there is very little on a technical basis that would have had people getting out of short positions on that day because you had no indication of a turn. You did have an indication on July 16th with that climactic day but then a week later, on the 23rd when that low was tested, there were not too many indicators that could tell you that this was an important shorterm bottom. With the cycles, whether you are using the time projections or the price projections, you know what your parameters are. You can say, this is right in the projection territory either timewise or pricewise so we should take a position on the long side here, get out of short positions, or reverse from short to long. With the price projections, you know where you are going to be wrong. If you have a projection that calls for that being the maximum downside plus or minus 30 points and then if you go down another 30 points on a closing basis, you are out of your position. A technician might have been able to look at a chart, maybe the RSI, stochastics or some shorterm indicator and say, "Wait a minute, we closed lower on the Dow on the 23rd than we did on the 16th so we have some potential divergence here." A technician always has to be careful with potential divergences because until they actually start moving in the other direction, you don't have a confirmation that a divergence is going to work out in your favor. For example, the Welles Wilder technique of using the RSI is not just to have a positive divergence, but to see the RSI get above the peak in between the two bottoms after that positive divergence The bottom line is that you really need to see prices move back up again off of what is an apparent low in order to confirm the fact that it was a bottom. That is where most technicians will take a position but you have already given up a few percentage points from the bottom waiting for that confirmation. Cycles, I maintain, give you the benefit of being able to actually attempt to pick the tops and bottoms. You are not always going to be successful but if you attempt to do that then you stand a far better chance in the long run because it gives you an advantage over the other technicians who have to wait for confirmation.

How many months or years would you say it took to develop a system that yielded profits on a regular basis?

I can't give you a time. I still believe along with everything else in life, the analytical work or any kind of work occurs in cycles too. That is one of the reasons you see all these bright lights in the stock market firmament; people who were very hot for a while all of a sudden get on the wrong track and stay on that track longer than they should. I think the important thing is we are learning lessons all the time and I have certainly learned some in the last two or three years because I have been almost steadfastly bearish in a time period that has been very bullish for the market. That has taught me the importance of flexibility. Probably one of the best markets that I call on a basis year in and year out is the gold market and that is because I have no emotional involvement with it. I haven't stuck my neck out and said, "I feel confident that this is going to happen or that is going to happen." I just look at the gold chart every day and do my projection work on it and then tell people what I see happening. I have no ax to grind. I don't care whether it goes up or down. Unfortunately with the stock market, when you get yourself into a place where you do have an ax to grind, that is when you start running into trouble. In retrospect, sometimes you will attempt to mold things into the way that you want them to turn out rather than being as objective as you possibly can in terms of your analysis.

Bob Gabele

214/ T<small>ECHNICALLY</small> S<small>PEAKING</small>

Bob Gabele was a stockbroker for seven years before calling it quits in 1982. While his brokerage career had been rewarding, it was less than emotionally satisfying. Following the call to establish a service which would provide useful financial information, he explored various avenues before settling on analyzing the buying and selling activities of corporate insiders. Thanks to the influence of two veteran insider analysts, this was an area he had passing familiarity with and one that made intuitive sense and appealed to his interest in human behavior. Through hard work and dedication to his goals, Mr. Gabele has distinguished himself as an authority on analyzing and interpreting corporate insider trading.

Perry Wysong and his partner Larry Unterbrink had served as mentors to Mr. Gabele early on and inspired him to follow in their footsteps. Recognized as a pioneer analyst in the field of insider trading and publisher of *The Consensus of Insiders* newsletter, Mr. Wysong had considerable experience analyzing insider transactions and willingly shared the mechanics of insider trading and methods of interpretation with Mr. Gabele. In 1983, Mr. Gabele founded the Investnet Group, a business which specializes in researching and analyzing insider stock transactions. Though the two businesses were separate, Mr. Wysong and Mr. Gabele continued their previous relationship which remained mutually beneficial. In exchange for the headstart, Mr. Gabele helped Mr. Wysong modernize his antiquated system for retrieving insider data. In the late 1970's, the only published source of insider transactions was a monthly government publication entitled "The Official Summary of Insider Transactions and Holdings." Waiting for these reports from one month to the next was nothing short of inefficient. Faster acquisition of data was needed so in 1983, Mr. Gabele "camped out" at the SEC headquarters in Washington, D.C., collecting daily insider filings as they were released, building a data base which he later shared with his mentors.

The analysis of insider activity is anything but surface deep and extends beyond a cursory review of purchases and sales. Attempts are made to screen every tidbit of data looking for consistent patterns of action. This "Sherlock Holmes" of insider trading probes deeply into the past and present investigating the "who, what, why, when, and how" of each and every insider transaction, looking for clues which might reveal an insider's ulterior motive for buying or selling. An additional benefit of insider analysis, one that is based on many years of observation, is the ability to use insider activity within a given industry to forecast future economic conditions.

Acquired in 1992 by CDA, the Investnet Group was subsequently renamed CDA/Investnet. Services range from comprehensive consulting to a weekly newsletter called *The Insiders' Chronicle*. For mavericks who wish to draw their own conclusions, access to insider data can be obtained from CDA/Investnet via the Internet. The company's subscriber constituency consists of money managers, stock brokers, individual investors and over 150 newspapers. Fielding questions from the financial press, analysts, and money managers consumes a great deal of Mr. Gabele's time. CDA/Investnet's service has been singled out as a provider of insider data to *Daily Graphs*, *Barron's*, and the *Wall Street Journal*.

Adhering to his early motto, "Don't compete, create," Mr. Gabele maintains a leading edge over his competitors because he searches constantly for innovative ways to monitor and interpret insider data.

For those who feel the inclination to blindly follow the lead of insiders, Mr. Gabele issues a few caveats which warn of potential pitfalls.

Why don't we start with some preliminary rules and regulations governing insider trading.

The Investment Act of 1934 mandated that insiders need to file evidence of their transaction activity or changes in ownership through a filing at the Securities and Exchange Commission (SEC). When I say transaction activity, I mean any change in holdings, not just purchases and sales. The filing is called a Form 4. An insider would be an executive officer, director, or anyone who owns 10% or more of a class of equities. Now be careful, because the minute I say 10% or more, people think this means the officer or director needs to own the 10% or more before they are considered an insider. That is not how the rule works. If you are a director or an officer, even if you hold no shares, you have to enter the SEC filing system by filing a Form 3. That is called the initial statement of ownership and tells the world that you are now a filing insider. Any changes from that initial statement would need to show up on a Form 4. Insiders have to file by the 10th of the month following any trade. Today is September 27th. If an insider bought on September 1st, their deadline for filing is October 10th. You have to file by the 10th of the month "*following*" your trade, so the largest period of time that insiders could stretch it before their filing has to hit the SEC would be from the first of one month until the 10th of the following month.

Will insiders typically wait the maximum time period to file?

When they are selling, they typically wait. When they are buying, they frequently file right away because they want everybody to see that they are buying as early as possible.

Where do stock options fit into the overall picture?

Let me tell you what has happened. Under the old rules, insiders had to show when they acquired stock or sold stock through the exercise of an option. The old rules did not require that the insiders disclose to the public their option grants or their option holdings. They did have to disclose to the public when they exercised options, but there was no way of telling how many options they still held after the exercise. In 1991, the SEC revised Section 16 of the Investment Act of 1934. One of the rules they changed was that insiders had to start filing evidence of their option grants and providing to investors what type of option holdings they held. In the pre-1991 era, you would have insiders exercising options and selling all their stock and yet still holding maybe millions of options which never showed up in the filings. The public never had any way of knowing about an insider's option holdings. Now, we not only know how many options they have but when they are exercisable as well. We also know when their options expire which helps us better understand their motives for exercising at times. The other thing that changed in 1991 was the fact that the SEC made a very subtle change in the designation of "executive officer." In the old days, they just said officers and directors had to file. In 1991, the SEC started saying that executive officers and "those in charge of policy making function" have to start filing. That was initially an attempt to refine the filing population but I think it broadened it a bit, because we have started seeing a lot more lab directors of biotech companies and people like that filing whereas we didn't have that before.

Does that skew the insider data?

Not at all because many times your most significant trades are not those of the most visible insiders. Sometimes your more subtle trades can be your most significant ones.

So at present, insiders legally have to disclose how many stock options they hold?

We now know what they hold in the form of options. Given the fact that so many insiders hold large option positions these days, I think it is significant for investors to know this in addition to how many shares are held by the insiders.

Perhaps we should stop and define the term "stock option."

These are not put and call options. These are incentive type stock options where, in addition to their regular compensation in terms of salary, insiders are granted options to purchase their company's stock, usually at a discount. Stock options provide some management incentive to increase the value of the stock plus sort of locks them in because options are usually not immediately exercisable. They usually have a vesting schedule attached to them which causes the insider to stick around for multiple years before exercising the options.

What is the typical vesting period?

It used to be about ten years and now we are seeing many five year programs being implemented.

After the options have been granted, when can an insider begin exercising?

Typically, in any option grant program, the most common waiting period before an insider can begin to exercise any of their options is usually a year, but not in every case.

In your analysis, don't you make the distinction between options that are in-the-money and options which are out-of-the-money?

That is a thing we watch very closely. When insiders are granted options they are typically out-of-the-money or at least close-to-the-money. Let's say I have a stock at $20.00 and I am granted options at $20.00. At $20.00, there is not much worth, but, if the stock were to go to $30.00, those options that were granted at $20.00 are now worth $10.00 per share. Typically, when an insider is granted options, the options exercise price or the strike price will be close to market value. The incentive there is, of course, for the insiders to work hard to get the share value up so their options are worth something. Now, I do make a distinction between insiders *holding* in-the-money options and out-of-the-money options. If all my options were close to market price, then there is not much risk sitting on those options. But if most of my options were for prices substantially lower than today's market price, then by not exercising those options, I am accepting market risk by sitting on them.

When you are analyzing insiders who hold in-the-money options, would you look at the market value of those options or would you look at the quantity they are holding?

I define options as a piece of an insider's holdings. When I define insider's holdings, I look at common stock plus options. I want to see what direction those insider's holdings are moving in. Are they going up or down? Are the insiders in a particular company trimming their holdings? Holding on to many options that are in-the-money is an indication that even though they haven't bought a lot of stock recently, insiders have a good stake in the company and they are accepting market risk. In other words, they don't necessarily think that stock is going to move lower in the near to intermediate term. If their holdings, as I define them, are dropping in either the area of common stock or options, and if it is happening more than in past years, then I am going to keep a closer eye on the situation.

Do you make the distinction between insiders holding in-the-money options and insiders making outright purchases?

Yes, I certainly will make the distinction. There are differences. But what I am saying is there are times when we learn from an insider's inactivity as much as we will learn from their activity. You are going to miss a lot of positive signals if you always look for insiders to buy because in many companies, insiders just don't buy. They don't buy because they hold so many options. I can tell you it's a fact—in some companies you will never get a buy signal if all you are looking for are insider purchases. For example, in June 1996, I pointed out in Insiders' Chronicle that even though Intel's share price was at a new all-time high, insiders were holding on tightly to both their shares *and* their options. Although there had been some selling by insiders in April, the numbers looked light compared to the typical levels of insider selling seen in past years. Our numbers showed that for 1984 through 1995, Intel insider selling averaged (split-adjusted) 970,970 shares for the period of January through May. For that same period in 1996, insiders had sold only 122,980 shares. Even more impressive was their propensity to hold not only stock, but in-the-money options as well, especially with the stock trading at historically high levels. This was a good clue that Intel insiders felt comfortable taking on market risk at that time. From their gestures, we inferred that there was a better chance the shares would head higher instead of lower. From June until December, the stock doubled in price. This is why looking at the options is an essential part of the analysis process.

What are the most common reasons for insider purchases and sales?

If asked why they are selling, most insiders will give you one of the following reasons—diversifying holdings, building a house, tax planning- those are the most commonly stated reasons for selling. When asked, insiders will never tell you specifically why they are selling. It is not reasonable to expect an answer that's precise nor will you get one. It has always been commonly assumed that insiders buy for one motive and that would be for profit. When we started working with the data back in 1983, it was fairly evident that there was another reason for insiders to buy and that would be an initial stock purchase by a new director who had just come on board. Lately, we have been faced with new challenges on the buy side, that is, other causes for insider buying activity. Certainly encouragement from the companies themselves cause insiders to buy shares. In some cases, companies are even loaning the insiders money to buy stock. You have to be very careful when analyzing insider buying to make sure that you are not falling into an orchestrated situation.

Corporations actually loan insiders money to buy stock. Does that aspect of the transaction become public knowledge?

It is not stated knowledge in the filings, although it should be. We have to do a lot more digging to understand which situation may fall into this camp. It tends to make me look for subtleties in the data as opposed to the obvious buying situations, where I suddenly see that 15 insiders have bought all at once, all near the same price. That "can" mean an orchestrated type situation where insiders maybe are being encouraged by the company to buy stock. Insiders have become much more cognizant of the public's perceptions of their actions. You have to be a lot more careful these days when analyzing the data.

Then you can no longer look at insider buying as a vote of confidence in their company?

You can, but you need to know what to look for. You should never simply look at an insider buy and blindly assume it was a vote of confidence nor should you ever look at an insider selling and assume the worst. Never! Interpreting insider actions has always taken a lot more work than the neophyte may assume. When I analyze insider buying, the first thing I want to do is put it into perspective. I want to see the track record of the acting insiders. For instance, there was a situation where insiders in a particular company were buying. The chairman was buying $50,000 worth of stock and three other executives were buying during the same period, spending between $15,000 and $30,000 apiece. They were buying shares, in the $30 range, that had dropped from the $40 level (where they had been six months prior). On the surface this buying looked good. When I looked at the insiders' past records, however, a different picture emerged. They all were very big sellers near the highs six months prior: The chairman had gotten out of over $4 million worth of stock. The other three had acted similarly as well. Once I saw this, I realized that these insiders were painting the tape. They were trying to instill confidence, hoping investors would follow their lead. The stock did, in fact move, but lower. It is trading in the low-to-mid $20's today. This is a good example why you need to look at the historical patterns of the insiders involved in order to put their most recent activity into perspective.

Which is a very time consuming process.

You need data bases to do this. Those who feel that they have the whole picture by looking at one transaction are very much short changing themselves. You rarely see the entire picture by looking at one trade or one set of trades that occurred in one given month. You need to understand what insiders at a particular company have been doing over time. We always look at who is acting at the time to see how today's actions stack up to their actions of the past. I would stress another thing here—always compare a company's insider to that company. Don't compare Apple Computer insiders to Compaq Computer insiders. Two different corporate cultures and insiders are involved.

Realistically, how far back would you have to look to spot a buying or selling pattern?

It depends on how old the company is. Some companies have long track records and some companies are very new. It is difficult to assume a great amount of significance in insider transactions in a company that has just recently gone public because you don't have a lot of track record to go by. The only track record you may have in a brand new company would be the individual track records of the insiders involved. In other words, if some of the insiders in that company have had affiliations with multiple boards over time, you can assess their track records by looking at their activities in the other companies that they have been involved in. Then you may be able to make some reasonable assumptions with regard to track records. But if you don't have any past history, it's very dicey. With new companies you have to be more patient and you really don't necessarily want to assume as much significance in any insider picture as you would into a company that is more seasoned. So typically, I would like to go back as far as I can. If I am looking at a Coca-Cola or a Pepsi or something like that, I am going to look as far back as my records go in order to understand if the current activity represents a true anomaly.

I can understand how it would be difficult to interpret insider maneuvers on an initial public offering (IPO) but what about companies that have been around for a year or so? For example, Netscape has been public a little over one year and one insider just recently sold 2.4 million shares of stock. Is that a significant move?

In new companies, we do watch the rate of increase or decline in the insider's holdings. In a fairly new company, if in a one to three year period insiders have managed to sell-off 30% or more of their holdings, I will be monitoring the situation. Netscape is not one of those. I do watch the rate of decline in their holdings.

IPO's and relatively new companies grab your attention if and when an insider unloads at least 30% of their holdings.

If they are dropping large percentages of their holdings, I am watching the situation very closely. I am just throwing out 30%. I have seen the numbers coming out as high as 90%. These are insiders who are dramatically trimming their holdings. Netscape is catching our eye a little bit more but that goes into another reason. All insider activity is relative. Any activity that's going on is relative to where a stock has been in the past. It is relative to what the insiders have done in the past. The selling by Netscape insiders stood out a bit in July 1996, because that was a period where not many insiders in the technology area were selling their shares, especially shares that had gotten as low as Netscape. Insiders were willing to let quite a few Netscape shares go in July at very low prices relative to where the stock had been. In August, the selling really revved up and still at prices well off the highs. Granted, there is not a lot of historical track record in the Netscape situation but their willingness to sell at lower prices well off the highs is at least a clue. Is it a huge red light? No, but it is something that investors should know about because this is a very new company and a new industry and people are trying to get valuation clues. Is it fair to assume that the insiders at Netscape have a good clue of their company's valuation in the stock market? No. Is it fair to read into the fact that because they are selling at lower prices than where the stock was a few months earlier that the price may not move back to the old prices? Maybe. I thought the sales at Netscape were somewhat noteworthy although not as significant as they would be had the company had a longer track record.

Those 2.4 million shares represented 14% of the insider's total holdings. That seemed like a pretty good chunk.

It's fairly typical to see insiders selling in a company that is fairly new. You have to expect it. For the investors who are new at this, they should realize that when the entrepreneurs who start these companies are finally able take them public, there is still a window of time within which they can't sell their stock. A lot of sweat equity went into these shares. When that window finally opens, you are going to see stock sold and don't get shook when you see it. A 14% holdings drop is not unusual in these instances.

If you saw one insider of an established company selling 30% of his holdings, would that be a red flag?

Chances are you wouldn't see that. Let me tell you how complex this gets. If that 30% drop in holdings is related to a person leaving the company, it's not significant. This is why I started out saying this is not as easy as looking at an insider buy and saying, "This stock is a buy." You have to ask a lot of questions in each situation. One of the first questions to ask is, "Is this person leaving?" Once you can identify that the person is not leaving, then you can take it further. Certainly in a Pepsi or a Coca Cola, if only one person is dropping 30% of their shares and that person is not leaving the company, it still could be for personal financial reasons. I am looking for situations where multiple people are dropping signficant chunks....and they are not leaving the company.

Can you give us a specific example detailing what you would look for?

One that we had been watching was Value Jet. The stock was already cheap when in September 1996, in classic sell-on-the-news fashion, five insiders dropped over 1.9 million shares into the bounce which occurred when the company announced it had received FAA's approval for its jets to fly again (after the Florida crash). Some of the selling insiders were dumping as much as 40% to 60% of their holdings in the $12 range. These prices were way down from the 1996 highs in the $35 range.

Had this distribution taken place over an extended period of time?

Yes, insiders had been selling Value Jet shares before that September period. Interestingly enough, they sold later as well.... and at lower prices. The shares dropped from the $12 range to the $7 to $8 area and they continued selling in December of 1996. This kind of action does not set our expectations very high for a return to higher prices soon at this company.

Do you compare insider selling within similar industries or sectors? For example, previously you said Netscape insiders were selling when few other insiders of technology companies were selling.

In July 1996, when the technology stocks got hit so hard, there was very little insider selling in the technology group. During a period like that, when you have such a storm going on in the market, the companies whose insiders did sell stood out. Value Jet did get a little more attention from us especially because the price of those shares were significantly down like the Netscape shares were. Netscape shares had fallen from their highs in the $86.00 dollar range and had rallied back to $75.00 by May of 1996. In the July period, there were quite a bit of insider sales in the 40's and that was well off the highs. The window had been open since February 1996 for Netscape insiders to sell. It wasn't like the window suddenly opened and they decided they were going to sell. In that particular period, given the fact that the tech stocks in general were getting hit so hard, I was looking at the relative situation. Insiders were not selling many tech shares at the time. Those corporate insiders that were selling during that market downdraft certainly stood out.

Though you were speaking about Netscape, you said that selling may not reflect an insider's view regarding the fundamental picture of the company. Why not?

Remember, Netscape was too new a company to read a lot into insider action. In other words, there are times when you really want to weigh the insider activity rather heavily. There are other times that you certainly want to pay attention to the insider activity but maybe not weigh it as much as you would in other situations. Netscape would be one of the second conditions. You want to pay attention to the selling you see in Netscape now, but I don't think you could weigh it as heavily as if it was a more seasoned company.

How long does a publicly traded company have to exist before the insider data can be meaningfully interpreted?

There is no magic number of years. As each year passes, we are going to see more and more data related to a particular company. For instance, in Netscape, we will see more and more insider activity and we will learn more about their behavior relative to how the stock is acting, relative to how the industry is acting, and relative to how the market is acting. As we go down the time line, we will gain more confidence in our ability to understand the data in that company.

What considerations should be given to the number of shares transacted versus the actual monetary value of the insider sale or purchase?

It's hard to ignore the dollar amount being moved around. Certainly, when somebody is putting up $300,000 or $500,000 to buy stock, it does and should get out attention. In some cases, I have to believe that the smaller buys can mean just as much. Let me say that I wouldn't want to base a decision on just one insider's action, even if that person did buy a lot of stock. Large dollar purchases, if they are surrounded by smaller dollar purchases by other insiders, do tend to be more interesting. I don't necessarily mean that all of those purchases have to show up in a week. I am talking about over a 90 day period of time or more. It is interesting when you look at insider transactions in terms of the dollar value. If a person is going to buy some stock, and they are willing to put up one-half million dollars, do you think they would buy before bad news? There is some intuitive logic involved here that says, "Chances are the news window is going to be okay for this company." Nothing works 100% of the time but logic would dictate that if I buy this stock at or around the price that this person paid, I should not get burned by some unexpected negative development, unless that person didn't know about it either. Take a utility stock insider for instance. What is the worst thing that can happen to you as a utility stock buyer? The dividend gets cut unexpectedly.

Now, if the insider has bought half a million dollars of that utility stock, if that insider just happens to be a director, I doubt if he sees any dividend cut coming in the next few quarters. So, yes, in some regards there is a certain amount of attention that should be paid to the large purchases. I think whenever we are talking about insiders or any tool, I think it needs to be said that the small investor or any investor should not base an entire decision just on insiders anyway. This is another tool for that tool box. The insider tool may say "go" but there may be other tools that say "no." That is up to the investor to figure out. We certainly get different clues from the insiders. Sometimes they are very strong, sometimes they are very subtle, but at all times, they are simply another tool to be using. Going back to the utility example, in that kind of situation where you have a group with relatively low volatility such as the utility stocks, a large insider purchase may mean a whole different thing than insider purchases in a volatile technology stock. Let's say the chairman of a technology company had made thirty million dollars by selling his shares near the highs in 1995. Then in July of 1996, when the market got hit hard, he stepped up and bought maybe one million dollars worth of stock—not an insignificant amount. But investors looking at this should be aware of the fact that the person pulled out thirty million dollars near the highs and put only one million dollars back to work at the lows. Because of the nature of the situation, I don't know if I would weight that one as highly as I would the utility situation. That chairman who pulled out thirty million dollars near the highs may feel an obligation to buy back a little bit of stock at the lows— "I'm chairman. I made a lot of money on this stock. I better buy a little bit more back here because this is the day of the class action suit." In some cases, I think some of these insiders are probably deciding to ante up a few bucks near the lows just because it looks good. I think investors have to be very aware and careful of this.

Regarding insider purchases and sales in general, are you looking at the actual number of shares being bought and sold, the dollar value, and the period of time the transaction occurs in?

It becomes relative to the situation at hand. It goes back to the old simple concept—insiders are acting. Why are they acting? Let's say their stock has just been hammered and they are buying. Why? The stock got cheap and they are bargain hunting. That's a fair reason I guess. Then you ask why has the stock been hammered? There has been some bad news. If it's bad news, what is the magnitude of their buying and how does it relate to their prior selling? You are looking for clues as to whether or not there is more bad news coming. Chances are, large volume buys will not occur near the lows until all the bad news is out. This does not mean the stock will rally right after the buys. In fact, it rarely does. Typically stocks that have been hit, because of the emergence of negative news, need some "healing time" before they are ready to move back up. In these cases, it is especially helpful to see persistent evidence of multiple insiders accumulating while the stock is down. How about buying near the highs, that is, buying on the way up? This is a whole different situation and has a whole different set of assumptions. Averaging up is a very bullish signal. Insiders usually average up because they feel that the stock is going up for a good reason. Some of our most bullish insider clues have come from insiders who have averaged up, over time, as their shares have appreciated in price. The other situation is when the stock is going sideways. Let's say a stock has been going sideways for 6 months, a year, 18 months or whatever and insiders start buying. They weren't buying before. What changed to cause them to want to buy now? You can turn this whole thing around for the sell side. A stock is going up. They want to take profits so they are selling. A stock is going down and they are selling. That could mean something different. It's not a good sign if you see insiders selling near the lows. Certainly if the same insiders who were selling at $40.00 are selling more stock at $30.00 and the stock goes down to $25.00—they are selling at successively lower prices—that is a very bad sign. Same thing applies to stocks going sideways. A stock has been going sideways for 6 months and suddenly insiders surface to sell. What caused that decision? The stock didn't move so you can't use the stock movement as a catalyst for the decision so what caused them to sell? It may have been something that happened internally or something going on in the industry or whatever, but something other than stock price is causing this action. So, you are not looking for any "thing." You are looking at insider action and asking, "What happened?"

Insider trades then have to be examined in context of the situation surrounding the transaction. Does your analysis have a starting point and sequence?

The first thing I do is pull out the charts and see where the stock has been. The second thing I have to do, if the stock has been moving, is to look at the news and see what has made the stock move and then try to understand which insiders are active. Then once I understand the movement in terms of the insiders, then I will look back at their track record to see what they have been up to. In other words, we look for breaks in historical buying or selling patterns, keeping in mind at all times the events surrounding the issue and stock price movement. For example, in November 1994, Intel experienced some problems with its new Pentium chip. At the time, we received a lot of calls from people wanting to know what the Intel insiders were doing with their stock in the wake of those problems. After looking at the split adjusted insider sales back to 1984, we found that insider selling looked normal. In fact, 1994 was historically one of the lightest sales years for Intel insiders. Based on the numbers, we found it hard to point to insider activity as evidence that there was a mountain of ice hiding beneath the Pentium "berg." At the time the Pentium trouble surfaced, the stock had been in a $28.00 to $35.00 trading range for over one year. Six months after the incident, the stock was trading around $78.00 per share. So I put together a lot of different pieces to come up with a decision, or at least a reasonable conclusion. These are not necessarily conclusions, it's just informed analysis. There is not one simple thing to look for. The old stock market saying has always been, "once everybody figures out the key, they change the locks." I think insiders are very similar.

Are you saying insiders "change the locks" to conceal their activities?

We have always been on the lookout for situations where insider silence tells a story. There are many companies where, year in and year out, insiders have sold as their share price rises. At times, we catch one of these company's shares going up but insiders have stopped selling. This has been a good signal that they see valid reason for the price rise and choose to hold on for the ride. We have published a number of commentaries along these lines. One day, we saw a company chairman issuing a press release trumpeting the fact that his company insiders were not selling any shares. Okay, this lock has changed for this company...time to find another key. Remember, frequently insiders want you to see, *and interpret*, their actions in a positive way. As the use of insider data has become more popular, it has become increasingly important to retain all objectivity and be as thorough as possible when evaluating this information. You need to do a lot of homework beyond just assuming an insider's action is simply positive or negative.

Is there more detective work?

I want to see what kind of following the stock has on Wall Street. Are analysts increasing or decreasing their estimates? We will look at situations where a stock has been doing nothing for a long time and notice that the Wall Street following is very low. They are down to just a couple of analysts following the stock and the estimates that are available are not very positive. The stock has been going sideways, yet insider buying has been picking up. This could be a signal that the news out of this company is going to get better. I can't tell you when the stock is going to move, but I can tell you that I think that the risks of that stock going lower are fairly low because Wall Street does not have a lot of expectation built into the stock. Insider expectations seem to exceed Wall Street's expectations and there may be a positive surprise coming. The converse is where insiders are selling regularly and the shares are going higher and higher and many analysts following the companies are looking for 20% or 30% growth rates. Selling insiders look wrong because the stock is so strong, yet, I get the feeling when I see some of these situations, that Wall Street's expectations may exceed the insider's expectations.

These incongruencies stick out like a sore thumb so to speak.

They become situations we monitor more closely. We dig deeper. The answer doesn't always come up right away. We have to watch over a period of time and try to understand if there are any changes in insider behavior that may affect their stock option holdings.

As a sentiment indicator, many technicians use the insider buy/sell ratio which takes into account the total insider purchases and sales for all publicly traded companies. The theory is that net insider buying is bullish and extreme insider selling is bearish. What are your views on using this indicator alone?

I don't think on an overall basis the insider buy/sell ratio is particularly prescient. There are times when it certainly screams "buy me" like in 1987 and 1990. In 1987, after the market crash, insiders bought stocks so the buy/sell ratio got very bullish. We backtested the buy/sell ratio and didn't find elegant correlation between it and market swings over the intermediate term. We use it in the newsletter to let people know what the overall picture looks like, but we usually warn them that we are not trying to time the market. Over a period of time, if I see insiders selling progressively more stock and the trend has been sustaining itself over an extended period of time, then I think that should be known, but it is very difficult to try to put a timing element into the market just based on this.

What are the parameters of the ratio?

Historically, the buy/sell has been 2:1 sells to buy. Anything above the 2.00 level would be bearish and anything below that would be on the bullish side. That is sort of the benchmark that a lot of people use.

In general, when many insiders from multiple corporations buy their stock, is it an indication of an oversold market or bullish outlook?

I think overall buying can indicate situations that a market has suddenly become oversold, just like we had in July 1996. There was quite a bit of insider buying then. Is that a bullish signal or is that a signal that the market is just very oversold? When the buying surfaced in July we weren't too surprised; I mean, the market had come down so far. To really get a bullish signal, you would want to wait and see if what we saw in July extended itself into a two to three month period of time like we saw back in 1994. That kind of buying in 1994 in a lot of big capitalization stocks was more of a signal to us, over time, that the market could be heading higher for the long haul than what we saw in July. Again, on an overall basis, it is very much like what I described earlier. Insiders are buying but the market got real cheap all of a sudden, so, of course they are going to come out and buy something. They are value players. Are the fundamentals in the economy supporting this type of buying? Only time is going to tell you. You can't say that the overall fundamentals in the economy, both macro and micro, have improved to a point where we are going to see a lot higher stock market 12 or 18 months out based on just one month of insider buying. What we saw in 1994, a steady, persistent level of insider buying in high quality companies that lasted on into early 1995, that was a bullish signal because it was a trend that held up over time.

In overall terms, the trend of buying or selling is extremely important.

It is extremely important and I really caution people trying to identify a trend too quickly, especially with this data.

From your perspective, how long is a trend?

The speed of light in insider analysis is 90 days in my opinion so I will start with 90 days. People who jump on a one month deal, fine—you may be right, you may be wrong. I would rather take it slow.

What is your interpretation of simultaneous insider sales and purchases within the same company?

That's a confusing picture. You can get buys and sells for any number of reasons. You can get buys and sells because the sellers are leaving the company and the buyers aren't. I tend to segregate the outsiders, what we call the beneficial owners, from the actual insiders. Generally, however, buys and sells, during the same time frame, show a "neutral" picture.

Who are the beneficial owners?

They are the 10% holders who are not operating as day to day insiders. Sometimes you will see those outsiders, the 10% holders, buying and insiders selling. I tend to discount the ten percenters then because they are not always part of the operations end of the company. They may not know the day to day operations of the company as well as the actual insiders. That would be a time when I segregate the two and say, "Okay, I am going to put more weight on the insiders that are buying than these outsiders who are selling." There will also be times when insiders are just flat out selling and buying at the same time. Now we can really get down to the fine points. There are times when it looks as if insiders are selling and they aren't really. One that comes to mind is Cirrus Logic (CRUS) back in early 1995. At the time,

President Michael Hackworth had sold 10,000 shares at prices just below $15 (split adjusted). The neophyte observer could easily have interpreted this as selling near the lows since the shares had dropped almost 60% before his sale. What he was actually doing, however, was *increasing* his holdings. The month prior to his buy, he had exercised options for 120,000 shares. He had probably sold the 10,000 in order to pay for his optioned-for shares. There were two other insiders exercising options and holding their shares at that time as well. Cirrus shares commenced a rally that didn't stop until they hit $120 later that year.

Is it likely that the portion of shares will be sold at the same time the options are being exercised?

Not necessarily. You asked the question about people buying and selling at the same time. Sometimes I will see situations where it looks like they are selling in the picture but the sellers are actually holding on to more than they are getting rid of and also there are some other insiders buying. That's a good picture even though it looks like there are some sellers on the surface. You need to be aware of what those sellers are doing when they are selling. Are they exercising all their options and then selling all their stock being exercised? That tells you one thing. Are they exercising "X" amount of options and selling maybe 20% of that? That is a different situation. When you have buyers and sellers, sometimes it is just a mixed picture. As I said before, when you have buyers and sellers together, sometimes the sellers are leaving the company. If you go back and check the corporate releases, you can see that the person is leaving. Sometimes the buyers are brand new—they are token purchases. These don't mean much either.

Is it a wash in those cases?

No, not necessarily. If there are buyers and sellers together and nobody is leaving the company and nobody is brand new, then it's a wash. If there are buyers and sellers and the buyers are not token buyers and the sellers are leaving the company, I am going to tend to lean toward the buy side. I may disregard the sells. It is more typical to expect selling from a person who is leaving. If I have buyers and sellers and the buyers are token, first time, new buyers and the sellers are not leaving the company, I am going to disregard the buys and look at the sells. This is not an exact science. There is even one more condition I want to touch on. Sometimes retirees, people who are leaving the company, are buying. They have to check a box in the filing that says they are leaving. If they are buying, that is a good sign. It is very rare but sometimes we see it. I remember a CFO at IBM was leaving the company and had been buying the stock as it moved up in price. The stock had already doubled and was in the 80's or 90's. It appeared to be a relatively high price to pay and yet, he was buying and holding. That looked good and proved, in fact, to be prescient. IBM shares moved much higher and have been as high as $170 since.

It is more bullish for insiders to buy stocks on the way up.

When a stock is moving up, you need to see either insider buying, or at least a lack of significant selling, in order to develop confidence that the stock is not becoming overvalued. I love situations where insiders buy at successively higher prices. This provides solid confirmation that fundamentals are moving up with stock price. There is an important assumption here, however.

What assumption is that?

If you are going to act using insiders as a tool, how much weight you give to those insider actions really depends on whether or not that stock is still at the levels it was when the insiders acted in the first place. I can't tell you how many times I have talked to people who get excited and tell me, "There is insider buying in that stock." Yes, there was insider buying at $13.00. The stock is a $20.00 stock now. The word spreads that insiders are buying but the stock is now up 50% or 60%. Insiders aren't buying now. They were buying then... before the stock's current move. That is why I talked about averaging up. Maybe the insiders bought at 13, 16, and 18. Now the stock is at 20, still within a stone's throw of where the insiders acted. That would be valid. So many times investors get messed up by hearing stories of insider buying or selling but they don't know at what prices. Let's say you are looking for returns in excess of 10%. If the stock has already moved that 10 or 15 percent, what are you looking for? You don't want to be jumping in at $15.00 based on that insider action at $12.00. It's really relative. If you are going to move related to insiders, you have to be moving at or around the prices where insiders acted.

When you see a lot of concerted insider buying or selling within a narrow window of time, can you make any sort of determination as to when their activity might show up in the price of the stock?

We have backtested stock performance after insider's actions. Typically, when a significant insider action occurs, your optimal performance on average will be five or six months out but in many cases it can go out as far as one year. It is not a quick thing. Some people think they have to act fast but it is just not that way.

Have you seen instances where insiders are buying or selling aggressively but their actions not impact the stock price at all?

Sure. Sometimes I have seen insiders aggressively buying and the stock has continued lower in the near term. Their timing is not that great. We look to them for "value" clues.

Do you think insider buying or selling is a better tool for undervaluation or overvaluation respectively rather than a timing tool?

We tend to look at it that way. There are times when it appears that the insider's timing was impeccable. Those are probably lucky situations. For instance, if the stock is coming down sharply, sometimes insiders will be among the first to buy and that can indicate that there may be no further bad news coming but it doesn't necessarily indicate the stock is going to turn around. A good example showed up in September 1996. Insiders bought ITT shares within a two week period after a sharp drop, picking up shares in the $47 to $48 range. After their buys, selling pressure continued which caused the shares to drop even lower. The stock touched $41 per share on a number of occasions and moved essentially sideways, at levels lower than the insider buys, until a bid from Hilton Hotels propelled the shares to as high as $60.

Will there be occasions where insiders will be wrong about their company?

Sure. You have to now be very wary of what the insiders are trying to project with their actions. I think this was always the case. Even Perry Wysong, my mentor in this game who started his newsletter back in 1962, was always wary of the fact that insiders may be trying to let you see what they want you to see. We have always been cautious about that side of the picture.

Does CDA/Investnet supply insider data to either Mansfield or Daily Graphs for use with their stock charts?

Daily Graphs.

If you look at the chart of a big cap company like General Motors or IBM in Daily Graphs, you frequently see insider sell symbols all the way across the bottom of the price chart. At first glance, one might think such intensive selling represented bearishness among the insiders. Should chartists try to decipher anything from this information?

At first glance it can look that way. You have to be aware that in a lot of your larger cap stocks, or a lot of companies whose insiders are compensated via the stock option route, that you are going to see more insider selling in those companies because insiders typically will exercise their stock options and sell the underlying shares. It is part of the compensation package and you have to become aware of it. Once aware of it, you have to understand how to gauge that type of activity. I am not saying I know how to do it in every case. When insiders are regular sellers in your larger cap stocks, the sell signals are much tougher to analyze.

Is it fair to say that the longer a company has been around, the more insider selling you are going to see because of the stock options?

The more mature the company, the more options that are going to be out there so you are going to see more selling. Don't forget we said the historical average for selling is two to one, sells to buy. That alone tells you that there is always a lot more selling than buying. You learn to expect it over time. When you are looking at insider data on the stock charts, you can't say insiders are selling; therefore, it is a sell. That is not how it works. Without filtering out the interference, the signals can be very garbled and unreliable.

Some of your research appears in the Wall Street Journal every Wednesday under "Insider Trading Spotlight" and in *Barron's* every Monday. Do you have any suggestions as to how readers can use these insider disclosures?

To correctly use any of this information that has been reported from us or someone else, it is important for a reader to put that into perspective and understand the situation surrounding it—the bigger picture. In *Barron's* we have included two different views. The first set of tables show the insider transactions that have occurred recently, the percentage change in holdings for the insiders that are acting, and the number of shares traded. The second picture is actually a six month window and I would advise people to keep an eye on that six month window in conjunction with the short window. The best suggestion I can give to anybody on how to use insider information is again, don't look at just the trade. Look at the sector situation, look at the charts on that company, and the news surrounding that company. Then try to assess the insider activity with these other things in mind as well. For instance, Staples had insider selling over the previous six months. If you went to the office supply sector during that period of time, you would have seen rather disappointing insider patterns in a number of the office supply stocks. If you looked at the oil and natural gas companies in 1995, especially the natural gas companies, you would have found a very positive insider picture.

What are the implications of buying or selling by insiders from multiple companies within a particular industry or group?

I look for sector confirmation. Don't fall into the trap of somebody painting the tape on you. Perry Wysong said back in the old days, "When you are looking at insiders you want to make sure you are looking at situations where many insiders are acting." The larger the number of insiders, the better, because that represents more decisions within a company. In other words, don't just act on one person's action. Weigh more heavily those situations where a number of insiders have acted. Now that is a good rule and we certainly adhere to that but the way to get around the risk of getting caught up in some company's orchestration is to follow the sector itself, not just the company. Once an insider's activity passes through some of the filters— the selling is not option related, a number of individuals are buying and they are insiders who don't buy all the time, the news around the company is interesting, the company is fundamentally healthy or not healthy—once you have satisfied all these little clues, and there are so many of them, the next tests that insider buying needs to pass are: "What does the industry look like? Are the insiders active in that industry? Is this the only company in the industry showing insider buying? Are there other companies in the industry showing insider buying? Are the other companies in this industry showing all selling and this is the only company that's buying?" As you dig deeper, you get more information on these things. I love a situation where there are twenty or twenty-five companies in an industry and many of them showing just one small insider buy and no sells—some kind of insider accumulation. When this happens, I may even like some of the companies that show no insider activity.

Zero insider activity is a good sign?

No activity on a sector basis can be a great clue. Let's just say there are twenty companies in, say the oil service industry and we'll say Schlumberger doesn't show insider buying but Schlumberger doesn't show any selling either. Let's say I like Schlumberger. It's a quality company and one of the best companies in the industry. I have insider buying in a number of oil service companies like Baker Hughs and Parker Drilling. I may decide that the water looks fine in the industry and I may want to buy the industry leader, even if it doesn't show insider buying. So, if I were a money manager, I may decide that the insiders are telling me that the oil service industry is a good one right now, therefore, I will pick the best company in that industry. I am not going to necessarily buy the company that insiders are buying. That is where sector activity can lead you to a sector where you may end up buying a company that has no insider activity. Let me take "no insider activity" back down to the individual stock level. Many times, companies will show on average 50 to 60 insider filings in a year. It may be more, it may be less. Once you have determined the average filing level for insiders in a particular company, there may be times when those filings just dry up. You don't see any insider signs at all; no purchases or sales—nothing. These can be situations where the company is in a quiet period for whatever reason and could be very interesting, especially if the stock is going up and insiders are not doing anything. In the past, insiders may have normally sold whenever their stock had gone up but now, nobody is doing anything. They are holding tight. Something very dramatic may be going on.

Meaning positive or negative?

Positive. If the stock is going up and they are not selling at all?

But they are not buying either.

They would be crazy to buy in front of the news I'm talking about. It could be a takeover coming. Don't forget, a lot of these people hold options so the fact that they are not doing anything on the surface doesn't necessarily mean they are not taking on risk because as a stock is rising, those options are becoming deeper and deeper in the money and yet, they are not exercising their options. So the inaction of insiders can lead you to some very positive confirmation signals. A recent rise in a company's stock may be justified for whatever reason. The stock has moved up 30%. What are the insiders thinking? Well, nobody is taking any profits. They are not afraid to hold on. Then if we look at their options, we see that they are sitting on a lot of options too. From the behavior of the insiders, they agree with what's going on with the price. We think this is a green light. That is a very classic way to look at insiders in terms of what they are thinking. That "inaction" part of the theory is something that we watch very closely.

Sector analysis does seem to have some safeguards.

The beautiful part of the sector analysis is that it is virtually impossible to orchestrate. It is totally ridiculous to assume that insiders in an industry are going to get together and say, "Let's make things look good and buy." It just spreads the risk. What we end up getting from sector analysis goes beyond simple confirmation as to which industries are doing well and which companies may be doing well within specific industries. We actually get some indication as to what the economy may be doing. Insiders in interest rate sensitive companies tend to behave "in mass" rather similarly, depending on their views as to what's going on with their own situations. For instance, electric utility insiders have been fairly good at predicting interest rate movements over the years. When the electric utility insiders are accumulating enough stock and selling little stock, the group moves up in our industry rankings. When this happens, we tend to not worry about interest rates going up. I have talked to utility insiders over the years about this. Some of them have told me, "I don't know what interest rates are doing. I just know if the economy is heating up in my local area." A director at a utility company told me that he watched the consumption demand; not the consumer power demand, but the commercial power demand. When he saw the power usage go up in the commercial accounts, he knew things were picking up in his local economy. This goes beyond watching the utility insider just to understand whether or not that dividend is going up or down for that company. If I have insider buying in the electric utility companies and also in insurance companies and banks, then I tend to feel better about interest rates. When I start seeing more buying in the retail area, restaurants, and apparel manufacturers, I get a little bit more concerned that things could be heating up, with regard to inflation.

Tell us more about how you use insider buying in sectors to judge the health of the economy.

The number one question we have had in 1996 is, "Where is the consumer?" We don't see much going on. The retail stocks rallied earlier in 1996 and the vast majority of retail concerns saw insiders selling into the move. They were taking advantage of what the market was giving them. We started noticing a pickup in insider buying in some very interesting areas in 1996. It started out in the more durable goods type areas. We started sensing it in the furniture manufacturers like Ethan Allen and some of the appliance makers like Maytag. Not just buying, but options exercising and lack of selling. Then we started seeing it in some of the smaller specialty steel companies, about a month later, it swung over to the chemical companies. We started putting together a picture in our minds of the possibility that consumers were actually doing more of their bigger ticket purchases this year. Whether or not that turns out to be right or wrong, only time will tell but we have seen an uptick in the housing numbers. We did sense that there was probably enough going on in some of these cyclical sectors that even though the retail numbers were really not showing that much, we probably had something going on in the heavier ticket items. That is taking the sector story to a level that goes beyond just what company(s) I like as an observer.

Do you ever see group insider buying in a weak sector?

Yes. An example of a very weak sector where we had strong insider buying were the bank stocks in 1989 and 1990. They bought the bank stocks but the bank stocks were decimated so you have to expect it. The same kind of logic needs to be applied to sector analysis. Did something occur to cause the stocks to become cheap or are things improving in the sector? Sometimes we will note that a sector is flat out improving in terms of insider buying without cheap prices suddenly surfacing to bring these people out. In other words, there was not a sudden downdraft in the stock price that made the entire group look cheap. In those situations, more often than not, there probably will be improving fundamentals, like we currently expect in the furniture stocks and steels.

Back in July 1996, you commented on the flurry of insider buying in REITS. What part of the economic picture does this group belong in?

Real estate investment trusts (REIT) are more interest rate sensitive. I expect to see insider buying in the REITs along with the banks and utility stocks. For the better part of 1996, we have been concerned about inflation. We have been on record talking about inflation but at the same time, the insider data has not looked terribly inflationary this year. We have seen other eras where the picture would draw us to a conclusion that would make us much more concerned about a demand type inflation than just say a commodity type inflation that we have been seeing lately.

How would the picture look if inflation were more demand driven rather than commodity driven?

The traditional demand type forces pushing up inflation are lots of disposable income and many people spending very freely. Department stores would be booming. We would see more insider activity on the buy side in the consumer related stocks. We are not seeing that yet. The buying that we are seeing right now is not in consumer type stocks. In fact, most of the buying recently has been spawned more by suddenly cheap prices in the stocks.

So we can follow your train of thought, would you run through a current scenario you have put together based on the activity of insiders?

Since late 1996, early 1997, insiders have continued to look positive in the utility stocks, as well as REITs. This, combined with the absence of activity in many of the consumer issues, tends to support the thesis that inflation will continue to remain under control for the intermediate term. If we were to assume, for the model, that the economy is not really booming at this time, the concern must be weighed whether or not we are in for a recession. To help answer this question, we have been able to determine, from our insider sector analysis, that there is activity out there in the economy—it's just that the disposable income is not going to the smaller ticket items. It may be going into items that are helping sectors where we see insider buying picking up. Apparel makers and retailers, cyclicals like steels and metal fabricators, and furniture companies come to mind. This seems to support the thesis of a slow growth economy that does not seem about to fall off the rails yet.

Cyclical corporations have their finger on the pulse of the economy because declining orders signal when the consumer has tapped out.

Right, and in my analysis I am discounting some of the companies that suddenly became cheap in July and insiders jumped in just because the price suddenly halved. I am looking for situations where insiders are basically buying all over the lot. They may have bought at the higher prices and then when stocks dipped, they may have bought more at lower prices.

Sometimes corporations will announce stock buy-backs for the corporate treasury. Do you track this type of stock repurchase?

Yes, we follow them as well as we can. This is a whole new area. Corporations don't have to file with the SEC when they make a repurchase so there is no filing associated with the action or the intent for that matter.

Won't corporate treasury repurchases show up on the balance sheets in the company's annual report?

They should but nobody gives a hoot what the company has already bought. They give a hoot what the company is going to buy next quarter or next year. People tend to focus on the new announcements that are being made. What is the percentage of people out there that you talk to who think corporate repurchases are a positive event?

I would say 95% of the people I know would think it was a positive event but personally speaking, I think it's a ploy to bolster the share price.

Right but it's not only a decoy, sometimes they have to do it. They have to. Companies are granting more stock options than ever before. It is at higher levels these years than in past years because in terms of the mix, companies are considering the options more of a component of the salary picture than they have before. Instead of getting all of your money in straight salary, they might give you 75% in salary and then 25% in stock options. These are the new deals and these new deals are causing increased demand for shares in order to cover the increasing amount of options that will be exercised in the next few years. I can tell you that from observing the data, there are a lot of companies that have doubled and tripled the level of their option grants in the last couple of years. I can tell you these are some of the very companies that are announcing repurchases right now because they have to get that stock somewhere for their executives to exercise their options. If companies don't have the stock in the treasury, they have only two choices— they either do a repurchase or they authorize more shares. The shareholders don't like seeing new shares being authorized because that is dilutive to earnings. If you look at the announcements out there these days, you will find they will say, it's for general corporate purposes or they will flat out say, it's for the executive stock incentive plan.

Sometimes they won't give any reason, will they?

A lot of times they don't. Right now, in a growing number of cases, shares are getting repurchased for general corporate purposes. Companies are not repurchasing stock because they are shrinking up the capitalization for the shareholders. They are not repurchasing stock because they think it is a great investment. They are doing it because they have to. They don't have enough shares to cover the insiders when they start exercising all their options.

So when there is not enough company stock in the treasury coffers to cover the options granted, corporations announce their intentions to repurchase shares in the open market.

Yes, and it is possible that this is going on in conjunction with insider selling. We are seeing a growing number of companies who have announced repurchases where there has been ongoing insider selling. We feel that individual or professional analysts should discount the significance of a company's repurchase activity when insiders are selling at the same time that the repurchase is going on.

Under what circumstances is corporate repurchasing a bullish sign?

There are many times when insiders are buying during the same time the company is buying. That is where we use the insiders to help validate the repurchase announcement. If it is significant looking insider buying and fits these different filters I have described, it can indicate a good situation where repurchase does mean something and the insider buying does mean something. Investors may really want to pay attention to these situations. The initial spirit of a repurchase was to enhance shareholder value. When I say initial spirit, I am going back into the 1970's and talking about Teledyne. Henry E. Singleton was actually shrinking up the capitalization of that company by retiring stock and that became sort of a textbook example of what a corporate repurchase is good for—the shareholder. After all, the shares you held would be worth more. These days, that is just not the case. That may be the fundamental question. Are the shares getting retired or are they going to remain out there in circulation? If they are going to remain in circulation because the insiders are exercising their options, it doesn't mean much.

Other than annual reports which has dated information, where can investors find current information on corporate repurchases?

To find sources of a company's repurchasing, all you have to do is look at any buy recommendation for any stock out on Wall Street. If an analyst follows the stock, repurchases are generally accepted as a positive event and the analyst would consider it significant enough to include in their work. If there is a repurchase going on, it will be in the analyst's buy recommendation.

Is there any single occurrence that will definitively point to a bullish or bearish scenario?

There is no one type of event that is always going to show up as most bullish or most bearish. Sometimes when it hits me between the eyes and I thought they were most bullish, nothing happened. I would venture to say though, that on the bearish side, I have seen the most problems occur when the same insiders are selling shares at successively lower prices down the time line. That has led to some real tank jobs. The most bullish cases would probably be what I saw in Noram Energy or Comp USA and that is, clusters of insiders continued to buy on the way up at higher prices—persistently buying at higher prices. I think those tend to be your best situations, at least the ones that look like they are "betable" strategies if you will. I would caution you on the insider buys, and I hate to throw caveats all over the place, but there is an increasing practice of corporations encouraging insiders to buy and in some cases, even loaning the insiders the money to buy the stock. Not that it is a negative to see this happen, but it is a concern. If they are buying stock; they are buying stock, so it is certainly hard to call it a negative but it takes something off the spin of the ball, if you will. It's not easy in every case for the analyst to determine whether the insider is really on the hook with the loan. About a year and a half ago, I saw a whole cluster of insider buys closely spaced and they were big. It prompted me to call the company and talk to somebody in the investor relations department. The person was very helpful and basically said that they were all on the hook and they were increasing their stakes in the company and it's very bullish. But the more we talked, the more I realized the insiders were getting bank loans to buy the stock. The company was cosigning the loan. Guess what the insiders were pledging for collateral on the loans? The stock. Give me a break. They were not on the hook. I don't want to finger the company but that stock was cheap in the first place. It was around a $4.00 a share and it went down to $2.00, so it halved in price. Now, let me tell you something else. I like successive or repetitive activity because there is always the risk that a one time cluster of insiders doing something is orchestrated. There was a company in the bank fiasco in 1989-1990, New England Bancorp. It was a classic example of how insiders could be wrong. A whole bunch of insiders jumped in and bought the stock as it was coming down. They only showed up once. In other words, a whole bunch insiders showed up to buy one time and the stock was like $12 or $13. If they liked it at $12 or $13, where were they at $8.00? Where were they at $7.00? Where were they at $6.00? Do you see what I mean? They didn't surface. They only came up that one time. This stock was a $130.00 stock back in the late 1980's. It's off the air now.

You certainly seem to leave no stone unturned in your analysis of insiders actions.

Sometimes the more you know, the less you know. We very rarely make comments unless we have done this type of work. Our comments are very short because we don't want to bore people and a lot of times people don't want to hear what's going on behind the scenes.

What is one of the most common misperceptions of insider trading?

People think that insider trading is something that affects the stock and it is not. Possibly the news of the insider data, once it gets out, may affect trading at times, but not all the time.

Paul Macrae Montgomery

When it comes to financial analysis, Paul Macrae Montgomery marches to a different beat. His avant garde methodologies have produced scores of prescient market calls attracting a clan of supporters that reads like a Who's Who in the financial markets—names like James Grant, Marty Zweig, Ned Davis, and Robert Prechter.

Though labeled as a bond market timer, Mr. Montgomery's reputation was first established in the gold market. In 1972, gold probably would have been voted the least likely investment to succeed, but that didn't alter his steadfastly bullish stance. Believing that bonds and stocks were mired in a longterm bear market, he saw a shining potential in gold, and the minute private ownership became legal in 1974, he recommended purchase long before its heady ride to $880.00 per ounce. In 1981, he achieved a remarkable feat by calling the exact low day in the bond market and went on to predict a secular bull market in both bonds and stocks that had not been seen in generations. Detecting signs of trouble brewing, he was one of the first to warn of the coming crisis in the savings and loan industry.

Mr. Montgomery entered the College of William and Mary with every intention of majoring in philosophy but eight o'clock classes and afternoon labs were such an anathema that he juggled his curriculum in an effort to avoid them. The end result was a triple major in philosophy, literature, and psychology, and later, an MBA.

Upon completion of his MBA, he returned to his family's real estate business but the diversity and fast-pace action of the financial markets lured Mr. Montgomery away from real estate. In the stock market, you could "take a position and have disclosure by the end of the day whether you were right or wrong whereas it might take 18 months to get an apartment project off the ground." Starting out as a stockbroker in 1971, he established roots at Legg Mason where he continues his work as market analyst and money manager. To keep his clients abreast of market conditions, he began writing reports customized to the needs of each client. Noticing repetitions emerging in each report, he later decided to write a general newsletter naming it *Universal Economics* to distinguish his opinions from those of Legg Mason.

With a business degree and background in real estate appraisals, he naturally gravitated to fundamental analysis first but his penchant for trading required a more timely approach. Convinced that psychology moves the markets more than the fundamentals, he turned to technical, psychological, and cyclical indicators as his mainstay for shortterm trading. However, from an investment standpoint, more emphasis is placed on monetary, economic, and fundamental factors. Mr. Montgomery divides his analysis into seven categories: trend, technical, psychological, monetary, economic, fundamental, and cyclical and then allocates his indicators accordingly. A stickler for interpreting indicators in the context of existing market conditions, he warns that an indicator's parameters should be adjusted beyond the normal limits during extreme bull or bear market moves.

Best known for creating the *Time* magazine cover indicator, Mr. Montgomery has many more indicators to his credit, particularly relating to the bond market. For nearly two decades, bonds went unnoticed and were given up for dead. Bond technicians became extinct. Characteristic of a true contrarian, Mr. Montgomery sensed a forthcoming resurgence in bonds and worked fast and diligently to develop operable indicators that would detect subtle changes in trend, positioning him ahead of the crowd. With his set of bond indicators in place, he waited to take advantage of the anticipated secular bull market in bonds. Thanks to his early vision and preparedness, events unfolded as forecasted, garnering a great deal of media attention. Although publicity most often links

Mr. Montgomery with the bond market, this perception is somewhat misleading as he is equally at home forecasting the outlook for stocks and gold.

Would you explain your interdisciplinary approach to market analysis?

Our work is divided into seven areas: technical, fundamental, trend, economic, psychological, monetary, and cyclic. The most original work we do involves the psychological and cyclic aspects of the market. With my background in real estate appraisals, I am very much aware of the fundamental approach to value. But, once you get into a public, double-auction market like the NYSE, with huge cash flows and various degrees of investor sophistication, securities assume a whole different set of characteristics. That is why I add the psychological and cyclic analysis.

Are your indicators integrated into a model?

I try to model everything. If you are a technician or a cycle theorist, you can always go through and pick a lot of indicators that make your point and then stop there, but the safest thing is to build a model. I have a laundry list of indicators and I will divide them into seven or eight categories like psychological indicators, technical indicators, fundamental indicators, and trend following indicators. Then within each category I utilize a number of tools. I will list half a dozen psychological indicators, half a dozen monetary indicators, half a dozen cycles, half a dozen technical indicators, and four banking statistics; things like that.

Is the model weighted or unweighted?

Some markets are fundamentally driven and some are psychologically driven so the ideal thing to do would be to shift the weights from one sector to the other, depending on what currently is driving the market. I haven't progressed to that point yet so for now, I leave the weights fixed. They aren't equal, but they are fixed. I might give 30% to the trend and 25% to psychology and 30% to the technicals and 15% to the banking statistics and so forth.

One of your psychological indicators that has received a lot of publicity is your *Time* magazine cover indicator. How far back did you test this?

I went back to the first day *Time* magazine was published, which was in March 1923. I looked at every cover from the early 1920's up until the early 1980's. Whenever there was a cover of apparent financial significance, I noted the price of the relevant security or market at that time and then checked the price three months, six months, and one year later. A little better than 50% of the time, the market or relevant security tended to move as the cover was suggesting for a month or so, but one year after the cover date, the market had moved significantly in the opposite direction in better than 85% of the cases.

Is the success of this indicator based on crowds being wrong at extremes?

The theory is that it is not earnings, dividends, sales or anything like this that pushes stock prices up. It's buying. Let's say I'm appraising a company. No matter how accurate my estimate of sales or earnings will be, that information is worthless if it is already disseminated to the public, because it will have already been reflected in the price structure. It will no longer be able to move prices. The great value of the *Time* cover indicator is that it shows the extent to which important information is already in the public domain and hence, reflected in the price structure. For example, I think in the fall of 1992 there was a *Time* magazine cover article that said, "Can GM Survive in Today's World," suggesting that General Motors might go bankrupt. You have to figure GM was having some difficulty at the time but once everybody getting a six-pack of beer or a package of Twinkies at the corner Seven-Eleven store has the cover of *Time* staring down at him saying, "Can GM Survive in Today's World," that means the story is really completely out. There is virtually nobody left to learn that story so you can safely assume that everybody who had any stock has already had the opportunity to sell. That is the great value of the indicator. It's not that the public is always wrong, but it shows the extent to which information is already in the public domain and hence fully reflected in market prices.

Can you think of other prominent magazine covers from the past that showed extreme pessimism or optimism?

One time IBM made the cover. The title was "The Colossus That Works." A month after that IBM was 138 and it went from there to somewhere in the 90's. Thirteen years later, in the summer of 1996, IBM was still below the price it was when that cover came out. Ted Turner made Man of the Year on the cover of *Time* and his stock, Turner Broadcasting, subsequently went up one point over the next couple of weeks to around $28.00. I don't think it has been that high since then. A great one was the housing market on the cover of *Newsweek*, which worked the same as the *Time* covers. It showed a picture with housing prices upside down and said, "The Real Estate Bust." The "V" on the roof was pointing down like an arrow implying housing prices were headed down and the housing industry was headed down. The next year, out of 89 S&P groups, the housing stocks were the third biggest performer after biotechs and brokerage houses.

The recurrent theme seems to be that if the cover projects a positive tone, you should be bearish and if it's negative, you should be bullish.

Correct. It is not for day to day trading purposes but over a period of several quarters, it is an extremely reliable indicator.

For a period of time, the stock of the featured company or related subject moves in accordance with the mood of the cover. How much time does it take to reverse course and move in the opposite direction?

Probably 60% of the time, the market has continued in the direction the magazine suggests for several weeks but then one year later, it has been opposite 85% to 90% of the time.

So for instance, if it's a bullish article, you will still have some time to sell your holdings?

Yes, you will sell into strength over the next several weeks.

Does the indicator have a good track record?

Better than 85%.

Many of your valuable indicators are proprietary. Why did you go public with this one?

I went public with this indicator 15 or 16 years ago because I figured I had gotten about as much enjoyment out of it as I could. I doubted that it would keep working but it has actually worked as well, or better, since it went public. Normally, indicators don't do that. Once they become public knowledge they stop working because everybody is using them. I think the reason this one continues to work is because nobody really has the courage to act off of it. It is interesting cocktail talk but nobody really has the courage to move millions of dollars based on this indicator. Some fund manager is not going to move $20 million dollars out of Microsoft because Bill Gates was on the cover of *Time*. He would get crucified if it didn't work out right. I don't mind that at all. I would be happy to move half of what I have off of a cover story like that.

That speaks volumes about your faith in this indicator. Can you rely strictly on the cover or is it necessary to read the underlying story?

Theoretically, you need to read the cover story to find out exactly what they are talking about, but if the cover is equivocal enough that you have to read the story to figure out what they are really saying, it's probably not highly reliable. The meaning needs to be obvious. I remember a few years ago there was a story that came out on the Midwest drought called "The Big Dry." That hit the stands virtually the day of the highs in the commodity market.

Other than *Time* and *Newsweek*, are there other magazine covers that produce equivalent results?

You can pick up similar signals from a lot of different magazines. The reason I focus on *Time* is because it has the longest history and the most samples to work with. *Business Week* has had some marvelous cover stories, just wonderful contra-indicators. They came out with an article called, "Trouble in the Government Bond Market" on May 28, 1984. It showed Uncle Sam riding a tandem bicycle looking like he was about to fall and crack up. Government bond yields hit 14% that day and went lower for the next 10 years.

Should you completely discount bullish or bearish covers appearing on Barron's, Forbes or other financial publications that normally write about subjects of a financial nature?

As I said, *Business Week* has had a lot of great covers. The problem is that if you are looking at a trade journal like *Business Week*, they have a business related cover just about every week so you constantly have to judge the significance of it. It is a lot of work and you get a lot of noise along with the good signals so it is harder to separate the wheat from the chaff. Whereas if you get a lay publication like *Time* and *Newsweek*, they could be writing about Madonna, O.J. Simpson, or a lot of other extraneous non-economic subjects. It's very rare that a business story makes the cover of *Time* magazine so you can be pretty sure it is an extreme.

The indicator works best when the subject is out of its natural element.

Yes, and just because something is on the cover of the *Wall Street Journal* doesn't mean it is going to go down because they have something about business every day. For example, in October 1929, there was a famous headline in *Variety* called "Wall Street Lays an Egg." Six months later, the market had actually retraced 50%. *Reader's Digest* in July 1996 came out with an article "How to Make a Million." Something similar came out in 1928. John Jacob Raskob wrote an article in the *Ladies Home Journal* called "Everybody Ought to Be Rich." When a non-business magazine starts trumpeting a business subject, that is when you can be sure the story has reached almost everybody so there is no way to profit from it except going the opposite way.

Have you backtested the indicator's return compared to the S&P 500?

Yes, but the problem is you don't have a signal all the time. When the magazine covers gave a signal, I think they had a rate of return 5 or 6 times as great as the S&P 500. A couple of years ago *Time* magazine had a smoker on the cover and everybody had a gun pointed at his head. It said, "Is It All Over for Smokers?" Phillip Morris was about $58.00 at the time and it went on to well over $100.00 in short order. If you had bought and sold GM off of the recent *Time* cover signals, you outperformed a buy and hold by about 10 to 1. When you get a signal, it is very reliable and outperforms the market by a significant amount, but you can't invest off that indicator alone because there are very long periods of time when it just simply doesn't have anything to say.

If your return in one trade was 50% or 60%, you could park those winnings in cash until the next opportunity.

That's true. I haven't gone through and tested it as if you had used that as your sole indicator. I don't think it would have been that spectacular because you would have spent a lot of time in cash when there weren't any signals. When the signals are in effect, they are four or five times greater than a buy and hold.

In the 1970's, you made a number of timely bullish calls on gold. Is gold still a market niche for you?

Yes, I probably make a significant portion of my income trading the gold stocks.

There used to be a link between bonds, the gold market and stocks. Within the last couple of years, the relationship seems to have unraveled somewhat. What are your thoughts?

There is a relationship but it is not what it used to be. Gold is essentially real money and interest rates are the rent on money. When gold was real money, that is, when we had the gold standard, almost by definition there was a correlation between the price of gold and interest rates. Once we got off the gold standard during the 1970's, we had a dramatic increase in the gold stocks, we had inflation, and interest rates went up. That is when gold went up to $880.00 per ounce. So statistically, if you look over long periods of time, there has always been a strong inverse correlation between gold stocks and the stock and bond market. I think the reason the connection hasn't been as good recently is that there used to be a very select group of people who invested in gold and gold stocks. These people were quite different from the people who invested in stocks and bonds. In fact, I remember in the 1970's, Cleveland Trust Company—they have changed their name now—ran articles warning banking clients not to invest in gold. You would get fired from a brokerage firm if you wanted to recommend gold stocks. I was very unusual in that Legg Mason allowed me to recommend anything I wanted. I was urging the sale of common stocks and the purchase of gold stocks in 1972 to 1974. In recent years, of course, gold stocks have become acceptable investments. There are now 40 gold stock mutual funds and brokerage houses issue research reports on them. They are legitimate investments for even banks and pension fund portfolios. Now you have a constituency that considers gold stocks the same as normal stocks so the inverse correlation has not been as apparent in recent years. For example, a lot of the gold stock funds ran up to all-time highs at the end of May 1996 with the NASDAQ and then they got smashed 20% down into mid-July with the NASDAQ. After mid-July, they went up 10% to 11% with the NASDAQ. As these stocks have become just like other stocks, they start taking on the same characteristics as the stock market, but I think eventually the former relationship will reassert itself.

There appears to be a lot of selling pressure in gold coming from many directions.

Supposedly, the central banks have done a lot of selling and all the Swiss accounts, which always used to recommend holding 10 to 15% of your assets in gold, are down to 1% or 2%. I am not sure how significant it is who's doing the buying and who's doing the selling. Gold demand is psychologically driven. I think the psychology is real important over the long term. With a wheat crop, you can wipe out the whole crop with a drought or flood whereas all the gold that has ever been mined is still here. The total supply doesn't change more than 1.5% a year. The amount we produce every year is very small compared to the outstanding stock. I think the psychological demand in the gold market is paramount rather than the supply, wherever it is coming from.

Psychologically, gold is supposed to be a haven during inflationary times and yet over the last year, while inflationary gauges such as the CRB index have been heating up, gold has barely budged.

That's true and I think it might be because in recent years, there are so many people who have been paying attention to gold that didn't used to. It is easy for gold to get overbought very quickly whereas something like soybeans, which nobody seems to care about anymore, has a much better chance to put on a stealth rally and take off before anybody realizes it. I think eventually gold will move because the capitalization of all the gold stocks in the world is probably one-third that of Coca-Cola. It wouldn't take much of an asset re-allocation to cause a dramatic rally. If gold does start going up now that people are aware of it and they decide it is prudent to have 5% of their portfolio in gold, there is not a big enough door for people to get through.

In your analysis of gold, do you use the London fixing price or the Comex price?

I look at both of them. I don't follow them closely on a daily basis because I don't do any day trading in gold. It is more longer term. The London weekly is fine for all I need.

What indicators do you watch to give you a feel for the trend of gold?

I look at the money flow into gold mutual funds.

As a contrarian indicator?

Yes. When you have had huge withdrawals or when you have four consecutive months of net withdrawals from the gold funds, that is a pretty safe buy. Same thing on net inflows. When you have had several months of big inflows, it's time to get out. That is a real good indicator.

Since the gold market is psychologically driven, you must keep some sentiment indicators.

The polling services are pretty good; Market Vane and Consensus. This is on bullion, not the gold stocks. I smooth the number by taking a 5 week moving average. Once that gets fairly high, it has been very dangerous to be in gold stocks. The time you want to be in gold stocks is when they are moving up and the metal is not doing anything and nobody cares about it. Once gold starts moving, that attracts the amateur crowd. People start calling their brokers wanting to know what gold is doing. That is not the kind of market to be in. When amateurs start getting interested in gold stocks, it is getting dangerous.

Are short interest ratios on individual gold stocks reliable contrarian indicators?

I used to do the short interest on the gold stocks but I stopped doing it years ago because a lot of the short interest was hedging. Another very valuable indicator is the value-weighted put/call ratio of the gold stocks. I don't use this now just because it is too much work. Rather than just looking at the volume or the open interest, I prefer to do a value-weighted put/call ratio. That means taking every option and multiplying the price times the volume or the open interest. If somebody wants to do the work, it is a very good tool.

Do cycles play a role in your analysis of gold?

I use cycles in my work as far as knowing whether I should pay attention to gold bullion or not. I don't base my trading decisions off of them. For example, gold has been underperforming for 15 years and the stock market has been going up for 15 years and there is a 15 to 16 year cycle. That doesn't mean that I am going to buy gold today, but it means I should consider shifting a lot of my analytic efforts and time and money into that group. Over time, cycles are probably the most accurate in the precious metals market because the supply of gold doesn't change and the demand for it is psychologically driven. It is not like food where you can have a huge demand. What is the demand for gold? People don't have to have it to fill their teeth. Nobody has to have gold. They just think they have to have it. When people think they have to have it, you get a panic. Gold is almost purely psychologically demand driven and so I use cycles to identify extremes in optimism and pessimism. The more a market is psychologically driven, the more accurate the cycles are.

Based on your experience, which cycles are the most reliable and useful?

A lot of cycle research has been done by the Foundation for the Study of Cycles. I would check with the Foundation because they do a lot of statistical analysis before they publish something so you get a sense of how reliable that cycle is. They have some reliable cycles; the 9 month cycle, the 33 month cycle, 5 years, and so forth. They primarily use sinusoidal cycles of equal length—33 years, 15 years, 5.58 years. The cycles that I use in my gold trading are proprietary and are not perfectly mechanical. Based on my background in psychology, I look for extremes in human emotion, enthusiasm or fear, and these cycles tend to come on an irregular basis. The cycles are predictable but it's like notes in a song; they don't always come the same distance apart. There are cycles of optimism and pessimism in the market place. Some people feel like they have to own gold, other times they don't want it at all. So cycles are very helpful in the gold and silver market because they address human emotions and gold is an emotional investment.

Is it fair to say that your major decisions to buy and sell gold primarily revolve around your cycle and Elliott Wave analysis?

Well, certainly on a short to intermediate-term basis. Over the long term, I do a lot of fundamental work on gold trying to figure out what its value is. The same thing for silver. Those things are important from a longterm perspective but as far as trading, gold stocks move 30% or more over a very short period of time and I don't want to be on the wrong side of any 30% move.

Regarding individual gold stocks, I believe you prefer staying away from the larger capitalization issues that big institutions clamor for?

I would rather find a gold stock that has a smaller capitalization. Barrick, and Placer Dome are virtually the entire XAU index. Barrick, for example, is the largest position in 25 different mutual funds. Where is the new buying going to come from? Portfolio managers are going to buy it if you get a huge inflow of public money into the funds but if you get that kind of inflow, it is because the gold stocks are running and the thinner stocks are going to do better. I like the gold stocks people don't own. I think you have a much better chance.

Is it safe to say that traditionally gold shares lead the price of gold bullion on the way up and on the way down?

They lead it on the way up and often on the way down. The one thing that I have found is that gold and gold stocks tend to make spike tops rather than smooth rounding tops. A lot of times you will get a spike top that occurs on one of my cycle days. There is a lot of enthusiasm and the stocks and bullion run up together. Occasionally you will get the bullion and the stocks topping together but typically, the stocks will move first and this is especially true at bottoms. Beginning in December 1973, American citizens could own gold. Bullion ran up a couple of days right before that but the gold stocks didn't follow at all. That was a big warning signal because they both really tumbled the next month. Gold stocks tend to lead at tops and bottoms but it is more reliable at bottoms because bottoms are slower forming and rounded. You often get spike tops in gold and gold related assets so very often there is not much, if any, lead time at the top from the stocks.

Is there a ratio which allows you to evaluate when gold stocks have become overpriced or underpriced relative to the price of gold bullion?

There are a couple of ways to do it. One of them is dividing the XAU by the current contract on the gold futures. Undervalued is 22:1 and overvalued is 28:1. You can also take the S&P gold mining index and divide it by COMEX gold. The range of normalcy is 44:1 to 56:1. I would say you would want to stay with the stocks as long as that ratio was going up and get out when it heads down irrespective of the level. I don't use these ratios myself but there is nothing wrong with it if you use them properly. Another way to do it is to look at the book value, the dividends, and the earnings of those S&P gold companies.

When the ratio is 44:1, that's saying gold mining stocks are undervalued relative to the price of gold and 56:1 indicates they are overvalued.

Yes. Right now it is 64 so according to that index, gold stocks are overpriced. The S&P gold mining group is currently trading around 240.00 so if you cut that in half, the XAU is about 120. You can double the XAU or you can use the S&P gold mining group, which is approximately twice the XAU. But if you use either one of these, you get exactly the same thing. The only difference is that one ratio is going to be twice as big as the other. What matters is the pattern and how it deviates from its historical range. Looking back at the ratio since 1979, gold stocks were cheap on January 21, 1980 because bullion had gotten to $880.00 but that wasn't a good time to buy gold stocks because bullion blew 200 points in a couple of days and then collapsed.

Judgment obviously seems to be a prerequisite when using these ratios.

That's the problem with the ratio. It is not like an on-off toggle switch. A ratio can be telling you any of 13 different things going on in the real world. Gold can be going up and the gold stocks can be going down, or they could both be going down but one could be going down faster than the other. They could both be going up but one is going up slower than the other. Just looking at the level per se doesn't tell a trader where he ought to have his money. That is why I don't use them.

Let's switch over to another investment arena you excel in—bonds. As a point of reference, what are your time horizons in bonds for the shortterm, intermediate-term, and longterm?

I look at four different time frames. What I define as shortterm is market movement between one and five weeks. Intermediate-term is one to five months. Longterm is six months to a few years. Then I also look at a time frame which some people say does not exist, the supercycle. I think it probably does but those are generational type moves, moves that last for 20 years or more. I look at all those time frames but you have to use different indicators for the different time frames. The shortterm is purely trading oriented and there I use primarily technical and psychological indicators. For the intermediate and longterm, indicators like the balance of payments might have an affect on longterm but you don't get the data until so late that it is not much help in forecasting a move that lasts a month or so.

Is it possible to use bond yields to forecast near-term economic conditions?

There is certainly a correlation between the economy and interest rates but I haven't studied that enough because I don't care what the economy is doing. My outlook is forecasting bond prices. I do know that the shape of the yield curve does tend to forecast the economy. You usually don't have a recession without an inverted yield curve and you don't have an inverted yield curve very long without a recession. I don't know if the level of interest rates forecasts the economy but the relationship between long rates and short rates certainly does have a bearing. In fact, at one time there was a market newsletter that offered market predictions based just on the shape of the yield curve.

Do you use the shape of the yield curve to make your bond market forecasts?

I studied this a lot and found it hard to use because the ratio between long rates and short rates is like the ratio between gold stocks and gold bullion. The ratio can go up or down for any of 13 different reasons. The shape of the yield curve can change by short rates going up and long rates going down, or they can both be going down but one is going down slower than the other, or they both are going up but one is going up faster than the other. It is a problematic situation but there are a couple of things I have found. Roughly speaking, a negative yield curve, or one that is getting worse, is poor for bonds. Also, I have found that when you have had a real wide spread, say 300 or 400 basis points between long rates and short rates, that has been a real good incentive for money to move into the bond market. When you have a wide yield curve like that and when the spread is rising, it attracts money into the bond market. When long rates lose half of their previous advantage over short rates, say the spread drops from 400 basis points to 200, some constituencies lose interest in the bond market. Say you have had a wide spread favoring longterm bonds and then the spread narrows but bonds still have a positive yield curve, that is, longterm rates still have higher yields than shorter rates. Once the yield curve has lost a lot of that spread, you tend to lose customers. The carry trade, for example, where you borrow short to lend long; the market becomes much less attractive for them so you start losing potential customers for the bond market once the yield curve contracts.

As the spread between short rates and long rates widen in favor of longterm rates, that is a bullish sign for bonds and as it contracts, that is a less bullish sign.

Yes, all other things being equal. You have to remember, sometimes if longterm bonds are just sitting there and all of a sudden out of the blue they drop two points (200 basis points) because of bad news, that is going to cause a widening of the spread unless short rates have risen the same amount. Generally speaking, that is why I said you can't just look at the curve. You have to look at the denominator and the numerator to see how it got there. A lot of people who weren't interested in bonds when there was only ½ point spread—say long bonds are 7% and short rates are 6½ % - would become buyers if all of a sudden there is a big spread between long rates and short rates. If they were going to get 8% or 8½ % instead of 6½ %, then you would start getting buyers moving from shortterm to longterm. Typically, narrow spreads are not very good for the bond market because there is really not much incentive to move money in them.

Can you quantify that a 400 basis point spread is sufficient to convert shortterm buyers to longterm buyers?

It's interesting, I have not found one particular level because people's memory is not so much on 100 basis points or 200 basis points. It is more like what they used to be able to get. If they used to get 100 basis points then 50 doesn't look so good. Or if they used to be able to get 400 and it drops to 200; 200 is still a pretty good spread but it is not 400, so you are going to start losing some interest in the bond market. It is the relationship between long rates and short rates rather than the actual level that I have found most helpful. Now I do a lot of these things on a spread basis and a ratio basis. With the spread basis you would subtract short rates from long rates.

Maybe we should stop and clarify what you use for short rates and long rates.

I usually use 30 year bonds versus 90 day Treasury bills. A lot of people say you ought to use the two year notes. Those things come and go as fads. I want a consistent series so I have taken this back to the Civil War. You can't get two year note prices back to the Civil War. I want to distinguish as clearly as possible between longterm, at-risk bonds and shortterm paper because that is where the big psychological difference comes in. It's whether people are worried about their balance sheet or their income statement. If they are very confident, they will worry about their income statement and will go as long as possible to get as much yield as possible. If they are scared, they will go as short as possible. That is what we are looking at—fear versus greed—the very longterm money versus instant access to your money.

You were in the process of explaining how you evaluate interest rate spreads.

There are two ways to judge these. If you have 7% long bonds and 3½ % short term money, that is a yield spread of 350 basis points. That is one way to look at it, but the one I pay more attention to is dividing long rates by short rates. So if you have a 7% long rate and a 3½ % short rate, that is a yield curve of 100 because you are getting 100% more to go long than to stay short. I find that is also helpful in doing historical work. If you go back to the 1940's when you had ¼ % and ½ % yields, spreads didn't mean that much but the ratios, the patterns, tended to hold up. In my historical analysis, I always use ratios. In 1980, when we had these dramatic interest rates we had never seen before—20% shortterm money and 15¼ % longterm governments—those numbers were unheard of but the ratios didn't get that much out of whack. The other thing to look for is a change in shape of the yield curve. One of the things that called the all-time low day in the bond market, which was September 28, 1981 or October 1, 1981, depending on which bond you look at, was the change in the shape of the yield curve. 1981 was a bear market year for bonds. Short rates had been up to something like 21%. Bond prices had been sinking since January but on October 1st, long rates and short rates were even. As I was saying, usually when the yield spread is even, there is not much incentive. For a couple of years, we had a negative yield curve and then all of a sudden, on October 1st, they crossed over. You could get one or two basis points more by going into the bond market. That day was the low day of the bond market. It was to some extent coincidence that it turned on that day, but the shape of the curve was moving dramatically in favor of longterm bonds. Previously, you had been able to get 600 basis points more by staying in shortterm paper but short rates started dropping and the spread narrowed to 500, then 400, then 300 and then finally by October. The yield curve is not always that precise a timing tool, but this is a classic example of the way things can work.

For the yield curve ratio, you are actually calculating the percentage difference between long rates and short rates. Are there particular circumstances where it is more appropriate to use the ratio versus the basis point spread?

Both the ratio and the difference is legitimate but if you look at them in historical terms, you get strange things periodically. Like at one very brief point during the Depression, Treasury bills had a negative yield. People were too afraid to put their money in banks or stocks or bonds so they would buy Treasury bills at 101 knowing they were going to be paid back only 100, but they knew their money would be safe. Treasury bills actually had a negative yield. There were long periods of time where yields were 1/8%. If you look at that on a ratio scale, you will get real big distortions if long-term rates were 7% and shortterm rates were 1/8%. If you did a ratio it would be 56:1, it would be off the chart. In a period like this, using the difference in basis points is better because 700 basis points difference would be not unreasonable. Both the ratio and the difference have their uses. It's just like, "How should you look at stock prices?" Should you use an arithmetic scale or should you use a semi-logarithmic scale. They both have value.

The implication of an inverted or negative yield curve is tight money, right?

Yes, and the implication for investors is that if you can get more interest on day to day deposits, why risk your money over 30 years. If I am going to tie my money up for a long time, I have to be paid some incentive to do it. If you are not getting paid any incentive to go long, it's a real disincentive to invest in the longterm bond market. You may as well just stay in shortterm paper.

If that's the case, why are investors queuing to buy 100 year Coca-Cola, IBM, or Disney corporate bonds with yields to maturity almost equal to 30 year bonds?

I don't know. I think it is smart of the corporations issuing the bonds. We are used to seeing long rates significantly higher than short rates because the logic is that if you are going to tie your money up for 30 years, you should get paid a lot more than for tying it up 30 days. You have that big risk premium to go long but for the first 20 or 30 years of this century, the thinking was the other way around. Short rates used to be consistently higher than long rates.

Consistently, regardless of economic conditions?

Yes, from the early 1890's to 1920. Their reasoning was that if they went longterm, they were guaranteed to earn a fixed interest rate for 30 years but if they went short, they would be forced to take their money back after 30 days and they wouldn't know what kind of interest rate they would get. It was like an insurance policy; the longer they would guarantee the return, the less interest you would be willing to accept. Those are facts. The yield curve used to be inverted most of the time before the 1930's and 1940's. Since the 1940's, it has rarely been inverted. I think the difference was our going off the gold standard. Back in the 1800's, everybody knew what the dollar was worth but once we went off the gold standard and Franklin Roosevelt invalidated the gold clause that was written in contracts, all of a sudden you never knew what your money would be worth in 20 years. It used to be that they would write into bonds and write into contracts that if you loaned someone $1,000.00, you would get $1,000.00 back in 20 years or the equivalent amount of gold. Whether you went for 20 days or 20 years, there wasn't any inflation risk because you knew the dollar would be as good as gold or you would get gold. Today, we don't have any idea what the dollar will be worth when we get our principal back in 20 years. It is all blips on a computer and there is no real currency anymore.

Speaking of inflation, to what extent will economic factors impact bond prices?

Inflation of course is critical. The problem with things that supposedly affect interest rates, like the unemployment rate and industrial production, is that those are lagging indicators. What causes interest rate movements is the supply and demand for money. If you look at a lot of these economic factors, you can get a feel for the supply and demand for money but it is late. These indicators tend to lag the interest rate movements themselves. Now, to the extent that you get trends in the economy, if you have long moves you can get on board for part of the move even if you are late. So these economic indicators aren't worthless but as far as any precise timing, they are invariably too late to be any good.

As the demand for credit increases, does it necessarily follow that interest rates will be forced higher?

No, because you have four factors. The demand for credit is just one of the factors. You have a demand and supply for both sides of the equation. You have a supply of money and demand for money which talks about the lending side and there is a supply of credit and demand for credit. For example, you would think that if you had a balance of payments deficit or a budget deficit, that interest rates would skyrocket because the government was spending more than they were taking in and had to borrow the difference, which they are. But for the last 20 or 30 years, there has been an inverse correlation with interest rates and the deficit. When the deficit has gone down, interest rates have gone up. When the deficit has gone up, interest rates have gone down. If you go back to the first part of the century, you will find that when budget deficits went up, interest rates went up 50% of the time and 50% of the time they went down. It was random. As I said, in recent decades there has actually been an inverse correlation between the deficit and the trend of interest rates because there are so many other factors, and they have more than offset them since the 1960's.

Can you go over some of the other factors?

The amount of new financing every year is tiny compared to the huge pool of bonds that are already outstanding. Let's say the government runs a big deficit one year. If everybody that owns all of these bonds just reinvests the coupons to buy more bonds, there would be more money coming into bonds than the government needs to finance its deficit. If people are really strapped for cash and are spending all of their interest coupons, there won't be a supply of buyers. The amount of debt already outstanding is huge compared to the new debt every year. If enough of the coupon payments on the old debt were reinvested, it would be more than enough to fund the new debt. I think that is one reason we had the unexpected inverse correlation between interest rates and deficits in recent years. Also, foreign central banks own so much of our debt now. When central banks want dollars, they don't buy the paper currency that we pass around with George Washington's picture on it. To get dollars, they will buy dollar denominated Treasury bills or two year notes or five year bonds. When we run a big balance-of-payments deficit, foreigners could put all this money and more back into the bonds that the government issues. So if foreigners, which are primarily the central banks, have a big net positive cash flow, they could be funding our deficit and then some. Interest rates could continue to go down even though we are running deficits.

If foreign central banks are buying dollars via government Treasury bills and notes, and they decided to sell their Treasury bill positions, could this action precipitate a sudden decline in the value of the dollar?

I think it is highly likely.

Do you measure the amount of new debt being coming into the bond market relative to the existing supply?

I don't and the reason is because the figures aren't immediately available. I have data on equity supplies versus prices on the NYSE going back fifty years and it is very instructive. I wish I had the same thing on the bonds, but I don't. When there have been long periods of dramatic, net reductions in the supply of equities—when companies have been buying back more of their stock than they have been issuing—the stock market has really taken off to the upside. When there has been significant new issuance of stock, the market has always run into heavy weather.

Regarding the supply of debt, what type of debt is actually included in those numbers?

Net debt is usually broken down into corporate and private. That is important because sometimes they will offset each other. Like in depressionary times, the public won't be borrowing. They will be paying down their debts so the public debt load will contract whereas government debt will expand to make up for the lost revenue and to try and stimulate the economy. People tend to break it into two separate categories because they oscillate back and forth.

In order to determine where interest rates are headed, is it more important to focus on the back end of the yield curve; that is, with 30 year bonds, rather than on the front end?

No. Two-thirds of the time, short rates and long rates move in the same direction and one-third of the time, they move in different directions. It is much easier for me to predict long rates than short rates. When people buy a Treasury bill at an auction, they usually will hold it until maturity. People who buy 30 year bonds don't hold them, especially nowadays. When people get scared, they will dump their gold, stocks, and bonds. People don't panic and run out and dump their Treasury bills when they are scared. They hold them and keep rolling them over. The only exception to that I can think of would be foreign investors. If they worried about the dollar, they would sell a lot of dollar denominated Treasury bills. You don't have a psychological panic in the front end of the debt market to the extent that you might in the long end. As far as the interest rate market is concerned, there are a lot of psychological tools that I can use in the bond market that really don't work in the T-bill market. If you own a 30 day T-bill, how much can you get hurt in the next 30 days? If you own a 30 year bond, you could get slaughtered. You could lose 15% of your assets in several months.

The further out you go on the yield curve, the more financial risk you incur.

You can see a significant depreciation of your assets if you own a 30 year bond.

In your opinion, the long end of the bond market is more predictable in terms of judging where interest rates might be headed.

The long end is more predictable because a lot of the psychological and cyclical factors which I use impinge on the bond market. If people are trying to make the biggest gains, they will chase anything. When people are scared, they just want liquidity. Sometimes people are worried about inflation so they will buy gold. Sometimes they are losing money and worried about their balance sheets. In that case, they will liquidate everything: gold, stocks and bonds. When people are really scared they will sell any kind of asset irrespective of the particular category, but you don't usually find people getting scared and dumping T-bills. You don't have the same psychological imperative of fear at the short end of the market that you do at the long end of the market. That is not always the case because sometimes people are just scared of being in cash or sometimes overseas investors will dump T-bills because they are afraid of the dollar. There are a lot of indicators that you can develop for the long end of the market that are not applicable to the short end.

Starting with the psychological indicators, is the put/call ratio on bond options an effective tool?

Yes, but I don't look at the volume or open interest on a raw basis. I calculate it on a dollar weighted basis. I take the price of every put and multiply it times the volume in that put and times the open interest. I do the same thing for the calls. So instead of saying there were X number of calls and Y number of puts, I get the actual dollar amount invested in all of the puts and in all of the calls. That is much more laborious but if you don't do that, you are giving a put that is selling for $5.00 the same weight as one that is selling for 50 cents. I want to know exactly how much money is invested in puts and how much is invested in calls. As a very rough rule of thumb, you can say that 50 to 200 is the range of normalcy. What that means is that you can have twice as much money in calls or twice as much money in puts on occasion, and that is within the bounds of normalcy. A number of 1000 would mean that there was ten times as much money in puts as in calls which is very dramatic. Those extremes are where you get major reversals at tops and bottoms in the market.

So extreme levels is the key.

There are two things that are important. One is the extreme level and the other is the pattern. As I said, between 50 and 200 is the range of normalcy. That means the puts and the calls are staying within the bounds of 2:1 of one another. Once you get way outside the bounds of 2:1, say you have four or five times as much money in puts or four or five times as much money in calls, then you get an extreme sentiment. The puts and calls are expiring all the time and you have new series coming out. For this reason, and because the parameters are naturally different in a bull market than in a bear market, I smooth the series. I determine those parameters by taking a 52 week moving average and a couple of standard deviations.

In essence, smoothing the ratio makes allowances for the fact that it is normal to see more call buying when a market is roaring ahead and an increase in put buying when the market is tanking.

Right, when you are in a bull market, the put/call ratio will stay lower than when you are in a bear market. A lot of people say if the put/call ratio is "this" it's too high, and if it's "that" it's too low. There is a certain truth to that but what number is high and low varies according to the market you are in. You can't say that any one level is always a buy or any one level is always a sell. I am trying to call turning points. So instead of just saying when the put/call is below 50 you have to sell bonds and when it is above 200 you have to buy them, I will take a 250 day moving average or a 55 day moving average and then a couple of standard deviations from that. That way, if you have some fundamental or cyclical change in the market that is taking everything to a higher or lower level, you won't get out of that market too soon. You need to adjust your parameters. I will take standard tools like the put/call ratio or yield spread and put standard deviations around them so I can adapt them for the current market environment.

What is your source for option data on bond futures and do you calculate the put/call ratio on a daily or weekly basis?

We get the data directly from the floor of the Chicago Board of Trade. *Barron's* has an abbreviated summary once a week. We have gotten in the habit of calculating it every day but you can do it once a week and it is very helpful.

Every week, Barron's publishes the polling service's sentiment figures for bonds. At one time, 70% and 30% were levels which signaled an imminent reversal. Are these still valid parameters?

It used to be that those numbers would swing widely. In recent years, they have become much more compressed. They usually stay between 40% and 60% instead of 70% and 30%. If you take the polling services, Market Vane or Consensus, in a bull market the numbers will stay higher than usual and in a bear market they will stay lower than usual. I did a study using 70% and 30% as buy/sell parameters on the bonds and then I did it again at 80% and 20%. I found that if you use just the raw numbers, it was actually worse than a buy and hold approach. Say your parameters are 80/20 or 70/30 and you start a major bull market like you did in the fall of 1981. After two or three explosive weeks up, you get a reading of 70% or 80% bulls and so you sell. The market sells off for a couple of weeks but the sentiment reading never gets down to 20% or 30%. It gets down to 40% or 50% and then it takes off again. If you are in a bear market and you buy at 30% waiting until 70% to get out, you will never get out because sentiment will never get up to 70% in a bear market. If you use those set parameters, 70/30, 80/20, or whatever, you will sell too early in a bull market and you will never get back in. In a bear market, you will buy too early and you will never get a sell signal. So 70% and 30% are good parameters but in a bull market, you sell on 70 and buy on 50 and in a bear market, you buy on 30 and sell on 50. 50% could be a sell signal in a bear market and a buy signal in a bull market. The width of the swings have changed in stocks and bonds but regardless of the numbers or the width of the swings, the principle has been consistent and that is, you can't use the same buy/sell parameters in a bull market and a bear market. In a bull market you have to raise your parameters and in a bear market you have to lower them; otherwise, you will get trapped into a position in a bear market you don't get out of or trapped on the sidelines in a bull market.

Does this mean you can't use it as a timing tool?

The only way to use it as a timing tool is to shift the parameters and in order to do that, you need to know whether you are in a bull market or a bear market. You can't use it alone. You have to use it in conjunction with another independent indicator that tells you something about the broader trend.

What other independent indicator would you use?

What I use is a total intermediate-term model but if you had to use just one thing, I would say use some monetary indicators, monetary meaning free reserves or the shape of the yield curve, things like that.

Free reserves have been net positive for so many years, it's not going to give many signals.

Yes, but you don't have to use the raw number. You can use standard deviations or you can take a 5 week average and subtract it from a 26 week average; something like that, so you get the trend rather than the level.

Are the cash levels of bond mutual funds a good sentiment gauge?

Yes. I created this indicator back in 1974 and it is something else you have to adjust for the shape of the yield curve. There is no one magic figure, like if it is below 4% it's bearish or if it's above 8% it's bullish. You can't use set parameters in bond funds but you can to some extent in stock mutual funds because in the stock market if you are running a growth fund, theoretically you are trying to get growth so managers will put the cash into stocks. If a stock manager has a lot of cash, it means he is negative about the stock market. If a bond fund manager has a lot of cash, it doesn't necessarily mean he is negative on the bond market. It might be because the yield curve is inverted. If long rates are yielding 8% and short rates are yielding 10%, the fund manager can actually get more income without running any risk by going to the front end of the market. For an income fund, it makes sense to go where the income is. Bond mutual fund cash positions just might reflect the shape of the yield curve. That is what happened in 1979 to 1981. Bond mutual fund cash levels got up to 20% or so. It wasn't because everyone was screamingly bearish on bonds. It was because shortterm rates were 22% and you could get more income with less risk by going to the front end of the market. If you are looking at the bond fund cash levels, you have to adjust them for the shape of the yield curve.

In other words, they look at the spread between 90 day Treasury bills and 30 year government bonds and judge which is the better deal?

Right. For example, if you are getting paid three times as much to go to the long end of the market, it makes sense to run your cash levels down to nothing. But say that short rates and long rates are just about even and they run their cash down to nothing; well, that's saying the bond fund managers are unreasonably optimistic. A few years ago, we had the widest spread between short rates and long rates that we have ever had. In that kind of environment, bond fund managers are not running their liquidity down because they are raving bulls. It's because they are getting paid 300% as much to go into the long end of the market as in the short end of the market. It makes sense for them to run their liquidity down to nothing so they can get those higher yields. But if long rates and short rates are pretty much even and people are running their liquidity down, then it becomes a very good indicator because it shows excessive bullishness. If bond fund liquidity were say 4%, that would mean one thing when the yield curve was extremely steep and something entirely different if the yield curve were flat.

Taking things in context, what are the bullish and bearish extremes for bond fund cash levels?

We don't have but about 20 years of history but in recent years, 4% to 12% have been the extremes.

Other than the shape of the yield curve, what other leading indicators help forecast the direction of interest rates?

It depends on the market. As I said, sometimes markets are purely psychologically driven. The 1990 to 1993 bond market was initially fundamentally driven or monetarily driven because you had a huge spread between long rates and short rates. Everybody borrowed money to buy bonds so they could pick up the positive carry between the cost of their debt and the yield on the bonds. At that time, the shape of the yield curve was a tremendous leading indicator for the bond market, but that was an unusual situation. At the end of that three year period, you still had a positive spread but then the psychological and technical factors took over because you had so many leveraged players. The huge drop in short rates made bonds fundamentally attractive to buy on a leveraged basis but then once you had so many leveraged players in the game, the least little fluctuations would wipe out your equity. Then it became a psychological and technical game. What the leading indicators are depends on the market. Some of them, like cycles, are always leading indicators. The psychological factors, like the put/call ratio, are leading indicators to some extent but the lead is not consistent. The technical indicators tend to deteriorate about the same time the market does so the technicals don't give you a whole lot of lead but they do give you some.

In order to predict bond prices, the first step is to determine which forces are driving the market, be it cyclical, technical, fundamental, monetary, or psychological.

Ideally that is what you would like to do but practically, it requires so much work and insight that you find the best you can do is to follow the numbers as they come in. You don't always figure it out ahead of time. Some of the numbers are almost always late. For example, if you follow Federal Reserve policy, you will catch the middle of the move but you always miss both ends of it because they are always late at tops and bottoms.

Specifically, what do you mean by Federal Reserve policy?

Changes in the discount rate, margin requirements, or Fed funds rate—things like that.

I thought the difference in the discount rate and the 90 day T-bill rate was always a reliable tool for predicting where shortterm rates were headed?

That's true but the Federal Reserve doesn't set the Treasury bill rate. I distinguish between T-bill rates and the discount rate. I consider T-bill rates a monetary factor and in some cases even a technical factor whereas the discount rate is an administered rate which I call Fed funds policy.

Things like the discount rate are virtually always late. If you are looking at T-bills, that is a free market rate and that can be a leading indicator. It used to be that if the T-bill rates were rising and they got within one point of crossing above the discount rate, that was negative. When T-bill rates went below the discount rate, that was positive. I used that for years but the formulas don't work as well going forward, maybe because a lot of people are watching them now that didn't used to.

When the T-bill rate rises above the discount rate, what is that saying about free market conditions?

Typically, it means that conditions are getting tighter. Supposedly, the discount rate is more of a penalty rate. You have to pay more if you need to borrow. If all of the free market rates are above the discount rate, it usually means that conditions have tightened making money more expensive. The leading rates are moving up but the lagging rates haven't caught up yet. I don't think raising the discount rate hurts the bond market. Of course, it hurts a lot of people that have loans tied to that. The discount rate is raised during conditions which are inimical anyway because you raise it usually to catch up with what is going on in the free market. The Fed doesn't drive interest rates around. I think the Fed is more of a trailer—it follows them.

Years ago you created an indicator which measured the average maturity of money market funds. Has its sensitivity in detecting a change in the trend of interest rates held up over time?

I was real enthusiastic about this when I first created it but it was primarily because it was my creation and it was something new, but I haven't found that it is that helpful. It's more confirming than leading because there are a lot of problems. First of all, it used to dance all over the lot. As the money market fund industry matured, the average maturity shortened. It used to be that people would go out 200 days and you can't do that anymore, so there have been secular changes. The actual number of days derives its significance from the context of the market you are in. Again, I take standard deviations and moving averages to see when there is too much enthusiasm or too much pessimism. I still plot it every week and it is a good confirmatory tool when the trend turns up or down, but you don't hit any real home runs; at least I haven't been making any great calls from it lately. I did a few years ago but never with just this indicator alone.

I followed it for several years and often you could see a trend in the process of changing.

That's true, it is helpful as a confirmatory indicator but as far as hitting the exact high or low day, I have done that only once and that was in conjunction with another indicator. Some cartoons came out in the comic papers talking about T-bills. It is very unusual to find something about money market rates on the family comics page. We happened to have an extreme in the money market maturities the same time the cartoon came out. I used that to call a precise turn in T-bill rates which worked, but I could not have called the turn just off of the money market maturity rate alone. I needed another indicator.

Barron's publishes these figures weekly. The number of days to maturity represents the length of time an investor is willing to tie up their money and reflects their outlook for interest rates. If the trend in days is declining, then that suggests that investors anticipate higher interest rates. If the number of days to maturity is rising, expectations call for a decline in rates.

Exactly. When they are sure rates are going to drop, they want to lock in the longest rate they can get.

That can be interpreted as bullish?

Right, and conversely when they are sure rates are going up, they want to shorten their maturity as much as possible so they can keep turning their money over to take advantage of rising rates. Like anything else, when you go to extremes, you are usually wrong but it requires a little bit of sophistication and history to know what an extreme is. There is no set number. Again, it depends on the market but it has been between 25 days and 70 days. If you are going to have a money market fund that is priced at the dollar, you have to meet certain requirements as far as how much paper you can have over so many days. So there are more restrictions now and those restrictions have changed the parameters somewhat.

Are the money supply figures included in your laundry list of indicators?

I don't use these as much as I used to because lately, most of the indicators that incorporate money supply figures have not been giving consistent or accurate buy and sell signals for the stock and bond market. I look at M2 and compare it with the Gross National Product (GNP). I look at M3, reduce it by the CPI, and smooth it to get the real rate of change in M3. A lot of the tools that I use-velocity of the money supply and the real M2, M3 and so forth—worked well in actual practice from the 1920's to the 1970's but in recent years, the figures have not been consistent and the tools based on them haven't been particularly helpful. I have heard explanations for all kinds of technical changes in the way we use our money that theoretically could account for it. I am sure there is some truth to these explanations, but I don't know enough about the theory of construction of these data series to make the proper adjustments and I haven't found anybody else that can either.

At one time, you tracked the relationship of money supply and loan demand.

I still look at whether banks are making loans or liquidating loans. I look at trends in lending activity; whether banks are putting all their money in the bond market like they did in late 1990 to 1993. Those trends seem to be consistent following the shape of the yield curve but as a percentage of the money supply or the algorithms that use the various M's, the numbers have been changing and they haven't been helpful.

In what capacity do you use bond futures to predict interest rates?

The sentiment figures and technical wave counts work well on bond futures and I think the reason is that in the futures market, there is a short for every long. If you get trends that extend for a few days, one side of the other is getting squeezed. You get fear, greed and panic in the futures market much more than in the cash market. For example, you rarely ever see Treasury bond futures move in the same direction as many as 5 or 6 days in a row because by the time the bond futures move that many days in a row, the margin clerk has killed that particular move by sending out margin calls. Whereas in the cash market, the advance/decline line of the New York bond exchange can go in the same direction 30 or 40 days in a row because nobody is forced to sell anything. The psychological, technical, and cyclical indicators work best in markets where you have a lot of forced buying and selling and where emotions are involved.

Will movements in bond futures signal pending moves in the cash market?

You can use the futures to some extent. Say you get a major turning point in the futures. If it is a valid turn, then the cash market, especially the NYSE corporate and high yield bonds, will tend to follow the futures. You get a lot of false moves in the futures because they whip around a lot but they also tend to lead by a little bit at major turning points.

One of your momentum measures calculates various rates of change between longterm rates and shortterm rates. With regard to time periods, does one particular rate of change provide a more timely signal than another?

When I am looking at long rates and short rates, I primarily look at 90 day Treasury bills versus 30 year Treasurys or something comparable. You don't want something like the Fed Funds rate which whips around for all sorts of strange reasons. You want to get the biggest dichotomy possible between the long end and the short end without any attendant artifacts. As far as the time periods for momentum measures, I use the same periods that I use in formulating moving averages. When you are using moving averages or a momentum measure, you want to make sure you are comparing prices at the same point in their respective cycles. There are cycles in the bond market from 10 days to 60 years. For that reason, when calculating momentum measures I will use 10 market days in the shorter term work, 21 market days, and as much as 126 market days in the longer-term work because there are cycles inherent in the bond market for those particular periods.

What is the implication of long rates exhibiting a faster rate of change than short rates?

First of all, short rates have a higher beta than long rates so for any given move, short rates will tend to move more. Short rates have a higher volatility but that is another reason for smoothing them. It is just like comparing utility stocks with technology stocks. In a bull market, the technology stocks will do better and in a bear market they will do worse. To some extent it is relative strength but it is also part of the beta. Technology stocks are inherently higher beta stocks than the utilities. The same thing is true in the shorter-term fluctuations of long and short rates. Theoretically, as long rates get higher compared to short rates, it's creating more incentive for hedge funds and investors to go long. As long rates come down and get closer to short rates, there is less incentive to go long on margin and more incentive to short the bonds. I don't particularly study the relative change between long rates and short rates in a derivative sense to see which one is gaining faster or slower. I look directly at the yield spread and the yield ratio between long rates and short rates.

You wrote a twenty page article titled "A Longer Term Perspective on the Bond Market" which clearly demonstrates your aptitude for original thought. In the text, you included a graph of the yield curve. Two levels are marked off, one at 33% contraction, which is considered bearish and the other at 50% contraction, which is very bearish. What is the significance of these two levels?

I found it very difficult to make money just looking at the yield curve because there are 13 different things that can be going on. You can have long rates rising and short rates falling. You can have long rates rising and short rates rising but long rates are rising faster than short rates. You can have them both rising but short rates are rising faster than long. Then you can have the reverse of that or you can have long rates level and short rates going up, or short rates level and long rates going up. If you look at a yield curve ratio and you have a number like 1.36, it sounds like you are saying something but as I said, there are actually 13 different combinations of conditions that this could be reflecting in the real world. It is very complex and for that reason, among others, I have never known anybody to be able to make any valuable predictions consistently from the yield curve ratio about the future performance of either of the two constituents of that ratio. But if you took the ratio of long rates to short rates, I did find a couple of rough rules of thumb. Other things being equal, it is more bullish when longer rates are higher than short rates and it is more bullish if long rates are gaining on short rates, that is, the spread between long rates and short rates is increasing. The reverse is true. It's negative when long rates are below short rates and it is bearish when the yield spread between long rates and short rates is contracting. I tried to get a little more precise. I wanted to know if the yield spread is contracting, how bad is bad? If short rates were 3% and long rates were 6%, long rates were 100% more than short rates. Let's say short rates stayed the same and long rates started coming down. The yield curve would be contracting because bond prices were going up. Well, bond prices didn't really get in trouble until they lost 50% of their former advantage over short rates. In this example, if short rates stayed at 3% and long rates dropped from 6% to 5%, they would still be attractive compared to short rates but if they went from 6% to 4½ %, they would have lost half of their advantage. Long rates had been 300 basis points or 100% higher than short rates but when they got to 4½%, they were only 150 basis points or 50% higher than short rates. Those levels, 50% and 33%, tended to correspond with a lot of tops in bond market rallies. The theory is that if you have a good yield over short rates, you are happy to hold bonds. As long as the spread is still significant, you are happy to stay in bonds but if it gets to a point where you give up half of your former gain, then a certain constituency will pull out of the market. They will say, "For 100% increase in income, I am willing to risk the bond market but if it's only 50%, it's not worth the risk." There is no magic number but I did find historically that the 50% factor was meaningful and the advantage of using those percents is that it works in all kinds of interest rate environments, whether short rates are 1% or 20%. Sometimes you may have a yield spread of 100 basis points and other times a yield spread of 600 basis points. Whatever the spread is, when you lose more than half of whatever level it started from, it is knocking one prop out from under the bond prices

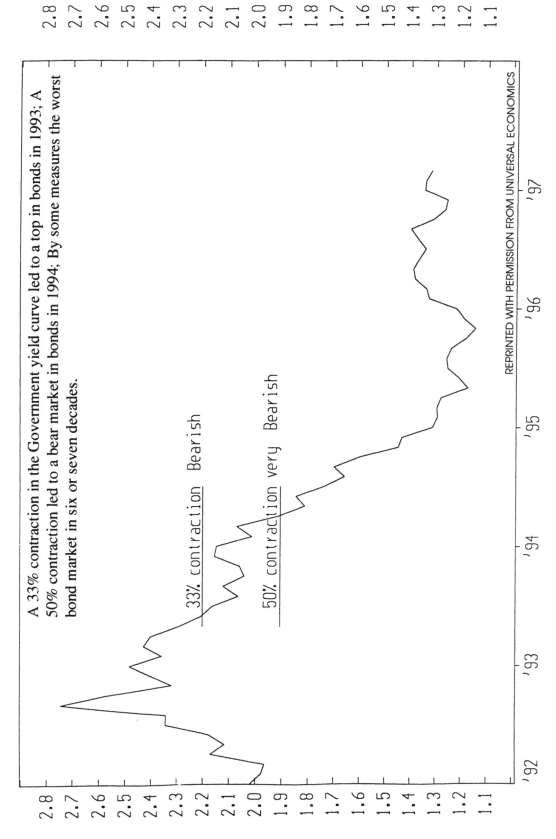

YIELD CURVE
30-YEAR BY 90-DAY TREASURIES

03/25/97

A 33% contraction in the Government yield curve led to a top in bonds in 1993; A
50% contraction led to a bear market in bonds in 1994; By some measures the worst
bond market in six or seven decades.

33% contraction Bearish

50% contraction very Bearish

REPRINTED WITH PERMISSION FROM UNIVERSAL ECONOMICS

because you are losing a certain constituency.

Do you just divide the 30 year Treasury bond by the 90 day Treasury bill and then plot the ratio on a chart?

Yes.

Since we are on the subject of ratios, let's switch to the bond yield/stock yield ratio.

In and of itself, this indicator is not a pinpoint timing tool but it can be if you combine it with other esoteric work like Elliott Wave analysis, cycle analysis or technical analysis. I like the ratio because it is the ultimate fundamental indicator. As the mood of the market changes, people want the guarantee of a bond that they will get their money back and they will get a certain income every period. Other times, they are content with the pocketful of promises from stocks. You don't have to agree to give me any of the money back. You don't have to agree to pay me any income. I'm just going to gamble that stocks are going to go up. Stocks pay dividends and bonds pay interest coupons. When you are discounting stock earnings or dividends, you have to use some factor and the appropriate factor would be the rate of return on alternate investments. The most logical alternate investment would be long dated bonds because you want something that has the same life expectancy as the investment you are considering. Since stocks are theoretically infinite, you want the longest-term bond you can have. By looking at the difference between the absolute level of the bond yield and dividend yield, you can see whether stocks are overpriced or underpriced fundamentally. You can look at the dividend yield on stocks and compare it to the yield on bonds and whichever is higher you can say, "Fundamentally bonds are cheap compared to stocks or fundamentally stocks are cheap compared to bonds." That's one way to look at it. But the behavior of the ratio is a great psychological tool to see whether people don't care about income or whether they are scared and that's the only thing they do want.

What do you use for your bond yield and dividend yield?

I use the S&P high grade bonds for the bond yield and the S&P Industrials for the stock yield. I use high grade bonds instead of the Treasury bond because if I am looking at corporate dividends, I want to compare it with something of comparable risk and that would be corporate bonds. A municipality can tax to meet interest payments and the Treasury can print money; create it out of thin air. Neither one of those options is available to a corporation. With the S&P Industrials, I am looking at the debt issue and the equity issue of the same company. Theoretically, the corporate risk is identical. I use the S&P Industrials instead of the S&P 500 because the S&P 500 includes utilities which are to some extent bond substitutes. A lot of people buy utilities instead of bonds for their yield. With this ratio, I am trying to determine the mood of the public. Are they in the mood for income or growth? If your goal is to distinguish between income and growth as accurately as possible, you don't want an equity index that is larded with a lot of bond substitutes. You don't want preferred stocks or utility stocks. You want industrials.

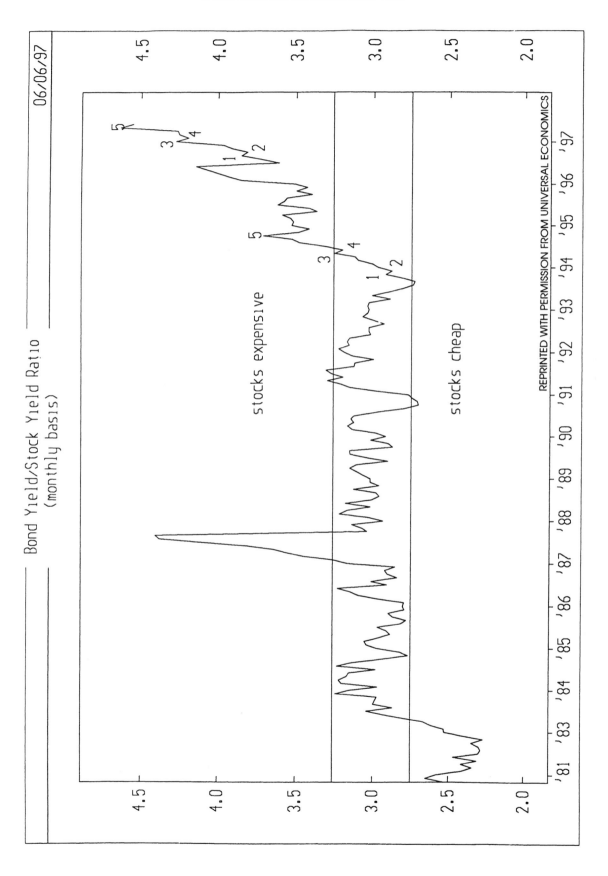

Bond Yield/Stock Yield Ratio
(monthly basis)

06/06/97

stocks expensive

stocks cheap

REPRINTED WITH PERMISSION FROM UNIVERSAL ECONOMICS

From a fundamental standpoint, is there a particular level where stocks become overvalued or undervalued relative to bonds?

The number should range a couple of standard deviations either side of 2.25. You can think about the ratio on a basis of earnings instead of dividends The stock earnings yield to bond coupons should be one to one. Historically, stocks don't pay out 100% of their earnings in dividends, they plow back 50%. In that case, if you are using dividends, a normal ratio would be two to one. You would want your bond income to be twice the dividend yield of stocks. The reason I am using 2.25 to 1.00 and a couple of standard deviations is I think earnings have become very misleading lately. Dividends are real whereas earnings are what your accountants tell you they are and then two years later they say, "No, we were wrong and then they write them all off." You can't restate dividends.

Are fundamental indicators helpful with regard to the bond market?

First of all, if you are looking at something like the inflation statistics or the budget deficit, they are too slow. The budget deficits have been contra-indicators for the last 20 or 30 years but they reflect what went on six months previously and then they are revised. If you have timely fundamental data and you can use it in a creative way, using rates of change, I certainly think fundamentals can be quite helpful but just looking at something like the Gross National Product or inflation statistics or the Flow of Funds doesn't seem to help.

Real interest rates are considered a fundamental indicator and are derived by subtracting the annual inflation rate from current interest rates. Which bond yield and measure of inflation do you plug into the formula?

I calculate it two ways. I use the CPI and the PPI just because that is what I have the greatest history on. I can take the PPI back to the 1770's so that is the most consistent. I won't argue with anybody that wants to use something else but I like the most history I can get. For the current yield, I use AAA longterm corporates or the equivalent but there again, because I have data back to the 1700's.

What are the drawbacks of following real interest rates?

You can say real interest rates are too high but does that mean interest rates are going to come down or that inflation is going to go up? You have the same problem that you have with the yield curve because you never know whether the long end is out of line or whether it is the short end that needs to adjust. In fact, one simple ratio such as real interest rates can be reflecting any one of 13 different things going on in the economy. If you look at the last 200 years, real interest rates have averaged 3¼ % but that doesn't mean if the real interest rate is 6% that nominal interest rates are going to drop by 3%. Rather, it could be that inflation is going to go up 3%. The other thing is that even though the average real rate might have been 3¼ %, if you look back historically, there have been huge departures from this average. In fact, between its extremes, the real rate of interest has fluctuated between about -30% and +30%. The people that popularized real rates of interest picked as their study period an 8 to 10 year period where real interest rates had been about 3% without fluctuating much on either side of that. That was probably the only stable period in the 200 year history of this country. If you look at all the time periods instead of that little slice of the pie, real interest rates are all over the lot. Real interest rates are only helpful if number one; you assume the relationship between inflation and interest rates will remain constant which it never has and two; if you are able to predict future inflation. I find it easier to predict interest rates than inflation. I use real interest rates in a fundamental model because I want to know what it is but I turned the weights down on them so much that by themselves, they are virtually never going to give a signal.

We have already discussed the yield curve and the fact that it serves multiple functions in terms of an indicator. When does it become a technical indicator?

There are a lot of ways to use the yield curve. When you are comparing two things, an indicator like that can be a technical indicator, a psychological indicator, a monetary indicator, or a fundamental one depending on how you use it. If a ratio is trending very strongly in one direction then it becomes a technical indicator and irrespective of the fundamentals, if you have a freight train going you want to get on it. The perfect example is the gold/silver ratio. People say short silver when the ratio is 15 and buy silver when the ratio gets to 40, because silver is fundamentally cheap at 40 times the price of gold or expensive at 15 times gold. That might be true but recently the ratio went from 15 to 20 to 40 and then it went to 101. My feeling is when that ratio is going up, you want to be in whichever of the two metals is stronger. Forget about the fundamentals. The same thing is true with stocks and bonds to a lesser extent. If you look at a spread or a ratio just as a snapshot in time, you get a fundamental value, and the bond yield/stock yield ratio is very helpful for a value investor. But the capital markets are dynamic, and from a trading perspective, one wants always to stay with the strongest asset category, which is indicated by whichever side of this ratio is strongest in the current market. And so this series is also a very valuable technical indicator. Also, if you find the ratios going to huge extremes; for example, if Treasury bill yields are actually negative because people are so afraid that they are willing to pay ¼% for the privilege of owning bills, then this ratio becomes a psychological indicator.

Are momentum (rate of change) indicators useful in the bond market?

Yes, because momentum usually turns before prices. If you are debating about getting out of the bond market, as long as the momentum measures are making new highs, you've got some extra time to sell your bonds. Once they start to trend down, that doesn't mean bond prices are going to fall but it means you have to start worrying about it. I determine whether momentum is uptrending or downtrending by performing standard technical algorithms on a momentum series. Momentum is say today's price compared with the price "X" number of days ago. Once you get that number, then you can do a moving average or do point and figure charts. A fairly good leading indicator for the stock market is looking at where shortterm interest rates are today versus where they were 13 or 26 weeks ago. People don't make their investment decisions based on where short rates are today versus where they were last Friday, but if you do a rate of change of Treasury bills, when rates are lower than they were 13 or 26 weeks ago, that's bullish for the stock market. When rates are higher than they were 13 or 26 weeks ago, it tends to be negative for the stock market. That is where you can use momentum in one asset category as a leading indicator for another asset category.

What is your technique for plotting momentum on a point and figure chart?

Suppose we are calculating momentum in basis points and you are comparing today's yield with the yield 10 days ago. If the yields are the same, the momentum figure today would be zero. If today's yield is one basis point higher, the momentum figure would be one. If it was four basis points higher, it would be four. So you plot the figures. Let's say momentum gets up to where rates are really flying, say interest rates today are 7% compared to 6.80% ten days ago. In that case, the momentum figure would be 20. Then say the next day bond rates uptick a little bit but because you are moving the data forward, instead of being 20 basis points higher than 10 days ago, it's only 17 basis points higher. Then the next day there is another surge in rates and they get up to maybe 21 basis points higher so that's a new high. Bond rates continue to go up but once momentum starts to break down—say it drops from 21 to 20 to 19 to 18 to 17 then to 16—when that momentum figure drops to 16, you get a point and figure sell because even though the rates are going up, the rate of change is slowing drastically. That gives you a sell signal on the momentum so I would grade the momentum studies as very negative but as long as bond prices were going up, I'd stay in the bonds but then the first time they didn't make a new high, I'd probably sell them. There's another method you can use. Instead of subtracting the yield 10 days ago from today's, you can divide it. That way you would have percentages instead of numbers—it would be 99% or 101% or 105%. So you take today's yield versus whatever your appropriate time horizon is, whether it's 10 days, 10 weeks, or whatever and you either get the ratio or you get the difference. Then you plot it and you will find technical patterns and point and figure breakouts.

For point and figure charting, what point value do you assign to each block?

I do a standard point and figure. I usually use three block reversals but you should change the scale enough so that the three block reversals give signals during the whole period that is pertinent to you. If you are a longterm trader, the blocks will have a bigger value than if you are a shortterm trader.

Will momentum indicators detect longterm changes in the bond market as well as shortterm changes?

They can be useful for longterm changes. The shortterm momentum indicators are good for fairly mechanical trading. With the longer-term ones, you will find a series of lower highs in momentum before a top. The longer-term ones are not as precise and require more interpretation.

Are you plotting momentum on various maturities?

I do it on a lot of things. I do it on 30 year bonds, T-bills, Eurodollars, and the bond buyer index. Then I do it on the net asset value of a dozen different bond funds because that is what I actually trade. Primarily, I use no-load funds for the money I manage so every day I want to look at everything I own or am thinking about owning. Rather than just plot the standard yields, I plot what I am actually trading because sometimes you get differences. The main differences, of course, are between risk spreads, that is, you get a big difference between government bonds and junk bonds in various parts of the cycle and in recent years, municipal bonds have had some leading characteristics. Government bonds will tend to lead corporate bonds so if you are trading government bonds or municipal bonds, you don't want to be looking at corporate yields because they are liable to be slow.

Can you say with some assurance that short rates will lead long rates at turning points?

I would say that historically, short rates lead at least 60% of the time. Eurodollars and utility stocks are helpful in forecasting long rates. If I am trying to figure out what the bond market is going to do and I've got the utility index doing one thing and the Treasury bill index doing another, I have found that in recent years the utility stocks have been better than T-bills or other shortterm rates. Maybe it is just in the current market environment where the same constituencies are interested in utility stocks and in long Treasurys, whereas the constituency interested in the short end of the market and the long end of the market are different. Typically both the Treasury bills and utilities lead bonds but when they have disagreed of late, utility stocks have been a better indicator than short rates.

Are there other interest rate sensitive groups which will confirm potential reversals in the trend of interest rates?

The primary indicators in my models are the New York Financial Index which includes every bank, insurance company, and broker listed. You don't pick up divergences there between the individual groups but I also page through several hundred mutual funds every night and I pick up the difference between regional banks, insurance stocks, and so forth. When the utilities, banks, and insurance companies are all going up together, usually the bond market is in pretty good shape because it takes a lot of money to move all those heavily capitalized sectors. When you start getting divergences among those sectors, it's a warning.

You look at the New York Financial index just to make sure it's moving in sync with the bond market?

Yes, and I also calculate the relative strength. If banks are going up and I am doing moving averages and momentum studies and banks keep making new highs I'll say, "That's great, the bond market is fine." That is one part of my analysis but I also divide the NYSE Financial stock index by the NYSE Industrial Stock index, because if the banks are making new highs but the relative strength keeps slipping, that is a serious warning sign for the bond market. S&P has indexes which are just as good and I look at all of them.

Moving averages are usually great timing tools for the stock market. Can the same be said for the bond market?

Moving averages on bond prices are very important. Not only do I calculate moving averages of prices and yields, I use them on ancillary indicators such as high/low ratios and advance/decline ratios, things like that. They are quite helpful. Moving averages are not particularly helpful on zero bonds. If you use a moving average on the junk bond index that is all you ever need to do to outperform 99.9% of the managers. The problem with using moving averages is that people with any kind of ego can't admit to the public, their clients, or themselves that all they are doing is following a mechanical line and if the price crosses this line I'll get in and if it crosses that one I'll get out. Clients would be mortified but the fact is that if you do that, you will outperform the vast majority of bond managers. People aren't willing to use just the moving averages because they always have to have an opinion. It's much more impressive to have some kind of rationale for what you do and it makes your clients feel comfortable but it doesn't really help your performance.

Are you implying that moving averages work best for junk bonds?

They are valuable for all bonds but deadly accurate for junk bonds. Not only are moving averages deadly accurate, they are vital for junk bonds. I would use moving averages for other bonds too, not for predictive purposes so much, but to protect your capital in case of a meltdown. Every now and then you get a dollar collapse or an inflation like we had in 1973-1974 and bonds just get killed. Even if moving averages are not predictive, they are very good ways to protect your capital because once price crosses below it, you sell and you get out with a 3% loss instead of suffering a 30% loss. Zero-coupon bonds are four to five times as volatile as normal full coupon bonds so the problem is that any moving average you pick will either cause a lot of whipsaws or be too insensitive. In my experience, moving averages don't work on zeros.

When you speak of moving averages, are you referring to a 10 week, 30 week, or 40 week moving average?

I have a lot of moving averages. The shortest one I use is a two week or a 10 market day. Then I use 252 days which is about a year. I use different moving averages in different models but the 10 day is the most sensitive I would ever use and as I said, they don't work on zero coupon bonds at all. Point and figure charts do work on zeros. I don't find that moving averages work well on the gold stocks, maybe because of the same volatility problems.

Have we skipped any technical indicators which are not proprietary?

I look at intermarket ratios like bonds versus gold, and silver versus housing prices but I don't look at them just in a static sense in terms of when something is cheap or expensive. I look at them in a dynamic sense using moving averages, Elliott wave counts, cycles, and so forth to try and figure out when the psychological dynamic is about to reverse and one asset category is about to outperform the other. I look at standard tools like moving averages, point and figure charts, stochastics, and MACD's but what's original about my work is that I will apply those not to just standard prices, but to all of these secondary things such as the ratio of silver prices to house prices or bond yields to stock yields. That is an all day job.

What is your analytical perspective on foreign interest rates?

I look at world interest rates but in the country's local currency, not in dollars. I want to see whether interest rates are going up in France and Germany and England and Spain while ours are going down. If that's the case, then our rates are probably going to turn around and go up rather than everybody else's rates turning around to follow us. I do an advance/decline line of world interest rates to see if most of the countries in the world are going up or down. If you find one or two countries out of step, they almost always join the pack rather than the pack joining them. That can be very helpful at times. Say we are having a bond market rally in this country that has been going on for 6 to 8 months and bonds have been rallying around the world. Then bonds in Germany, France, and England start to head down while ours are still going up. We might all be happy but if you have an advance/decline line of the world bond markets, it would be headed down because all the rest of the countries are going down and the United States is going up. That is a pretty good sign it's time to get out of the bond market.

Despite the difference in currency valuations, a close correlation exists between bond markets around the world?

Yes. There is certainly a relationship between currency and the bond market but I haven't figured it out because it is not a consistent relationship. Forget about exchange rates and just look at what nominal interest rates are doing in every country of the world and then go with the majority because if one or two countries are out of step, they invariably join the rest.

How many countries are included in your advance/decline line?

I follow twelve or thirteen countries.

When one country raises or lowers interest rates, that is going to trigger a chain reaction in the others?

Right, and very interestingly, they often move in cycles at the same time. I think cycles are universal psychological events so they ought to show up in Japan and England as well as this country.

John Murphy

John Murphy describes his career path as a "series of accidents" and "a lot of luck." His interest in technical analysis began by being in the right place at the right time. Starting out in the late 1960's with a liberal arts degree and no destination other than Wall Street, he searched for a position in a Wall Street firm not because of any particular interest in the financial markets themselves but because he intuitively knew Wall Street was a good place to be. Ironically, what began as a routine job developed into a fascination and thirty year affair with technical analysis.

Mr. Murphy's first position was with CIT Financial Corporation. They had a job opening and he needed a job. Hired as an assistant to the portfolio manager, he charted stocks held in the company's portfolio. In his view, this was merely an interim position. His next calculated move was to break into the fundamental side of the business. However, he connected intellectually with the many facets of technical analysis and began reading everything available on the subject. The more he read the more his interest intensified. In the early 1970's, stocks entered a bear market and his position at CIT became redundant. Merrill Lynch had an opening in their commodity department. Having no interest in commodities but again, needing a job, he took the position with plans to ride out the bear market in stocks for a couple of years and then migrate back toward the equity market. Two years turned into ten years. As Mr. Murphy explains, "Commodities were red hot at this time." With the recent advent of financial futures such as stock indexes, bonds, and currencies it was an exciting time to be in the commodity markets. He was promoted to the post of Director of Technical Analysis for the commodity department at Merrill Lynch, later moving into money management.

In the 1980's, Mr. Murphy branched off on his own doing consultant work and teaching evening courses at the New York Institute of Finance. During his teaching stint at the NYIF, he had the opportunity to work with the author of his favorite book on technical analysis, William Jiler, who wrote *How Charts Can Help You in the Stock Market.* Suggestions were made that Mr. Murphy write his own book covering the material he was teaching in the classroom. The NYIF course, Technical Analysis of the Futures Market, eventually became the title of his very first book. Still popular today, this landmark book comprehensively covers the field of technical analysis as it relates to the futures market.

Mr. Murphy served as a technical consultant and writer for the Commodity Research Bureau for about seven years. When the New York Futures Exchange decided to launch their new futures contract on the CRB index they called upon Mr. Murphy's expertise to help research the project. These two experiences, combined with his work in commodities at Merrill Lynch, laid the groundwork for an area of analysis which has become his trademark intermarket technical analysis. While working with the various commodity markets day in and day out, Mr. Murphy witnessed a relationship between stocks, bonds, and commodities. The interplay between these markets was displayed in such a manner that allowed him to define a sequential movement from one market to another. Ten years of research in this market niche culminated in his second book, *Intermarket Technical Analysis,* one of the most comprehensible and well-researched books on the subject of technical analysis. Currently, he uses intermarket analysis as a tool for asset allocation.

For the last five years, Mr. Murphy has been headquartered at CNBC as their resident technical analyst. For great advice on how to make money in the market, catch Mr. Murphy every Monday, Wednesday, and Friday at scheduled times. Five years of feedback and fielding questions from CNBC's viewer audience relating to his segments on the show provided the impetus for his latest book, *The Visual Investor.* This book seeks to simplify the concepts of technical analysis for the average investor as it relates to mutual funds, sectors, and global investing.

Mr. Murphy joined forces with Greg Morris, a software developer for twenty years, to form MURPHY MORRIS, Inc. which was created to produce educational software and on-line services for investors. The website is www.murphymorris.com. Somewhere in his harried schedule, Mr. Murphy manages to squeeze in time to work on computer software projects and give lectures at seminars around the world.

Staunchly defending his brotherhood of technicians, he argues that technicians are relegated to the financial equivalent of a caste society. Technicians, treated like black sheep, are seldom given recognition for their prescient calls and more often than not are denigrated for inaccurate forecasts while economists and fundamentalists are revered as gods and quickly forgiven for their judgment errors. This perception is generated and perpetuated by the media. On June 27th, 1996, a reporter for the Wall Street Journal interviewed four technical analysts and then prefaced the article with the following statement: "Some people deride technical analysis as the stock market equivalent of voodoo." What better evidence is needed to substantiate Mr. Murphy's claims.

With almost 30 years of market experience to his credit, Mr. Murphy warns investors against blithely accepting the conventional wisdom that emanates from Wall Street because it is nearly always self-serving. Watch the markets instead. Let the markets tell you when and where to put your money.

Is technical analysis an art?

To call it an art seems to imply that it is purely subjective—that there are no rules. There is a body of rules but they can be interpreted in different ways. Someone said to me recently, "Technical analysis works because all of the technical analysts make it work." People who aren't familiar with it have a simplistic view of it. It's an amazingly diverse and complicated area. There are as many different approaches as there are analysts. It's like medicine. Two different doctors can arrive at two different diagnoses but that doesn't mean there is no science involved. Proof that it is not an art is that computers can now interpret indicators according to a body of rules. For example, suppose an investor wants to look at the relative strength index (RSI) on IBM. They call up their IBM chart which displays the RSI at the bottom of the screen. They can move their cursor and click on RSI and their computer will interpret the RSI. It will say the market is overbought or the market is oversold. There is no art involved. It is just a computer interpreting a body of rules. I don't like the word art. There is a body of rules and art is involved in how you interpret those rules but I think maybe skill is a better word. It's a combination of art, science, and skill.

Technical analysts are constantly being challenged by the fundamental camp to produce a fundamental equivalent of a Warren Buffet or a John Templeton, and of course, we always hear the jibe, "I have never met a rich technician." Why all of the negative press?

There are lots of very wealthy people out there who use technical analysis. I honestly don't understand why technical analysts are always put on the defensive. If a fundamental analyst is caught on the wrong side of a stock, it is simply reported that the analyst downgraded the stock. No one is criticized and yet the technical community is always criticized when they get a forecast wrong. In July 1996, one semiconductor stock announced disappointing earnings and the stock price plunged 8 points the next day—a drop of 25%. The following day, one of the fundamental analysts downgraded the stock from a near-term outperform to a longterm outperform. That's horrible. This analyst screwed up but nothing more was said—no criticism, nothing. I see fundamental analysts getting by with this all the time. I think there are a lot of fundamental analysts out there who are closet technical analysts masquerading as fundamental analysts. I say this because I have noticed so often that after a stock does something significant that's technical, the next day we get 3 or 4 fundamental downgrades. Isn't it amazing that every time a stock breaks its moving average we get fundamental upgrades and downgrades. About two years ago, we had the biggest collapse in the bond market in a half a century. I was one of the people who predicted it. It was very obvious on the charts that this was happening. The economic community throughout the entire period of time said, "This isn't happening." They missed this big collapse and yet I never heard one word of criticism. They missed the whole last recession and yet the media persists in interviewing economists despite the fact that their forecasting record is so horrible. This year is another example. We had been pointing out that the drop in commodity prices and various other intermarket factors were pointing to economic weakness. All of the other economists were saying, "No, no it can't be happening." Now they are reporting signs of economic weakness and the media keep interviewing these same people. I keep asking, "Why don't you interview the people who were right?" It's mind boggling to me how fundamental analysts and economists are allowed to get away with murder and yet technical analysts seem to be held to a much higher standard.

What is the source of all this criticism?

The academic, economic, and journalistic communities. These people are very anti-technical for one simple reason—they don't understand it. People you deal with in the media are financial writers for the most part. They don't trade the market. They don't analyze the markets. They write about the markets after the fact. For decades, the academic community has been telling us that the market is a random walk and you can't predict it but people have been making a pretty good living doing it. The minute you are referred to as a technical analyst you are pigeonholed and not taken seriously. Sometimes technical analysts cause their own problems. You have to speak English and you have to make sense to people. I am acutely aware of this working on television where I have gotten a lot of reactions from television viewers. When you flash a chart up on the television screen and advise people to buy a stock because of a MACD crossover or a stochastic crossover, the average person doesn't have a clue what you are talking about. They are saying, "You think I'm going to go out and buy this stock just because two lines are crossing?" A lot of technical analysts talk in jargon. It sounds very artificial and the average investor who isn't attuned to all of these indicators just turns off. You have to make an attempt to explain to people what you are talking about.

Isn't it true that mutual funds and institutions have resident technical analysts or hire analysts as consultants to advise them regarding the technical situations of the market?

Of course. Because of intense competition and the incredible flood of money flowing in, mutual funds have to always be performing. The result is that money comes out of one stock sector and goes into another and the name of the game has been sector rotation. If you move out of technology you have to move into something else. This is all timing. People call it momentum investing. Call it whatever you want but it strikes me as being purely technical. It has very little to do with the fundamentals because the fundamentals don't change all that much. They are using various timing measures to help them determine when they want to move out of one sector and into another. Now, if you were to ask them, "Are you using technical analysis?" they would probably say, "No, we don't even have a technical analyst on our staff." What about that guy over in the corner? "Well, he's our quantitative analyst." Many quantitative analysts are nothing more than technical analysts. Part of the problem is the term itself. I hate the term technical analysis. What does the term "technical" mean. It means nothing. It scares people. I prefer the term "market analyst." It's much broader.

Does technical analysis have an edge over fundamental analysis?

Yes. You can't trade off the fundamentals because they change too slowly. My job is to see things beforehand and to try and predict things. The minute something becomes a big piece of news, I have no interest in it. My job is to predict it. About one month before the Sumitomo copper scandal, we covered the breakdown in copper and copper stocks and warned people it was a good time to get out. When the news broke a month later, there was nothing left for me to say. It's the classic argument between fundamental and technical analysis. By the time the thing happens, it is too late to do anything with the information. Another good example occurred in the semi-conductor stocks during the 3rd quarter of 1995. The tech stocks were going through the roof. I was getting all kinds of negative readings. The relative strength was breaking down and the volume was turning negative. I commented on the air that it was a good time to get out and yet all the fundamental analysts who came on CNBC were bullish as hell. I distinctly recall one analyst in particular who was very bullish. The anchor host said to him, "Our technical analyst John Murphy says the group doesn't look good technically—the charts are breaking down. How do you respond to that?" The fundamental analyst laughed and said, "Look, charts tell you where you have been but they can't tell you where you are going." Let the record show that in the next 3 months that group lost almost 50% of its value. Not only that, in January and February of 1996, these very same people who were saying "buy" earlier had now turned negative and I went on the air and said, "This is the time to buy." They were ignoring the market's message. The fundamentalists had stayed bullish and watched the market drop 50% and then when the bearish news came out, they then turned bearish right at the bottom. This is a classic example of the difference between technical and fundamental analysis. The market itself votes on the fundamentals every day. Maybe we don't know what the fundamentals are at that moment but the market tells us. If the general trend of prices is toward higher levels, that tells me that demand is greater than supply and the fundamentals are positive. If the market or a stock is going up and the fundamentals are bearish, something doesn't make sense. If the fundamentals are bullish and the stock or group starts to break down then clearly the market is telling us that something is wrong. The market ultimately decides. It's basic economics. When supply exceeds demand, prices drop. When demand exceeds supply, prices rise. The market tells us which way the supply demand equation is moving.

In the last two to three years, strong and swift break-outs and breakdowns have been occurring with more regularity. Is there a possible cause for these distortions in momentum?

With futures and options, you are getting a lot of focus on shortterm activity. A lot of professionals are technically oriented. A stock breaks a support level and it attracts some immediate selling. On a very shortterm basis, I think you have technical traders trading against technical traders. It could be the fast dissemination of news. The minute a report comes out or a rumor of a report it's on CNBC and you can see an immediate reaction in the price of the stock. We see this all the time.

So it's not necessarily because there is a larger percentage of the investing public using technical analysis?

I think that's part of the reason. Technical analysis is growing as never before. You can pick up an incredibly sophisticated software package for under $500.00 and then get live feed data for pennies a month. It's very hard for the average investor to do fundamental analysis. How in the world can you track 3,000 stocks? It's very easy to track stocks on a computer screen. Investors who trade mutual funds are now discovering they can move in and out of funds simply by charting. This may be contributing to some of the shortterm volatility.

Do you think a lot of investors today are more shortterm oriented than in the past?

I think they are becoming more shortterm oriented. They start off being longterm investors but that is a myth. People are longterm investors as long as the stock market is going up 20% a year but history doesn't support that view. Right now, people are being conditioned to buy the dips and it has always worked. That's going to end. There is a whole generation who thinks putting money in mutual funds is like putting money in the bank. These people got a rude awakening during the bond market collapse in 1994. They are going to discover one day that they have lost 30% of their money in the stock market.

How do you approach the market?

My approach to the markets is a top down approach. I look at individual stocks but my real focus is on sectors of the market. Sectors are the way to play the game. There is an enormous amount that goes on beneath the surface. Many of the exchanges have launched all kinds of sector indexes such as drug stocks, biotech, semiconductors, and telecommunications to name a few. There are mutual funds that match up with almost every one of them. People ask me how did the market do? What do you mean by the market? The Dow was up and NASDAQ was down. The tech stocks are breaking down badly yet the oil stocks are going up. It depends on where you are in the market. When commodity prices pick up showing signs of economic strength, you want to rotate toward the economically sensitive stocks like the aluminums, papers, oils, and copper. When people start questioning the strength of the economy, money flows toward defensive stocks such as the foods, drugs, and tobacco. It is not just a case of should I be in the market or should I be out of the market. It's knowing where to be in the market at any given time.

What technique do you use to pinpoint and time which sector to be in?

If I had to pick one indicator it would be simple relative strength analysis. I am not referring to the relative strength index. That's something else. I look at about 80 different industry groups, the S&P industry groups for the most part. I find it more meaningful to look at the strength of each index relative to the S&P 500. I simply take the various industry groups and divide each group by the S&P 500 index. I plot the ratios so I can see what each group is doing relative to the market. For example, I was looking at the index of auto stocks which includes the big three auto makers—Ford, Chrysler, and General Motors. If you calculate a ratio of the auto group compared to the S&P 500, going back over the last couple of years you would have seen that the ratio line was dropping. On a relative strength basis, this meant that during this time auto stocks were underperforming the market. In the beginning of 1996, the line started to move up. This indicated to me that the autos, which had been out of favor, might now be a good place to invest. I spend a lot of time on relative strength analysis. It's the most useful tool I use right now.

Once you plot the ratios do you observe just the directional movement of the lines?

You can apply almost any indicator to these relative strength lines. You can use an oscillator to determine when it is overbought and oversold. I don't get into that because I think it's overkill. Once in a while I will use moving averages. I mostly apply simple trend line analysis using trendlines. When it looks like the relative strength is starting to break down you rotate out of that group and into a group that is beginning to move up. If I have six different charts and they are all moving up, then I am looking for the one group moving up the fastest. Relative strength analysis helps you isolate those areas within the stock market that are doing well versus those that aren't doing well. Why put your money into a group that is underperforming? There are layers and layers of this. Once you find a group then you can choose which stock within the group shows the highest relative strength. Going back to Chrysler, Ford, and GM, you can divide their individual stock price by the auto index to determine which one is the weakest and which one is the strongest. You are not only looking for the strongest industry, you are looking for the strongest stocks within each industry. I find that this is becoming my main tool. This is a very simple indicator. Almost any software package lets you do this and some actually rank the industry groups so you can see which ones have been the strongest in the last week versus three months ago. Relative strength analysis is highly reliable but nothing works every single time. That's why I use it in conjunction with a lot of other things. I am just trying to spot the direction of the relative strength line for some indication of a change in trend telling me it is time to rotate into or out of a sector depending on which way the line is going. I keep it simple.

How far back do you normally go in looking at ratio analysis?

Normally I will go back six months, maybe a year. I am looking for changes in the trend. The main reason I follow relative strength is to pinpoint changes within the market character itself. For example, in the first quarter of 1996, we had tremendous strength in the NASDAQ index and technology stocks and we had tremendous buying in the cyclical stocks. Then right around the beginning of the second quarter the relative strength line showed a distinct change. The cyclical stocks and the NASDAQ technology stocks started to break down on a relative strength basis. It didn't really show up on the charts themselves but on a relative strength basis we noticed that for the first time the tech stocks and cyclicals were starting to underperform. We started to notice money rotating toward the defensive and consumer staples stocks; like cosmetics, household products, drugs, food, tobacco, and soft drinks. This entire group started to outperform the market on the upside at the very time that the cyclicals and the tech stocks were starting to break down. That suggested a significant shift in the market. It's just a matter of looking for changes in the trend. It's the turns that I am looking for. The work is really shortterm because we are trying to advise people who are in the stock market and who trade sector funds so the real focus is the last 3-6 months.

Is it necessary to jump on board at the first signs of strength or weakness or can you still come in midway of a move and still make money?

You want to get in as soon as possible because many times these rotations within the market last only a few months. You have to spot the changes early. That's why I chart these ratios. For example, back in May 1996, I showed a relative strength chart of NASDAQ versus the S&P 500 on CNBC. Over the previous three to four months, NASDAQ had been outperforming the S&P 500 by a very wide margin because the technology stocks were surging. When you looked at the relative strength line you could see it had reached a resistance level set in September 1995. We suggested that the rally in the tech stocks was probably over for now and it might be a good time to take some money off the table. That was about a week before the index itself peaked. Peaks and troughs and support and resistance apply the same for relative strength lines as they do for individual stocks. By the time a group's strength or weakness becomes obvious or they report it in the papers, it's usually too late. A month after my coverage the guys at work asked, "John, is this a good time to start getting out of the technology stocks?" and I said, "No, the time to get out of the technology stocks was a month ago when I first mentioned this." The only way this works is if you spot it very early and the only way you can do that is with charts. This is why I try to use trendlines. It's always best to catch the exact top or exact bottom but the bottom line is that you never do. The ratio line bounces a little bit in a downtrend or it slips a little bit in an uptrend. You are never really sure if it's a reversal or just a pullback. There is still judgment involved.

Is relative strength analysis applicable to foreign markets?

Yes. For example, over the last five to six years the Japanese market had been underperforming the U.S. on a relative strength basis. In the middle of 1995, for the first time in almost 5 years, the Japanese market started to outperform the U.S. market on a relative strength basis. We did a story on Japanese auto stocks in 1996. The relative strength of the Japanese autos was outperforming the Japanese market. If you wanted to put some money in Japan, I would have said the autos should have been one of the areas you looked at because it was one of the strongest sectors. I rely heavily on relative strength analysis.

It sounds like you apply the same conventional rules of interpretation to relative strength lines as you would for traditional trendlines?

Exactly. Relative strength charts look like any other chart—a line going up or down. Going back to the case of the NASDAQ versus the S&P, it was simply a matter of reaching a previous peak. If you had looked at just the individual charts, NASDAQ was at an all time new high and the S&P 500 was at an all time new high. There was no benchmark. Yet, if you looked at the relative strength line, you could see that the line actually reached a previous high that it had set about six months earlier which indicated to me a resistance level. Relative strength lets you see a lot of things before they become evident on the actual charts themselves.

What are your techniques for constructing a trendline?

I happen to like trendlines quite a bit. One of the old rules of trendline analysis is that you need two points to draw a line. It should be tested a third time and then you know you have a valid trendline. A lot of times when I draw a trendline it's been touched only twice. I'm aware of the fact that it may not be a valid trendline but at that particular point in time I don't have the luxury of three points. I take artistic license on occasion. The slope of the trendline is a subjective thing. The steeper the trendline, the less reliable it is. I guess the best trendlines are generally 45 degree slopes. If it is too much steeper than that I tend to be suspicious of it. If it is much flatter than that I am even more suspicious of it. I don't sit there with a protractor and measure it but I have a good sixth sense as to which trendlines are more reliable. I look at many different trendlines from daily to longterm.

Do you use longterm charts to confirm the shorter term picture?

I like to know where the longer term trends are so I begin by looking at charts going back twenty years. They may or may not have any great bearing on what is happening today but I like to know if we are near longterm support and resistance levels. You can tell any story, bullish or bearish, if you pick the right chart. For example, you can look at a price chart of a stock setting a 52 week high. Maybe it doesn't look overly exciting but if you go back you discover that you are breaking a major downtrend line that has been in effect for 5 years or you are breaking a three year old resistance level. I did a story on the Japanese yen. The yen had been dropping but was approaching a little support level. A monthly chart of the Japanese yen going back ten years showed the price sitting at a ten year uptrend line. I do like to look at very longterm charts. When you work backwards you start running into a lot of surprises. I think it is better to start with a 15 or 20 year chart. All you have to do is glance at them, work your way up and then do your real analysis on a 52 week chart or 2 year chart.

In your day to day work do you lean more toward daily charts or weekly charts?

If I had to pick one chart it would probably be the last 52 weeks because then you kind of get a sense of, "Is this important?" I try not to get caught up in the very shortterm swings. I look at them closely but the basic audience I talk to are not traders. They are investors for the most part so I try to concentrate on the important trends. The chart I use the most is the last 52 weeks but then very often I will go in both directions from there—looking at a chart of less than one year and maybe a four or five year chart and then I will zero in on the chart telling the best story.

If you are looking at a longterm trend and it tends to be stalling, what sort of signals do you wait for, other than the obvious trendline break, to confirm that the trend has changed?

I do some Elliott Wave analysis. I look at volume very closely. Are we near a longterm resistance level that maybe was set 10 or 15 years earlier? I look at On-Balance-Volume to see if the last move up was confirmed by the volume. If not, then I may turn more negative. I look at stochastics and the RSI to see if we are in an overbought condition. I also look at what that stock or group is doing relative to the overall market. I tend to form an opinion on something long before it starts to break down. A lot of what I do is anticipatory but then some of it is reactive as well.

Are there any particular chart patterns that you think are more reliable than others?

Yes. The patterns I look for the most are head and shoulders reversal patterns, double tops and double bottoms, and triangles. I really like triangles because not only are they very easy to spot, they are normally continuation patterns. Part of my work includes Elliott Wave analysis. If I can identify a triangle, in Elliott wave terms, that's normally a fourth wave which means if you are in an untrend, there is another up leg coming but it may be the last one. Sometimes if I am having trouble with an Elliott Wave interpretation, finding a good triangle usually helps me determine where we are in the trend. So I find triangles very helpful. I really don't get too caught up in saucers, flags, and pennants. I have never found these to be terribly helpful.

What types of "triangles" are you referring to?

Generally, symmetrical triangles, but, also, if I can see a good descending or ascending triangle I will use it. My favorites are the symmetrical triangles because they are usually continuation patterns.

Stocks that break the neckline on a head and shoulders formation and then immediately reverse closing above the neckline ultimately appear to take off to the upside with a high degree of momentum.

One of the most positive patterns is a head and shoulders top that doesn't work. The Dow in May of 1996 had an apparent head and shoulders topping pattern. On May 8, 1996, the Dow broke below its neckline support level intraday. It had all the earmarks of a big breakdown, but later in the day it came back and closed very strong. It was a classic key reversal day. It opened lower, it broke support, and then it closed above support on very heavy volume. It was just obvious that it was not a head and shoulders top. In Elliott Wave analysis, the "abc" pattern is the corrective phase. When you get that third "c" wave down it is very often the latter part of what appears to be a head and shoulders top. I always ask myself when we are breaking that neckline, "Is this really a breakdown or is this just the "c" wave; the final wave of a correction?" If it is a "c" wave then it is a very bullish pattern. Very often the signal will be whether the close is under the neckline. If a stock dips under the neckline but then closes up I immediately switch to a different interpretation. This is not a head and shoulders pattern. This is just a completion of an "abc" correction in which case we should at least go up and re-test the old highs again.

You allow some leeway just in the event these formations don't materialize?

Absolutely. You have to be careful how you use these terms. Someone says, "This looks like a head and shoulders top" and I am always reluctant to say "yes" because it is not a head and shoulders top until we break the neckline. A lot of times when a certain stock is testing a previous peak, I am asked on the air, "Is this a double top?" My response is that it is always possible it could be a double top but let's not call it a double top. Normally if a stock re-tests an old high, maybe 80% of the time it is going to back off from that and then go right through it. When it backs off you can't say it's a double top. There isn't enough evidence yet.

When a stock breaks its neckline and then reverses, is it more credible for the price to close above the neckline on the same day of the break?

It's easier that way because then you know right off the bat that it is not a head and shoulders top but sometimes we may close a little bit below it. In fact, this is one of the reasons I am reluctant to mention specific numbers. If I say a stock closing under 30 would break the neckline and it closes at 29 7/8—it's not convincing. We say these patterns work most of the time but sometimes you will get fooled. It will slip under the neckline and then turn around and go right back up again and you get caught. The close to me is the most important price of the day. Let's assume a stock closes under the neckline and it looks like a head and shoulders break. A lot of times you will get a bounce right back up to the neckline. The real key is that if on the subsequent rebound it closes back above the neckline then you know something is wrong. It just shouldn't do that.

Nothing's perfect.

People say charting doesn't work a lot of the time. I would say, "Yes, that's absolutely right but a lot of times fundamentals and economics don't work." I am very much a defensive trader in the sense that I am always looking to see what would have to happen to tell me I am wrong. One of the tremendous benefits of charting is that if you do take a position in a stock and then something goes wrong, the charts tell you very quickly that you have made a mistake. You have the option of either liquidating your position or at least not buying any more or selling any more. In futures, this is very easy. You simply get out of your position very quickly. But for stock investors maybe it's not that simple. Nobody likes to be wrong. That's why I always advise people to do things in stages rather than all at one time. If it looks like maybe we are forming a head and shoulders top, I don't like to wait for the breakdown. If there is not enough evidence to say for certain that this is a head and shoulders top or a double top yet other indicators are negative, then I might say, "Take some profits" in anticipation of breaking the neckline. If it does break the neckline, more can be sold. You may take a little loss on that position but all things considered you may still make money on the trade if you sold some of the shares at a higher level. If it doesn't break down but starts moving up and you still have half of your position you might even consider reinstating the other half. You do it in stages. From my days as a trader, if I think a stock has moved up too far or is testing longterm resistance or I see an Elliott Wave 5 or whatever, there may not be enough evidence to sell all of the stock but I will begin selling some of it. If I see a stock in what I think is a basing pattern I may start accumulating this stock in small amounts in anticipation of what could be an upturn. If it does turn up you can buy some more. It's a combination of anticipating and reacting.

So this is your personal investment strategy?

Yes, I think so. I don't think you should make a full commitment to anything at any one time. There are always a series of retests and reconfirmations and this and that so you do a little bit at a time. If a stock gets overbought you sell a little bit of it. If it breaks its 50 day moving average maybe you sell a little bit more. You do everything in stages.

What measures of breadth do you watch?

I look at all the A/D lines, the new highs and lows, the McClellan oscillator, and the McClellan Summation Index. At least once a week, I will glance at the percentage of stocks above their 10 and 30 week moving averages.

Let's talk about some of the specifics of your analysis. What are your favorite indicators?

A lot of the work I do is very simple. Over the years I have experimented with every technique and every indicator. I have gradually simplified what I do because I literally follow everything; international markets, commodities, currencies, indexes, and individual stocks. Using about 80 indicators it isn't possible to do an elaborate analysis of everything so I have narrowed my work down. I must admit that a lot of what I do is very simple trend following. I ask myself, "What is the trend?" I use trendlines and simple support and resistance analysis and some of the patterns that we talked about. I also look at moving averages and volume. On-Balance-Volume is one of my favorite indicators. It has shortcomings but I find it still works quite well for me.

Are we talking about Joe Granvilles's On-Balance-Volume?

Yes. A lot of software programs now let you overlay On-Balance-Volume right on top of a price chart of a stock. The old programs had the line along the bottom. If I see price going up but the volume is not confirming it, then I know there is a problem. I always like to look at what the On-Balance-Volume is doing.

There are a lot of arguments out there claiming it doesn't take into account the price moves during the day. Have you modified Granville's original concept?

There are some arguments that a stock may close down one tick on a given day and all that day's volume is counted as negative. I understand that but I think it balances out. I am interested in the overall trend of the On-Balance-Volume, especially when you overlay it on top of the prices, not a one or two day move in one direction. There are many ways you can modify it. I am suspicious of a lot of the refinements. I have experimented with some of them but I am most comfortable with the simpler version. It's certainly not perfect but it has worked very well for me so I have gravitated toward it. It tells you whether or not the volume flow is moving in the same direction as the price action and that's all I'm concerned about.

How do you use the On-Balance-Volume line?

It's a background indicator. I don't make specific trading decisions using it. It tells me whether or not things are in sync at the moment. Is the volume confirming the price action? If the On-Balance-Volume is moving up faster than the price action, which you can see very clearly on the computer screen, I take this as a positive sign. If it is below the price action, I take that as a negative. You may notice that a stock may move to a new high but its On-Balance-Volume line forms a double-top. On-Balance-Volume is also very helpful in topping or basing patterns. For example, if we are in a trading range and the On-Balance-Volume breaks out to the upside, instead of having to wait for the break-out, I might be inclined to be more aggressive or if I get a break-out to the upside on a stock and the On-Balance-Volume doesn't confirm it, it might make me more cautious. The On-Balance-Volume line tells me when to be careful. During the second half of 1996, IBM had a tremendous run to the upside. One of the indicators that helped me correctly anticipate the rally was a very strong OBV line for IBM.

What other volume indicators do you use?

I don't spend a lot of time looking at volume bars. I know there are some very fancy indicators out there that look at internal volume, money flow, and things like that. I glance at them once in a while but I keep coming back to On-Balance-Volume. It's such a simple indicator. I just want to see the On-Balance-Volume line confirming the price action. When I see a major divergence then I become concerned about it.

You said earlier that you use moving averages. Which ones do you use?

I do use moving averages quite a bit but again nothing fancy. I use the 20 day, 50 day, 100 day, and 200 day moving averages. Each one tells me something different. For very shortterm work I use a 20 day and for more severe corrections I use the 50 day. For longer term work I use a 100 day and a 200 day. I also use Bollinger Bands in conjunction with moving averages to help me determine support and resistance levels. When you use Bollinger Bands on a daily chart, normally they are constructed as two standard deviations around a 20 day moving average. That 20 day moving average becomes critical to support and resistance. I use Bollinger Bands on daily charts but one overlooked area is that they are also very helpful on weekly and monthly charts, weekly charts in particular. You can apply the same technique to weekly charts except that instead of using a 20 day moving average you are using 20 weeks. If you are using a monthly chart you would use 20 months. Since I am a little longer term oriented, my favorite way to use Bollinger Bands is on a weekly chart with a 20 week moving average. I find that the 20 week moving average works as a very good support and resistance line. If you are looking at a daily chart and you want to translate the 20 week line to the daily chart, you have to use a 100 day moving average because that is the equivalent of 20 weeks. Breaking the 100 day moving average line is very significant.

Are there any other standard indicators you favor?

I use Welles Wilder's relative strength index (RSI) and stochastics for overbought and oversold readings. As far as overbought and oversold situations are concerned, I place more emphasis on the weekly charts than I do the daily charts. The MACD, the moving average convergence-divergence, is probably my favorite indicator because it is both a trend following indicator and an overbought/oversold oscillator—the best of both worlds. The MACD histogram is also very helpful, especially on weekly charts.

What advantage does the weekly chart have over the daily chart for these overbought/oversold indicators?

I am very careful when I use these to not just look at the very shortterm. I like to look where these indicators are on a weekly basis because weekly is more important and sometimes even monthly. I've noticed that many traders following the buy and sell signals on a daily stochastics chart get whipsawed a lot. They aren't aware of the fact that they got a buy signal on the daily but the weekly was giving a sell signal. I think you should always look at the weekly first. If the weekly stochastics are negative then the buy signals on the daily are not going to work. You have to use the weekly as a filter.

The bottom line is that you get fewer whipsaws.

I find that stochastics is one of the more reliable indicators if you use the weekly but you don't act on every signal. I never advise anyone to blindly follow any signal. You use it as one of the filters. It tells you when something is starting to lose momentum. It warns you of a possible trend change. You have to use it in conjunction with other things. Another good indicator that isn't used by too many people is the average directional movement index (ADX). It helps me determine when a market is in a trend or in a trading range and suggests which approach to use—a trend following approach or a trading approach?

Does market imply that you can use the ADX for stocks, bonds, indexes, and commodities?

You can use it for anything. If the ADX line is moving up, it basically means that there is a strong trend going on at that particular time. It doesn't tell you the direction of the trend, just that there is a trend. You would then employ a trend following technique of some type, like a moving average. If the ADX line is dropping, that means the market is entering a choppy phase where there is no real trend. In those instances moving averages don't work well. You have to switch to a more trading type of indicator like an oscillator or something like that. We have a lot of indicators, like moving averages, that work well in a trending environment but not in a trading range. The toughest thing is to decide which market you are in—a trading range market or a trending market. The ADX line helps you to determine that. I keep an eye on this on a weekly basis because I like to know when it is turning.

Any others?

I dabble a little bit in other things. I use some Elliott wave analysis, cycle analysis, and I like to play around with Fibonacci retracements but they are more background. I would say these half dozen or so things are probably the major indicators I watch.

Take us step by step through your process of choosing a stock, the criteria you use to screen a stock.

My analysis is not complicated. First of all, before I even look at a stock, I have already looked at which sectors of the market are doing well and which sectors aren't doing well. Then I look at the groups. At the end of each day, I sit down at my computer and look at about 80 group charts. I scan them to see what's turning up and what's turning down. I am looking for only those groups which are technically attractive. After I have zeroed in on five or six groups that look attractive, I will look at their relative strength. I am not so much interested in groups that are in the middle of a move. There is no point focusing on a group that has been going up for three months. It may go up further but I am looking for something that is just beginning to turn up or just beginning to turn down. I want to spot these as early as possible. I pick the group or groups first and then I will look at maybe a dozen or so stocks in those groups to see which ones I like. I don't just pick stocks randomly. I start by looking at a 52 week chart just to get a sense how the stock's acting. Is it going up, is it going down, is it basing, or is it topping? I like to know where the stock price is in relation to its 40 week moving average. If I find a stock that looks interesting, maybe it's breaking out to the upside or maybe the pattern looks attractive, then I will print a copy. By the end of the day, I might have printed charts on 5 or 6 stocks that look attractive. Then I'll examine them in more depth using technical indicators. I will look at the volume flow, the weekly MACD, and maybe I'll take a look at a longer term chart. Before I ever begin to really analyze a chart, I have already looked at maybe 50 others and picked the best looking ones from a group standpoint and then from a standpoint of general attractiveness. I look at a lot of data each day and to be perfectly honest a lot of it is just very visual. I think that over the course of years everybody develops a certain eye for these things. I go through a lot of stuff very fast. Maybe that's not the right way to do it but that's the way I do it.

When you are choosing the best stocks, does your decision ever take into account a projected return?

Not really but that's why I look for stocks or groups that are just beginning to turn. I am not looking for a short turn. I am looking for important turns. You want something that is going to last maybe several months and you want to get in as early as possible. If something has been going up for a while and is approaching a resistance level there's no point in buying it. But no, I don't sit there and calculate the return.

Does any kind of fundamental analysis enter into your methodology?

It does in the sense that I try to keep an eye on what's going on in the economy. If I see weakness in the cyclicals or in technology stocks, this would indicate that investors are getting more pessimistic about the economy. When that happens, they normally buy defensive issues such as bonds, utilities, and consumer staples. I keep an eye on interest rates and inflation. Is that fundamental analysis? I don't know. With the intermarket work, I must admit it's hard to put a name on it. If the dollar is moving up against the Japanese yen, that is one of the factors that makes me positive about the Japanese stock market. That's fundamental. I also like to know when there are earnings reports coming out and how the markets react to those reports. How the market reacts to an earnings report tells you a lot about the technical strength or weakness of a market. If a good earnings report comes out and a stock doesn't react well, that is normally a very bad sign. I don't think what I do is purely technical.

What is intermarket technical analysis?

It's nothing more than pure economic analysis, except there is only one difference—we are not using economic indicators; we are using the markets—the bond market, the stock market and the commodity market. It comes back to one of the premises of technical work and that is, the markets themselves are always leading indicators. The economic indicators are always late. For example, wages are not a leading indicator of inflation. They generally turn up well after commodity prices turn up. The markets are always leading and therefore early. We simply use charts and traditional technical analysis to make economic judgments.

How did you get started using intermarket technical analysis?

It was evolutionary. When I first started technical analysis, it was in the stock market. Then I went into the futures market. The world of futures trading includes commodities, currencies, bonds, and stock indexes. Futures traders become used to following all of these things together; they treat the stock market like any other market whereas stock traders are trained to study just the stock market. After working with these long enough you begin to see all kinds of correlations between the markets. Noticing these relationships I gradually started working with them more and more. The next thing you know it developed into a whole form of analysis.

How many different markets are involved in intermarket analysis?

The whole premise of intermarket work is that you follow everything. The real key is the relationship between commodities and bonds. Historically there has been a very close, inverse relationship between commodity prices and bond prices. Rising commodity prices are usually an early indication of some inflationary pressure which is normally negative for bonds. This is the most important link. The next logical link is the relationship between bonds and the stock market. The stock market is very sensitive to movements in interest rates. I use the bond market as a leading indicator for the stock market. Bonds tend to peak and trough about six months ahead of the stock market.

What are some other relationships?

I also look at the international markets quite a bit. I like to see what the global bond markets and global stock markets are doing. I look at the dollar but I don't give that much weight. The real guts of what I do is the relationship between commodities, bonds, and stocks. I use commodities to help predict what bonds are doing and I use bonds to predict what stocks are doing.

Following so many markets, is there a starting point and sequence for your intermarket analysis?

There is a lot that goes into it. You don't actually start anywhere because it's an ongoing thing. I'm looking at the stock market, the bond market, the dollar, utilities, gold, and other commodities all the time. Let's work backwards. If I am analyzing the stock market, I want to know the direction of bonds because bonds affect stocks. You have to look at bonds before you look at stocks. In order to do bonds I have to look at commodities so I start with the commodity trends. I look at various commodity indexes. I look at individual commodity charts trying to figure out the direction of commodity prices. Some are more important than others. The key commodities I follow are the oil market, copper, the grain markets, and the precious metals. If I had to pick one commodity which I think is the most important it would be the oil

CRB Index and T-bond prices

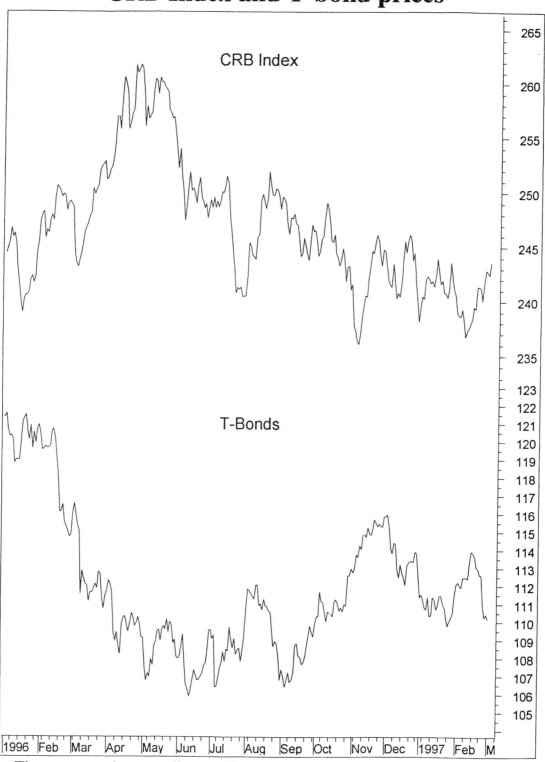

These two markets usually trend in opposite directions. Bond prices do much better when the CRB Index is falling.

market. I try to get a sense of the general trend of commodity prices. If I can get a good handle on that, it will tell me a lot about the direction of interest rates in the sense that if commodity prices have entered a bull market that should put upward pressure on interest rates. There is a very close link between the direction of interest rates and commodity prices. From there I do my analysis of the bond market. If commodity prices are rising and I am getting some bearish readings on bonds that seems to confirm the idea that rising commodity prices are taking their toll on bonds. When bonds, utilities, and some of the other interest sensitive areas start to break down, I take a look at the stock market. In order to determine if the intermarket forces are working, you have to divide the stock market into many sectors. Certain sectors, like the utilities, tend to peak earlier than others. For example, in the early stages of a stock market top, if bonds have peaked, the whole interest rate sensitive stocks area, like the utilities and banks, usually start to break down. The most prominent and reliable are the utilities. At the same time, you begin to see weakness in the interest rate sensitive sectors of the market, you will see strength in many of the economically sensitive stocks, like the cyclical stocks. When I begin to see a rotation in the market out of the utilities and interest rate sensitive stocks and into cyclical stocks, stocks that actually benefit from rising inflation like copper and oil, that confirms that we are near a market top. A breakdown in the interest rate sensitive stocks while the oil stocks are holding up is a very late cycle phenomenon and very symptomatic of a top in the market. This is the point to rotate out of interest sensitive stocks and into oil stocks or maybe even gold stocks. Whenever you hear or read about the stock market, it's always prefaced with what the bond market is doing. Newspapers and television programs talk about the stock market being held hostage to the bond market. Five years ago there was a controversial debate about the link between stocks and bonds. Now it is so routine that no one even disputes it anymore. It is a complicated mechanism and there are many stages you go through but that's sort of the way I look at it.

If I recall from your book, you follow various measures of commodity price behavior.

You really have to follow a number of indexes to get a good reading on what commodity prices are doing because the indexes are constructed differently. For example, the Commodity Research Bureau index (CRB) is about half agricultural markets whereas the Journal of Commerce (JOC) index is composed of industrial prices. Supposedly the JOC is a better indicator of trends in the economy. I look at both of them. To be convinced that a trend has been established in the commodity market, I like to see both indexes moving in the same direction. If they are both moving up then we have something more sustainable.

You not only look at the CRB and JOC indexes but each individual commodity as well?

Well, not necessarily each one. I look at certain key commodities. I want to see where the strength is coming from. If the CRB index is rising and it's being caused just by grain prices to me that doesn't carry a lot of weight. If oil prices are going up too then it carries a lot more weight. If just the grain markets alone were pushing up the CRB, you can't ignore it but it's not as important as if the copper and oil and markets were rising.

Which other indexes do you track?

There are all kinds of indexes I follow to see if they are confirming one another. Some of the ones

Bond prices and the S&P 500

A rising bond market has a positive impact on stocks. A falling bond market usually coincides with a correction or consolidation in stocks.

I watch are the XOI oil market index and the Goldman Sach's commodity index, which is 50% energy related. I look at the XAU gold index and the BKX, which is the bank index.

Does gold lead the other commodities?

Believe it or not, one of the first leading indicators in the commodity market is lumber because it is so interest rate driven. Traditionally lumber moves first, then gold. These are the two main leading ones. Although oil is a very important commodity, I would categorize oil and copper as coincident indicators.

The price behavior of gold has confounded many analysts.

Historically gold has been a leading indicator but it hasn't worked this time around. Gold stocks were breaking out in late 1995 and gold started to make a strong move and reaching a five year high in early 1996. I thought everything was kicking in beautifully and then it just fell apart. This really puzzled me because the precious metals, normally leaders, are not participating in any way in the commodity rally we are having and I don't totally understand why. Gold is also very useful in that gold shares generally have a negative correlation with the stock market. We have been in a major bull market in stocks since 1982 so gold is out of favor. I have noticed the last couple of months that every time the stock market has sold off sharply you have had a big jump in the gold shares. Let's say bonds have topped and so bonds are not a good place to be and then stocks begin to fall and people become convinced that maybe the stock market isn't a great place to be. There aren't a lot of places you can invest. Maybe it will take the perception that stocks have topped and are in a bear market before gold really takes off. I don't know.

Gold almost feels as if it is being manipulated?

To me, it is not important why it happens. I have heard all of the theories like central banks selling gold. Whatever the reason, gold hasn't responded to my intermarket work. On a day to day basis when I am trying to predict the market, there is no point in saying that the dollar is down today so gold should bounce because it hasn't been happening. I am one of those people who believes that the market is always right. I have been bullish on gold for the last two years. I was wrong. I keep saying gold should be going up, and people tell me, "Well, maybe it's artificial" and I say, "Yes, maybe it is but I can't use that." I can't say I am wrong because the central bankers are holding it down. To me that's a cop out. Someday we may find out there is a story behind this. It may be that we aren't wrong, we were just early. Maybe this is a temporary situation. Maybe that relationship will kick back in again at some point. What I find frustrating is that everyone wants everything to happen immediately. If bonds are coming down and stocks are going up, people ask, "Why isn't intermarket analysis working?" People sometimes forget that these are longterm trends. You can't always explain these relationships on a day to day basis.

To pinpoint which markets are outperforming in your intermarket work, are you relying on relative strength or ratio analysis?

Yes. There are all kinds of intermarket influences I pay attention to and a lot of it can be done with ratio analysis. Most software packages allow you to do ratio analysis. I am astounded that something so simple is not more widely used because I think it's a very powerful tool and you can use it in so many different ways.

Give us some examples.

Well, I do all kinds of ratios. I look at the CRB index versus bonds because that tells me at any given time whether you should be in commodities or bonds. To calculate the ratio I usually use the 30 year Treasury for bond prices but I don't think it makes too much of a difference because all the bond markets generally move together. All you are trying to do is see which market is stronger at a particular time. I place a lot of importance on the ratio between the CRB index and bonds prices. It has worked very well over the years. When the ratio is rising, that indicates commodity prices are outperforming bond prices. Normally this is indicative of a pickup in inflationary pressures and a stronger economy. Historically when that ratio is rising it has been negative for stocks as well as bonds. Over the last decade, the ratio had been dropping because we have been in a kind of disinflationary period where financial assets were outperforming hard assets. That ratio peaked in mid-1996. That indicated that investors should be out of commodities or inflation sensitive stocks and in bonds and interest rate sensitive stocks. There are many stock groups that are very sensitive to the action in the individual commodities. I look at the relationship of commodities to their respective stock groups then I look at those stock groups relative to the overall market. Copper stocks, for example, are very sensitive to what happens in copper. When we had the collapse in copper prices in May 1996, because of the Sumitomo scandal, copper stocks, which had been outperforming the market, started to break down about the same time clearly confirming the negative activity in copper.

Will individual stock issues ever lead the underlying commodity?

Very often they do. In this particular case it wasn't true. Copper broke down first.

Do you compare the individual commodities, such as copper, to a commodity index like the CRB or to a market index like the S&P 500?

I very often look at what the group is doing relative to the market. I also look at things like gold stocks versus gold.

What is the relationship there?

Generally speaking, gold stocks tend to lead the price of gold.

Gold mining shares usually lead the price of the metal itself? Can you quantify an average lead time?

A ratio of the CRB Index and T-bond prices

CRB Index / T-Bond Ratio

A falling ratio favors bonds and stocks over commodities. A falling ratio also favors rate sensitive and consumer stocks. A rising ratio favors cyclicals and inflation-sensitive stocks.

No, not really. We have had many rallies in the gold stocks and gold really hasn't followed. Everything else in 1996 has worked well. At the start of 1996, commodities rose, bonds were down, utilities fell, stocks slipped, oil and gold shares went up. The price of gold refused to budge and this was puzzling. Every time gold gets near the $400.00 level we hear about producer and central bank selling? There is a ratio which measures when gold stocks become too expensive relative to the price of gold. You divide the Barron's gold mining index by the price of gold. Generally speaking, when the ratio rises above 2.00 that means that the gold shares are too high relative to the price of gold and you would sell the shares. When it drops under 1.50 it means that gold shares are a buy relative to the price of gold. It's a benchmark. Earlier in 1996 gold stocks took off and got up well above the 2.00 level. As a result they sold off. I don't follow the ratio religiously but anytime it gets above 2.00 it means the spread between the two is too wide and one of two things has to happen; either the price of gold has to go up or gold stocks have to come down. The latter is what happened in 1996. At some point in this whole scenario the price of gold should start moving up.

It's well accepted that utilities lead stocks by about nine months. Given that bonds lead stocks by about six months, does it follow that the utility average leads bonds?

Utilities and bonds usually move very closely together. Weakness in utilities are a leading indicator of higher interest rates. If the utilities start to drop sharply, everybody knows that is generally bearish for stocks. That is the historical rule. If you get really weak action in the utilities, especially the electric utilities, then within six to nine months we should run into problems. A lot of times the utilities will lead the bonds by a little bit but I don't look so much for a lead time, I just want them to confirm one another.

The interest rate sensitive utilities have historically been a leading indicator for the stock market. Do you expect deregulation of the utility industry to uncouple this link?

I am suspicious of that argument because I have been hearing it ever since 1994 and so far it doesn't seem to have made a difference. Every time the utilities do something negative I point out that it is interest rate driven. About a dozen analysts show up and say it has nothing to do with interest rates, it's because of deregulation. Despite all of the talk about deregulation, the link between utilities and the bond market is still remarkably close. If you look at a chart of utilities and bonds, you can't tell them apart. As long as it works I will continue to use it. When it stops working, I won't use it anymore.

The dollar is possibly the least accurate link in your intermarket analysis, right?

Yes, I think so.

Don't you start your analysis there?

Not so much anymore. Many of the relationships of the dollar that worked very well in the past have not worked that well over the last couple of years. For example, one of the historic relationships we have seen over the prior decade is the inverse relationship between gold and the dollar. We really haven't seen that lately. Another rule of thumb is that when the dollar goes up that's bullish for bonds. We hear this all the time but the fact of the matter is that recently one of the things pushing the dollar higher is rising U.S. interest rates. Rising interest rates are bearish for bonds. The dollar is a very complicated mechanism. I do look at it but it becomes less and less important in my intermarket work.

How critical is the number "three" in the Three Steps and a Stumble Rule?

What I find is a lot of these old cliches like "Three Steps and a Stumble" and "Two Tumbles and a Jump" are just things people have accepted over the years. I don't think there is anything magical about "three" steps or "two" tumbles. It is recognition of the fact that interest rates affect stocks. When the Fed starts raising interest rates, at some point the stock market suffers. The Three Steps and a Stumble rule is constructed in a very precise way. Three Fed tightenings could mean anything. The way the Fed moves now isn't the way they moved thirty years ago. They are much more subtle in doing things. I suspect in the old days they moved in much bigger increments whereas now they move in one-eighth and quarter point increments. To me it is the intent. I generally don't follow the letter of those rules. I know what they mean—that multiple Fed tightenings generally hurts the market. Whether its two or four, that's a judgment call.

Generally speaking, will international stock markets move directly with U.S. equity markets?

I have been stressing more and more to watch the global correlations. Some of the markets are more closely correlated than others. We tend to correlate very closely with the United Kingdom, Canada, and the other more developed countries. One country which has been very much out of step with us over the last five years has been Japan. Latin America and Mexico have very low correlations to the U.S. For those who are concerned about our markets being overextended and who want to diversify don't put your money into developed countries whose markets correlate with the U.S. I have been suggesting the Japanese or Mexican markets. They would tend to work better for global diversification.

What type of charts do you use for your intermarket analysis?

I always like to keep a longer term perspective. There is a fantastic service that I like very much called "The Business Picture" (Gilman Research, Oakland, CA). They give you a chartbook full of very large charts of all the major stock averages, bond yields, Treasury bills, the CRB index, global markets, and a lot of indicators that go back 30 years. Periods of economic strength and recessions are marked in. You can overlay one chart on top of the other to compare what happens to bond yields when the dollar has gone up or what has happened historically to the stock market when yields have gone down. This is extremely helpful for the intermarket work I do. When people say things like, "This situation in interest rates is similar to what happened in 1966," you can very easily go back, take out your T-bill chart or bond yield chart comparing it to what happened in 1966 to see if it really is the same. It's very easy to make historic comparisons with these charts.

You follow futures as well as equities. Is it difficult to make the transition from one to the other?

I don't think there is that much of a difference in the overall techniques. My work in the futures area tends to be much more shortterm oriented. I think shorter term analysis works better in the futures area maybe because so many futures traders are technical analysts. I don't know. I find that in the equity area, because I have such a heavy background in futures, I have to force myself to take a longer term perspective. Sometimes I try to interpret every little wiggle in the stock market.

What is your opinion of trading systems?

I don't think too much of systems. Technical analysis seems to have attracted a lot of former engineers. These people are very statistically advanced but they don't really understand the markets so they have to mechanize it by putting their indicators into a system. Over the years I guess I have spoken at every computer conference in the world at one time or another. You get so many people there that have all of the latest software programs. They are very sophisticated. They know all the latest indicators and formulas but if you show them what I consider the basics of technical analysis, I discover they really don't understand it. I think you have to start at the bottom and learn how the markets work. You have to go through the whole classical education eventually working your way up to the computers and all the fancy indicators. Unfortunately, a lot of people start in the other direction. Lately, I have found that at seminars I just want to talk about the basics of charting. Everyone else is talking about the fancy indicators but yet no one has explained to people that you really don't need all the fancy indicators out there. They are nice if you have them but they really become secondary if you understand how the markets work. Because of the fact that I literally follow so many markets, I can't possibly do an in-depth analysis of everything so over the last few years I have really simplified what I do. Quite frankly, I think my work has been a lot better since I have gotten back to the basics using simple trendline analysis, moving averages, support and resistance, and percentage retracements.

One of the nightmares of trading systems is the potential for whipsaws?

Well that's the problem. These systems have 50 or 60 indicators. Many of them overlap and conflict with one another. If you studied all the indicators you would never have time to trade. If you look at 20 indicators, six of them might be saying buy, six say sell, six are neutral and the other two you can't figure out. You get indicator paralysis. My feeling is that it comes down to—"Is the line on the chart going up or down?" That doesn't mean to say that I don't use these indicators. Occasionally I will sit down and go through the whole arsenal. After doing technical analysis for a long period of time you learn to recognize from a simple price chart whether a stock is overbought or oversold without having to look at an oscillator. Having worked with these things over the years I actually do a lot of this subconsciously.

A seat of the pants approach?

Yes. That's just something that comes with time and experience.

Do you have any words of wisdom that you would like to pass on related to your investment experiences?

Yes, *If you are right on the market, most people will disagree with you.* If I am right, almost everybody who comes into CNBC that day will totally disagree with me. I feel very content in that. When everybody is saying the same thing that I am saying then I'm usually wrong. Most of the world the security analysts, the economists, the journalists who cover the market—they are still 90% fundamentally oriented. If you go back to the idea that the charts really do lead the fundamentals and if I'm reading the charts that means I am going to be ahead of the fundamentalists and they are all going to disagree with me. Appearing to be wrong is something you have to learn to live with. Early in your career I think it bothers you. It's a tough thing to accept but eventually you will be proven right. I am extremely comfortable being alone. In fact, I assume that if I am right, I will be alone.

Martin Pring

Martin Pring has made innumerable contributions to the field of technical analysis, especially with regard to education. His books, videos, and CD ROMs have been instrumental in generating interest in technical analysis, helping to bring it to the forefront. I cut my investment teeth on *"Technical Analysis Explained,"* now in its third edition, and consistently recommend this book as a first choice for novices interested in learning the rudiments of technical analysis. By the spring of 1997, McGraw-Hill hopes to release Mr. Prings CD ROM/book combination as a basic course in technical analysis. For the more seasoned analyst, three other titles are available *"Martin Pring on Market Momentum," "The All-Season Investor,"* and *"Investment Psychology   Explained."*

A native of England, Mr. Pring began his financial career as a stock broker in Canada. Reading a copy of Edwards and Magee's *"Technical Analysis of Stock Trends"* piqued his interest enough to explore the subject further. Growing increasingly dissatisfied with the fundamentally based research his brokerage firm produced, he converted to technical analysis. Soon thereafter, he began part-time consulting work for the Bank Credit Analyst (BCA) in Montreal, Canada until he joined them full-time in 1974. Leaving in 1980 to start his own firm, The International Institute for Economic Research, he continued consultant work for the BCA and with their assistance, launched his first newsletter, *The Pring Market Review*.

To better serve the needs of clients, the 48 page *Pring Market Review* was later divided into two separate monthly publications, a twelve page newsletter renamed the *Intermarket Review* and the *Intermarket Global Chart Book*, a unique 38 page historical perspective of the world's principal financial markets. Weekly updates of the *Intermarket Review* are available via E-mail. More recently, the newsletter has undergone some technological revisions and is now available in multimedia form on the world wide web at www.pring.com. Separately on the web, Mr. Pring is producing a fully interactive weekly, five minute course on technical analysis.

There seems to be no end to Mr. Pring's innovation. Creating user friendly educational tools for aspiring technical analysts has consumed the better part of his time over the last few years. He has worked with Equis International to produce training videos and CD ROM tutorials to be used in conjunction with their Metastock software for technical analysis. The CD ROM offers a five minute presentation describing the use and function of each one of twenty five indicators, including his own KST indicator. In addition, he has developed templates for the Metastock program enabling users to create their own trading systems. Pushing himself to the limit, he is working concurrently on writing an eight module CD ROM course providing ninety minutes to two hours of technical analysis instruction per CD as well as a CD ROM program for Telescan users. Much of his own research and analysis has been relegated to the back burner until these projects are complete.

Just so you are not side-tracked by his educational endeavors, Mr. Pring has made some timely forecasts. In *Barron's* alone he made three bullish calls which materialized as predicted. There was a bullish article on commodities in the May 4, 1987 issue, gold in the November 13, 1989 issue, and bonds in December 10, 1990 issue. Other articles have appeared in the *International Herald Tribune*, *Futures Magazine*, and *Technical Analysis of Stocks and Commodities*. His speaking engagements carry him to audiences of technical analysts around the globe.

Mr. Pring is also a principal of Pring Turner Capital, a money management firm with a global investment perspective.

Regarding methodologies, is there one particular aspect of your work which is your "trade-mark" so to speak?
As far as technical analysis is concerned, the KST system that I use is probably unique.

What does the KST stand for?

Know Sure Thing.

Is the KST system a composite of indicators?

It's a weighted, smoothed, momentum indicator. Any price, at any time, is determined by a number of interacting cycles of different lengths. If you just look at a rate of change indicator, you are just picking up one or two of those cycles, maybe the longer ones or the shorter ones. The KST takes four different rates of change, smooths them with a moving average, adds them up together, and weights them. The biggest time span gets the greatest weight. The KST does this for three different types of trend—the shortterm trend, the intermediate trend, and the longterm trend. So you have three different KST indicators all operating at the same time because you would like to know when the first shortterm buy occurs in the first longterm bull market. So the longterm has big swings and gives you perspective when you are at the beginning of a major move and when you are in a topping out phase. Then you can look at the intermediate-term and the shortterm KST's to help you determine the timing. Obviously, you are not going to be buying a shortterm move when the longterm KST is topping out or declining because what you would be doing is buying at a market top or a bear market rally. We put the short, intermediate, and longterm KST's on a chart to gain perspective.

What are you taking the rate of change of?

Anything. It could be the stock market, bonds, or gold.

You are treating the KST as a momentum oscillator.

Absolutely.

What is the interpretation if the KST is below the zero axis?

All you can say is that momentum is in a downtrend.

If it's above the zero axis, is it in an uptrend?

Well, I should say that if it's going down below zero, it's in a downtrend. If it's going down above zero, it's also in a downtrend.

Once it crosses the zero axis to the upside, after having been below it, is it then considered an uptrend?

Yes, but I don't really regard crossing the axis as significant.
Does the zero axis serve any purpose at all?

It does in a sense that if the KST is going up and it's below zero, it's a low risk type of position. If it's going up and above zero, obviously the risks get higher.

Since the KST is a charted line, are you primarily looking at the "trend" of the indicator as well as patterns for all three time horizons?

Trendlines, double tops, double bottoms, divergences—everything.

Divergences meaning between the three time periods?

Divergences between the individual KST indicators and the price.

Is the KST indicator incorporated into Metastock's software program?

No, it's not. You can put custom formulas in yourself or they sell one of my modules that you insert into Metastock. It's an add on.

Are cycles in general part of your analysis?

Not a great deal because I find it is such an imperfect science. I am aware of them. The KST doesn't include all the cycles by any means but it is an attempt to try and include more than one cycle.

What range of cycle lengths are included in the KST indicator?

For the longterm cycle, we are looking at the four year business cycle. We take the 9 month rate of change, the 12 month rate of change, 18 month rate of change, and a 24 month rate of change and then we smooth those with moving averages, weight them, add them up, and divide by 10 because it is the sum of the weights. The idea is that you can put the smoothed, 24 month rate of change onto a chart and see that in most markets it will reflect the bull and bear cycle quite well. The problem is when something reflects a longterm cycle, which is what this is, it's usually late in giving signals. If you are looking at the shortterm KST, then you use time spans based on daily data but the principle is the same. In other words, we take say a 6 day, 10 day, 20 day, and 25 day rate of change, smooth those out, and weight them and that would be our shortterm KST indicator. The intermediate would be somewhere in the middle of the short to longterm time frame. By including the shorter term cycles, it speeds up the turning points and doesn't offer you too much in the way of whipsaws.

It sounds like you use the shorter term KST to call attention to an impending turn of greater significance?

Well, it helps to turn it quicker, yes, without losing the regularity of the swings.

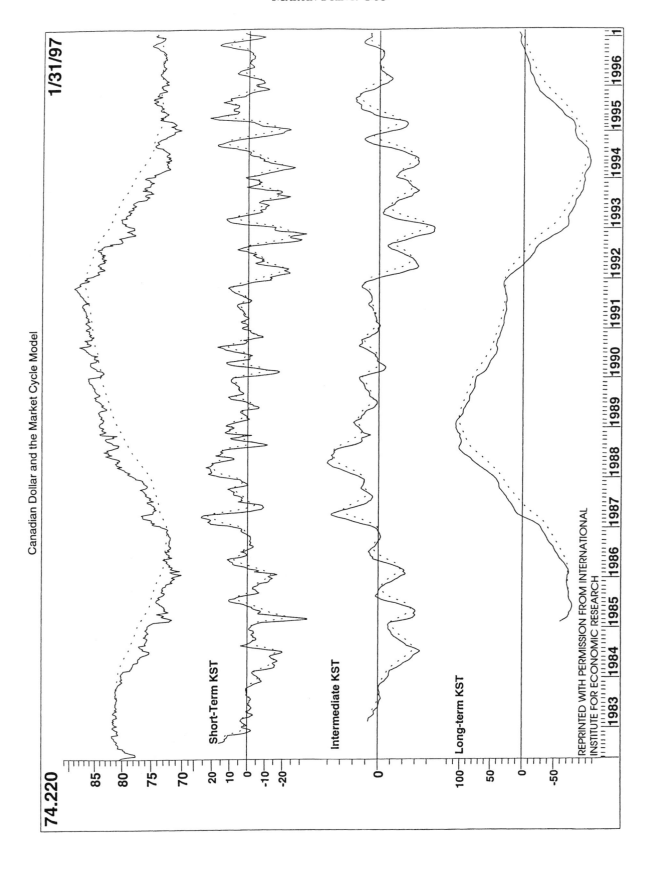

Canadian Dollar and the Market Cycle Model

At one time, the business cycle was an integral part of your analysis. Is this still the case?

Yes, that's right, but that's not technical analysis. You can use technical analysis to help you figure out where you are in a business cycle. But the business cycle work itself is really economic. The other unique thing that I do is that I use a six stage business cycle.

Six stages within the typical four year time period?

Yes. The idea is that the business cycle keeps repeating. It extends approximately four years from trough to trough. A chronological sequence of events take place during a business cycle. In an economic sense, there are a lot of different economic indicators that move chronologically. Starting with say first of all, the money supply and then working into housing starts- which is the first actual hard asset, if you will, that starts to bottom out during a cycle—and then moving all the way through the cycle to capital expenditure. So there are a lot of different events that take place during a business cycle and usually they follow each other pretty religiously. Occasionally, one might fall out of kilter but you use the others to check what is going on. There are three markets: bonds, stocks, and commodities. Each of these markets also undergo a chronological sequence starting first with bonds, then stocks, and finally commodities. Since there are three markets, we have six turning points and hence six stages. We have a top in the stock market and a bottom in the stock market, a top and bottom in the bond market, and a top and bottom in the commodities market.

If I understand you correctly, you are saying that each of those three markets top and later bottom, all within a four year period. Can one assume that this cyclical rotation will occur with a fair degree of regularity?

Yes. Taking it back to the beginning of the 19th century, it has worked pretty well in every cycle, but there are some notable exceptions. I mean, if it were that easy, everyone would be following it. That is why I use technical analysis to help me determine the current stages. I also have models which are called barometers. We have, let's say, 10 or 12 indicators that have pretty good records for analyzing bull and bear markets in stocks but none of them are perfect. So we take these indicators and each time one is positive, it goes in the plus column. When more than 50% of the indicators are positive, the whole barometer turns bullish which tells us that our combination of technical, economic, and financial indicators are pointing to a positive backdrop for equities and vice versa. Then we do that for industrial commodity prices and also for bonds. It is important to take industrial commodity prices as opposed to agricultural commodity prices.

Why is that?

Because industrial commodity prices are driven by the business cycle and agricultural commodities generally are more influenced by weather.

Wouldn't agricultural prices impact the business cycle in terms of inflation or deflation?

Well, they might have some impact but they don't act in the same way that the industrial commodity prices act. We are trying to use something which is purely economically driven and purely business cycle driven which is industrial commodity prices. Now, sometimes you have things like cotton, which is actually an agricultural product, included in industrial commodities so even that isn't pure.

Do you look at industrial commodity prices individually or collectively in a group?

Primarily as a group. There are two indexes I follow. They are the Commodity Research Bureau (CRB) spot raw industrial material index and the Journal of Commerce (JOC) raw material index. They are slightly different. The JOC includes energy and the CRB spot does not include energy.

You mentioned the use of a barometer. Are indicators from the various markets lumped together as a group in one barometer or are there separate barometers for the stock market, the commodity market, and so forth?

Yes well, there may be two or three economic indicators and two or three financial indicators and two or three technical indicators. Then we have some chronological indicators. We know that bond prices peak after commodity prices bottom. So we might include bond prices as an indicator. In other words, if we can prove that bond prices have peaked because they have crossed their nine month moving average, we'll say that is obviously bullish for commodities because that is a condition that has to be met before commodity prices move up.

In *"Technical Analysis Explained,"* **you wrote about the Kondratieff cycle of 50-54 years. Based on the end of the last cycle in 1929, the next cycle seems to be a little behind schedule.**

Well, you have to look upon it as a cycle of inflationary and deflationary forces rather than prices because there has been no corrective wave in terms of prices. Prices have continued to go up but if you look at things like the bond market you can see that there has been a definite longterm decline in yields from 1981 to 1992, when it bottomed out. So, I think the cycle is still alive and well. The question is, "Has it bottomed out?" and it is too early to say from a technical aspect.

At one time, wasn't it possible to go back historically and make a case for the Kondratieff cycle to occur with a fair degree of accuracy every 50 to 60 years?

I think you still can, except you must not look at it in terms of consumer and wholesale prices, which is what some of the earlier work did. You have to look at it in terms of inflationary and deflationary forces. A good measure of that might be yields on longterm bonds.

Can you use industrial commodity prices as a measure of inflationary forces?

Yes, but they haven't corrected like the bond yields have. We are more likely to get a better signal from the bond yields than from the industrial commodities because they have just been moving sideways since 1981.

Do you look at a rate of change in longterm bonds and industrial commodities and then compare the two?

Yes, we look at smoothed rates of change.

Are there any ratios you use which compare interest rates and commodities?

Yes, bond prices relative to commodities. One of our favorite indicators is the inflation versus deflation groups in the stock market. Inflation groups are those that react positively to inflationary forces like mines and energy—aluminum, gold, and oil. Deflation groups are those that react favorably to declining interest rates such as electric utilities, insurance companies, and so forth. We take about four groups in each category and make an index of deflation groups and inflation groups and then calculate a ratio of inflation divided by deflation. This ratio helps to tell you where you are in the cycle. If inflation is beating deflation then that tells you that you are in the right hand part of the cycle and vice versa. The reason we do four groups rather than just one group is that sometimes you get some really unusual things happening within an industry that distorts the industry from its normal cyclical behavior. We had that about 10 or 15 years ago in the agricultural machinery index. They went through a real depression. As a result, during the inflationary part of the cycle, this group didn't rally very much. That was an inflation sensitive group. That is why we take four groups rather than one group. We could just use gold and electric utilities, but if there are certain regulatory actions being taken on electric utilities, that might distort the group for a particular cycle.

If utilities are considered a "flight to safety" vehicle of investing, wouldn't a lot of money coming into utilities distort the indicator?

Well no, that helps it because that is when people are scared. That means you are in a deflationary part of the cycle, so that's good from an analytical point of view. It's when you get something abnormal from the cyclical that distorts it.

Abnormal meaning what?

If you are in a deflationary part of the cycle, and we will say that there is a massive public relations campaign to regulate utilities, then that may depress the utility stocks when they should be going up. So in other words, you have an unusual factor which is distorting what should be a positive cyclical period. That is why you take several different groups. Most of the time nothing is affected by these special factors but sometimes it is.

7.4200

1/31/97

Moody's AA Corporate Bond Yield Vs The Inflation/Deflation Index

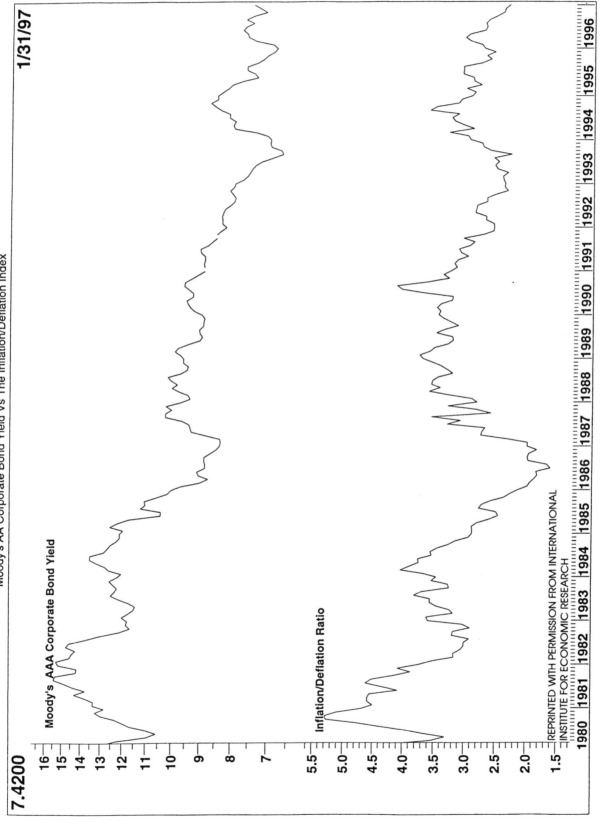

Moody's AAA Corporate Bond Yield

Inflation/Deflation Ratio

REPRINTED WITH PERMISSION FROM INTERNATIONAL
INSTITUTE FOR ECONOMIC RESEARCH

Once you have calculated the ratio, how do you interpret it?

If it is going up, it's positive for inflation sensitive stocks and that tells you that you are in the inflationary part of the business cycle. If it is going down, it tells you that you are in the deflationary part of the cycle and also that deflation sensitive groups are outperforming inflation sensitive stocks. You determine whether it is going up or down by looking at it in relation to its 12 month moving average or sometimes you can draw trendlines or price patterns or use some other trend determining technique. An eclectic approach.

This is an auxiliary indicator, one which you would look at separately from the other indicators in your barometer?

That's right. Another ratio we look at is consumer non-cyclicals to consumer cyclicals. Consumer non-cyclicals are things like food stocks, tobacco stocks—that sort of thing. They tend to be defensive stocks that do well early in the cycle. The non-cyclicals are things like auto parts and autos and these stocks tend to do better in the latter part of the cycle. So they too have a bit of a sequence going on with them. They can both be going up at the same time but when you take a ratio of the two, it becomes pretty clear which one is doing better than the other. That is another thing we look at to try and figure out where we are.

When the consumer cyclical stocks are moving up, that signals a move into a more inflationary environment?

Yes.

Are there any other ratios you use?

Stocks versus bonds. Generally speaking, when bonds outperform stocks on a trend basis, it is the beginning of a bear market because bonds have already gone down quite a bit because they lead stocks. At that point, stocks begin to fall quite sharply. So that means that the stock/bond ratio falls. This is often a sign that a bear market in stocks is getting underway.

For the denominator portion of the ratio, do you use the current value of the 30 year Treasury bond?

They would have to use a 30 year price against the stocks, like the S&P 500. It is best done if you can get a total return series. In other words, stocks including dividends and bonds including interest because that is really what the asset position is about.

How difficult is it to obtain the total return data for the 30 year bond and the S&P 500 index?

Most of the data bases now have a total return stock index and a total return bond index. The problem is, the history is not very long. It is maybe four or five years. My data goes back about 50 years.

Given that inflation is a negative harbinger for the stock market, are these ratios leading, coincident, or lagging in terms of timing?

If you are crossing a 12 month moving average, I think the signals themselves always come after the fact. By definition, there has always been some time that has elapsed.

Do you use a 12 month moving average for all of these ratios?

Twelve months seems to work as a compromise. Nothing works perfectly in all situations and I would say that the 12 month moving average works less imperfectly than the rest. But you use that and look back and see whether it has been reliable or not in the past. Some series will whip across a 12 month moving average every six months or so but others are much smoother. If it has worked well in the past, one would give it a greater weighting when it crosses the 12 month moving average. If it does so when you are breaking a trendline at the same time, then you can be pretty sure the trend is turning. If you have momentum turning at the same time—you just build up a weight of the evidence approach using the different indicators.

Could you just as easily determine the trend by calculating a single biweekly or monthly ratio rather than calculating a moving average?

Yes. Most of these ratios are done on a monthly basis anyway so you could by definition, look at it only once a month. But you can get an idea in the middle of the month what's going on by looking at the weekly data for the same things.

Are there any specific economic indicators you use?

A very simple one is taking a 12 month moving average of the discount rate. When the discount rate is above its 12 month moving average, that indicates that the trend of shortterm interest rates is positive and vice versa.

You follow international markets. What is your approach?

I basically look at the markets individually and try and assess if there is any commonality to them. In other words, if you have all of the markets bottoming out or all the markets topping out then that becomes a lot more reliable than if you just have one or two bottoming out or topping out. We use the usual indicators—the longterm KST's. I use monthly rates of change—9, 12, 18, and 24 month rates of change and smooth those with moving averages. To some degree, I use relative strength as well. I don't measure the breadth of the foreign markets because I don't have the data.

In terms of breadth, do foreign bourses keep advance/decline statistics within their own home markets?

Some of them do. I have done a lot of work on the Italian market and they have the A/D breadth data and I know it is available in Canada and the United Kingdom.

Does your scope of analysis include emerging countries?

A little bit yes, now that the data is becoming available. You can pretty well get data on any country in the world now.

Can you recommend a source?

There are a number of different sources. Dow Jones has a good international country data base. Though the history is not very great, Telescan has a very large data base of international stock issues. There is an Australian company called Proview which offers a lot of international interest rates which I can't find anywhere else.

I believe you track foreign interest rates also. Will foreign interest rates move in relationship to U. S. interest rates?

There is a bit of a global cycle, yes, but within the global cycle individual countries can move independently.

With so many foreigners holding so many dollars, would a change in U.S. interest rates trigger a response in foreign interest rates?

All interest rates impact through the currency. In other words, if the currency is going down and against the wishes of the establishment, then government concerns are forced to tighten monetary policy. That pushes up interest rates so there is a relationship there. Also, if U.S. rates are going up then they become more competitive relative to other countries so that other things being equal, helps to push the dollar up.

Other countries raising their interest rates simply to protect their currency could be acting alone, not in unison with other countries.

Right.

With regard to stock markets in developed countries, what correlations have you observed and is there a tendency for one country to lead?

The United Kingdom has had an historical record of leading the United States. Italy seems to have a record of moving counter to everybody else. I don't know of any other relationships like that except in the natural resource markets, which tend to do better at the end of a global business cycle. Toronto has good relative strength at the end of the cycle relative to the United States and vice versa. That sort of thing would be true of Australia and of South Africa but that is only the resource based stocks in those indices. Canada has banks, so the banks will still act the same way as the banks in the United States. That is another thing, the industry groups around the world tend to move, I wouldn't say in tandem, but closely together. In other words, a European bank, an American bank, and a Canadian bank are usually in a bull market together.

And the resource stocks tend to move together?

Very much so in the resource stocks because their products are priced in dollars.

Other than oil, what other natural resource commodities are priced in dollars?

If you sell copper, you are going to be selling it in dollars. It doesn't make much difference if it is produced in Chile or Canada, they are still getting dollars for it. If the dollar price goes up, the mines go up. Even on the London Metal Exchange, the dollar contracts for copper and aluminum are very popular.

Around the world, daily prices for gold bullion differ somewhat? Which price more accurately reflects the true supply/demand picture?

I look at the afternoon (P.M.) fixing price in London as the key determinant but obviously gold prices move fairly close together. The thing about the afternoon fix in London is that it's physical gold. The COMEX is all futures contracts. The afternoon fix is consistent. A lot of volume occurs each day at the P.M. fix so that's a good price. I don't think you get much better results using the P.M. fix as opposed to using the New York COMEX close but it is something that we have a good history on, so that's what I use. I use this in conjunction with the Philadelphia gold and silver share index (XAU) and the Toronto Stock Exchange (TSE) gold and silver share index. I also follow the Financial Times gold share index which is an index of South African gold stocks. All of these would be adjusted for U.S. dollars to make them consistent.

The price of gold is "fixed" twice daily in London, once in the morning and once in the afternoon. Why is there more volume in the afternoon?

Because the New York gold market is open then. The afternoon fix in London is at 3:30 p.m which is 10:30 in the morning in the U.S.

Are there other types of analysis you perform on the various gold indexes other than charting them and observing the trend?

I am looking at the technical aspect of all these things and interrelating them. Gold shares typically lead gold at market bottoms. The shares make a bottom, then gold makes a bottom, then the shares make a higher bottom, and then gold makes a lower bottom. That's a good sign and vice-versa. Although at peaks, it's the divergences that you look for. Sometimes the shares peak after the gold and sometimes the gold peaks after the shares, but at bottoms, it's usually the shares that lead the gold.

Do you look at any gold ratios?

Yes, the gold/silver ratio.

You are calculating the ratio by dividing the price of COMEX gold by COMEX silver?

Yes.

Are you looking for comparisons in relative fundamental value?

I don't really look at that. I look more at the trends. I don't think there is such a thing as over and undervaluation between gold and silver.

Specifically, what are you looking for?

The trend of gold versus silver. I want to determine which one is the better one to be in. If the trend is up and it's a gold/silver ratio, then you would be in gold. If the trend is down you would be in silver. When the line is going up, it means gold is outperforming silver and when the line is going down, it means silver is outperforming gold.

I thought the precious metals tended to move somewhat together?

No, I wouldn't say that. Over the long haul, they do move together but there is always a leader in a group and that is what you want to be in, the leader. They may both be going up but one is going up faster.

Can we depend on gold and gold stocks to move inversely with the stock market?

No. Gold actually fits in somewhere between bonds and commodities because gold tends to discount commodity price moves. Since 1978, it has discounted pretty well every major move in industrial commodity prices.

Would you explain what you mean by "discounted"?

It anticipates moves in commodity prices. In other words, gold prices bottomed in the beginning of 1993 and commodity prices bottomed at the end of 1993. If gold is coming down, it is saying that the rise in commodity prices is limited.

This theory should hold true on the upside as well as the downside?

Yes. But it is not precise. The leads and the lags differ and so do the magnitudes.

Is there an average period of time in which gold leads commodities?

It can be misleading if you rely on an average time. Sometimes it is quicker and sometimes it is longer. The important thing is to identify a reversal in gold. If you can see that gold is in an uptrend and commodities are going down, the next thing to look for is a turnaround in commodities. In fact, I would say that a rally in gold is almost a prerequisite for a rally in commodities and vice versa.

Would this apply to all commodities?

Industrial commodities. Since bond yields move with commodities, of course, there is a relationship there too. I look at a ratio of commodities to bonds. You can put a chart up and show that gold leads bond yields.

What is the order of movement?

Gold leads commodities which leads bonds. Gold bottoms out, then commodities, and then bond yields. In other words, gold bottoms out, commodities bottom out, and bonds prices peak, so in a sense you can say that there are eight stages to the business cycle.

Do you place more credence on the economic aspects of your work rather than the technical?

I think they both go hand in hand.

From a technical perspective, what indicators do you follow?

The Relative Strength Index (RSI). I take a nine day RSI and smooth it with an eight day moving average.

Then do you use the standard parameters—70 as overbought and 30 as oversold?

It is more 75/25 because the shorter the RSI, the more it swings.

If beginners start using the RSI, would you advise them to wait for extreme levels before taking action?

Oh definitely, yes.

Are there other technical indicators?

The McClellan Oscillator and the A/D line. New highs are an important indicator. I look at that on both a daily and weekly basis.

At one time you recommended "advancing" a moving average. Do you still use this technique?

Not as much as I probably should do. It is a good technique.

How much do you advance the moving average?

It depends on the average. I would advance a 25 day average somewhere between 3 and 7 days.

So roughly 25% of what you are using as an average.

Normally a little less than that.

In *"Technical Analysis Explained,"* you were speaking about a penetration of a neckline in a head and shoulders pattern and you mentioned that it was essential to wait for a 3% penetration. Do you still feel that this is the case?

In the old days, people were looking at longterm charts so 3% in a primary bull or bear market is a reasonable number, but in a day to day situation, it is a ridiculous number. If you are looking at shortterm moves, like Eurodollars, 3% can often be the whole move. You can't really use 3%. Three percent is supposed to be a decisive breakout but you can't say whether it is 1% or ½ % because each item you are measuring has different volatility. What's considered a big move for utilities is nothing for gold shares which have a higher volatility. You have to use common sense.

If you were going to select a stock, what technical criteria would you use?

If you are looking at an item in isolation, you would look at the market cycle model (KST)—the longterm KST, the intermediate term KST, and the shortterm KST. Then you would relate those to some trend following signals and the price itself—trendline breaks, the 40 week moving average crossover—that type of thing. For individual stocks, I use the top down approach where I look at the market. Is the market in a buying mode? What is the group doing? What is the stock within the group doing?

Let's say you have found three or four candidates but can make only one choice. Which indicators would you use in your final analysis?

I would look at the longterm KST to make sure the momentum is below zero and possibly rising. By definition, the longterm KST is going to be bottoming out after the short and intermediate term KST's. Let's say you've had the shortterm KST go up which is the actual bottom in the market or an individual stock and then it reacts. On a shortterm or intermediate term reaction, that is the point where the longterm has started to turn up so that may be another possibility there. In other words, you are looking at the first reaction in a bull market because then you have everything going for you. The other thing to look at is relative strength. You do a market cycle model of the relative strength of the stock against the market. KST's work very well for relative strength. They work better in a "relative" sense than on an absolute basis because the "relative" is more cyclical. You look at the market cycle model (KST) of the relative strength line.

Do you ever use stochastics?

Not very often because I don't have a great deal of confidence in stochastics. Most of these indicators that you see are all a variation on a theme anyway. Basically, they all act in a very similar way and it is just a different shade of gray. There is no holy grail. That is why I stick to rate of change and to some degree, the RSI, and the KST, which is a sort of sophisticated rate of change. I feel comfortable using them. Anything else you look at is all basically a statistical manipulation of price. The only one that is different is volume. Volume is a totally different, independent variable so we look at rates of change in price oscillators which are smoothed trend deviations in volume.

Can you be more specific?

You take a moving average of volume and another moving average of volume and divide the short one by the long one. You can use a 5 day moving average of volume divided by a 25 day moving average of volume, or a 10 day divided by a 25 day and relate that to a similar measure for price. If you have volume going up and price going up then that's a good sign but if price momentum is going up and the volume momentum is going down, then that is bad because you haven't got the enthusiasm.

Do you look at individual volume on days when breakouts occur?

Yes, but that is rate of change in a visual sense because if you get a breakout and the volume bars expand, by definition you relate those volume bars to the previous 10 days or the previous 20 days and you have a rising rate of change. So in other words, you have a visual effect of the rate of change. But the problem with the volume bars is that sometimes there is a rate of change which you don't perceive because it is more subtle. The rate of change, or the price oscillator approach (trend deviation approach), will pick that kind of thing up.

If you use the trend deviation approach with a 10 day/ 25 day rate of change, will that provide a signal in a timely manner?

Sometimes, yes. Like all of these indicators, sometimes the price will move ahead of the indicator but that is why you don't rush after every situation. In other words, you might see a good signal from a rate of change in volume and a rate of change in price that occurs pretty close to the low so you take action on it. But if you get the signal where price is a long way from the low, then you say, "Okay, it has given the signal but it is too far away and too risky for me to do anything now. I will look around for another situation."

That is where common sense fits in?

Well, it's more discipline than common sense.

You also work with industry groups. Is there a set pattern of movement for certain equity groups at tops and bottoms?

Well, there is a rotation. I look at relationships such as the ratio of a leading group like the financials to a lagging group such as energy to see if they are trading places. Energy does well at the end of the cycle. Obviously, things that are interest rate sensitive, like electric utilities and financials, tend to do well at the beginning of the cycle, sometimes even before the stock market bottoms out. The electric utilities and financials usually peak ahead of the market. The energy stocks usually lag at both ends. There is a definite rotation but, unfortunately, you can't classify every group in that rotation process because it doesn't always work out that way. Banks should peak early in the cycle because they are financials but in 1973, banks did very well at the end of the cycle. So even the early leaders can be late leaders. As a general rule, you have your interest sensitives doing well at the beginning of the cycle and the inflation and economically driven basic industry and cyclical groups doing well at the end of the cycle.

Phil Roth

Phil Roth has officially been involved with the financial markets since 1967 but his interest in the market precedes this date by several years. At the age of 12, Mr. Roth went to work for the local baker scraping floors and cleaning pans. After a couple of months of employment, the baker informed Mr. Roth that he was wasting his money and announced that he was putting him on a $5.00 per week allowance and convinced him to invest the balance of his earnings in a mutual fund. Not only was his employer helping to ensure Mr. Roth's financial future, he was determined to provide him with the necessary tools to make wise financial decisions. These tools were derived from technical analysis. As odd as it may sound, his first introduction to technical analysis came from a German immigrant baker.

Mr. Roth's employer avidly traded both stocks and commodities exclusively using technical analysis. Having an interest in the markets was never an option in this particular bakery. Employees were assumed to have an interest in the markets or soon would have by simple indoctrination. Excluding his employer, there were five other bakers, all German immigrants. Each and every one of them were interested in the financial markets and all conversation revolved solely around this subject. The radio remained on throughout the day broadcasting the market action, albeit infrequently. At 5:00 p.m. the *World Telegram Sun Newspaper* would arrive with that day's closing stock prices. Flour was brushed away from the bench, and charts stained with doughnut jelly were spread out in preparation for their daily updates. This was 1956, the pre-computer era when stocks were kept by hand and the markets closed at 3:30 p.m. Mr. Roth continued to work in the bakery throughout high school learning all of the nuances of investing via technical analysis.

Guided by his market savvy mentors, Mr. Roth accumulated a respectable nest egg during his five years of labor in the bakery. He envisioned being a proprietor of a bakery. When he was seventeen, a bakery in his neighborhood surfaced for sale. He came "extremely close" to buying the bakery and skipping college but the circumstances of the time persuaded him otherwise. This was the Vietnam era, a time in which you had to "plan your life around the draft." Had he purchased the bakery and then been drafted, he could have lost his business.

With the risks outweighing the benefits, he made the decision to attend college and graduated with a BA in Economics. He continued his education by enrolling in graduate school. Tired of borrowing money, he discontinued his graduate study and began mailing out a "zillion" resumes to Wall Street firms. He heard from exactly one firm, Merrill Lynch. He entered their research training program in 1967 accepting a salary that was barely enough to live on.

There were several stages within the training program. Trainees initially began their experience at the wire desk providing information to clients. The next step was the correspondence unit. Responsibilities at this level included providing research information upon request. The final post was the position of portfolio analyst, not to be confused with the portfolio analysts of today. At this post, the trainee would analyze the portfolios of clients who had cash balances sitting in their accounts. They would make stock or bond recommendations based on a "menu" or formula constructed by Merrill Lynch. The time spent in the training program averaged a year or so after which time the trainee had the opportunity to choose between technical analysis, fundamental analysis, or portfolio management. As fate would have it, the first opening for Mr. Roth appeared in the technical analysis department. He confesses that had he to do all over again he would have chosen to spend some time as a fundamental analyst.

Mr. Roth's first job in the technical analysis department was as an assistant to the "official tape watcher." His boss started out as a floor clerk on the New York Stock Exchange in 1928. Starting with no money, he made $100,000 as a 17 year old in 1928 when manipulators ran Radio Corporation, known today as RCA, from $50.00 a share to over $500.00. In those days, stocks could be traded without margin as long as they were bought and sold within the same day. He later lost it all in the Crash of 1929. As you can imagine, he learned a great deal from his employer. Mr. Roth's very first duty as an assistant was changing the paper tape on the ticker machine. When one roll was reaching the end, he had to be standing in place, ready to feed the new tape in before the old tape ran out. This was no easy feat. His finicky boss wouldn't allow the ticker to be turned off because that would result in some lost trades. There was the occasional mishap which necessitated turning off the ticker tape. This sent his boss over the edge because he missed a few prints. Once overcoming the hurdles of changing the tape, the job became terrific.

From Merrill Lynch, Mr. Roth moved to Loeb Rhodes and later to E.F. Hutton. In 1988, E.F. Hutton was acquired by Shearson Lehman. He is currently chief technical analyst and Senior Vice President at Dean Witter Reynolds, Inc. Mr. Roth takes a top down approach to market analysis determining first the health of the overall market from a longterm perspective and then gradually works his way down to the shorter term. His indicators are organized within four categories which correspond with the various trends in the market. They are the secular, cyclical, medium term, and shortterm. Referring to himself as an "indicator junkie," he has more than 150 indicators in his repertoire but does not track all of them on a daily basis. I would like to point out that during the interview we were speaking off-the-cuff but each time we completed a category, he reviewed his list of indicators to make certain he wasn't omitting something of great importance. I thought this showed a high degree of conscientiousness.

When Mr. Roth first began developing indicators, computers and portable calculators were non-existent. Charts were kept by hand. Creating an indicator thirty years ago was a very labor intensive process. Other than by hand, the only means of performing mathematical computations was with an electrically operated calculator called the "Addressograph Multigraph." Speed was not its strong point. Calculations literally took one second per decimal point. Collecting historical data necessitated spending long hours at the library looking through back issues of ***Barron's*** and the ***Wall Street Journal***. Ironically, as tedious and arduous as these tasks were, it was this intensive research surrounding the creation of an indicator which made technical analysis more intriguing and interesting for Mr. Roth. Despite the barriers and handicaps, Mr. Roth speaks fondly of this time recalling the tremendous amount of satisfaction derived from seeing his efforts rewarded with the discovery of an indicator that was highly useful. Today, he still finds time to create new indicators.

Does your analysis take the form of a top down or bottoms up approach?

I do both. With a top down approach my market indicators will answer questions like, "Do stocks make sense at all relative to other forms of investment?" Are bonds more attractive? Is gold more attractive, etcetera?

So you follow those markets as well?

Yes, and there is an important reason for that. I will throw that out up front. When you are analyzing the supply and demand picture for equities, changes in valuation of equity alternatives will affect the supply and demand for stocks. In other words, all other things being equal, if bonds go up in price, it means they are less attractive relative to stocks. If bonds went down in price, they would be cheaper and therefore relatively more attractive compared to equities. I am looking at the commodity markets, the bond markets, and the currency markets. These tell me in general whether equities are attractive or not. My macro indicators point me toward sectors of the equity market that might make sense. If interest rates are falling, I might want to buy interest rate sensitive stocks. If commodity prices are rising, I might want to buy commodity type stocks. The macro indicators will also point me specifically toward industry groups. If I think the market looks quite vulnerable, and I am looking for a defensive haven, I might want to be buying higher yielding electric utility stocks. The macro indicators point me not to specific stocks but to groups and sectors and tells me whether or not the equity market makes sense at all. Then I look at as many chart patterns as I can, as often as I can. I am expecting to get the same message on individual stocks. If my macro indicators say oil stocks are attractive then I am expecting to see good looking charts in the energy area. Now when those two things diverge it tells me I have to rethink things. Often the stock charts will change before the macro indicators because stocks are a leading economic indicator and commodities are a coincident economic indicator. Oil stocks are probably going to change direction before oil prices do. I continually have to look at the chart patterns to see if the macro message is still correct or if it is changing.

When you say macro indicators what are you referring to?

When I use the word macro indicator I mean "market indicators." I use more than 150 different indicators for different time periods: shortterm, medium term, longterm and what I call the secular trend. I don't follow 150 indicators every day because some indicators are longer term indicators and they don't change very often. I use the word "macro" when I am looking at the market as a whole. When I talk about micro indicators I am talking about looking at a myriad of individual stocks to try and come up with the same kind of judgment about the market that you would get by looking at market indicators.

Do you look at your macro indicators individually or in a model?

I don't have a black box. In other words, I don't turn bullish on the market if 80 of them happen to be bullish and 70 of them are bearish. Different indicators are important for different time periods. I have to decide in every cycle, "What is critical to this cycle? What is motivating investors? What is driving the market in this cycle?" Some things are going to be more important than others.

Starting with your longest time period, what you call the secular trend, describe the indicators which correspond with this time frame?

I use that term to describe the trend that encompasses two or more economic cycles and two or more stock market cycles. A market cycle and an economic cycle are normally four or five years so the secular trend is a couple of those and can be 20 or 30 years. The indicators that work best on a secular basis are asset allocation indicators. In other words, what percentage of financial assets do people have in stocks, bonds, and cash? At the beginning of a secular uptrend, people will own very little stock and have most of their money in cash and bonds. As the secular trend persists, more money shifts from cash and bonds into equities. As the secular trend gets old you will have an overwhelming position in equities. The general rule, for both institutions and individuals, has been 40% is low for equities and 60% is high. At the beginning of the cycle in the 1980's it was at the 40% level. People had very little equity. Now we are passing the 55% level, the bearish side of neutral, but quite far from a fully negative reading.

What would you consider fully negative?

I would say 60% but again it might go to 70%. These are general guides that give me some measure of confidence in the secular trend. If people have an historically large percentage of their assets in equities they aren't going to be buying much more.

Where can readers dig up data on asset allocation?

Data on asset allocation can be obtained from the "Flow of Funds" statistics published by the Federal Reserve. The Fed tells you the asset allocation by economic sector. They report it for life and other insurance companies, state and local government retirement funds, and pension funds. They give you a total financial asset picture for each of those sectors and the equity percentage of total assets. Valuation indicators are another secular indicator.

Fundamental valuations?

Valuation indicators are not fundamental indicators. That is one of the biggest misconceptions. People think that indicators like yields, multiples and the price to book are fundamental indicators. They are not. They are technical indicators. Why did stocks sell at 8 times earnings in 1982 and 22 times earnings in 1992? Because people were bearish on the equity market in 1982 and they were bullish on the equity market in 1992. Valuations are measures of people's confidence in stocks. Why are people willing to buy and hold the S&P 500 today with a yield of 2.3%? Because they are very bullish on the appreciation prospects for equities. If they weren't the yield would not be at a record low by historical standards. Now, I want to make it clear that I would not get bearish on the equity market if people had 60% of their assets in equities and yields were at record low levels because the market can remain at high valuations levels. They are very longterm indicators that don't change very often. They can stay bullish or bearish for long periods of time. They are not going to tell you what month or even necessarily what year the market will turn down. They are only going to tell you that stocks are high and that the cycle is old. You need to use intermediate-term and shorter term indicators for timing.

Which valuation indicators receive your primary attention?

Multiples and yields. Price to book measures are of less importance because book values are only calculated once a year and usually with a six month lag. In other words, we won't know the book value of 1996 until the middle of 1997. I am interested in it but it comes out so infrequently and with a long lag. Multiples and yields on the other hand are calculated every day.

What are the normal parameters that signal over and under valuation for these indicators?

Historical bounds on yields—under 3% would be low or bearish, above 6% would be high or bullish. For multiples I would say above 20 would be high or bearish; below 10 would be low or bullish. I would say the average for yields should be maybe 4 to 4½ % and 14 to 15 for multiples. Let me mention one other thing. In terms of valuation indicators, I also watch the payout ratios. Yields might be low but are payout ratios high or low? If you have declining yields and declining payout ratios, one ameliorates the other. Very low yields implies a tremendous amount of optimism towards stocks but that notion is diluted somewhat by a very low payout ratio.

Given that utilities typically have high pay out ratios, do you look at payout ratios based on an average for all corporations or do you look at each industry separately?

Standard and Poors reports the payout ratio for the S&P 500. That's what I watch. Historically, the range usually has been between 40% and 60%.

From the secular trend do you move on to the cyclical trend?

I use the word cycle to mean a four or five year trend. Indicators that work particularly well on a cyclical basis are cash flows and cash. How much cash do institutions have and what are the cash flows? In this past 1990 cycle the most important indicator has been cash flow from the public indirectly buying equities through mutual funds. Cash flows into mutuals funds are what happens to be driving this cycle. It's certainly not earnings or interest rates. Earnings have been good and bad. Interest rates have gone up and down. The one thing that has persisted has been a massive flow out of cash and bonds into equities. That has been the whole story. In my opinion, when that ends the market is in trouble. The naive way of looking at it is to say, "When we see evidence that the public has stopped buying, the market is going to go down." In reality the market is going to go down first and then the public is going to stop buying. You probably read in the paper that there were mutual fund redemptions last week.

About four billion dollars worth if I recall.

Well, that happened after a 10% decline in the market. That is not an early warning signal. Now, if redemptions persist that's a big story. There are two ways a bull market ends. One is the public stops buying. The other is professionals decide not to invest the cash. The market has gone up because the public has bought mutual funds *and* fund managers have immediately put it into equities. They have immediately invested all of the money coming from the public refusing to let any cash build up. If professionals decide that cash is more attractive, then the bull market would be in trouble especially if you have institutions trying to raise cash at the same time the cash flow from the public is abating. The two indicators I am paying the most attention to from a cyclical standpoint are the flows from the public, which I don't expect to be a leading indicator, and what professionals are doing with that money.

How can readers determine whether professionals are buying or not buying stocks?

The Investment Company Institute (ICI) reports monthly the net fund sales to the public, the cash positions of mutual funds, the portfolio transactions of portfolio managers, and the switching the public is doing from fixed income funds to equity funds. We get a pretty good picture of what is going on.

Wouldn't you have to look at cash and cash flows for a period of time to see a trend?

Sure. Remember this is a cyclical indicator that works on a four or five year basis. It would take a number of months to see a trend and to spot a reversal in the trend.

As you just pointed out, mutual fund redemptions are obviously not a leading indicator but couldn't you make the case that mutual fund cash levels could be a leading indicator?

Yes, but they are a very longterm lead. Cash levels have been at multi-year lows for several years. Cash has not been the story in this cycle. Cash flow has been the story. The last time there was high institutional cash was in late 1990 after the Persian Gulf War and it was a buy signal. By 1992, cash was very low. If institutional cash was the only indicator you had, you would have been bearish since 1992. Professionals have been forced to buy stocks. Something like 80% of professional money managers underperformed the market in 1995. They had to invest the massive cash flow. In a rising market, if they let any cash build up, they would have underperformed even more.

What is the range for mutual fund cash?

My trading rule on mutual fund cash is under 9% low, above 12% high. It is 6.7% right now. The last time it was meaningfully under this level was in the 1960's. Mutual fund cash was less than 5% but I never expect it to get that low again because now the fund business is entirely different. Now you have fund switchers. Mutual funds have to keep more cash because the flows are much more rapid than they were in the 1960's so we are never going to see those levels again. Cash flow is a demand indicator. On the other side we have the supply indicators—new equity financing. Is the equity supply growing or contracting? Is it high or low?

Are you talking about initial public offerings and secondaries?

Yes, but you also have existing corporations selling new stock. That is not an IPO but that is equity financing. So you have that supply. I also follow corporate repurchases which is a contraction in the supply indicator.

Corporations from time to time will announce stock buy backs. How do know it is not a move which is designed to attract attention to the stock?

I don't follow the announced plans. Just because they announce a buy back doesn't mean they are ever going to do it. I watch the "Flow of Funds" figures from the Federal Reserve. Every quarter, they give you a net supply figure; that is, equity financing minus buy backs.

Do you look at the trend or actual numbers?

Both. I am interested whether the numbers are positive or negative and whether they are growing or contracting.

A contracting supply is bullish and a growing supply is bearish?

Right. At a cyclical bottom in the market you see corporate repurchases exceeding equity financing. That would be a bullish cyclical indicator. It's bearish when new equity financing dwarfs buy backs. Even though the market was rising in the fourth quarter of 1995, the supply number went from positive to negative indicating that the equity supply was contracting—a very bullish indication. It has changed dramatically in 1996.

You mentioned that the ICI keeps statistics on fund switching. Do you monitor this and if so, what does it tell you?

I am watching it because it is part of the cash flow. I wouldn't use this indicator by itself. If fund switchers are moving from fixed income funds to equity funds it tells you that they are bullish. That is one piece of information. I add that to the net sales to the public, including reinvested dividends, and keep a total cash flow number.

Do you use ever use ICI fund switching statistics to get a handle on market sentiment? In other words, if investors are switching out of conservative mutual funds into more aggressive funds, would you interpret this as speculative?

I watch the cash flow in and out of the total equity funds and in and out of the aggressive growth funds. The total would better reflect investment attitudes by the public and the aggressive growth funds would better reflect more speculative attitudes.

So you do use them as a gauge of sentiment?

Yes. You might think it odd but in actuality the two are almost always giving the same picture. As investors buy mutual funds in general they tend to buy aggressive growth funds. When they buy a lot of equity funds in general, they tend to buy a lot of aggressive growth funds. Looking at the parts hasn't really shown anything different than looking at the total.

What else do you look at in a cyclical time frame?

Money supply. Historically, there has been a strong positive correlation between money supply growth and stock prices. Having said that, it has not been helpful at all in this cycle. Money is being redefined so I am not paying a lot of attention to it.

What do you mean by redefined?

If you go back ten years ago, there was an M1 and an M2 and that was it. Now there is an M3, M4, and M5. The M's are not particularly useful because there is a muddling of what's cash and what's investment. Also, international flows have grown dramatically in the last ten to fifteen years.

Any more cyclical indicators?

Foreign buying and selling of U.S. stocks and U.S. purchase or sale of foreign stocks is another cyclical supply/demand indicator. I am interested in finding out whether U.S. investors are spending more money abroad than foreigners are spending here. If they are, which is the case now, it would be a negative supply/demand indicator. I get this information from the Securities Industry Association (SIA). They have it country by country and I put it together and get some aggregates.

When you are assimilating these aggregates, does one country receive more weighting than another?

I actually don't even do it country by country. I do it region by region. In most countries the numbers are insignificant. There are only a handful that actually influence the total very much. In fact, Europe is mainly the United Kingdom. Japan is the biggest factor in the Far East. I am actually only interested in the total.

The simple fact that money is coming or going is more important than which particular geographical region is receiving or losing those funds?

Clearly where U.S. dollars are going tells you something about how speculative the demand is by Americans. If a rising portion of U.S. buying of foreign stocks is going into emerging markets, it indicates confidence and speculation. I am interested in strictly one thing. Is money flowing net in or out? The pendulum has swung. For most of the financial history of the U.S., we have been the net benefactor of international flows. That has changed. In the last few years, U.S. investors are spending more money abroad than foreigners are spending here. Everybody talks about the wonders and miracles of international investing and how it reduces risk. What they don't talk about is that we are spending more money abroad then they are spending here. We are net losers in this game.

If we have exhausted your supply of indicators from the cyclical time frame, let's move on to the intermediate term.

The medium term for me is a three to six month horizon. It is the most important one to me for two reasons. First, it is the horizon that most people operate in. Professionals perform quarter by quarter. Secondly, most of my indicators happen to be in the intermediate time frame. In my opinion, the types of indicators that work best in the intermediate term are measures of psychology. How bullish and how bearish are different market participants? The basic premise is that investors make bottoms and traders make tops. Over the intermediate term, if the market has been trending down, I am going to be looking for signs of increasing investment buying and increased trader liquidation to indicate a forthcoming bottom. There are two kinds of sentiment indicators—polls and transactional indicators. Polls tell us whether people are bullish or bearish. Transactional indicators tell us what these different classes of investors are actually doing in the market.

Should we start with the polls first?

The polls are very popular. Because all the polls are polls of aggressive participants and aggressive participants tend to be too bearish at bottoms and too bullish at tops, they are considered contrary indicators. I watch four polls which come out every week. They are all reported in **Barron's**. There is a poll of investment club participants conducted by the American Association of Individual Investors (AAII). You might think these investors are conservative but as it turns out, it represents aggressive individuals. The general parameters I use on the AAII poll ranges between 3 to 1 bears to bulls at a bottom and 3 to 1 bulls to bears at a top. An overenthusiastic or bearish reading would be 60% bulls to 20% bears. The opposite, 60% bears and 20% bulls, would be overly pessimistic and may be an indication of a bottom. This poll has been around maybe 10 years. The poll that has been around the longest is conducted by Investor's Intelligence. They poll over 130 market letter writers. They have a method for determining whether the letter writer is bullish or bearish. Sometimes it is difficult to tell, people hedge. Market letter writers tend to be rather shortterm oriented. Even though they profess to be giving longterm advice they really aren't. That is why this poll works on a contrary basis. I have two indicators on this poll. I watch the bear percentage by itself. When that gets to 20% or less, it is a bearish indicator. It is a bullish indicator when bears reach a reading of more than 60%. I have that 60-20 rule on the bears. I also watch bulls as a percentage of bulls + bears. I divide bulls by bulls plus bears. In theory, that percentage can run from zero to 100%. Under 25% would be bullish, above 75% would be bearish. There are two polls of stock index futures traders which we know have shortterm views. One is conducted by Market

Vane and the other by Consensus Incorporated. I use a 65-35 rule on these polls and a 4 week moving average of the bullish percent. When the bullish percentage reaches 65% on a four week basis, that is bearish. When it reaches 35% or less on a four week basis, then I consider that a bullish signal. On all the polls I use a four week moving average to smooth the readings. I don't want one week to be overly influential.

What mistakes do you see investors making in the interpretation of these polls?

In my opinion sentiment indicators are only useful when they are at extremes. Take Market Vane as an example. Let's say it is 50% bulls one week, which is in the middle of a neutral reading, and the next week it goes to 60%. Some people would look at that and say, "Too many bulls or the bulls have increased therefore the indicator has turned negative." While going from 50% to 60% might be going in a bearish direction, 60% in my opinion is not a bearish reading. Most of the time sentiment measures can be in the middle. You don't want to overly rely on them. When it is moderately high and goes a little higher, well, that is not particularly important. Excessive pessimism and excessive optimism are important.

Would you use one extreme reading as a signal or do you require two consecutive extremes?

You can't use sentiment indicators without considering what the market is doing. The stronger the market the more lead time you are going to get from sentiment indicators because when a market is real strong, everybody knows it and a lot of people are going to be bullish and right. A top or bottom in the market, in my opinion, is never going to be indicated simply by a sentiment indicator alone. You need to see the three components of a bottom—1) traders liquidating 2) investors buying and 3) stability. A bottom is that point in a downtrend when prices stop going down because investment demand offsets trader liquidation. You need trend, investment activity and speculative activity. You need those three elements in making a bottom. Regardless of how bearish or how bullish a sentiment indicator was, I wouldn't necessarily act on that. It depends on other indicators and what the market was doing.

What are the lead times for sentiment indicators?

It is important to realize that tops form over time and sentiment indicators can lead a final top in the averages by a long periods of time. Most stocks start off strong and as an uptrend matures, you start to lose stocks and trends narrow. The peak bearishness in the sentiment indicator or the excessive optimism will generally occur when the vast majority of stocks are doing well. In fact, early in a bull market, you might get a negative sentiment reading because everybody recognizes that the trend is strong. Sentiment is just one element in looking for a top or bottom.

Do sentiment indicators lead at bottoms as well?

Bottoms are different than tops. Tops and bottoms are not mirror images of one another. Stocks tend to bottom out together but not top out together. Bottoms tend to form more quickly. When people get bearish, pessimism tends to build more quickly and sentiment indicators usually give less lead at a bottom. A sentiment indicator could lead by three or four months at a top. It is unlikely to lead by more than a few weeks at a bottom.

How often will simultaneous confirming signals occur from all three polls?

I would say that at major market bottoms the polls would generally all have turned bullish sometime during the decline but not necessarily at exactly the same time. We had major bottoms in 1987 and 1990. All the polls were bullish on both of those bottoms. Obviously, the more important the bottom, the more likely you get all the indicators in sync. You would get less confirmation at a weaker bottom. The chances of all the polls being most bearish at the absolute market high is remote. At a final top in the market, the majority of stocks are already going down. Money moves from the broad list to the narrow list of blue chips which dominate the averages. So almost always, a final top in the market will be made with a shrinking minority of stocks carrying the averages. The sentiment polls are rarely excessively optimistic at that point because people have been losing money already. Polls are what people are saying, but of course, what they are saying doesn't necessarily conform to what they are doing. You really need to watch both the polls and the transactional indicators. I like to have both pointing in the same direction, for example, traders talking bearish and acting bearish. I have more confidence in a particular indicator if this occurs.

Investors putting their money where their mouth is so to speak.

The most important transactional indicator as far as public investment attitudes go would be our internal business here at Dean Witter. There is really no good information available to the general public on individual investment activity in the market, at least not very current. For example, the mutual fund figures tell you something about individual investment attitudes but it comes out once a month with a one month lag. The "Flow of Funds" statistics from the Federal Reserve comes out quarterly with a couple of months lag. These are not really useful from a timing standpoint. I do have access to our internal figures here. Every morning, I know what our customers did the day before.

How do you use your internal figures?

I have it broken down by margin account versus cash account. Obviously, a cash account would reflect a more conservative attitude than a margin account. I look at our business on the NYSE versus the OTC market, the former being more conservative or investment oriented whereas the latter would be more speculative. An ideal sentiment bottom based on the public sentiment statistics at our firm would be cash account buying on the NYSE, margin account selling on the NYSE, and selling in the OTC market. That combination would tell me that we are getting investment buying and trader liquidation. You don't often get that but at important turns you do. The last time we had this combination was at the major market bottom in 1990. Since then, the figures have been either neutral or negative. I watch a 10 day moving average of the data. There are different ways of measuring internal business. You can watch the shares, the transactions, and the dollar value. I know the number of shares our customers are buying, I know the number of transactions, that is, buys versus sells, and I know the amount of money that is going toward buying and selling. I have access to all three numbers but the number I have the most confidence in is transactions rather than dollars so I watch the transactions.

Why?

Because transactions give me an indication of the number of investors. A large number of buy transactions is more important than a lot of money because one big buyer could distort the money. If I get a preponderance of buy transactions and sell transactions then I know I am getting a broader sample of what the business is. I create a buy/sell ratio on my internal business indicator. The rule is when the NYSE cash account business reaches 1.2 buys to sells on a 10 day basis, that's a buy signal but it is just one element. For the margin accounts, I use the mirror image of this. A buy/sell ratio of 0.8 on a 10 day basis would be a bullish signal. A favorable bottom configuration would be a 1.20 10 day NYSE cash and a 0.8 10 day NYSE margin. The opposite would be a top. The numbers are more volatile in the OTC market. There I use 1.30 and 0.70. A ratio above 1.30 for OTC buying would be a negative signal and below 0.7, bullish. Violent swings in the market will produce violent swings in the figures so that's why I use a 10 day moving average. These are just the figures from Dean Witter. Occasionally, I talk to technicians at other firms. When I see extremes you can pretty much rest assured the other firms will see it also. I can't recall times when they were vastly different. Because they are just a sample, I can't rely heavily on these numbers by themselves. I use this indicator as a confirming tool.

Is there a substitute that readers could use like the margin debt figures reported in Barron's?

No. Unfortunately, the NYSE changed the margin data a number of years ago. Now, they include bond margin as well as equity margin. Therefore, when the margin debt is going up we can't tell if they are buying more stocks or buying more bonds. In fact, maybe they are just margining the account to buy a new car. When margin debt goes up, all you know is that they are borrowing money on their accounts. You have no idea what they are doing with it. I mean it still does what you would expect it to do. In a bull market it is growing. The only sources of public investment activity would be internal cash account business within brokerage firms, the mutual fund figures which you see once a month, and the "Flow of Funds" figures which you see once a quarter. Those pretty much reflect the investment attitudes of the public.

What about the attitudes of traders?

There are a lot more indicators available on trading attitudes. The transactions on derivative securities tend to be very good barometers of the attitudes of public traders because derivatives are basically bought and sold by traders, not investors. Not that investors don't do it but the vast majority of activity in options and futures is done by traders. Since I am making the presumption that traders tend to be wrong at turning points, I am expecting to see high put/call ratios at market bottoms and low put/call ratios at market tops. I am expecting to see stock index futures selling below theoretical values at bottoms and well above theoretical values at tops. Now, let's just go into that for a moment starting with options. I keep a lot of put/call indicators. I keep "activity" measures of options activity meaning volume. I look at put volume relative to call volume. The first thing I watch is the total of all put and call activity on the Chicago Board of Exchange (CBOE) which is comprised of index option activity and equity option activity. By itself, the total is not too important but when it is very high or very low it is. I am using a 10 day moving average on all of these ratios. The rule on the total CBOE put/call ratio is 1.0 and over is bullish, under 0.6 is bearish. You rarely see put activity equalling call activity. There is almost always more call activity. When it gets to even, especially on a 10 day basis, that is clearly a bullish signal. Then I look at the index options. The majority of index option activity occurs in the S&P 100 (OEX) index. Before I give you my trading rule, let me explain something. There has been a tremendous increase in hedging using options in recent years. Of course, hedging is not the same as an outright speculative transaction so it tends to dilute the utility of the indicator. Increased hedging activity has produced a secular rise in the put/call ratio on the OEX. For this reason, I have had to raise my trading rule over the years. Right now, the rule I am using is on a 10 day basis, 1.30 and above is bullish; under 0.9 is bearish.

How do you know how much to adjust your parameters?

Well, I don't. I am eyeballing the chart over time and I see a secular rise in that indicator. In other words, this last market bottom had a higher ratio than the previous bottom and this market top had a higher ratio than the previous top. Unfortunately, I don't know if the next bottom will have a higher ratio. This is one of the problems with analyzing the option data. It's a little bit of guesswork and I have a feeling that my parameters are probably too low. Let me say this—all other things being equal—if you are hedging and you are increasing your hedging, you are bearish. The fact that it is a hedge does not negate the fact that it still reflects some kind of pessimism.

What else do you monitor?

I look at the equity options. The equities also have been having a secular rise but less so. Right now I am using 0.65 or higher as a bullish reading and 0.35 or lower as a bearish reading on a 10 day basis.

Why do you segregate the OEX options from equity options?

Basically, because it's different people. I think professionals tend to operate in index options and individuals tend to operate in equity options. If I get a high "index" put/call ratio and a not so high "equity" put/call ratio, it tells me that professionals are more bearish than the public. Now, I am expecting both professional traders and individual traders to be too bearish at bottoms. Traders are traders. I like to see one confirming the other. I keep what I call the "other index ratio." The total CBOE options would be the equities, plus the OEX, plus all the other index options. There are other index options many of which have very low activity. So I just add everything together. My trading rule on that has been above 2 to 1 is bullish, below 1 to 1 is bearish. Of my option activity indicators, I consider the CBOE equity and the OEX to be the most important.

Where can readers get this option data?

That's the good part about this indicator, the data is readily available. I get it off my quote machine but it comes out in the newspapers every day. In fact, the CBOE has a telephone recording that gives you the data on the hour and half-hour for that day. I take samples intraday. Depending on what the market is doing, a very, very high reading intraday reading might be important.

Are option premiums included in your analysis?

Yes. Every week I get a report from the Options Clearing Corporation (OCC) which gives me the average premium on puts and the average premium on calls. Now, that is all calls and all puts, those in-the-money, out-of-the-money, and at-the-money. There is a lot of garbage in there. Option premiums are affected by attitudes and interest rates but if you watch a ratio of the two, interest rates don't matter. Using a ratio is a simple way of washing out interest rates. I keep a four week moving average of the total put premium divided by the total call premium. It has worked rather well. The OCC reports the premiums for index options, equity options, currency, and fixed income options. I keep only the premium put/call ratios on the indexes and the equities. The parameters are, on a four week basis, under 0.5 is bearish and above 1.5 is bullish.

When the OCC reports these premium figures, are they an average for the week or on a closing day basis?

The level is as of the day's close for the reporting week. Any option purist would tell you that an average is a bad number but having looked at it for a number of years, it seems to work well. If I had the time, I would try to look at the in-the-money options, out-of-the-money options, and at-the-money options separately because you might get a different picture. When I was at E.F. Hutton, we did a lot of naked option business and that was very useful. If you assume that option traders have a shortterm horizon, naked option players have a real short horizon. People are always selling naked puts and naked calls but, at market bottoms, you would have an explosion of people selling naked puts. It was an unbelievable bottom and top indicator. Unfortunately, I don't have that indicator anymore because Dean Witter discourages naked call and put trading.

What other transactional sentiment measures do you watch?

Short sellers tend to be motivated late in market declines. Twenty five years ago, there wasn't much of an option market. Traders had to short stocks when they were bearish. Shorting indicators were quite useful and important but over time they have become less important. Most traders these days buy puts and calls rather than shorting stock. Most of the shorting that is done has nothing to do with pessimism. It has to do with arbitrage and hedging. I watch a lot of shorting indicators and I don't have a lot of confidence in most of them for this reason. Having said that, the ones that seem to work best are coming from the NYSE which breaks down the shorting by specialists, NYSE members, and the public. I watch four ratios from that weekly series. The first two are "quantitative" measures of shorting; the second two are "qualitative" measures of shorting. First, I watch total shorting as a percentage of NYSE volume. Even though there has been an increase in hedge shorting, that percentage hasn't changed too much over time because the total volume in the NYSE has gone up a lot as well. Under 6% would be low or negative, above 10% would be high or positive. That 6% to 10% rule has worked for many years and it is still a reasonably good rule. The next ratio I keep is public shorts as a percentage of total short volume. The public shorting number has changed dramatically over the years, so much so I don't even know what is a good number anymore. When I started in the business, a 2% ratio was very bullish. It has been 4% or 5% recently and the market, of course, is not making a bottom. In any case, I am watching that number because I am hoping that ultimately I may get something out of it. I also watch NYSE member shorts as a percentage of total shorting and specialist shorts as a percent of total shorting. In theory the lower the member short ratio, the more bullish it would be because it would mean that the public percentage would be higher. But that has been dropping dramatically over time. The bottom line is, of those four ratios, the only one that still seems to work reasonably well is the total shorts relative to volume.

I thought the specialist ratio still had some merit?

It does but unfortunately I don't know the level anymore. The reason the indicator works is not because the specialists are geniuses. It's because by definition, they have to be a buyer at market bottoms and a seller at market tops. They are forced by their job to be most bullish at the right time and most bearish at the right time. In other words, if there are no other sellers and the specialist is the only seller that is pretty close to a top. It means the public is as bullish as they are ever going to get. The bottom line is that I want to keep an eye on it because maybe the hedging activity will level off and we will be able to read it again.

What other sentiment indicators do you watch?

Public investors tend to be buyers at bottoms. All kinds of traders tend to be bearish at bottoms. Professionals more or less make the market go up and down. You aren't going to get much of a lead from professionals so I consider institutions to be more or less coincident indicators. The typical portfolio manager is forced to perform quarter to quarter and isn't going to be bearish too long into a rising market or vice versa. I watch the large block statistics, those of 50,000 or more. They are reported in **Barron's** every week. I create a 10 day moving average of the ratio of upticks to downticks. When the ratio is rising, institutions are in an accumulation mode and that is positive. When the ratio is declining, institutions are in a liquidation mode and that is negative. Because of a relatively short lead, peak block buying tends to occur within a month or two of tops. Peak selling tends to occur within a week or two of bottoms. I look for extremes in the large block uptick/downtick ratio. Once you get an extreme on the high side then you want to look for a top and vice versa. When the ratio is rising by +.20 or more in a 10 day period, that is considered positive. In other words, if the ratio has gone from .8 to 1.0 in a 10 day period, up 0.20, it is in a positive mode. The opposite, a decline of 0.20 or more, would be negative. Let's say the ratio gets down to 0.60

which indicates very heavy selling and it moves to 0.80, it would probably do that pretty close to a bottom. It is a good indicator for catching the turns so that's how I use it.

Are we talking about shortterm turns?

I use it on an intermediate term basis and occasionally it will give you a strong signal shortterm as well. What I look for is a high or low extreme and then a turn. Having said that, we haven't had an overbought or oversold extreme in the last couple of years. As odd as that might sound with all the institutional buying, we haven't had an important signal from this indicator. It's been neutral most of the time ranging between 0.8 and 1.2 which is sort of modest buying and modest selling. You want to know what professionals are doing over the short run and this sample of large block activity is one of the few ways you have of making a guess at it.

What other professional sentiment measures do you monitor?

Corporate insider activity. It is both a medium term and cyclical indicator. Insiders tend to be right. I keep an eight week ratio of sells to buys on transactions which I get from Vickers. When the ratio gets to 3 to 1 that is bearish. When it is under 1.25 to 1 that is bullish. If it actually goes under 1.00 we get net insider buying on an eight week basis. That is very unusual and even more bullish. This indicator works pretty well but it usually leads by long periods of time. It is usually more beneficial as a longer term, cyclical indicator rather than a medium term indicator. It might be useful from a shorter term standpoint when you get real extremes. When it gets to real extremes, especially on the low side, that is a pretty good buy signal. It doesn't work well at tops because insiders tend to sell for long periods of time in an up market. It works better at bottoms.

Speculation reflects sentiment. How do you evaluate speculative interest in the market?

Bottoms in the market are made when there is a total lack of speculative interest and tops are made when there is tremendous speculative interest. We are always looking for ways to gauge this. We talked about equity financing earlier. This is a measure of speculative interest. One that we didn't talk about is relative volume; that is, volume in the OTC market relative to volume on the NYSE. At a bottom, you would expect less volume in the OTC market on a relative basis and at a top or late in a bull market, you would expect high relative volume. There has been a secular rise in volume on the OTC market relative to the NYSE. Even though that ratio is high at peaks and low at troughs, the peaks and troughs have all been higher now going back ten or fifteen years. One reason for this might be because of the major technology companies, like Intel and Microsoft, who have chosen to stay listed on the OTC exchange rather than move to the NYSE. Twenty years ago anytime a company got big enough to be on the NYSE, it most assuredly moved from the OTC market. Now, there has been less of that. That has distorted this indicator somewhat. Nevertheless, peaks in the market tend to correspond with peaks in the OTC to NYSE volume ratio. Troughs in the market tend to have troughs in that ratio.

You calculate this by dividing the OTC daily volume by the NYSE daily volume?

Yes. I keep it monthly and I also keep a 10 day moving average. In the spring 1996, it got to about 145-150% when the market was topping out. 1994 was the first year that OTC volume surpassed NYSE volume. This year it's running 134% of the NYSE volume year to date. This is remarkable considering that in 1994 the figure was 101% and in 1989 it was 80%. In 1981, it was 66%. Although there has been a secular rise, it is still a useful indicator. It tends to peak and trough at market peaks and troughs. For example, if the market tops out and goes down and this ratio doesn't drop, it may be one reason to believe you are not at a bottom yet.

Given this longterm secular rise in the relative values, how can readers evaluate what is speculative and what is conservative?

You can't really have a rigid percentage. I have made a channel over a long period of time connecting troughs and peaks. I'd say that the bottom in that channel now is probably around 100%. I would expect the next important trough in the market to be something like 100%. Now it's 134%, down from 150%. The parameters are constantly moving up but it is still a reasonably good measure of speculative intensity. I used to watch the American Stock Exchange volume as well. In the late 1960's, upon occasion, AMEX volume was 50% to 100% of the NYSE. It is now 5%. The opposite has been true on the AMEX which has been coming down over time. Nevertheless, peaks and troughs in it have been reasonably good market indicators. The peaks and troughs are now probably 8% to 9% for the high side and 4% or 5% for the low side. That's volume. Relative price is also a measure of speculation. One way of measuring this that people have been using for many years is the S&P high grade stock index compared to the S&P low priced stock index. Standard and Poor's publication *OUTLOOK* has this data going back to about 1926. The S&P low priced index is a speculative stock index. The S&P high grade index is a quality stock index. I divide the low priced index by the high grade index. That ratio rises during bull markets and declines during bear markets. You expect the ratio to be high going into a market peak and low going into a market trough because speculative stocks tend to go up more and down more.

Do you look at specific numbers?

From the 1940's through the 1970's, the ratio tended to go up and down within a flat band during bull markets. When it got to 2:1 or higher, it was a top. When it got to 1:1 or lower, it was a good bottom signal. This indicator went bananas in the 1980's getting over 4:1. The reasonable parameters now are 2.00 to 2.50:1.00 is low and 4.00 to 4.50:1.00 is high.

What are some of the other measures of speculative interest?

The average price of the most active list is a measure of speculative intensity. This number tends to get low at market tops and high at market bottoms. During a bull market, the average price of the active list usually falls because more speculative stocks tend to fill at lower prices than high quality stocks. In recent years, with the tendency toward stock splits, the precise number has become trickier to read. Therefore, all stocks have a somewhat lower average price than they did thirty or forty years ago. The precise number is not important. The average has been in the range of $30.00 to $40.00. Under $30.00 is low and above $40.00 is high or bullish. At the bottom of 1987, it was $65.00, which was a good bottom signal. At the top in 1987, it got down to around $30.00. The theory is that the leadership of the market will tend to get more speculative and one way that's reflected is a lower priced active list. I also watch the volume in the active stocks and the performance of the active stocks as well. If the average price is declining and the volume on the active stocks relative to the total is rising, and the breadth is strong in the active stocks, all of these would be sort of an ideal top configuration. The opposite would lead to a bottom type configuration—price gets high—the relative volume gets low—and the breadth becomes poor. I watch the average price, the average volume, and the performance of the active stocks as a measure of speculation. Another measure of speculation, or lack of it, the volume in the 30 Dow stocks compared to the NYSE volume. That would tend to go down as the market goes up and up as the market goes down. Tops and bottoms are not mirror images of one another so you tend to get the major stocks bottoming first but they don't top first, they top last. What happens during the cycle is that people go from quality to speculative stocks until speculative stocks break. The quality stocks hang in there so you get another spate of relative strength usually late. That is one argument for the breadth of the market topping out before the DJIA and it's an argument for indexes like the Russell 2000 and the Value Line index topping out before the Dow.

To what extent do you follow IPO's or stock splits in relation to speculative activity?

In the 1980's there was a corporate trend toward reducing the price of a stock. There were a lot of stock splits regardless of what the market was doing. I haven't really paid a lot of attention to this since. I watch IPO's as a percentage of new equity financing. This is more of a cyclical indicator. The ***Investment Dealers Digest*** does a thorough quarterly summary of the IPO data. In a maturing cycle, not only does equity financing go up and not only does IPO financing go up, but IPO's become a greater percentage of the total. Prior to 1996, the peak in total financing was in 1993. New equity financing was $102 billion in 1993 and IPO's were 59% of that. That 59% figure has been exceeded only once in the previous 25 years so not only was the total high for new equity financing, the IPO percentage was a near record as well. It came down in 1994 and 1995, but it has ballooned again in 1996. We will make a new peak this year. I just look for record levels. Since the 1960's, IPO's have never been above 60% of the total new equity financing. It just about got there in 1993, came down and now it's jumped back up this year. To me, the equity financing total is more important than the IPO total anyway.

Let's move on to your shortterm indicators?

The internal dynamics of the market are really the only thing you have to analyze the shortterm. These are trend and momentum indicators such as price, volume, breadth, and relative strength. The most important is price. There are technicians out there that will tell you volume is more important or that volume leads. I don't believe that. The bottom line is, if you buy a stock and it goes up, you make money. Whenever I am analyzing the trend, I always start with price. Price is a "*quantitative*" measure of trend. I use volume, breadth, and other momentum measures as confirming rather than leading indicators. Volume and breadth are "*qualitative*" measures of trend and are of secondary importance. If my price indicators are strong and my breadth and volume measures are strong I have more confidence in the trend. Shortterm indicators primarily tell you the direction and strength of a trend but they don't tell you where you are in the trend.

Why do you differentiate between qualitative and quantitative measures of the trend?

The reason I call it qualitative is that the stronger the breadth picture and volume picture, the more confidence I have in the trend; in other words, the higher the quality of the trend. If the DJIA is rising and the daily A/D line is rising, what does that mean? It means that the majority of stocks are more or less performing in line with the DJIA. If the DJIA is rising and the daily A/D line is falling, it means that a minority of stocks are moving in the direction of the Dow. Does that mean the market can't go up? No, but it means that I have less confidence in the trend. If breadth is rising and volume is rising and prices are rising, that is a trend that is not likely to end abruptly. Before a trend ends, you will usually get volume or breadth to falter before price.

With regard to indexes, which measures of price do you use?

There are many measures of price. Most people think in terms of the DJIA but that happens to be a very poor measure of price. It is thirty blue chip stocks and it's an arithmetic index. I watch it because that is what most people look at but I don't really do any analytical work on it. Most of my analytical work is done on the NYSE Composite Index because it is a capitalization weighted index and is very broad based. I watch the S&P 500 because the typical institution is going to be using this index to measure their performance. Since the S&P 500 index is about 85% to 90% of the NYSE Composite, it moves virtually identically with it. I look at the NASDAQ composite index because it is a measure of glamour type stocks. I look at the Russell 2000 as a measure of secondary stocks. I look at the Value Line geometric index because that is a measure of the average stock. I watch different indexes because they tell you about different segments of the market but for the market as a whole, I use the NYSE Composite. To measure price momentum, we use moving averages.

Do you have a favorite time period?

There are as many moving averages as there are analysts following them. In general, I use short-term moving averages for shorter term trends and longer moving averages for longer term trends. There is no "perfect" moving average. It's basically just a device to smooth the trend. I remember once discussing this indicator with another analyst and mentioned I used a 10 day moving average. He said, "You know, I tested that and found that an eleven day works better." To me, that was such a ludicrous comment. Maybe it did work better and maybe tomorrow it will be nine and next year it will be twelve. I use a lot of 10 day moving averages because they are easy to calculate. You don't have to divide. You just move a decimal point. The spread between a price index and its moving average tells you about momentum. If the spread is wide on the positive side, that means over-bought but it also means powerful momentum on the upside. If the index is well below its moving average line, it means it's oversold but it's also telling you that downside momentum is being generated. The spread between several moving averages, like the 10 day and 30 day, tells you the same thing. If a price index is rising and it is above a rising 10 day moving average and the 10 day moving average is above the 30 day moving average, we are now talking about a trend that seems to be very persistent. The spread between the 10 day and the 30 day also tells you something about momentum. Another sign of an overbought market in an uptrend is when the spread widens between two moving averages. The difference between an index and a moving average or between one moving average and another moving average is a measure of the intensity of the trend.

What about moving average crossovers, that is when a shorter term moving average line crosses paths with a longer term moving average?

You can look at a moving average line crossovers. Let's define a shortterm uptrend by saying the shortterm trend is up if the price is above the 10 day moving average and the 10 day moving average is above the 30 day moving average and they are all rising. What is the first thing that can happen to change? The price itself can go down. In other words, the 10 day is still rising, the 30 day is still rising, but now the daily price has fallen. If the daily price falls under the 10 day moving average, that would be another sign of weakness. The 10 day moving average is still rising but the daily price has fallen under it. The next thing that will happen is that the 10 day will flatten out. Now we have another signal of weakness. The price has fallen below the 10 day, the 10 day has turned down but the 30 day is still rising. The next thing that happens is that the 10 day moves under the 30 day—another sign of weakness. The 30 day is still rising though. At some point, you have the price falling and it is below a falling 10 day and the 10 day is below a falling 30 day and now we've got the opposite configuration of where we started. Each of those changes is a sign of a weakening trend. The price weakens, then the 10 day moving average weakens and then the 30 day moving average weakens. I don't really operate with rigid rules based on this but they are useful trailing indicators. I have kept a 10 day and a 30 day on the NY Composite Index for 30 years. As a general rule, when the NY Composite is rising and it's above its 10 day and the 10 day is above its 30 day, that is positive sign on an intermediate term basis. The 10 day moving average line crossing the 30 day moving average line has worked very well as a trend following indicator. It's not perfect. Abrupt changes in the market will make the moving average crossover indicator work less well. You will get some whipsaws. If you are long the index only when the 10 day is above its 30 day and you are short the index when the 10 day is below the 30 day, you will outperform a buy and hold strategy on the NYSE Composite by a tremendous amount. Even though there are going to be lots of crossovers that will produce whipsaws, you will still outperform the NYSE Composite. The reason this simple trading rule works is because you are short or out during declines.

What are some other techniques for smoothing the trend of the market?

You can create exponential moving averages and front end weighted moving averages. They tend to be more sensitive. I don't really do much with them because I don't think it really helps your trading per se to front end load a moving average. You can adjust your tactics and work just as well with an arithmetic moving average.

Isn't it possible that if you weight a moving average you can end up getting whipsawed more often?

Yes, exactly. The more sensitive it is the more whipsaws you get. There is always a trade off between the number of signals and whipsaws. You have to decide what your time horizon is. The more shortterm oriented you are the more whipsaws you have to be willing to accept. I don't know of any way around that. You can't eliminate a whipsaw. Least squares is another way of measuring the trend. My Composite Trend Indicator is calculated by a least squares method rather than a moving average method. I calculate a least squares line and then calculate the change in slope of that line. It tends to be more continuous. Directional changes are less frequent with the least squares method than with moving averages. In other words, the data you take off today can affect the moving average more than the data you are adding. To avoid this problem, you can front end weight a moving average or you can use the least squares method. The moves tend to be smoother and the end points are not as significant on a least squares calculation as they are with moving averages. The precise way you measure the trend and the slope of the trend is not as important as the discipline; that is, following the particular rules you have set.

What are your guidelines on volume?

Volume tends to mirror price. During a trend you expect to see volume gradually building in an advancing stock and gradually declining and in a declining stock but you often get big increases in volume at the ends of both an uptrend and a downtrend. I look at volume a little differently than most people. Most people think that rising volume in a rising trend means demand is picking up. It also means supply has picked up. Let's say a stock which is in a rising trend trades 50,000 shares a day and then suddenly starts trading 100,000 shares a day. Well we know demand has picked up but we also know that supply has picked up. You are now able to sell more. Sellers are becoming more active. My rule on volume is that once volume starts to rise, it has to continue to stay high or get higher to maintain that trend because now the supply has picked up. That is why a big change in volume is often a sign that you are late in that trend. In a declining trend, a big pick up in volume would mean that buyers are becoming more active or are able to become more active. For example, if a stock has gone up for six months and volume has expanded from say 100,000 a day to 200,000 a day and then suddenly started trading 500,000 a day, I would conclude that we might be running into resistance especially if prices ceased moving ahead. Big changes in volume tend to occur with changes in the trend. If you have a stock that is rising on a modest rise in volume and suddenly there is a very big change in volume, that is probably a sign that the uptrend is coming to a close. The same thing is true of the downside. A big pick up in volume can be the end of a decline. While declining volume usually accompanies a decline in trend, a big pickup could mark an end to that downtrend.

As in blow-off moves and selling climaxes?

Right. Another general rule is that big stocks tend to bottom out on high volume and small stocks tend to top out on high volume. The larger the capitalization of the stock, the less likely it is going to show big volume at a top and the more likely it is going to show huge volume at a bottom. In order to stem a decline in the big capitalization stocks, they need to be accumulated over a long period of time; therefore, I would expect large capitalization stocks to build bigger bases and show higher volume near a bottom. Speculative stocks can't be accumulated in a basing pattern because to buy them you have to mark them up. Speculative stocks tend to make much smaller bases and build volume right away during an advance. They tend to top out on high volume because that is the only way to distribute them. I would expect small stocks to have high relative volume at a top compared to bigger stocks. Because there are 10,000 stocks, there are many exceptions but those are the general rules.

Any particular characteristics you look for to detect churning?

There are two elements to a top. One is a big change in volume. The other is no price movement. I wouldn't get bearish simply because there was a big change in volume as long as the stock is moving up; but, once it tends to stall and the volume remains high, then I would consider that bearish and the opposite bullish—big volume and the price stops going down.

In other words, in declining markets you don't expect a lot of volume on the downside unless possibly the trend is getting ready to change?

I would not be looking for big volume to mark the end of a decline. If it did occur it might be a signal the decline might be ending. Declines often end with stabilization in price and very little change in volume. I don't know the odds but it certainly happens often.

Do you think upside volume is more important than downside volume as a confirming indicator?

Generally stocks have to be pushed up but can sink of their own weight. It would be most unusual for a stock to have a major advance without rising volume. The opposite, where volume is light and stocks continue to sink, is common. For the market as a whole, most of the time volume tends to peak before price. One sign of a speculative market is usually higher volume. Markets rarely peak at the point of maximum speculation. They usually peak later. In fact, in a trend you tend to get major stocks doing well at the beginning. Then somewhere along the line there is a phase of increasingly better action in more speculative stocks but before the market goes down, there is usually a move back into the major stocks. Since the secondary stocks attract higher volume to move up, you often get a volume peak before a price peak. As a general rule, you can expect to see the highest volume three to six months ahead of a price peak. It doesn't work all the time but it works much of the time. I also watch turnover. Turnover is volume on the NYSE divided by the total shares outstanding. This is a monthly statistic. Often a rise in volume for the market over a long period of time reflects lots of new shares being lifted rather than increased trading activity; therefore, you want to look at both turnover and volume. Usually they look the same but occasionally turnover can be flat and volume can be rising if there are a lot of new stocks being listed. In fact, that has been the case in this cycle. There has been a huge increase in listings on the NYSE. In

1994 and 1995, volume was rising quite a bit but turnover didn't rise very much. In 1996, turnover did rise as well as volume so that tells me that there was a pickup in speculative intensity in 1996.

When you were at E.F. Hutton you kept an upside/downside volume indicator?

I still do. This can be calculated different ways. You can look at all the volume in advancing stocks and compare that to all the volume in declining stocks. You can also define upside/downside volume by looking at the total volume on upticks versus the total volume on downticks but it is harder to get your hands on that data. Over time though, I haven't noticed any great difference in these two. Of course, there is the net—the difference between upside volume and downside volume. On the upside: downside volume, I keep a 10 day moving average of total upside volume on the NYSE and a 10 day moving average of the total downside volume on the NYSE as well as a 10 day moving average of the net difference between the two. The net difference can rise because upside is rising more than downside or upside is rising and downside is falling or upside is flat and downside is falling. The fact that the net is rising is useful but you really need to know why. That is why I look at the other two components. I want to know if a rally is a function of increased demand or falling supply. I use 10 day upside volume as a proxy for demand and 10 day downside volume as a proxy for supply. I am always looking at the two and making some conclusion about what is happening. I also calculate Joe Granville's On-Balance-Volume (OBV). During any particular time period, if the price is higher you consider the volume positive, if the price is lower, you consider the volume negative. You can do it on a daily basis or a weekly basis. I have kept it for 30 years on an hourly basis on the NYSE Composite Index. It is one of my favorite shortterm charts. Ironically, whether you use upside/downside, upticks/downticks, or Joe's OBV technique, they all usually look about the same. There are always differences but not that much difference.

How is its track record with regard to shortterm signals?

The OBV tends to lead price. For example, if price has been going sideways and the OBV line is rising, that would be a bullish divergence. There tends to be somewhat of an upside bias in the index because stocks tend to trade more volume when they are going up than they do when they are going down so OBV lines are going to rise more often than price. A bullish divergence has to be tempered with the notion that there is an upward bias. Since there is an upward bias, it would be more significant if you get a negative or bearish divergence. It is usually a good signal when the OBV line fails to confirm a higher price. That doesn't happen very often on the NYSE Composite index. Use OBV to look for confirmations and divergences between the price action and the volume.

Have you incorporated any modifications to the original concept of OBV?

I take the hourly volume and if the index is up during that period I consider that positive volume. If it is down I consider that negative volume. Since there are not an even number of hours in the trading day, I calculate the period from 12:30 to 2:00 as one hour because this period usually has the lightest volume for the day. So even though there are 6½ hours in the trading day, I only keep a 6 hour chart.

Looking at upside volume and downside volume individually is more important to you than the ratio of upside to downside volume?

I keep the ratio as well but I only keep the volume ratio for one thing and that is to calculate the trading index. When I am doing my volume work, I am looking at 10 day totals of upside volume, downside volume, and net volume rather than the ratio. Both are useful but I think total volume is more important than the ratio because changes in the total volume are more important to me than relative volume changes. A day with very low volume would be less significant than a day with very high volume. I want to know if a rally is a function of increased buying power or decreased selling pressure or a combination of the two. People say that the markets are oversold when the net volume gets deeply in the minus side but sometimes it's not. It could be underbought. In other words, sometimes that number becomes negative not because of a particularly large rise in downside volume but because there has been a big drop in upside volume. In my opinion, underbought markets are different than oversold markets. They are not as important. In an uptrend, a market will get underbought rather than oversold. It is a sign of strength.

What kind of work do you do with the trading index or ARMS index?

The ARMS index is another volume indicator. It is the average volume in declining stocks divided by the average volume in advancing stocks. If there is no particular extreme on an intraday or daily basis, I don't consider it to be an important number. For the market, I keep a 10 day moving average of the ARMS index. The 10 day moving average is important and tends to move between .80 and 1.20. These bounds would be neutral. Above 1.20 is getting oversold and below .80 is getting overbought. The trading index tends to lead much more than other qualitative trend measures. An overbought trading index, let's say under .80, often occurs very early in advancing markets. So an overbought trading index is usually a bullish signal rather than a bearish signal. Big oversolds are usually close to bottoms. For the OTC market my parameters are .70 and 1.30.

The wider spread on the OTC market is to account for additional volatility?

Right. The OTC market swings more widely.

Other than volume, what other qualitative trend measures do you use?

I watch the numbers of new highs and the number of new lows. Basically the more stocks that are making new highs in an uptrend, the more confidence I have in that trend. Like a lot of other qualitative trend measures, new highs tend to peak well before the final peak in the averages. I keep a 10 day moving average of daily new highs and lows and I also keep weekly new highs and new lows. Another indicator I keep is a 10 day moving average of new highs divided by {new lows plus new highs}.

Is the weekly computation based on a 10 day moving average?

No. I simply chart the net difference between the new weekly highs and lows. These statistics are in

Barron's. More often than not it is going to show you the same thing that the daily does. I look at it because sometimes it's different and when it's different it might be important. It is conceivable that you could have 100 new highs every day on the NYSE and 100 new highs for the week meaning the exact same 100 stocks made new highs every day. You could also have 100 new highs every day and 500 new highs for the week which means that you have a totally different list each day. In reality, it is going to be something in between but if you find an extreme like this it would be very important. I do a similar thing with what I call break-outs or price alerts. I keep a computer screen which looks at the last 75 days of price action. I keep track of the number of stocks that are making new highs and new lows over that 75 day period. I treat it the same way I do the "new high" list in the paper keeping a 10 day moving average of the net. This is a more short to medium term indicator. This list is also a source of trading ideas. A stock can't go up or down without appearing on the list.

Are there additional shortterm trend indicators in your arsenal?

The different components of a trend are price, volume, and breadth. I keep what I call a Composite Trend Indicator and Composite Momentum Indicators. They are unweighted or geometric indexes. My Composite Trend Indicator is a composite of a price measure, a breadth measure, and a volume measure. In the Composite Trend Indicator, my price measure is the NYSE Composite index. The NYSE cumulative breadth is my breadth indicator, and OBV is my volume measure. For OBV, I take the hourly and the last reading of the day. I multiply the NY composite index by the breadth measure times the OBV volume measure and then I take the third root of that which becomes my Composite Trend Indicator. This is the daily reading. My Composite Momentum Indicators are calculated by using least squares rather than moving averages. I take the 10 day, 30 day, 10 week, 30 week, and 30 month of the daily readings. Though I use the same procedure for all of them, let's just talk about the 10 day. To get my 10 day Composite Momentum Indicator, I calculate the least squares line for the last 10 days of data. I calculate the slope of the least squares line. I compare that to the slope of the 10 days through yesterday. Every day I have a running or cumulative 10 day period as you would do for a moving average, but I take the 10 points instead of using a moving average. I just compare the slope of the least squares line. Fifteen years ago I did an experiment to see if least squares would be a smoother way of looking for trend reversals and momentum changes than moving averages. I go through all this machination now because as it turned out, it is smoother. Somebody can create something that looks like my model. They couldn't come up with the same number because they wouldn't know what my base was but it wouldn't matter.

What about one of the most common measures of breadth, the A/D line?

The traditional A/D line that most people use looks at the total number of stocks on the NYSE. The total number of stocks is up 50% from the early 1980's. We have gone from 2,000 issues to over 3,000 issues. There are closed-end bond funds, preferred stocks, and foreign stocks in these totals which mucks up the A/D line. Not only are there more stocks listed but a lot of them aren't even stocks. Bond funds aren't stocks. They trade like common stocks but they are bonds. It is my feeling that the breadth line is becoming less and less relevant. I have started keeping my statistics also on just the breadth of the S&P 500 component stocks. These are all operating companies. You would expect it could look considerably different from the total based on its makeup and it does. It has been far weaker longterm.

Will the average reader have access to the S&P 500 advance/decline figures?

No. I have talked to the NYSE and asked them to release just the figures for domestic operating companies, that is take out bond funds, preferreds, and foreign stocks. They could do it easily but I have had no luck. I have seen S&P breadth mentioned in the papers occasionally but it is certainly not there on a regular basis. I don't like to use a lot of indicators that other people don't have access to but I have to use this for analytical purposes. I am starting to keep a number of indicators on just the S&P 500 index, like upside/downside volume and the TRIN.

Do you have any favorite chart patterns that you look for?

I have some thoughts about that. If you start with a basic text, like Edwards and Magee, what the book trains you to do is "pattern recognition" but I think you can't see the forest for the trees if you do that. If you are looking for head and shoulders patterns, you will find 10,000 of them or none. To my knowledge, I don't think I have ever seen a perfect head and shoulders pattern but I have seen thousands of imperfect ones. Beauty is in the eye of the beholder. There is only one thing about patterns that is important and that is "Is the pattern a continuation pattern or a reversal pattern?" When a stock has been in a trend and suddenly stops advancing or stops declining, it is now doing something else. Is that pattern likely to lead to a move in the same direction or to a move in the opposite direction? My first rule is that the longer a stock spends in the pattern the more likely it is to be a reversal pattern. Stocks that are going up, go up. They don't stop going up too long. Pattern identification is not important to me.

Where do commodities and bonds fit into your work?

The other markets obviously affect my opinion on the equity market and the equity market affects my opinion on those other markets. Stocks are a leading economic indicator. Commodities are a coincident economic indicator. Bonds are a lagging economic indicator. The relationship between these markets is always telling me something about the economy. My first comment is that it is a mistake to think that all you need is bonds going up and then stocks go up. I read in the financial press that stocks and bonds move together then they de-link for a while and then re-link. This drives me nuts because they don't link and de-link. Stocks and bonds are both manifestations of the economic cycle. Stocks lead bonds because stocks are a leading economic indicator and bonds are a lagging economic indicator. For example, if stocks are rising and bonds are rising and commodities are rising, what's going to happen? If all three markets are rising, what do we know about the economy? Well, the commodity markets are going up. They are a coincident indicator so the economy must be strong. Stocks are going up. Stocks are a leading economic indicator, so stocks are reacting to current expectations that future conditions are going to be favorable. Bonds are going up. Bonds shouldn't go up for long in that environment. Bonds have to turn down so we know that we are at the end of the rope for bonds. If all three markets are rising you look to sell bonds. If all three markets are declining, what do you do? You look to buy bonds.

Do you use the CRB index as a measure of commodity prices?

The CRB index is not a perfect measure of inflation nor a perfect measure of commodity prices. I use the CRB in a general sense to talk about commodity prices but it is not a good index. It is heavily weighted toward grains. It is possible for the CRB to go up while industrial commodity prices are going down. If that is happening it's not telling you about a strong economy. It's telling you that the weather in Iowa is bad. I watch a number of commodity indexes. I watch the CRB index, the Goldman Sachs commodity index, the Dow Jones commodity index, and I watch raw industrial prices by themselves. Most of the time, the CRB is going to give you the same picture. If you are trying to simplify things, look at the CRB index.

Let's assume that the indexes which measure commodity prices continue to inch ahead and stocks are still moving up, at some point the two are going to diverge, right?

It depends. Rising commodity prices could be a measure that inflation is picking up. It's not simply a function of a decent economic environment. If rising commodity prices are having a big, negative effect on bonds, stocks are probably going to go down. If commodity prices are rising and the bond market is meandering sideways, stocks are going to go up because then stocks will be reacting to the positive aspect of better earnings, not the negative aspect of lower valuations because of rising interest rates.

Now that we know what indicators you follow, can you tell us how you tie the secular, cyclical, intermediate, and shortterm together?

My top down analysis will tell me whether or not I want to own stocks at all relative to other forms of investment. I believe the longterm trends drive the shortterm trends. I have the most confidence when I am looking for shortterm buy ideas when the medium term trend and when the longterm trend is up. You don't often get everything going the same way but when you do it is good for confidence. The longest trend, the secular trend, is pretty much irrelevant from a tactical standpoint. It is most important at either the beginning or end of a cyclical trend. If I think the secular trend is very strong but the cyclical trend is topping out, all other things being equal, I am not going to be as bearish. The same thing applies when I are comparing the cyclical to the medium term. If the cyclical trend is up strongly, I am less concerned about an intermediate term setback. If the intermediate term looks good and the cyclical looks bad, obviously I am going to be much more cautious. If the medium term trend is up, I am not going to be as concerned about a shortterm setback. When I am looking for a buy idea in an individual stock, I like to see a group that has not been outperforming the market for several cycles or more. Groups tend to be in favor, on a relative basis, for several cycles. Rarely is it just one. The intermediate term, a three to six month horizon, is where I start and from there I move to the shortterm and then to the longterm. I focus more on the intermediate term than the other time horizons for two reasons. Institutions and individuals operate in that horizon. There is not a respectable money manager I know who is going to sit out a three to six month swing even though he says he has a two to five year horizon. I think the same thing can be said for the public. Secondly, I have more indicators at work in that time horizon. I use the shortterm for timing my decisions as to what or what not to buy.

Would you throw out the names of a few groups that lead at bottoms and peak at tops?

Most of the time the bond market will be improving before the stock market so interest rate sensitive stocks like consumer staples, utilities and to a lesser degree, financials, would tend to show relative strength prior to a bottom and early in an advance. During an advance, you get economically sensitive areas doing well. That includes both consumer cyclicals as well as industrial cyclicals-like capital goods and technology. The groups to play last are generally the commodity driven groups which would be energy and basic materials. Every cycle has exceptions and these are just very general guides. Gold stocks as well as other inflation type stocks tend to do well at the end of an uptrend and often as the market is rolling over.

Could you differentiate between consumer staples and consumer cyclicals?

Consumer staples are stable growth stocks. This would include groups like foods, beverages, tobacco, household products, health care, and pharmaceuticals. These are the defensive or stable growth areas. Consumer cyclicals are consumer spending stocks—retail, automobiles, housing, media, entertainment, and gaming. Consumer staples tend to do well very early, prior to a bottom. Consumer cyclicals tend to pick up next.

What valuable advice would you pass on to readers?

My primary trading rule is that you make money if you don't lose money. Risk control is the name of the game. Technical analysis brings risk control to the table. Fundamental analysis has a very difficult time dealing with risk. If a fundamental analyst likes a stock at $30.00 a share and the stock goes down to $25.00, he must like it more because it's cheaper. Maybe it's more attractive, maybe it isn't. The technician treats weakness as a reason for caution, not as a reason for optimism. The stock has gone down so let's investigate why. Averaging down is usually a mistake. In my opinion, there is only one time when you can average down and that is when you are damn sure the next move is up. You have to be more sure when you are averaging than when you bought the stock the first time. Ironically, most people are less certain when they average down than when they bought it the first time. The only reason they buy more is because it's down. They are trying to lower their average cost when the market might be giving you a message that maybe something has turned sour. Risk control is critical and technical analysis is very useful in determining risk because we can look at support areas, trendlines, gaps, and moving averages. There are many ways of identifying the trend and deciding when the trend has been broken or when it has reversed. I would not buy a stock simply because I was confident it was going up. I always look for a favorable profit to risk ratio. Unless I can identify and quantify the risk, I am not going to buy a stock. If I am a trader, from a shortterm standpoint, I am willing to accept relatively modest profits. I want to have a profit to risk ratio of at least 2:1 on a shortterm commitment. If I am an investor with a medium term horizon, I am looking for bigger profits and will accept more risk. Generally, as an investor I will look for a 3:1 profit to risk ratio. If I am looking for a 10% return on a "trade," then I am not going to accept more than 5% risk. If I am an investor looking for 30% or more profit, I am going to accept a 10% risk. The profit to risk ratio has to be more for the investment than for the trade.

Do you use stops to limit your risk?

In the words of Alan Shaw, Smith Barney's chief technical analyst, there are four things that can happen to you when you buy a stock. It can go up a little, go up a lot, go down a little, or go down a lot. The fourth thing you absolutely have to prevent. You have to use stops to limit your losses. I frequently hear people who are afraid to use stops comment, "What happens if I get whipsawed? What happens if the stock just goes ¼ or ½ point under my stop and then reverses?" There is this fear of being whipsawed which I find ironic because if you don't use a stop what happens? You could take a big loss. Whipsaws are small losses that prevent big losses. A whipsaw means you have now accepted a small loss and so be it; now you move on to the next trading idea. We have to get out of our head this fear of being whipsawed because a stop prevents the big loss. Successful trading and investing entails taking a lot of small losses.

If you had to describe the ideal entry point based on risk: reward, what would the scenario look like?

I like to buy stocks where I can identify a small amount of risk, such as stocks coming out of bases. Let's say I like a stock at $30.00. It has recently advanced across a base built in the $20.00 to $30.00 range. I have a lot of confidence that the pattern between $20.00 and $30.00 is a base and I conclude that the pattern will produce a $40.00 target. If I look at the pattern and the stock has gone straight up from $20.00 to $30.00, my comment would be that this stock is not a great buy because I can only count it to $40.00 and it could have risk to $20.00. There is as much risk as there is potential in this situation. I like to see a stock that stalls under a resistance level and consolidates. I would then look for some backing and filling or stabilization in the $27.00 to $30.00 range establishing a support area nearby. Obviously, I want to try to buy it closer to $27.00 than $30.00 but I am willing to pay $30.00 because now I have a stop at $27.00 and a $40.00 target. With the stock at $30.00, I have 10 points of potential and 3 points of risk. I have a 3:1 profit to risk ratio. Now the stock looks good to me. The most important thing to me is a good profit to risk ratio. I don't care how strong the chart looks.

Do you have any rules as to how many times the price has to touch $27.00 to be considered reliable support?

I can't give you rules like that. Chart interpretation is highly subjective. That really depends on whether we are talking about a stock from a two week horizon, a two month horizon, or a two year horizon. The volume the stock is trading and changes in volatility will affect my interpretation of how long it needs to spend in a base pattern. I look for a drop in volatility and volume after an advance to indicate a consolidation. To the technician, volatility is it's intraday range relative to its price. I am expecting the range to contract during a consolidation. My normal "trading" horizon is one to two months. For that time period, I would be looking for at least a couple of weeks of consolidation to make a judgment.

What is the most difficult psychological or emotional barrier that technicians have to deal with?

Admitting error. People don't sell because it is an admission of a mistake. If you have made an error you have to get beyond the notion that if you don't sell a stock then you don't have to accept the fact that you made an error. Taking losses is a normal course of doing business. You have to be objective and admit errors frequently.

Lance Stonecypher

Ned Davis Research is a prestigious investment advisory firm, highly regarded for their innovative methods of analyzing traditional indicators. Established in 1980 by Ned Davis and partner Ed Mendel, the firm has evolved into a major "think tank." Eleven analysts cover the broad equity markets, credit markets, foreign currency markets, international markets, and specific industry groups. As many as eight different market newsletters are published summarizing the results of their analyses.

Lance Stonecypher is responsible for many of the creative studies and indicators which emerge from Ned Davis Research. A magna cum laude graduate (BBA) of the University of San Diego, Mr. Stonecypher joined Ned Davis as his research assistant in 1986 and worked in the trenches creating hundreds of indicators and writing newsletters before later becoming Managing Director of Selection Services.

As a teenager, Mr. Stonecypher chose photography as a hobby. For a while, he set his sights on becoming a commercial photographer until he realized that photography demanded perpetual infusions of cash. Choosing not to be penniless for the rest of his life, he examined other options. In retrospect, his experiences with photography taught him a technical skill and inspired him to be creative, two things which would later be helpful to him as a research analyst. Another interest, which he shared with his father, was the stock and commodities markets and by the time he entered college, he had determined that his career would center on some aspect of the financial markets. With a penchant for research and aptitude for quantitative and statistical analysis, he decided to become an investment research analyst. With a clear course of direction, he moved toward his goal overlooking one small detail—evaluating the demand for his expertise. After spending months looking for a position, he was directed to Ned Davis Research and offered a job. Seizing the opportunity, he packed all of his belongings, drove cross-country from California to Florida, and has been with the firm ever since.

At least 90% of the work at Ned Davis Research is objective and based on historical precedent. Their timely and unbiased market commentary is always supported by a host of indicators with a proven track record. Over 2,000 technical, fundamental, monetary, and economic indicators have been converted to chart form, which are available individually or as a complete set in a bound edition.

From 1968 to 1978, Ned Davis earned a great deal of recognition within the investment community for his remarkable ability to consistently forecast the markets; however, at the close of each year, after the results were tallied, the profit column didn't seem to measure up to those spectacular forecasts. Why wasn't he getting rich following his own advice? Upon closer inspection, he discovered a number of causes such as failure to cut losses, lack of discipline, emotional responses, and refusing to accept personal responsibility for being wrong. To eliminate these hurdles, major reforms were made in his investment strategy between 1979 and 1980.

Today, risk management is the name of the game at Ned Davis Research and making money for their large base of institutional clients now takes precedence over forecasting the market. From a massive data base of indicators that have been extensively tested, various models have been constructed in a scientific and mathematical format for the purpose of generating objective and disciplined investment decisions.

In the following pages, Mr. Stonecypher discusses the investment philosophy at Ned Davis Research and presents a sampling of their indicator models, two essential building blocks which have attributed to the success of the firm.

Since the investment credo at Ned Davis Research is a major contributing factor to the firm's enviable track record, why don't we start with that.

When we develop indicators and models, there are a number of principles which we try to adhere to. After studying forecasts of the financial markets for nearly 16 years, our firm hasn't found any one person or any single indicator that could consistently and reliably forecast an uncertain world- we haven't found the holy grail.

It's good to have the truth right up front.

While no one is right in their forecasts year in and year out, there are a number of advisors who seem to make money year in and year out, such as Marty Zweig and Dan Sullivan. These are investment winners who, according to Mark Hulbert, have consistently made money, at least since 1980. Of course, there are a number of investment legends like John Templeton, Warren Buffet, Peter Lynch, and Paul Tudor Jones who have also consistently made money. All of these people rely on different investment philosophies, ranging from Benjamin Graham longterm valuation techniques to "in and out" commodity trading. That includes dollar cost averaging and buying stocks with high yields to market timing—buying stocks that are relatively strong but with almost no yield. This clearly demonstrates that a variety of techniques can make money. But despite their varied and sometimes contradictory styles, these winners shared four key characteristics which are the basis of our philosophy at Ned Davis Research.

And what are those four key characteristics?

First, they all used objectively determined indicators rather than gut emotions to trade. Ned has a riddle he shares with clients relating to this. There is a room with three people in it. One is a high-priced lawyer, another is a low-priced lawyer, and the third is the tooth fairy. In the middle of them is a one hundred dollar bill. Suddenly, the lights go out and then come back on. The $100.00 has disappeared. The question is, "Who took the one hundred dollar bill?" The answer is the high-priced lawyer because the other two are simply figments of the imagination. The point is that we want to make sure that what our indicators are saying are really factual rather than a figment of our imagination. It is absolutely critical that we stick with objectively determined indicators. The second characteristic is that all of these winners are very disciplined in their approach. They stay with their system through good times as well as bad. In classical Greek tragedies, the hero is always ruined in the end by some psychological character flaw. We often use this as an analogy because a common flaw of many investors is that they let their ego or personal feelings become involved in their market views, which makes it extremely difficult to admit mistakes. Discipline allows us to control our mistakes. The third key characteristic is that while disciplined, all of these people were flexible enough in their approach to change their minds whenever the evidence shifted. I remember back to the crash of 1987. Marty Zweig had done a study which showed that in every case, following a stock market decline of 30% or more, the economy always sank into a depression or severe recession. And yet within days after the crash, when his indicators turned very bullish, Marty turned bullish as well despite a lot of his fears. So he was flexible enough in his mindset that he shifted his outlook based on his objective indicators. The fourth characteristic is that all of these people are extremely risk averse. Ned Davis once asked Paul Tudor Jones what he did at work all day. He said, "The first thing I do is try and figure out what could go wrong and then I spend the rest of the day trying to cut my risks." Now, here is a commodity trader who is known as a risk taker, but I say he is risk averse. So, these four tenets: objectivity, discipline, flexibility, and risk management are the cornerstones of our investment philosophy.

What is your strategy for controlling or limiting risk?

We emphasize that this is a business of making mistakes. If we all make mistakes, what is it that separates the winners from the losers? The answer is simple—winners end up making small mistakes while the losers make huge ones. The winners cut their losses short. Our company has two mandates—one, we are trying to make money and two, we are trying to stay out of big trouble. Back in 1991, Ned Davis wrote a book entitled ***"Being Right or Making Money."*** Being right is a lot of fun when your forecasts are correct but we think it is more important to concentrate on making money. We tell our clients that the art of forecasting is something we do only for fun, but making money is something that we are dead serious about and we try to approach it in as scientific a manner as possible. For the most part, we view ourselves as risk managers.

More as risk managers than stock pickers?

Yes, definitely. One of the differences between professionals and amateurs is that amateurs tend to look toward the potential rewards while professionals ask, "What are the risks?" Most of our work is geared toward a broader, macro overview of the markets. We will try to assess risk in the S&P 500 and the Dow rather than picking individual stocks.

And you rely on your models to alert you to risk or opportunity?

Yes. As a hypothetical example, if we had a model composed of say, 10 indicators, and all those indicators were bullish, then obviously we would be extremely bullish. Then let's say 2 indicators turn bearish—that's 8 indicators bullish and 2 bearish. We would still stick with the investment but we might take about 20% of the chips off the table, just out of respect for the higher risk. The markets are not a black and white world, either bullish or bearish. They are really composed of shades of gray—degrees of bullishness and bearishness. That is a very critical point for us at Ned Davis Research.

Will you wait for the set parameters in your models to issue buy and sell signals or is there some subjective evaluation that eventually enters into the decision process?

We do both. For the most part, our models are objective anchors giving us discipline to our work but we often like to prescribe some interpretation to them. For example, right now our primary model, (the composite longterm investment guide) BIG MO, is at 45%, a low neutral position. That means that 45% of the indicators in the model are bullish. BIG MO contains clusters of indicators from various areas. One area might be monetary, another sentiment, another one valuation, and another the economy; however, the primary overriding factor in BIG MO is the tape action. For years now, we have seen the valuation aspect of the model read extremely bearish and yet the tape action has been extremely bullish. A critical interpretation there is the fact that you have a divergence within the model—valuations are at bearish extremes while the tape is still positive. To use a popular analogy, you have one foot in a bucket of hot water and another in a bucket of cold water. On average, everything appears fine—no, it's not fine. There is a very high risk going on right now. That is the way we might prescribe some interpretation to our indicators but we would use the model as an anchor. We look at 2,800 indicators in charts and offer our opinion after looking at all those different objective indicators. Knowing our interpretation, clients might be a bit quicker pulling the trigger if something should develop. The bottom line is that our models are designed with one foremost thought in mind and that is controlling risk. We want to limit the really big mistakes.

If that's the case, then your models must be programmed to capture major trend reversals and not the day to day price blips?

Exactly. Because we are an institutional service, we are focused on trying to catch the big moves because that is where the big money is made.

What advantages will investors gain by using a model?

Because our focus at Ned Davis Research is on modeling the financial markets, this is probably one of the first questions that arises from our clients. For the most part, there are essentially three very good reasons for using models. As we talked about before, the models give us objectivity. It's not that we have anything against judgment, but we just like the fact that our models are mathematically able to quantify our favorite indicators, thereby providing an objective sounding board devoid of any emotional errors in judgment. The second thing that we like about our models is that they provide a discipline. You can watch these models deteriorate or improve but when they start switching signals from positive to negative, it becomes a real strong force to get in line with the model. Also, our models are specifically designed to focus on risk. As the indicators deteriorate and the risks rise, that is when we begin to cut back our investment position. Again, objectivity, discipline, and risk management are some of the better reasons for using models.

Would you walk us through the eight charts included here?

These eight charts illustrate the way we build models but most of our major composite models are much more complex than this. For example, BIG MO, our primary trend model, has about 800 different indicators in it. We also chart a lot of indicators separately because we like to see exactly what is going on with the "inner workings" of the composite models.

These charts seem to cover a span of 27 years. Is that the typical time frame you would use in your models?

These charts go back to 1968 but many of our models will go back a lot further than this. Many of

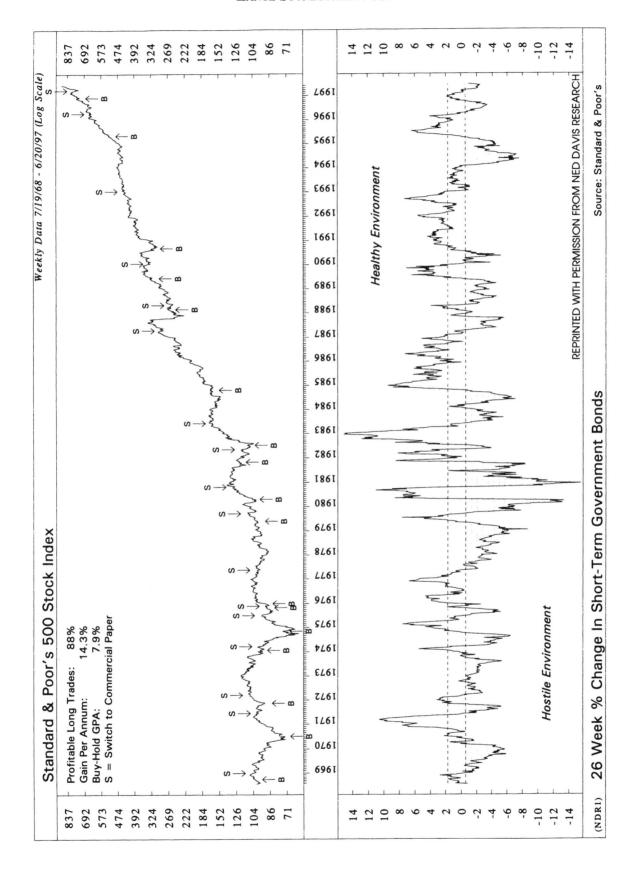

Standard & Poor's 500 Stock Index

Weekly Data 7/19/68 - 6/20/97 (Log Scale)

Profitable Long Trades: 88%
Gain Per Annum: 14.3%
Buy-Hold GPA: 7.9%
S = Switch to Commercial Paper

Healthy Environment

Hostile Environment

(NDR1)   26 Week % Change In Short-Term Government Bonds

REPRINTED WITH PERMISSION FROM NED DAVIS RESEARCH   Source: Standard & Poor's the economic models go back to the 1940's. We have data that goes all the way back to 1900 and a few indicators even go back to the 1800's, but most of our weekly data starts around 1960 to 1965. First of all, let me orient you to the charts. In the lower left hand corner of each chart there is a chart number. These charts are numbered NDR 1 through NDR 8. On all of these charts, with maybe the exception of one, the top clip shows the market we are trying to forecast or assess risk in. In this case, it is the S&P 500 which is the standard for institutional clients. Plotted in the lower clip of chart NDR 1 is the 26 week rate of change in shortterm government bonds, which is what we are using to derive the buy and sell signals in the top clip. The up arrow or "B" site in the top clip is where this indicator is telling us to "buy" and the "S" arrow pointing down is where we would sell and switch to commercial paper. One of our main rules is "Don't fight the Federal Reserve." For staying on the right side of monetary or interest rate trends, the 26 week rate of change in shortterm government bonds is a good indicator to use. To calculate this, you simply use Standard and Poor's shortterm government bond index of 2 to 4 year government notes and determine if the index is higher or lower than it was six months ago. If shortterm government notes are higher by 1.8% or more, that's a buy signal. If shortterm bonds have declined by 0.5% from 26 weeks ago, the model generates a sell signal. More specifically for our purposes, the indicator has to rise above the top horizontal dashed line. Once that is exceeded, a buy signal is generated. Likewise, a drop below the lower dashed line generates a sell signal. Our computer program can assess the accuracy of these indicators or "batting average" as we call it. As it turns out, 88% of all buy signals shown in the top clip of this chart were accurate and profitable, which is a good batting average. By buying the S&P 500 at the buy signals and then switching into risk-free money market vehicles on the sell signals, you would have made 14.3% per annum during this 28 year period. Buying and holding the S&P 500 over this same time period would have resulted in only a 7.9% return. So by not fighting the Federal Reserve you would have more than doubled the buy and hold approach. But even with an indicator that is as good as this one, we would still rather use a "tree" of indicators rather than hang out on any single limb. Monetary trends and Federal Reserve policy are just one limb of that tree.

What do the other limbs look like?

Our first rule is to respect the primary trend but we also use other types of indicators relating to monetary factors and sentiment that help us to do some early top and bottom spotting and risk assessment of the market. The first chart (NDR 1) shows the liquidity that the Federal Reserve board provides for the economic and financial systems but we also like to look at liquidity within the stock market itself. The theory is that when everyone is extremely optimistic they tend to be fully invested and when they are extremely fearful, they raise cash. When a lot of fear has built up, there is potential demand for stocks on the sidelines. Take a look at chart NDR 2. This shows the percentage of bullish advisors divided by the quantity of bullish plus bearish advisors from Investor's Intelligence. This indicator usually swings between 30% when the crowd is extremely bearish, up to about 90% where the crowd is extremely optimistic. The rule that we developed for this indicator is "Beware of crowds at extremes." We created some buy and sell signals that are shown on this chart but to be perfectly honest, the track record is rather mixed at best. The problem is that during extended moves, the crowd actually tends to be right for a period of time. During those periods of time, sentiment indicators such as these won't work very well because they are often too early. Chart NDR 3 takes a look at what happens when the advisory service sentiment indicator is combined with the shortterm government bond momentum indicator

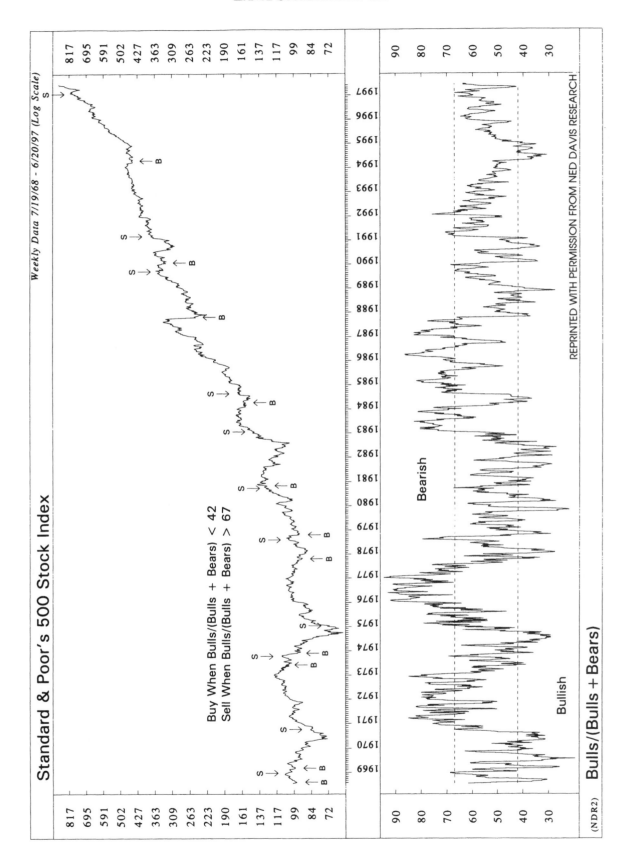

Standard & Poor's 500 Stock Index

Weekly Data 7/19/68 - 6/20/97 (Log Scale)

817
695
591
502
427
363
309
263
223
190
161
137
117
99
84
72

Buy When Bulls/(Bulls + Bears) < 42
Sell When Bulls/(Bulls + Bears) > 67

Bulls/(Bulls + Bears)

(NDR2)

Bearish

Bullish

REPRINTED WITH PERMISSION FROM NED DAVIS RESEARCH

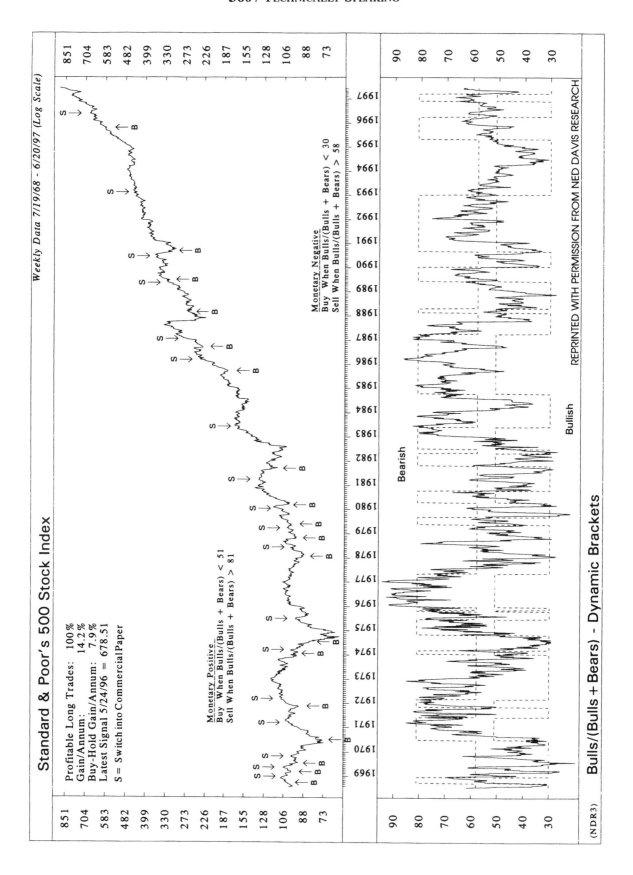

Standard & Poor's 500 Stock Index

Weekly Data 7/19/68 - 6/20/97 (Log Scale)

Profitable Long Trades:	100%
Gain/Annum:	14.2%
Buy-Hold Gain/Annum:	7.9%
Latest Signal 5/24/96 =	678.51

S = Switch into Commercial Paper

Monetary Positive
Buy When Bulls/(Bulls + Bears) < 51
Sell When Bulls/(Bulls + Bears) > 81

Monetary Negative
Buy When Bulls/(Bulls + Bears) < 30
Sell When Bulls/(Bulls + Bears) > 58

REPRINTED WITH PERMISSION FROM NED DAVIS RESEARCH

Bearish

Bullish

Bulls/(Bulls + Bears) - Dynamic Brackets

(NDR3)

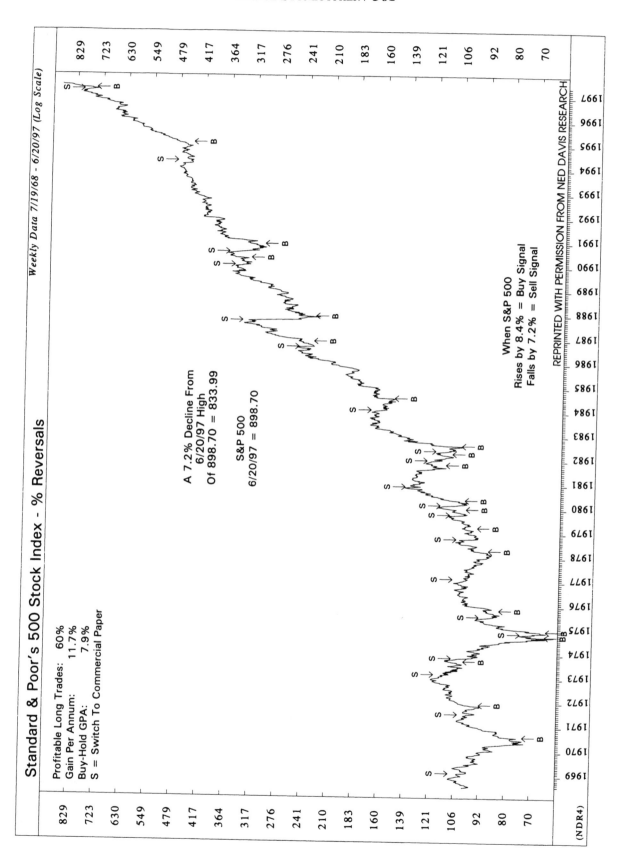

Standard & Poor's 500 Stock Index - % Reversals

Weekly Data 7/19/68 - 6/20/97 (Log Scale)

Profitable Long Trades: 60%
Gain Per Annum: 11.7%
Buy-Hold GPA: 7.9%
S = Switch To Commercial Paper

A 7.2% Decline From
6/20/97 High
Of 898.70 = 833.99

S&P 500
6/20/97 = 898.70

When S&P 500
Rises by 8.4% = Buy Signal
Falls by 7.2% = Sell Signal

REPRINTED WITH PERMISSION FROM NED DAVIS RESEARCH

(NDR4)

that we saw in the first chart (NDR 1). This combined indicator assumes that when monetary conditions are "favorable," *less* pessimism is needed to describe a bullish condition and *more* optimism is required to describe a bearish condition. Conversely, when monetary conditions are "unfavorable," you are going to need a whole lot more pessimism to reach a good bullish bottom and much less optimism to reach a bearish top. Chart NDR 3 illustrates this effect in what we call our "dynamic brackets." When the bond momentum indicator describes monetary conditions as positive, these brackets shift upward while the opposite occurs when the indicator describes monetary conditions as negative. It turns out that through a strategy of switching into commercial paper on the sell signals, 100% of the closeout trades shown on this chart would have been profitable.

Are your figures in chart NDR 2 a combination of polling services or exclusively Investor's Intelligence?

These sentiment numbers here are derived strictly from Investor's Intelligence. We just use the bullish investment advisors and the bearish advisors and exclude the correction category. The third area where we have put the most weight basically says, "Don't fight the tape" or "The trend is your friend." Chart NDR 4 shows an indicator that we developed to be trend sensitive or tape sensitive so that we can stay in harmony with the market. I like to describe this indicator as a caboose on a train. Using the end of week close for the S&P 500 stock index, when the S&P 500 rises by 8.4% from a bottom, we know that the train is confirmed going north and we get a buy signal at that point. When the S&P 500 falls by 7.2% from a peak, the train is confirmed heading south and a sell signal is generated. The negative point about indicators such as these is the accuracy rate. Historically, trend following indicators have numerous whipsaws which produce a lot of small losses. In fact, with regard to buy signals, this indicator has been right only 60% of the time. The odds are only a little bit better than flipping a coin. You might ask, "Why use it?" From our testing, we have learned that the big money is made on the big moves; therefore, we use it because if there is a major extended move, you are almost guaranteed to be on the right side of it. You are not going to sit through a major bear market, like the 1968-1970 style bear market at the beginning of this chart, very long. Trend sensitive indicators such as these provide a stop-loss, ensuring that you are not going to be on the wrong side of any big move. Had you followed this model you would have made 11.7% per annum, beating the buy and hold return of 7.9%. Chart NDR 5 illustrates another method of generating trend sensitive signals. This indicator simply uses the 30 week rate of change of the Value Line Composite Index.

Do you smooth the 30 week rate of change with a moving average?

No, we simply take the 30 week rate of change based on the weekly close of the Value Line Composite Index. To generate a buy signal, the rate of change has to improve from an oversold condition rising to -1%. In order to generate a sell signal, the indicator must deteriorate from an overbought condition down to +15%. With an accuracy rate of 94% on the buy signals and an overall gain of 11.5% per annum, the track record on this trend sensitive indicator happens to be much better than the one in chart NDR 4. We tell clients that this is a business of making mistakes and that everyone makes mistakes. The real difference between the winners and the losers in the stock market, and the *only* difference, is that the losers make big mistakes that they can't recover from while winners cut their losses short.

Thank you for making that critical point.

So tape sensitive or trend sensitive indicators are extremely important in our work. In fact, even if their track records are not the best, and quite often they are not, we still insist that any model used to determine our core invested position be at least 50% weighted with trend sensitive indicators. There will be a lot of little whipsaws that eat away at the batting average but when you use indicators that involve interest rates, you get great accuracy but there are times when interest rates are declining and the stock market will decline as well. This was the case in the 1930's. In a situation like that, the interest rate model doesn't have an objective means to get you out of the market. That is why you need the trend sensitive indicators. Chart NDR 6 represents our composite model, which includes a combination of the sentiment and monetary indicators in charts NDR 1 and NDR 3 along with two tape or trend sensitive indicators. In this particular model, we bought on the buys but "sold short" on the sell signals. When the composite indicator is above zero, the weight of the evidence is positive and a buy signal is generated. When the weight of the evidence is negative, we get a signal to sell short. The batting average of this indicator is 70% meaning that about 2/3 of all signals were profitable. Through testing, we would have made about 7.3% per annum versus 7.9% from a buy-hold basis.

The buy and hold strategy seems to have a slight lead over the trading strategy.

When you use the riskier strategy of going long and selling short, testing has indicated that you slightly underperform a buy and hold approach. In a bull market such as we've had, it's very difficult to make money using a shortselling strategy. But in a bear market, this indicator will signal you to sell short and you can really rack up the gains, outperforming a buy and hold approach. Chart NDR 7 is comprised of the same four indicators in chart NDR 6 but this time we divided it into what we call modes or stratums. The bullish mode means that the model is at least net positive by two indicators. When the indicators are mixed, we are in a neutral mode and when the model is net negative by at least two indicators, then we are in a bearish mode. Notice that most of the time the indicators are mixed but during the periods of time when at least two are net positive, the S&P 500 rises at an annual rate of about 34.4%—an incredible return. In the neutral mode, the S&P 500 gains about 8.1% which is fairly close to the 7.9% return based on a buy and hold approach. When the indicator shifts to a bearish mode, the market drops at a 15.4% annual rate. This is the type of risk analysis that we can do with our models. By looking at the different modes, you can gauge if the market is bullish and low risk or bearish and high risk.

What alternative is there for investors who don't want to sell short?

For our clients who don't want to sell short or take a lot of risk, we have put together an asset allocation model. An example of this is on chart NDR 8. The only thing that we are allocating is how much money we want to put in the stock market. When all four of the indicators are bullish, we put a higher percentage of money in the stock market because the returns in that mode are so great. If only two are net positive, we still stay in a buy mode but we reduce our risk to the point that we are only 75% invested in stocks. When the net result is at zero, we are going to be 50% invested in stocks. When all four indicators are negative, we are out of stocks entirely and safely tucked away in risk-free money market funds.

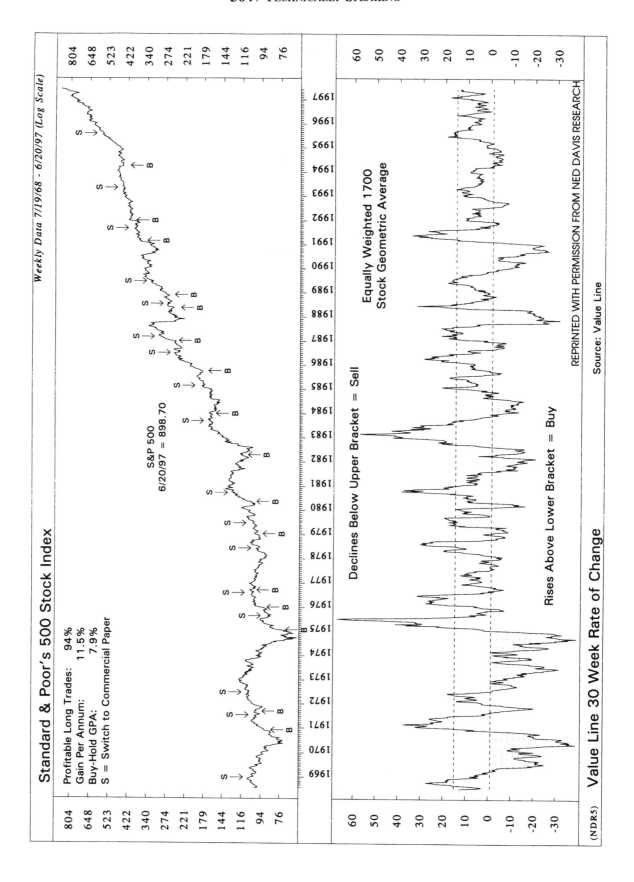

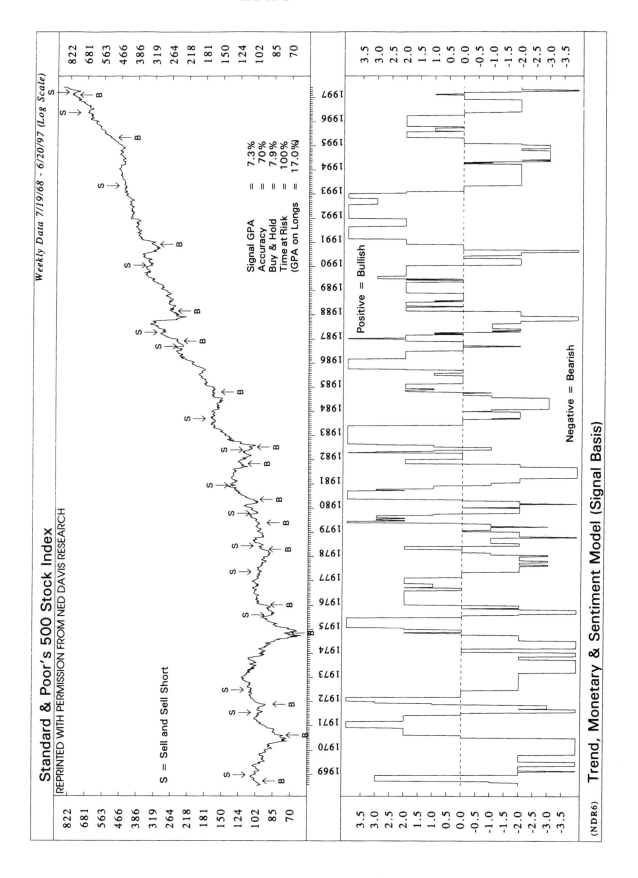

Standard & Poor's 500 Stock Index

Weekly Data 7/19/68 - 6/20/97 (Log Scale)

REPRINTED WITH PERMISSION FROM NED DAVIS RESEARCH

S = Sell and Sell Short

Signal GPA	=	7.3%
Accuracy	=	70%
Buy & Hold	=	7.9%
Time at Risk	=	100%
(GPA on Longs	=	17.0%

Positive = Bullish

Negative = Bearish

(NDR6) **Trend, Monetary & Sentiment Model (Signal Basis)**

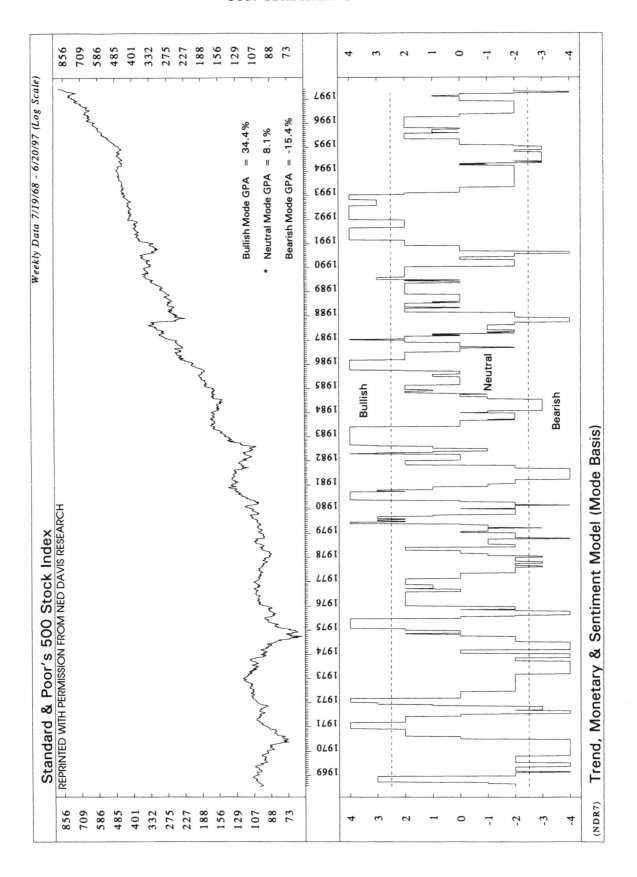

Standard & Poor's 500 Stock Index

REPRINTED WITH PERMISSION FROM NED DAVIS RESEARCH

Weekly Data 7/19/68 - 6/20/97 (Log Scale)

Bullish Mode GPA = 34.4%

* Neutral Mode GPA = 8.1%

Bearish Mode GPA = -15.4%

Bullish

Neutral

Bearish

(NDR7) Trend, Monetary & Sentiment Model (Mode Basis)

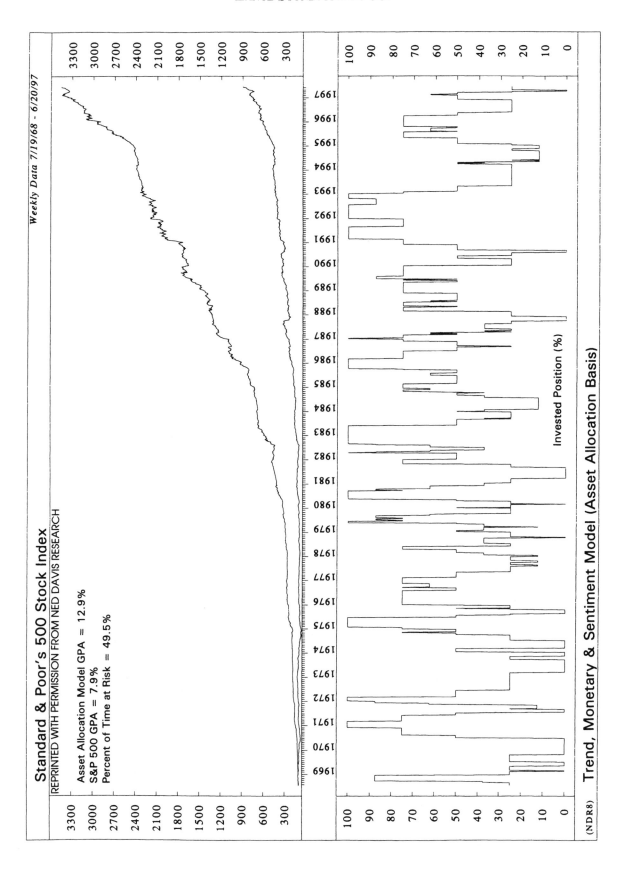

Standard & Poor's 500 Stock Index

REPRINTED WITH PERMISSION FROM NED DAVIS RESEARCH

Weekly Data 7/19/68 - 6/20/97

Asset Allocation Model GPA = 12.9%

S&P 500 GPA = 7.9%

Percent of Time at Risk = 49.5%

Invested Position (%)

(NDR8)   Trend, Monetary & Sentiment Model (Asset Allocation Basis)

So you incrementally scale into investment positions as the market strengthens and out of positions as the market deteriorates?

Yes and when we are 75% invested in stocks, the balance, 25%, goes into commercial paper. When we are 50% in stocks, we are 50% in commercial paper. When 25% of our investment capital is in stocks, 75% of our money is in commercial paper. Starting with an adjusted rate of 100 in 1968, the S&P 500 has risen to almost 900 since that time. However, the top line of chart NDR 8 shows what you would have done by following the asset allocation model—$100.00 invested in 1968 would now be worth over $3,400.00. That gives you a 12.9% yearly gain versus 7.9% on a buy and hold basis. You are able to beat a buy and hold strategy by almost 2:1 without the risk of a buy and hold because half of the time your money is safely tucked away in relatively risk-free commercial paper. So, the three philosophies behind our work are: "Don't fight the Federal Reserve Board," "Be aware of crowds at extremes," and "Don't fight the tape."

In your indicator arsenal at Ned Davis Research, you have several monetary, economic, and valuation indicators which have well defined buy and sell parameters and are easy to calculate. One such indicator is the rate of change in the Fed funds rate.

Monetary indicators are some of the most powerful tools in our arsenal and with the exception of the deflationary cycle of the 1930's, they have tested out extremely well historically. In the 1930's, even though interest rates went down, monetary indicators failed to work during that cycle. The rate of change in the Fed funds interest rate uses raw monthly data and you just calculate the percentage change in the Fed funds rate versus the rate 16 months ago. The upper bracket is at 26% and the lower bracket is at -7%. The interpretation of this indicator is a little different. When the Fed funds rate falls from a high level crossing through +26%, that generates a buy signal and when the Fed funds momentum is at a low level and starts rising above -7%, that is going to give a sell signal.

In terms of a rate of change, sixteen months is a rather long period of time. Should the signals from this indicator be viewed as the beginning of a longterm trend?

Certainly the frequency of the signals tend to be years in duration. Everyone has their own definition of short, intermediate and longterm but I would classify this as a longer term monetary indicator.

As far as shortterm interest rates go, the ratio of the 90 day Treasury bill to the discount rate appears to be a good leading indicator for calling turns in the S&P 500.

Yes. For this indicator, we simply divide the yield of the 90 day Treasury bill by the discount rate. The parameters are at 96.58 and 109.03. When this indicator rises above 109.03, it generates a sell signal because the 90 day T-bill yields are too high relative to the discount rate, perhaps implying that banks are selling their Treasury bills in order to increase liquidity. When the indicator drops below 96.58, it generates a buy signal.

Shortterm Treasury bill yields are expressed in two ways, the average discount yield or the yield to maturity. Which one is used in this calculation?

We use the yield to maturity.

Isn't the ratio of the Fed funds rate to the discount rate an equally valuable monetary indicator?

Yes and historically, when the Fed funds rate is 113% of the discount rate, we become bearish. If it is 105% of the discount rate, we are bullish. According to our testing, when the indicator has been at 105% or below, the Value Line Composite has gained at an annual rate of 34.1%. At a level above 113%, the Value Line has declined at a 3.4% annual rate. That's a big difference and once again it attests to the power of monetary indicators.

Doesn't the S&P 500 stock earnings yield minus the 90 day Treasury bill yield have a good track record for detecting major trend reversals?

Yes, this indicator has tested well historically. You have two elements working for you here— valuation and interest rates and you are weighing the evidence between the two. It is a bullish indication when this indicator rises above 1.4 and a bearish sign when it declines below -0.5.

Are there other indicators which look at valuation levels in relation to interest rates?

The ratio of longterm Treasury bond yields versus the earnings yield for the S&P 500. Using the S&P longterm government bond index as our longterm Treasury bond yield, we calculate the ratio and then we go one extra step and take a 26 week rate of change. The lower parameter is at -8.9% and the upper parameter is at 8.7%. Historically, longterm government bonds have declined at a 8.7% annual rate whenever the 26 week rate of change in the bond yield to stock earnings yield ratio is above 8.7%. When the 26 week rate of change has dropped below -8.9%, longterm government bonds have gained at an annual rate of 7.4%.

An economic indicator with a knack for pinpointing market tops and bottoms is consumer confidence.

Economic indicators don't always analyze well because of the lag time involved in reporting the data and because of revisions in the data, but this indicator is a good one as far as economic indicators go. Consumer confidence is a measure of consumer expectations, which are important because consumer spending is somewhere around 2/3 of all economic activity. The Conference Board surveys several thousand households each month asking questions based on general business conditions and the job outlook. About 40% of the survey involves questions relating to current conditions while 60% is weighted with future expectations—do consumers feel that the economy will be better or worse six months from now? The results of the survey are compiled and then released monthly by the Conference Board as "consumer confidence." For our purposes, we take a 5 month smoothing of consumer confidence. To test this indica-

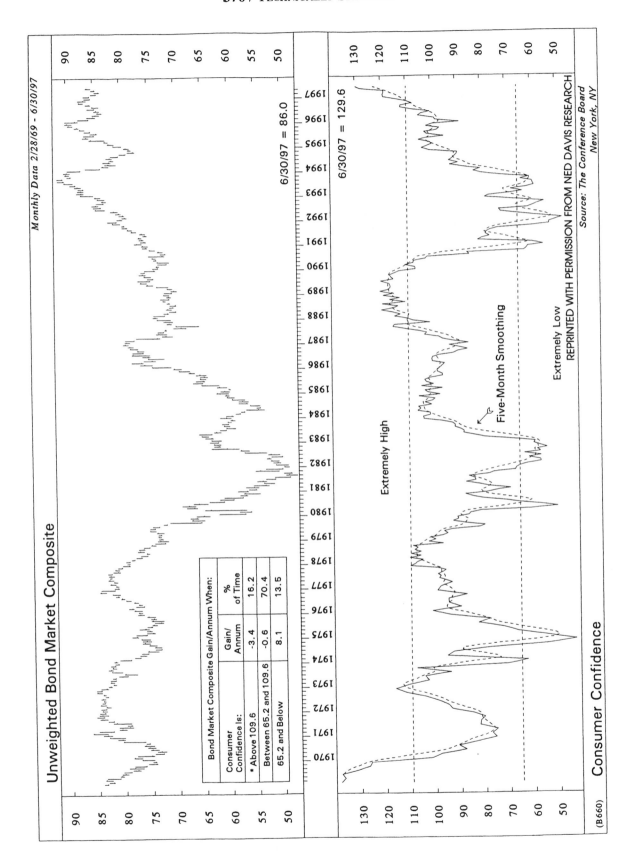

Unweighted Bond Market Composite

Monthly Data 2/28/69 - 6/30/97

Bond Market Composite Gain/Annum When:		
Consumer Confidence Is:	Gain/Annum	% of Time
* Above 109.6	-3.4	16.2
Between 65.2 and 109.6	-0.6	70.4
65.2 and Below	8.1	13.5

6/30/97 = 86.0

6/30/97 = 129.6

Extremely High

Five-Month Smoothing

Extremely Low

REPRINTED WITH PERMISSION FROM NED DAVIS RESEARCH

Source: The Conference Board
New York, NY

Consumer Confidence

(B660)

tor, we developed a measure called the "unweighted bond market composite." We found that at a level above 109.6, bond prices have declined at a 3.4% annual rate. At a level below 65.2, bond prices gain at an 8.1% annual rate.

To smooth the indicator, are you taking an average of the raw numbers for five consecutive months?

Yes, just a simple moving average or moving mean.

Since the bond market is used as a benchmark to test the indicator's performance, does this mean that consumer confidence impacts the bond market more than the stock market?

Not necessarily. We test a lot of our economic indicators with the bond market because there is often a strong correlation between economic activity and interest rates. There are definitely correlations and trends with the stock market also, but we just haven't gotten around to testing all of the economic indicators relative to the stock market. Recently, we have been focusing more on applying the economic data to specific industry groups rather than the broad market. For example, we might look at consumer confidence versus a retail stock group.

Inflation usually has a negative impact on the stock market. Is it helpful to track the year to year change in the CRB index?

Yes, because this indicator tells you when the market is in a low-risk mode and a high-risk mode. The calculation is simply a year to year rate of change in the weekly CRB cash price in the form of a ratio. In other words, we take Friday's close for the CRB cash price and divide it by the CRB cash price 52 weeks earlier. Then we smooth the ratio by taking a three week average. The parameters are 96 and 108.2. Inflation is considered low below a level of 96 and high when it's above 108.2. When this indicator has risen above 108.2, the Dow Jones Industrials have declined at a 4.7% annual rate. When the three week moving average of the ratio has been below 96, the Dow has gained 19.7% on an annual basis.

Dan Sullivan

Dan Sullivan began investing in the stock market in the eighth grade, purchasing shares in Gotham Hosiery at $10.00 per share. His rationale for selecting this particular stock was twofold. It was cheap, and it had experienced the most drastic decline in the past year compared to other listed stocks. In the end, this strategy proved unsuccessful. Though burned by this first experience, determination propelled him to search for new answers. Several years later after his initial venture in the market, he read two books that completely reversed his original investment philosophy of buying at the lows—*Battle for Investment Survival* by Gerald Loeb and *How I Made Two Million in the Stock Market* by Nicholas Darvas. Both authors advocated buying stocks that were already moving up rather than buying stocks at their absolute lows and then waiting for them to move. In other words, buy high and sell higher. Adopting this new methodology drastically improved his investing habits, and despite the changes in the market since his revelation 25 years earlier, it still remains his modus operandi.

A prolific reader, few investment books have missed his scrutiny. In his spare time, he frequented used book stores scouting for investment books of every description, both current and out-of-print. Buying their entire inventory was not an unusual move. Interestingly, he observed that during bear markets, used book stores would be brimming over with discarded investment books whereas during bull markets, the shelves would be virtually empty. This intensive search for knowledge has left him with an impressive book collection.

With a few years of market experience under his belt, Mr. Sullivan felt prepared to share his views and recommendations with others, and seriously contemplated starting a stock market newsletter. Possessing the knowledge but uncertain of his writing skills, he practiced writing a few newsletters comparing his to the ones brokerage firms distributed to clients. The content and lingo were similar. So in 1969, he left his responsibilities as proprietor of a liquor store and focused on publishing a stock market newsletter, *The Chartist*. Based on the ratings by Hulbert Financial Digest, *The Chartist* has gained a compounded annual return of 16% over the last fifteen years. In 1988, he began a second monthly newsletter targeting mutual fund investors called *The Chartist Mutual Fund Timer*.

Mr. Sullivan then turned his attention to money management. However, before risking other people's money, he successfully managed his own and his mother's. This family account became the basis for the "actual cash account" found in each issue of *The Chartist*. Designed to serve as a personal track record, the "actual cash account" replicates with real money each buy or sell recommendation the newsletter issues to subscribers. In short, he "puts his money where his mouth is"—a bold stance that signals confidence in his investment style and a trait which separates him from many of his contemporaries. Although quick to acknowledge the difficulties an investment advisor faces when his own money is on the line, he believes that the advantages outweigh the disadvantages, especially for the client. There is the issue of accountability. Your record is exposed. If you are wrong, you can't gloss over it. You experience the same profits or losses as your clients.

With regard to portfolio management, Mr. Sullivan's primary objective is to choose stocks exhibiting the highest relative strength. In most instances, these would be aggressive growth stocks but there are some periods where "blue chips" best meet his criteria. Two critical elements of his investment style are taking losses quickly and letting profits run.

Though his trend and momentum models are proprietary, Mr. Sullivan does share a couple of momentum indicators which he invented that have a near flawless track record. In the past, one of his inventions, the 90% Plus Momentum Thrust Ratio, was klept by another technician. To prove ownership, he offered a reward in *The Chartist* to anyone who could produce a back issue which contained the original introduction of this indicator. An alert subscriber soon produced the needed evidence.

What sparked your interest in technical analysis?

It's the price action of the market itself. I would see stocks moving ahead of the fundamentals. A positive or negative write-up on a stock doesn't necessarily mean it's going to move in that direction. I remember one of my best stocks was Resorts International. *Barron's* ran three articles in a row saying how bad that stock was and that there were criminal elements involved. Of course, everybody sold it short and then it took off.

Did you own it before the negative publicity or did you buy it after?

I had bought it just before the publicity came out but I held it. I worried about the stock after the third article. There were three featured articles in a row but actually that is what brought in all the short sellers. I don't have the exact numbers but in six months it was up like 500%. It just really moved.

From an analytical standpoint, do you start by determining the overall trend?

Yes, I am always looking at the different stock charts but first I am trying to figure out which way the market is going. The direction of the market is the primary goal and then I go to the stocks. The stocks I am looking at are the stocks which are leading; that is, high relative strength stocks that are out in front of the market.

Do you pay much attention to groups at all?

No. I use relative strength and it seems that the leaders will be in a similar industry but I don't zero in on a particular group.

Your strategy is to pick stocks with the strongest relative strength. Will you ever short stocks displaying the weakest relative strength?

I have developed a short selling methodology, but it is not for individual stocks. It's for using the Rydex URSA fund that can go short the S&P 500. The fund moves in the opposite direction of the S&P, so if the S&P goes down, the Rydex URSA will go up a comparable amount. I haven't used it yet in actual practice and the profits from it weren't overwhelming. The signals averaged 6% profit per trade but there weren't that many trades. I went back to 1964 and I think there were only eight trades. I don't think a lot of money is made on the short side but I think it will be a useful tool. The only thing that could be dangerous about it is that they use derivatives.

With only eight signals in 32 years, there is certainly no danger of getting whipsawed. You group your indicators in a model, right?

Yes. Right now, I have three models—monetary, trend, and momentum. When two out of the three models are positive, you have a buy signal. As far as selling, it is a little different in that you can be taken out with momentum or trend but not with the monetary model. I have just found that the market doesn't necessarily fall apart once the monetary model turns negative. In fact, sometimes it keeps going up. So, I use trend to get us out or if the momentum model turns negative I will get out. There have been times where the monetary model will turn negative and the market will collapse soon after, but I just prefer to wait for the trend to take us out.

Is it possible to start with the monetary model and discuss a few of the indicators in this model?

Well, it is proprietary but it is the trend of interest rates that we are following. It is a combination of longterm and shortterm rates.

How about the trend and momentum models?

Both of those are proprietary also but the trend is just the trend of the market. On the momentum model, I can tell you one of my indicators that I use that worked really well for a number of years and that is the 10 day moving average of advancing stocks versus declining stocks on the NYSE. Ned Davis uses a version of this. When the moving average of the ratio goes above 2.00 to 1.00, it is an excellent time to buy. Three months after a 2:1 reading, the market advanced an average of 10.38% and six months later it was 17.93% ahead. There have been many instances where this has worked and worked really well. One reason that I missed the 1995 rally in the market is because this particular indicator never did kick in. It worked in 1990. I remember back on August 26th, 1982, it was a record 2.64. In 1982, a lot of people just didn't really believe it because the market had been going down for so long. It worked great at that time but now everybody is pretty aware of these thrust indicators so I don't know how well it's going to work next time. I invented this 2:1 momentum thrust ratio but now everybody has copied it and changed it.

Your momentum thrust ratio allows you to spot the resumption or beginning of bull markets?

Yes, but previously people always used it as an overbought/oversold indicator and they would say, "Oh, the indicator is over 2.00. The market is overbought." But it is just the opposite. Usually it's the beginning of a new bull market. This indicator hasn't worked in years. It hasn't failed, but it just hasn't given a buy signal.

How do you calculate the A/D momentum thrust ratio?

It is a 10 day moving average of advances versus a 10 day moving average of declines. You add up all the advances for the last ten days and you have the total. Then you add up the declines. To get the ratio, you divide the advances by the declines. When you get a ratio of over 2:1, it's a roaring buy.

Is there any way a bear market rally could generate a 2:1 reading on the A/D ratio?

It could but it never has in the past. It's amazing. All throughout 1973 and 1974, there were some really good rallies but not one plus 2.00 reading. Not one the whole time. It didn't produce a positive 2.00 reading until 1975. In 1991, we had the 90% rule and the momentum ratio both kick in and that was a really powerful market. I was up 71% that year.

What is the 90% rule?

It is more of a shortterm momentum indicator. When 90% of the stocks on the NYSE move above their 10 week moving averages, that is a buy signal. It has never failed. When 90% of stocks rise above their 10 week moving average line, it indicates that the market has generated enough thrust to continue rising for many more months. It is hard to buy because on every occasion, the market appeared heavily overbought and vulnerable. All the stocks are participating in the rally but the market has always gone higher over the next 3, 6, 9, and 12 months. It has a perfect track record. There have been only 8 readings since 1970. Between the initial signal and the 4th week, the market has been higher eight out of eight times. Ian McAvity used to chart this in his newsletter going back years and years. I spotted that whenever the line got above 90%, it was a good time to buy. As always, there are caveats. The ill-fated 1973 bear market rally witnessed a reading in excess of 89% in the number of stocks above their 10 week moving averages. It was only by a hair's breadth that the 90% plus reading failed to give a buy signal during that period. If a 90% plus reading had been generated at that time, it would have been a monumental failure for this indicator because during the next 12 months, the Dow proceeded to give up some 400 points.

Zero whipsaws.

It has never failed. It hasn't given a buy signal in years but when it does, it has a good record. The last one was on February 15, 1991. Past bull markets that were accompanied by such excessive momentum have not ended until many months have passed. In all instances, the market has been higher 4, 12, 26, and 52 weeks after the initial 90% reading. When all of the periods are combined, the S&P was higher 29 out of 30 times. The only time it was lower was back in 1980, when it lost 5.65% between the 26th and 52nd week. Putting it another way, the market has been higher 96.6% of the time.

I have seen CNBC occasionally flash on the screen the number of stocks above their 10 week and 30 week moving averages. Is there another source that you know of?

This is available from *Investor's Intelligence*.

At one time, you gave recognition to the 80/60 rule. What is it and how is it used?

That is one indicator that I follow. I was on Wall Street Week and talked about that and I have written a lot on it. It tells you when to sell but like a lot of indicators, they work well and then they don't. It seemed to work really well up until the last five years but it hasn't worked in a while. The 80/60 rule looks at stocks above their 30 week moving average. *The Chartist* 80/60 rule dictates that whenever the number of stocks on the NYSE above their own 30 week moving averages reaches 80% and then proceeds to drop to 60% or lower, it is a warning flag. On eleven of the twelve times that this has happened, the 30 week series did not reach 80% again until it had dropped below 30%. So even if it tries to turn back up again after it drops below 60%, the series usually moves below 30% before it turns back up. It hits 30% before it will hit 80% again. But this in itself might not mean anything because individual stocks can still go up. In July 1996, I think it did go under 30% but then the market didn't fall apart all that much.

Is it fair to say that once the indicator rises above 80% that the market is very overbought?

Not necessarily. The theory was that when it dropped that much, the back of the bull market was broken. There was something wrong. You had fewer and fewer stocks that were bucking the trend on a fairly longterm basis—a 30 week moving average. Although you might have a rally, you wouldn't go to new highs. We do not use it as a sell signal because it is often early and on one occasion, it didn't work at all.

Is there a strategy that can be implemented when the figure reaches 30%?

It's not necessarily a buy signal. This is certainly not a precise timing indicator. When it flashes a warning, we do not necessarily head for the exit and sell all our stocks nor do we take the signal lightly. Over the years we have found that its greatest strength has been to keep us from doing any further buying. Whenever a caution signal is generated by the 80/60 rule, we stop buying. Even after a caution signal, a bull market can take several weeks to unwind. Sometimes it is early by several months and sometimes it's late. Don't be impatient. Its redeeming quality is that it keeps you from getting sucked in at the top.

You wouldn't recommend that the indicator be used as a buy signal when it dips below 30% and starts heading back up?

Well, it could but I have never used it for that because sometimes it will go up and then go back down again. I guess some people consider 30% oversold but I have seen it go down to 5% when a market is really getting hit. Like 1987, if you look at a chart I'm sure it went right down to the bottom of a chart.

You can get the percent of stocks above their 30 week moving average from *Investor's Business Daily* and *Investor's Intelligence*?

Yes, I know *Investor's Intelligence* has the 30 week series.

Do you use MACD?

I don't use it but it is a good trend following methodology and it works.

Other than your momentum thrust ratio, do you do anything unusual with breadth?

I watch the daily A/D line. It is really important that it confirm the rest of the averages. When the averages break out, the A/D line should not necessarily be making a new high but the overall market should be participating.

Relative strength is an integral part of your analysis, right?

Relative strength is really important.

Are you looking at the relative strength line that appears on stock charts?

I have a certain methodology. I have relative strength ratings I use which are proprietary.

Can the relative strength ratings in *Investor's Business Daily* be used?

The ones I use are a lot like the ones in *Investor's Business Daily*. Those are really good relative strength ratings and can be used.

Do you use any fundamentals at all in your work?

Although they are very important, I'm a technician and a chartist so I don't look at the fundamentals. Personal prejudices creep into the picture when you know a lot of fundamental details on a company. Fundamental reasons behind a stock being overvalued or undervalued manifest themselves in the price of the stock. The fundamentals can be great and the stock can be going down.

Do you follow sentiment?

I look at sentiment and talk about sentiment a lot but I have never used it for making a decision. It seems that the market always goes contrary to what everybody expects but then there are periods where people can be right for a long time in both directions.

What are you thoughts on volume?

For my stock selection, I look at volume because I want the stock to be actively traded.

Do you want to see volume increasing as stocks are moving higher?

It helps but it is not going to deter me from buying a stock if it isn't. Every bull market seems to live on a dramatic increase in volume. Each cycle has more volume. That was the case in 1982.

What is most unique to you with regard to your investment style?

I can go from 0% to 100% invested overnight. I also can go from 100% invested to being completely out of the market. This shakes people up. I might wait a long time before doing anything then go in, find out I'm wrong, and then get out. I think I can nip my mistakes really quickly. I know when I am wrong, especially on the downside. I get out really fast. One of my cardinal rules is that when the market or a stock is going against you, you have to cut your losses really quickly. Another thing that would be different is that once I am in the profit column, I will gamble with paper profits which means there are going to be times when I am going to overstay a stock and give up a good portion of the profits. I only have two core stocks now that have been held for a long time, those are Microsoft and United Healthcare. They both have their ups and downs but United Healthcare is still down selling at 41 today and it was as high as 69 not too long ago. So I have given up a lot of profit sticking around on that one. But then Microsoft is up and has made a new high. I do overstay but I think you should risk your paper profits.

I am sure you are overstaying for a reason; that is, the technical picture still looks positive.

When I first start out buying, I act like a trader, then once I have established good paper profits then I become more longterm oriented on those individual stocks. So when I first start out, I want to cut losses quickly if I am wrong. Sometimes I will cut losses and then the market will turn right around. You have to be willing to get back in again. In 1990, I was shaken out right at the beginning of the bull market. We were in before the Gulf War and the market was going up. Then it sold off in January, and I was shaken out. A week later, we were back in. This isn't the norm but you have to be willing to do it. Usually, I don't really do that much buying and selling. I am not trying to scalp a few points. I am looking for the big 100% or 300% move but at the start I am acting as a trader in that I am going to cut losses quickly if I am wrong.

Your initial intent is not to force a trade?

I am hoping that everything is going to work out great and my stocks are just going to keep going up forever.

What signal do you need to get you out of a stock?

A break in the moving average line or breaking below a support area. The 200 day moving average is one of my favorites.

If you are trying to ride a stock for the long term looking for the big moves, are you basing your buy and hold decisions using a ten year chart?

I don't have any set time frames. Like the two stocks I mentioned, I have held those since 1991. The idea is to hold them as long as possible. Some stocks will live through two or more cycles but there are not too many like that. If you are fortunate enough to get a couple of good ones, they can make up for a lot of losers.

I don't know how long you have actually held Microsoft but let's just say, theoretically, you have held it for five years. What has to happen to convince you to throw in the towel and sell your entire position?

As long as the longterm chart pattern is favorable I will stay with it.

What type of chart constitutes longterm?

It would be a pattern measured in months.

Over a period of five years, a stock can have several different levels of old support. Which level are you going to look at?

I am just much more liberal on those types of stocks than I would be on something I just bought in this cycle. In fact, as we go along, we could even scale back some more.

Just to make this crystal clear, would you go over your basic investment strategy again?

I go in 100% at the outset of the cycle. I try to get in the profit column and then I will take some profits on the way up. When in my opinion the market is ready for a correction, I will cut back to 50% invested but I will risk my paper profits on the remaining portion.

So you scale back as you are going up so that you are not risking 100% of your profits at the top.

Exactly.

Don't you expose your personal capital to your own recommendations?

Yes.

I think that is very unique. I don't know of too many other analysts who put their money where their mouth is.

That's right, I forgot to mention that. I risk my own money. A lot of people say you can't be objective, but I think it makes you very objective because you are really watching things closely. You are not asking your subscribers to do anything you are not willing to do yourself.

Do you follow any mutual fund indicators, like the cash levels or the inflows?

We have a mutual fund letter and the cash levels are important and part of my decision making process. I think it is worrisome now that the cash level is down so low. When the bull market began it was around 13%. Now it's like 7% so you know its late in the bull market. It is just taking more and more money to keep this market going. I think it is going up because people are buying mutual funds and mutual funds are buying stocks regardless of valuations. A lot of people are going to be in for a real shock when they find out that a stock can go down. Everybody is conditioned to buy on dips. It looks like a money machine to people. It's going to unravel. There is no question about it and it's going to be brutal.

Were you involved with the market in 1968 during the last mutual fund mania?

No, but I have read a lot about it. I started my newsletter in 1969. Actually, I came in at a good time because it was when stocks were going down. They went down for about six years until late 1974. Although the Dow made new highs, the Value Line Composite didn't make a new high. The two periods are very similar except in this one there is just so much more money involved. There are so many mutual funds being created on a daily basis.

What is one of your favorite stock patterns?

I like a stock that consolidates and retraces maybe 1/3 of the ground that it gained on the previous up cycle. If it can do that fairly quickly, say within 8 weeks, and then breakout to new highs, it is a very strong pattern. I will look for that.

So you like to buy breakouts from bases that occur after a stock has already begun moving higher?

Yes.

Is all of your work done on bar charts?

Yes. I don't use candlesticks or point and figure.

Do you look at bonds in relation to stocks?

Yes. I think the bond market is extremely important in relationship to the stock market. It is a good sign when the bond market is acting well. I like to see my bond model on a buy signal. Lots of times bonds will turn favorable ahead of the market.

Let's say you were going to choose a stock. What would be the primary technical things to look for?

I want an actively traded stock, one that is breaking out of a base and hasn't run up too much. You want the stocks that are along the lines of what Gerald Loeb wrote about in ***Battle for Investment Survival***. He liked to go with the stocks that were actively traded and leading the parade.

What do you mean by actively traded? Are you speaking of the number of shares outstanding?

It is the volume and the number of shares outstanding. I try to stay away from thinly traded stocks.

What are some important psychological rules which you follow?

I am really a stickler for cutting losses quickly. I practice this. With the money I have managed, no one has ever lost any serious money because I get out. You have to go with the flow. You have to be willing to admit when you are wrong and change your position.

Let's say you get into the market and then you are taken out. Will you wait a while to make sure you don't get taken out a second time?

I am following my models. They get me out and then I will get back in again if they go positive.

Strictly adhering to your models takes the emotional aspect out of the market.

You just have to have a game plan. It's not that I don't change things—I do. Over the years you do evolve but you have to know what you are going to do ahead of time. You take your positions and then you decide that you are going to do such and such if this happens. You have a game plan mapped out and you really have to follow it. I have different trading rules that I follow.

What are they?

They mainly revolve around the models which are proprietary but there are a couple that I did share—the momentum thrust indicator and when you have 90% of the stocks above their 10 week moving average line. You want to try and concentrate on the stocks that are going up and not try to guess the bottom. A lot of amateurs like to buy low and sell high but I like to buy high and sell higher.

If I understand you correctly, you are not a bottom picker. You are not going to buy a stock until after a trend has been established.

I am not a bottom picker. Hopefully I will come in, off the bottom, when the trend is established.

Will you enter a position after seeing a particular technical pattern, such as a double bottom, or will you wait for a percentage move up off the lows?

The stocks that I am concentrating on are already up. They are even up during a bear market because they are resisting the trend. They are in their own private bull market. So as soon as I am convinced that the market has turned and we are going up, then I will concentrate on the leaders which invariably will look overpriced—they always do. They look like they have gotten ahead of themselves.

But you buy them anyway instead of waiting for a pullback?

If the market from that point on turns back down then they have indeed gotten ahead of themselves and they are going to get hit. That is why you have to get out quickly with high relative strength stocks.

It sounds like relative strength is your pet indicator.

It is.

Jim Tillman

Jim Tillman entered Clemson University with the idea of obtaining a degree in electrical engineering when a class project in Economics 101 altered his ambitions. The project, which involved creating a hypothetical stock portfolio, triggered an immediate interest in the financial markets and more specifically, in technical analysis, because in order to efficiently select the strongest, healthiest stocks, he had relied on what was most familiar to him as an engineering student- charts. Anxious to become involved with the financial markets, he halted his engineering studies, opting to pursue a career as a stock broker instead. Unfortunately, legal age restrictions detained him from fulfilling his goal before age twenty-one.

By 1961, technical analysis had only a limited following and the subject was still regarded as somewhat taboo in most investment circles; however, a devotee of technical analysis, Mr. Tillman found an open-minded and flexible brokerage firm who accepted his preference for this form of analysis and allowed him to use it as a basis for investment advice. After becoming a branch manager and having his firm bought out during the brokerage consolidations of the late Sixties and early Seventies, he settled with Interstate Securities in Charlotte, North Carolina, as an institutional broker in 1971. In that same year, he began writing a weekly market newsletter for institutional clients called *Cycletrend*. Now published every three weeks, *Cycletrend* focuses on market timing and is available to individuals as well as institutions.

The foundation of Mr. Tillman's analysis is built upon an integration of three complimentary methodologies: cycle analysis, Elliott wave analysis, and centered moving averages. Centered moving averages are valuable in that they can be used to project the completion of an uptrend or downtrend, often in terms of both time and price. Like many other technicians, Mr. Tillman respects the fundamentals and recognizes that a primary trend is established and remains in force based upon the fundamental outlook for a stock. But when technical analysis and fundamental analysis send conflicting messages, the technicals always take precedence. In cases where stocks reach extremes in valuations, technical analysis becomes indispensable.

According to Timer Digest, Mr. Tillman's forecasts for stocks, bonds, and gold since 1990 have consistently earned him a position in the top ten rankings. A quick rundown of his more prominent forecasts reveals why. In October 1974, investors faced a stock market that had been plunging since July of that year, with secondaries losing as much as 80% from their 1968 highs. Two events occurred that October convincing him that the market was on the verge of changing direction—the dominant four year cycle turned up and price objectives from centered moving averages reached their downside objectives. The next issue of *Cycletrend* announced, "The Bear is Gone," precisely catching the start of a long awaited bull market. Then in 1977, as a result of following the 60 year Kondratieff wave, he began heralding the commencement of a bull market of major proportions slated to begin between 1981 and 1983. In contrast to the trading environment of the Seventies, he emphasized that the best strategy for the Eighties would be a buy and hold approach. Soon after the crash of 1987, Mr. Tillman was interviewed on FNN and stated that over the next three to four months, the market would turn up. After the magnitude and severity of the market's collapse on October 19th, it was difficult to be bullish, but his cycle work indicated new highs extending into 1989 or 1990. The host, Bill Griffeth, pointed out the comparisons with 1929 but, relying on the convincing evidence before him, he stood firm and reiterated that his cycle work projected new stock market highs in the coming months. By June 1990, the Dow stood at 3,000.

Appearing on the Ira Epstein show, he projected a hard market decline to 2100 or 2200 by the year's end. As predicted, the market dropped until October 10, 1990, bottoming at 2353. On the eve of the U.S. invasion of Kuwait, January 16, 1991, he appeared on CNBC, outlining a bullish scenario. The market exploded upward the following day barely looking back for the next six years.

One of the first chartered market technicians (CMT), Mr. Tillman remains an active participant of the Market Technician's Association lecturing at their seminars and contributing to their quarterly journal. Today, Mr. Tillman works independently as a consultant for institutional clients and as editor of *Cycletrend*.

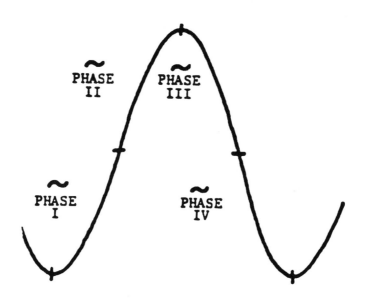

PHASE II

PHASE III

PHASE I

PHASE IV

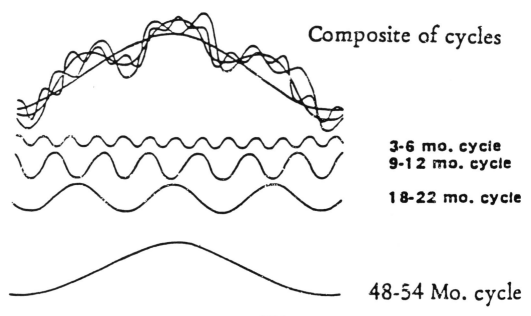

Composite of cycles

3-6 mo. cycle
9-12 mo. cycle

18-22 mo. cycle

48-54 Mo. cycle

How are cycles different from more traditional forms of technical analysis?

Cycles are a form of pattern recognition that I think is very helpful for people to understand how all chart patterns can be traced to the combination of cycles. The classic example is the large, perfect head and shoulders formation of the DJIA for each four year cycle from 1966 to 1974. The left shoulder is the first 18 month cycle high, the head was the second 18 month cycle and also the four year cycle peak, and the right shoulder was the third 18 month cycle high with the four year cycle going down hard. I think everything gets its foundation from the combination of the cycles and that is why I like them so well.

Your cycle analysis includes surveillance of 10 week cycles, 20 week cycles, 40 week cycles, 80 week cycles, 4 year cycles continuing up to the 60 year Kondratieff cycle. In terms of a starting point, what are your suggestions for investors beginning cycle analysis for the first time?

When I am looking at a chart, the first thing to do is find the last major low that is visible on a chart. If you are looking at a very longterm chart, the best thing to do is to find one point that could be classified as a four year cycle bottom, the largest cycle that tends to operate in the stock market. Because it can vary, find a low that is approximately three to four years from the previous low.

All starting points for cyclical analysis should begin at minimum with a four year cycle?

I believe so. If you are concentrating on where you are in a major trend, if you are two years away from a major low, then you should start thinking about a larger cycle high occurring which will change your investment method. Once you have had a major cycle low, you have wiped the slate clean. That is the reason you try to find a wash-out low. If you can find a four year cycle bottom or a major low which you think has occurred, then you can start observing the pullbacks that occur at 10 weeks, 20 weeks, and 40 weeks later. In other words, you can wait for your sequence of cycle lows to occur following a major four year cycle bottom. If you are a shortterm trader, use the 10 week cycle pullbacks to buy. If an intermediate investor, use the deeper 20 and 40 week cycle lows that occur two or three times each year to buy. That assumes that the four year cycle is up.

When did the last major cycle low occur prior to 1996?

From a four year cycle perspective, it was 1994 and then 1990.

In one of your market newsletters, you mentioned that 1889 was your "model" year. Is this still relevant?

Various markets from the past have served as models at different times. In the early 1970's, for example, I chose a period from 1908 to 1915-1916 as a model that the stock market cycles would go by. Sure enough, it was an exact profile. The market did repeat the pattern of that time period from about the early 1970's into the 1978-1979 period. That is where I got the idea that the market would change from its traditional four year cycle spike low and double bottom in the 1978-1979 period because that is what happened back in the 1910-1915 period, being just prior to and leading up to the 1920's bull market. Later, there was another time period that caught my eye and that was 1887 to 1890, which was almost an exact model for 1987 to 1990. It served its purpose as an excellent road map for a good three years. Because it looked like we were on a 100 year repeating cycle, it made me become prematurely cautious in 1993. Of course, we didn't collapse in 1993 as we did in 1893. Different time periods from the past will set up the market exactly like the cycles were then but you have to be careful about following them 100%. Be aware that they can change. There are good patterns and models that you can simply pick out in the past where cycles were similar and they will work for a while but then they will dissipate at some point. We then have to go back to our current cycle analysis.

Once you enter a particular decade, is there a series of weeks or months that a cycle will follow consistently or is it random?

From the perspective of cycles, you should always be conscious of where you started from a major low that could have been a once in a generation kind of low. All through the 1800's and early 1900's, the clearest cycle is 17 to 18 years, but you never look at one cycle by itself. You would ask, "Where is the force coming from? What is the current trend?" In the 1950's, you had such a strong uptrend that your pullbacks occurred every 52 to 53 months. During that particular time, the market had small four year cycle corrections because the 17 year trend was so strong. The market went from bottom to top in 17 years, from the 1949 low to the 1966 high. From 1966 on, the four year cycle from low to low shortened to 48 months and then to 43 months indicating a change in the longer term trend support. The big change occurred after the uptrend had been broken in 1966 to 1968, proving that a cycle had rolled over. In the mid-1970's, it was tough to find out where the four year cycle was. You entered a large sideways market where the lows became slightly shorter. The point is that the longterm view should be kept in perspective but from a practical viewpoint, you simply go to the most dominant low that you see on a chart. If it is four years, then you can quickly start the sequence of looking for smaller and smaller cycles.

As a point of reference, would you define what you consider to be shortterm, intermediate-term, and longterm?

I would define longterm as approximately two years—from the low to the high of a four year cycle. I would classify intermediate as 6 months to 9 months, which is half of the dominant 12 month (40 week) or 18 month (80 week) cycles from the bottom to the top. In either one of those time frames, your stock may go six months or longer from low to high. Shortterm cycles run 10 to 20 weeks, the optimum shortterm trade tends to be 23 market days from bottom to top.

Is cycle analysis more difficult in raging bull markets?

When the trend is so powerful as it has been in the 1980's, yes. You get translation of the cycles in a strong trend because you are dealing with extremely longterm cycles. The biggest cycle is the predominant influence and the smaller cycles become less visual. First of all, it is good to have the big monthly picture in mind, then the weekly picture, and then the daily picture because you are dealing with monthly, weekly, and daily cycles. In the 1970's, it was a lot of fun to measure the four year cycle high to high in stocks and then go from intervening low and invariably the stock would try to make that four year cycle low right where you would expect it to. That was extremely helpful when the market was going sideways through the late 1960's and all through the 1970's. Even though you have been in a powerful uptrend since 1982, if you measure obvious highs and then go from an intervening low, the next lows you will find are in that general area. It is something you just keep playing with but if you are looking for an entry point on a stock, especially one that has been going through a huge correction—it is not unusual for a stock to go from 50 down to 7 or 8 in a bear market—by using the monthly picture you get an idea of where a cycle low is going to occur just by measuring the high points. It doesn't always work but it's good to have as a tool. You can then apply other tools or a simple trendline break in that time frame to confirm a bottom may have occurred.

Do you think it will be trickier doing cycle analysis if and when we ever have a major correction?

Well, you only have two alternatives. One is that you have a downtrend similar to the uptrend, in which case, yes, it will be tricky. The alternative is that the market goes sideways like it did in the 1960's or 1970's. You had a strong uptrend and then when the major cycles reached their peak and started going sideways or turning down, it produced a flat market period. When we look at the 200 year history, the market has always been up on a longterm basis but it goes sideways sometimes for many years. It is when the market is going sideways that your three to four year cycle begins to show through and is very helpful.

The four year cycle becomes more apparent in a longterm sideways consolidation pattern?

Yes, that is its *forte*. This is when the value of the weekly and daily cycles increases because you can measure highs and begin to see that the lows start to occur on schedule.

What are your suggestions for spotting cycle lows on charts?

A quick and dirty approach is using two fingers. Find two previous lows and put a finger on each low. Lift your fingers up and move them forward to see if a time period for another low is coming due or, measure two previous highs and then measure forward from an intervening low. Quite often I use Hurst's suggestion of taking a strip of paper and with a pencil, make a little mark between two lows and then slide the strip of paper across the chart to see where other additional lows occur. Where you continue to find additional pullback lows at previous cycle bottoms, you form a cluster of little black marks or "synchronicity" on the right hand side of your strip. Projecting that into the future from some important low that occurred several weeks ago gives you a very quick method of looking for the next cycle bottom. You can do a dozen different stocks and often you will find that the commonality between lows of all those stocks occur within a window of about one week. Sometimes you can use that as the market's cycle. But be aware that quite often when your stock is going into the final high of an intermediate cycle, those little marks out in the future may turn out to be a high instead of a low. For this reason, a system to stay with the trend as long as possible may also be used. This tends to happen in the late stage of a move and past the optimum combination of the bullish cycles. In another technical method, called Elliott wave, these extended moves tend to occur near the top of a wave 3, which is usually the longest and strongest portion of an advance. For those familiar with Elliott wave, if you measure time from the bottom of wave 1 to the end of wave 2, that distance is often when wave 3 ends at a top. The principle being that wave 3 is longer than wave 1, sometimes 1.618, and so timewise you might go low to low from the bottom of wave 1 and the bottom of the wave 2 pullback and then you may go low to high from the bottom of wave 2 to the top of wave 3.

What is the cycle sequence that you use?

The majority of cycles break up into two's—the 10 week, the 20 week, the 40 week and so forth-but I have always used 3, three week cycles to equal one 10 week cycle and three, 18 month cycles to equal one four year cycle.

You are coming just a little bit shy of the exact cycle period?

Right. I use three, 3 week cycles to equal one nominal ten week cycle. A 3 week cycle averages out to be 13 to 17 market days from cycle low to cycle low. Your 10 week cycle peak would occur after the second 3 week cycle has turned up. Half of 13 is 6.5 days, so if you had bottomed correctly in 13 days for a 3 week cycle low, 6½ days up from there or around 19 days, you could possibly be at the next 3 week and 10 week cycle high. Many moves end anywhere from 18 to 23 market days from low to high because it is the top of the second three week cycle and you are coming into the top of the 10 week cycle. When you extend into the high right on a chart longer than 10 weeks, it is because you have a very strong 20 week cycle or a very strong trend, period. You are translating to the high right on your chart from the strength of the other cycles. You will find however, that your oscillators will still try to turn down at the same points.

Will the strip of paper method work on a weekly chart as well as a longer term chart?

You can do all of this with weekly and monthly charts but it's always good to at least have looked at a monthly chart to see if the lows you are looking at are a four year cycle low, a two year cycle low, or a one year cycle low. First, see which direction those cycles might be moving in. When you are looking at a one year daily chart, if you have started to break trendlines that are six or eight months in length, you immediately know that a longer cycle is changing direction.

For those unfamiliar with the principles of Elliott wave, could you give us your rendition?

wave 1 is your first rally which breaks up into 5 smaller waves. This is how you tell which direction the true trend is in. On a daily chart, little wave one of five is called an impulsive wave and should be a clear, strong advance. It may be only several days in duration but stocks or indexes start breaking downtrend channels and volume increases. This is an indication of a definite change in trend and that the cycles have turned up. After the five waves, then you have an "a-b-c" correction of around 50% that takes the form of a zig-zag pullback or sideways consolidation. Either one is perfectly acceptable.

Countertrend moves are designated by letters instead of numbers, thus an a-b-c pullback is a countertrend move in an uptrend. That move is called wave 2. From there, the next advance would be called wave 3. After wave 3, there is another normal correction called wave 4 that pulls back an equivalent of .23 to .38 of your previous advance. The wave 4 correction could be a sideways consolidation or a zig-zag pullback but under the principle of alternation, if wave 2 is a zig-zag correction then wave 4 is a sideways consolidation. You won't get the same pattern in wave 2 and 4. Robert Prechter's book, ***The Elliott Wave Principle***, is the best book around on Elliott wave analysis.

The third wave is the longest part of the move and the fifth wave is the final phase of the move.

Correct.

You once said that one of the benefits of cycles is that they present a "contrary view at proper times." Would you expand on that statement?

By empirical observation, they have found through the years that people tend to be most bullish at tops and most bearish at bottoms. Market tops and bottoms, in terms of bullish or bearish sentiment, basically line up with the cycles but sentiment is such a general indicator that it is most useful at four year cycle turning points. For example, when the market is at a high and a 4 year or 18 month cycle is entering its high mode, it is helpful to look at sentiment. This is when speculative juices are flowing the most and sentiment runs to enthusiastic levels. When a cycle is bottoming, sentiment is most bearish.

In other words, if you went back to a period where the sentiment numbers were extremely high or low and then compared that time period with the four year cycle time period, you would often find the cycle bottoming and topping about the same time sentiment numbers are reaching extremes?

Yes, sentiment should be making its extreme at a four year cycle low or high, but you can't count on it 100%. Frankly, I don't use sentiment very much because people follow these sentiment indicators so much that sometimes you are second guessing the second guessing but you have to be aware of them. I had rather look at the cycle objectives that come from the centered moving averages forming a focal point in the past. If they all formed a focal point at the center of an Elliott wave 3 and you know that you are going into a broadening trading range or top, you can figure that this is a wave 5. Then look at the cycle time periods, like the 4 year cycle or the 18 month cycle, averaging about 78 weeks. It was 78 weeks from the bottom in November 1994 to the top in July 1996. In a case like that where the market had been going straight up into that point, I don't think of a cycle low occurring. If a market is at a high during a time period where a cycle bottom is due to occur, I would immediately reverse my thinking and say it looks like the next longer cycle is dominant.

The prevailing trend should always override what the cycle is telling you?

Right, unless the market goes down at a cycle low, it is not a cycle bottom. Maybe you developed your framework several months ago but if the market keeps on going up into the cycle time frame and your other indicators would have you long, don't be a fool and fight the tape. Be aware of the cycle time frames but also be aware that the next longer cycles will not roll over until you break what Hurst referred to as a valid trendline. For example, you won't break two 20 week cycle bottoms unless the next longer cycle is turning down. This is helpful for individual stocks because people can draw trendlines very easily.

What was Hurst's definition of a valid trendline?

The trendlines that Hurst indicated as valid would connect two cycle bottoms approximately 10 weeks apart. Then you would extend that trendline into the future. When that line is broken, it would prove that the 20 week cycle is rolling over, that is, turning down. It may also prove that cycles longer than that are turning down. When you are drawing your trendlines, you need to think in terms of cycles.

If a trendline connecting two 10 week cycle bottoms is broken, that is telling you that the 20 week cycle is down. Does it follow that a broken trendline connecting two 20 week cycle bottoms indicates that the 40 week cycle is down?

Yes, it does. In this case, you would begin to sell intermediate positions as they also break trendlines or anticipate selling into strength near the next 10 week cycle high.

To locate where a 10 week cycle begins, would you simply find two previous low points on a chart that are approximately 10 weeks apart?

Yes, you would simply look back within the time frame of the last 20 weeks to find two bottoms that appear to be 10 week cycle bottoms and then connect those two points with a trendline.

If you are using a 52 week daily chart, realistically, the only repeating cycles visible would be the 10 week and 20 week, right?

Yes. If you are a longterm investor and interested in the four year cycle, then you would have to switch to a weekly chart which would give you at least three years because you are actually looking for a move that will last for two years, which is bottom to top of a four year cycle. It is best to use weekly charts instead of daily, unless you are a trader. The Mansfield charts are very good including their relative strength line. You will see relative strength change after you have broken the trendline because you are losing momentum.

With regard to cycle periods, is there one time where relative strength is more crucial than another?

I think it is most important at cycle tops. You can do the same thing with trendlines but relative strength is a good, quick method of seeing which stocks are becoming weaker earlier than the market. The other time relative strength is good is when you have made an important low like a 40 week cycle or more. Some people say go with the highest relative strength stocks at a market bottom but through the years, that has gotten me in a lot of trouble. The highest relative strength stock could be a utility and it doesn't go anywhere. In fact, when you are at an intermediate and longterm cycle bottom, I think it's best to choose the weakest shortterm relative strength stock but one that has good longterm monthly relative strength still intact. You are coming at it from two cycle viewpoints. A longer term relative strength indicates a four year cycle or longer trend is still up while on a shortterm basis, the weakest relative strength might indicate that you have cleaned this stock out. The relative strength line on a monthly longterm SRC chart is also very good at intermediate bottoms. After there has been a fairly sizeable correction, go to those stocks that have positive relative strength on a monthly basis. Years ago, I developed the swing factor to compare two time frames based on cycles to detect a slight change in relative strength. I would get buy signals on a stock or a group when other people were having to sell out because the relative strength had begun to fade. It was the exact opposite to what other methods of relative strength were doing and it worked beautifully.

What is the swing factor?

It is the second derivative of relative strength. Testing data of 20 years, I had come up with various cycles for different groups but in general, I took two time periods. I compared the relative strength of a group for the last year with the relative strength of the previous year. It detected a change in the current one year cycle versus the previous one year cycle. If the current one year cycle had better relative strength than the previous one year cycle, then the swing factor would be positive. Theoretically, once you have passed the centerpoint of that two year downtrend, you were coming into a four year cycle bottom. If I could detect a positive change in relative strength before it became noticeable on a chart, then I was detecting a bell curve bottoming versus the previous one year bell curve that had been topping and coming down to the centerpoint. My swing factor would go positive while the stock was still at a cycle low. I got away from using it in the 1980's but I used it in the 1970's because we were in such a trading market.

Is it only useful in a trading range market like the 1970's?

No, it is helpful for spotting a change in any longterm trend, but it is best in rotational markets when major groups are changing. For example, in October 1980, I was running my swing factor and the top five negative stock groups were all oils and gold and the top ten positive groups were all consumer stocks, department stores, retailers; stock groups that people had ignored for years. I could not understand what was going to happen to make the change. When President Reagan was elected, charts show that was the top in oils and the bottom for consumer stocks. The market, in its infinite wisdom, detected Reagan for what he was, free enterprise and pro-business. The oils were topping on inflation and the retailers and department stores and others became the darlings for the next several years. In the long trending market, the big monthly relative strength or swing factors continued to work but not as well because we did not have big swings back and forth like you have in a flat or sideways market.

Will the swing factor work again in the future?

Yes, we will go back into a time when it is very important. Now of course, in a trending market such as we have had, relative strength lines are good to look at to confirm the trend. Both price and relative strength should trend together. Relative strength usually will break a trend first and this is an alert to sell.

Going back to trendlines, there seems to be a very close relationship between the actual trendline and the cycles. If a valid trendline is broken, is it always true that the next longer cycle is turning down?

Yes, under the theory of cycles, once a trend is intact, it should only be broken when the cycle supporting that trend changes direction. Suppose, for example, you find a chart with a trendline that is six months in length. The market has respected that trendline on every correction and then the trendline is finally broken. Since it is six months in length, you have to consider that at least a one year or longer cycle has begun to turn down. The cycle turning down is longer than the time frame of the trendline. That is your first valid proof that a cycle is beginning to turn down. During the strong uptrend of 1996, it was difficult at times to find shortterm cycle bottoms because every correction held on a good longterm trendline drawn from December 1974. You didn't know if some of those touches were a 10 week, 20 week, or even a 40 week cycle because none of the trendlines were broken. That's a problem as far as validating which cycle bottom was where. As long as a trend is so strong that it almost completely ignores shortterm cycles with large amplitude. You just really have to stay with the trend and figure that the dominant cycle is one year or maybe even four years in length. This is a phenomenon that occurs when all of your centered moving averages are basically riding right on top of one another. They are forming a straight trend right through the center of all prices as almost a single line because all of the cycles are within one channel. In those cases, it is best to put your hands in your pockets and stay with the trend because a topping formation, or proof that the cycles are rolling over, obviously will not occur until a trendline is broken. Period. Until the trend is broken, one can use pullbacks to the trendline 8 to 10 weeks apart as buy signals.

When you say stay with the trend, are we basing the trend on the trendline emanating from the original two low points that were eight to ten weeks apart?

Yes, and then draw a 20 week trendline when time from a major low allows. They are often the same. Stay with the longer trend unless you are a trader. A pullback 17 to 23 weeks from an intermediate low qualifies for a 20 week cycle low.

Then the number "twenty" is not cast in stone?

It's always a nominal term and the cycle period actually averages between 17 and 23 weeks.

Let's say a 10 week valid trendline is broken. In order to stay in tune with the longer term trend, would you then need to draw another trendline connecting two 20 week cycle lows?

Yes, but not until it is proven to be a 20 week cycle low. For example, you could break the 10 week valid trendline briefly and that proves your 20 week cycle has turned down, but it does not tell you that the cycle will bottom and immediately turn back up. It just helps you identify that the 20 week cycle is down. Similarly, if you have a trendline connecting two 20 week cycle lows, if that trend is broken, you assume the 40 week cycle is down. However, if it is only briefly broken and it is 39 to 40 weeks from a previous low, you may also assume it may have bottomed and you may use this as a buy point.

If a break occurs in a 20 week or 40 week trendline, is that more significant than a break in the 10 week trendline?

It depends on your time frame of investing. If you are a shortterm investor, you are generally always interested in the 10 week cycle trendline. A broken trendline tells you that the next longer cycle is rolling over but that doesn't mean it's "just" started rolling over. It may be already bottoming just as your trendline is being broken. That's one of the tricky points. As I said, you would measure from your previous low. If you were 39 or 40 weeks from that low and the trendline is just barely broken then immediately reverses back up, that identifies it as a possible 40 week cycle bottom. The break identified that the cycle is down but it doesn't tell you whether or not you have more weeks of downward pressure. Let's use another example, this time with a 20 week trendline. If you are 15 weeks from a previous 20 week low and you break a valid 20 week cycle trendline, you know there is the possibility of 4 to 5 more weeks until you reach a 20 week cycle bottom. The trendline break proves that the market was becoming weaker not only from a 20 week cycle perspective but perhaps from even longer term cycles. Where you break the trendline in time in relation to where the cycle began helps determine how weak the market has become.

In other words, it's necessary to know where each previous cycle low occurred in order to project how much time is left until the next bottom. What other indications could you look for that might indicate a cycle bottom?

Actually, a full analysis of cycles requires knowing where all of the cycles are—the 10 week, the 20 week, the 40 week, the 80 week, and so forth. These trendline breaks are somewhat of a road map that keep telling you where you are. Yes, a trendline break is a caution flag but did you then get an oversold condition consistent with a 20 week and a 10 week cycle bottom? You can look back at the oscillators and compare oversold conditions at the previous 10 week and 20 week cycle bottoms. Cycles are not the end all. You have to use a combination of other tools to go with cycle analysis.

If I understand you correctly, you will use traditional forms of technical analysis first and then use cycles to corroborate or negate what your other indicators are telling you?

Yes. Cycles are helpful to keep things in perspective. You can look back at four year cycle lows in the past and in some cases, compare the statistics of oversold conditions or even sentiment at those times. I think it is more meaningful when you compare statistics for similar cycle time periods.

When you say compare statistics, what do you mean?

In the 1970's, the 18 month and four year cycle lows would be your most bearish time periods on an intermediate and longterm basis. So the 1974 low should compare in sentiment to the 1970 low. More recently, the 1984 low, the 1987 low, and the 1990 low were all somewhat 3 to 4 years apart so they are similar cycles. 1994 was different. Ninety percent of the time I use the Dow in my cycle analysis but other indexes can show the cycle influence as well. Looking at the November 1994 time period, the utilities, the advance/decline line, and bonds were all down 25% from their highs in September 1993. The Dow did not look like a normal four year cycle bottom from the 1990 low. By November, it had not even gone below its previous low of April or May 1994. This is where synchronicity, as it is referred to, comes in. If you concentrate on the Dow exclusively, it can throw you off. You have to look at the internal market also. So 1994 was as valid a four year cycle bottom as any other. It was not visible in the Dow but it was visible in other indexes.

When you don't get confirmation from all indexes or averages showing the same cycle patterns, how do you resolve the picture?

Commonality. In Hurst's book, he suggested running cycles on a portfolio of stocks and coming up with a time period which was common to the majority. I think that is a valid point because as I said, things which are not in the Dow Jones Industrial Average like secondaries, utilities, or bonds may in fact be getting washed out and forming a very clear cycle bottom, and yet the Dow does not follow suit. Obviously, the easiest cycle bottoms to identify are those where the Dow and the major averages have the profile you would expect; that is, a very long and steep decline. From a chart viewpoint, the period of 1978-1979 was also very different. Although it had been four years from the four year cycle bottom in 1974, it was a difficult time period to call because there was a double bottom—a low in the spring of 1978 and a low in the spring of 1979. For the previous 30 years, every bear market had simply been a nice clean wash-out, spike low. When there is a double bottom or a double top, you should consider that there might be a cycle changing direction half-way between those two points. In 1978, the centered moving averages finally defined where the four year cycle had bottomed and it bottomed basically on schedule, four years from the 1974 bottom.

In most cases, will cycles bottom with a spike low or wash-out low in price?

Yes, that is what you would normally look for as a sign that all cycles have bottomed together.

What's a good method for spotting commonality among stocks and indexes?

As you are analyzing stocks from a cyclical viewpoint and measuring highs and lows, if you keep notes or make marks on the chartbook, you will begin to see individual stocks topping or bottoming, or due to top or bottom, in the same time frame. I use this method as a cross check to see what the internal market is doing versus the Dow or other indexes. You can even see cycles change by looking at relative strength. For example, in the last two years, the one year or 40 week cycle has tended to work very well for the OTC

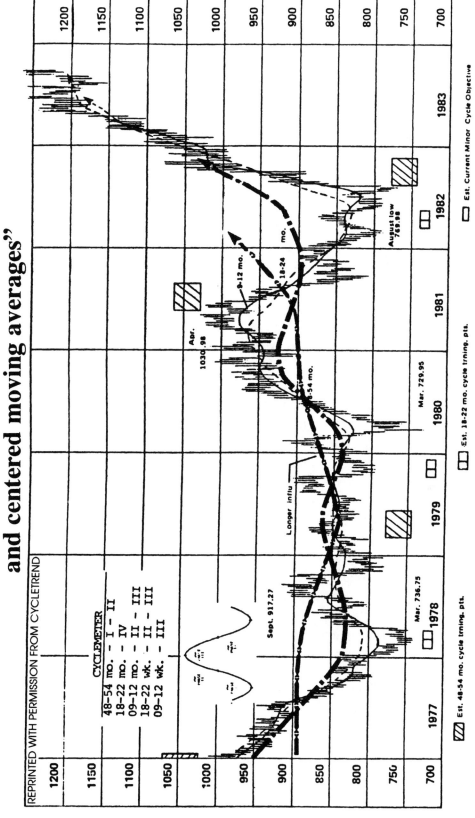

"Cyclemeter showing cycle turning points and centered moving averages"

market. While the 40 week cycle was down, the relative strength on the OTC market was very poor but once the 40 week cycle turned up in November to December of 1994, then the relative strength improved. The OTC market, at least for the last several years, tends to be more sensitive to the one year cycle so you could avoid OTC stocks when that cycle is down and then consider the more volatile OTC stocks when the 40 week cycle turns up. You can also see that change in the relative strength line, which is a helpful clue that the 40 week cycle is working.

Investors must be resigned to the fact that individual indexes and particular sectors are going to be staggered in terms of cycle tops and bottoms.

That has always been the case and this is where the relative strength studies become important. Relative strength is one way you can tell whether a cycle is having an effect or not. For example, at the 1974 low, the best longterm relative strength group was the steels. There were very few others. In October and November of 1974, the market had tanked into the four year cycle bottom. Steel stocks made a large double bottom on monthly charts but were unable to go below their low of a year earlier in December 1973, while the market averages were substantially lower. Their longterm relative strength showed a very positive trend and they became the leaders of the new bull market.

There are different time periods of relative strength. What is the minimum you recommend using?

I think all analysis should start with longterm monthly charts to get the bigger, overall picture. A sector will tend to go through longterm changes in relative strength. Sometimes it almost takes 7 to 9 years for their relative strength to turn around. Strong relative strength stocks get to excessive prices and tend to top out last and relative strength always tends to go with the sector that is in vogue during a four year cycle. During the 1972-1973 period, it was the "Nifty-Fifty" stocks. Stocks like Xerox and Eastman Kodak were selling at 60 times earnings. These stocks made their highs in September 1973, after the Dow had already topped out in January. When the "Nifty-Fifty" stocks topped out in 1973, they had poor relative strength versus the other averages and sectors for the next six years, until the spring of 1979 when the 4 year cycle bottomed. If you look at monthly charts of the "Nifty-Fifty" stocks, all of them had created a five wave advance from the low that began in the mid-1960's. 1973 was their fifth wave blow-off move in the third, four year cycle top. You see, three, four year cycles would be 12 years but to the top of the third, four year cycle would be approximately nine years. So nine years tends to be a common time period for major moves from bottom to top. Three 4 year cycles, can produce a major 5 wave pattern in longterm charts.

As a shortterm guide, can readers use the relative strength found on daily charts or the numerical values of relative strength from *Investors Business Daily*?

Yes, and the relative strength from *Investors Business Daily* would bring in another technical method—the cup with handle approach from William O'Neil's book, *How To Make Money in Stocks*. If a stock rallies, forming a small double top, then has a pullback ½ to 1/3 of the previous advance, what you have is a rounding bottom that looks like a cup and the pullback looks like the handle of a cup. Basically the stock is bottoming on a cycle. A trader looking at this stock might see a double top but when the stock pulls back, it doesn't pull back very much. If the relative strength line holds steady while the stock is correcting, then the stock tends to breakout on the next advance. If the relative strength line holds during a correction, some investors will buy before the breakout but I like to make sure that the longer term moving average is up. If you buy on the breakout, O'Neil recommends to buy within 10% of the breakout point and use a 7% stop-loss strategy. Positive relative strength and a double top pattern with a shortterm rounding bottom are all positive signs. If a 30 week or 200 day moving average is turning up, these indicate the longer term cycles are becoming stronger.

If you look at relative strength nine years back then you must use very longterm charts.

In 1978 to 1979, I started writing about a 61 to 63 year cycle that was due to bottom in 1981 to 1983. Instead of trading, as we had done in the 1970's, where market timing was important, I said that the 1980's would be a decade when a buy and hold approach would be the most important. Those concepts came from looking at 40 year charts. In the case of the blue chip stocks, you could go back and look at charts from the 1940's to the 1960's and draw a clear top to top longterm trendline that produced an upper trendline of a major parallel channel. That is where the Dow topped out in the mid-1960's. Then you could draw a parallel line from the 1942 low or maybe from the 1946 low to produce a longterm channel. By 1979 to 1981, many stocks like American Telephone, General Motors, Borden, Campbell Soup, had been out of favor for so long that none of them had made new highs in 17 years. They had worked sideways until they were at the bottom of their longterm upward channels. These were the stocks that began to move first at the 1982 bottom and were, of course, leaders for most of the decade in the 1980's. That prediction came from very longterm trends. I think someone should be aware of trends at least 10 years or longer in length.

Am I correct in assuming that you use charts from Securities Research Corporation?

Yes. I think they are an excellent source. Arithmetic charts in a long move become exaggerated. Shorter term, you can use arithmetic charts but the longer term channels that I am talking about become quite accurate with semi-logarithmic charts such as the SRC charts.

"Centered moving averages," which are a twist on the more traditional moving averages, are your mainstay and correlate with your cycle periods. How are they constructed?

First of all, you create moving averages of the stock or index prices that you want to analyze. Choose a moving average that is one-half of the cycle period that you want to observe. If you are looking at a four year cycle, you would use a two year moving average. A two year moving average will track a four year cycle. Then you place the two year moving average ½ span back on your charts, in other words, you lag it one year on your charts. If you are looking at a 20 week cycle, you would use a 10 week moving average and place that average five weeks back on the chart. Every moving average that I use is one-half the length of the cycle and displaced one-half span.

What is the purpose of displacing the moving averages ½ span back on the chart?

Because mathematically, that is tracking the exact cycle. You want to see visually how the cycle was unfolding in the past. You would think that putting them in past time is of little value but there is an interesting phenomenon that occurs with centered moving averages. When you have three or more centered moving averages on a chart, you will find that they will tend to go through one central price on the chart. Usually this is the middle of a nice acceleration move to the upside or downside. Amazingly, you will be able to tell quite often where that focal point is going to form days or weeks in advance from hourly charts. You don't have to wait for the daily and the weekly centered moving averages to tell you what the center of the move is. In the 1987 crash, the downward move formed a focal point in hourly centered moving averages and several months later, the monthly and weekly centered moving averages came through that same price. In other words, once the hourly cycles had formed a focal point and that objective had been met, it indicated that the downside move was basically over.

You are calling a convergence of several centered moving averages a focal point?

Yes, because it becomes the central point of several cycle channels.

How can you predict the resolution of a trend by looking at the focal point formed by something as short as hourly moving averages?

Hourly charts tend to form a focal point that your daily and even weekly centered moving averages possibly will go through later. This gives you an early idea of a daily or even weekly objective. You wouldn't apply hourly centered moving averages to a longterm weekly chart. I use the same centered moving averages on an hourly basis that I do on a daily chart. I use a 7 hour centered moving average, 13 hour, 25 hour and then I have a 50 hour centered moving average. I never use anything less than "hourly" for centered moving averages although they work for any time frame.

From what you have just described, these focal points appear to be very powerful timing tools.

Yes. The reason for the focal point is twofold. You can develop a time and price objective from previous lows by using that focal point to create a mirror image on the other side because cycles tend to unwind as they began. Measuring from a previous low to the focal point is the halfway point of a move so the second half of the move should equal the first and that will give you a price objective. It does not always work but if you see it unfolding, it is very helpful. For example, on September 3, 1996, a low occurred in the Dow Jones Industrial Average at 5550. Hourly centered moving averages crossed on September 11th at 5754 and the close and low for that day was at 5750. The previous low was 5550, a 200 point difference. Adding 200 points to the focal point at 5750 gives you a price target of 5950. When I switched to daily charts, the daily centered moving average lines pointed to the same 5750 area, the same price target as the hourly centered moving averages. The daily centered moving averages were just a few days behind the hourly but they came through the same focal point at 5750. The daily focal

Centered Moving Averages Converging to Form Focal Point
Dow Jones Industrial Average

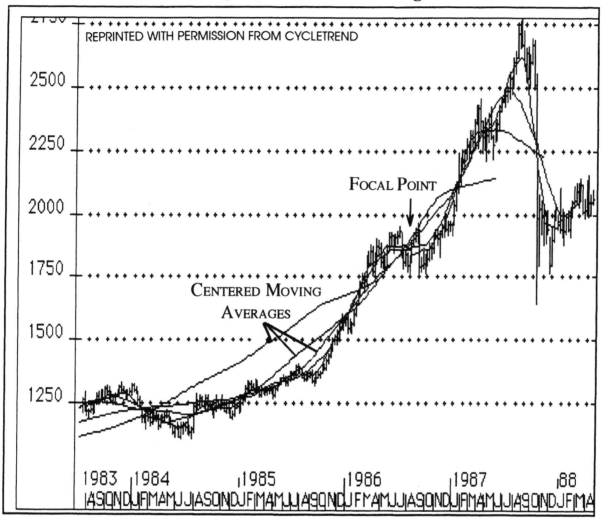

REPRINTED WITH PERMISSION FROM CYCLETREND

FOCAL POINT

CENTERED MOVING AVERAGES

points, hourly focal points, and even the weekly focal points (formed in mid-1995), all meshed together giving a price target in the area of 5950. I had objectives at 5922, 5924, 5956, and 5986. The 5986 came from measuring the hourly Elliott wave pattern of little wave 1 up. Since wave 5 is equal to wave 1, that gave me 5986. You can do the cycles and the Elliott wave measurements and generally come up with a "zone" of price targets.

For an upside price objective, you measure from the previous low to the focal point and double that distance?

Draw a straight line from a previous low through the focal point and extend the line on out. Take a caliper or two fingers, and measure from the low to the focal point and double it along that line. Put a little crosshatch at the top where the distances are equal between the focal point to the top and the focal point to the previous low. Don't do this more than three times because when three centered moving averages have gone through one point, you are tracking three cycles. You would not want to go beyond three price or time objectives.

How would you obtain the time objective using this technique?

You measure the distance in time from a previous low to the focal point, and then project that same time frame forward.

In your previous example, you demonstrated that centered moving averages are clearly helpful in providing price objectives for the DJIA. Is this technique equally effective with individual stocks and bonds?

It is just as important in individual stocks and bonds.

In order to have a trustworthy focal point, would you recommend using a minimum of three centered moving averages?

Yes, I think so and it comes somewhat from Elliott's five wave principle.

How do they relate?

Your focal point is usually going to occur at the center of wave 3. First you have a wave 1 move up, followed by a pullback or sideways correction for wave 2, during which time your centered moving averages will try to bottom and then turn up slowly. Next you will have a wave 3 up, reach a high, and then go sideways, working into wave 4. By that time, your centered moving averages have come through the center of wave 3 and if you measure from that point back to the bottom of wave 1, generally you will get a price objective for wave 5. You will notice that before that final push up in wave 5, your centered moving averages will have gone through wave 3, still trending up strongly and about the time that they touch the bottom of the sideways consolidation in wave 4, the market takes off in wave 5. In other words, they are

"Price Objective of 7242 Using the Focal Point at 6256 and Cycle Low of 5270"

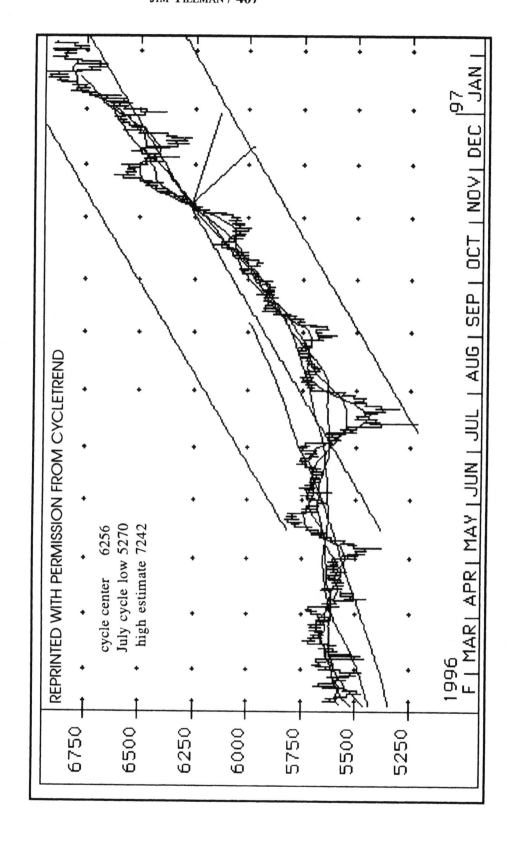

REPRINTED WITH PERMISSION FROM CYCLETREND

cycle center 6256
July cycle low 5270
high estimate 7242

about to form a focal point through the sideways portion of wave 4. The correction is over and the market takes off in wave 5. If you look back at the 1974-1975 market, you had a correction from June/July of 1975, sideways into December and you will notice that all centered moving averages were up strongly and had come through the center of wave 3, indicating that the consolidation should have been about over by December. The market exploded in January 1976. This was a very classic case but you will see it time and again on individual stocks. It helps you determine that wave 5 is over.

If you have a major focal point in the center of wave 3, can you draw a line from previous lows to obtain projections for time and price?

Yes, each time centered moving averages form a focal point, a line drawn from a previous low (if in an uptrend) through the focal point gives a good estimate of a price and time objective. The main focal point occurs in the center of the longest portion of an advance, generally wave 3. Three lines can be drawn through this point from recent lows. For the first objective, draw a line from the bottom of wave 2 (the last low) and extend it through the focal point. This generally will confirm the price and time objective for wave 3. Drawing a line from the very bottom of wave 1 through this same point at the center of wave 3 will give you the objective for wave 5—generally.

And that is both in price and time?

Yes, generally both price and time. Time will slip one way or the other a little in wave 5 because your peak of momentum stops at the top of wave 3, so from that point forward, the cycles have already started the process of rolling over.

At the "peak" of wave 3?

Yes. You will lose momentum from that point forward. Wave 4 will take about one-third longer to unfold because the uptrend is not quite as strong as it was at the bottom of wave 2. If it took two weeks for wave 2 to unfold then it might take 3 weeks for wave 4 to unfold. It may take longer but that would be a general rule. Now, remember that the centered moving averages are lagged in time. Day by day they continue to crawl up and about the time they touch wave 4, you are ready to advance in wave 5. You can draw your trendline through the center of wave 3 and wave 4 and that's going to be the center of your channel. Extend that trendline into the future and that's about where wave 5 will go to in the future because it is the centerline of the channel.

What are your suggestions for using centered moving averages?

You have to realize that you are generally near your upper price objective when all of the centered moving averages are crossing each other. People might ask, "What good is that?" Well, it basically tells you that this move is over so that you can expect a move to unfold in the opposite direction. When the price or time objective is met, then you simply start looking in the other direction. That's the value of the centered moving average approach. It tells you that the move is over and gives you confidence that you have met an objective. When you reach an upper objective, get ready to sell. You can bring in other indicators such as oscillators, diverging sell signals, trendline breaks, moving average line breaks; anything that confirms that the move is over. The same thing is true on the downside. When you have had a focal point and you are meeting all of your objectives, that is when you would start looking for a reversal to the upside. It fits perfectly together if you are at a 10 week, 20 week or 40 week cycle time frame for a low. From January of 1984 until mid-year, the Dow went through a correction. All of the longer term moving averages of the Dow were in an extremely strong uptrend but the 10 day, 20 day, and 40 day centered moving averages, though small, formed a perfect focal point at the halfway point during a correction so shortterm objectives were being met. The longer term uptrend was still very strong and you had no change in momentum. So you simply used that as an intermediate buy point. I might mention something else. In the crash of 1987, many people were very bearish thinking that we had started another 1929. In comparing 1987 with 1929, it was important to know where the focal point was. There was one key difference in the focal points of those two periods. In 1987, the longer term moving averages that had not crossed through the focal point were still below the focal point and *rising*. What would it take to force them through that focal point? It would take a *higher* market "in the future" for them to go through that same focal point that the lesser moving averages had gone through (see chart of DJIA 1983-1988). In 1929, the longer term centered moving averages were *above* the focal point on the charts so what would it take to pull those longer term moving averages down through the focal point? It would take lower prices in the future. That is one of the subtle, but important key points about centered moving averages. When you are using centered moving averages, you have to think forward in time.

That example illustrates the importance of looking at longer term centered moving averages in relation to shorter term centered moving averages.

I think the magnet is strong enough to attract the longer averages through a focal point that is already formed.

So once you have pinpointed a focal point, is there much risk that the centered moving averages will reverse course and miss the focal point altogether?

They will if the market reverses because of unexpected news, but that is not normal. The worst thing that you can do is to obey them without caution. Let's say that you have several moving averages that you think should continue to rise through a focal point. That would be a good indication that your uptrend would continue but if a double top starts forming, that is an automatic clue to be cautious because a cycle can turn down halfway between a double top. The cycle centered moving averages will come up through the focal point, but then stall and go sideways before turning down halfway between a double top. This indicates a larger cycle is turning down. A double top is always possible so you have to watch for them. Since a final rally is usually over quickly in wave 5, stalling near a previous high is usually a warning to go ahead and take profits.

For best results, I believe you use 5 or more centered moving averages. Is that for longer term work?

If used on monthly charts, they provide longer term perspective but they may also be used on daily or hourly charts for shorter term perspective. For example, longterm monthly centered moving averages intersected right through the center of the entire advance from 1949 to 1966. I said in the late 1960's that this was important because all of the longterm focal point objectives were met at a Dow level of 1,000. Once you meet major, longterm cycle objectives on the upside, what happens? The market either goes down or sideways. From 1966 until 1982, the market went sideways. There was a similar flat market from 1906 to 1914 and I was using that period as a comparison to the 1960's and 1970's.

In a situation like that, are there other indicators to give you advance warning as to whether the market would go down or sideways or do you have to wait and see how it resolves?

Other indicators are always used but here we are talking about cycles which are so large that you want to switch to more useful centered moving averages for shorter term cycles, such as the four year, 18 month, or one year. You are just keeping the big time frame and the big cycles in the back of your mind because they are not useful for anything except developing a major strategy.

That is, for determining the longterm secular trend?

Correct.

In your own analysis, which centered moving averages do you rely on?

I use a 7 week centered moving average for tracking a cycle that is anywhere from 10 to 13 weeks. Then I use a 13 week average which tracks a 20 to 26 week cycle. Each moving average works as both a half-span and a full-span picture on your chart. For example, a 13 week moving average is going to show you the trend and profile of the 26 week cycle but it is also the full-span moving average of the 10 to 13 week cycle. It is the half-span moving average of the 26 week cycle and the full moving average of the 10 to 13 week cycle. At one glance it tells you the direction of the 20 week cycle and through its half-span measurement, it gives the price objective of that cycle from where it passes through the focal point. So I use 7, 13, 25, and 49 "days or weeks" for the moving averages. I shorten the number by one to make it an odd number because when I did charts by hand, this placed the average between the price bars exactly where they should be.

So far you have been talking about price targets for the upside. Will you get accurate downside objectives if you draw a line from a cycle peak down through a focal point?

Yes, but since cycles tend to bottom together, you have to allow for "overshoot." Shortterm cycles in a steep downtrend will temporarily overshoot more general longer cycle objectives. That is why cycle mirror images don't work as well at bottoms. These give you an approximation of price but you should be prepared for an overshoot because you have more than one cycle occurring at the same time. You tend to get a better mirror image objective at the high.

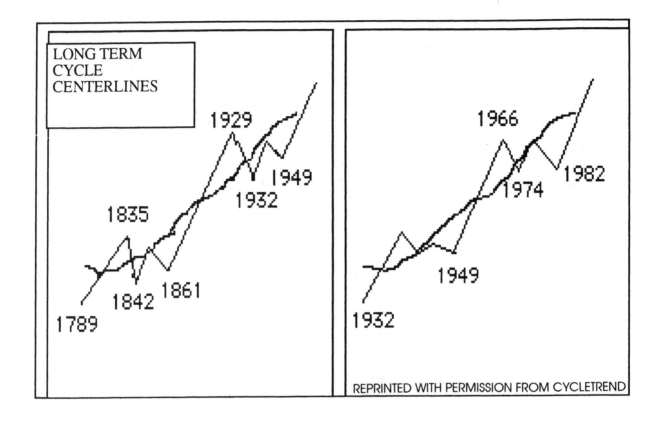

LONG TERM
CYCLE
CENTERLINES

1929

1949

1932

1835

1861

1842

1789

1966

1974

1982

1949

1932

REPRINTED WITH PERMISSION FROM CYCLETREND

What do you mean by mirror image?

Mirror image is a very valid cyclical phenomenon. A pattern will often unfold at the top similar to how it was created at the bottom. Picture a sine wave going from its trough to the peak. When an advance is underway, the focal point of the centered moving averages helps to determine the halfway point of the move. You can then draw a straight line from previous lows through the focal point and project into the future. Measuring along these lines from the focal point gives you both a sense of time, pattern, and price for the expected high. I don't go beyond using three lows because cycles combine either in two's or three's. Three companion cycles or three tangent cycles generally produce the majority of the move for that time period. If you take the very first low prior to the centerpoint you will get your very first high, then you go back and maybe you had a previous low prior to that and you project your second high. Then you would connect the first low, normally at the bottom of wave 1, through the focal point and that would tend to point at the top of Elliott wave 5.

Would the actual chart pattern look similar also?

Yes. In fact, some computer programs allow you to flip or reverse chart patterns for this reason.

Using tracing paper, if you trace out the bottom of a pattern and mark the focal point, can you then rotate the paper, line up the focal point, and project how the pattern will appear at the top?

Yes, that's a good way. Flip it upside down and put that at the focal point of the centered moving averages. That is just as valid as using the centered moving averages.

Are there software programs which can calculate centered moving averages?

Nowadays, almost any program that people use has the capability of centering moving averages. All of the popular programs allow you to put your moving average wherever you want to.

Earlier, you mentioned using oscillators as a confirming tool for cycle tops and bottoms. What type of oscillator are you referring to?

Simple rate of change. In other words, taking the difference in today's price from the price 7 days ago, however, I smooth the rate of change with a 3 day moving average. Actually, I use a 3 day moving average of a 4 day rate of change. It gives me the same profile as a 7 day rate of change but it is more reliable and the reversal is not as sharp.

How are the oscillators constructed?

Construct a rate of change equal to ¼ of the length of your cycle if you want divergences at your cycle high and low or ½ if you want to see the profile of the cycle. I like to use a rate of change that is ¼ of the cycle

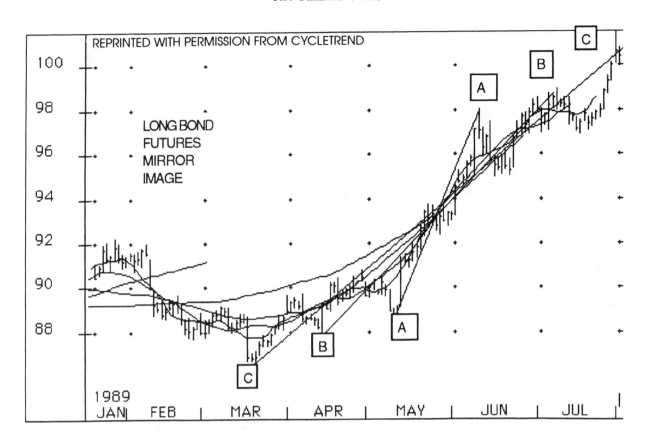

period because I am visually accustomed to looking for divergences. For example, if you are looking at a 28 day cycle, you would use a 7 day oscillator. What occurs is a divergence at the bottom of the 10 week cycle and a divergence at the top of the 10 week cycle for somewhat mechanical buy and sell signals.

Would you describe what to look for in such divergences?

A divergence is any momentum oscillator that does not confirm a new high in the item it is tracking in an uptrend or a new low if in a downtrend. A cycle has to lose momentum before it changes direction so you want to see this momentum change. In an uptrend, making a second higher high in price with the downtrend over two oscillator peaks, produces a good sell signal as soon as the tightest uptrend on price lows is broken. This will generally occur near the top trend of a channel. You would expect to get the next positive divergence near the bottom of this channel approximately 4 to 5 weeks later.

Does this scenario only hold true if the parallel channel is trending up?

No, in fact, if you have the correct oscillator tracking a cycle, a flat trend would theoretically give perfect buy and sell signals at cycle turning points. The trend of the next longer cycle causes left or right translation in a cycle, which can cause signals to vary slightly.

Going back to divergences at the top and bottom of 10 week cycles, can traders take positions based on these divergences?

Yes, because in a ten week cycle, upmoves tend to last approximately 23 market days. Through the years, the most common has been approximately 23 days but it can vary to as high as 30. In 1996, we had 32 to 33 days from low to high but those were unusual. Generally, whenever you are in a strong move you will find an hourly 5 wave advance from the bottom of a 10 week cycle to the top of the 10 week cycle. You are going to have minor focal points occur at the center of wave 3 and then you get a divergence in your oscillator at the top of the 10 week cycle. It fits together perfectly.

Of course, the same guidelines for keying in these momentum oscillators would apply to all cycle time periods?

Yes. If you are looking at a 20 day or 20 week cycle, you would use a rate of change oscillator of ½ of the cycle period which would be 10 days or 10 weeks to get the profile of the cycle. Theoretically, the center point of your rising sine wave is within the first five days of a 20 day cycle. Then in the second five days, or at day 10, the oscillator would have gone down and then back up, perhaps making a lower peak than prices. Therefore you have a negative divergence and you can use that as a mechanical sell signal. When that oscillator turns down the second time, just go ahead and sell because you know that you are into your cycle peak. Same thing at a bottom. When you get a positive divergence, you buy. I like an oscillator because if your trend is extremely strong, the oscillator may make a new high the second time causing you to hold until you have a negative divergence. Wait until you get another new high in the stock

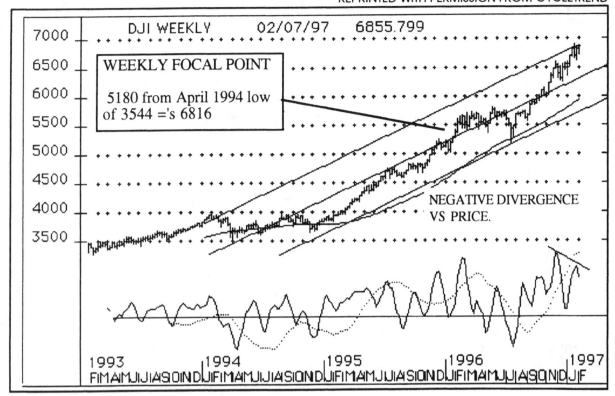

and the oscillator makes a lower high. In that case, you can recognize that it might have made a five wave advance. It has gone up for wave 1, pull back for wave 2, up in wave 3, the trend is strong so it pulls back a little in wave 4, and then goes to a higher high in wave 5 and you get your divergence there instead of earlier in the cycle.

Breaking one 10 week cycle into three 3 week cycles allows you to identify where the rallies and corrections will occur. During which phase does the new high occur after the corrective pullback?

Following a 10 week cycle low, the first pullback is normally a three week cycle around 13 market days and you can generally figure that you are about at the halfway point in your rise. Then the stock may go to a new high, to make a 3 and 10 week cycle peak. When the oscillator turns down the second time from a lower peak and price is at a new high, that is a negative divergence and you sell. Signals through the years tend to occur 18 to 23 market days from a buy point because if the three week cycle were to pull back into the 13th day and then rise into the 18th day, that is five days up. That is just about where you would normally get a diverging sell signal, but if a new high occurs in the oscillator along with price, that tells you the trend is very strong and to stay with it a little longer. You might put a stop under a minor pullback, but stay with it. When it finally goes up into the 23rd day and you get a divergence, use that as a sell signal. It's just a mechanical approach. I remember in 1984, the 18 month cycle was due to bottom in June to July. On the pullback, weekly charts were giving positive divergences and then daily charts gave positive divergences giving a clue that intermediate and shortterm cycles were bottoming together. The most conservative and more accurate signals occur when you have a weekly divergence first and then a daily divergence.

Is this the only momentum measure that you use?

Yes, but any method used will work if it is based on the correct cycle.

As far as divergences are concerned, will the oscillators generate signals for longterm cycles such as the four year cycle?

Definitely. If you want a divergence at the four year cycle peak you would use a one year oscillator. To view the cycle itself, use a two year oscillator. If you want divergences, use ¼. If you want a full cycle, use one-half. You could run them both and that way you would have somewhat of a confirmation.

Will they conflict?

No, generally they will work together. Sometimes your eye misses the ½ oscillator slowly rolling over. The divergence with the ¼ oscillator just pulls your eye to it more quickly.

Will these oscillators work well for individual stocks?

That is where it is so valuable because if you get lazy, you can actually just go with the oscillator by itself. I wrote the programs to give me diverging sell signals or buy signals automatically both on daily and weekly charts and it just works beautifully.

Are there periods of synchronicity in cycles, in other words, will a 10 week cycle coincide or intersect with a 20 week cycle and a 40 week cycle at peaks or troughs?

Yes, this is how you rank the importance of a cycle low or high. If you are looking for a 40, 20, and 10 week cycle to bottom together, you expect it to be much more important than say a 10 week by itself.

According to cycle analysis, the major trend is determined by drawing a trendline through two focal points formed by smaller cycles. Are those smaller cycles the 10 week and the 20 week cycles?

If you were on a daily chart, the focal point would be the 10, 20, and 40 week cycles. The center of wave 3 is usually where the focal point is formed. As the price works sideways in wave 4, it forms another focal point which may be less clear. You draw your trendline connecting the focal points at the center of wave 3 through the center of wave 4. That determines your major trend. Then you can draw an outside boundary trendline between the bottom of wave 2 and wave 4 and when that is broken, you will know that your 5th wave has passed.

Is that your method of constructing parallel channels?

Yes, the centerlines will always go up through the center of a parallel channel. You can first form your centerline through the focal points and then draw the parallel outside boundaries. You can draw straight line channels or channels that follow cycle centerlines. If you sketch in 3 or 4 channels following different centerlines, it is a great way to see how cycles mingle together.

After wave 4, what scenario would unfold telling you that the end of an uptrend was over?

Assuming you have created about 4 waves of an expected 5 wave pattern, a focal point is already visible near the center of the last strong advance (wave 3) and the stock may be in a consolidation (wave 4). The next rally will generally stall at the centerline of your channel. You don't often reach the upper boundary of the channel in wave 5. You will have confirmation that it is a wave 5 if the stock or index goes up and touches the centerline and then falls, breaking the lower boundary of the parallel channel.

Would you wait until the lower parallel channel trendline is broken before reacting?

That depends. Generally, you give up a good 10% from the top of wave 5 before the trendline or moving average is broken. If you are convinced that you have gone up in five waves, you have a nice clear channel, a clear centerline and your last high was on the centerline at which point a negative divergence in momen-

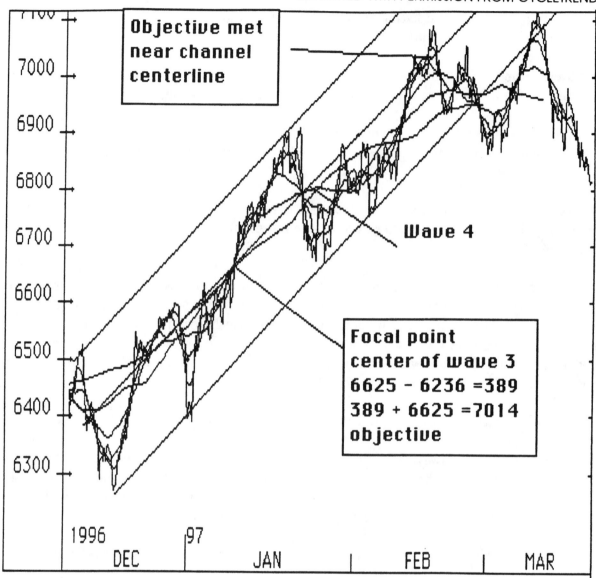

Objective met near channel centerline

Wave 4

Focal point center of wave 3 6625 − 6236 =389 389 + 6625 =7014 objective

tum occurred, you have as much evidence as you could possibly need to sell there and not wait for a trendline break.

What you have just described is a "when to sell" strategy. Is there a reciprocal plan for "when to buy"?

Using the reverse method, stocks will generally complete a 5th wave down at a new low but stopping at the down channel centerline. A positive divergence should confirm this is a completed 5 wave pattern but a trigger could be the simple 1-2-3 method that traders use.

What is the 1-2-3 method?

Imagine a stock making a bottom, rallying, and then pulling back halfway. You would put a # 1 at the bottom. After the stock rallies, then that first little high off the bottom is a #2. If the stock pulls back and then moves higher than #2, then circle that point and put a # 3 there. Traders try to keep it simple so when a stock or index goes above point 2, that is their buy point. Now, don't confuse this with Elliott. Point 2 or the first rally peak will probably top against a parallel downtrend channel. The pullback to point 3 is generally a retest of the channel centerline. As the stock goes back up, it will be breaking out of the channel. You can use the old 1-2-3 method, the breakout method, or buy in Elliott terms—wave 1 is up, wave 2 is the pullback, and by the time you break the previous high, you are in wave 3. Using any of these methods, your first price objective is double the width of your previous down channel. You measure from the bottom trendline of the channel to the top trendline of the channel. This method is also like the old measured move. Once you have broken out of the downtrend channel, pulled back to the center line, and then turned back up, you can start a new preliminary upchannel with those two lows.

How is the measured move different from what you just described?

Let's approach it from an "a-b-c" pullback in Elliott terms. Let's suppose that a stock or the market has gone up in a nice upward channel in five waves. Your first correction from the top is generally called an "a" pullback. Quite often a stock will break its uptrend channel and bottom shortly thereafter. Usually that becomes a halfway point from the centerline of the channel to the bottom of the channel. A stock moves that distance again but that is not the measured move, that is just the "a" wave down. A "b" rally will quite often go back just underneath the trendline break. This is the "b" move. The next decline, which would be wave "c" down, would generally be equal to the first decline. Therefore, "a" down and "c" down are equal measured moves, quite often both in time and price. Measuring from high to high from the top of five to the top of wave "b" in distance and then from the low of "a" over to the low of "c" in distance is sometimes exactly the same in price and time. The "b" move is that little corrective or "kickback" rally usually caused by a very shortterm cycle. This is generally the three week cycle rally in the down phase side of the 10 week cycle. Let's say the 10 week cycle was up for 5 weeks and now it is going to be down for 5 weeks so your second three week cycle would try to rally somewhere around the 6 to 6½ week period. That is where you would normally have a kickback rally within your downtrend of the 10 week cycle.

What type of overbought/oversold oscillators do you use?

For years I have done the exact same 10 day overbought/oversold oscillator that is on the back page of Trendline. I take the net advances and declines for 10 days and keep that on a running total basis and that is your oscillator. For example, let's say you had 10 days with the following net difference between advances and declines: +404, -113, -99, + 418, -313, +227, +503, +107, -145, -992. For that 10 day period, the plurality would be -3 issues. You keep this on a cumulative basis. You can use an oscillator of this type for divergences or as a shortterm trading tool. I plot the oscillator right under the Dow Jones Average and at tops and bottoms it will often diverge, just like a momentum oscillator. You should reach a very oversold condition at a 20 week cycle bottom and you could use the A/D oscillator as an indication that the market is oversold.

How would you know for sure that you had a buy signal?

If the oscillator is deeply oversold and it has been 20 weeks from a previous low when a break in the trendline occurs, you can figure that you are at a 20 week cycle bottom. If so, you could buy on any shortterm positive divergence. If however, it is only 15 or 16 weeks into a 20 week cycle and a stock breaks a trendline, a more serious decline is perhaps underway. In this case, odds favor waiting for the market to become oversold nearer a projected low time period. Under those conditions, breaking a trendline is a sell signal.

Are there any other helpful breadth measures in your toolbox?

In 1970, I created what I call the volume/issues ratio or Tillman's VIR indicator. The VIR indicator is the volume ratio minus the issues ratio. The volume ratio is obtained by taking a 10 day total of all up volume and dividing it by a 10 day total of down volume. I do the same thing for the issues ratio—a 10 day total of up issues divided by a 10 day total of down issues. Then I simply substract the issues ratio from the volume ratio. For example, if the volume ratio was .95 and the issues ratio was .96, the VIR would be -1 (.95 - .96). I buy the first day VIR goes positive from zero or below. My stop is that day's low. You would expect your issues ratio and volume ratio to move closely together but I observed many years ago that when the market is advancing, volume increases and the difference between the ratios goes up. On the NYSE in an up market, the ratio seldom reaches a net difference of 50 points and in a down market, it seldom returns to zero. For years it was a buy signal when the net difference between the volume issues ratio was zero. That signal often turned out to be the bottom day. Through the years, it has changed a little and has started staying under zero maybe two or three days after a deep oversold condition, but as soon as it popped back up above zero, the market turned up. It is a good buy signal. The reason for this is that volume tends to expand during a wash-out condition; some of the stocks hold while volume increases. That means that you are getting to a capitulation stage so the VIR ratio falls to zero or below.

If a move below zero indicates an oversold market, what level is considered overbought?

For the NYSE, when the ratio difference rises above 35 and then falls back under 30, it has led to tops in the past. Sometimes in a screaming market the number will go to 40 or 50 and I have seen it as high as 70 before it begins to fall. Generally you are going to find this occurring within a 10 or 20 week cycle. The market usually starts topping out on less volume and the number of up issues will decline. Being very sensitive to either issues or volume, the oscillator will start down. Perhaps it is coincidental but often it will fall below the 30 level right around the high point.

Is there a particular analytical sequence that you go through each day?

If I were to come back off of a long vacation and wanted to catch up, the first thing I would do is bring the averages up to date. I would calculate the 10 day breadth oscillator and the cumulative advance/decline line to look at the basic health of the market. Then I would create the centered moving averages on a chart of the DJIA to see where the market was in relation to a previous move. Those three things, the breadth oscillator, the A/D line, and centered moving averages on the Dow, would give me a feeling of how healthy the market was and whether some price objectives had been met. After determining the general health of the Dow, I then scan about 1,000 stocks in Trendline for a feeling of the consensus pattern of individual issues. Next, I would focus on measuring 10 week, 20 week, and 40 week cycles for individual issues, very often by hand, to find stocks that I am interested in purchasing or selling short.

What factors determine whether you will go long or short?

I would first determine what phase the cycles are in. If the Dow is reaching a price objective, than nine times out of ten individual stocks will appear the same way. For opportunities to go short, I would scan for stocks that look like the Dow and have met their price objectives and their 10 week and/or 20 week cycles are beginning to turn down. On the long side, you want to see an oversold condition. It is just a matter of watching stocks that fit the pattern of the Dow and once the 10 week cycle has met its downside objective, getting a positive diverging buy signal from the momentum oscillator would compliment the picture. If you have a diverging buy signal that is usually good enough. To refine the signal to a daily basis, I have added a positive candlestick as added confirmation. Quite often the low day has a positive candlestick or on a chart that has the opening prices, the stock will open down on the low day, wash-out, and close up from the opening. I don't care whether it closes higher than the previous day's close. We can look at the big picture and talk about that all we want but on every chart, whether it is daily, weekly or monthly, there is "one" bar that is the high or low day. For years, I may have bought one or two days early looking for a cycle low only to get stopped out so I looked for one simple indication of a turn and the candlestick one day reversal works well. The principle is that a cycle low or high is an extreme and will produce a blow-off top or a key reversal. When all of the cycles are going down together and one of them is in a very strong "c" wave decline, or when you get a stock that has been down for 7 days in a row and it goes up on the 8th day, you have had a wash-out. You can use the standard MACD indicator as an additional tool. When the two lines cross, you are past the cycle low.

For your own investing purposes, you would want each of these indicators to be saying the same thing?

Yes. The combination of a positive divergence, a positive candlestick, crossover of centered moving averages toward the downside are just three of the simplest things that you can use to go long. It would help if you are looking at an "a-b-c" Elliott wave pattern or if there had been a 50% correction of the previous advance. Through the years, I have tried a lot of sophisticated things and probably every system known and yet, quite often it can boiled down to these very simple things. There are number of simple tools that from a cyclical viewpoint, adds some measure of knowledge about whether a cycle is bottoming or topping but if you can become familiar with the very basics, such as how the trendline channels and the centered moving averages operate together, you can go a long way with just those tools.

This is a lot of material for people to digest. Will Hurst's book fill in any gaps that we might have left out or if they need clarification.

Yes, definitely.

Stan Weinstein

In a world that is still dominated by fundamental analysts, Stan Weinstein has succeeded in gaining recognition as one of Wall Street's most respected technicians. When he speaks, people listen.

Mr. Weinstein's market initiation was not entirely different from other novices first taking the plunge. In 1961, while attending college, he invested all of his Bar Mitzvah money in the stock market. Fitting in context with his background in economics, he used fundamental analysis as the basis for his decisions. A bear market hit in 1962 and nearly wiped him out. This experience spurred him toward searching for an alternate, more profitable game plan. After reading *Technical Analysis of Stock Trends*, he tested the precepts and found they had merit. He made the switch from fundamental analysis to technical analysis and from that point on, he has been 100% technically oriented.

Undeterred by this negative start, Mr. Weinstein headed immediately for the brokerage business after receiving his degree in economics. He was a stock broker for seven years before he began writing buy and sell orders for the now defunct Walston and Company. Earning a considerable sum of money in this position, he decided to change gears, leaving behind a sure thing and reaching toward uncertainty. In 1970, he made the transition from broker to technical editor for *Indicator Digest*. Three years later, he left this job and joined fellow technician Justin Mamis as a partner in the *Professional Tape Reader*, a stock market newsletter still in its infancy stage. Then in 1976, he acquired Mr. Mamis' stake in the business and focused on building his subscriber base. In a few short years, he saw his business grow from about 200 subscribers to over 10,000.

Mr. Weinstein is drawn to the market by two distinct forces, challenge and excitement. He finds the market sometimes frustrating but never boring. Technical analysis, in his opinion, is not work. It is the "ultimate fun." According to Mr. Weinstein, there are three necessary prerequisites for success in the market as well as in life—organization, discipline, and pragmatism. It is an absolute necessity to prioritize your work, segregating the urgent from the unnecessary-first things first. Do what's most important first and least important last. As he says, "If you don't have time for stochastics, you can still get by." In order to obtain a more disciplined, less emotional approach to investing, he has constructed a proprietary model containing 50 indicators which he calls "Weight of the Evidence." As the name implies, each indicator is assigned a different "weighting" or degree of importance. Though frequently pirated by other technicians, let the record show that Mr. Weinstein was the first to coin this phrase.

His workaholic lifestyle (a portion of this interview was conducted via cellular phone at Mr. Weinstein's insistence and expense) is filled with the duties of editor and publisher of the *Professional Tape Reader*, a biweekly market newsletter. A second service is offered to institutional clients called *Global Trend Alert*. He has offered seminars for all levels of investors on subjects ranging from simple moving averages to the virtues of capital preservation. Based on his earlier experiences with losses, he strongly advocates the use of stops and in fact, his newsletter subscribers have been spared serious losses in the past as a result of using predefined stops.

Impressed by Mr. Weinstein's technical expertise, I wrote to him in 1989 expressing an interest in working with him as an assistant. Very shortly thereafter, I received a package containing two articles- a rejection letter and a copy of his book, *Secrets for Profiting in Bull and Bear Markets*. Inscribed within was a personalized message of hope and encouragement. This benevolent gesture is universally characteristic of Mr. Weinstein's attitude toward humanity. From among hundreds of investment books, his book was voted "Best Investment Book of the Year" by *Stock Trader's Almanac* and should be required reading for all market participants. I encourage you to read this premier book for more in-depth coverage of what is discussed here, excellent guidelines on risk management, and methods for calculating price projections.

Mr. Weinstein's market views have appeared in the *Wall Street Journal*, *Barron's*, *USA Today*, the *New York Times*, and *Investors Business Daily* just to name a few. He has been a frequent guest on *Wall Street Week* and *Nightly Business Report*, as well as many other leading financial programs.

Profiled in *Millionaire* magazine, Mr. Weinstein's financial success confirms that his methodologies work. Over the last 17 years, with the exception of August 1985, he has correctly predicted every major bull and bear market. His prescient calls have earned him the "Stock Timer of the Year for Stocks" award presented by *Timer Digest*.

Every technical analyst has his own distinctive style of analyzing the markets. Is there any one aspect of your analysis you deem to be unique in relation to your fellow technicians?

I would say nothing is totally unique but I feel my approach is somewhat different. One is that I truly am 100% technical. I have totally learned to put the fundamentals 100% on the side. A lot of people consider themselves technicians. I'll read their work and suddenly I will see things being thrown in like "if the Fed does this or the Fed does that." To me it is 100% supply and demand. So, I don't just talk it, I walk it. That's number one. Number two, I really do believe in sticking to my principles and keeping my analysis relatively easy. I know all the different games—candlestick charts, point and figure, bar charts, etcetera. I have tried them all but I found out that the more things you use the more you will get conflicting answers—three things are bullish, one thing is bearish. It fouls you up. I have learned to stick by my system, refine it, and basically listen to the chart itself. I very much believe in moving averages. I think they are a great help in defining trends in charts. Years ago, I developed a proprietary indicator called the NYSE Survey. It is the percentage of stocks that are technically healthy; that is, in stages I and II. From an indicator point of view it is unique. My NYSE Survey has done a great job over the years of foreshadowing important market tops. For example, in late 1972, early 1973, even though the Dow was moving to a new all-time high, this indicator was showing significant weakening. This negative pattern also appeared in late 1976 (before the 1977 bear market) and again in the summer of 1987 before the October 1987 crash. When I get past the charts of individual stocks, one thing that has helped is my proprietary "Weight of the Evidence" approach. I use 50 indicators, each singularly have a good track record. I'm not putting anybody down, because whatever works for you is terrific—this is a tough game—but I see a lot of people have a favorite two or three indicators to call the market. I listen to what the majority of my indicators are saying at any point in time. Another thing that is distinctive to my methodology is my "forest to the trees" approach. The last thing which I have always stressed and had in my book is that I think it is smart for everybody to treat their portfolio as a hedge fund. Some markets are transitional markets, not bullish or bearish, and money can be made on both sides of the tape at such times.

From an analytical point of view, do you begin with your "forest to the trees" approach?

Yes, the first thing I look at is the major trend of the market. That is the "forest." Before I pick up my Mansfield chart book, I want to know, "What is the likely trend over the next 6 to 12 months?" That is an important starting point. I try to keep it simple. If the market is real bullish I don't want to be short; I want to be a buyer. Then I work toward the trees. The trees are the sectors. I want to get into the individual groups which look best. I don't want to buy laggards, I want to buy leaders. The little leaves on the trees are individual stocks. When I am looking at individual stocks, it sounds crazy, but I really think the individual stocks are the least important of all. Going back historically, if you catch the major moves, like buying almost anything when we turned bullish in July or August of 1982 or selling almost anything when we turned bearish in August 1987, it's hard to be wrong. So the market is the most important determinant, the sectors are second, and stocks are certainly important but in a pecking order, they are the third thing I look at. Then you can say, "Okay, the market is bullish, this XYZ sector is the best sector and within the XYZ sector, this is the best stock." Conversely, when the market is turning negative, you look for the most negative sectors and then the weakest or most vulnerable stocks within that sector. Determining the trend is the starting point but you really have to keep an open mind. I am never going to get bagged into a scenario. One of my strengths is that if I am wrong I admit it. Believe me, I have been wrong and I will be wrong again in the future. That is a part of the market. I know I am going to have interceptions but I think I am going to throw more touchdowns than most anybody else. I just want to keep the interceptions to a minimum. If I have made a mistake, I want to cut it quickly and get back into the game. After I go through my "forest to the trees" approach, even though I have a little scenario going on in my head, I let the charts talk to me. There have been a couple of times over the years where I may have been bearish but as I look through the charts, I see more and more stocks shaping up. So I simply switch gears and become more positive.

With regard to analyzing charts, is there a particular time horizon you prefer to use?

Absolutely. I don't think anybody should look at less than a one year chart. Ideally, I would like to see two years. Forget looking at a chart that is three to six months because you could be getting a break-out but if you look at the previous action, the price could be coming into supply. When I first go through the Mansfield charts I kind of feel like a major league scout looking at the guys who have been put in the minor league. After my staff and I go through thousands of Mansfield charts, we may narrow it down to something like the 100 best and the 100 worst. This is a starting point. Then on those, you look at Horsey charts (monthly charts that go back 8 to 10 years) in order to spot major support and resistance areas. Let's say I have picked out six stocks in great groups that meet all of my criteria. Then I will start playing timing games with things like stochastics, MACD, and relative strength. Of these six stocks, maybe two are overbought on a stochastic basis. They may be a good pick 30 days from now after they correct. The stochastics on the other four are oversold. So from a timeliness, trading point of view, these four would be better. You can't do this much analysis on all the charts or you'd be like Rip Van Winkle. For the average person, if they will just look at the market, then the sectors, then stocks in the sectors, this will be enough. They should use common sense. You don't buy stocks that are ridiculously far from support. I would rather miss something than pay too much for it. I am kind of neurotic this way. So if stock XYZ is breaking out at 20, I don't mind paying 20½ to 21—that's no big deal. But if stock XYZ should be bought at 20 1/8 and people are paying 26, those are the kind of people that lose a lot of money and say, "Charts don't work." You have to buy it relatively close to the ideal breakout point to keep your risk factor down.

With so many momentum players in the game today, do you buy a stock immediately as it is breaking out or do you wait for it to pull back?

I do both. I mention this in my book. If you are a trader, I think you should go for it but if you are an investor, which most people are, I think the smartest thing to do is to buy half a position on the breakout and the other half on the pullback. If 20 1/8 is a breakout and the stock closes at 19½, forget it. But if it closes at the end of the day at 20¼ on a valid breakout and the volume has picked up, I would buy half of a position on the breakout and then when it gets a good distance away, say 22 or 23 and pulls back and holds at 20¼ or 20½, I would buy the other half. That is a good one-two punch. If you strictly buy only the pullback, which is safer, you are going to miss too many good stocks because when the momentum players start taking stock away from you, you'll never get any. The reality is that if momentum players are going to be making the charts you have to adjust to what's going on. Over the years, the market "gets" all of the different types of market players. In one cycle, it will be technicians while at another time the market will level the buy and hold people. Right now, momentum players have been the heroes over the last three to four years. If I'm right, over the next year or so they are going to get it. When they go out of style that will help us to be able to buy stocks more easily.

You mentioned that you looked for areas of support and resistance on 8 to 10 year charts. Realistically, how viable are old levels of support and resistance?

A lot of people think after a year or two resistance is not there but I disagree. I definitely factor in resistance back 6 to 12 months. You don't have to be a genius to know that nearby resistance is far more potent then resistance 10 years ago but I will go back on the charts up to 10 years. Resistance is resistance. I think you should know it's there. It becomes less and less important because a lot of people have already taken losses. To give you an example, a stock breaks out at 20 and gets really extended and goes to 32. I say, "Where is it likely to stop?" I'll take a look at the Horsey charts and see that seven years ago it had a high of 34. You figure nobody is still in it from seven years ago. You know what? It stops at 33½. It's amazing, so I still respect old resistance levels but you have to know that resistance dissipates in strength as time goes by. Twelve month resistance is very potent.

Do you have any specific techniques for constructing a trendline?

First know that I think trendlines are less important than moving averages. I am probably disagreeing with a lot of other technicians but I use trendlines and I use moving averages. Of the two, I think moving averages are more important. You can take any two points and you have a trendline but if you are using a two point reversal trendline, they better have been good sharp rallies off of those two bottoms. Connect intraday lows rather than closes. The intraday price to me is much more important. Make sure the two points you are connecting are good, valid points, reasonably far apart, ideally at least two weeks apart and maybe even a couple of months apart. In an ideal world, if I can lay my ruler on a chart and find three points on a chart over 3 to 5 months that it hits, I know I am dealing with an important trendline. When you extend that trendline out into the future, it's amazing what happens. I remember in my book I had Skyline as an example. I think it hit the trendline six times over a year and a half. I bring common sense into the equation. I look at some people's charts and they look like spider webs. I can't even read the charts because there are so many lines. You'll go nuts with all those conflicting signals. It should be obvious—this is a good chart, that's a bad chart. Probably one of the greatest mistakes that I have seen over the years is that people overwhelm themselves with trying to do too much. Try to keep things simple and pick one really clear line that has been hit 3 or 4 times over the last couple of months. The other thing is don't be silly. Sometimes I see people drawing trendlines that go up at a 60 degree angle. If a slope is real sharp, you can break a trendline easily. I would say the trendline should usually be under 45 degrees to be meaningful. The flatter the trendline, the more meaningful the break. Just realize that if you have a very steep trendline it is only showing a slowing down of momentum, it's not a bear signal.

I thought a steeply sloped trendline was exhibiting powerful momentum?

It does. I am talking about a break in a steeply sloped trendline. The fact that it has a sharp, rising slope showed it was a very aggressive upmove and after the break maybe it will now rise at a slower rate of ascent. Picture this. Let's say a stock or the market is going up at a 60 degree angle and it breaks the trendline. That doesn't necessarily mean it's a sell. Maybe now it will start moving up at a 40 degree angle instead of a 60 degree angle. There is no doubt that it is showing a slowing down of momentum. The closer you get to a horizontal line, the more serious it is. If you have a line that is rising at only 10 or 15 degrees, and it has been hit a couple of times and then you break below it, that's not just a slowing down. I think you are ready to head south.

Earlier, you mentioned your preference for moving averages. Let's delve into this subject a bit deeper.

The two moving averages that I have found historically to be the most helpful are the 10 week and 30 week moving averages. Plenty of chart services use 40 week moving averages. I have tried 40 week, 30 week, and 20 week. I have found that the 20 week moving average is nice and early but you get a tremendous amount of whipsaws. The 40 week moving average, which the great preponderance of Wall Street uses, has minimum whipsaws but you are late. I try to be a real world person. I realize life isn't perfect and the stock market isn't perfect and the technicals aren't perfect. I try to see what works most of the time and come down the middle. The 30 week moving average comes down the middle very nicely. You get minimum whipsaws, not a whole lot more than the 40 week, and it turns earlier. It is amazing how many times I will put out a buy/sell signal and I will see 4 to 8 weeks later market advisory services using a 40 week moving average jump on board. I think the 30 week moving average is very important for investors. The 10 week moving average, while it is not real important for the investor, is absolutely crucial for traders. I think investors and traders should learn to use both the 10 week and the 30 week moving averages. I strongly believe in bringing common sense to this equation. It is a mistake for people to lock themselves into "I'm an investor" or "I'm a trader." Even an investor should learn if stock XYZ has had a tremendous run from 10 to 30 and then even though it is longterm bullish, if the 30 week moving average is say at 15 and you have doubled the longterm moving average, you don't have to be a genius to know you have a correction coming. If you start breaking below the 10 week, which is perhaps say at 28, I would certainly never tell them to blow the whole position but I think even the longterm investor should shave the position a little—take a few chips off the board. Profit taking is not a dirty word. You see that within the last year, the markets have developed incredible volatility. I think this is one of the things that my institutional clients, even the fundamentalists have learned. You've got to have a little bit of trading aspect to you. I'm not talking shortterm but intermediate-term—two to three months. If something is real extended, I think investors should take some profits when you break the 10 week moving average. A trader's case is another thing. They should sell more aggressively.

Does the market have to be in a clear cut uptrend or downtrend for the moving averages to be useful?

Useful is the wrong word. The moving average is always useful even if it's to tell you that you are in a whipsaw environment. To be really "profitable" you need a strong trend—not even a question. The moving averages are most helpful in a market that has a clear cut trend. For example, a lot of charts broke down below their 10 week and 30 week moving average lines in May and early June 1996. Then you had that tremendous sell-off into mid-July. In early August, a lot of stocks started moving back above their 10 week moving averages. When you are oversold and start moving above the 10 week moving averages, you want to be less short. In some cases stocks moved above their 30 week moving averages. It was a better rally than we expected so we quickly made adjustments. The most profitable times are when you are coming out of a longterm bear market, like 1982 to late 1983. All of the stocks were above their moving averages for about a year and a half. Same thing coming off of late 1994. For all of 1995 and in most cases, the first half of 1996, all were very bullish. Conversely, if you go back in history and study 1973-1974, in many cases stocks stayed below their moving averages for close to two years. It is more profitable and easier to trade when you have a trend behind you. This environment that we are in is very difficult because you are getting a lot of whipsaws. People put down moving averages saying they can lead to whipsaws. Even though it's annoying to get whipsawed, I think it is a small price to pay so that you don't ever get killed. I would rather have 3 or 4 whipsaws in a row than to hold onto something, having no idea where the hell to get out, and get bombed on the long or short side.

So this is a stage when the phrase "when in doubt, stay out" becomes applicable?

I love it. "The bigger the top the bigger the drop." Those are good phrases and we are putting in some pretty big tops here. You don't have to bet on every race. Right now, this is not a real high probability bet. I think we are in a very toppy, whippy phase. In my fax to institutional clients—I was kidding around but somewhat serious—I said, "It almost makes you a believer in random walk." When the market is so trendless as this, trades don't work very well. The trend will become definable again. I may see a couple of interesting things but I definitely wouldn't be betting as heavily as in January through May of 1996. To me that was a slam dunk on the long side. June and July were a slam dunk on the short side. There is nothing wrong with saying, "I'm not going to play, I'm going to take it easy." There are some races that are better to bet on than others.

What are your thoughts on the spreads between 10 week and 30 week moving average lines?

This is a little bit subjective because the more volatile a stock is the wider the spread. Cisco Systems is going to have a much bigger spread than say a stock like General Motors. A person should just use common sense. Look at a chart over a two to three year period and you can gauge what the average spread is for different stocks. You will see that historically every time it gets to say 5 or 6 points away from its moving average line, that turns out to be an overbought or oversold signal. Conversely, a very volatile four letter aggressive stock might be 15 or 20 points away from its moving average line. The bottom line is that this is all pattern development. It's kind of like kids have personalities—charts have personalities. I wouldn't act strictly off of this but when you put the whole deal together, it works.

Don't you categorize market indexes and individual stocks in four distinct stages—I, II, III, and IV?

Right, and I'll quickly define the stages. Stage I is the basing phase while Stage II is the exciting, advancing phase. Eventually, after an upmove, a stock moves into Stage III, which is the topping phase and once it breaks down from support and starts trending lower it is in the destructive Stage IV declining phase. To illustrate with numbers, let's say stock XYZ has fallen from 20 down to 8. As long as a stock is below its 30 week moving average you are in stage IV. Then let's say it moves between 8 and 10 and starts to form a constructive base. If the 30 week moving average is still far away, say at 15, I still consider it late stage IV. It is a little bit subjective but if we continue building this base and the 30 week moving average drops down to 10½, that is, if it gets within spitting distance of the price, I will say we are early in a stage I base. You know for sure that you are in late stage I when the stock physically moves above the 30 week moving average or the 30 week moving average stops declining or becomes almost flat. Once you move above the 30 week moving average, even if a stock hasn't broken out of a valid base, you are in stage I. Now let's say you are in stage I and the stock goes between 8 and 10. Eventually, maybe six months after this sideways base movement, you break out above resistance at 10½ and it breaks above its 30 week moving average, now you are in stage II. That is the momentum phase. Go for it. I don't care what the fundamentals are saying, I want you to be bullish on the stock. While you are in stage II, longterm investors should just stay with the stock. There will be plenty of corrections along the way but they all happen above rising 30 week moving averages. Forget the trading aspect and just ride it. Let's say a year later the stock price is up to 22 and it starts going sideways, whipping a little below the 30 week moving average which is flattening out. You are now in a stage III distributional top. Traders blow it out. Investors should lighten up, selling maybe a quarter to a third of a position. When you break below the bottom of the trading channel, let's say it's 20, that is stage III turning into stage IV. When it breaks below 20, you are in stage IV. Nobody should be holding a stage IV stock. We all know that you get the heck out and stay out of the way. I would like to stress that before a person becomes a winner, they have to eradicate the most losing techniques. I have said this for years in my speeches and I believe it sincerely. So the first thing that you should do is never hold a stage IV stock. If you can get everybody to do this they will be well on their way to success. When I give speeches I kid around by saying, "Today's going to be like an AA meeting, you are going to take the oath—we are never going to hold or average down in another stage IV stock." If what I have just said can be eradicated, I think even some of the crummiest market players will take a quantum leap forward.

Get rid of the bad habits.

Absolutely. Everyone has bad habits but they spend time blaming everyone else. It's the broker's fault or the news media's fault or the market letter writer's fault. Some people are confirmed losers. They will lose no matter who they follow. If somebody comes up and says, "Stan, I don't have time to go through all this analysis, give me your best stock that's going to double in the next thirty days," I know that person is a loser because he's not ready to do serious work.

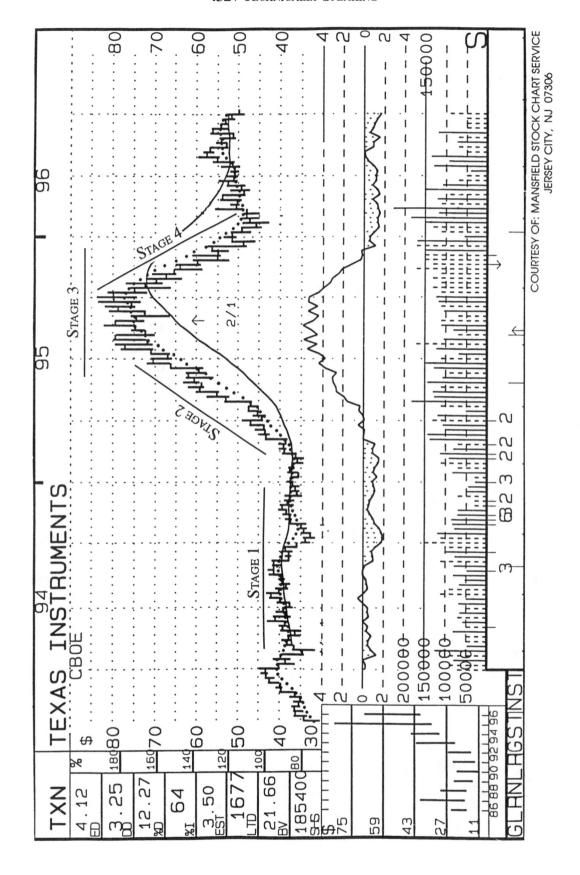

When you spot a stock breaking out of a base and moving from stage I to stage II, how do you distinguish between a stock making a false breakout and the start of a true, legitimate uptrend?

First of all, you really can't totally until after the fact but we can at least have a hint into which one is more likely. If the volume doesn't pick up considerably, you have a big chance of a false breakout.

Should we expect average daily volume to double?

At minimum a double. Historically, if you go back the big winners have at least triple volume on the daily charts. I would say you are very unlikely to get a false breakout if you have double volume on a weekly chart and triple on a daily chart. The other thing that will help keep the false breakouts down is to make it close above the breakout. If you can give me these two things at the end of the day it would cut down the chance of a false breakout. Let's say a stock broke out at 20 1/8, went up to 20½ and closed at 19 7/8 and the volume didn't pick up. The odds, and that's all we are dealing with is probabilities, are that this could be a false breakout if you get this type of thing. I don't like to buy a stock at 9:42 in the morning. I like to see how it's going to close at the end of the day.

So you want a stock to close at its intraday high when it breaks out?

It doesn't necessarily have to close at its daily high but it has to close above the breakout. If the breakout was at 20 1/8, it should close above that. The higher in the day the better.

Let's say you sit down with your new Mansfield chartbook in an attempt to find a stock candidate for purchase. What major characteristics would you look for?

I do it instinctively. It's almost like Gestalt where you are not even thinking about it. It's the sum total of all you have been trained to see but let me try to break it down. First of all, I do my group work. I'm going to be paying attention to stocks that are in strong groups. The second thing I want to look for is a good chart pattern I want something that preferably hasn't broken out or has recently broken out and is about to pull back. I don't want a stock that is like "mission impossible"—20 points away from the break-out and real extended. I want timeliness. I want something that can soon pull back to the breakout or it is about to breakout. When it does breakout, I don't want to have a lot of resistance nearby. If it is going to break out at 20 1/8 and at 22 I have supply, that is not going to thrill me. But if I see one that breaks out into virgin territory and it's at a new all time high, that turns me on a lot. New all time highs tingle me. I like this situation better because there is no theoretical supply. Nobody has a loss in the stock and has to get out. Another big factor is risk:reward. I want a stock where I can see that the risk:reward is in my favor. Let's say the stock broke out at 20 1/8 and it's at 22. Then I say, "If it breaks back below 19 or 18 7/8 I'm going to lose 3 points but if it works, it's going to go to 30." At least I can see some risk:reward in my favor. I like 3:1 as my risk:reward ratio—3:1 if I'm right versus I'm wrong. I want to have 3 points up for every one point down. Let's hypothesize that it could go to 29. It's now at 22. It probably has 7 points to the upside and I could lose three before I get stopped out. That is a little better than 2:1. I don't love it. I find another stock that is at 22. There is no supply and I think it could go to 32 and I can get stopped out at 20 7/8 because there is a prior bottom there. I might have a risk:reward of 5:1 in my favor. When I first go through my charts, I make a mental calculation of risk to reward. I don't do all of the mathematics. When I look at a chart for the first time I am just making a list—here are good stocks in good groups. Let's say I have 20 stocks from certain groups. Then I start to whittle them down and say, "If I get stopped out with this one I am going to lose 4 points and maybe I am only going to make 8 points, it's 2:1—fair." This one is 3:1—very good. Then I start looking at other factors. All things being equal, I like bigger bases because I believe bigger accumulations lead to bigger moves. I like very little or no overhead supply nearby. I like good relative strength, and obviously if I see volume building up even before the breakout, that's usually a tell-tale sign strength is sneaking in. I like to see some volume characteristics and volume confirmation.

Of course, the stock price should be positioned above its moving average lines.

That goes without saying. If all of this is going on below a declining 30 week moving average line, I am not going to be paying attention to it. The moving average has to be right. In an ideal world, the best scenario would be a stock that was breaking out with no supply, it's near or above the 10 week moving average, and the breakout will also take the stock above its 30 week moving average. That is really a kind of super proposition.

In other words, when you see a stock getting ready to move above its 10 and 30 week moving average, that is a pretty good buy signal even though there might be some resistance overhead?

Sure. But I am making this first run through and will get a whole bunch of stocks. Then I narrow them down by saying, "This is an A-, this one is a B+, here's an A+." In an ideal world I'd like minimum or no resistance but maybe there is no such animal in this batch. I'd like to be very close to the break-out and I'd like to have a relatively close stop point. If the stop point is going to be like 20% away, forget it.

So you make a general list of stocks and then cull the least attractive candidates?

Yes. That's the way you should do it. It can make you nuts if you try to do it right the first time. The first time should really be instinctive.

Just a quick visual interpretation?

You should just look for basically good patterns. On the first run through you cut down, say 1,000 charts, to 20 or 30. On the second run through you should really start to sweat it a little, thinking about risk:reward and playing all the games I have just alluded to. When I get excited about a chart it should just pop out. I think, "Wow, that's a Picasso," then I can start quantifying it later.

You stressed that moving averages, pattern recognition, and group strength are your primary technical tools with regard to culling a large groups of stocks. Let's say you have narrowed the list of twenty stocks down to four. You can only buy one. Moving in order from most impor-

tant to least important, what other indicators would you use to make your final decision?

When you are fine tuning your work I would say resistance is the next important thing. You have to look at longterm charts and see where the resistance is. Let's say you have four A+s here and to make it easy, make believe they are all at $12.00 but one of them is in virgin territory and another one has resistance at 14. We know we are going to throw out the one with nearby resistance at 14 and concentrate on the one that has no overhead supply. Whenever you break down below a support level that you think is important and then boom, you move back above it, or you break out of a top congestion area and then you move back below it; that is how tops and bottoms start to form.

When you say longterm, is a three year chart sufficient?

Yes, that would be fine but, I look at Horsey's 10 year charts. The minimum chart investors should look at would be 3 or 4 years. Longterm resistance still counts. I can't tell you how many times I have looked at longterm charts and seen a stock approaching a high from 10 or 12 years ago. It's almost like looking for an excuse to stop and it stops near there. It is really good if people do look at longterm charts to get an idea of where they could run into trouble.

What else do you use in your final analysis?

You should also look at relative strength. All things being equal, one has neutral relative strength, another looks like it has much stronger relative strength. Another important factor I use to make my cuts is risk:reward. I think too many times people only look at the upside potential of a stock. To keep it simple, let's say you have narrowed it down to two stocks. Both are in virgin territory, they both look great, and they have good relative strength. How do I choose between these two? One of them is at 12 and it has support at 8. The stop you can realistically put at 7. I will end up taking a 40% loss if I am wrong. The other stock is at 12 and support is at 11. I can put a meaningful stop at 10 3/8. It's a no brainer—I'll go with the second stock. Too many people only look at the fact that the pattern is good and that's great but you have to look at your risk:reward because once in a while we all know we are going to be wrong. I don't want any one stock to hurt me. I would never pick a stock where the stop is more than 15% away and ideally I would really like it to be 10% or less away. If you can show me a stock with a 10% stop, close to support, no resistance, and good relative strength—go for it.

Mansfield collates their individual stock charts by group or industry. Separately, they also print charts showing the performance of particular groups. When you weed out the weak and strong groups, do you look first at the group charts or individual charts within a group?

For the average person, if they look at the group charts in the front of Mansfield that really is a tremendous help. But I do a second thing. If you have the time, looking at the individual charts within a group can raise you to a higher level. Sometimes groups are very narrowly defined, that is, some of those groups represent only 3 or 4 stocks. If one stock is a takeover or something like that, it totally distorts the group. In the old days, I didn't understand this. I would say, "This group looks great" and then I would go through Mansfield and see 22 charts within that group and only one looked good. The group didn't look that good. When I go through my work I like to take a naive approach. I forget what I previously thought about groups and focus on today—what looks problematic and what looks good? I like to see the charts individually pop up with no prejudice. I like to see agreement between the groups and individual charts. So that's the second thing. Here's a good case. When we put out the buy recommendation several months ago on the banks, the S&P bank group on a relative basis looked okay but it wasn't that super. But a lot of individual stocks like Bank of America, Nation's Bank, looked very, very good. I think there was a lot of junk in the group but the leaders were breaking out and going topside. I think that the individual stocks were ahead of the group at that point. I remember when I did my work that night, that suddenly I had 22 buys and 11 of them were banks. Even though the group had only been so-so you didn't have to be a genius to say, "Hey this is looking very good." The same thing happened recently with drugs where the group itself looked just okay but I saw Warner-Lambert shaping up and Abbott breaking out. A lot of individual drug stocks were looking very good. Individual charts and groups should agree and when they don't, something is usually wrong.

If groups and individual charts disagree, would you pay more attention to the individual chart?

Without question, I would definitely pay more attention to the individual chart. But I pick stocks more in terms of where they both agree. For example, the bank charts shouldn't be giving a sell signal as a group and then a stock like Bank America is heading topside. That would bother me. If a bank group chart is just okay, like a B but not an A, and I see a lot of A+'s in the individual charts, that's okay with me. Of the two, you are recommending a stock, not the group. For the average person, if they can do only one, I think if they use the groups probably 80% of the time it's going to give them almost the same answer.

What are you thoughts on buying or shorting stocks that buck the major, overall market trend?

I think that it is great. Some people can't do this. For those people who have the temperament and are really serious, I think that it's a good discipline if everybody runs their own hedge fund. I do this a lot of times myself. We all get sloppy and say, "Ah, it's a bull market" and you only look at the good stocks and you can miss some very good moves on the downside. For example, I put out a sell signal in August/September of 1995 on the technology sector and I actually had bigger profits on the short side with sells. In the middle of the bull market, we recommended shorting Micron Technology. So I think that everybody should treat their accounts as a hedge fund. If things are very bullish, there is nothing wrong with saying, "I'm 98% bullish and I have only one short so I'm 2% short." Conversely, it's good discipline not to be 100% short in a bear market so you don't become too prejudiced and root against the market when it starts turning up. A hedge fund helps you move with the market flow. For example, 3 or 4 months ago, the hedge fund should perhaps have been 95% long and 5% short. As you moved into June, I would have dropped to 65% long and 35% short. If I were running a true hedge fund tonight, I think there would be nothing wrong with being 50% long, 50% short. I think you could make money on both sides. My 50% long would be the nifty-fifty big cap stocks and the 50% short position would be four and five letter OTC stocks. I disagree with those people who are bullish on Monday and suddenly turn bearish on Tuesday. If you are doing this right, and you go back over the month, you are 90% bullish, you are 80%, you are 70% and so on. As more charts keep breaking down or going "topside," you keep moving in the proper direction so that you are in position before the official signal is given.

In other words, you are staying with the trend but your asset allocation is shifting?

Right. We are actually going with the trend. It is nice and easy when you know what the trend is. For example, coming off of a bottom like 1982, you obviously know what the trend is. Coming off a big decline like 1962 or 1973-1974, you know what the trend is. But right now, what is the trend? It's up in terms of the averages. Individually, more stocks are down than up. The drugs and the banks can be making the S&P look much more bullish while individual stocks are blowing up in your face. Right now I think there is a lot of distribution going on under the cover of Dow strength. I think a lot of people are going to be deluded on the downside when this whole thing rolls over and turns bearish. In this kind of market it would be crazy to be 100% long. This is why I like my NYSE Survey. When the NYSE Survey is very bullish and I see five stocks breaking out for every one breaking down, I know where my slant should be but I should still look at the one that is breaking down because in a bull market, there is something wrong there. When you are in a bull/bear environment, I think it's really great to have longs and shorts. If you do this right, anyone who looks at a broad spectrum of charts should move incrementally rather than making a big judgment.

On or around July 16th, 1996, a large majority of stocks broke below both their 10 and 30 week moving averages and then quickly reversed above them. A novice thinking that a break below the 30 week moving average line signaled stage IV would have sold out and been whipsawed.

If a stock breaks below the 30 week moving average, if the 30 week moving average is still rising, it is more likely that it is in stage III than if you break below a horizontal or a declining 30 week moving average. That is number one. Number two is a little bit subjective. If the stock breaks its 30 week moving average and in addition, it also breaks below an area of congestion, whether I get whipsawed or not, I have to put that in stage IV. Let's say you have been going between 23 and 26 and the 30 week moving average line is flat and at 24. You break 24 and then you break below 23, which has been support for the last 3 or 4 months, that is stage IV. If a stock was recently at a new high, went below its 30 week moving average which may even still be rising, and then moved back above it—unless it goes to new highs, a big stage III top is being built. Maybe it even holds up for a couple of more months thereafter. If you go back and look at the charts in 1973, you had a lot of stocks that broke below moving averages and whipped several times back and forth but they never really went topside above that range. The whole thing was part of a stage III top which is the most difficult part of the cycle to handle. "Whipping" comes during transitional periods, usually between a stage I and stage III. It doesn't take a genius to figure out that this isn't a stage I bottom we are experiencing here. As long as you haven't violated an actual area and you haven't broken below a clear cut range and if the moving average is still rising, we have to assume it is probably stage III.

A "warning sign" for impending stage III tops seems like a good explanation for this type of behavior.

Yes, it's a warning sign. This is where a lot of people screw up technicals—they expect it to be like surgery. Even surgery in the real world isn't perfect. Doctors kill people. Life isn't perfect. There are going to be whipsaws. That is part of the game. You can't be looking for an excuse to put down technical analysis. Don't think that just because the price broke below the 30 week moving average one time and then went back that the game is nonsense. You have to accept that this is a very valid tool but be warned that this tool isn't perfect. If you come in with a fair and open mind and learn how to use it properly, it will work probably 80% of the time. A break in the 30 week moving average line is a warning and that warning should be respected.

Are moving average crossovers used for shortterm signals?

No, the exact opposite. This may be contradictory from what other people say but as I see it crossovers (for example 10 week moving averages moving above or below the stock's 30 week moving average) are a longer term <u>confirmation</u> or reinforcement of a major trend. Some people trade strictly off of this. I am not saying you can't do it but I find it a very slow, lagging indicator and it is going to be late. There are ways of being much earlier. For a person looking for a 6 to 12 month kind of move and is already in the stock, you can press your bet when the crossing happens. But to first wait until that point to make the bet, I think you are already in the fifth inning of the game. When you really turn out to be right it's just good money management to press your bet. It is the same thing as in Black Jack. When you are on a roll, bet more aggressively than when you are cold. So when you have a good pattern working your way, it's a good thing to press the bet.

How do you interpret moving average crossovers?

It will be late but it is a confirming signal that a major, major turn is taking place when the 10 week moving average crosses the 30 week moving average. This is the sequence: a terrific stock starts going into a stage III top. It breaks below the 10 week moving average and then eventually breaks below the 30 week. Maybe the 10 week moving average is still above the 30 week moving average. You had the sharp drop and then it rallies back. The 10 week breaks the 30 week and they often stall at that point where they are converging. If you get it, this is a good point to do some short selling. Again, I wait for this signal and when you see that, it is a very strong confirmation. The flip on the bottom is good too for a bullish signal. Let's say a stock breaks out at 15, goes up to 20, and pulls back to 15 or 16. You have already bought some of your initial position. The 10 week moving average is coming underneath and up through the 30 week moving average. That is a bullish confirmation and makes me feel even stronger that I want to add to the position. I don't think it is a good idea to initiate trades off of crossovers but I do think it is a good longer term confirmation of major trend changes up and down so I use it for confirmation and to add to positions.

Which crossover is more significant—the 10 week moving above or below the 30 week or the 30 week moving average moving above and below the 10 week?

I see the 10 week moving average coming through the 30 week moving average up and down as more significant. The 10 week moving average turns quicker than the 30 week. The two most meaningful for me are—if the 10 week moving average has been below the 30 week moving average for a long time and it moves above it—good positive confirmation. You will notice that it is usually going to be accompanying a pullback. Conversely, when the 10 week has been above the 30 week for a long time and then the 10 week starts breaking below the 30 week, that's a good negative confirmation. You have already had other signals and patterns that probably came along before this which have made you feel bullish or bearish. I see a crossover as a confirming kind of deal that your formation was correct.

You follow the differences in stocks making new highs versus lows on both a daily and a weekly basis. Will the daily differential generate a trend reversal first?

Absolutely, not even a question. By definition, the daily will generate it first but know that each one has a plus or minus. Over the longer range, the daily will more likely give you a couple of whipsaws. The weekly is not as likely to whipsaw so that is more meaningful. The daily will generate a reversal first and then if it is a real good signal, maybe three or four weeks later, the weekly should be confirming it. Even though the daily has a shorter term feel to it and it is definitely a tremendous necessity for traders, the daily can even be used on a longer term basis. You can look back on a chart, like we have had in this case over the past year and a half, and you will see lower peaks on the daily even though the Dow has gone higher. You can see that pattern forming. The weekly has some longterm advantages but the daily serves its purpose for shorter trading. I think both of them should be used.

Your proprietary indicator, the NYSE Survey, allows you to ascertain the overall health of the market by categorizing individual stocks within four stages based on the stock's price in relation to it's 30 week moving average line. How well does your indicator correlate with Investor's Intelligence percentage of NYSE stocks above their moving average line?

I would think that there is a definite correlation but it is not a one to one correlation. I would say it is about a 75 to 80% correlation. But you are not going to see the NYSE getting super bullish and the other indicator very bearish. I think my gauge is finer tuned because we put patterns in there along with the moving averages. If you use just the moving averages, you could theoretically break below a moving average and it immediately becomes negative. So it's not perfect. The other indicator doesn't make a differentiation between whether the moving average is rising, not rising, falling or whatever. I think that is where my indicator has an advantage.

There will be a lot of people who won't have the time or inclination to go through hundreds of individual charts.

There is no question that the average person is not going to have time to look at each chart individually. If they are not going to make the wise choice to subscribe to the *Professional Tape Reader* and we can't rectify that error, then I think failing that, they should definitely look at the percentage of stocks above or below their moving average line.

You created the "eleven o'clock" and "last hour" indicator. Can you tell me about these and what is significant about those time periods?

First we started out with the last hour indicator. Understand that I always work in reverse. A lot of people think, "Hey this seems to make sense" and then they try to prove the point. I think that is backwards. I just take a look at all these different indicators and patterns and as I see what works, then I start reflecting. You might ask me, "What is the theory behind this?" To be perfectly honest, I don't give a hoot why things work—it's just that they do work. I am the ultimate pragmatist. The reality is that we charted all the different hours and the first one that I saw that had a really good correlation was the last hour, between 3:00 p.m. and 4:00 p.m. That was easy to justify because people I knew on the floor of the exchange would tell me how specialists in the last hour often adjust their books before they go home for the day. Also, a lot of shortterm traders want to be flat for the night and then they will come in trading again for the next day. So how they position themselves in the last hour is very important. It made sense intellectually but it also worked on a longterm basis. Then we tried it for all other hourly time frames. Eleven o'clock to noon turned out to be very interesting. In some respects, the more work I did I found that the eleven o'clock indicator was even better than the last hour. That really surprised me because I really thought the last hour would be the best tip-off. For whatever reason, I found that the 11:00 a.m. to 12:00 p.m. time frame seems a tad more longer term oriented while the last hour I found better for the intermediate-term. There is usually a reason for things but I just don't care too much about it. I started talking with a lot of people on the floor who told me that both of these time periods really make sense. The reason for the 11:00 a.m. to noon hour is: Let's face it, when the market opens I don't want to be in there because there are a lot of overnight orders, odd-lots, foreign orders—things like that. It usually takes an hour to an hour and a half before that stuff blows itself out. About 10:30 a.m. or 11:00 a.m., traders often start putting on positions after they see the fluff is out of the way. Then, at noon, people are taking time out for lunch—the ones that aren't drinking Maalox. So I think that between 11:00 a.m. and noon you are getting a snapshot of where they are initiating trades of the day. Between 3:00 p.m. and 4:00 p.m. you are certainly getting an insight and a snapshot into how they are feeling at the end of the day, initiating or closing out positions. Those two things are symmetrical in some respects. The two together, especially when they are both moving in the same direction, are very helpful indicators.

If readers wanted to start charting these two indicators, could they just jump right in or would they have to collect some back data?

They can get started very easily. Just like with an advance/decline line, as long as you scale it off, net up or net down, you can start at any point in time. It's not like you have to go back a year before. This will start working for you after a few months of history. Obviously, the more data you have, the better off you are.

To calculate the indicators, do you just subtract the 11:00 a.m. level of the DJIA from the noon level and the 3 p.m. level from the 4 p.m. level?

It's so easy. Take the differential between the two times periods for the DJIA, obviously plus or minus. It's cumulative so each day add on or subtract off the current numbers from the previous total.

Make a daily graph. A lot of times you get thrown off by keeping a table with a couple of good or bad days. Start charting it because you will start to see a trend and it is very helpful. For example, the 11:00 a.m. was fantastically bullish from late in 1994 until about May 1995. It has been weak the last couple of months. Even now, with the slight little bounce up it had, it really isn't coming back commensurate with the market which reinforces that there is a tremendous disparity in this rally. Over the past year and a half, all the other rallies were good. This time it is rallying but rallying poorly which makes me feel like we are topping out. You can do this with stocks too. If somebody is really serious and they have a few pet stocks, I have found this to be fantastically helpful with individual stocks. It's really laborious but if you have the time to do it, it works well.

You keep two separate charts on these?

Keep two separate charts because from time to time they tell you something very different which is currently happening. The ideal is when the two of them are in gear. That is a slam dunk. For all of 1995, the two of them were clearly in gear together. They started splitting off in either April or May. Now you are starting to get a divergence where the last hour is still favorable but the eleven o'clock isn't terrific. It is getting a shortterm rally within a longterm negative pattern and it is well below it's prior peak. The eleven o'clock indicator is usually earlier turning than the last hour.

Would it be helpful to compute a ratio dividing the volume for each of these hourly periods by the total day's volume?

I shouldn't talk because I haven't done it. If you haven't done it, you are just giving your own two cents. Somebody could try that but I would think that volume might be less helpful than the price. I think price is the most important thing. I use volume to confirm price. You can get thrown off a lot if you just look at volume and chart the volume. You don't know if it was an up or down day. I don't think the pattern is going to be as helpful. When you do the price you know, "that was down big, they were really scared" or "that was up big, they really got excited." I am not going to be dogmatic about this but my gut instinct says that it is not going to be nearly as helpful.

On a shortterm basis, what other indicators would you use to judge the trend of the overall market?

One should definitely use the call/put ratio. It's the same thing as the put/call ratio, it's just the inverse.

Why do you invert the ratio?

I started doing it that way years ago. I'm just used to it. One way is not any better than the other. However you use it, just make sure you interpret it properly. I like the call/put ratio because it is very easy for the average person to understand. The relevant numbers for me are: at 3.00 and higher you have to start looking for shortterm tops. Start looking for shortterm bottoms at 2.00 and lower, especially below 2.00. Anything in between is neutral. In July, when you put in that important intermediate bottom, you had approximately 1.4 calls for every one put being purchased. That was very low. That is almost equal and historically you rarely have them equal. That showed a lot of pessimism. When you go back to May, before the decline, the ratio got to an exceedingly high 4 to 1. That was a lot of optimism. There were four calls being purchased to every one put. That was one of the highest readings I have seen in years. The call/put ratio told you that there was way too much optimism in May and way too much pessimism in July. In late August, early September, the market had that sell-off going from about 5700 down to 5560. The pessimism built up incredibly fast. The call/put ratio dropped down to 1.9. This was the little kicker that told me the Dow was probably going to break out to new highs even though a lot of the other averages wouldn't confirm.

Regarding the call/put ratios, do you look at the equities, indexes, or both?

First of all, I am not calculating it myself anymore. I used to do it out of **Barron's**. **Barron's** has the C.B.O.E. and other exchanges and I used to average them together. Now I use the one on my Bridge system and they are doing it off of the equity. I think the equities are far more meaningful than the indexes.

The C.B.O.E. has a toll free number available to get the put/call data on the hour and half-hour from that exchange only. The equity put/call ratio is actually pre-calculated.

That's fantastic. It's ridiculous to spend two hours doing eighteen different things to one indicator. I really believe in the acronym KISS, "keep it simple stupid." I have found that with a lot of indicators, once you track them for a while you will start to see where the turns occur. My call/put numbers may be say 3.00 and 2.00 and the C.B.O.E. may be 2.8 and 1.8. The exact numbers I use may be off by magnitude a little bit but they can use the C.B.O.E. and it will correlate. If people can call in and get the numbers without a lot of calculation, they should do it and keep it simple.

After all, the objective is to spot the extreme readings.

That's right. The extremes are what they really want to spot and also unusual patterns. Sometimes you are not at an extreme. The top and bottom extremes were obvious in May and July. In late August, early September, there wasn't a wild extreme but the fact that the Dow was so near the high and you had a lot of pessimism, that was a shortterm bell ringer telling you that you were probably going to break out and go topside. If the call/put ratio drops from 3.00 to 2.00 and the market has had only a very small fall, the pessimism is coming in too quickly and that I think is more meaningful than if it had dropped 500 points. If the market dropped this much I would expect to see the ratio drop to 2.00. Sure, you will probably get an oversold bounce. If you look at the extremes, you will be 1000% right for sure but the numbers in relation to what's happening in the market are also important. If the ratio changes too quickly on either side, that is very meaningful. The call/put is especially good for the intermediate-term and isn't as good for the short-term.

What other indicators do you look at on a shortterm basis?

The percentage of bearish advisors. The fact that this indicator got up to 45% to 46%, the highest in a year and a half, confirmed what we saw in July with the call/put ratio. They dovetailed nicely. Also, I like the Investor's Intelligence overbought/oversold oscillator—the number of stocks above or below their 10 week moving averages. That also got wildly oversold in mid to late July.

What are the parameters of the Investor's Intelligence overbought/oversold oscillator?

I would say 70% becomes overbought and 30% is oversold. You can't be totally mechanical about these things. You have to tie it in with what the market it doing. If you have a market that is very strong and you have reached 70% but the charts aren't showing any signs that the rally is ending-fine—it's a little overbought but I am not going to take that too seriously. That is a real early signal. Conversely you've had a big rally and you start to see signs of churning. If that number gets above 70% and then starts to dip down, I might take some chips off the table. Every 70% isn't the same. Part of their rule is if it gets above a number then you want to see at least one week where it flags a little lower. It could be 75 one week, 72 the next, then 70 the next. You want to know that this indicator is starting to top out. It is a three part deal. First you want to get close to plus or minus 70. Secondly, you want to see if the rally is showing signs of at least getting tired and then the third part is that you want to see this indicator come down. To put it together, let's say you went up to 71% last week and the market is starting to get a little churny. The next week it is 69%. You don't bet the whole ranch on it but that's telling me that it's an overbought reading. That is one thought. A second thought is that you have to be a little more aggressive for the oversold number. I have seen the overbought number lead by a good several weeks. There are a lot of cases where you get above 70% but the market doesn't go down for another six to eight weeks. The oversold number usually correlates more closely with actual turns. When you get an oversold reading you will usually be within a week or two of an important short to intermediate bottom. That is another little subtlety of their indicator. I think it is a big mistake for people to become totally mechanical. You have to develop a feel in technical analysis. Some 70% readings lead to a B minus decline, some lead to an A+ correction. Same thing happens with stochastics. If you sell your stock on every overbought signal you are going to get whipsawed. When it fits in with the other things we talked about it is a good fine tuning indicator. Another good indicator is the 10 day and 30 day moving averages of the advance/decline line (A/D). When the 10 day A/D line gets extremely overbought, above plus 300, or oversold, below minus 300, and the 10 day A/D moving average line crosses above or below the 30 day A/D, that is a confirming deal. If the market gets really oversold like it did in July 1996 dropping 600 points and then if the 10 day A/D moving average line crosses and moves up through the 30 day A/D line, that is a very good bullish confirmation. It doesn't happen too often. Conversely, if the 10 day A/D is like +400 and the 10 day A/D moving average breaks down below the 30 day A/D moving average line, that is a good confirmation that you are going to get a correction.

Would you explain your overbought/oversold readings on the 10 day advance/decline in a little more detail?

It's an oscillator. All you are doing is taking the net differential of advances minus declines for 10 straight days. Let's say today you have 1,000 advances and 700 declines. That's plus 300. You can keep a running total of the net difference for 10 straight days or you divide the total by 10 and make it a moving average. You can do it either way as long as you are consistent. When you get to plus 300 or 400, or in the case of the total, plus 3,000 to plus 4,000, that is historically overbought.

Conversely minus 300 to minus 400 is oversold. For those you want to be a bit more sophisticated, there is another little game that you can play. Let's say one week an overbought signal gets to +380. You say, "Fine, I will take a few chips off the table because the market is extended." Two weeks later the 10 day A/D moving average starts heading down and breaks below the 30 day moving average of advance/declines. Let's hypothesize that the 30 day moving average is at +200 and the 10 day moving average drops below the 30 day moving average at +200. This is a very important short to intermediate-term sell signal. When the 10 day moving average violates the 30 day moving average, that usually leads to a decline for a good couple of weeks. Conversely, on the bottom, let's say you have been down to -320. It's oversold so you are covering a few shorts. The 10 day moving average moves above the 30 day which we'll guess is at -200. That is telling you that the rally is going to be a little bit better than you expected so you had better cover some more shorts. That is a good short to intermediate term confirming indicator. Anytime the 10 day A/D moving average breaks above or below the 30 day it has meaning and is important but if you look back historically, the most significant corrections or rallies are signaled by the 30 day being far away from the zero line of the oscillator. The higher the 30 day is when the break comes the more meaningful it is. This is another subtlety. Just to make this clear, let's say the 10 day A/D is at + 400 and the 30 day is near the zero line and the 10 day A/D breaks below the zero line. There's going to be a little decline but it's not as serious as if the 30 day A/D moving average line had been higher on the oscillator chart. If the 30 day is at least in the +150 or +200 zone when the break occurs, that will produce a more meaningful sell-off then if it is near the zero line. For example, let's say the 10 day A/D moving average has been well above the 30 day moving average and then it breaks below it at a point where the 30 day is well above the zero line, say as high as +200, you will have a more meaningful sell-off. Conversely, if you get the reverse signal at a market bottom, that is, an oversold signal with the 30 day at -150 to -200 and then the 10 day A/D moving average crosses above it, that will give a more meaningful rally signal than if the 10 day crosses up through the 30 day when the 30 day is near zero.

Is this the extent of your trend following indicators?

I will give you one more helpful indicator—the TRIN gauge. Keep it simple. Don't do it intraday. Do a 10 day moving average of the closing TRIN. If you drop to .80 or lower, you are usually overbought. Conversely, if you go to 1.20 or higher, that is oversold. Look at the TRIN in relation to what the market is doing for subtleties. In late August, early September period in 1996, the TRIN didn't quite make 1.20 to get fully oversold. It got to about 1.16. This was very unusual because the market was still near the top so that was a sign that a lot of individual stocks were building up bearishness even though the whole market didn't. That is another sign of extreme pessimism and coming at too soon a point. It's not like the oversold reading was coming after a 500 point fall. If an indicator doesn't get to 1.20, that is, if it only gets to 1.10 and there is not a big sell-off, that is meaningful. If investors follow these indicators they will be pretty well tuned in.

To bring things together, would you classify your overbought and oversold indicators according to shortterm or intermediate-term?

There is a difference between the indicators I use for the stock market and for individual stocks. For the market in general, the 10 day A/D is very good as an intermediate-term indicator. For those who are more sophisticated and have their own computer systems, I think MACD and stochastics are as good as it gets shortterm. The stochastics turn earlier than the MACD but give you more whipsaws. The MACD has less whipsaws and is a little bit later. Again, we are talking very shortterm. When you use the two together I think they are very good for both the market and individual stocks. Using 10 day moving average line crossovers of the A/D line is very good shortterm work to confirm your opinion. For the intermediate-term I think the TRIN and the call/put ratio are excellent but people need to separate these indicators. When people get confused sometimes they will say something is very oversold because the 10 day A/D is oversold. They don't realize that the TRIN or the call/put ratio is not so oversold. I have seen the A/D oversold for a long time. When you get the really meaningful bounces, you are going to first get the shortterm indicators oversold and then you get the intermediate ones oversold. Like in July 1996, they all came together—the TRIN, the call/put, and your shortterm indicators like the 10 day A/D. When they all coalesce, that really gives you something.

So it is perhaps better, especially for the inexperienced, to wait until they all simultaneously give the same signal?

I think so. It's one thing if you have a lot of experience, then you can do it sequentially. But for the average person, they are going to start seeing oversold levels and it will be like "there is a communist under every bed." I see this all the time. I think beginners should move incrementally on a learning curve. You don't want to bet every race. Initially, just do the big easy bets. Then as you become a little sharper, you can trade around that. There are usually only a couple of extremes a year. In 1996, where did these indicators all come together? They all came together at the May top and at the July bottom.

Which indicators do you use to measure momentum?

I would say you measure momentum by looking at where the market and the averages are in relation to their 30 week moving average. How far is the stock above its 30 week moving average? Obviously, if you start getting pretty far above it, you have built up a lot of momentum. When an individual stock is getting too far above its 30 week moving average and especially its 10 week, it's showing good positive momentum longterm. Each stock has its own historical characteristic. When you start getting to a certain point on the chart, like doubling the moving average or something, even though that is showing tremendous momentum, it is also overbought shortterm. Another good momentum gauge is stochastics because it is a rate of change and that is a perfect measure of momentum. It's even better than MACD. For individual stocks, I think you should use stochastics and MACD to measure momentum.

MACD and stochastics are primarily shortterm, right?

Stochastics and MACD are not strictly scalping tools. They are shortterm but depending on the computer system, you can adjust them and the same concept can be used on a weekly chart. I use the intermediate-term MACD and stochastics on weekly charts. When you are using 6 day and 12 day stochastics, that is obviously shortterm. But then when you start doing it on a weekly basis, 6 weeks and 12 weeks on weekly charts, the intermediate term signals are very meaningful. Those signals are giving you moves that often last 3 to 6 months. The last thing I use to measure momentum is relative strength. Especially with individual stocks, I think this is outstanding.

Are you talking about the relative strength index?

Yes. I would suggest using the relative strength index two ways. Use the shorter term relative strength index for daily charts and then there is a weekly relative strength index which is definitely important for intermediate to longterm. At extremes it can also be used as a trading tool. When it gets up as high as it can get, you know it's a top or if it is down to 10%, it's very oversold. The relative strength index and stochastics both tend to be early. Mansfield charts have a different way of weighting relative strength. When relative strength starts increasing and going above the Mansfield zero line, I have found that to be meaningful. The relative strength index is a shorter term measure of momentum, more for trading, whereas the relative strength line has a longer term orientation.

When you are trying to judge the overall market trend, on which major indexes do you keep tabs?

Those people who are only going to look at the Dow— forget it. If you look at the Dow, the S&P 500, the NASDAQ composite, the Dow Transportations, the Dow Utilities, and the A/D line you will be in great shape. Through almost all of 1995, all of those were in gear on the upside. When they are in gear don't argue, just go with it. Conversely, if you take a look you will see since late May, early June 1996, you are getting a lot of disparity. Some are going to new highs, some aren't going to new highs. That is a sign that you are putting a top in here. When they are all in gear, don't worry about whether they are too high or too low, just go with the trend. When you start to see things getting out of gear, that is a sign of a trend reversal. The sequence usually goes in this order— first you have the utilities go. Then usually you start to usually see the Transportations go. The A/D line should come next. Then the speculative issues should top out. The last thing to top out are usually the blue chip averages. Usually at the end, investors go to quality because they don't have a lot of confidence. When these are out of gear you can make money but you have to play it carefully because that means something.

How do you measure speculation?

An easy measure is what I call my "speculation index." This is so easy to calculate. You can get the numbers from *Barron's* every week. It is the weekly volume for NASDAQ divided by the weekly volume of NYSE. Historically, you get more NYSE volume than OTC volume. When the OTC volume gets very low, like 70% or 75% of NYSE volume, that is usually an important sign that nobody wants to speculate. That is near a bottom. That happened in late 1994. Conversely, when it gets high and you start getting above 1.20 and 1.30 showing that for every one share traded on the NYSE you are trading 1.20 or 1.30 shares on NASDAQ, then you are starting to get speculation. In late May of 1996, when I really turned negative on the aggressive stocks, we set a new all time high. I think the number was something like 1.80. You got almost two shares of OTC stock traded for every one share on the NYSE and that said it all. I don't care how high the Dow goes, I think you will see that the speculative stocks topped out in late May, very coincident with this speculation index. Now this is a good longterm speculation gauge. A good shortterm measure of speculation is the call/put ratio.

You spend a lot of time with industry groups. Have you observed a definable sequence regarding group rotation at market tops and market bottoms?

I would say that historically, starting a move, investors usually go first to quality—good blue chips-and then will fan out to the wildly speculative stocks, the $1.00 and $2.00 OTC stocks. At the end of the game it becomes wildly blue-chip again. This to me is a clearer sign than saying, "When Group A moves that's the start and when Group B moves that's the end." Historically, copper or the oils move at the end but it doesn't always turn out to be true. These kinds of things can be a claptrap. People are going to decide that this is the rule and in the next cycle suddenly they will see the mobile homes leading first. Every cycle is somewhat different. These things change like fads. What is most likely to hold true is at first, when investors are not sure if this is the real deal, they go into the blue chips. Then as they start to become more emboldened, they invest more aggressively in OTC speculative stocks. At the end when you see the speculative issues starting to lag and top out while the Dow makes a new high, that to me is a pretty clear sign that you can take it to the bank. That is more important than my telling you, "Because copper has moved, sell stocks." I don't believe in that so much.

Bonds and financial stocks usually move in the same direction but there were occasions during 1996 when the two diverged. Is this a rare occurrence?

Yes, but here is where a lot of people have all these rules etched; "if bonds are good then gold has to be bad" or "if bonds are good, bank stocks have to be good" etcetera, etcetera. Yes, those things usually hold but there are times they diverge. The bottom line is that it happens rarely but it is happening now. People say, "Stan, how can you be at all concerned about the market when historically we know if the financials are okay the market is usually okay." My answer is that maybe this is one of the few times it can uncouple. I always go back and say, "Is there a time it was like this?" If you go back to 1962, the bond market was just fine and they crashed the stock market. 1977 wasn't as fine but bonds weren't a problem and interest rates were benign. The stock market had a bear market. The same thing happened in 1990 when you had that junior bear market in stocks and bonds were again benign. So it is certainly not without precedent. Too many times people learn the rules so to speak. The rules might work 75% of the time, but if you are getting a divergent answer, you have to be open and accept that this might be the 25% of the time it's not working. That is one of the things that I find so annoying about Wall Street. They always know the "answer." If the Fed does this, the market can't possibly do that. It is ridiculous. If it were that easy, we would all make a million tomorrow.

So in situations where there are divergences, you fall back on the tape for the answer?

Absolutely. At the top of my newsletter I have the logo, "the tape tells all." I really believe this.

When I think back, the times when all of us make mistakes is when we don't listen to the tape. Over the years, I have had myself hit over the head enough times to know the market is smarter than I.

I certainly can relate to those experiences.

All of us can. I'm sure if you are honest with yourself the times you were most wrong was when you thought something out intellectually. This is where the charts can help you the most, when they diverge from what everybody is thinking. There are times when I have made up great stories in my head— "this should happen, that should happen" and it blows up in my face unless the chart agrees with me. The technicals are not Nancy Reagan astrology. When a doctor looks at a cardiogram, if he has never met you or me, he can make a certain guesstimate about our health or lack thereof. The same thing with blood testing. That is what we are doing with charts—running cardiograms of the market, which is supply and demand. And if you will learn to listen to the cardiograms, you will have a much better chance of being right then selling yourself on an intellectual proposition.

It's difficult not to anticipate the resolution of a chart pattern rather than letting the chart tell us what it is doing.

That is what we all have to learn. Most people don't even get to chart patterns. They read something in the paper that says XYZ has good earnings so the stock should go up. If you look at the chart, that stock's pattern is a horror show. That is why I became a technician. I started out getting a degree in economics and saying, "Now this is the way the market should act." It never worked that way and I lost a lot of money. I decided there had to be a better way. Some people aren't open. They continue to hit their head against the wall and they don't understand why the wall doesn't move. I know if something isn't working there has to be a better way so I start looking.

You follow roughly 50 indicators in your "Weight of the Evidence" approach. Are these indicators equally weighted?

Definitely not. I think that certain indicators are more important than others. I always kid around and say that if I were stuck on a desert island and could only have two indicators, I think the two I would want would be my NYSE Survey and the advance/decline line. A third indicator would be the Dow with some other average in relation to its 30 week moving average. I will definitely weight these much higher because I think they are more important. Forget weightings. I think it is more important for people to separate what is an early warning indicator and what is a confirming indicator, that is, coincident with what's going on. I think this is where people foul up. For arguments sake, right now if you take a look, new highs are improving. Well, they should. The stock market is going up. But conversely, if you take a look at the NYSE Survey, which is usually early, it is not showing as much strength as it should on this rally. Anytime you see that you have a problem 3 to 4 months out. Divergences can be wildly early. Rather than be worried about weighting, I think people should start putting. We know tops are the toughest times in the cycle. We are making a stage III top which is a transitional stage. It is not obvious in the Dow but it is obvious in a lot of stocks. So how should a top form? First, you should have the bonds and the utilities top out well ahead of the market. They topped out in January/February 1996. They are usually very early by

6 to 9 months. Then you should have a speculative top next. The speculation index reached its highest point in May. When we had the June/July sell-off, they should have killed the "specs" and they did. The Dow was down only 10% and the OTC Composite was down 25%. Boom, that did it. Then after you put in a bottom in July and started coming back up, there should be less confidence. They shouldn't go right back to the specs, it should become nifty-fiftyish. Well, it is. A lot of OTC four and five letter stocks under $20.00 that were the big leaders up until May aren't lifting with almost a 600 point Dow rally. The A/D should top out ahead of the Dow. I think it has. That was one of the things that was wrong with the May top. There were no divergences in May in the A/D line. Everything was pretty confirmed then but now you are getting a lot of divergences—classic things where the Dow is at a new high and the Transportations are not. All these things are really coming to the fore the way they should when you are putting in a top. Sometimes it can be fast like 1987, other times it can go on for a year like 1972. When you are putting in a top and all the things are happening in textbook fashion the way they should, it just takes a long time and you get a lot of false moves and it is very annoying. This is one of the most complex tops I have seen in my 35 years in the market but I think if we step back, most of the things that are supposed to happen, which we just outlined, are sequentially happening.

What was the most painful lesson the market taught you and what did you learn from it?

The market has taught me a lot of painful lessons. First of all, no matter how sure you are of something, never bet the whole ranch. The first lesson I learned was back in late 1961—early 1962. At that time, I was in school getting my economics degree. I was believing in the fundamentals. I was getting a lot of fundamental stock services telling me about all these great stocks. I bet my whole Bar Mitzvah money on the stock market and the 1962 crash came along and it wiped out all of my money. At that time, it was a lot of money to me. The lesson I learned was that fundamentals don't work, at least fundamentals by themselves. Fundamentals are important when you are putting them together with the chart. That was lesson number one and that is really what propelled me to become a technician. After that, I remember going to the school library and getting Edwards and Magee's book *Technical Analysis of Stock Trends* and saying, "What the heck is all this?" I started doing some charting. I am not going to say I made money right away but I lost less. I found that there was really something to technical analysis and it was interesting. I saved up the next little bit of money and started out the second time and got much better. The second lesson I learned was not having stop losses. In 1962, stocks came down so much that I sold at the bottom because it looked like they were going to go down forever. When I look back, they were good companies. Some of them had tremendous falls. I didn't realize first starting out that good companies could get whacked. When I started looking at charts, I realized that no stock should ever fall by half and lose that much money. Remember I told you to look at two charts and see which one has less risk? Going back to that initial experience, I am very risk averse. We never get past those experiences. It's like people who were tainted by the depression. Before I look at how much I can make, I first say, "How much can I lose?" I think that is important. You realize that once you learn this game you can have a lot of small losses and still come back to fight another day but when you are on margin and you take a big hit like I did in 1962, it takes a long time until you put the money together and come back. It was a painful lesson but it was a good thing. I always believe that something positive can come out of something negative. That did it. I'm a technician today and I learned to always cut my losses.

That experience was your tuition for learning.

I agree. I don't think most people who become successful in the market can just walk into the market and become successful anymore than somebody can walk onto a tennis court and start whacking the ball. You really have to pay some dues. Some people have a faster learning curve than others. Some people go through life and never learn. They blame their brokers or their stock market letter writers. You have to pay your tuition.

What are the most essential psychological traits for successful investing?

I think the first thing is to admit to yourself that you are emotional and then to be able to put your emotions on the side. That is another reason I use stop losses. I can be as emotional as the next person. We all believe when a stock is rocketing it is going to 100 and when it starts down it's going to zero. That is the nature of human beings. When you learn how to properly use stop losses and to move the stops, they insulate your emotions from your stock market decisions. Discipline is one of my strong traits. When something goes against me I say, "I was wrong" and that's it. If you can see your emotions for what they are and say, "How am I going to handle this?" I am going to be disciplined. I am going to follow my stop losses. I am not going to guess, "This time it's different." I wrote in my book and I believe it—those people who learn how to properly take a loss can become the biggest winners. One of the most crippling traits that I have seen in people is—I'll wait for a stock to come back to get out even. People who can't take losses, who pull their stops, or don't want to put stops in—they are going to get whacked. It's just a matter of when and in what market. They are going to get killed because the stock is going to go against them and at some point it has gone too far against them and they are finished. Can you take a loss? Can you be disciplined? Can you say, "Fine, I'm going to be whipsawed now and then but that's better than losing 50% or 60% in a stock?"

When your forecasts don't materialize, do you ever go back and analyze the situation?

I do, absolutely—it's painful but very important. I always try to figure out what went wrong. For example, I stuck my neck out when the market topped out in May 1996 and said that was going to be the high initially for the Dow and all the averages. At 5180 I covered shorts and called for the rally but I only called for 5600. I didn't call for 6500 so I amended that in August saying I thought the Dow could make a marginal new high. When I looked back, you know what was wrong there? There were no divergences. We have had only two or three cases in the whole 20th century where a market has topped out with no divergences. I had just looked at so many bearish charts that I said, "This is it." I really didn't pay enough attention to the fact that the odds were that we were not going to end without divergences. That is why I feel better about this second rally as a double top is forming. This fits in more with classical theory of divergences. In the old days, I used to keep a dairy of what I thought the mistake was. I think everybody should keep a diary and you will soon see a pattern develop. Everybody has patterns. Some people's pattern will be that they take profits too quickly. Another person's pattern may be that they never take losses. You will see what your pattern is and then you have to learn to deal with it. I guarantee you that if a person is losing a lot after they get good technical skills, they have a character thing to deal with. They should find out what their pattern is because it is correctable. Sometimes you will take a look and say if you had to do it over again, I'd do it. It's a perfect call, it just didn't work. If it's that I would just forget about it. It's just a cost of doing business.

Do you have any favorite quotes?

"The tape tells all" and "Don't bet every race." A lot of times people say to me, "This time the market is wrong." I have always come back with, "The market is never wrong. The market is the ultimate reality. We are wrong." Another thing I have said is, "It's not un-American to sell short." I think everybody should learn to sell short. In essence, not being willing to sell short is kind of like driving a car with no reverse on it.

Newton Zinder

Newton Zinder was hoping to become a physician when World War II interrupted his plans. Taking a leave of absence from an accelerated pre-med program of study, he enlisted in the Navy to serve his country. When the war was over, he returned home only to find the medical schools crowded and flooded with applicants. He was turned away. In his own words, he "floundered for a while" before discovering that he was interested in the financial markets. He attended evening classes in economics, accounting and investing to acquire a background in finance.

In 1953 while still going to school in the evening, Mr. Zinder obtained a position as a fundamental analyst and for the next eight years of his career, his analysis was based purely on the fundamentals. In 1960, he transferred to E.F. Hutton as a fundamental analyst. Joe Granville was the resident technical analyst there at the time. More flamboyant in his earlier years than now, Mr. Granville would often run up and down the halls at E.F. Hutton yelling, "Major break-out, major break-out." Despite his eccentricities, Joe Granville was an excellent technical analyst and made some very valuable contributions to the study of technical analysis, not the least of which was his first book *A Strategy of Daily Stock Market Timing for Maximum Profits.* With their desks in close proximity of one another, the gregarious Mr. Granville developed a friendship with Mr. Zinder and it wasn't long before he began sharing his technical work. Joe Granville wrote a technical market letter for E.F. Hutton on a daily basis. In the summer of 1962, Mr. Granville went on vacation. Robert Stovall, head of the research department at this time, noticed that Granville had been showing Mr. Zinder a few "tricks of the trade." Wanting to maintain the continuity of these daily market letters, Mr. Zinder was approached and asked to assume this writing task during Mr. Granville's two week absence. He was reluctant to tackle the job because he considered it "crazy" to try and predict the market on a day by day basis but company loyalty won out over feelings of inadequacy. One year later Mr. Granville left for another two week vacation and Mr. Zinder was once again temporarily tapped to fill in as technical analyst. On his first day back from vacation, Mr. Granville handed in his resignation. Forced upon him by circumstances, Mr. Zinder found himself inheriting the position and overnight was transformed from a fundamental analyst to a technical analyst. That was 1963. From that time until his retirement in 1992, he continued practicing technical analysis and writing a daily market letter.

Mr. Zinder adapted well to technical analysis but having started with fundamental analysis, he still paid attention to the fundamentals. His predecessor would have disagreed. Joe Granville didn't believe in integrating the technicals and the fundamentals. Mr. Zinder recalls Granville posing the question, "What do earnings have to do with stock prices?" followed by a prolonged and exaggerated response of, "Nothing."

Mr. Zinder was at E.F. Hutton from 1960 until 1988 at which time they were acquired by Shearson Lehman. He was with Shearson until his retirement in 1992. During his career as a technician, he created the "Labor Day Week" seasonal indicator which received much acclaim from the *Stock Trader's Almanac.*

In 1987, my stock broker transferred to E.F. Hutton. Knowing of my intense interest in technical analysis, he saved Mr. Zinder's "internal" daily market letters and then mailed me fifty or sixty at a time. Even though the letters were dated, reading Mr. Zinder's insightful market commentary and his blow by blow descriptions of market action greatly improved my prospects as a fledgling technician.

What are some of the signs that you look for in market tops and market bottoms?

In terms of a market bottom, one area would be the sentiment indicators. This could be the survey of advisory services published by *Investor's Intelligence*, the put/call ratios, or *Market Vane's* survey of stock index futures traders. These indicators should show an extreme negative outlook toward the market. Some observers consider it a good sign when volume is relatively light and the market is in a downward phase. I do not. I think that you can get nickeled and dimed to death on relatively light volume. Light volume is more an indication of an absence of buyers. At any given moment there is stock that has to be sold. It may be that individuals want to finance a house, send a kid to school, or go on a vacation. On the other hand, there is not necessarily buying that has to be done at a particular moment. All things being equal, I feel sellers outnumber buyers. If volume is very light the chances are the market will decline. I am not talking about light volume during a shortterm correction in an uptrend. At that time, light volume would be okay but if the market is in a bear phase or in an obvious intermediate term correction, light volume is not a bullish sign. It is only when volume picks up that a bottom may be in sight because a pick up in volume could be an indication that buyers are finally willing to step to the plate. That could be an indication of an impending bottom. You need buyers to stop a decline so when you see volume picking up on a decline it is often a sign that the decline is nearing an end. This would be a second indication I would look for.

Do you ever view light volume as a sign of indifference or indecisiveness?

It could be either, but indifference also increases the chance that stocks are going to fall of their own weight. I am talking about a market which is in an obvious downward phase. In that situation I do not view light volume as a bullish or positive sign. You hear people say, "The market was down today but it was on light volume." If the stock goes down, you can lose money whether it's light volume or heavy volume. As the market declines, if you see fewer issues making new lows, that would be a sign that you are approaching some kind of bottom. The averages may be making lower lows but more individual issues begin to hold above prior lows. An additional sign may be where you get some bad news and the market really doesn't react any further on the downside to this bad news. The thing to remember is that bottoms are not the opposite of tops. When you get very heavy volume and the stock or market refuses to make additional progress, it suggests that buyers and sellers are coming into balance. Heavy volume and lack of further upside progress is one sign of a top. Going back to sentiment, you see extreme bullishness. The majority thinks the market has to go higher and that is evident in the put/call ratios, advisory services, *Market Vane*, or other indicators of sentiment.

What are the differences between tops and bottoms?

Usually a bottom occurs rather abruptly. It is not long and drawn out and the first rally off the bottom can be quite dramatic. Tops, unlike bottoms, tend to be drawn out. A top doesn't occur over a few days. It is more often over a few months or longer period. One other sign of tops and bottoms would be a variety of non-confirmations. At a possible bottom some averages make lower lows while other averages hold above prior lows. Here you have to be careful about the breadth because the chances are that cumulative breadth will make a lower low even after most of the averages have bottomed out. On the other hand, at a top, cumulative breadth will tend to peak well before the averages. Technical analysis is not just about the Dow Jones Industrial Average which some people and the news media still equate with "the market." You hear, "The market was up 21 points." That means the Dow was up 21 points and often only 3 or 4 stocks contributed to that 21 point gain. When the bulk of the market is actually doing nothing or going down that is certainly a warning. I pay a lot of attention to the technology stocks because these are the stocks traders gravitate into. They are volatile. You can buy them quickly and sell them quickly. If they are acting well, I think it is a positive sign for the market. If they are not, I view that as a negative sign. On an overall longterm term basis, the Dow is a good indication of what the market is doing. On a very shortterm basis it can be a very misleading one. Sometimes you have indications in terms of specific groups. Utilities, for example, tend to peak well ahead of the market and bottom out well ahead of the market. The same is true for many other stocks such as financials that fall under the category of being interest rate sensitive. They tend to lead the overall market. In the last couple of decades, interest rates have had such a big impact on the market that these stocks often give you a clue to changes in interest rates or the fact that interest rates are not going any higher or lower.

Based on your many years of observing the markets, would you say bonds and utilities more or less move together?

Utilities tend to lead bonds. Usually if you see strength in utilities that would be a sign that interest rates may not be going much higher and may even start to turn down which, of course, means bonds would get stronger. Stocks tend to be a leading indicator and bonds are really a coincident or lagging indicator. On a day by day basis you will see the bond market definitely having a big impact on stocks. If you come in one morning and bonds are down sharply, chances are stocks are going to open lower.

When the DJIA experiences a sharp up day and then quickly gives up its gains later in the session, how can you determine if this pattern is a shortterm correction or the start of a bear market?

You really can't be sure. The first decline in a bear market is going to look like a normal correction in an ongoing bull market. Let's say you made a top yesterday and you are starting to go down today. It looks like the first correction yet that top may never be bettered again. The first rally off of a bottom is still going to look like a bounce which may not last, yet you never see those lows again. As I said, tops tend to be drawn out so you get a broadening formation. I would point out though that what used to take two months to occur now takes place in two hours. Cycles are becoming more and more compressed.

In your daily market letter, you would occasionally mention that the markets reacted emotionally. What are the characteristics of an emotional move?

I think it is usually the volatility of the move. Very often, violent changes in both directions over a very short period of time is an indication of a change in the market's overall direction. July 16, 1996 is an example of this. I think the extreme moves that occurred early that day, down so sharply, up and then down again and then up was an indication that the decline that had started a few weeks earlier had just about run its course. A week later, you got the test of that low which, to be frank, sort of fooled me at that point because I didn't expect a test to occur so quickly. I probably would have been whipsawed. I thought the market would rally, hold a few weeks, and then come down gradually but you had the test a week later and I really didn't believe it. In hindsight, I should have believed it because you then had that strong rally off the late July test. The whole day had heavy volume which suggested there was a big tug of war between the buyers and the sellers and the buyers won. There are always hooks. This is still an art, not a science. You have to be flexible. Another example of an emotional reaction was the reaction in tobacco stocks to a recent court decision. I thought they would bounce back very quickly and yet they didn't. In fact, they went to even lower lows. This court decision was really something different than just stating that cigarettes are dangerous for you. There was the addiction thing that companies knew about but didn't warn consumers about. Sometimes an emotional reaction tends to be the more realistic one.

Typically, won't the Dow stocks lead at market bottoms and then be the last ones to tank at the top?

Yes, big capitalization, stable type of stocks often lead. People go into them at or near a market bottom because they are still nervous. They want to get involved in the market but they are certainly not going to buy a secondary or tertiary stock.

What is your interpretation of large moves either up or down that occur late in the trading day?

You have to determine if there was a reason for it. Did some news or earnings come out or did some brokerage house make a bullish or bearish comment? I have found that many market moves are much more random now than they were twenty or thirty years ago. This may be heresy as far as some technical analysts are concerned. My experience is that you are getting some very big moves in the market in the last half hour or hour that will have no relationship to what's going to happen the next day. From the 1960's through a good part of the 1980's, I used to feel, and rightly so, that if the market finished strong one day there was a good chance it was going to open strong the next day. If we finished weak one day, there was a good chance it was going to continue, at least early the next day, to the downside. That is not the case anymore. You can have the Dow gain 30 points in the final half-hour of the day. You might think, "Gee, good close, we should have a good open tomorrow." Forget it. It doesn't have that much significance anymore.

What is the reason for that?

I can give you a few reasons. One is that a lot of trading late in the day is related to futures and options which can have an exaggerated impact late in the day. Two, the whole structure of the market is different now then it was thirty years ago. At that time you had just the NYSE. When we closed that day, that was the market until early the next day when it opened again. Now I use the phrase "the market is around the clock and around the world." Even recently you have seen that stocks have big moves in the third market after New York closes. They trade in Japan afterwards. Bond futures continue to trade in Chicago at night. Markets start off in London with many U.S. stocks trading early the next day before New York opens. Trading is almost a 24 hour affair which therefore negates the potential that a strong or weak close in New York will have some follow through the next day. Late in my career, I found that writing about the market on a day to day basis was almost an exercise in futility. The first thing I would do at 6:00 in the morning was to turn on the radio to hear what the dollar was doing in Europe, what U.S. stocks were doing in Europe, and what bonds were doing in Europe because these were going to affect our market at the opening, not how we closed the previous day.

So you can't place much credence in what happens in the last hour or half-hour?

No. Let's go back to the July 16th day where you had a down-up, down-up move. This kind of move, especially if you finish strong after being down very sharply earlier in the day, should have some kind of follow through the next day. That is more of a special case. In the normal trading range type of market, a strong or weak close is not a particularly good indication of what necessarily will happen the following day.

Aren't multiswing days also a signal of a directional change in trend?

Yes, a shortterm change in trend.

Do you watch how the market responds to news?

Yes, but it is different news in each cycle. I remember we used to be on pins and needles Thursday afternoon when the money supply figures came out. Now most investors probably don't know what the money supply is. Now we worry about the Fed having a meeting or you worry about whether the PPI or CPI will be 0.1% higher or lower than what is forecasted. Response to the news is important. As you know, the Fed left interest rates unchanged recently. Someone was quoted as saying, "The news was very good yesterday and the market didn't really respond." Well, everybody and his brother knew that the Fed was going to leave interest rates alone. That was the expectation so obviously that was in the market. The market will move when something happens that is contrary to its expectations. The consensus was that the Fed would leave interest rates unchanged. If they lowered rates or raised rates, that would have been a surprise. People who thought the market was going to go up because the Fed left rates unchanged were naive. It was ridiculous to think that way because the expectation was that the Fed was not going to do anything that day as far as rates were concerned.

So if news is already out, you don't pay too much attention to that.

No. First of all, it's always, "What is the market expecting?" When changes in expectations occur, that impacts the market. For example, let's say that the Fed raised rates yesterday and the market didn't go down. That would have been a very bullish sign. That is one example of how the news could have given you a clue about the market's internal condition.

The same is true of a surprise earnings announcement. If stocks react to lower earnings by holding steady or moving higher, that is a bullish sign.

Yes, or it means that the bad news is already in the stock price.

What sort of working relationship do you see between the dollar and the stock market?

A strong dollar will have some impact on Dow Jones type of companies because most of them are multi-national companies. If the dollar is quite strong, their earnings could be negatively impacted. The strong dollar also could be implying that people feel interest rates are going to move up and that could also have some impact. It is one of the factors you take into consideration.

What are your thoughts on the relationship of U.S. markets and foreign markets?

If I hear that the British market is very strong without any specific reason, that is, they haven't changed interest rates in London or anything like that, we will probably follow them early that day. But even now, you are never sure when the British market is strong whether it is following us from the previous day or we are going to follow them when our market opens.

Though there are several aspects of the original Dow Theory, many people still maintain that the Dow Transports must confirm the Dow Industrials and vice versa. Is this still a necessary prerequisite?

Writing a daily letter, I had to be focused on very shortterm trends and the Dow Theory is not designed for shortterm work. It is more applicable to longer term trends. You can get your Dow Theory signal after the Dow is already down 400 points. So you say, "What good is that? It finally gave me a signal that we are in a bear market. I knew about it for some time." As far as I am concerned, it has less and less validity. Also, I think the market has changed over the last 25 years. It is much less homogeneous than it used to be. Now you can have stocks and groups in bull markets and stocks and groups in bear markets almost at the same time. Going back into history you had long sweeping trends in the market which you really don't have now. Volatility and divergences have picked up.

What are your favorite measures of momentum?

There are a lot of them that you can use but I basically use just three: the 10 day advance/decline figures, 10 day advancing volume versus 10 day declining volume which is called On-Balance-Volume, and the 10 day trading (ARMS) index. Momentum indicators will tend to peak ahead of a price peak and bottom ahead of a price bottom.

Your description of On-Balance-Volume sounds a bit different from Joe Granville's original concept.

It is sort of a take off on that. Joe did it primarily on individual stocks, I do it just on the overall market. You add up the last 10 days of advancing volume and subtract from that the last 10 days of declining volume.

You are going to get a number, say 322 million for example. I plot that number on a chart. You will get tops and bottoms, that is, peaks and troughs in momentum. A lower peak in momentum when the averages are at a higher high could be a sign that momentum may be waning. But I have found that volume indicators are somewhat less reliable nowadays. I think the volume figures can be distorted because of a lot of double counting. I am sure NASDAQ has double counting.

What do you mean by double counting?

Let's say you are going to buy 1,000 shares of Chrysler at the market on the NYSE and you put your order in at the same time as I put in an order to sell 1,000 shares at the market. Our orders get matched down on the floor and 1,000 shares of Chrysler go by on the tape. That is 1,000 shares which will be part of Chrysler's total volume for the day. Now let's say you decide you want to buy 1,000 shares of Amgen, an OTC stock and I decide I want to sell 1,000 shares. Your 1,000 shares are going to be sold by your broker, perhaps through a dealer who is a market maker in Amgen. It's going to show 1,000 shares. My sell order will also go to a dealer who will execute my order. Again it will show 1,000 shares. In other words, two separate 1,000 share trades which will add 2,000 shares to the total volume in Amgen that day. So when you see now that NASDAQ volume is so much greater than NYSE volume you have to keep in mind that there is a lot of double counting. People who are unaware of this are making the case that there is a big speculative binge in the market now since NASDAQ volume is so much higher than the NYSE volume. Considering that NASDAQ is actually a bigger market than the NYSE with more stocks traded, if you take away the double counting, the volume is really not that much more and is actually less.

Do you look at the On-Balance-Volume for indexes and individual stocks?

I use it for the NYSE. Some people keep OBV for NASDAQ as well. I don't just because I have enough things to keep. I don't use it for individual stocks which, as I said, is basically what Joe Granville does.

What calculations do you do with breadth?

I keep a 10 day cumulative figure on the daily A/D statistics and I chart it. Trendline has the A/D line underneath the averages on their charts. I also watch the weekly A/D figures but not with the same emphasis that I watch the daily. I have found that the daily has a downward bias and the weekly has an upward bias. I pay more attention to the daily because I have always focused on very shortterm trends. Breadth will tend to peak ahead of the averages but you don't know how far ahead. It may be two months or six months. To give you an example let's say the market has been advancing and the 10 day breadth figure shows +4,000 advances. There have been 4,000 more advances over the last 10 days than declines. Then the market reacts and rallies again. It may make a higher high in terms of the averages and yet the momentum never gets above say +3,000 on a 10 day basis. This tells you that this last advance, even though it made higher highs in the averages and may have looked good on the surface, came with diminished upside momentum. That can be a warning sign that an advance is losing steam. The reverse would work on the downside. Another momentum indicator is the ARMS indicator. It is a ratio of two ratios—advances divided by declines; divided by; advancing volume divided by declining volume. This is a good indicator of overbought and oversold levels. When it gets below .80, the market is considered overbought. Above 1.20 the market is considered oversold. Everything in between is neutral. You can chart this too and see little trends developing.

You once wrote in your market letter that if breadth is not overbought on a 10 day basis but the ARMS index is, then that suggests that the advancing volume is being concentrated in a very narrow base of stocks.

Yes. You don't often see that but it is a good sign to look for.

I recall reading in one of your market letters that a market shows signs of strength when it can neutralize an overbought reading without a correction.

That's right. Neutralizing an overbought reading without much of a setback means the market is essentially moving sideways. This is usually a good sign that it is going to resume the advance once the overbought condition has been neutralized. I used to say, "The bears have neutralized the overbought condition but have nothing to show for it," because the market was still up but no longer overbought. Any pullback off that overbought condition provides another buying opportunity. You can say the same thing about an oversold condition.

Would the market or an individual stock exhibit weakness if it fell and then neutralized its oversold condition by moving sideways?

Yes. If it could not rally from a big oversold and it neutralizes the oversold condition by moving sideways, that usually means another downleg is coming. That brings up another point here. After you neutralize an overbought condition and then the market rallies again but it does not become as overbought as it was earlier, that is a sign that momentum is starting to peak. Momentum tends to peak before the price peaks. The peak of the second rally may have gotten above the peak of the first rally but the fact that the market didn't get as overbought as it did the first time would be a sign that the advance is starting to lose momentum. The same thing works on the oversold. Even though the averages or the market make lower lows, the fact that the market didn't become as oversold on the second leg down as it did during the first leg is often a sign that a decline is losing momentum.

Do you pay attention to changes in average daily volume on the NYSE?

Not really. There is a secular uptrend in volume right now. Volume is useful for individual stocks. A change in an existing volume pattern often precedes a change in price. Let's say you see a stock that is trading every day around 100,000 shares and it really isn't doing anything pricewise. Suddenly you get a few days where it is trading 500,000 shares and it's still not doing anything. That could be a sign that something is going to happen. What I have just said is more useful in terms of individual stocks, not the market as a whole. You also have to take seasonal factors into account. August tends to be a light volume month. It is a big vacation month. Almost all of Europe is on vacation in August so you are getting very little trading from overseas.

Speaking of seasonality, are there any particular time segments which you have found to be historically stronger or weaker than others?

A lot of early work was done on seasonal factors. I don't think they work as well as they used to. There was almost a given that the market would rally before a three day weekend. I don't think this is as common now. We used to have particular days that were typically strong like the two days before Good Friday. Another example is the day after Thanksgiving, the Friday that is sandwiched between the holiday and the weekend. Many market participants are absent that day and this sort of created a dearth of supply. The market usually does very well on light volume that day but it had no real significance. The following week the market often declined. Another example is that the market is usually higher on the second or third trading day of the New Year than it was on the day before Christmas, though there are often a couple of down days between the two holidays. I also discovered a Labor Day week forecasting pattern that was written up in the *Stock Trader's Almanac*. If the Dow is down for the four day week after Labor Day chances are very good that it would be lower a month after the end of that week. Of course it could be higher in the interim. If the Dow was up the week of Labor Day, chances were very good that it would be higher a month later but it could be lower in the interim. You get all these statistics and say this worked sixteen out of the last twenty times which is a good record but it is not going to do you any good if you have one of the four times it didn't work.

What are the weakest and strongest months?

We had a couple of massacres in the late 1970's as well as in 1987 in October so that month has been viewed with some trepidation but it is not that bad historically. Markets tend to do better in the winter and summer than in the spring and the fall. May tends to be a down month but historically it was also often the month where either a bear market or an intermediate decline ended. In reference to May, I remember one analyst used to say, "When the flowers begin to bloom the market often fades." September, October, and May tend to be among the more difficult months. There are statistics that show that the market has an upward bias between the time of the political conventions and the election. If it doesn't happen this year, 1996 will be one of the exceptions.

Would you run through your procedure for picking a stock?

To begin, you have to relate it to the whole market environment at a given time. If you are in a trading range environment and you wait for the breakout of the range, very often much of the move has already happened and you don't get much follow through. In other words, the breakouts or the breakdowns don't mean as much. If you are going to buy a stock in a trading range market, it is perhaps better to buy it toward the bottom of its own individual trading range using the actual bottom of the range, or slightly below it, as a protective stop. That is generally the case in a trading range market. If, however, you are in more of a trending market where you are moving in one direction with just brief set-backs, then I think chart breakouts, do have validity and a chance for a follow through. When you have chart breakouts you like to see something more than 1/8 of a point. As one old trader used to tell me, "Beware of a new high by just an 1/8 of a point" because that is often a bad sign. I also think you have to relate a stock to the group it is in. I would rather buy a weak stock in a strong group than a strong stock in a weak group because I find that more often than not the group will eventually affect the stock. If I am in a strong group and I see a stock that is lagging or weak, I might feel more confident that the weak stock will have some kind of a catch-u move. A strong stock in a weak group is often an aberration and usually the group trend, especially if t' group trend is weak, will eventually overcome the existing strength in that particular stock.

Do moving averages influence your stock decisions?

Moving averages, especially the longterm ones, do have validity because they tend to act as supp resistance points, at least initially. Longterm moving averages also tell you the general trend of the You can make a case that if a stock is way above its moving average, then the stock is overbough could be vulnerable to a partial retracement toward the moving average. It is certainly not a good point. At the same time if a stock in a downtrend is oversold and way below its moving averag sometimes you can get a reflex move toward the moving average that might provide a trading oppor If the stock is too far below its moving average, it is probably no longer a good short.

Are inside days and outside days significant?

They were at one time but I think they are less so now. The outside days do have possible cance only if they occur after a big move in one direction or another. In other words, aft advance if you get a negative outside day that would possibly signal a shortterm top. Aft decline if you get a positive outside day that could signal a possible shortterm reversa upside. Inside days don't have very much significance. Usually, you will never get more t inside days in a row. Even two days are not very common. If you have already had two insi you should try to figure out whether the next move will be up or down because the chances there is not going to be another inside day. Futures traders use inside and outside days mu than stock traders.

Did you ever follow futures?

I followed interest rate futures and stock index futures only to the extent that I felt t'e affecting the stock market. I found for a long time that the stock index futures took their'm the bond futures. I think the traders were just on different sides of the room watching e'er. When the market is extremely sensitive to the trend of interest rates, you will find that 'tle move in the bond futures is almost magnified in the stock index futures and then further magr the stock market through program trading.

You personally knew Gerald Loeb. Did you pick up any good investment habits from'

He did not believe in diversification. He made the famous statement, "Put all of your eggs ir basket and then watch the basket." He believed if you did diversify you got nowhere because the stocks would offset the good stocks. He felt that the only way to make money was by betting on one or two stocks. The big thing he believed in was to have an exit point. Loeb used to say, in terms of numbers of losses, he was the biggest loss taker at E.F. Hutton. Most of his trades were losing trades but the ones that he made the money on were really big winners. That is the way he was successful. If he bought a stock in the morning and it started to go against him even slightly in the afternoon, he would sell the stock. If the stock started to look better later in the afternoon, he might even buy it back again before the market closed. He was a very active in and out trader. Commissions were much lower then than now. Most of his clients were wealthy people. He had no reluctance to take a lot of small losses to protect his clients capital hoping that the few big gains would more than offset the many small losses. That was something that he always emphasized. He made money because he rarely took a big loss.

Based on your experience in the market, what is the most important rule of investing?

The most important rule is to have an exit point. Setting an exit point is the hardest thing for people to do. If people have a loss in the stock they say, "Well, it's down a little, I will wait a little longer." It goes down a little bit more and before you know it, the stock is down 50%. When I taught classes to trainees I used to ask, "If a stock goes down 50% what are you going to do with it?" They would say to me, "I'll wait until I get back even and then I will sell the stock." People don't realize that if a stock goes down 50% it has to double before you break even again. It is simple arithmetic. So then I would say, "If you think it's going to double why don't you buy the stock now?" They would say, "Oh, no, I can't buy anymore right now." This means that they have become paralyzed in their investment decisions. You have to limit your losses and you have to have an exit point. Futures traders set exit points all the time. They have to be very disciplined. One futures trader used to tell me, "Never go in until you are sure where you are going to get out." That is a key point. You have to realize that you are going to be wrong at times. Everything may point to a higher market. All the indicators you have are positive and yet for one reason, or perhaps for no reason, the market will go down. You have to protect yourself. People will ask, "How much should I limit my loss?" The number that I often gave would be 15% at most. Then they say, " I just sold it and took a 15% loss and then the stock turned around right after I sold it and doubled in price." I would answer them, this is the insurance you pay. You pay auto insurance every year but that doesn't mean that you wasted your money because you didn't have an accident or your car wasn't stolen during the year." You pay for it to protect you and your insurance premium is your loss. On the other side of the coin, people are often reluctant to take gains. They are always sighting the tax problem. I have one basic rule, "Don't let a tax consideration govern an investment decision." The stock market couldn't care less about your particular tax situation. There's the old story about the guy who is up 50% in 11 months. If he waits another month he can get a longterm capital gain out of this. Meanwhile, the market looks terrible, the stock is starting to look terrible, but he still waits another month. His big gain turns into a loss because he waited one more month. You find this happening with many doctors and lawyers and yet I have never seen a doctor or lawyer turn down a higher fee because he is going to be in a higher tax bracket. When it comes to investments he suddenly becomes very tax conscious.

Think back to your beginnings as a technician, what is one of the biggest traps awaiting the unwary?

I think a lot of market forecasters, whether they are technicians or not, tend to make a forecast first and then look to the indicators to back up that forecast. In the biggest bull market there will always be some bearish indicators and in the worst bear market there will always be some indicators that are giving bullish readings. If a person is bullish and the market is going down, they will always cite those few bullish indicators ignoring the fact that the market is going down. I think you have to use the "weight of the evidence." Stan Weinstein of the ***Professional Tape Reader*** coined this phrase years ago. If you look at 100 indicators, 70 may be positive and 30 may be negative. You have to decide which are the most important at that particular time. One trap that people can get into is that you will probably find that the indicator that called or confirmed the last two or three bull markets will give you a misleading reading on the next one. Don't put too much faith in one indicator just because it was correct the last two or three cycles. It probably will give you a false reading this time and trap you because everybody thought that indicator gave such a good signal the last time. If everybody is looking at that one indicator, the chances are that it is not going to work this time. You have to look at a wide range of indicators. It is important to look at everything. You don't add up 2 and 2 and say this is 4 and therefore this has to go this way. It doesn't work that way. Market forecasting is not a science. There is a subjective assessment that goes into every forecast.

It is easy to get locked into our expectations of where we think the market is going and it's hard to switch gears when we are wrong.

That's true. That happens with individual stocks. A stock breaks out at 20 and you say, "Now it's going to go to 28 or 30." At 24 or 25 it starts to act lousy and the market is also acting lousy giving you all the clues that maybe you should get out but you don't. You are still trapped in that original forecast of 28 or 30 but the stock never gets there. It falls back to 20 and before you know it you have a loss.

How do you feel about these dramatic market forecasts that seem to be the hallmark of technical gurus?

The media is not interested if you tell them the market isn't going to do much or it's going to stay in a trading range but just say the market is going down 2,000 points or it's going up 2,000 points and you will get interviews all over the place. That's the kind of story they want. It almost seems that some of the forecasts are prompted by individuals trying to grab some publicity or media attention. I like to use the old forecasting rule—"Give them a number but don't give them a date. If you give them a date, don't give them a number." I may think the market is going to 10,000 but I don't know when or that the market is going to be higher next year than this year, but I don't have any specific figure. I give them either the number or the date, but I am not going to give them both.

Reference
Charts

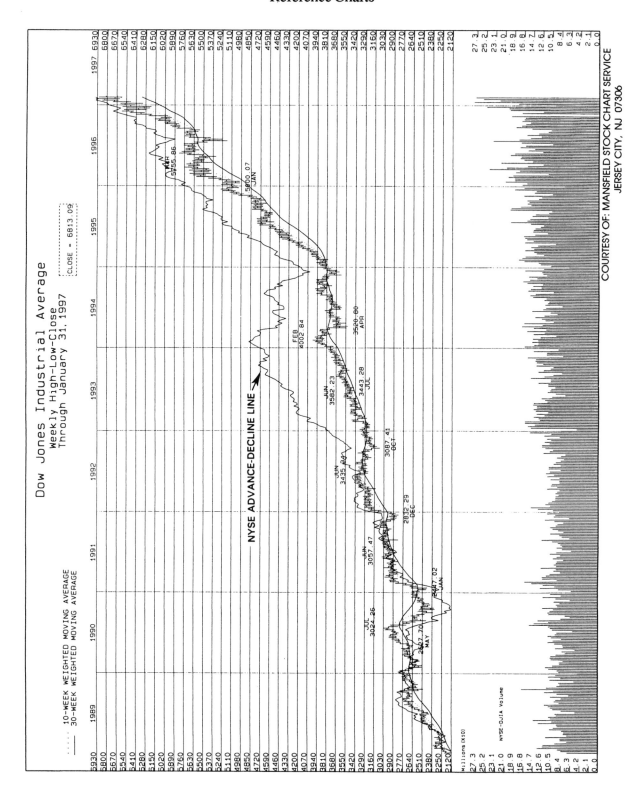

Dow Jones Industrial Average
Weekly High-Low-Close
Through January 31, 1997

CLOSE = 6813.09

..... 10-WEEK WEIGHTED MOVING AVERAGE
——— 30-WEEK WEIGHTED MOVING AVERAGE

NYSE ADVANCE-DECLINE LINE

COURTESY OF: MANSFIELD STOCK CHART SERVICE
JERSEY CITY, NJ 07306

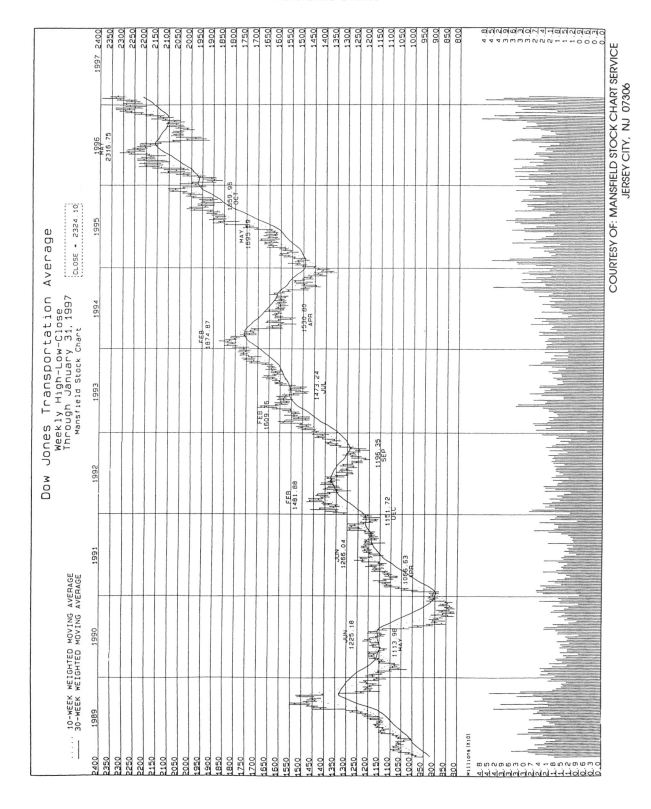

Dow Jones Transportation Average
Weekly High-Low-Close
Through January 31, 1997
Mansfield Stock Chart

CLOSE = 2324.10

...... 10-WEEK WEIGHTED MOVING AVERAGE
——— 30-WEEK WEIGHTED MOVING AVERAGE

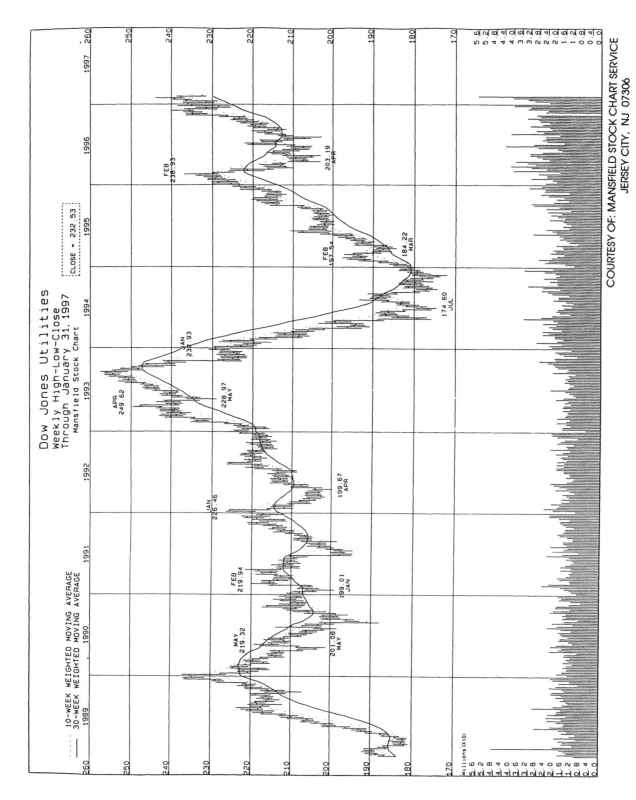

Dow Jones Utilities
Weekly High-Low-Close
Through January 31, 1997
Mansfield Stock Chart

CLOSE = 232.53

10-WEEK WEIGHTED MOVING AVERAGE
30-WEEK WEIGHTED MOVING AVERAGE

COURTESY OF: MANSFIELD STOCK CHART SERVICE
JERSEY CITY, NJ 07306

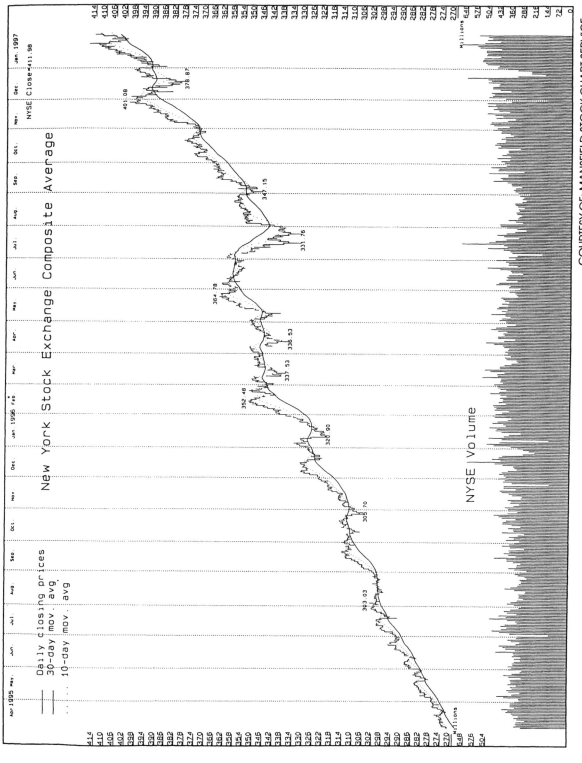

New York Stock Exchange Composite Average

Daily closing prices
30-day mov. avg.
10-day mov. avg

NYSE Close=411.98

NYSE Volume

COURTESY OF: MANSFIELD STOCK CHART SERVICE
JERSEY CITY, NJ 07306

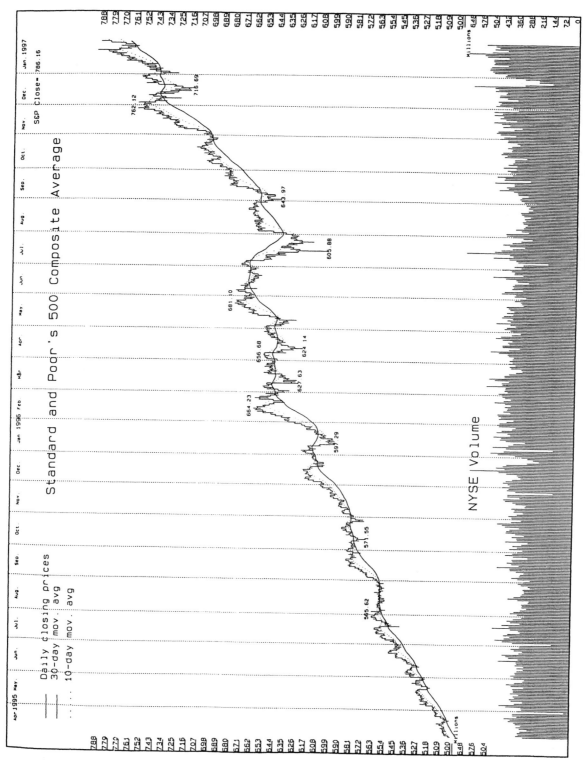

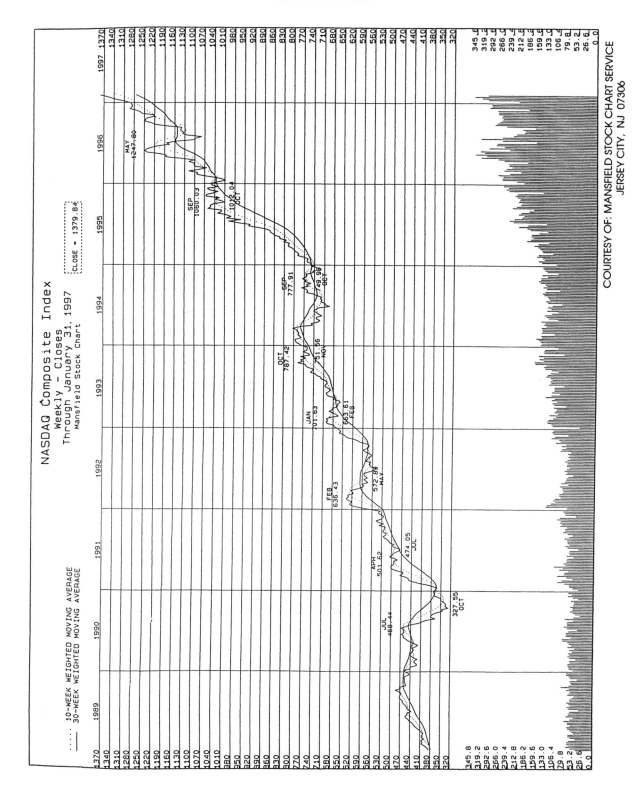

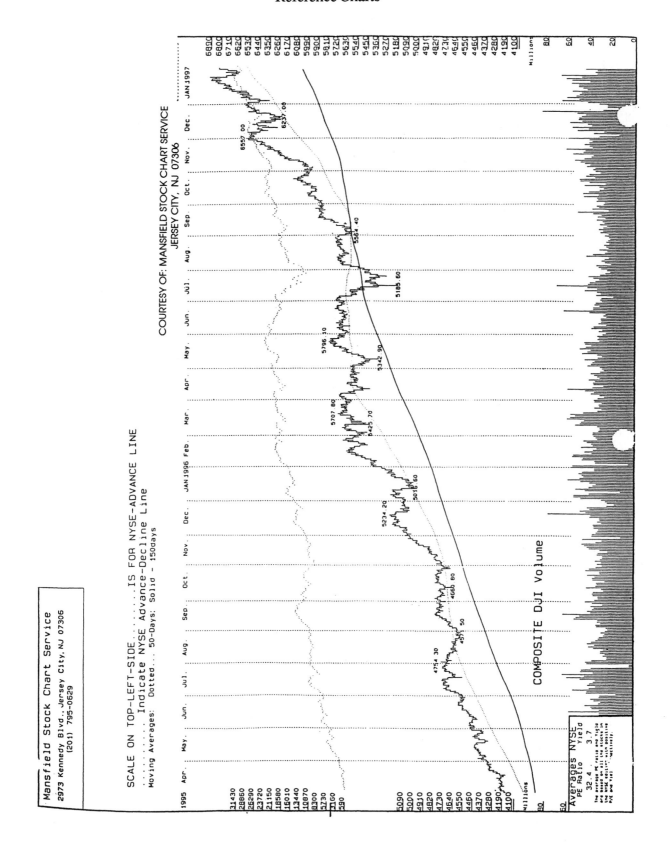

Mansfield Stock Chart Service
2973 Kennedy Blvd., Jersey City, NJ 07306
(201) 795-0629

SCALE ON TOP-LEFT-SIDE.......IS FOR NYSE-ADVANCE LINE
...........Indicate NYSE Advance-Decline Line
Moving Averages: Dotted... 50-Days; Solid - 150days

COURTESY OF: MANSFIELD STOCK CHART SERVICE
JERSEY CITY, NJ 07306

COMPOSITE DJI Volume

Averages NYSE
PE Ratio   Yield
32.4   3.7

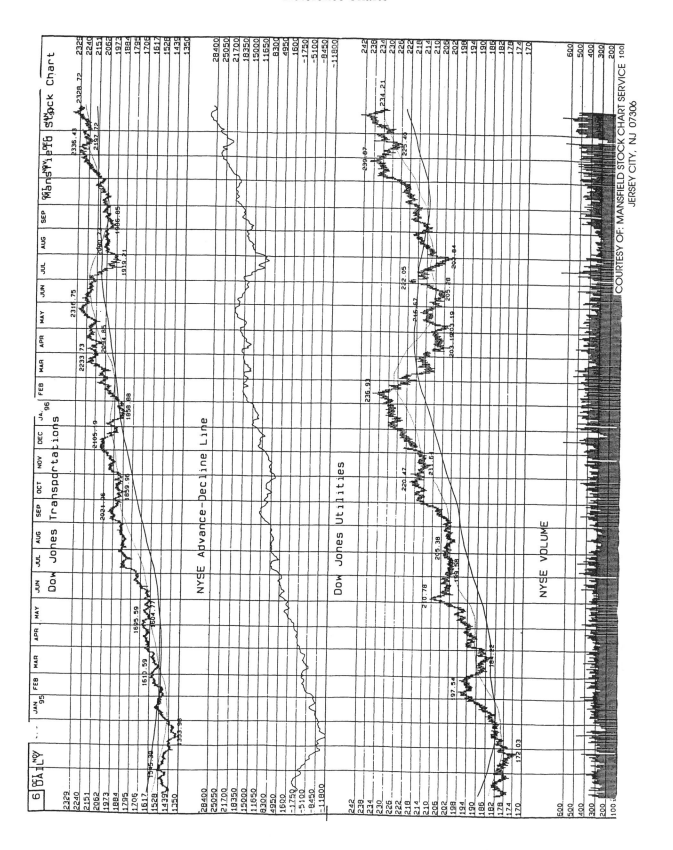

Information
Resources

AIQ Systems
P.O. Box 7530
Incline Village, Nevada 89452
800-332-2999

American Association of Individual Investors (AAII)
625 North Michigan Avenue
Chicago, Illinois 60611
312-280-0170

Barron's
200 Burnett Road
Chicopee, Massachusetts 01020
800-544-0422

Conference Board Incorporated
845 Third Avenue
New York, New York 10022
800-872-6273

Chicago Board of Exchange (CBOE)
400 South LaSalle Street
Chicago, Illinois 60605
800-678-4667

Chicago Board of Trade (CBOT)
141 West Jackson Boulevard
Chicago, Illinois 60604
800-572-3276

Concensus Incorporated
1735 McGee Street
Kansas City, Missouri 64108
816-471-3862

Daily Graphs
P.O. Box 66919
Los Angeles, California 90066-0919
800-472-7479

Gilman Research Corporation
P.O. Box 20567
Oakland, California 94620
510-655-3103

Federal Reserve Board
Publication Services
Mail Stop 127
Washington, D. C. 20551
202-452-3244

Federal Reserve of St. Louis
P.O. Box 66946
St. Louis, Missouri 63166
314-444-8444

Foundation for the Study of Cycles
900 West Valley Road
Suite 502
Wayne, Pennsylvania   19087
800-477-0741

M.C. Horsey and Company
P.O. Box H
Salisbury, Maryland 21801
410-742-3700

Investment Company Institute (ICI)
1401 H Street NW
Washington, D.C. 20005
202-326-5800

Investment Dealer's Digest
2 World Trade Center
18th Floor
New York, New York 10048
212-227-1200

Investors Business Daily
12655 Beatrice Street
Los Angeles, California 90066
800-835-0714

Investors Intelligence
30 Church Street
P.O. Box 2046
New Rochelle, New York 10801
914-632-0422

Mansfield Chart Service
2973 Kennedy Boulevard
Jersey City, New Jersey 07306
201-795-0629

Market Technician's Association (MTA)
1 World Trade Center
Suite 4447
New York, New York 10048
212-912-0995

Market Vane
P.O. Box 90490
Pasadena, California 91109
818-395-7436

McClellan Market Report, The
P.O. Box 4126
Glendale, California 91222
800-872-3737

Metastock
Equis, International
3950 South 700 East
Suite 100
Salt Lake City, Utah 84107
800-882-3040

Options Clearing Corporation (OCC)
440 South LaSalle Street
Chicago, Illinois 60605
800-537-4258

Rydex Series Trust
6116 Executive Boulevard
Suite 400
Rockville, Maryland 20852
800-820-0888

Securities and Exchange Commission (SEC)
450 Fifth Street, N.W.
Washington, D.C. 20549
202-272-2800

Securities Industry Association (SIA)
120 Broadway
New York, New York 10271
212-608-1500

Securities Research Company (SRC)
101 Prescott Street
Wellesley Hills, Massachusetts 02181
800-369-0118

Standard and Poor's
25 Broadway
New York, New York 10004
212-208-8786

Technical Analysis of Stocks and Commodities
4757 California Avenue S.W.
Seattle, Washington 98116
800-832-4642

Traders Press
P.O. Box 6206
Greenville, South Carolina 29606
800-927-8222

Trendline Daily Action Stock Charts
25 Broadway
New York, New York 10004
800-221-5277

Wall Street Journal
200 Burnett Road
Chicopee, Massachusetts 01020
800-568-7625

Martin Zweig
Zweig Forecast
P. O. Box 360
Bellmore, New York   11710
800-633-2252

Contributors
Addresses

Names and Addresses
of
Technicians

Stan Berge
Dominick and Dominick
2 Charles Street
Providence, Rhode Island   02904
401-521-8610

Ralph Bloch
Raymond James and Associates
880 Carillon Parkway
St. Petersburg, Florida   33716
800-237-5643

John Bollinger
Bollinger Capital Management, Inc.
P.O. Box 3358
Manhattan Beach, California   90266
310-798-8855
E-mail: bbands@ix.netcom.com
http://www.margin.com/bollinger

Marc Chaikin
Instinet
875 Third Avenue
28th Floor
New York, New York   10022
212-303-1992

Paul Desmond
Lowry's Reports
631 U.S. Highway 1
Suite 305
North Palm Beach, Florida   33408
561-842-3514

Peter Eliades
Stockmarket Cycles
P.O. Box 6873
Santa Rosa, California 95406
800-888-4351

Bob Gabele
CDA/Investnet
1355 Piccard Drive
Rockville, Maryland 20850
301-975-9600

Paul Macrae Montgomery
Legg Mason
600 Thimble Shoals Boulevard
Suite 110
Newport News, Virginia   23606
757-873-3300

John Murphy
MURPHYMORRIS, Inc.
9500 Forest Lane
Suite 550
Dallas, Texas   75243
214-342-9364
http://www.murphymorris.com

Martin Pring
The International Institute for Economic Research, Inc.
P.O. Box 624
Gloucester, Virginia   23061
800-221-7514
http://www.pring.com

Phil Roth
Dean Witter Reynolds
Two World Trade Center
63rd Floor
New York, New York   10048
212-392-2222

Lance Stonecypher
Ned Davis Research
P.O. Box 1287
Nokomis, Florida   34274
941-484-6107

Jim Tillman
Cycletrend
P.O. Box 667787
Charlotte, North Carolina   28266
704-588-6129

Dan Sullivan
The Chartist
P.O. Box 758
Seal Beach, California   90740
310-596-2385

Stan Weinstein
The Professional Tape Reader
P.O. Box 2407
Hollywood, Florida   33022
800-868-7857

Newton Zinder
1734 Roland Avenue
Wantagh, New York   11793

Published by Traders Press, Inc.®

ID#	ISBN#	TITLE	LIST PRICE
1840	0934380740	12 Habitudes of Highly Successful Traders by Ruth B Roosevelt	19.95
301	093438018X	A Comparison of 12 Technical Trading Systems by Lukac & Brorsen	25.00
38	0934380589	A Complete Guide to Trading Profits by Alexander Paris	19.95
1394	093438049X	A Professional Look at S&P Day Trading by Don Trivette	29.00
2100	0934380651	A Treasury of Wall Street Wisdom by Schultz and Coslow	24.95
1494	0934380511	Ask Mr. Easy Language by Sam Tennis	49.00
263	0934380317	Astro-Cycles: The Trader's Viewpoint by Larry Pesavento	49.00
1116	0934380376	Beginners Guide to Computer-Assisted Trading by Peter Alexander	29.95
1401	0934380503	Channels and Cycles: A Tribute to J M Hurst by Brian Millard	45.00
889	0934380287	Chart Reading for Professional Traders by Michael Jenkins	75.00
1722	0934380635	Charting Commodity Market Price Behavior by L Dee Belveal	34.95
1500	0934380562	Cyclic Analysis: A Dynamic Approach to Tech. Analysis by JM Hurst	19.95
2700	093438083X	Dynamic Trading by Robert Miner	97.00
3150	0934380937	Essentials of Trading by Pesavento & Jouflas	35.00
1470	0934380546	Exceptional Trading: The Mind Game by Ruth B Roosevelt	39.95
1098	0934380368	Fibonacci Ratios with Pattern Recognition by Larry Pesavento	49.00
1300	0934380481	Futures Spread Trading: The Complete Guide by Courtney Smith	49.95
888	0934380279	Geometry of Stock Market Profits by Michael Jenkins	50.00
390	0934380333	Harmonic Vibrations by Larry Pesavento	49.00
277-B	0934380759	How to Trade in Stocks by Jesse Livermore/Richard Smitten	29.95
962-A	0934380643	Investing by the Stars by Henry Weingarten	29.95
3600	093438097X	Investor Skills Training by Rob Ronin	24.95
2250	0934380864	It's Your Option by Marvin Zelkin	29.95
3800	0934380996	Keeping a Cool Head in a Hot Market by Ruth B Roosevelt	10.00
1287	0934380430	Magic of Moving Averages by Scot Lowry	29.95
3450	0934380953	Market Beaters by Art Collins	40.00
1700	0934380619	Market Rap by Art Collins	24.95
329-S	0934380538	Mind Over Markets: Power Trdg with Mkt Generated Info by J.Dalton	29.95
3500	0934380961	Option Strategies for Sophisticated Traders by Mitch Crask	34.95
3050	0934380910	Overcoming 7 Deadly Sins of Trading by Ruth B Roosevelt	24.95
1514	093438052X	Pit Trading: Do You Have the Right Stuff by Hoffman & Bacetti	39.95
336	0934380325	Planetary Harmonics of Speculative Markets by Larry Pesavento	49.00
538-A	0934380309	Point and Figure Charting: The Complete Guide by Carroll Aby	35.00
1162	0934380384	Point and Figure Commodity & Stock Trading Techniques by K.Zieg	35.00
3400	0934380945	Precision Trdg with Stevenson Price & Time Targets by JR Stevenson	49.00
2500	0934380813	Private Thoughts from a Trader's Diary by Pesavento & MacKay	40.00
72-S	0934380260	Professional Commodity Traders by Stanley Kroll	19.95
32	093438004X	Profitable Grain Trading by Ralph Ainsworth	25.00
77-A	0934380627	Profit Magic of Stock Transaction Timing by JM Hurst	25.00
1388	0934380473	Profitable Patterns for Stock Trading by Larry Pesavento	49.00
3000	0934380856	Roadmap to the Markets by Tom Busby	24.95
3200	0934380880	RSI: The Complete Guide by John Hayden	34.95
1600	0934380600	Short Term Trading with Price Patterns by Michael Harris	69.95

1208	0934380414	Stock Patterns for Day Trading by Barry Rudd	95.00
2000	0934380686	Stock Trading Techniques Based on Price Patterns by Michael Harris	95.00
2900	0934380848	Taming Complexity by Dennis McNicholl	29.95
914	0934380457	Technical Trading Systems for Commodities & Stocks By C. Patel	50.00
1115	0934380392	Technically Speaking by Chris Wilkinson	39.00
1524	0934380597	The Amazing Life of Jesse Livermore by Richard Smitten	29.95
3700	0934380716	The Complete Guide to Non-Directional Trading by Weber/Zieg	39.95
551	0934380236	The Crowd/Extraordinary Popular Delusions by Lebon & MacKay	19.95
3100	0934380872	The Handbook of Global Securities Operations by Jerry O'Connell	65.00
800	0934380708	The Opening Price Principle by Larry Pesavento	29.95
195-A	0934380244	The Taylor Trading Technique by Douglas Taylor	25.00
5	0934380031	The Trading Rule That Can Make You Rich* by Edward Dobson	29.95
1165	0934380406	Trading Secrets of the Inner Circle by Andrew Goodwin	49.00
580	0934380252	Understanding Bollinger Bands by Edward Dobson	8.00
3300	0934380902	Understanding E-Minis by Jerry Williams	24.95
43-A	0934380082	Understanding Fibonacci Numbers by Edward Dobson	5.00
174	0934380139	Wall St. Ventures and Adventures thru 40 Years by Richard Wyckoff	24.95
2400	0934380767	When Supertraders Meet Kryptonite by Art Collins	35.00
2800	0934380821	Winning Edge 4 by Adrien Toghraie	69.00
175	0934380120	Winning Market Systems: 83 Ways to Beat the Mkt by Gerald Appel	39.95

Wholesale Discount Schedule

1-9 copies	30% discount
10-25 copies	44% discount
26-50 copies	48% discount
51-100 copies	55% discount
101 plus copies	60% discount

Traders Press Inc.®
703 Laurens Road
Greenville, SC 29607

Phone: 800-927-8222 or 864-298-0222
Fax: 864-298-0221
http://www.traderspress.com